4th Workshop on Statistical Machine Translation 2009

(WMT 09)

Held in Conjunction with EACL 2009

Athens, Greece
30-31 March 2009

ISBN: 978-1-61738-558-2

Printed from e-media with permission by:

Curran Associates, Inc.
57 Morehouse Lane
Red Hook, NY 12571

Printed by Curran Associates, Inc. (2010)

For permission requests, please contact the Association for Computational Linguistics at the address below.

Association for Computational Linguistics
209 N. Eighth Street
Stroudsburg, Pennsylvania 18360

Phone: 1-570-476-8006
Fax: 1-570-476-0860

acl@aclweb.org

Additional copies of this publication are available from:

Curran Associates, Inc.
57 Morehouse Lane
Red Hook, NY 12571 USA
Phone: 845-758-0400
Fax: 845-758-2634
Email: curran@proceedings.com
Web: www.proceedings.com

Introduction

The EACL 2009 Workshop on Statistical Machine Translation (WMT09) took place on March 30 and 31 in Athens, Greece, immediately preceding the 12th Conference of the European Chapter of the Association for Computational Linguistics (EACL), which was organized by the Greek National Centre for Scientific Research, with support from Athens University of Economics and Business – Department of Informatics, and the Institute for Language and Speech Processing.

This is the fifth time this workshop has been held. The first time was in 2005 as part of the ACL 2005 Workshop on Building and Using Parallel Texts. In the following years, the Workshop on Statistical Machine Translation was held at HLT-NAACL 2006 in New York City, US, at ACL 2007 in Prague, Czech Republic, and at ACL 2008 in Columbus, Ohio, US.

The focus of our workshop was to evaluate the state of the art in machine translation (MT) for a variety of languages. Recent experimentation has shown that the performance of machine translation systems varies greatly with the source language. In this workshop, we encouraged researchers to investigate ways to improve the performance of MT systems for diverse languages.

Prior to the workshop, in addition to soliciting relevant papers for review and possible presentation, we conducted a shared task that brought together machine translation systems for an evaluation on previously unseen data. The shared task also included a track for evaluation metrics and system combination methods.

The results of the shared task were announced at the workshop, and these proceedings also include an overview paper for the shared task that summarizes the results, as well as provides information about the data used and any procedures that were followed in conducting or scoring the task. In addition, there are short papers from each participating team that describe their underlying system in some detail.

Like in previous years, we have received a far larger number of submission than we could accept for presentation. This year we received 21 full paper submissions. 12 full papers were selected for oral presentation.

We received 3 short paper submissions for the evaluation task, 5 short paper submissions for the system combination task, and 20 short paper submissions for the translation task. Due to the large number of high quality submission for the full paper track, shared task submissions were presented as posters. The poster session gave participants of the shared task the opportunity to present their approaches.

The invited talk was given by Martin Kay (Stanford University and Saarland University).

We would like to thank the members of the Program Committee for their timely reviews. We also would like to thank the participants of the shared task and all the other volunteers who helped with the manual evaluations.

Chris Callison-Burch, Philipp Koehn, Christof Monz, and Josh Schroeder

Co-organizers

Organizers

Organizers:

Chris Callison-Burch, Johns Hopkins University (USA)
Philipp Koehn, University of Edinburgh (UK)
Christof Monz, University of Amsterdam (The Netherlands)
Josh Schroeder, University of Edinburgh (UK)

Invited Talk:

Martin Kay (Stanford University and Saarland University)

Program Committee:

Lars Ahrenberg, Linköping University (Sweden)
Yaser Al-Onaizan, IBM Research (USA)
Necip Fazıl Ayan, SRI (USA)
Thorsten Brants, Google (USA)
Chris Brockett, Microsoft Research (USA)
Francisco Casacuberta, University of Valencia (Spain)
David Chiang, ISI/University of Southern California (USA)
Colin Cherry, Microsoft Research (USA)
Stephen Clark, Cambridge University (UK)
Trevor Cohn, Edinburgh University (UK)
Brooke Cowan, MIT (USA)
Mona Diab, Columbia University (USA)
Andreas Eisele, Saarland University (Germany)
Marcello Federico, FBK-irst (Italy)
George Foster, Canada National Research Council (Canada)
Alex Fraser, University of Stuttgart (Gemany)
Michel Galley, Columbia University (USA)
Jesus Gimenez, Technical University of Catalonia (Spain)
Keith Hall, Google (USA)
John Henderson, MITRE (USA)
Rebecca Hwa, University of Pittsburgh (USA)
Doug Jones, Lincoln Labs MIT (USA)
Damianos Karakos, Johns Hopkins University (USA)
Katrin Kirchhoff, University of Washington (USA)
Kevin Knight, ISI/University of Southern California (USA)
Shankar Kumar, Google (USA)
Philippe Langlais, University of Montreal (Canada)
Alon Lavie, Carnegie Mellon University (USA)
Adam Lopez, Edinburgh University (UK)
Daniel Marcu, ISI/University of Southern California (USA)
Lambert Mathias, Johns Hopkins University (USA)
Bob Moore, Microsoft Research (USA)
Smaranda Muresan, Rutgers University (USA)
Franz Josef Och, Google (USA)
Miles Osborne, Edinburgh University (UK)

Kay Peterson, NIST (USA)
Mark Przybocki, NIST (USA)
Chris Quirk, Microsoft Research (USA)
Antti-Veikko Rosti, BBN Technologies (USA)
Holger Schwenk, LIUM (France)
Jean Senellart, Systran (France)
Libin Shen, BBN Technologies (USA)
Wade Shen, Lincoln Labs MIT (USA)
Michel Simard, National Research Council Canada (Canada)
David Talbot, Google (USA)
Jörg Tiedemann, University of Groningen (The Netherlands)
Christoph Tillmann, IBM Research (USA)
Dan Tufiş, Romanian Academy (Romania)
Clare Voss, Army Research Labs (USA)
Taro Watanabe, NTT (Japan)
Andy Way, Dublin City University (Ireland)
Jinxi Xu, BBN Technologies (USA)
Richard Zens, Google (USA)

Additional Reviewers

Nicola Bertoldi, FBK-irst (Italy)
Mauro Cettolo, FBK-irst (Italy)
Jeffrey Micher, Carnegie Mellon University (USA)

Table of Contents

Conference Program

Monday, March 30, 2009

9:00–9:15 Opening Remarks

Overview of the Shared Tasks

9:15–9:45 *Findings of the 2009 Workshop on Statistical Machine Translation*
Chris Callison-Burch, Philipp Koehn, Christof Monz and Josh Schroeder

Shared Task: Evaluation and System Combination

9:45-10:15 Boaster Session

10:15-11:30 Poster Session: Shared Evaluation Task

Syntax-Oriented Evaluation Measures for Machine Translation Output
Maja Popović and Hermann Ney

A Simple Automatic MT Evaluation Metric
Petr Homola, Vladislav Kuboň and Pavel Pecina

Machine Translation Evaluation with Textual Entailment Features
Sebastian Padó, Michel Galley, Daniel Jurafsky and Christopher D. Manning

10:15-11:30 Poster Session: Shared System Combinations

Combining Multi-Engine Translations with Moses
Yu Chen, Michael Jellinghaus, Andreas Eisele, Yi Zhang, Sabine Hunsicker, Silke Theison, Christian Federmann and Hans Uszkoreit

CMU System Combination for WMT'09
Almut Silja Hildebrand and Stephan Vogel

The RWTH System Combination System for WMT 2009
Gregor Leusch, Evgeny Matusov and Hermann Ney

Machine Translation System Combination with Flexible Word Ordering
Kenneth Heafield, Greg Hanneman and Alon Lavie

Monday, March 30, 2009 (continued)

Incremental Hypothesis Alignment with Flexible Matching for Building Confusion Networks: BBN System Description for WMT09 System Combination Task
Antti-Veikko Rosti, Bing Zhang, Spyros Matsoukas and Richard Schwartz

11:30-12:30 Invited Talk by Martin Kay

12:30-14:00 Lunch break

14:00-14:30 Panel Discussion

Shared Task: Translation

14:30-15:30 Boaster Sesssion

15:30-17:30 Poster Session

The RWTH Machine Translation System for WMT 2009
Maja Popović, David Vilar, Daniel Stein, Evgeny Matusov and Hermann Ney

Translation Combination using Factored Word Substitution
Christian Federmann, Silke Theison, Andreas Eisele, Hans Uszkoreit, Yu Chen, Michael Jellinghaus and Sabine Hunsicker

NUS at WMT09: Domain Adaptation Experiments for English-Spanish Machine Translation of News Commentary Text
Preslav Nakov and Hwee Tou Ng

The Universität Karlsruhe Translation System for the EACL-WMT 2009
Jan Niehues, Teresa Herrmann, Muntsin Kolss and Alex Waibel

The TALP-UPC Phrase-Based Translation System for EACL-WMT 2009
José A. R. Fonollosa, Maxim Khalilov, Marta R. Costa-jussà, José B. Mariño, Carlos A. Henráquez Q., Adolfo Hernández H. and Rafael E. Banchs

Deep Linguistic Multilingual Translation and Bilingual Dictionaries
Eric Wehrli, Luka Nerima and Yves Scherrer

MATREX: The DCU MT System for WMT 2009
Jinhua Du, Yifan He, Sergio Penkale and Andy Way

Monday, March 30, 2009 (continued)

LIMSI's Statistical Translation Systems for WMT'09
Alexandre Allauzen, Josep Crego, Aurélien Max and François Yvon

NICT@WMT09: Model Adaptation and Transliteration for Spanish-English SMT
Michael Paul, Andrew Finch and Eiichiro Sumita

Statistical Post Editing and Dictionary Extraction: Systran/Edinburgh Submissions for ACL-WMT2009
Loïc Dugast, Jean Senellart and Philipp Koehn

Experiments in Morphosyntactic Processing for Translating to and from German
Alexander Fraser

Improving Alignment for SMT by Reordering and Augmenting the Training Corpus
Maria Holmqvist, Sara Stymne, Jody Foo and Lars Ahrenberg

English-Czech MT in 2008
Ondřej Bojar, David Mareček, Václav Novák, Martin Popel, Jan Ptáček, Jan Rouš and Zdeněk Žabokrtský

SMT and SPE Machine Translation Systems for WMT'09
Holger Schwenk, Sadaf Abdul Rauf, Loïc Barrault and Jean Senellart

Joshua: An Open Source Toolkit for Parsing-Based Machine Translation
Zhifei Li, Chris Callison-Burch, Chris Dyer, Sanjeev Khudanpur, Lane Schwartz, Wren Thornton, Jonathan Weese and Omar Zaidan

An Improved Statistical Transfer System for French-English Machine Translation
Greg Hanneman, Vamshi Ambati, Jonathan H. Clark, Alok Parlikar and Alon Lavie

The University of Maryland Statistical Machine Translation System for the Fourth Workshop on Machine Translation
Chris Dyer, Hendra Setiawan, Yuval Marton and Philip Resnik

Toward Using Morphology in French-English Phrase-Based SMT
Marine Carpuat

MorphoLogic's Submission for the WMT 2009 Shared Task
Attila Novák

Monday, March 30, 2009 (continued)

Edinburgh's Submission to all Tracks of the WMT 2009 Shared Task with Reordering and Speed Improvements to Moses
Philipp Koehn and Barry Haddow

Tuesday, March 31, 2009

Full Papers Session 1: Use of training data

9:00–9:30 *Mining a Comparable Text Corpus for a Vietnamese-French Statistical Machine Translation System*
Thi Ngoc Diep Do, Viet Bac Le, Brigitte Bigi, Laurent Besacier and Eric Castelli

9:30–10:00 *Improving Arabic-Chinese Statistical Machine Translation using English as Pivot Language*
Nizar Habash and Jun Hu

10:00–10:30 *Domain Adaptation for Statistical Machine Translation with Monolingual Resources*
Nicola Bertoldi and Marcello Federico

10:30-11:00 Coffee break

Full Papers Session 2: Reordering

11:00–11:30 *Chinese Syntactic Reordering for Adequate Generation of Korean Verbal Phrases in Chinese-to-Korean SMT*
Jin-Ji Li, Jungi Kim, Dong-Il Kim and Jong-Hyeok Lee

11:30–12:00 *A Quantitative Analysis of Reordering Phenomena*
Alexandra Birch, Phil Blunsom and Miles Osborne

12:00–12:30 *A POS-Based Model for Long-Range Reorderings in SMT*
Jan Niehues and Muntsin Kolss

12:30-14:30 Lunch break

Tuesday, March 31, 2009 (continued)

Full Papers Session 3: Linguistic modeling

14:30–15:00 *Disambiguating "DE" for Chinese-English Machine Translation*
Pi-Chuan Chang, Daniel Jurafsky and Christopher D. Manning

15:00–15:30 *A Systematic Analysis of Translation Model Search Spaces*
Michael Auli, Adam Lopez, Hieu Hoang and Philipp Koehn

15:30–16:00 *A Deep Learning Approach to Machine Transliteration*
Thomas Deselaers, Saša Hasan, Oliver Bender and Hermann Ney

16:00-16:30 Coffee break

Full Papers Session 4: Error metrics and tuning

16:30–17:00 *Stabilizing Minimum Error Rate Training*
George Foster and Roland Kuhn

17:00–17:30 *On the Robustness of Syntactic and Semantic Features for Automatic MT Evaluation*
Jesús Giménez and Lluís Màrquez

17:30–18:00 *Fluency, Adequacy, or HTER? Exploring Different Human Judgments with a Tunable MT Metric*
Matthew Snover, Nitin Madnani, Bonnie Dorr and Richard Schwartz

Findings of the 2009 Workshop on Statistical Machine Translation

Chris Callison-Burch
Johns Hopkins University
ccb@cs.jhu.edu

Philipp Koehn
University of Edinburgh
pkoehn@inf.ed.ac.uk

Christof Monz
University of Amsterdam
christof@science.uva.nl

Josh Schroeder
University of Edinburgh
j.schroeder@ed.ac.uk

Abstract

This paper presents the results of the WMT09 shared tasks, which included a translation task, a system combination task, and an evaluation task. We conducted a large-scale manual evaluation of 87 machine translation systems and 22 system combination entries. We used the ranking of these systems to measure how strongly automatic metrics correlate with human judgments of translation quality, for more than 20 metrics. We present a new evaluation technique whereby system output is edited and judged for correctness.

1 Introduction

This paper presents the results of the shared tasks of the 2009 EACL Workshop on Statistical Machine Translation, which builds on three previous workshops (Koehn and Monz, 2006; Callison-Burch et al., 2007; Callison-Burch et al., 2008). There were three shared tasks this year: a translation task between English and five other European languages, a task to combine the output of multiple machine translation systems, and a task to predict human judgments of translation quality using automatic evaluation metrics. The performance on each of these shared task was determined after a comprehensive human evaluation.

There were a number of differences between this year's workshop and last year's workshop:

- **Larger training sets** – In addition to annual increases in the Europarl corpus, we released a French-English parallel corpus verging on 1 billion words. We also provided large monolingual training sets for better language modeling of the news translation task.
- **Reduced number of conditions** – Previous workshops had many conditions: 10 language pairs, both in-domain and out-of-domain translation, and three types of manual evaluation. This year we eliminated the in-domain Europarl test set and defined sentence-level ranking as the primary type of manual evaluation.
- **Editing to evaluate translation quality** – Beyond ranking the output of translation systems, we evaluated translation quality by having people edit the output of systems. Later, we asked annotators to judge whether those edited translations were correct when shown the source and reference translation.

The primary objectives of this workshop are to evaluate the state of the art in machine translation, to disseminate common test sets and public training data with published performance numbers, and to refine evaluation methodologies for machine translation. All of the data, translations, and human judgments produced for our workshop are publicly available.[1] We hope they form a valuable resource for research into statistical machine translation, system combination, and automatic evaluation of translation quality.

2 Overview of the shared translation and system combination tasks

The workshop examined translation between English and five other languages: German, Spanish, French, Czech, and Hungarian. We created a test set for each language pair by translating newspaper articles. We additionally provided training data and a baseline system.

[1] http://statmt.org/WMT09/results.html

Proceedings of the Fourth Workshop on Statistical Machine Translation, pages 1–28,
Athens, Greece, 30 March – 31 March 2009.

2.1 Test data

The test data for this year's task was created by hiring people to translate news articles that were drawn from a variety of sources during the period from the end of September to mid-October of 2008. A total of 136 articles were selected, in roughly equal amounts from a variety of Czech, English, French, German, Hungarian, Italian and Spanish news sites:[2]

Hungarian: hvg.hu (10), Napi (2), MNO (4), Népszabadság (4)

Czech: iHNed.cz (3), iDNES.cz (4), Lidovky.cz (3), aktuálně.cz (2), Novinky (1)

French: dernieresnouvelles (1), Le Figaro (2), Les Echos (4), Liberation (4), Le Devoir (9)

Spanish: ABC.es (11), El Mundo (12)

English: BBC (11), New York Times (6), Times of London (4),

German: Süddeutsche Zeitung (3), Frankfurter Allgemeine Zeitung (3), Spiegel (8), Welt (3)

Italian: ADN Kronos (5), Affari Italiani (2), ASCA (1), Corriere della Sera (4), Il Sole 24 ORE (1), Il Quotidiano (1), La Republica (8)

Note that Italian translation was not one of this year's official translation tasks.

The translations were created by the members of EuroMatrix consortium who hired a mix of professional and non-professional translators. All translators were fluent or native speakers of both languages. Although we made efforts to proofread all translations, many sentences still contain minor errors and disfluencies. All of the translations were done directly, and not via an intermediate language. For instance, each of the 20 Hungarian articles were translated directly into Czech, English, French, German, Italian and Spanish. The total cost of creating the test sets consisting of roughly 80,000 words across 3027 sentences in seven languages was approximately 31,700 euros (around 39,800 dollars at current exchange rates, or slightly more than $0.08/word).

Previous evaluations additionally used test sets drawn from the Europarl corpus. Our rationale behind discontinuing the use of Europarl as a test set was that it overly biases towards statistical systems that were trained on this particular domain, and that European Parliament proceedings were less of general interest than news stories. We focus on a single task since the use of multiple test sets in the past spread our resources too thin, especially in the manual evaluation.

[2]For more details see the XML test files. The `docid` tag gives the source and the date for each document in the test set, and the `origlang` tag indicates the original source language.

2.2 Training data

As in past years we provided parallel corpora to train translation models, monolingual corpora to train language models, and development sets to tune parameters. Some statistics about the training materials are given in Figure 1.

10^9 word parallel corpus

To create the large French-English parallel corpus, we conducted a targeted web crawl of bilingual web sites. These sites came from a variety of sources including the Canadian government, the European Union, the United Nations, and other international organizations. The crawl yielded on the order of 40 million files, consisting of more than 1TB of data. Pairs of translated documents were identified using a set of simple heuristics to transform French URLs into English URLs (for instance, by replacing *fr* with *en*). Documents that matched were assumed to be translations of each other.

All HTML and PDF documents were converted into plain text, which yielded 2 million French files paired with their English equivalents. Text files were split so that they contained one sentence per line and had markers between paragraphs. They were sentence-aligned in batches of 10,000 document pairs, using a sentence aligner that incorporates IBM Model 1 probabilities in addition to sentence lengths (Moore, 2002). The document-aligned corpus contained 220 million segments with 2.9 billion words on the French side and 215 million segments with 2.5 billion words on the English side. After sentence alignment, there were 177 million sentence pairs with 2.5 billion French words and 2.2 billion English words.

The sentence-aligned corpus was cleaned to remove sentence pairs which consisted only of numbers or paragraph markers, or where the French and English sentences were identical. The later step helped eliminate documents that were not actually translated, which was necessary because we did not perform language identification. After cleaning, the parallel corpus contained 105 million sentence pairs with 2 billion French words and 1.8 billion English words.

Europarl Training Corpus

	Spanish ↔ English		French ↔ English		German ↔ English	
Sentences	1,411,589		1,428,799		1,418,115	
Words	40,067,498	41,042,070	44,692,992	40,067,498	39,516,645	37,431,872
Distinct words	154,971	108,116	129,166	107,733	320,180	104,269

News Commentary Training Corpus

	Spanish ↔ English		French ↔ English		German ↔ English		Czech ↔ English	
Sentences	74,512		64,223		82,740		79,930	
Words	2,052,186	1,799,312	1,831,149	1,560,274	2,051,369	1,977,200	1,733,865	1,891,559
Distinct words	56,578	41,592	46,056	38,821	92,313	43,383	105,280	41,801

10^9 Word Parallel Corpus

	French ↔ English	
Sentences	22,520,400	
Words	811,203,407	668,412,817
Distinct words	2,738,882	2,861,836

Hunglish Training Corpus

	Hungarian ↔ English	
Sentences	1,517,584	
Words	26,114,985	31,467,693
Distinct words	717,198	192,901

CzEng Training Corpus

	Czech ↔ English	
Sentences	1,096,940	
Words	15,336,783	17,909,979
Distinct words	339,683	129,176

Europarl Language Model Data

	English	Spanish	French	German
Sentence	1,658,841	1,607,419	1,676,435	1,713,715
Words	44,983,136	45,382,287	50,577,097	41,457,414
Distinct words	117,577	162,604	138,621	348,197

News Language Model Data

	English	Spanish	French	German	Czech	Hungarian
Sentence	21,232,163	1,626,538	6,722,485	10,193,376	5,116,211	4,209,121
Words	504,094,159	48,392,418	167,204,556	185,639,915	81,743,223	86,538,513
Distinct words	1,141,895	358,664	660,123	1,668,387	929,318	1,313,578

News Test Set

	English	Spanish	French	German	Czech	Hungarian	Italian
Sentences	2525						
Words	65,595	68,092	72,554	62,699	55,389	54,464	64,906
Distinct words	8,907	10,631	10,609	12,277	15,387	16,167	11,046

News System Combination Development Set

	English	Spanish	French	German	Czech	Hungarian	Italian
Sentences	502						
Words	11,843	12,499	12,988	11,235	9,997	9,628	11,833
Distinct words	2,940	3,176	3,202	3,471	4,121	4,133	3,318

Figure 1: Statistics for the training and test sets used in the translation task. The number of words is based on the provided tokenizer and the number of distinct words is the based on lowercased tokens.

In addition to cleaning the sentence-aligned parallel corpus we also de-duplicated the corpus, removing all sentence pairs that occured more than once in the parallel corpus. Many of the documents gathered in our web crawl were duplicates or near duplicates, and a lot of the text is repeated, as with web site navigation. We further eliminated sentence pairs that varied from previous sentences by only numbers, which helped eliminate template web pages such as expense reports. We used a Bloom Filter (Talbot and Osborne, 2007) to do de-duplication, so it may have discarded more sentence pairs than strictly necessary. After deduplication, the parallel corpus contained 28 million sentence pairs with 0.8 billion French words and 0.7 billion English words.

Monolingual news corpora

We have crawled the news sources that were the basis of our test sets (and a few more additional sources) since August 2007. This allowed us to assemble large corpora in the target domain to be mainly used as training data for language modeling. We collected texts from the beginning of our data collection period to one month before the test set period, segmented these into sentences and randomized the order of the sentences to obviate copyright concerns.

2.3 Baseline system

To lower the barrier of entry for newcomers to the field, we provided Moses, an open source toolkit for phrase-based statistical translation (Koehn et al., 2007). The performance of this baseline system is similar to the best submissions in last year's shared task. Twelve participating groups used the Moses toolkit for the development of their system.

2.4 Submitted systems

We received submissions from 22 groups from 20 institutions, as listed in Table 1, a similar turnout to last year's shared task. Of the 20 groups that participated with regular system submissions in last year's shared task, 12 groups returned this year. A major hurdle for many was a DARPA/GALE evaluation that occurred at the same time as this shared task.

We also evaluated 7 commercial rule-based MT systems, and Google's online statistical machine translation system. We note that Google did not submit an entry itself. Its entry was created by the WMT09 organizers using Google's online system.[3] In personal correspondence, Franz Och clarified that the online system is different from Google's research system in that it runs at faster speeds at the expense of somewhat lower translation quality. On the other hand, the training data used by Google is unconstrained, which means that it may have an advantage compared to the research systems evaluated in this workshop, since they were trained using only the provided materials.

2.5 System combination

In total, we received 87 primary system submissions along with 42 secondary submissions. These were made available to participants in the system combination shared task. Based on feedback that we received on last year's system combination task, we provided two additional resources to participants:

- Development set: We reserved 25 articles to use as a dev set for system combination (details of the set are given in Table 1). These were translated by all participating sites, and distributed to system combination participants along with reference translations.

- n-best translations: We requested n-best lists from sites whose systems could produce them. We received 25 100-best lists accompanying the primary system submissions, and 5 accompanying the secondary system submissions.

In addition to soliciting system combination entries for each of the language pairs, we treated system combination as a way of doing *multi-source* translation, following Schroeder et al. (2009). For the multi-source system combination task, we provided all 46 primary system submissions from any language into English, along with an additional 32 secondary systems.

Table 2 lists the six participants in the system combination task.

3 Human evaluation

As with past workshops, we placed greater emphasis on the human evaluation than on the automatic evaluation metric scores. It is our contention

[3] `http://translate.google.com`

ID	Participant
CMU-STATXFER	Carnegie Mellon University's statistical transfer system (Hanneman et al., 2009)
COLUMBIA	Columbia University (Carpuat, 2009)
CU-BOJAR	Charles University Bojar (Bojar et al., 2009)
CU-TECTOMT	Charles University Tectogramatical MT (Bojar et al., 2009)
DCU	Dublin City University (Du et al., 2009)
EUROTRANXP	commercial MT provider from the Czech Republic
GENEVA	University of Geneva (Wehrli et al., 2009)
GOOGLE	Google's production system
JHU	Johns Hopkins University (Li et al., 2009)
JHU-TROMBLE	Johns Hopkins University Tromble (Eisner and Tromble, 2006)
LIMSI	LIMSI (Allauzen et al., 2009)
LIU	Linköping University (Holmqvist et al., 2009)
LIUM-SYSTRAN	University of Le Mans / Systran (Schwenk et al., 2009)
MORPHO	Morphologic (Novák, 2009)
NICT	National Institute of Information and Comm. Tech., Japan (Paul et al., 2009)
NUS	National University of Singapore (Nakov and Ng, 2009)
PCTRANS	commercial MT provider from the Czech Republic
RBMT1-5	commercial systems from Learnout&Houspie, Lingenio, Lucy, PROMT, SDL
RWTH	RWTH Aachen (Popovic et al., 2009)
STUTTGART	University of Stuttgart (Fraser, 2009)
SYSTRAN	Systran (Dugast et al., 2009)
TALP-UPC	Universitat Politecnica de Catalunya, Barcelona (R. Fonollosa et al., 2009)
UEDIN	University of Edinburgh (Koehn and Haddow, 2009)
UKA	University of Karlsruhe (Niehues et al., 2009)
UMD	University of Maryland (Dyer et al., 2009)
USAAR	University of Saarland (Federmann et al., 2009)

Table 1: Participants in the shared translation task. Not all groups participated in all language pairs.

ID	Participant
BBN-COMBO	BBN system combination (Rosti et al., 2009)
CMU-COMBO	Carnegie Mellon University system combination (Heafield et al., 2009)
CMU-COMBO-HYPOSEL	CMU system comb. with hyp. selection (Hildebrand and Vogel, 2009)
DCU-COMBO	Dublin City University system combination
RWTH-COMBO	RWTH Aachen system combination (Leusch et al., 2009)
USAAR-COMBO	University of Saarland system combination (Chen et al., 2009)

Table 2: Participants in the system combination task.

Language Pair	Sentence Ranking	Edited Translations	Yes/No Judgments
German-English	3,736	1,271	4,361
English-German	3,700	823	3,854
Spanish-English	2,412	844	2,599
English-Spanish	1,878	278	837
French-English	3,920	1,145	4,491
English-French	1,968	332	1,331
Czech-English	1,590	565	1,071
English-Czech	7,121	2,166	9,460
Hungarian-English	1,426	554	1,309
All-English	4,807	0	0
Multisource-English	2,919	647	2184
Totals	**35,786**	**8,655**	**31,524**

Table 3: The number of items that were judged for each task during the manual evaluation.

that automatic measures are an imperfect substitute for human assessment of translation quality. Therefore, we define the manual evaluation to be primary, and use the human judgments to validate automatic metrics.

Manual evaluation is time consuming, and it requires a large effort to conduct it on the scale of our workshop. We distributed the workload across a number of people, including shared-task participants, interested volunteers, and a small number of paid annotators. More than 160 people participated in the manual evaluation, with 100 people putting in more than an hour's worth of effort, and 30 putting in more than four hours. A collective total of 479 hours of labor was invested.

We asked people to evaluate the systems' output in two different ways:

- Ranking translated sentences relative to each other. This was our official determinant of translation quality.

- Editing the output of systems without displaying the source or a reference translation, and then later judging whether edited translations were correct.

The total number of judgments collected for the different modes of annotation is given in Table 3.

In all cases, the output of the various translation outputs were judged on equal footing; the output of system combinations was judged alongside that of the individual system, and the constrained and unconstrained systems were judged together.

3.1 Ranking translations of sentences

Ranking translations relative to each other is a reasonably intuitive task. We therefore kept the instructions simple:

> *Rank translations from Best to Worst relative to the other choices (ties are allowed).*

In our the manual evaluation, annotators were shown at most five translations at a time. For most language pairs there were more than 5 systems submissions. We did not attempt to get a complete ordering over the systems, and instead relied on random selection and a reasonably large sample size to make the comparisons fair.

Relative ranking is our official evaluation metric. Individual systems and system combinations are ranked based on how frequently they were judged to be better than or equal to any other system. The results of this are reported in Section 4. Appendix A provides detailed tables that contain pairwise comparisons between systems.

3.2 Editing machine translation output

We experimented with a new type of evaluation this year where we asked judges to edit the output of MT systems. We did not show judges the reference translation, which makes our edit-based evaluation different than the Human-targeted Translation Error Rate (HTER) measure used in the DARPA GALE program (NIST, 2008). Rather than asking people to make the minimum number of changes to the MT output in order capture the same meaning as the reference, we asked them to edit the translation to be as fluent as possible without seeing the reference. Our hope was that this would reflect people's understanding of the output.

The instructions that we gave our judges were the following:

> *Correct the translation displayed, making it as fluent as possible. If no corrections are needed, select "No corrections needed." If you cannot understand the sentence well enough to correct it, select "Unable to correct."*

Each translated sentence was shown in isolation without any additional context. A screenshot is shown in Figure 2.

Since we wanted to prevent judges from seeing the reference before editing the translations, we split the test set between the sentences used in the ranking task and the editing task (because they were being conducted concurrently). Moreover, annotators edited only a single system's output for one source sentence to ensure that their understanding of it would not be influenced by another system's output.

3.3 Judging the acceptability of edited output

Halfway through the manual evaluation period, we stopped collecting edited translations, and instead asked annotators to do the following:

> *Indicate whether the edited translations represent fully fluent and meaning-equivalent alternatives to the reference sentence. The reference is shown with context, the actual sentence is* **bold**.

In addition to edited translations, unedited items that were either marked as acceptable or as incomprehensible were also shown. Judges gave a simple yes/no indication to each item. A screenshot is shown in Figure 3.

3.4 Inter- and Intra-annotator agreement

In order to measure intra-annotator agreement 10% of the items were repeated and evaluated twice by each judge. In order to measure inter-annotator agreement 40% of the items were randomly drawn from a common pool that was shared across all annotators so that we would have items that were judged by multiple annotators.

INTER-ANNOTATOR AGREEMENT

Evaluation type	$P(A)$	$P(E)$	K
Sentence ranking	.549	.333	.323
Yes/no to edited output	.774	.5	.549

INTRA-ANNOTATOR AGREEMENT

Evaluation type	$P(A)$	$P(E)$	K
Sentence ranking	.707	.333	.561
Yes/no to edited output	.866	.5	.732

Table 4: Inter- and intra-annotator agreement for the two types of manual evaluation

We measured pairwise agreement among annotators using the kappa coefficient (K) which is defined as

$$K = \frac{P(A) - P(E)}{1 - P(E)}$$

where $P(A)$ is the proportion of times that the annotators agree, and $P(E)$ is the proportion of time that they would agree by chance.

For inter-annotator agreement we calculated $P(A)$ for the yes/no judgments by examining all items that were annotated by two or more annotators, and calculating the proportion of time they assigned identical scores to the same items. For the ranking tasks we calculated $P(A)$ by examining all pairs of systems which had been judged by two or more judges, and calculated the proportion of time that they agreed that $A > B$, $A = B$, or $A < B$. Intra-annotator agreement was computed similarly, but we gathered items that were annotated on multiple occasions by a single annotator.

Table 4 gives K values for inter-annotator and intra-annotator agreement. These give an indication of how often different judges agree, and how often single judges are consistent for repeated judgments, respectively. The interpretation of Kappa varies, but according to Landis and Koch (1977), $0 - .2$ is slight, $.2 - .4$ is fair, $.4 - .6$ is moderate, $.6 - .8$ is substantial and the rest almost perfect.

Based on these interpretations the agreement for yes/no judgments is *moderate* for inter-annotator agreement and *substantial* for intra-annotator agreement, but the inter-annotator agreement for sentence level ranking is only *fair*.

We analyzed two possible strategies for improving inter-annotator agreement on the ranking task: First, we tried discarding initial judgments to give

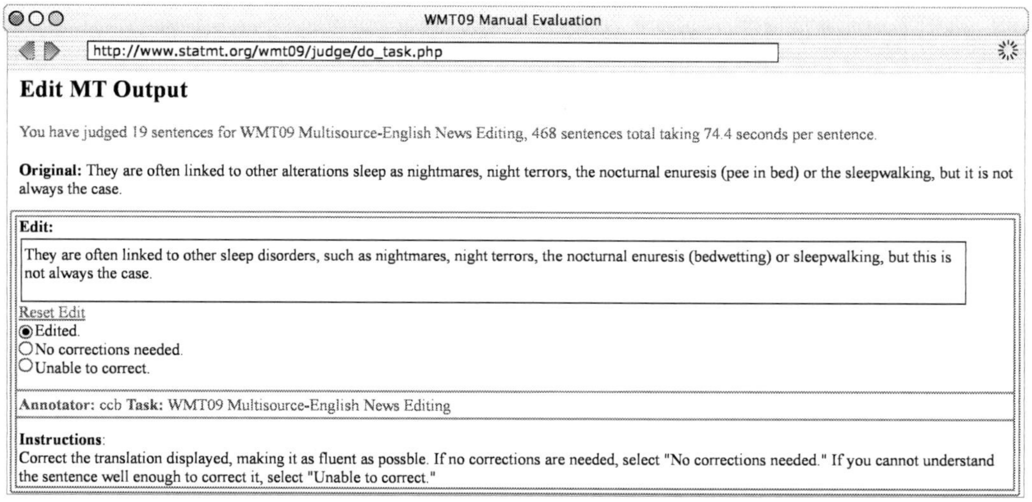

Figure 2: This screenshot shows an annotator editing the output of a machine translation system.

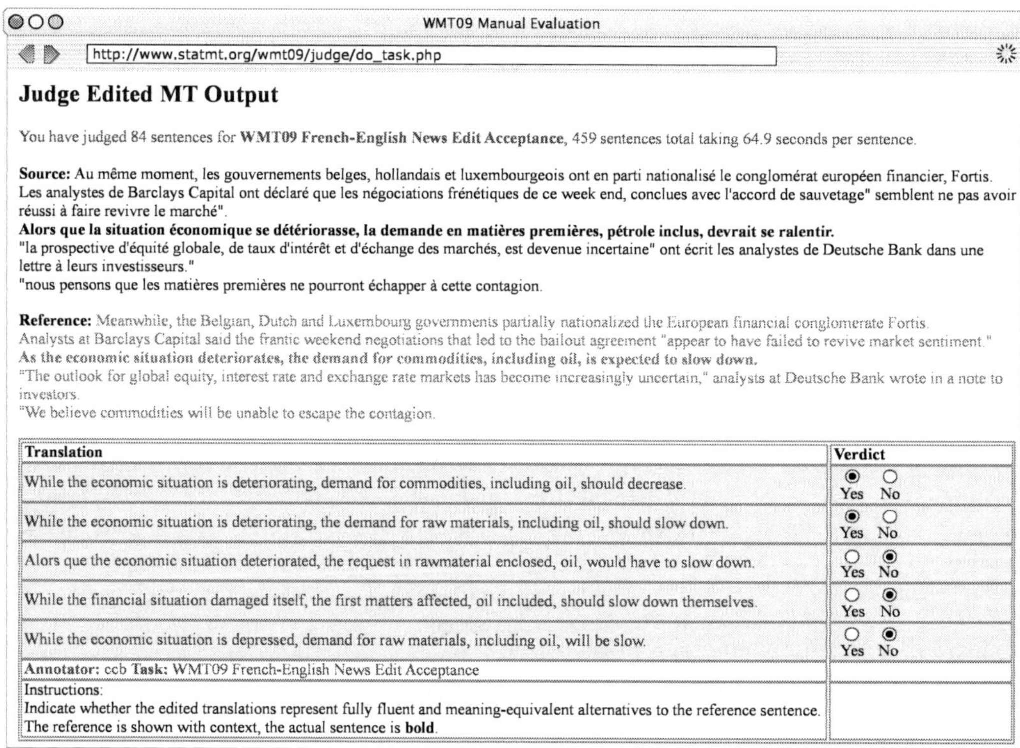

Figure 3: This screenshot shows an annotator judging the acceptability of edited translations.

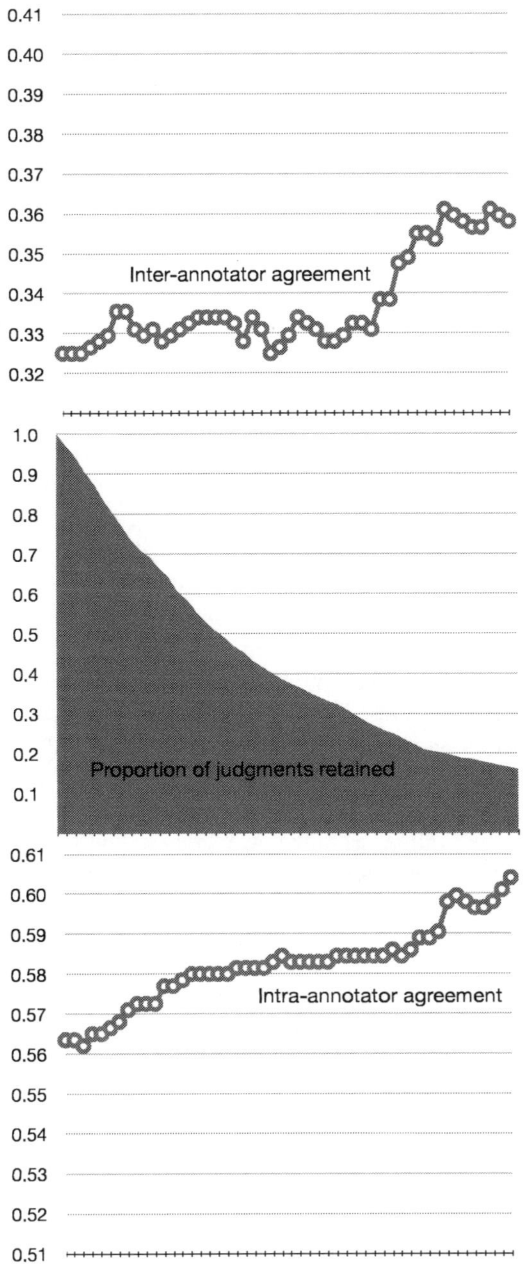

Figure 4: The effect of discarding every annotators' initial judgments, up to the first 50 items

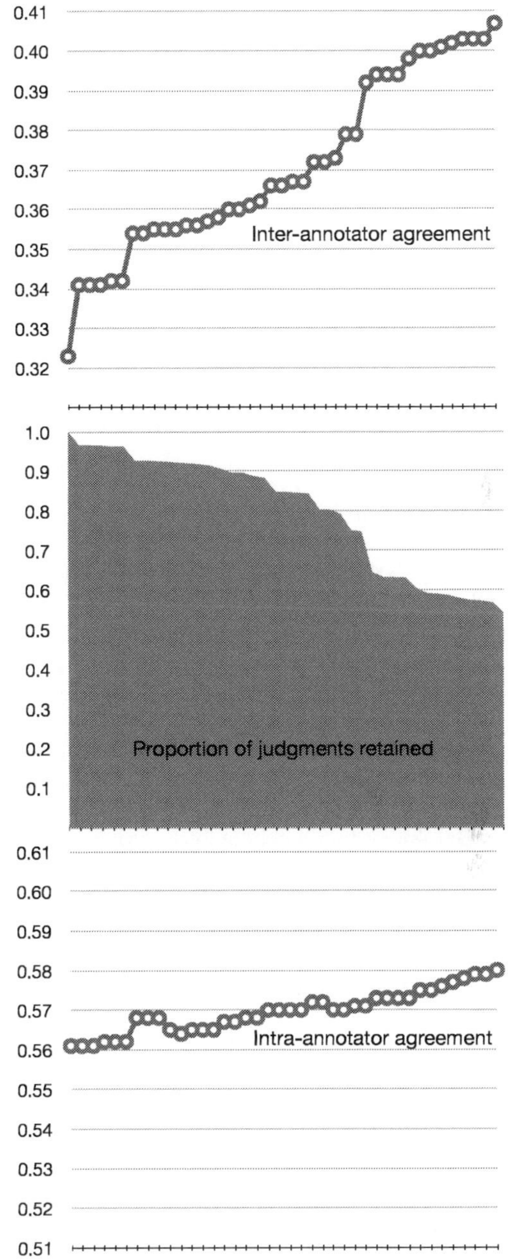

Figure 5: The effect of removing annotators with the lowest agreement, disregarding up to 40 annotators

annotators a chance to learn to how to perform the task. Second, we tried disregarding annotators who have very low agreement with others, by throwing away judgments for the annotators with the lowest judgments.

Figures 4 and 5 show how the K values improve for intra- and inter-annotator agreement under these two strategies, and what percentage of the judgments are retained as more annotators are removed, or as the initial learning period is made longer. It seems that the strategy of removing the worst annotators is the best in terms of improving inter-annotator K, while retaining most of the judgments. If we remove the 33 judges with the worst agreement, we increase the inter-annotator K from *fair* to *moderate*, and still retain 60% of the data.

For the results presented in the rest of the paper, we retain all judgments.

4 Translation task results

We used the results of the manual evaluation to analyze the translation quality of the different systems that were submitted to the workshop. In our analysis, we aimed to address the following questions:

- Which systems produced the best translation quality for each language pair?
- Did the system combinations produce better translations than individual systems?
- Which of the systems that used only the provided training materials produced the best translation quality?

Table 6 shows best individual systems. We define the best systems as those which had no other system that was statistically significantly better than them under the Sign Test at $p \leq 0.1$.[4] Multiple systems are listed for many language pairs because it was not possible to draw a statistically significant difference between the systems. Commercial translation software (including Google, Systran, Morphologic, PCTrans, Eurotran XP, and anonymized RBMT providers) did well in each of the language pairs. Research systems that utilized only the provided data did as well as commercial vendors in half of the language pairs.

The table also lists the best systems among those which used only the provided materials. To determine this decision we excluded *unconstrained systems* which employed significant external resources. Specifically, we ruled out all of the commercial systems, since Google has access to significantly greater data sources for its statistical system, and since the commercial RBMT systems utilize knowledge sources not available to other workshop participants. The remaining systems were research systems that employ statistical models. We were able to draw distinctions between half of these for each of the language pairs. There are some borderline cases, for instance LIMSI only used additional monolingual training resources, and LIUM/Systran used additional translation dictionaries as well as additional monolingual resources.

Table 5 summarizes the performance of the system combination entries by listing the best ranked combinations, and by indicating whether they have a statistically significant difference with the best individual systems. In general, system combinations performed as well as the best individual systems, but not statistically significantly better than them. Moreover, it was hard to draw a distinction between the different system combination strategies themselves. There are a number of possibilities as to why we failed to find significant differences:

- The number of judgments that we collected were not sufficient to find a difference. Although we collected several thousand judgments for each language pair, most pairs of systems were judged together fewer than 100 times.
- It is possible that the best performing individual systems were sufficiently better than the other systems and that it is difficult to improve on them by combining them.
- Individual systems could have been weighted incorrectly during the development stage, which could happen if the automatic evaluation metrics scores on the dev set did not strongly correlate with human judgments.
- The lack of distinction between different combinations could be due to the fact that

[4] In one case this definition meant that the system that was ranked the highest overall was not considered to be one of the best systems. For German-English translation RBMT5 was ranked highest overall, but was statistically significantly worse than RBMT2.

Language Pair	Best system combinations	Entries	Significantly different than best individual systems?
German-English	RWTH-COMBO, BBN-COMBO, CMU-COMBO, USAAR-COMBO	5	BBN-COMBO>GOOGLE, SYSTRAN, USAAR-COMBO<RMBT2, no difference for others
English-German	USAAR-COMBO	1	worse than 3 best systems
Spanish-English	CMU-COMBO, USAAR-COMBO, BBN-COMBO	3	each better than one of the RBMT systems, but there was no difference with GOOGLE, TALP-UPC
English-Spanish	USAAR-COMBO	1	no difference
French-English	CMU-COMBO-HYPOSEL, DCU-COMBO, CMU-COMBO	5	no difference
English-French	USAAR-COMBO, DCU-COMBO	2	USAAR-COMBO>UKA, DCU-COMBO>SYSTRAN, LIMSI, no difference with others
Czech-English	CMU-COMBO	2	no difference
Hungarian-English	CMU-COMBO-HYPOSEL, CMU-COMBO	3	both worse than MORPHO
Multisource-English	RWTH-COMBO	3	n/a

Table 5: A comparison between the best system combinations and the best individual systems. It was generally difficult to draw a statistically significant differences between the two groups, and between the combinations themselves.

there is significant overlap in the strategies that they employ.

Improved system combination warrants further investigation. We would suggest collecting additional judgments, and doing oracle experiments where the contributions of individual systems are weighted according to human judgments of their quality.

Understandability

Our hope is that judging the acceptability of edited output as discussed in Section 3 gives some indication of how often a system's output was understandable. Figure 6 gives the percentage of times that each system's edited output was judged to be acceptable (the percentage also factors in instances when judges were unable to improve the output because it was incomprehensible).

The edited output of the best performing systems under this evaluation model were deemed acceptable around 50% of the time for French-English, English-French, English-Spanish, German-English, and English-German. For Spanish-English the edited output of the best system was acceptable around 40% of the time, for English-Czech it was 30% and for Czech-English and Hungarian-English it was around 20%.

This style of manual evaluation is experimental and should not be taken to be authoritative. Some caveats about this measure:

- Editing translations without context is difficult, so the acceptability rate is probably an underestimate of how understandable a system actually is.
- There are several sources of variance that are difficult to control for: some people are better at editing, and some sentences are more difficult to edit. Therefore, variance in the understandability of systems is difficult to pin down.
- The acceptability measure does not strongly correlate with the more established method of ranking translations relative to each other for all the language pairs.[5]

Please also note that the number of corrected translations per system are very low for some language pairs, as low as 23 corrected sentences per system for the language pair English–French.

[5]The Spearman rank correlation coefficients for how the two types of manual evaluation rank systems are .67 for de-en, .67 for fr-en, .06 for es-en, .50 for cz-en, .36 for hu-en, .65 for en-de, .02 for en-fr, -.6 for en-es, and .94 for en-cz.

French–English
625–836 judgments per system

System	C?	≥others
GOOGLE •	no	.76
DCU ⋆	yes	.66
LIMSI •	no	.65
JHU ⋆	yes	.62
UEDIN ⋆	yes	.61
UKA	yes	.61
LIUM-SYSTRAN	no	.60
RBMT5	no	.59
CMU-STATXFER ⋆	yes	.58
RBMT1	no	.56
USAAR	no	.55
RBMT3	no	.54
RWTH ⋆	yes	.52
COLUMBIA	yes	.50
RBMT4	no	.47
GENEVA	no	.34

English–French
422–517 judgments per system

System	C?	≥others
LIUM-SYSTRAN •	no	.73
GOOGLE •	no	.68
UKA •⋆	yes	.66
SYSTRAN •	no	.65
RBMT3 •	no	.65
DCU •⋆	yes	.65
LIMSI •	no	.64
UEDIN ⋆	yes	.60
RBMT4	no	.59
RWTH	yes	.58
RBMT5	no	.57
RBMT1	no	.54
USAAR	no	.48
GENEVA	no	.38

Hungarian–English
865–988 judgments per system

System	C?	≥others
MORPHO •	no	.75
UMD ⋆	yes	.66
UEDIN	yes	.45

German–English
651–867 judgments per system

System	C?	≥others
RBMT5	no	.66
USAAR •	no	.65
GOOGLE •	no	.65
RBMT2 •	no	.64
RBMT3	no	.64
RBMT4	no	.62
STUTTGART •⋆	yes	.61
SYSTRAN •	no	.60
UEDIN ⋆	yes	.59
UKA ⋆	yes	.58
UMD ⋆	yes	.56
RBMT1	no	.54
LIU ⋆	yes	.50
RWTH	yes	.50
GENEVA	no	.33
JHU-TROMBLE	yes	.13

English–German
977–1226 judgments per system

System	C?	≥others
RBMT2 •	no	.66
RBMT3 •	no	.64
RBMT5 •	no	.64
USAAR	no	.58
RBMT4	no	.58
RBMT1	no	.57
GOOGLE	no	.54
UKA ⋆	yes	.54
UEDIN ⋆	yes	.51
LIU ⋆	yes	.49
RWTH ⋆	yes	.48
STUTTGART	yes	.43

Czech–English
1257–1263 judgments per system

System	C?	≥others
GOOGLE •	no	.75
UEDIN ⋆	yes	.57
CU-BOJAR ⋆	yes	.51

Spanish–English
613–801 judgments per system

System	C?	≥others
GOOGLE •	no	.70
TALP-UPC •⋆	yes	.59
UEDIN ⋆	yes	.56
RBMT1 •	no	.55
RBMT3 •	no	.55
RBMT5 •	no	.55
RBMT4 •	no	.53
RWTH ⋆	yes	.51
USAAR	no	.51
NICT	yes	.37

English–Spanish
632–746 judgments per system

System	C?	≥others
RBMT3 •	no	.66
UEDIN •⋆	yes	.66
GOOGLE •	no	.65
RBMT5 •	no	.64
RBMT4	no	.61
NUS ⋆	yes	.59
TALP-UPC	yes	.58
RWTH	yes	.51
RBMT1	no	.25
USAAR	no	.48

English–Czech
4626–4784 judgments per system

System	C?	≥others
PCTRANS •	no	.67
EUROTRANXP •	no	.67
GOOGLE	no	.66
CU-BOJAR ⋆	yes	.61
UEDIN	yes	.53
CU-TECTOMT	yes	.48

Systems are listed in the order of how often their translations were ranked higher than or equal to any other system. Ties are broken by direct comparison.

C? indicates constrained condition, meaning only using the supplied training data and possibly standard monolingual linguistic tools (but no additional corpora).

• indicates a **win** in the category, meaning that no other system is statistically significantly better at p-level≤0.1 in pairwise comparison.

⋆ indicates a **constrained win**, no other constrained system is statistically better.

For all pairwise comparisons between systems, please check the appendix.

Table 6: Official results for the WMT09 translation task, based on the human evaluation (ranking translations relative to each other)

Given these low numbers, the numbers presented in Figure 6 should not be read as comparisons between systems, but rather viewed as indicating the state of machine translation for different language pairs.

5 Shared evaluation task overview

In addition to allowing us to analyze the translation quality of different systems, the data gathered during the manual evaluation is useful for validating the automatic evaluation metrics. Last year, NIST began running a similar "Metrics for MAchine TRanslation" challenge (MetricsMATR), and presented their findings at a workshop at AMTA (Przybocki et al., 2008).

In this year's shared task we evaluated a number of different automatic metrics:

- Bleu (Papineni et al., 2002)—Bleu remains the *de facto* standard in machine translation evaluation. It calculates n-gram precision and a brevity penalty, and can make use of multiple reference translations as a way of capturing some of the allowable variation in translation. We use a single reference translation in our experiments.

- Meteor (Agarwal and Lavie, 2008)—Meteor measures precision and recall for unigrams and applies a fragmentation penalty. It uses flexible word matching based on stemming and WordNet-synonymy. meteor-ranking is optimized for correlation with ranking judgments.

- Translation Error Rate (Snover et al., 2006)—TER calculates the number of edits required to change a hypothesis translation into a reference translation. The possible edits in TER include insertion, deletion, and substitution of single words, and an edit which moves sequences of contiguous words. Two variants of TER are also included: TERp (Snover et al., 2009), a new version which introduces a number of different features, and $(\text{Bleu} - \text{TER})/2$, a combination of Bleu and Translation Edit Rate.

- MaxSim (Chan and Ng, 2008)—MaxSim calculates a similarity score by comparing items in the translation against the reference. Unlike most metrics which do strict matching, MaxSim computes a similarity score for non-identical items. To find a maximum weight matching that matches each system item to at most one reference item, the items are then modeled as nodes in a bipartite graph.

- wcd6p4er (Leusch and Ney, 2008)—a measure based on cder with word-based substitution costs. Leusch and Ney (2008) also submitted two contrastive metrics: bleusp4114, a modified version of BLEU-S (Lin and Och, 2004), with tuned n-gram weights, and bleusp, with constant weights. wcd6p4er is an error measure and bleusp is a quality score.

- RTE (Pado et al., 2009)—The RTE metric follows a semantic approach which applies recent work in *rich textual entailment* to the problem of MT evaluation. Its predictions are based on a regression model over a feature set adapted from an entailment systems. The features primarily model alignment quality and (mis-)matches of syntactic and semantic structures.

- ULC (Giménez and Màrquez, 2008)—ULC is an arithmetic mean over other automatic metrics. The set of metrics used include Rouge, Meteor, measures of overlap between constituent parses, dependency parses, semantic roles, and discourse representations. The ULC metric had the strongest correlation with human judgments in WMT08 (Callison-Burch et al., 2008).

- wpF and wpBleu (Popovic and Ney, 2009) - These metrics are based on *w*ords and *p*art of speech sequences. wpF is an n-gram based F-measure which takes into account both word n-grams and part of speech n-grams. wpBLEU is a combnination of the normal Blue score and a part of speech-based Bleu score.

- SemPOS (Kos and Bojar, 2009) – the SemPOS metric computes overlapping words, as defined in (Giménez and Màrquez, 2007), with respect to their semantic part of speech. Moreover, it does not use the surface representation of words but their underlying forms obtained from the TectoMT framework.

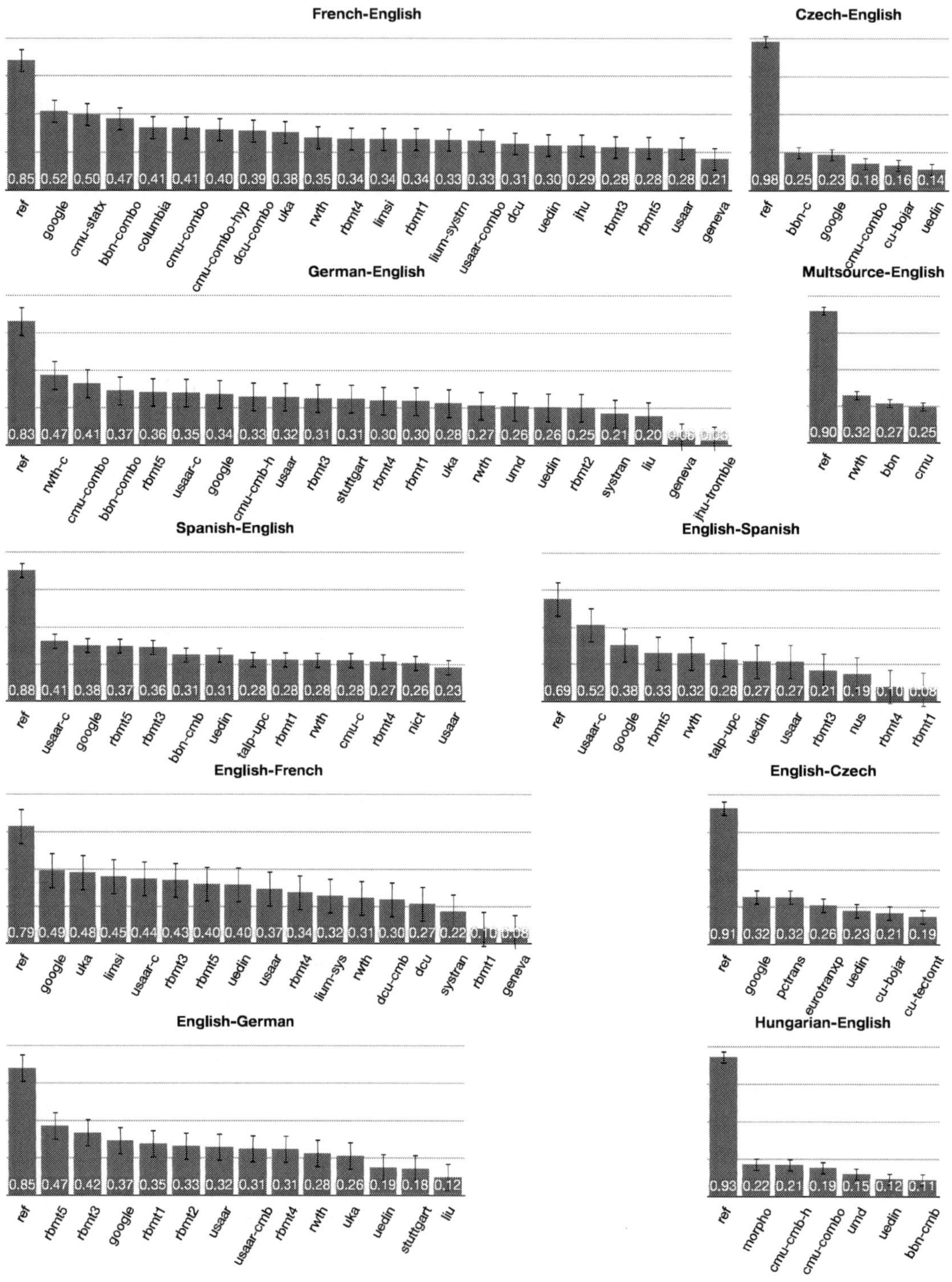

Figure 6: The percent of time that each system's edited output was judged to be an acceptable translation. These numbers also include judgments of the system's output when it was marked either *incomprehensible* or *acceptable* and left unedited. Note that the reference translation was edited alongside the system outputs. Error bars show one positive and one negative standard deviation for the systems in that language pair.

5.1 Measuring system-level correlation

We measured the correlation of the automatic metrics with the human judgments of translation quality at the system-level using Spearman's rank correlation coefficient ρ. We converted the raw scores assigned to each system into ranks. We assigned a human ranking to the systems based on the percent of time that their translations were judged to be better than or equal to the translations of any other system in the manual evaluation.

When there are no ties ρ can be calculated using the simplified equation:

$$\rho = 1 - \frac{6 \sum d_i^2}{n(n^2 - 1)}$$

where d_i is the difference between the rank for system_i and n is the number of systems. The possible values of ρ range between 1 (where all systems are ranked in the same order) and -1 (where the systems are ranked in the reverse order). Thus an automatic evaluation metric with a higher absolute value for ρ is making predictions that are more similar to the human judgments than an automatic evaluation metric with a lower absolute ρ.

	de-en (21 systems)	fr-en (21 systems)	es-en (13 systems)	cz-en (5 systems)	hu-en (6 systems)	Average
ulc	**.78**	.92	.86	**1**	.6	**.83**
maxsim	.76	.91	**.98**	.7	.66	.8
rte (absolute)	.64	.91	.96	.6	**.83**	.79
meteor-rank	.64	**.93**	.96	.7	.54	.75
rte (pairwise)	.76	.59	.78	.8	**.83**	.75
terp	-.72	-.89	-.94	-.7	-.37	-.72
meteor-0.6	.56	**.93**	.87	.7	.54	.72
meteor-0.7	.55	**.93**	.86	.7	.26	.66
bleu-ter/2	.38	.88	.78	.9	-.03	.58
nist	.41	.87	.75	.9	-.14	.56
wpF	.42	.87	.82	**1**	-.31	.56
ter	-.43	-.83	-.84	-.6	-.01	-.54
nist (cased)	.42	.83	.75	**1**	-.31	.54
bleu	.41	.88	.79	.6	-.14	.51
bleusp	.39	.88	.78	.6	-.09	.51
bleusp4114	.39	.89	.78	.6	-.26	.48
bleu (cased)	.4	.86	.8	.6	-.31	.47
wpbleu	.43	.86	.8	.7	-.49	.46
wcd6p4er	-.41	-.89	-.76	-.6	.43	-.45

Table 7: The system-level correlation of the automatic evaluation metrics with the human judgments for translation into English.

5.2 Measuring sentence-level consistency

Because the sentence-level judgments collected in the manual evaluation are relative judgments rather than absolute judgments, it is not possible for us to measure correlation at the sentence-level in the same way that previous work has done (Kulesza and Shieber, 2004; Albrecht and Hwa, 2007a; Albrecht and Hwa, 2007b).

Rather than calculating a correlation coefficient at the sentence-level we instead ascertained how consistent the automatic metrics were with the human judgments. The way that we calculated consistency was the following: for every pairwise comparison of two systems on a single sentence by a person, we counted the automatic metric as being consistent if the relative scores were the same (i.e. the metric assigned a higher score to the higher ranked system). We divided this by the total number of pairwise comparisons to get a percentage. Because the systems generally assign real numbers as scores, we excluded pairs that the human annotators ranked as ties.

	en-de (13 systems)	en-fr (16 systems)	en-es (11 systems)	en-cz (5 systems)	Average
terp	.03	-.89	-.58	**-.4**	**-.46**
ter	-.03	-.78	-.5	-.1	-.35
bleusp4114	-.3	.88	.51	.1	.3
bleusp	-.3	.87	.51	.1	.29
bleu	-.43	.87	.36	.3	.27
bleu (cased)	-.45	.87	.35	.3	.27
bleu-ter/2	-.37	.87	.44	.1	.26
wcd6p4er	.54	-.89	-.45	-.1	-.22
nist (cased)	-.47	.84	.35	.1	.2
nist	-.52	.87	.23	.1	.17
wpF	-.06	.9	.58	*n/a*	*n/a*
wpbleu	**.07**	**.92**	**.63**	*n/a*	*n/a*

Table 8: The system-level correlation of the automatic evaluation metrics with the human judgments for translation out of English.

SemPOS	.4	BLEU_{tecto}	.3
Meteor	.4	BLEU	.3
$\text{GTM(e=0.5)}_{tecto}$	.4	NIST_{lemma}	.1
$\text{GTM(e=0.5)}_{lemma}$	.4	NIST	.1
GTM(e=0.5)	.4	BLEU_{lemma}	.1
WER_{tecto}	.3	WER_{lemma}	-.1
TER_{tecto}	.3	WER	-.1
PER_{tecto}	.3	TER_{lemma}	-.1
F-measure_{tecto}	.3	TER	-.1
F-measure_{lemma}	.3	PER_{lemma}	-.1
F-measure	.3	PER	-.1
		NIST_{tecto}	-.3

Table 9: The system-level correlation for automatic metrics ranking five English-Czech systems

6 Evaluation task results

6.1 System-level correlation

Table 7 shows the correlation of automatic metrics when they rank systems that are translating into English. Note that TERp, TER and wcd6p4er are error metrics, so a negative correlation is better for them. The strength of correlation varied for the different language pairs. The automatic metrics were able to rank the French-English systems reasonably well with correlation coefficients in the range of .8 and .9. In comparison, metrics performed worse for Hungarian-English, where half of the systems had negative correlation. The ULC metric once again had strongest correlation with human judgments of translation quality. This was followed closely by MaxSim and RTE, with Meteor and TERp doing respectably well in 4th and 5th place. Notably, Bleu and its variants were the worst performing metrics in this translation direction.

Table 8 shows correlation for metrics which operated on languages other than English. Most of the best performing metrics that operate on English do not work for foreign languages, because they perform some linguistic analysis or rely on a resource like WordNet. For translation into foreign languages TERp was the best system overall. The wpBleu and wpF metrics also did extremely well, performing the best in the language pairs that they were applied to. wpBleu and wpF were not applied to Czech because the authors of the metric did not have a Czech tagger. English-German proved to be the most problematic language pair to automatically evaluate, with all of the metrics having a negative correlation except wpBleu and TER.

Table 9 gives detailed results for how well variations on a number of automatic metrics do for the task of ranking five English-Czech systems.[6] These systems were submitted by Kos and Bojar (2009), and they investigate the effects of using Prague Dependency Treebank annotations during automatic evaluation. They linearizing the Czech trees and evaluated either the lemmatized forms of the Czech (*lemma*) read off the trees or the Tectogrammatical form which retained only lemmatized content words (*tecto*). The table also demonstrates SemPOS, Meteor, and GTM perform better on Czech than many other metrics.

6.2 Sentence-level consistency

Tables 10 and 11 show the percent of times that the metrics' scores were consistent with human rankings of every pair of translated sentences.[7] Since we eliminated sentence pairs that were judged to be equal, the random baseline for this task is 50%. Many metrics failed to reach the baseline (including most metrics in the out-of-English direction). This indicates that sentence-level evaluation of machine translation quality is very difficult. RTE and ULC again do the best overall for the into-English direction. They are followed closely by wpF and wcd6p4er, which considerably improve their performance over their system-level correlations.

We tried a variant on measuring sentence-level consistency. Instead of using the scores assigned to each individual sentence, we used the system-level score and applied it to every sentence that was produced by that system. These can be thought of as a metric's prior expectation about how a system should preform, based on their performance on the whole data set. Tables 12 and 13 show that using the system-level scores in place of the sentence-level scores results in considerably higher consistency with human judgments. This suggests an interesting line of research for improving sentence-level predictions by using the performance on a larger data set as a prior.

7 Summary

As in previous editions of this workshop we carried out an extensive manual and automatic evaluation of machine translation performance for translating from European languages into English,

[6] PCTRANS was excluded from the English-Czech systems because its SGML file was malformed.

[7] Not all metrics entered into the sentence-level task.

	fr-en (6268 pairs)	de-en (6382 pairs)	es-en (4106 pairs)	cz-en (2251 pairs)	hu-en (2193 pairs)	xx-en (1952 pairs)	Overall (23152 pairs)
ulc	**.55**	**.56**	.51	.50	.51	.51	**.54**
rte (absolute)	.54	.56	.51	.50	.55	.51	.53
wpF	.54	.55	.50	*.47*	*.48*	.51	.52
wcd6p4er	.54	.54	*.49*	*.48*	*.48*	.50	.52
maxsim	.53	.55	*.49*	*.47*	.50	*.49*	.52
bleusp	.54	.55	*.49*	*.47*	*.46*	.50	.51
bleusp4114	.53	.55	*.48*	*.47*	*.46*	.50	.51
rte (pairwise)	*.49*	*.48*	**.52**	**.53**	.55	**.52**	.51
terp	.52	.53	*.48*	*.46*	*.45*	*.48*	.50
meteor-0.6	.50	.53	*.46*	*.48*	*.47*	*.47*	*.49*
meteor-rank	.50	.52	*.46*	*.48*	*.47*	*.47*	*.49*
meteor-0.7	*.49*	.52	*.46*	*.48*	*.47*	*.47*	*.49*
ter	*.48*	*.47*	*.43*	*.41*	*.40*	*.42*	*.45*
wpbleu	*.46*	*.45*	*.46*	*.39*	*.35*	*.45*	*.44*

Table 10: Sentence-level consistency of the automatic metrics with human judgments for translations into English. Italicized numbers fall below the random-choice baseline.

	en-fr (2967 pairs)	en-de (6563 pairs)	en-es (3249 pairs)	en-cz (11242 pairs)	Overall (24021 pairs)
wcd6p4er	**.57**	*.47*	.52	*.49*	**.50**
bleusp4114	.57	*.46*	.54	*.49*	.50
bleusp	.57	*.46*	.53	*.48*	*.49*
ter	.50	*.41*	*.45*	*.37*	*.41*
terp	.51	*.39*	*.48*	*.27*	*.36*
wpF	.57	*.46*	**.54**	n/a	**.51**
wpbleu	.53	*.37*	*.46*	n/a	*.43*

Table 11: Sentence-level consistency of the automatic metrics with human judgments for translations out of English. Italicized numbers fall below the random-choice baseline.

	fr-en (6268 pairs)	de-en (6382 pairs)	es-en (4106 pairs)	cz-en (2251 pairs)	hu-en (2193 pairs)	Overall (21200 pairs)
Oracle	.61	.63	.59	.61	.67	.62
rte (absolute)	.60	.61	**.59**	.57	**.65**	**.61**
ulc	**.61**	**.62**	.58	**.61**	.59	.60
maxsim	**.61**	**.62**	**.59**	.57	.61	.60
meteor-rank	**.61**	.61	**.59**	.57	.61	.60
meteor-0.6	**.61**	.61	.58	.57	.60	.60
rte (pairwise)	.56	.61	.57	.59	.64	.59
terp	.60	.61	**.59**	.57	.56	.59
meteor-0.7	**.61**	.61	.58	.57	.55	.59
ter	.60	.59	.57	.55	.51	.58
wpF	.60	.59	.57	**.61**	*.46*	.58
bleusp	**.61**	.59	.56	.55	*.48*	.57
bleusp4114	**.61**	.59	.56	.55	.46	.57
wcd6p4er	**.61**	.59	.57	.55	*.44*	.57
wpbleu	.60	.59	.57	.57	*.43*	.57

Table 12: Consistency of the automatic metrics when their system-level ranks are treated as sentence-level scores. Oracle shows the consistency of using the system-level human ranks that are given in Table 6.

	en-fr (2967 pairs)	en-de (6563 pairs)	en-es (3249 pairs)	en-cz (11242 pairs)	Overall (24021 pairs)
Oracle	.62	.59	.63	.60	.60
terp	.62	.50	.59	**.53**	**.54**
ter	.61	**.51**	.58	.50	.53
bleusp	.62	*.48*	.59	.50	.52
bleusp4114	.63	*.48*	.59	.50	.52
wcd6p4er	.62	.46	.58	.50	.52
wpbleu	**.63**	**.51**	**.60**	n/a	**.56**
wpF	**.63**	.50	.59	n/a	.55

Table 13: Consistency of the automatic metrics when their system-level ranks are treated as sentence-level scores. Oracle shows the consistency of using the system-level human ranks that are given in Table 6.

and vice versa.

The number of participants remained stable compared to last year's WMT workshop, with 22 groups from 20 institutions participating in WMT09. This year's evaluation also included 7 commercial rule-based MT systems and Google's online statistical machine translation system.

Compared to previous years, we have simplified the evaluation conditions by removing the in-domain vs. out-of-domain distinction focusing on news translations only. The main reason for this was eliminating the advantage statistical systems have with respect to test data that are from the same domain as the training data.

Analogously to previous years, the main focus of comparing the quality of different approaches is on manual evaluation. Here, also, we reduced the number of dimensions with respect to which the different systems are compared, with sentence-level ranking as the primary type of manual evaluation. In addition to the direct quality judgments we also evaluated translation quality by having people edit the output of systems and have assessors judge the correctness of the edited output. The degree to which users were able to edit the translations (without having access to the source sentence or reference translation) served as a measure of the overall comprehensibility of the translation.

Although the inter-annotator agreement in the sentence-ranking evaluation is only fair (as measured by the Kappa score), agreement can be improved by removing the first (up to 50) judgments of each assessor, focusing on the judgments that were made once the assessors are more familiar with the task. Inter-annotator agreement with respect to correctness judgments of the edited translations were higher (moderate), which is probably due to the simplified evaluation criterion (binary judgments versus rankings). Inter-annotator agreement for both conditions can be increased further by removing the judges with the worst agreement. Intra-annotator agreement on the other hand was considerably higher ranging between moderate and substantial.

In addition to the manual evaluation criteria we applied a large number of automated metrics to see how they correlate with the human judgments. There is considerably variation between the different metrics and the language pairs under consideration. As in WMT08, the ULC metric had the highest overall correlation with human judgments when translating into English, with MaxSim and RTE following closely behind. TERp and wpBleu were best when translating into other languages.

Automatically predicting human judgments at the sentence-level proved to be quite challenging with many of the systems performing around chance. We performed an analysis that showed that if metrics' system-level scores are used in place of their scores for individual sentences, that they do quite a lot better. This suggests that prior probabilities ought to be integrated into sentence-level scoring.

All data sets generated by this workshop, including the human judgments, system translations and automatic scores, are publicly available for other researchers to analyze.[8]

Acknowledgments

This work was supported in parts by the EuroMatrix project funded by the European Commission (6th Framework Programme), the GALE program of the US Defense Advanced Research Projects Agency, Contract No. HR0011-06-C-0022, and the US National Science Foundation under grant IIS-0713448.

We are grateful to Holger Schwenk and Preslav Nakov for pointing out the potential bias in our method for ranking systems when self-judgments are excluded. We analyzed the results and found that this did not hold. We would like to thank Maja Popovic for sharing thoughts about how to improve the manual evaluation. Thanks to Cam Fordyce for helping out with the manual evaluation again this year.

An extremely big thanks to Sebastian Pado for helping us work through the logic of segment-level scoring of automatic evaluation metric.

References

Abhaya Agarwal and Alon Lavie. 2008. Meteor, M-BLEU and M-TER: Evaluation metrics for high-correlation with human rankings of machine translation output. In *Proceedings of the Third Workshop on Statistical Machine Translation*, pages 115–118, Columbus, Ohio, June. Association for Computational Linguistics.

Joshua Albrecht and Rebecca Hwa. 2007a. A re-examination of machine learning approaches for

[8] http://www.statmt.org/wmt09/results.html

sentence-level MT evaluation. In *Proceedings of the 45th Annual Meeting of the Association for Computational Linguistics (ACL-2007)*, Prague, Czech Republic.

Joshua Albrecht and Rebecca Hwa. 2007b. Regression for sentence-level MT evaluation with pseudo references. In *Proceedings of the 45th Annual Meeting of the Association for Computational Linguistics (ACL-2007)*, Prague, Czech Republic.

Alexandre Allauzen, Josep Crego, Aurélien Max, and Fran cois Yvon. 2009. LIMSI's statistical translation systems for WMT'09. In *Proceedings of the Fourth Workshop on Statistical Machine Translation*, Athens, Greece, March. Association for Computational Linguistics.

Ondřej Bojar, David Mareček, Václav Novák, Martin Popel, Jan Ptáček, Jan Rouš, and Zdeněk Žabokrtský. 2009. English-Czech MT in 2008. In *Proceedings of the Fourth Workshop on Statistical Machine Translation*, Athens, Greece, March. Association for Computational Linguistics.

Chris Callison-Burch, Cameron Fordyce, Philipp Koehn, Christof Monz, and Josh Schroeder. 2007. (Meta-) evaluation of machine translation. In *Proceedings of the Second Workshop on Statistical Machine Translation (WMT07)*, Prague, Czech Republic.

Chris Callison-Burch, Cameron Fordyce, Philipp Koehn, Christof Monz, and Josh Schroeder. 2008. Further meta-evaluation of machine translation. In *Proceedings of the Third Workshop on Statistical Machine Translation (WMT08)*, Colmbus, Ohio.

Marine Carpuat. 2009. Toward using morphology in French-English phrase-based SMT. In *Proceedings of the Fourth Workshop on Statistical Machine Translation*, Athens, Greece, March. Association for Computational Linguistics.

Yee Seng Chan and Hwee Tou Ng. 2008. An automatic metric for machine translation evaluation based on maximum similary. In *In the Metrics-MATR Workshop of AMTA-2008*, Honolulu, Hawaii.

Yu Chen, Michael Jellinghaus, Andreas Eisele, Yi Zhang, Sabine Hunsicker, Silke Theison, Christian Federmann, and Hans Uszkoreit. 2009. Combining multi-engine translations with moses. In *Proceedings of the Fourth Workshop on Statistical Machine Translation*, Athens, Greece, March. Association for Computational Linguistics.

Jinhua Du, Yifan He, Sergio Penkale, and Andy Way. 2009. MATREX: The DCU MT system for WMT 2009. In *Proceedings of the Fourth Workshop on Statistical Machine Translation*, Athens, Greece, March. Association for Computational Linguistics.

Loïc Dugast, Jean Senellart, and Philipp Koehn. 2009. Statistical post editing and dictionary extraction: Systran/Edinburgh submissions for ACL-WMT2009. In *Proceedings of the Fourth Workshop on Statistical Machine Translation*, Athens, Greece, March. Association for Computational Linguistics.

Chris Dyer, Hendra Setiawan, Yuval Marton, and Philip Resnik. 2009. The University of Maryland statistical machine translation system for the fourth workshop on machine translation. In *Proceedings of the Fourth Workshop on Statistical Machine Translation*, Athens, Greece, March. Association for Computational Linguistics.

Jason Eisner and Roy W. Tromble. 2006. Local search with very large-scale neighborhoods for optimal permutations in machine translation. In *Proceedings of the Human Language Technology Conference of the North American chapter of the Association for Computational Linguistics (HLT/NAACL-2006)*, New York, New York.

Christian Federmann, Silke Theison, Andreas Eisele, Hans Uszkoreit, Yu Chen, Michael Jellinghaus, and Sabine Hunsicker. 2009. Translation combination using factored word substitution. In *Proceedings of the Fourth Workshop on Statistical Machine Translation*, Athens, Greece, March. Association for Computational Linguistics.

Alexander Fraser. 2009. Experiments in morphosyntactic processing for translating to and from German. In *Proceedings of the Fourth Workshop on Statistical Machine Translation*, Athens, Greece, March. Association for Computational Linguistics.

Jesús Giménez and Lluís Màrquez. 2007. Linguistic features for automatic evaluation of heterogenous MT systems. In *Proceedings of ACL Workshop on Machine Translation.*

Jesús Giménez and Lluís Màrquez. 2008. A smorgasbord of features for automatic MT evaluation. In *Proceedings of the Third Workshop on Statistical Machine Translation*, pages 195–198.

Greg Hanneman, Vamshi Ambati, Jonathan H. Clark, Alok Parlikar, and Alon Lavie. 2009. An improved statistical transfer system for French-English machine translation. In *Proceedings of the Fourth Workshop on Statistical Machine Translation*, Athens, Greece, March. Association for Computational Linguistics.

Kenneth Heafield, Greg Hanneman, and Alon Lavie. 2009. Machine translation system combination with flexible word ordering. In *Proceedings of the Fourth Workshop on Statistical Machine Translation*, Athens, Greece, March. Association for Computational Linguistics.

Almut Silja Hildebrand and Stephan Vogel. 2009. CMU system combination for WMT'09. In *Proceedings of the Fourth Workshop on Statistical Machine Translation*, Athens, Greece, March. Association for Computational Linguistics.

Maria Holmqvist, Sara Stymne, Jody Foo, and Lars Ahrenberg. 2009. Improving alignment for SMT by reordering and augmenting the training corpus. In *Proceedings of the Fourth Workshop on Statistical Machine Translation*, Athens, Greece, March. Association for Computational Linguistics.

Philipp Koehn and Barry Haddow. 2009. Edinburgh's submission to all tracks of the WMT2009 shared task with reordering and speed improvements to Moses. In *Proceedings of the Fourth Workshop on Statistical Machine Translation*, Athens, Greece, March. Association for Computational Linguistics.

Philipp Koehn and Christof Monz. 2006. Manual and automatic evaluation of machine translation between European languages. In *Proceedings of NAACL 2006 Workshop on Statistical Machine Translation*, New York, New York.

Philipp Koehn, Nicola Bertoldi, Ondrej Bojar, Chris Callison-Burch, Alexandra Constantin, Brooke Cowan, Chris Dyer, Marcello Federico, Evan Herbst, Hieu Hoang, Christine Moran, Wade Shen, and Richard Zens. 2007. Open source toolkit for statistical machine translation: Factored translation models and confusion network decoding. CLSP Summer Workshop Final Report WS-2006, Johns Hopkins University.

Kamil Kos and Ondřej Bojar. 2009. Evaluation of Machine Translation Metrics for Czech as the Target Language. *Prague Bulletin of Mathematical Linguistics*, 92. in print.

Alex Kulesza and Stuart M. Shieber. 2004. A learning approach to improving sentence-level MT evaluation. In *Proceedings of the 10th International Conference on Theoretical and Methodological Issues in Machine Translation*, Baltimore, MD, October 4–6.

J. Richard Landis and Gary G. Koch. 1977. The measurement of observer agreement for categorical data. *Biometrics*, 33:159–174.

Gregor Leusch and Hermann Ney. 2008. BLEUSP, PINVWER, CDER: Three improved MT evaluation measures. In *In the Metrics-MATR Workshop of AMTA-2008*, Honolulu, Hawaii.

Gregor Leusch, Evgeny Matusov, and Hermann Ney. 2009. The RWTH system combination system for WMT 2009. In *Proceedings of the Fourth Workshop on Statistical Machine Translation*, Athens, Greece, March. Association for Computational Linguistics.

Zhifei Li, Chris Callison-Burch, Chris Dyer, Juri Ganitkevitch, Sanjeev Khudanpur, Lane Schwartz, Wren Thornton, Jonathan Weese, and Omar Zaidan. 2009. Joshua: An open source toolkit for parsing-based machine translation. In *Proceedings of the Fourth Workshop on Statistical Machine Translation*, Athens, Greece, March. Association for Computational Linguistics.

Chin-Yew Lin and Franz Josef Och. 2004. Automatic evaluation of machine translation quality using longest common subsequence and skip-bigram statistics. In *Proceedings of the 42nd Annual Meeting of the Association for Computational Linguistics (ACL-2004)*, Barcelona, Spain.

Robert C. Moore. 2002. Fast and accurate sentence alignment of bilingual corpora. In *Proceedings of the 5th Biennial Conference of the Association for Machine Translation in the Americas (AMTA-2002)*, Tiburon, California.

Preslav Nakov and Hwee Tou Ng. 2009. NUS at WMT09: Domain adaptation experiments for English-Spanish machine translation of news commentary text. In *Proceedings of the Fourth Workshop on Statistical Machine Translation*, Athens, Greece, March. Association for Computational Linguistics.

Jan Niehues, Teresa Herrmann, Muntsin Kolss, and Alex Waibel. 2009. The Universität Karlsruhe translation system for the EACL-WMT 2009. In *Proceedings of the Fourth Workshop on Statistical Machine Translation*, Athens, Greece, March. Association for Computational Linguistics.

NIST. 2008. Evaluation plan for gale go/no-go phase 3 / phase 3.5 translation evaluations. June 18, 2008.

Attila Novák. 2009. Morphologic's submission for the WMT 2009 shared task. In *Proceedings of the Fourth Workshop on Statistical Machine Translation*, Athens, Greece, March. Association for Computational Linguistics.

Sebastian Pado, Michel Galley, Dan Jurafsky, and Christopher D. Manning. 2009. Machine translation evaluation with textual entailment features. In *Proceedings of the Fourth Workshop on Statistical Machine Translation*, Athens, Greece, March. Association for Computational Linguistics.

Kishore Papineni, Salim Roukos, Todd Ward, and Wei-Jing Zhu. 2002. Bleu: A method for automatic evaluation of machine translation. In *Proceedings of the 40th Annual Meeting of the Association for Computational Linguistics (ACL-2002)*, Philadelphia, Pennsylvania.

Michael Paul, Andrew Finch, and Eiichiro Sumita. 2009. NICT@WMT09: Model adaptation and transliteration for Spanish-English SMT. In *Proceedings of the Fourth Workshop on Statistical Machine Translation*, Athens, Greece, March. Association for Computational Linguistics.

Maja Popovic and Hermann Ney. 2009. Syntax-oriented evaluation measures for machine translation output. In *Proceedings of the Fourth Workshop on Statistical Machine Translation*, Athens, Greece, March. Association for Computational Linguistics.

Maja Popovic, David Vilar, Daniel Stein, Evgeny Matusov, and Hermann Ney. 2009. The RWTH machine translation system for WMT 2009. In *Proceedings of the Fourth Workshop on Statistical Machine Translation*, Athens, Greece, March. Association for Computational Linguistics.

Mark Przybocki, Kay Peterson, and Sebastien Bronsart. 2008. Official results of the NIST 2008 "Metrics for MAchine TRanslation" challenge (MetricsMATR08). http://nist.gov/speech/tests/metricsmatr/2008/results/.

José A. R. Fonollosa, Maxim Khalilov, Marta R. Costa-jussá, José B. Mariño, Carlos A. Henráquez Q., Adolfo Hernández H., and Rafael E. Banchs. 2009. The TALP-UPC phrase-based translation system for EACL-WMT 2009. In *Proceedings of the Fourth Workshop on Statistical Machine Translation*, Athens, Greece, March. Association for Computational Linguistics.

Antti-Veikko Rosti, Bing Zhang, Spyros Matsoukas, and Richard Schwartz. 2009. Incremental hypothesis alignment with flexible matching for building confusion networks: BBN system description for WMT09 system combination task. In *Proceedings of the Fourth Workshop on Statistical Machine Translation*, Athens, Greece, March. Association for Computational Linguistics.

Josh Schroeder, Trevor Cohn, and Philipp Koehn. 2009. Word lattices for multi-source translation. In *12th Conference of the European Chapter of the Association for Computational Linguistics (EACL-2009)*, Athens, Greece.

Holger Schwenk, Sadaf Abdul Rauf, Loic Barrault, and Jean Senellart. 2009. SMT and SPE machine translation systems for WMT'09. In *Proceedings of the Fourth Workshop on Statistical Machine Translation*, Athens, Greece, March. Association for Computational Linguistics.

Matthew Snover, Bonnie Dorr, Richard Schwartz, Linnea Micciulla, and John Makhoul. 2006. A study of translation edit rate with targeted human annotation. In *Proceedings of the 7th Biennial Conference of the Association for Machine Translation in the Americas (AMTA-2006)*, Cambridge, Massachusetts.

Matthew Snover, Nitin Madnani, Bonnie Dorr, and Richard Schwartz. 2009. Fluency, adequacy, or HTER? exploring different human judgments with a tunable MT metric. In *Proceedings of the Fourth Workshop on Statistical Machine Translation*, Athens, Greece, March. Association for Computational Linguistics.

David Talbot and Miles Osborne. 2007. Smoothed Bloom filter language models: Tera-scale lms on the cheap. In *Proceedings of the 2007 Joint Conference on Empirical Methods in Natural Language Processing and Computational Natural Language Learning (EMNLP-CoNLL)*, Prague, Czech Republic.

Eric Wehrli, Luka Nerima, and Yves Scherrer. 2009. Deep linguistic multilingual translation and bilingual dictionaries. In *Proceedings of the Fourth Workshop on Statistical Machine Translation*, Athens, Greece, March. Association for Computational Linguistics.

A Pairwise system comparisons by human judges

Tables 14–24 show pairwise comparisons between systems for each language pair. The numbers in each of the tables' cells indicate the percentage of times that the system in that column was judged to be better than the system in that row. Bolding indicates the winner of the two systems. The difference between 100 and the sum of the complimentary cells is the percent of time that the two systems were judged to be equal.

Because there were so many systems and data conditions the significance of each pairwise comparison needs to be quantified. We applied the Sign Test to measure which comparisons indicate genuine differences (rather than differences that are attributable to chance). In the following tables ⋆ indicates statistical significance at $p \leq 0.10$, † indicates statistical significance at $p \leq 0.05$, and ‡ indicates statistical significance at $p \leq 0.01$, according to the Sign Test.

B Automatic scores

Tables 26 and 25 give the automatic scores for each of the systems.

	GENEVA	GOOGLE	JHU-TROMBLE	LIU	RBMT1	RBMT2	RBMT3	RBMT4	RBMT5	RWTH	STUTTGART	SYSTRAN	UEDIN	UKA	UMD	USAAR	BBN-COMBO	CMU-COMBO	CMU-COMBO-HYPOSEL	RWTH-COMBO	USAAR-COMBO
GENEVA		**.76‡**	.08‡	**.63†**	**.54**	**.69†**	**.73‡**	**.83‡**	**.78‡**	**.49⋆**	**.77‡**	**.75‡**	**.74‡**	**.57†**	**.74‡**	**.69‡**	**.75‡**	**.84‡**	**.60**	**.84‡**	**.71‡**
GOOGLE	.15‡		.03‡	.23†	**.50**	.43	.24†	.39	**.42**	.39	.43	.33	.27⋆	.29⋆	.38	**.48**	**.57⋆**	**.44**	.32	.35	.36
JHU-TROMBLE	**.75‡**	**.90‡**		**.77‡**	**.81‡**	**.84‡**	**.91‡**	**.94‡**	**.88‡**	**.79‡**	**.83‡**	**.83‡**	**.93‡**	**.89‡**	**.92‡**	**.90‡**	**.94‡**	**.90‡**	**.95‡**	**.91‡**	**.83‡**
LIU	.29†	**.65†**	.12‡		**.49**	**.63**	**.63⋆**	**.57**	**.63⋆**	.41	**.49**	**.46**	**.50**	**.49**	**.50**	.41	**.66†**	**.53**	**.59‡**	**.62†**	**.53**
RBMT1	.32	.43	.11‡	.46		.42	**.46**	**.50**	**.61†**	.34	**.46**	**.58**	**.51**	.42	.42	**.56**	**.47**	**.53**	**.49**	**.58**	**.54**
RBMT2	.25†	**.46**	.09‡	.37	**.45**		.33	.45	.23†	.3	.28	.47	.42	.31⋆	.34	.39	**.49**	**.61**	.4	.32	.29⋆
RBMT3	.17‡	**.59†**	.02‡	.26⋆	.35	**.46**		.27	**.45**	.27	.36	.46	**.42**	.43	.26⋆	**.49**	.4	.48	**.58**	.29	.31
RBMT4	.12‡	**.47**	.07‡	.37	.4	.45	**.52**		**.60⋆**	.39	**.39**	**.45**	.39	.31⋆	.29†	.44	**.54**	**.45**	.37	.43	.30
RBMT5	.13‡	.34	.07‡	.30⋆	.24†	**.57†**	.41	.29⋆		.31	**.50**	.34	.3	.28†	.43	.30	**.49**	**.57**	.3	**.49**	.21
RWTH	.21⋆	**.55**	.10‡	.41	**.49**	**.55**	**.46**	**.46**	**.60**		**.44**	**.57**	**.48**	**.51⋆**	**.41**	**.56**	**.64‡**	**.54**	**.56⋆**	**.74‡**	**.59⋆**
STUTTGART	.17‡	.43	.13‡	.39	.43	**.55**	**.39**	.36	.33	.34		.38	**.42**	**.52**	**.42**	**.49**	**.49**	.28	.35	**.56**	**.46**
SYSTRAN	.11‡	**.63**	.06‡	.42	.37	.47	**.50**	.32	**.58**	.34	**.55**		.36	**.44**	.35	.43	**.61†**	**.46**	.41	.33	.44
UEDIN	.10‡	**.50⋆**	.03‡	.35	.49	**.46**	.39	**.52**	**.55**	.29	.39	**.52**		.35	.33	**.42**	**.58⋆**	**.43**	**.56**	**.59†**	**.55**
UKA	.29†	**.58⋆**	.04‡	.32	**.47**	**.63⋆**	**.55**	**.54⋆**	**.64†**	.24⋆	.28	.39	**.50**		.29	**.50**	**.48**	.36	**.57⋆**	**.45**	**.45**
UMD	.16‡	**.53**	.08‡	.38	**.49**	**.43**	**.63⋆**	**.68†**	**.49**	.38	.39	**.41**	**.50**	**.49**		**.46**	**.54**	**.44**	.38	**.46**	**.50**
USAAR	.19‡	.44	‡	.41	.34	**.49**	.4	.44	**.33**	.36	.33	**.45**	.39	.32	.41		**.46**	**.41**	.31	.42	.11
BBN-COMBO	.14‡	.31⋆	.06‡	.26†	.44	.44	**.48**	.36	.38	.23‡	.35	.26†	.29⋆	.34	.36	.37		.32	.23†	**.38**	.32
CMU-COMBO	.10‡	.36	.07‡	.37	.37	.36	.48	.40	.30	.28	**.53**	.41	.4	**.43**	.28	.34	**.50**		.33	**.53**	.44
CMU-COMBO-H	.3	**.46**	‡	.10‡	.39	**.43**	.40	**.48**	**.57**	.27⋆	**.41**	**.47**	.28	.26⋆	.38	**.49**	**.65†**	**.46**		.41	**.47**
RWTH-COMBO	.06‡	**.38**	‡	.19†	.36	**.54**	**.43**	.43	.30	.10‡	.33	**.56**	.22†	.27	.23	.42	.32	.31	.41		.29
USAAR-COMBO	.20‡	**.55**	.17‡	.3	.39	**.57⋆**	**.45**	**.59**	**.32**	.27⋆	.33	**.47**	.32	.33	.27	**.16**	**.55**	.44	.4	**.50**	
> OTHERS	.22	.51	.06	.38	.44	.52	.49	.49	.50	.33	.44	.48	.44	.42	.41	.47	**.56**	.48	.46	.51	.43
>= OTHERS	.33	.65	.13	.50	.54	.64	.64	.62	**.66**	.50	.61	.60	.59	.58	.56	.65	.68	.63	.62	**.70**	.62

Table 14: Sentence-level ranking for the WMT09 German-English News Task

	GOOGLE	LIU	RBMT1	RBMT2	RBMT3	RBMT4	RBMT5	RWTH	STUTTGART	UEDIN	UKA	USAAR	USAAR-COMBO
GOOGLE		.34†	**.56**	**.51**	**.55**†	.44	**.56**†	.37	.41	.42	.45	.45	**.43**
LIU	**.58**†		**.62**‡	**.55**†	**.55**⋆	**.61**‡	**.59**†	.37	.38	**.47**	**.43**	**.58**†	.44
RBMT1	.39	.33‡		**.56**†	**.44**	**.50**⋆	**.57**†	.41	.32‡	.37⋆	.35†	.45	.42
RBMT2	.35	.34†	.34†		**.43**	.37⋆	.40	.25‡	.25‡	.31‡	.36†	.37⋆	.32†
RBMT3	.31†	.35⋆	.41	.35		.37⋆	.41	.24‡	.25‡	.33‡	.43	**.49**	.36⋆
RBMT4	**.48**	.33‡	.33⋆	**.56**⋆	**.55**⋆		**.47**	.37	.35†	.34‡	**.45**	**.44**	.38
RBMT5	.36†	.35†	.33†	**.50**	**.53**	.33		.36†	.32‡	.35†	.31‡	.25‡	.32‡
RWTH	**.51**	**.46**	**.50**	**.60**‡	**.65**‡	**.51**	**.60**†		.38	**.47**	**.48**	**.52**	**.54**
STUTTGART	**.50**	**.47**	**.62**‡	**.65**‡	**.64**‡	**.57**†	**.62**‡	**.46**		**.52**†	**.54**†	**.66**‡	**.53**
UEDIN	**.50**	.37	**.53**⋆	**.64**‡	**.62**‡	**.60**‡	**.55**†	.45	.28†		**.41**	**.53**	.35
UKA	**.47**	.42	**.57**†	**.58**†	**.46**	.44	**.62**‡	.35	.32†	.36		**.46**	.41
USAAR	**.46**	.36†	**.46**	**.55**⋆	.42	.42	**.48**‡	.42	.28‡	.39	.44		.41
USAAR-COMBO	.37	**.45**	**.54**	**.55**†	**.55**⋆	**.53**	**.61**‡	.39	.40	**.39**	**.46**	**.52**	
> OTHERS	.44	.38	.48	**.55**	.53	.47	.54	.37	.33	.39	.42	.48	.41
>= OTHERS	.54	.49	.57	**.66**	.64	.58	.64	.48	.43	.51	.54	.58	.52

Table 15: Sentence-level ranking for the WMT09 English-German News Task

	GOOGLE	NICT	RBMT1	RBMT3	RBMT4	RBMT5	RWTH	TALP-UPC	UEDIN	USAAR	BBN-COMBO	CMU-COMBO	USAAR-COMBO
GOOGLE		.21‡	.40	.40	.41	.38	.23‡	.35	.31†	.25‡	**.36**	.14	.21
NICT	**.74**‡		**.52**	**.53**	**.63**‡	**.64**‡	**.55**†	**.61**‡	**.65**‡	**.59**†	**.62**‡	**.78**‡	**.66**‡
RBMT1	**.56**	.40		.34	**.44**	**.46**	.35	**.48**	.42	.42	**.57**†	**.52**	**.54**
RBMT3	.40	.39	**.40**		.34	.36	.42	.4	**.55**	**.50**	**.57**⋆	**.48**	**.62**†
RBMT4	**.55**	.32‡	.41	**.46**		**.47**	.39	**.49**	**.49**	**.48**	**.54**	**.57**⋆	**.54**
RBMT5	**.54**	.30‡	.35	**.44**	.38		.45	**.50**	**.49**	.23	**.51**	**.51**	**.66**‡
RWTH	**.64**‡	.29†	**.50**	**.53**	**.53**	**.49**		**.42**	**.46**	.43	**.44**	**.51**	**.58**‡
TALP-UPC	**.48**	.24‡	.44	**.47**	.41	.36	.39		.36	.32⋆	**.47**	**.45**	**.50**
UEDIN	**.61**†	.16‡	**.48**	.42	.41	.46	.44	**.43**		.44	**.49**	**.51**	**.41**
USAAR	**.69**‡	.28†	**.47**	.44	.38	**.35**	.43	**.60**⋆	**.48**		**.64**†	**.58**‡	**.56**⋆
BBN-COMBO	.35	.20‡	.32†	.36⋆	.39	.37	.36	.39	.32	.31†		**.50**	**.40**
CMU-COMBO	**.19**	.15‡	.33	.39	.32⋆	.37	.36	.31	.37	.21‡	.35		**.31**
USAAR-COMBO	**.23**	.20‡	.42	.31†	.39	.25‡	.27‡	.35	.35	.32⋆	.36	.29	
> OTHERS	.50	.26	.42	.42	.42	.42	.39	.44	.43	.37	.49	.49	**.50**
>= OTHERS	**.70**	.37	.55	.55	.53	.55	.51	.59	.56	.51	.64	**.70**	.69

Table 16: Sentence-level ranking for the WMT09 Spanish-English News Task

	GOOGLE	NUS	RBMT1	RBMT3	RBMT4	RBMT5	RWTH	TALP-UPC	UEDIN	USAAR	USAAR-COMBO
GOOGLE		.39	.21‡	**.49**	.36	**.48**	.34⋆	.39	.33	.36⋆	.21
NUS	**.50**		.11‡	**.62**†	**.51**	**.51**	.35	.25	**.47**	.36	.43
RBMT1	**.76**‡	**.80**‡		**.79**‡	**.79**‡	**.83**‡	**.64**‡	**.76**‡	**.80**‡	**.67**‡	**.64**‡
RBMT3	.42	.31†	.16‡		.30⋆	.43	.34	.29‡	**.56**	.24‡	.32
RBMT4	**.47**	.32	.11‡	**.52**⋆		**.49**	.38	.36	**.51**	.39	.38
RBMT5	.42	.40	.11‡	**.49**	.35		.31†	.39	**.47**	.18†	.47
RWTH	**.59**⋆	**.52**	.26‡	**.54**	**.51**	**.61**†		**.46**	**.56**†	.39	**.55**†
TALP-UPC	**.49**	**.41**	.17‡	**.63**‡	**.52**	**.51**	.29		**.45**⋆	.39	.41
UEDIN	**.50**	.32	.17‡	.36	.37	.46	.30†	.29⋆		.32†	.36
USAAR	**.58**⋆	**.56**	.23‡	**.67**‡	**.53**	**.47**†	**.51**	**.49**	**.61**†		**.58**⋆
USAAR-COMBO	**.31**	**.45**	.21‡	**.54**	**.49**	**.50**	.30†	**.43**	**.43**	.33⋆	
> OTHERS	.50	.45	.17	**.56**	.47	.53	.38	.42	.52	.37	.43
>= OTHERS	.65	.59	.25	**.66**	.61	.64	.51	.58	.66	.48	.61

Table 17: Sentence-level ranking for the WMT09 English-Spanish News Task

	CMU-STATXFER	COLUMBIA	DCU	GENEVA	GOOGLE	JHU	LIMSI	LIUM-SYSTRAN	RBMT1	RBMT3	RBMT4	RBMT5	RWTH	UEDIN	UKA	USAAR	BBN-COMBO	CMU-COMBO	CMU-COMBO-HYPOSEL	DCU-COMBO	USAAR-COMBO
CMU-STATXFER		.37	**.44**	.17‡	**.63**†	**.47**	**.46**	**.58**†	.34	.32	.25†	.42	**.48**	**.46**	.28	.38	**.58**‡	**.47**	**.39**	.41	.35
COLUMBIA	**.56**		**.56***	.37	**.71**‡	**.48**	**.56**‡	**.35**	**.45**	.28*	**.38**	.42	**.41**	**.33**	**.58**	**.50**	**.64**†	**.52**	**.64**†	**.71**‡	**.58**†
DCU	.27	.29*		.15‡	**.67**‡	**.45**	.33	.34	.29	.31	.29	.27*	.24	**.37**	.21†	.39	**.61**‡	.4	.36	.37	.1
GENEVA	**.76**‡	**.54**	**.73**‡		**.71**‡	**.65**‡	**.73**‡	**.62***	**.66**‡	**.76**‡	**.46**	**.79**‡	**.57**	**.74**‡	**.72**‡	**.67**†	**.69**‡	**.52**	**.71**‡	**.67**‡	**.64**†
GOOGLE	.23†	.17‡	.12‡	.13‡		.21‡	.35	.09‡	.20‡	.27†	.31†	**.44**	.16‡	.21‡	.33	.27*	**.28**	.30	.34	.37	.16‡
JHU	.40	.26	.38	.22‡	**.60**‡		.31	**.44**	.27	.37	.29†	.41	.33	.37	**.48**	.48	**.53**	**.47**	.31	**.47**	.29
LIMSI	.4	.16‡	**.38**	.19‡	**.56**	**.49**		.29	.37	.27	.20‡	.38	.23*	.33	.29	.38	**.61**†	.47	.31	.36	.26*
LIUM-SYSTRAN	.23†	.30	**.42**	.33*	**.61**‡	.27	**.45**		**.48**	.31	**.41**	**.44**	.32	.35	**.41**	**.39**	**.54**†	**.61**†	.24	**.67**†	.36
RBMT1	**.53**	.23	**.42**	.19‡	**.57**‡	**.46**	**.51**	.45		**.47**	.33	**.46**	.33	.41	.30	**.61**	**.77**‡	**.51**	**.41**	**.50**	.41
RBMT3	**.57**	**.63***	**.55**	.15‡	**.69**†	**.44**	**.57**	**.52**	.41		.22‡	**.38**	**.51**	**.43**	.43	.31	**.57***	**.46**	**.47**	.38	**.55**
RBMT4	**.58**†	.35	**.51**	.36	**.67**†	**.60**†	**.63**‡	.35	**.41**	**.59**‡		**.40**	**.55**	**.50**	**.71**‡	**.52**†	**.63**†	**.65**†	**.65**†	**.66**†	.38
RBMT5	.42	**.49**	**.54***	.09‡	.38	**.49**	**.49**	.37	.27	.29	.34		.38	.39	**.51**	.18	.42	**.58**	**.48**	**.50**	**.60**‡
RWTH	.38	.39	**.45**	.32	**.63**‡	**.46**	**.51***	**.34**	**.56**	.39	.32	**.52**		**.48**	**.46**	**.46**	**.66**‡	**.62**†	**.61**‡	**.66**‡	**.54***
UEDIN	.41	.21	.31	.19‡	**.68**‡	**.46**	**.42**	.35	.41	.38	.31	**.46**	.33		.34	.41	**.41**	.35	**.44**	**.63**‡	.37
UKA	**.40**	.31	**.54**†	.19‡	**.51**	.37	**.44**	.33	**.52**	**.51**	.17‡	.27	.32	**.49**		.34	**.39**	**.53**	**.36**	**.44**	.29
USAAR	**.44**	.43	**.52**	.26†	**.62***	.48	**.46**	.30	.30	**.58**	.17†	**.24**	.44	**.47**	**.41**		**.65**‡	**.52**	**.70**‡	**.55**	.41
BBN-COMBO	.21‡	.21†	.12‡	.23‡	.26	.32	.28†	.23†	.12‡	.26*	.22†	**.49**	.09‡	.34	.23	.19‡		**.44**	**.49**†	.28	.21‡
CMU-COMBO	.41	.36	.4	.28	.30	.35	.47	.21†	.29	.42	.23†	.31	.17†	**.49**	.25	.42	.31		**.37**	**.29**	.25
CMU-COMBO-H	.24	.21†	**.38**	.23‡	**.37**	**.39**	.31	.24	.31	.41	.28†	.31	.14‡	.33	.34	.24‡	.18†	.3		.29	.27
DCU-COMBO	.41	.13‡	**.42**	.20‡	.37	.29	**.50**	.19†	.44	**.49**	.23†	.46	.20‡	.21‡	.37	.39	**.31**	.26	**.46**		.19‡
USAAR-COMBO	**.41**	.25†	**.18**	.28†	**.66**‡	**.53**	**.52***	**.48**	.41	.38	**.53**	.17‡	.21*	**.42**	**.42**	**.47**	**.58**‡	**.58**	.47	**.63**‡	
> OTHERS	.40	.31	.41	.23	**.56**	.43	.46	.36	.37	.41	.30	.40	.33	.41	.40	.40	.50	.47	.46	.49	.36
>= OTHERS	.58	.5	.66	.34	**.76**	.62	.65	.60	.56	.54	.47	.59	.52	.61	.61	.55	**.73**	.66	.71	.67	.57

Table 18: Sentence-level ranking for the WMT09 French-English News Task

	DCU	GENEVA	GOOGLE	LIMSI	LIUM-SYSTRAN	RBMT1	RBMT3	RBMT4	RBMT5	RWTH	SYSTRAN	UEDIN	UKA	USAAR	DCU-COMBO	USAAR-COMBO
DCU		.12‡	.39	**.47**	**.44**	.33	**.44**	.27	**.45**	.24*	**.49**	.24	**.46**	.26†	**.39**	.33
GENEVA	**.62**‡		**.73**‡	**.69**‡	**.80**‡	**.50***	**.71**‡	**.50***	**.52***	**.56**†	**.66**‡	**.46**‡	**.56**‡	**.57**	**.74**‡	**.84**‡
GOOGLE	**.46**	.15‡		.28	.42	.26	**.44**	.26†	.34	.29*	**.44**	.24	.32	.29	**.36**	.32
LIMSI	.25	.16‡	**.45**		**.48**	.23*	**.43**	.30	**.45**	.27	**.42**	**.34**	.4	.36	**.53**†	**.38**
LIUM-SYSTRAN	.24	‡	**.45**	.32		.17†	.29	.17†	.21†	.38	.29	.17‡	.35	.17†	.41	**.41**
RBMT1	**.39**	.25*	**.51**	**.51***	**.53**†		**.46**	**.40**	.29	**.52**	.36	**.60***	**.63**‡	**.41**	**.44**	**.60**†
RBMT3	.36	.11‡	.37	.37	**.52**	.24		.25*	.27*	.31	**.44**	.43	.32	.27*	**.53**	**.44**
RBMT4	**.36**	.19*	**.58**†	**.37**	**.57**†	.23	**.61***		**.42**	.32	**.50**	.22	.39	**.44**	**.53**	**.56***
RBMT5	.41	.17*	**.53**	.39	**.61**†	**.38**	**.58***	.30		**.41**	**.52***	.41	**.48**	.13	**.54**	**.60**
RWTH	**.59***	.21†	**.63***	**.50**	**.47**	.29	**.44**	**.37**	.31		.37	**.35**	**.51**	.16†	**.50**‡	**.57**†
SYSTRAN	.35	.20‡	.33	.39	**.38**	**.40**	.22	.29	.26*	**.44**		**.47**	.33	.32	**.60***	**.45**
UEDIN	**.38**	.11‡	**.41**	.28	**.77**‡	.33*	**.51**	**.44**	**.49**	.32	.37		**.30**	.31	**.56**	**.56**‡
UKA	.36	.09‡	**.46**	.4	**.45**	.23‡	**.50**	.39	.29	.29	**.47**	.26		.19‡	.41	**.56**†
USAAR	**.66**†	.27	**.52**	**.49**	**.70**†	.31	**.61***	.29	**.32**	**.64**†	**.62**	**.51**	**.61**‡		**.76**‡	**.65**‡
DCU-COMBO	.32	.11‡	.30	.18†	**.45**	.22	.29	.33	.29	.13‡	.27*	.26	.41	.12‡		.21
USAAR-COMBO	**.40**	‡	**.39**	.17	.26	.17†	.28	.20*	.28	.20†	.39	.04‡	.06†	.08‡	**.39**	
> OTHERS	.41	.15	.47	.39	**.52**	.29	.45	.32	.35	.35	.45	.34	.42	.28	.51	.49
>= OTHERS	.65	.38	.68	.64	**.73**	.54	.65	.59	.57	.58	.65	.60	.66	.48	.74	**.77**

Table 19: Sentence-level ranking for the WMT09 English-French News Task

	CU-BOJAR	GOOGLE	UEDIN	BBN-COMBO	CMU-COMBO
CU-BOJAR		**.54**‡	**.44**	**.45**‡	**.52**‡
GOOGLE	.28‡		.32‡	.18‡	.23
UEDIN	.38	**.51**‡		**.38**	**.45**‡
BBN-COMBO	.31‡	**.39**‡	.32		**.38**‡
CMU-COMBO	.28‡	**.29**	.27‡	.24‡	
> OTHERS	.31	**.43**	.34	.31	.40
>= OTHERS	.51	**.75**	.57	.65	**.73**

Table 20: Sentence-level ranking for the WMT09 Czech-English News Task

	CU-BOJAR	CU-TECTOMT	EUROTRANXP	GOOGLE	PCTRANS	UEDIN
CU-BOJAR		.31‡	**.45**‡	**.43**‡	**.48**‡	.30‡
CU-TECTOMT	**.51**‡		**.54**‡	**.56**‡	**.58**‡	**.42***
EUROTRANXP	.35‡	.26‡		.39	**.38**	.29‡
GOOGLE	.31‡	.30‡	**.42**		**.43***	.26‡
PCTRANS	.33‡	.27‡	.36	.38*		.30‡
UEDIN	**.42**‡	.37*	**.52**‡	**.50**‡	**.53**‡	
> OTHERS	.38	.30	.46	.45	**.48**	.31
>= OTHERS	.61	.48	.67	.66	**.67**	.53

Table 21: Sentence-level ranking for the WMT09 English-Czech News Task

	MORPHO	UEDIN	UMD	BBN-COMBO	CMU-COMBO	CMU-COMBO-HYPOSEL
MORPHO		.21‡	.28‡	.24‡	.27‡	.28‡
UEDIN	**.70**‡		**.59**‡	**.45**‡	**.55**‡	**.50**‡
UMD	**.61**‡	.26‡		.21‡	.29	**.38**
BBN-COMBO	**.67**‡	.23‡	**.48**‡		**.41***	**.52**‡
CMU-COMBO	**.59**‡	.25‡	**.35**	.29*		**.42**
CMU-COMBO-HYPOSEL	**.55**‡	.15‡	.34	.27‡	.34	
> OTHERS	**.62**	.22	.41	.29	.37	.42
>= OTHERS	**.75**	.45	.66	.54	.62	**.68**

Table 22: Sentence-level ranking for the WMT09 Hungarian-English News Task

	GOOGLE$_{CZ}$	GOOGLE$_{ES}$	GOOGLE$_{FR}$	RBMT2$_{DE}$	RBMT3$_{DE}$	RBMT3$_{ES}$	RBMT3$_{FR}$	RBMT5$_{ES}$	RBMT5$_{FR}$	BBN-COMBO$_{CZ}$	BBN-COMBO$_{DE}$	BBN-COMBO$_{ES}$	BBN-COMBO$_{FR}$	BBN-COMBO$_{HU}$	BBN-COMBO$_{XX}$	CMU-COMBO-HYPOSEL$_{DE}$	CMU-COMBO-HYPOSEL$_{HU}$	CMU-COMBO$_{CZ}$	CMU-COMBO$_{HU}$	CMU-COMBO$_{XX}$	DCU-COMBO$_{FR}$	RWTH-COMBO$_{DE}$	RWTH-COMBO$_{XX}$	USAAR-COMBO$_{ES}$
GOOGLE$_{CZ}$		**.61***	**.54***	**.47**	**.52**	**.51**	**.47**	**.61***	.42	.38	**.52**	**.55**	**.54**	.11‡	**.51**	.48	.34	**.49**	.32	**.53**	**.52**	**.50**	**.59**	**.53**
GOOGLE$_{ES}$	.33*		.42	.37	.38	.41	.35	**.49**	.45	.11‡	.39	.25	.36	.18‡	.26*	.36	.22‡	.32	.18‡	.38	.4	.4	.38	.22
GOOGLE$_{FR}$	.27*	.42		.26†	.36	.43	**.47**	.33	.35	.29*	.23†	**.50**	.23	.14‡	.29†	.21†	.11‡	.17‡	.22‡	**.39**	**.48**	.32	.36	.27
RBMT2$_{DE}$	.33	**.49**	**.61**†		.41	.43	.25†	**.52**	.38	.33	.41	.4	**.55**	.20‡	**.66***	**.62***	.18‡	**.55**	.35	.35	**.58**	**.54**	**.61***	**.57**†
RBMT3$_{DE}$	.37	**.60**	**.54**	.41		.42	.38	.45	**.61**	**.48**	.39	.40	**.63**‡	.32	.43	.25†	.35	.35	.25†	**.56**	**.69**†	**.46**	**.49**	**.46**
RBMT3$_{ES}$	.34	**.52**	**.46**	**.51**	**.54**		.43	.36	.38	.30*	**.54**	.41	.47	.25*	**.50**	.42	.26*	.43	.27†	**.52**	**.57**	.47	**.46**	.26*
RBMT3$_{FR}$	.40	**.58**	.37	**.63**†	**.53**	**.57**		**.54**	**.50**	.36	**.64***	.44	**.55**	.13‡	**.60**	**.64***	.4	**.53**	.31	**.46**	**.48**	.44	**.52**	**.42**
RBMT5$_{ES}$	.29*	.41	**.55**	.31	**.48**	.36	.33		.39	.16‡	.44	**.50**	**.68**†	.23†	.35	**.48**	.38	.37	.41	**.60**†	**.51**	**.51**	**.65***	.32
RBMT5$_{FR}$	**.47**	**.52**	**.45**	**.50**	.33	**.51**	.34	**.42**		.29	**.59**	.44	**.49**	‡	**.49**	**.61***	.28*	.19‡	.35	**.58**†	**.60***	.27	**.59**	**.57**
BBN-COMBO$_{CZ}$	**.41**	**.74**‡	**.65***	**.55**	.44	**.67***	**.56**	**.80**‡	**.46**		.46	**.58**	**.70**‡	.22†	**.73**‡	**.63**†	.32	**.38**	.48	**.65***	**.72**‡	**.66**‡	**.70**‡	**.58**
BBN-COMBO$_{DE}$	.39	**.54**	**.58**†	.41	**.49**	.44	.31*	.44	.28	**.49**		**.49**	**.52**	.16‡	**.52**	.36	.22*	.38	.33*	.41	**.68**†	.34	**.52**	**.56**
BBN-COMBO$_{ES}$	.38	**.40**	.41	**.43**	**.47**	**.55**	**.46**	.25	**.51**	.31	.43		**.44**	.20†	**.50**	**.42**	.30†	.32	.29*	.36	**.62**	.47	.44	**.38**
BBN-COMBO$_{FR}$	.38	**.52**	**.35**	.36	.27‡	**.53**	.40	.26†	.33	.24‡	.44	.36		.12‡	**.47**	**.47**	.32	.44	.27†	**.41**	.42	.33	**.60**‡	.35
BBN-COMBO$_{HU}$	**.84**‡	**.75**‡	**.78**‡	**.60**‡	**.57**	**.70***	**.71**‡	**.62**†	**.84**‡	**.65**†	**.72**‡	**.63**†	**.85**‡		**.78**‡	**.69**†	**.60**‡	**.71**‡	**.50**	**.85**‡	**.78**‡	**.87**‡	**.86**‡	**.75**‡
BBN-COMBO$_{XX}$	.4	**.54***	**.63**†	.34*	**.50**	.47	.32	**.45**	.39	.20‡	.39	.45	.41	.14‡		.24‡	.21‡	.3	.21‡	**.46**	**.40**	.47	**.41**	**.41**
CMU-CMB-HYP$_{DE}$	.48	**.43**	**.68**†	.29*	**.64**†	**.46**	.31*	.30	.30*	.23†	**.41**	.39	.32	.19†	**.74**‡		.21‡	.32	.31	**.50**	**.74**‡	.38	**.56***	**.53**
CMU-CMB-HYP$_{HU}$	**.63**	**.75**‡	**.78**‡	**.70**‡	**.55**	**.63***	**.46**	**.58**	**.59***	**.50**	**.61***	**.70**†	**.59**	.13‡	**.68**‡	**.69**‡		**.65**‡	.39	**.75**‡	**.71**‡	**.82**‡	**.80**‡	**.68**†
CMU-COMBO$_{CZ}$	.32	**.59**	**.81**‡	.36	**.50**	**.46**	.41	**.50**	**.60**‡	.28	**.54**	**.52**	**.47**	.20‡	**.55**	**.56**	.26‡		.13‡	**.55**	**.69**†	**.57**	**.66***	**.55**
CMU-COMBO$_{HU}$	**.62**	**.76**‡	**.69**‡	**.58**	**.68**†	**.67**†	**.59**	**.54**	**.54**	.48	**.67***	**.64***	**.70**†	.32	**.74**‡	**.60**	**.50**	**.77**‡		**.66**†	**.72**‡	**.61**	**.82**‡	**.82**‡
CMU-COMBO$_{XX}$	.4	**.50**	.33	**.51**	.37	.43	.44	.29†	.24†	.32*	**.56**	**.43**	.39	.13‡	.39	.39	.16‡	.30	.32†		.39	.4	**.46**	.4
DCU-COMBO$_{FR}$	.44	**.57**	.29	.32	.25†	.29	.26	.35	.27*	.19‡	.23†	.38	.42	.15‡	.34	.20‡	.12‡	.19†	.17‡	**.50**		**.55**	**.49**	.30*
RWTH-COMBO$_{DE}$	.41	**.43**	**.52**	.37	.39	**.53**	**.50**	.35	**.53**	.25‡	**.40**	.47	**.54**	.10‡	.47	**.41**	.07‡	.38	.30	**.53**	.38		**.56**	**.49**
RWTH-COMBO$_{XX}$	.31	.38	**.44**	.26*	.41	.39	.31	.26*	.32	.18‡	.29	.44	.19‡	.10‡	.36	.25*	.11‡	.28*	.15‡	.39	.42	.28		.44
USAAR-COMBO$_{ES}$	.37	**.37**	**.54**	.21†	.4	**.58***	.39	**.47**	.31	.32	.34	.28	**.55**	.11‡	.38	.38	.20†	.38	.18‡	**.44**	**.67***	.43	.44	
> OTHERS	.41	.54	.54	.43	.45	.49	.41	.44	.44	.32	.46	.46	.50	.16	.51	.45	.26	.40	.29	.52	**.57**	.48	.55	.47
>= OTHERS	.52	.67	**.70**	.55	.55	.57	.52	.58	.58	.43	.57	.59	.62	.27	.62	.58	.37	.52	.36	.63	.68	.59	**.69**	.62

Table 23: Sentence-level ranking for the WMT09 All-English News Task

	BBN-COMBO	CMU-COMBO	RWTH-COMBO
BBN-COMBO		.37	**.40**‡
CMU-COMBO	**.41**		**.44**‡
RWTH-COMBO	.32‡	.34‡	
> OTHERS	.36	.35	**.42**
>= OTHERS	.62	.58	**.67**

Table 24: Sentence-level ranking for the WMT09 Multisource-English News Task

	RANK	BLEU	BLEU-CASED	BLEU-TER	BLEUSP	BLEUSP4114	MAXSIM	METEOR-0.6	METEOR-0.7	METEOR-RANKING	NIST	NIST-CASED	RTE-ABSOLUTE	RTE-PAIRWISE	TER	TERP	ULC	WCD6P4ER	WPF	WPBLEU
German-English News Task																				
BBN-COMBO	0.68	0.24	0.22	–0.17	0.29	0.31	0.51	0.55	0.6	0.41	7.08	6.78	0.13	0.1	0.54	0.63	0.31	0.45	0.36	0.31
CMU-COMBO	0.63	0.22	0.21	–0.19	0.28	0.29	0.49	0.54	0.58	0.4	6.95	6.71	0.12	0.09	0.56	0.66	0.29	0.47	0.35	0.29
CMU-COMBO-HYPOSEL	0.62	0.23	0.21	–0.19	0.28	0.3	0.49	0.54	0.57	0.4	6.79	6.5	0.11	0.09	0.57	0.66	0.29	0.47	0.35	0.3
GENEVA	0.33	0.1	0.09	–0.33	0.17	0.18	0.38	0.43	0.44	0.30	4.88	4.65	0.03	0.04	0.71	0.86	0.22	0.58	0.25	0.17
GOOGLE	0.65	0.21	0.20	–0.2	0.27	0.28	0.48	0.54	0.57	0.39	6.85	6.65	0.11	0.11	0.56	0.65	0.29	0.48	0.35	0.28
JHU-TROMBLE	0.13	0.07	0.06	–0.38	0.09	0.1	0.34	0.43	0.41	0.29	4.90	4.25	0.02	0.02	0.81	1	0.19	0.61	0.22	0.12
LIU	0.50	0.19	0.18	–0.22	0.25	0.27	0.46	0.51	0.54	0.38	6.35	6.02	0.06	0.05	0.61	0.72	0.27	0.49	0.33	0.26
RBMT1	0.54	0.14	0.13	–0.29	0.20	0.21	0.43	0.50	0.53	0.37	5.30	5.07	0.04	0.04	0.67	0.76	0.26	0.55	0.29	0.22
RBMT2	0.64	0.17	0.16	–0.26	0.23	0.24	0.48	0.52	0.55	0.38	6.06	5.75	0.1	0.12	0.63	0.70	0.29	0.51	0.31	0.24
RBMT3	0.64	0.17	0.16	–0.25	0.23	0.25	0.48	0.52	0.55	0.38	5.98	5.71	0.09	0.09	0.61	0.68	0.29	0.51	0.32	0.25
RBMT4	0.62	0.16	0.14	–0.27	0.21	0.23	0.45	0.5	0.52	0.36	5.65	5.36	0.06	0.07	0.65	0.72	0.27	0.52	0.30	0.23
RBMT5	0.66	0.16	0.15	–0.26	0.22	0.24	0.47	0.51	0.54	0.37	5.76	5.52	0.07	0.06	0.63	0.70	0.28	0.52	0.31	0.24
RWTH	0.50	0.19	0.18	–0.21	0.25	0.26	0.45	0.50	0.53	0.36	6.44	6.24	0.06	0.03	0.60	0.74	0.27	0.49	0.33	0.26
RWTH-COMBO	0.7	0.23	0.22	–0.18	0.29	0.30	0.50	0.55	0.59	0.41	7.06	6.81	0.11	0.07	0.54	0.63	0.30	0.46	0.36	0.31
STUTTGART	0.61	0.2	0.18	–0.22	0.26	0.27	0.48	0.52	0.56	0.38	6.39	6.11	0.1	0.06	0.60	0.69	0.29	0.49	0.33	0.27
SYSTRAN	0.6	0.19	0.17	–0.22	0.24	0.26	0.47	0.52	0.55	0.38	6.40	6.08	0.08	0.07	0.60	0.71	0.28	0.5	0.33	0.26
UEDIN	0.59	0.20	0.19	–0.22	0.26	0.27	0.47	0.52	0.55	0.38	6.47	6.24	0.07	0.04	0.61	0.70	0.27	0.49	0.34	0.27
UKA	0.58	0.21	0.2	–0.20	0.27	0.28	0.47	0.52	0.56	0.38	6.66	6.43	0.08	0.04	0.58	0.69	0.28	0.48	0.34	0.28
UMD	0.56	0.21	0.19	–0.19	0.26	0.28	0.47	0.52	0.56	0.38	6.74	6.42	0.08	0.04	0.56	0.69	0.28	0.48	0.34	0.27
USAAR	0.65	0.17	0.15	–0.26	0.23	0.24	0.47	0.51	0.54	0.38	5.89	5.64	0.06	0.05	0.64	0.71	0.28	0.52	0.31	0.24
USAAR-COMBO	0.62	0.17	0.16	–0.25	0.23	0.24	0.47	0.51	0.55	0.38	5.99	6.85	0.07	0.06	0.64	0.70	0.28	0.51	0.32	0.25
Spanish-English News Task																				
BBN-COMBO	0.64	0.29	0.27	–0.13	0.34	0.35	0.53	0.57	0.62	0.43	7.64	7.35	0.16	0.13	0.51	0.61	0.33	0.42	0.4	0.35
CMU-COMBO	0.7	0.28	0.27	–0.13	0.33	0.35	0.53	0.58	0.62	0.43	7.65	7.46	0.21	0.2	0.51	0.60	0.34	0.42	0.40	0.36
GOOGLE	0.70	0.29	0.28	–0.13	0.34	0.35	0.53	0.58	0.62	0.43	7.68	7.50	0.23	0.22	0.5	0.59	0.34	0.42	0.41	0.36
NICT	0.37	0.22	0.22	–0.19	0.27	0.29	0.48	0.54	0.57	0.39	6.91	6.74	0.1	0.1	0.60	0.71	0.3	0.46	0.36	0.3
RBMT1	0.55	0.19	0.18	–0.24	0.25	0.26	0.49	0.54	0.57	0.40	6.07	5.93	0.11	0.12	0.62	0.69	0.3	0.49	0.34	0.28
RBMT3	0.55	0.20	0.2	–0.22	0.26	0.27	0.50	0.54	0.58	0.41	6.24	6.08	0.13	0.14	0.60	0.65	0.31	0.48	0.36	0.29
RBMT4	0.53	0.2	0.19	–0.22	0.25	0.27	0.48	0.53	0.57	0.4	6.20	6.03	0.10	0.11	0.60	0.67	0.3	0.48	0.35	0.28
RBMT5	0.55	0.20	0.2	–0.22	0.26	0.27	0.5	0.54	0.58	0.40	6.26	6.10	0.12	0.11	0.6	0.65	0.31	0.48	0.36	0.29
RWTH	0.51	0.24	0.23	–0.16	0.3	0.31	0.49	0.54	0.58	0.4	7.12	6.95	0.11	0.08	0.56	0.68	0.31	0.45	0.37	0.32
TALP-UPC	0.59	0.26	0.25	–0.15	0.31	0.33	0.51	0.56	0.6	0.41	7.28	7.02	0.13	0.11	0.54	0.64	0.32	0.44	0.38	0.33
UEDIN	0.56	0.26	0.25	–0.15	0.32	0.33	0.51	0.56	0.60	0.42	7.25	7.04	0.16	0.1	0.55	0.64	0.32	0.43	0.39	0.34
USAAR	0.51	0.2	0.19	–0.22	0.25	0.27	0.48	0.54	0.57	0.4	6.31	6.14	0.11	0.09	0.62	0.67	0.3	0.48	0.34	0.28
USAAR-COMBO	0.69	0.29	0.27	–0.13	0.34	0.35	0.53	0.58	0.62	0.43	7.58	7.25	0.20	0.13	0.51	0.6	0.34	0.42	0.4	0.35
French-English News Task																				
BBN-COMBO	0.73	0.31	0.3	–0.11	0.36	0.38	0.54	0.59	0.64	0.45	7.88	7.58	0.14	0.12	0.2	0.20	0.36	0.40	0.41	0.37
CMU-COMBO	0.66	0.3	0.29	–0.12	0.35	0.36	0.53	0.58	0.63	0.44	7.72	7.57	0.15	0.12	0.24	0.26	0.35	0.41	0.41	0.37
CMU-COMBO-HYPOSEL	0.71	0.28	0.26	–0.14	0.33	0.35	0.53	0.57	0.61	0.43	7.40	7.15	0.1	0.08	0.31	0.33	0.34	0.42	0.4	0.35
CMU-STATXFER	0.58	0.24	0.23	–0.18	0.29	0.31	0.49	0.54	0.58	0.40	6.89	6.75	0.08	0.07	0.38	0.42	0.31	0.46	0.37	0.32
COLUMBIA	0.50	0.23	0.22	–0.18	0.29	0.30	0.49	0.54	0.58	0.40	6.85	6.68	0.07	0.07	0.36	0.39	0.31	0.46	0.36	0.31
DCU	0.66	0.27	0.25	–0.15	0.32	0.34	0.52	0.56	0.61	0.42	7.29	6.94	0.09	0.07	0.32	0.34	0.33	0.43	0.38	0.34
DCU-COMBO	0.67	0.31	0.31	–0.11	0.36	0.37	0.54	0.59	0.64	0.44	7.84	7.69	0.14	0.12	0.21	0.22	0.35	0.41	0.42	0.38
GENEVA	0.34	0.14	0.14	–0.29	0.21	0.22	0.43	0.49	0.52	0.36	5.32	5.15	0.05	0.05	0.54	0.52	0.26	0.53	0.29	0.22
GOOGLE	0.76	0.31	0.30	–0.10	0.36	0.37	0.54	0.58	0.63	0.44	8	7.84	0.17	0.13	0.17	0.2	0.36	0.41	0.42	0.38
JHU	0.62	0.27	0.23	–0.15	0.32	0.33	0.51	0.56	0.6	0.41	7.23	6.68	0.08	0.05	0.33	0.36	0.32	0.43	0.37	0.32
LIMSI	0.65	0.26	0.25	–0.16	0.30	0.32	0.51	0.56	0.60	0.42	7.02	6.87	0.09	0.07	0.35	0.36	0.33	0.44	0.38	0.33
LIUM-SYSTRAN	0.60	0.27	0.26	–0.15	0.32	0.33	0.51	0.56	0.60	0.42	7.26	7.10	0.10	0.06	0.33	0.36	0.33	0.43	0.39	0.35
RBMT1	0.56	0.18	0.18	–0.25	0.24	0.25	0.48	0.53	0.57	0.4	5.89	5.73	0.07	0.06	0.51	0.45	0.3	0.50	0.34	0.26
RBMT3	0.54	0.2	0.19	–0.22	0.25	0.27	0.48	0.53	0.56	0.39	6.12	5.96	0.07	0.06	0.45	0.45	0.30	0.49	0.35	0.28
RBMT4	0.47	0.19	0.18	–0.24	0.24	0.26	0.48	0.52	0.56	0.39	5.97	5.83	0.07	0.06	0.46	0.45	0.3	0.49	0.34	0.27
RBMT5	0.59	0.19	0.19	–0.24	0.25	0.26	0.49	0.54	0.57	0.40	6.03	5.9	0.09	0.07	0.46	0.43	0.31	0.49	0.35	0.28
RWTH	0.52	0.25	0.24	–0.16	0.30	0.32	0.5	0.55	0.59	0.40	7.09	6.94	0.07	0.03	0.35	0.39	0.32	0.44	0.38	0.32
UEDIN	0.61	0.25	0.24	–0.16	0.31	0.32	0.50	0.55	0.59	0.41	7.04	6.85	0.08	0.04	0.35	0.38	0.32	0.44	0.38	0.33
UKA	0.61	0.26	0.25	–0.15	0.31	0.33	0.51	0.55	0.6	0.41	7.17	7.00	0.08	0.04	0.34	0.37	0.32	0.44	0.38	0.34
USAAR	0.55	0.19	0.18	–0.24	0.24	0.26	0.48	0.54	0.57	0.4	6.08	5.92	0.07	0.06	0.46	0.44	0.3	0.49	0.34	0.26
USAAR-COMBO	0.57	0.26	0.25	–0.16	0.31	0.33	0.51	0.55	0.59	0.41	7.13	6.85	0.08	0.02	0.33	0.35	0.32	0.44	0.38	0.33
Czech-English News Task																				
BBN-COMBO	0.65	0.22	0.20	–0.19	0.27	0.29	0.47	0.52	0.56	0.39	6.74	6.45	0.24	0.3	0.52	0.60	0.29	0.47	0.34	0.29
CMU-COMBO	0.73	0.22	0.20	–0.2	0.27	0.29	0.47	0.53	0.57	0.39	6.72	6.46	0.34	0.34	0.53	0.60	0.29	0.47	0.35	0.29
CU-BOJAR	0.51	0.16	0.15	–0.26	0.22	0.24	0.43	0.5	0.52	0.36	5.84	5.54	0.26	0.28	0.61	0.69	0.26	0.52	0.31	0.24
GOOGLE	0.75	0.21	0.20	–0.19	0.26	0.28	0.46	0.52	0.55	0.38	6.82	6.61	0.32	0.33	0.53	0.62	0.29	0.47	0.35	0.28
UEDIN	0.57	0.2	0.19	–0.23	0.25	0.27	0.45	0.50	0.54	0.37	6.2	6	0.22	0.25	0.56	0.63	0.27	0.49	0.33	0.27
Hungarian-English News Task																				
BBN-COMBO	0.54	0.14	0.13	–0.29	0.19	0.21	0.38	0.45	0.46	0.32	5.46	5.2	0.16	0.18	0.71	0.83	0.23	0.55	0.27	0.2
CMU-COMBO	0.62	0.14	0.13	–0.29	0.19	0.21	0.39	0.46	0.47	0.32	5.52	5.24	0.28	0.22	0.71	0.82	0.23	0.55	0.28	0.2
CMU-COMBO-HYPOSEL	0.68	0.14	0.12	–0.29	0.19	0.21	0.39	0.45	0.46	0.32	5.51	5.16	0.25	0.25	0.71	0.82	0.23	0.55	0.27	0.2
MORPHO	0.75	0.1	0.09	–0.36	0.15	0.17	0.39	0.45	0.46	0.32	4.75	4.55	0.34	0.49	0.79	0.83	0.23	0.6	0.26	0.17
UEDIN	0.45	0.12	0.11	–0.32	0.18	0.19	0.37	0.42	0.43	0.30	4.95	4.74	0.12	0.12	0.75	0.87	0.21	0.58	0.27	0.19
UMD	0.66	0.13	0.12	–0.28	0.18	0.2	0.36	0.44	0.45	0.30	5.41	5.12	0.21	0.13	0.68	0.85	0.22	0.55	0.27	0.18

Table 25: Automatic evaluation metric scores for translations into English

	RANK	BLEU	BLEU-CASED	BLEU-TER	BLEUSP	BLEUSP4114	NIST	NIST-CASED	TER	TERP	WCD6P4ER	WPF	WPBLEU
English-German News Task													
GOOGLE	0.54	0.15	0.14	–0.29	0.20	0.22	5.36	5.25	0.62	0.74	0.54	0.3	0.23
LIU	0.49	0.14	0.13	–0.29	0.2	0.21	5.35	5.18	0.65	0.78	0.54	0.3	0.23
RBMT1	0.57	0.11	0.11	–0.32	0.17	0.19	4.69	4.59	0.67	0.81	0.57	0.28	0.21
RBMT2	0.66	0.13	0.13	–0.30	0.19	0.21	5.08	4.99	0.62	0.75	0.55	0.30	0.23
RBMT3	0.64	0.12	0.12	–0.29	0.2	0.21	4.8	4.71	0.62	0.76	0.54	0.31	0.25
RBMT4	0.58	0.11	0.10	–0.33	0.17	0.18	4.66	4.57	0.7	0.84	0.57	0.27	0.2
RBMT5	0.64	0.13	0.12	–0.3	0.19	0.20	5.03	4.94	0.64	0.79	0.55	0.3	0.23
RWTH	0.48	0.14	0.13	–0.28	0.2	0.21	5.51	5.41	0.62	0.78	0.53	0.3	0.23
STUTTGART	0.43	0.12	0.12	–0.31	0.18	0.20	5.06	4.82	0.67	0.79	0.55	0.29	0.21
UEDIN	0.51	0.15	0.15	–0.27	0.21	0.23	5.53	5.42	0.63	0.77	0.53	0.31	0.24
UKA	0.54	0.15	0.15	–0.27	0.21	0.22	5.6	5.48	0.62	0.75	0.52	0.31	0.24
USAAR	0.58	0.12	0.11	–0.33	0.18	0.19	4.83	4.71	0.69	0.8	0.57	0.28	0.21
USAAR-COMBO	0.52	0.16	0.15	–0.27	0.21	0.23	5.6	5.39	0.62	0.75	0.52	0.31	0.24
English-Spanish News Task													
GOOGLE	0.65	0.28	0.27	–0.15	0.33	0.34	7.27	7.07	0.36	0.42	0.42	0.37	0.31
NUS	0.59	0.25	0.23	–0.17	0.30	0.31	6.96	6.67	0.48	0.59	0.44	0.34	0.28
RBMT1	0.25	0.15	0.14	–0.27	0.20	0.22	5.32	5.17	0.55	0.66	0.51	0.24	0.16
RBMT3	0.66	0.18	0.17	–0.18	0.28	0.3	5.79	5.63	0.49	0.59	0.45	0.33	0.27
RBMT4	0.61	0.21	0.2	–0.20	0.26	0.28	6.47	6.28	0.52	0.64	0.47	0.31	0.25
RBMT5	0.64	0.22	0.21	–0.2	0.27	0.29	6.53	6.34	0.52	0.64	0.46	0.32	0.26
RWTH	0.51	0.22	0.21	–0.18	0.27	0.29	6.83	6.63	0.50	0.65	0.46	0.32	0.26
TALP-UPC	0.58	0.25	0.23	–0.17	0.3	0.31	6.96	6.69	0.47	0.58	0.44	0.34	0.28
UEDIN	0.66	0.25	0.24	–0.17	0.30	0.31	6.94	6.73	0.48	0.59	0.44	0.34	0.29
USAAR	0.48	0.20	0.19	–0.21	0.26	0.27	6.36	6.16	0.54	0.66	0.47	0.30	0.24
USAAR-COMBO	0.61	0.28	0.26	–0.14	0.33	0.34	7.36	6.97	0.39	0.48	0.42	0.36	0.31
English-French News Task													
DCU	0.65	0.24	0.22	–0.19	0.29	0.30	6.69	6.39	0.63	0.72	0.47	0.38	0.34
DCU-COMBO	0.74	0.28	0.27	–0.15	0.33	0.34	7.29	7.12	0.58	0.67	0.44	0.42	0.38
GENEVA	0.38	0.15	0.14	–0.27	0.20	0.22	5.59	5.39	0.68	0.82	0.53	0.32	0.25
GOOGLE	0.68	0.25	0.24	–0.17	0.30	0.31	6.90	6.71	0.62	0.7	0.46	0.40	0.36
LIMSI	0.64	0.25	0.24	–0.17	0.3	0.31	6.94	6.77	0.60	0.71	0.46	0.4	0.35
LIUM-SYSTRAN	0.73	0.26	0.24	–0.17	0.31	0.32	7.02	6.83	0.61	0.71	0.45	0.40	0.36
RBMT1	0.54	0.18	0.17	–0.23	0.24	0.26	6.12	5.96	0.65	0.76	0.5	0.35	0.29
RBMT3	0.65	0.22	0.20	–0.20	0.27	0.28	6.48	6.29	0.63	0.72	0.48	0.38	0.33
RBMT4	0.59	0.18	0.17	–0.24	0.24	0.25	6.02	5.86	0.66	0.77	0.50	0.35	0.3
RBMT5	0.57	0.20	0.19	–0.21	0.26	0.27	6.31	6.15	0.63	0.74	0.49	0.36	0.31
RWTH	0.58	0.22	0.21	–0.19	0.27	0.28	6.67	6.51	0.62	0.75	0.48	0.38	0.32
SYSTRAN	0.65	0.23	0.22	–0.19	0.28	0.29	6.7	6.47	0.63	0.74	0.47	0.39	0.34
UEDIN	0.60	0.24	0.23	–0.18	0.29	0.30	6.75	6.57	0.62	0.71	0.47	0.39	0.35
UKA	0.66	0.24	0.23	–0.18	0.29	0.30	6.82	6.65	0.61	0.71	0.46	0.39	0.35
USAAR	0.48	0.19	0.18	–0.23	0.24	0.26	6.16	5.98	0.66	0.76	0.5	0.34	0.29
USAAR-COMBO	0.77	0.27	0.25	–0.15	0.32	0.33	7.24	6.93	0.59	0.69	0.44	0.41	0.37
English-Czech News Task													
CU-BOJAR	0.61	0.14	0.13	–0.28	0.21	0.23	5.18	4.96	0.63	0.82	0.01	n/a	n/a
CU-TECTOMT	0.48	0.07	0.07	–0.35	0.14	0.16	4.17	4.03	0.71	0.96	0.01	n/a	n/a
EUROTRANXP	0.67	0.1	0.09	–0.33	0.16	0.18	4.38	4.26	0.7	0.93	0.01	n/a	n/a
GOOGLE	0.66	0.14	0.13	–0.30	0.20	0.22	4.96	4.84	0.66	0.82	0.01	n/a	n/a
PCTRANS	0.67	0.09	0.09	–0.34	0.17	0.18	4.34	4.19	0.71	0.90	0.01	n/a	n/a
UEDIN	0.53	0.14	0.13	–0.29	0.21	0.22	5.04	4.9	0.64	0.84	0.01	n/a	n/a
English-Hungarian News Task													
MORPHO	0.79	0.08	0.08	–0.37	0.15	0.16	4.04	3.92	0.83	1	0.6	n/a	n/a
UEDIN	0.32	0.1	0.09	–0.33	0.17	0.18	4.48	4.32	0.78	1	0.56	n/a	n/a

Table 26: Automatic evaluation metric scores for translations out of English

Syntax-oriented evaluation measures for machine translation output

Maja Popović and Hermann Ney
RWTH Aachen University
Aachen, Germany
popovic,ney@informatik.rwth-aachen.de

Abstract

We explored novel automatic evaluation measures for machine translation output oriented to the syntactic structure of the sentence: the BLEU score on the detailed Part-of-Speech (POS) tags as well as the precision, recall and F-measure obtained on POS n-grams. We also introduced F-measure based on both word and POS n-grams. Correlations between the new metrics and human judgments were calculated on the data of the first, second and third shared task of the Statistical Machine Translation Workshop. Machine translation outputs in four different European languages were taken into account: English, Spanish, French and German. The results show that the new measures correlate very well with the human judgements and that they are competitive with the widely used BLEU, METEOR and TER metrics.

1 Introduction

We proposed several syntax-oriented automatic evaluation measures based on sequences of POS tags and investigated how they correlate with human judgments. The new measures are the POSBLEU score, i.e. the BLEU score calculated on POS tags instead of words, as well as the POSP, the POSR and the POSF score: precision, recall and F-measure calculated on POS n-grams. In addition to the metrics based only on POS tags, we investigated a WPF score, i.e. an F-measure which takes into account both word and POS n-grams.

The correlations on the document level were computed on the English, French, Spanish and German texts generated by various translation systems in the framework of the first (Koehn and Monz, 2006), second (Callison-Burch et al., 2007) and third shared translation task (Callison-Burch et al., 2008). Preliminary experiments were carried out on the data from the first (2006) and the second task (2007) – Spearman's rank correlation coefficients between the adequacy and fluency scores and the POSBLEU, POSP, POSR and POSF scores were calculated. The POSBLEU and the POSF score were shown to be the most promising, so that these metrics were submitted to the official shared evaluation task 2008. The results of this evaluation showed that these metrics also correlate well on the document level with another human score, i.e. the sentence ranking. However, on the sentence level the results were less promising. The possible reason for this is the main drawback of the metrics based on pure POS tags, i.e. neglecting the lexical aspect. Therefore we also introduced a WPF score which takes into account both word n-grams and POS n-grams.

2 Syntactic-oriented evaluation metrics

We investigated the following metrics oriented on the syntactic structure of a translation output:

- POSBLEU
  The standard BLEU score (Papineni et al., 2002) calculated on POS tags instead of words;

- POSP
  POS n-gram precision: percentage of POS n-grams in the hypothesis which have a counterpart in the reference;

- POSR
  Recall measure based on POS n-grams: percentage of POS n-grams in the reference which are also present in the hypothesis;

- POSF
  POS n-gram based F-measure: takes into account all POS n-grams which have a counter-

Proceedings of the Fourth Workshop on Statistical Machine Translation, pages 29–32,
Athens, Greece, 30 March – 31 March 2009. ©2009 Association for Computational Linguistics

part, both in the reference and in the hypothesis.

- WPF
  F-measure based both on word and POS n-grams: takes into account all word n-grams and all POS n-grams which have a counterpart both in the corresponding reference and hypothesis.

The prerequisite for all metrics is availability of an appropriate POS tagger for the target language. It should be noted that the POS tags cannot be only basic but must have all details (e.g. verb tenses, cases, number, gender, etc.).

The n-gram scores as well as the POSBLEU score are based on fourgrams (i.e. the value of maximal n is 4). For the n-gram-based measures, two types of n-gram averaging were investigated: geometric mean and aritmetic mean. Geometric mean is already widely used in the BLEU score, but is also argued not to be optimal because the score becomes equal to zero even if only one of the n-gram counts is equal to zero. However, this problem is probably less critical for POS-based metrics because the tag set sizes are much smaller than vocabulary sizes.

3 Correlations between the new metrics and human judgments

The syntax-oriented evaluation metrics were compared with human judgments by means of Spearman correlation coefficients ρ. Spearman's rank correlation coefficient is equivalent to Pearson correlation on ranks, and its advantage is that it makes fewer assumptions about the data. The possible values of ρ range between 1 (if all systems are ranked in the same order) and -1 (if all systems are ranked in the reverse order). Thus the higher value of ρ for an automatic metric, the more similar it is to the human metric. Correlation coefficients between human scores and three well-known automatic measures BLEU, METEOR and TER were calculated as well, in order to see how the new metrics perform in comparison with widely used metrics. The scores were calculated for outputs of translation from Spanish, French and German into English and vice versa. English and German POS tags were produced using the TnT tagger (Brants, 2000), Spanish texts were annotated using the FreeLing analyser (Carreras et al., 2004), and French texts using the TreeTagger[1]. In this way, all references and hypotheses were provided with detailed POS tags.

Experiments on 2006 and 2007 test data

The preliminary experiments with the new evaluation metrics were performed on the data from the first two shared tasks in order to investigate Spearman correlation coefficients ρ between POS-based evaluation measures and the human scores adequacy and fluency. The metrics described in Section 2 (except the WPF score) were calculated for all translation outputs. For each new metric, the ρ coefficient with the adequacy and with the fluency score on the document level were calculated. Then the results were summarised by averaging obtained coefficients over all translation outputs, and the average correlations are presented in Table 1.

2006+2007	adequacy	fluency
BLEU	0.590	0.544
METEOR	0.598	0.538
TER	0.496	0.479
POSBLEU	**0.642**	**0.626**
POSF gm	*0.586*	**0.551**
am	*0.584*	**0.570**
POSR gm	0.572	0.576
am	0.542	0.544
POSP gm	0.551	0.481
am	0.531	0.461

Table 1: Average system-level correlations between automatic evaluation measures and adequacy/fluency scores for 2006 and 2007 test data (gm = geometric mean for n-gram averaging, am = arithmetic mean).

Table 1 shows that the new measures have high ρ coefficients both with respect to the adequacy and to the fluency score. The POSBLEU score has the highest correlations, followed by the POSF score. Furthermore, the POSBLEU score has higher correlations than each of the three widely used metrics, and all the new metrics except the POSP have higher correlations than the TER. The POSF correlations with the fluency are higher than those for the standard metrics, and with the adequacy are comparable to those for the METEOR and the BLEU score.

[1] http://www.ims.uni-stuttgart.de/projekte/corplex/TreeTagger/

Table 2 presents the percentage of the documents for which the particular new metric has higher correlation than BLEU, METEOR or TER. It can be seen that on the majority of the documents the POSBLEU metric outperforms all three standard measures, especially the correlation with the fluency score. The geometric mean POSF shows similar behaviour, having higher correlation than the standard measures in majority of the cases but slightly less often than the POSBLEU. The POSR has higher correlation than the standard measures in 50-70% of cases, and the POSP score has the lowest percentage, 30-60%. It can be also seen that the geometric mean averaging of the n-grams correlates better with the human judgments more often than the artimetic mean.

Experiments on 2008 test data

For the official shared evaluation task in 2008, the human evaluation scores were different – the adequacy and fluency scores were abandoned being rather time consuming and often inconsistent, and the sentence ranking was proposed as one of the human evaluation scores: the manual evaluators were asked to rank translated sentences relative to each other. RWTH participated in this shared task with the two most promising metrics according to the previous experiments, i.e. POSBLEU and POSF, and the detailed results can be found in (Callison-Burch et al., 2008). It was shown that these metrics also correlate very well with the sentence ranking on the document level. However, on the sentence level the performance was much weaker: a percentage of sentence pairs for which the human comparison yields the same result as the comparison using particular automatic metric was not very high. We believe that the main reason for this is the fact that the metrics based only on the POS tags can assign high scores to translations without correct semantic meaning, because they are taking into account only syntactic structure without taking into account the actual words. For example, if the reference translation is "This sentence is correct", a translation output "This tree is high" would have a POS-based matching score of 100%. Therefore we introduced the WPF score – an F-measure metrics which counts both matching POS n-grams and matching word n-grams.

The ρ coefficients for the POSBLEU, POSF and WPF with the sentence ranking averaged over all translation outputs are shown in Table 3. The correlations for several known metrics are shown as well, i.e. for the BLEU, METEOR and TER along with their variants: METEOR-r denotes the variant optimised for ranking, whereas MBLEU and MTER are BLEU and TER computed using the flexible matching as used in METEOR. It can be seen that the correlation coefficients for all three syntactic metrics are high. The POSBLEU score has the highest correlation with the sentence ranking, followed by POSF and WPF. All three measures have higher average correlation than MTER, MBLEU and BLEU. The purely syntactic metrics outperform also the METEOR scores, whereas the WPF correlations are comparable with those of the METEOR scores.

2008	sentence ranking
BLEU	0.526
MBLEU	0.504
METEOR	0.638
METEOR-r	0.603
MTER	0.318
POSBLEU	0.712
POSF gm	0.663
am	0.661
WPF gm	0.600
am	0.628

Table 3: Average system-level correlations between automatic evaluation measures and human ranking for 2008 test data.

Table 4 presents the percentage of the documents where the particular syntactic metric has higher correlation with the sentence ranking than the particular standard metric. All syntactic metrics have higher correlation than the MTER on almost all documents, and on a large number of documents than the MBLEU score. The correlations for syntactic measures are better than those for the BLEU score for more than 60% of documents. As for the METEOR scores, the syntactic metrics are comparable (about 50%).

4 Conclusions

The results presented in this article suggest that the syntactic information has the potential to strenghten automatic evaluation metrics, and there are many possible directions for future work. We proposed several syntax-oriented evaluation metrics based on the detailed POS tags: the POSBLEU score and POS-n-gram precision, recall and

2006+2007	adequacy BLEU	adequacy METEOR	adequacy TER	fluency BLEU	fluency METEOR	fluency TER
POSBLEU	77.3	58.3	75.0	81.8	83.3	83.3
POSF gm	72.7	58.3	75.0	63.6	75.0	83.3
am	68.2	58.3	75.0	63.6	66.7	68.1
POSR gm	63.6	75.0	58.3	68.1	66.7	58.3
am	54.5	75.0	58.3	63.6	58.3	50.0
POSP gm	63.6	50.0	75.0	45.4	50.0	58.3
am	54.5	41.7	66.7	36.4	50.0	58.3

Table 2: Percentage of documents from the 2006 and 2007 shared tasks where the particular new metric has better correlation with adequacy/fluency than the particular standard metric.

2008	BLEU	MBLEU	MTER	METEOR	METEOR-r
POSBLEU	71.4	85.7	92.8	57.1	64.3
POSF am	64.3	78.6	92.8	50.0	50.0
gm	64.3	78.6	92.8	57.1	50.0
WPF am	57.1	64.3	100	42.8	50.0
gm	57.1	64.3	92.8	42.8	50.0

Table 4: Percentage of documents from the 2008 shared task where the new metric has better correlation with the human sentence ranking than the standard metric.

F-measure, i.e. the POSP, POSR, and POSF score. In addition, we introduced a measure which takes into account both POS tags and words: the WPF score. We carried out an extensive analysis of the Spearman's rank correlation coefficients between the syntactic evaluation metrics and the human judgments. The obtained results showed that the new metrics correlate well with human judgments, namely the adequacy and fluency scores, as well as the sentence ranking. The results also showed that the syntax-oriented metrics are competitive with the widely used evaluation measures BLEU, METEOR and TER. Especially promising are the POSBLEU and the POSF score. The correlations of the WPF score are slightly lower than those of the purely POS based metrics – however, this metric has advantage of taking both syntactic and lexical aspect into account.

Acknowledgments

This work was realised as part of the Quaero Programme, funded by OSEO, French State agency for innovati on.

References

Thorsten Brants. 2000. Tnt – a statistical part-of-speech tagger. In *Proceedings of the 6th Applied Natural Language Processing Conference (ANLP)*, pages 224–231, Seattle, WA.

Chris Callison-Burch, Cameron Fordyce, Philipp Koehn, Christof Monz, and Josh Schroeder. 2007. (Meta-)Evaluation of Machine Translation. In *Proceedings of the ACL Workshop on Statistical Machine Translation*, pages 136–158, Prague, Czech Republic, June.

Chris Callison-Burch, Cameron Fordyce, Philipp Koehn, Christof Monz, and Josh Schroeder. 2008. Further Meta-Evaluation of Machine Translation. In *Proceedings of the Third Workshop on Statistical Machine Translation*, Columbus, Ohio, June.

Xavier Carreras, Isaac Chao, Lluís Padró, and Muntsa Padró. 2004. FreeLing: An Open-Source Suite of Language Analyzers. In *Proceedings 4th International Conference on Language Resources and Evaluation (LREC)*, pages 239–242, Lisbon, Portugal, May.

Philipp Koehn and Christof Monz. 2006. Manual and automatic evaluation of machine translation between european languages. In *Proceedings on the Workshop on Statistical Machine Translation*, New York City, June.

Kishore Papineni, Salim Roukos, Todd Ward, and Wie-Jing Zhu. 2002. BLEU: a method for automatic evaluation of machine translation. In *Proceedings of the 40th Annual Meeting of the Association for Computational Linguistics (ACL)*, pages 311–318, Philadelphia, PA, July.

A Simple Automatic MT Evaluation Metric

Petr Homola
Charles University
Prague, Czech Republic

Vladislav Kuboň
Charles University
Prague, Czech Republic

Pavel Pecina
Charles University
Prague, Czech Republic

{homola|vk|pecina}@ufal.mff.cuni.cz

Abstract

This paper describes a simple evaluation metric for MT which attempts to overcome the well-known deficits of the standard BLEU metric from a slightly different angle. It employes Levenshtein's edit distance for establishing alignment between the MT output and the reference translation in order to reflect the morphological properties of highly inflected languages. It also incorporates a very simple measure expressing the differences in the word order. The paper also includes evaluation on the data from the previous SMT workshop for several language pairs.

1 Introduction

The problem of finding a reliable machine translation metrics corresponding with a human judgment has recently returned to the centre of attention. After a brief period following the introduction of generally accepted and widely used metrics, BLEU (Papineni et al., 2002) and NIST (Doddington, 2002), when it seemed that this persistent problem has finally been solved, the researchers active in the field of machine translation (MT) started to express their worries that although these metrics are simple, fast and able to provide consistent results for a particular system during its development, they are not sufficiently reliable for the comparison of different systems or different language pairs.

The results of the NIST evaluation in 2005 (Le and Przybocki, 2005) have also strengthened the suspicion that the correlation between human judgment and the BLEU and NIST measures is not as strong as it was widely believed. Both measures seem to favor the MT output created by systems based on n-gram architecture, they are unable to take into account certain factors which are very important for the human judges of translation quality.

The article (Callison-Burch et al., 2006) thoroughly discusses the deficits of the BLEU and similar metrics. The authors claim that the existing automatic metrics, including some of the new and seemingly more reliable ones as e.g. Meteor (cf. (Banerjee and Lavie, 2005)) "...they are all quite rough measures of translation similarity, and have inexact models of allowable variation in translation." This claim is supported by a construction of translation variations which have identical BLEU score, but which are very different for a human judge. The authors identify three prominent factors which contribute to the inadequacy of BLEU – the failure to deal with synonyms and paraphrases, no penalties for missing content, and the crudeness of the brevity penalty.

Let us add some more factors based on our experiments with languages typologically different than English, Arabic or Chinese, which are probably the languages most frequently used in recent shared-task MT evaluations. The highly inflected languages and languages with a higher degree of word-order freedom may provide additional examples of sentences in which relatively small alterations of correct word forms may have a dire effect on the BLEU score while the sentence still remains understandable and acceptable for human evaluators.

The effect of rich inflection has been observed for example in (Týnovský, 2007), where the author mentions the fact that the BLEU score used for measuring the improvements in his experimental Czech-German EBMT system penalized heavily all subtle errors in Czech morphology arising from an out-of-context combined partial translations taken from different examples.

The problem of the insensitivity of BLEU to the variations of the order of n-grams identified in reference translations has already been mentioned in

Proceedings of the Fourth Workshop on Statistical Machine Translation, pages 33–36,
Athens, Greece, 30 March – 31 March 2009.

the paper (Callison-Burch et al., 2006). The authors showed examples where changing a good word order into an unacceptable one did not affect the BLEU score. We may add a different example documenting the phenomenon that a pair of syntactically correct Czech sentences with the same word forms, differing only in the word order whose n-gram score for $n = 2, 3$, and 4 differs greatly. Let us take one of the sentences from the 2008 SMT workshop and its reference translation:

When Caligula appointed his horse to the Senate, the horse at least did not have blood on its hoofs. — Když Caligula zvolil do senátu svého koně, neměl jeho kůň aspoň na kopytech krev.

If we modify the Czech reference sentence into *Když svého koně do senátu zvolil Caligula, jeho kůň aspoň neměl na kopytech krev.*, we destroy 8 out of 15 bigrams, 11 out of 14 trigrams and 12 out of 13 quadrigrams while we still have sentence with almost identical meaning and probably very similar human evaluation. The BLEU score of the modified sentence is, however, lower than it would be for the identical copy of the reference translation.

2 The description of the proposed metric

There is one aspect of the problem of a MT quality metric which tends to be overlooked but which is very important from the practical point of view. This aspect concerns the expected difficulties when post-editing the MT output. It is very important for everybody who really wants to use the MT output and who faces the decision whether it is better to post-edit the MT output or whether a new translation made by human translators would be faster and more efficient way towards the desired quality. It is no wonder that such a metric is mentioned only in connection with systems which really aim at practical exploitation, not with a majority of experimental MT system which will hardly ever reach the stage of industrial exploitation.

We have described one example of such practically oriented metric in (Hajič et al., 2003). The metric exploits the matching algorithm of Trados Translator's Workbench for obtaining the percentage of differences between the MT output and the reference translation (created by post-editing the MT output). The advantage of this measure is its close connection to the real world of human translating by means of translation memory, the disadvantage concerns the use of a proprietary matching algorithm which has not been made public and which requires the actual use of the Trados software.

Nevertheless, the matching algorithm of Trados gives results which to a great extent correspond to a much simpler traditional metric, to the Levenshtein's edit distance. The use of this metric may help to refine a very strict treatment of word-form differences by BLEU. A similar approach at the level of unigram matching has been used by the well-known METEOR metric (Agarwal and Lavie, 2008), which proved its qualities during the previous MT evaluation task in 2008 (Callison-Burch et al., 2008). Meteor uses Porter stemmer as one step in the word alignment algorithm. It also relies on synonymy relations in WordNet.

When designing our metric, we have decided to follow two general strategies – to use as simple means as possible and to avoid using any language dependent tools or resources. Levenshtein metric (or its modification for word-level edit distance) therefore seemed to be the best candidate for several aspects of the proposed measure.

The first aspect we have decided to include was the inflection. The edit distance has one advantage over the language independent stemmer – it can uniformly handle the differences regardless of their position in the string. The stemmer will probably face certain problems with changes inside the stem as e.g. in the Czech equivalent of the word *house* in different cases *dům* (nom.sg) — *domu* (gen., dat. or loc. sg.) or German *Mann* in different numbers *der Mann* (sg.) — *die Männer* (pl.), while the edit distance will treat them uniformly with the variation of prefixes, suffixes and infixes.

As mentioned above, we have also intended to aim at the treatment of the free word order in our metric. However this seems to be one of the major flaws of the BLEU score, it turned out that the word order is extremely difficult if we stick to the use of simple and language independent means. If we take Czech as an example of a language with relatively high degree of word-order freedom, we can still find certain restrictions (e.g. the sentence-second position of clitics, their mutual order, the adjectives typically, but not always preceding the nouns they depend upon etc.) which will definitely influence the human judgment of the acceptability of a particular sentence. These restrictions are language dependent (for example Polish, the language very closely related to Czech, has different rules for congruent attributes, the adjectives stand much more often to the right of the governing noun) and they are also very difficult to capture algorithmically. If the MT output is compared to a single reference translation only, there is, in fact, no way how the metric could account for the possible correct variations of the word order without exploiting very deep language dependent information. If there are more reference translations, it is possible that they will provide the natural variations of the word order, but it, in fact, means that if we want to stick to the above mentioned requirements, we have to give up the hope that our metric will capture this important phenomenon.

2.1 Word alignment algorithm

In order to capture the word form variations caused by the inflection, we have decided to employ the following alignment algorithm at the level of individual word forms. Let us use the following notation: Let the reference translation **R** be a sequence of words r_i, where $i \in <1, \ldots, n>$. Let the MT output **T** be a sequence of words tj, where $j \in <1, \ldots, m>$. Let us also set a threshold of similarity $s \in <0, 1>$. (s roughly expresses how different the forms of a lemma may be. The idea behind this criterion is that a mistake in one morphological category (reflected mostly by a different ending of the corresponding word form) is not as serious as a completely different lexeme. This holds especially for morphologically rich languages that can have tens or even hundreds of distinct word forms for a single lemma.) Starting from t_1, let us find for each t_j the best r_i for $i \in <1, \ldots, n>$ such that the edit distance d_j from t_j to r_i normalized by the length of t_j is minimal and at the same time $d_j < s$. If the r_i is already aligned to some t_k, $k < j$ and the edit distance $d_k > d_j$, then align t_j to r_i and re-calculate the alignment for t_k to its second best candidate, otherwise take the second best candidate r_l conforming with the above mentioned conditions and align it to t_j. As a result of this process, we get the alignment score A_{TR} from **T** to **R**. $A_{TR} = \frac{\sum(1-d_i)}{m}$ (for $i \in <1, \ldots, n>$) where $d_i = 1$ for those word forms t_i which are not aligned to any of the word forms r_j from **R**. Then we calculate the alignment score A_{RT} using the same algorithm and aligning the words from **R** to **T**. The similarity score **S** equals the minimum from A_{TR} and A_{RT}. The way how the similarity score **S** is constructed ensures that the score takes into account a difference in length between **T** and **R**, therefore it is not necessary to include any brevity penalty into the metric.

2.2 A structural metric

In order to express word-order difference between the MT output and the reference translation we have designed a structural part of the metric. It is based on an algorithm similar to one of the standard sorting methods, an insert sort. The reference translation **R** represents the desired word order and the algorithm counts the number of operations necessary for obtaining the correct word order from the word order of the MT output **T** by inserting the words t_i to their desired positions r_j (t_i is aligned to r_j). If a particular word t_i is not aligned to any r_j, a penalty of 1 is added to the number of operations.

2.3 A combination of both metrics

The overall score is computed as a weighted average of both metrics mentioned above. Let L be the lexical similarity score and M the structural score based on a word mapping. Then then overall score S can be obtained as follows:

$$S = aL + bM$$

The coefficients a and b must sum up to one. They allow to capture the difference in the degree of word-order freedom among target languages. The coefficient b should be set lower for the target languages with more free word-order. Because both then partial measures L and M have values in the interval $<0, 1>$, the value of S will also fall into this interval.

3 The experiment

We have performed a test of the proposed metric using the data from the last year's SMT workshop.[1] The parameters a, b, and s have been set to the same value for all evaluated language pairs, no language dependent alterations were tested in this experiment:

Parameter	Value
s	0.15
a	0.9
b	0.1

[1]The data are available at http://www.statmt.org/wmt08.

The values for the parameters have been set up empirically with special attention being paid to Czech, the only language with really rich inflection among the languages being tested.

We have performed sentence-level and system-level evaluation using the Spearman's rank correlation coefficient which is defined as follows:

$$\rho = 1 - \frac{6 \sum d_i^2}{n(n^2 - 1)}$$

where $d_i = x_i - y_i$ is the difference between the ranks of corresponding values X_i and Y_i and n is the number of values in each data set.

The following scores express the correlation of our automatic metric and the human judgements for the language pairs English-Czech and English-German. The sentence-level correlation ρ_{sent} is the average of Spearman's ρ across all sentences.

Language pair	Metric	ρ_{sent}	ρ_{sys}
English-Czech	proposed	0.20	0.50
English-Czech	BLEU	0.21	0.50
English-German	proposed	0.91	0.37
English-German	BLEU	0.90	0.20

3.1 Conclusions

The metric presented in this paper attempts to combine some of the important factors which seem to be neglected by some generally accepted MT evaluation metrics. Inspired by the fact that human judges tend to accept incorrect word-forms of corectly translated lemmas, it employs a similarity measure relaxing the requirements on identity (or similarity) of matching word forms in the MT output and the reference translation. At the same time, it also incorporates a penalty for different length of the MT output and the reference translation. The second component of the metric tackles the problem of incorrect word-order. The constants used in the metric allow to set the weight of its two components with regard to the target language properties.

The experiments performed on the data from the previous shared evaluation task are promising. They indicate that the first component of the metric succesfully replaces the strict unigram measure used in BLEU while the second component may require certain alteration in order to achieve a higher correlation with human judgement.

Acknowledgments

The presented research has been supported by the grant No. 1ET100300517 of the GAAV ČR and by Ministry of Education of the Czech Republic, project MSM 0021620838.

References

Abhaya Agarwal and Alon Lavie. 2008. *Meteor, M-BLEU and M-TER: Evaluation metrics for high correlation with human rankings of machine translation output.* In Proceedings of the Third Workshop on Statistical Machine Translation, pages 115-118. Columbus, Ohio, Association for Computational Linguistics.

Satanjeev Banerjee and Alon Lavie. 2005. *Meteor: An automatic metric for MT evaluation with improved correlation with human judgments.*. In Workshop on Intrinsic and Extrinsic Evaluation Measures for MT and/or Summarization, Ann Arbor, Michigan.

Chris Callison-Burch, Miles Osborne, Philipp Koehn. 2006. *Re-evaluating the Role of BLEU in Machine Translation Research.*. In Proceedings of the EACL'06, Trento, Italy.

Chris Callison-Burch, Cameron Fordyce, Philipp Koehn, Christof Monz, Josh Schroeder. 2008. *Further Meta-Evaluation of Machine Translation.*. In Proceedings of the Third Workshop on Statistical Machine Translation, pages 70-106, Columbus, Ohio. Association for Computational Linguistics.

George Doddington. 2002. *Automatic evaluation of machine translation quality using n-gram co-occurrence statistics.* In Proceedings of the second international conference on Human Language Technology Research, San Diego, California,USA

Jan Hajič, Petr Homola, Vladislav Kuboň. 2003. *A Simple Multilingual Machine Translation System.*. In Proceedings of the MT Summit IX, New Orleans, USA.

Kishore Papineni, Salim Roukos, ToddWard, and Wei-Jing Zhu. 2002. *Bleu: A method for automatic evaluation of machine translation.*. In Proceedings of ACL 2002.

Audrey Le and Mark Przybocki. 2005. *NIST 2005 machine translation evaluation official results.*. Official release of automatic evaluation scores for all submissions.

Miroslav Týnovský. 2007. *Exploitation of Linguistic Information in EBMT.*. Master thesis at Charles University in Prague, Faculty of Mathematics and Physics.

Textual Entailment Features for Machine Translation Evaluation

Sebastian Padó, Michel Galley, Dan Jurafsky, Christopher D. Manning[*]
Stanford University
{pado,mgalley,jurafsky,manning}@stanford.edu

Abstract

We present two regression models for the prediction of pairwise preference judgments among MT hypotheses. Both models are based on feature sets that are motivated by *textual entailment* and incorporate lexical similarity as well as local syntactic features and specific semantic phenomena. One model predicts absolute scores; the other one direct pairwise judgments. We find that both models are competitive with regression models built over the scores of established MT evaluation metrics. Further data analysis clarifies the complementary behavior of the two feature sets.

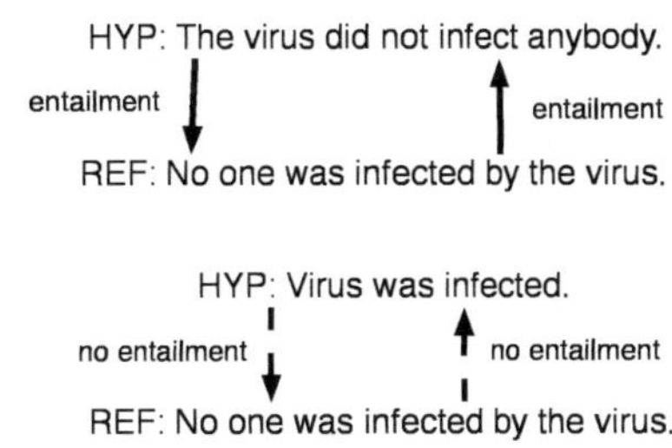

Figure 1: Entailment status between an MT system hypothesis and a reference translation for good translations (above) and bad translations (below).

1 Introduction

Automatic metrics to assess the quality of machine translations have been a major enabler in improving the performance of MT systems, leading to many varied approaches to develop such metrics. Initially, most metrics judged the quality of MT hypotheses by *token sequence match* (cf. BLEU (Papineni et al., 2002), NIST (Doddington, 2002). These measures rate systems hypotheses by measuring the overlap in surface word sequences shared between hypothesis and reference translation.

With improvements in the state-of-the-art in machine translation, the effectiveness of purely surface-oriented measures has been questioned (see e.g., Callison-Burch et al. (2006)). In response, metrics have been proposed that attempt to integrate more linguistic information into the matching process to distinguish linguistically licensed from unwanted variation (Giménez and Màrquez, 2008). However, there is little agreement on what types of knowledge are helpful: Some suggestions concentrate on *lexical* information, e.g., by the integration of word similarity information as in Meteor (Banerjee and Lavie, 2005) or MaxSim (Chan and Ng, 2008). Other proposals use *structural* information such as dependency edges (Owczarzak et al., 2007).

In this paper, we investigate an MT evaluation metric that is inspired by the similarity between this task and the *textual entailment* task (Dagan et al., 2005), which suggests that the quality of an MT hypothesis should be predictable by a *combination* of lexical and structural features that model the matches and mismatches between system output and reference translation. We use supervised regression models to combine these features and analyze feature weights to obtain further insights into the usefulness of different feature types.

2 Textual Entailment for MT Evaluation

2.1 Textual Entailment vs. MT Evaluation

Textual entailment (TE) was introduced by Dagan et al. (2005) as a concept that corresponds more closely to "common sense" reasoning than classical, categorical entailment. Textual entailment is defined as a relation between two natural language sentences (a premise P and a hypothesis H) that holds if *a human reading P would infer that H is most likely true.*

Information about the presence or absence of entailment between two sentences has been found to be beneficial for a range of NLP tasks such as Word Sense Disambiguation or Question Answering (Dagan et al., 2006; Harabagiu and Hickl, 2006). Our intuition is that this idea can also be fruitful in MT Evaluation, as illustrated in Figure 1. Very good MT output should entail the reference translation. In contrast, missing hypothesis material breaks forward entailment; additional material breaks backward entailment; and for bad translations, entailment fails in both directions.

Work on the recognition of textual entailment (RTE) has consistently found that the integration of more syntactic and semantic knowledge can yield gains over

[*]This paper is based on work funded by the Defense Advanced Research Projects Agency through IBM. The content does not necessarily reflect the views of the U.S. Government, and no official endorsement should be inferred..

Proceedings of the Fourth Workshop on Statistical Machine Translation , pages 37–41,
Athens, Greece, 30 March – 31 March 2009. ©2009 Association for Computational Linguistics

surface-based methods, provided that the linguistic analysis was sufficiently robust. Thus, for RTE, "deep" matching outperforms surface matching. The reason is that linguistic representation makes it considerably easier to distinguish admissible variation (i.e., paraphrase) from true, meaning-changing divergence. Admissible variation may be lexical (synonymy), structural (word and phrase placement), or both (diathesis alternations).

The working hypothesis of this paper is that the benefits of deeper analysis carry over to MT evaluation. More specifically, we test whether the features that allow good performance on the RTE task can also predict human judgments for MT output. Analogously to RTE, these features should help us to differentiate meaning preserving translation variants from bad translations.

Nevertheless, there are also substantial differences between TE and MT evaluation. Crucially, TE assumes the premise and hypothesis to be well-formed sentences, which is not true in MT evaluation. Thus, a possible criticism to the use of TE methods is that the features could become unreliable for ill-formed MT output. However, there is a second difference between the tasks that works to our advantage. Due to its strict compositional nature, TE requires an accurate semantic analysis of all sentence parts, since, for example, one misanalysed negation or counterfactual embedding can invert the entailment status (MacCartney and Manning, 2008). In contrast, human MT judgments behave more additively: failure of a translation with respect to a single semantic dimension (e.g., polarity or tense) degrades its quality, but usually not crucially so. We therefore expect that even noisy entailment features can be predictive in MT evaluation.

2.2 Entailment-based prediction of MT quality

Regression-based prediction. Experiences from the annotation of MT quality judgments show that human raters have difficulty in consistently assigning absolute scores to MT system output, due to the number of ways in which MT output can deviate. Thus, the human annotation for the WMT 2008 dataset was collected in the form of *binary pairwise preferences* that are considerably easier to make (Callison-Burch et al., 2008). This section presents two models for the prediction of pairwise preferences.

The first model (ABS) is a regularized linear regression model over entailment-motivated features (see below) that predicts an absolute score for each reference-hypothesis pair. Pairwise preferences are created simply by comparing the absolute predicted scores. This model is more general, since it can also be used where absolute score predictions are desirable; furthermore, the model is efficient with a runtime linear in the number of systems and corpus size. On the downside, this model is not optimized for the prediction of pairwise judgments.

The second model we consider is a regularized logistic regression model (PAIR) that is directly optimized to predict a weighted binary preference for each hypothesis pair. This model is less efficient since its runtime is quadratic in the number of systems. On the other hand, it can be trained on more reliable pairwise preference judgments. In a second step, we combine the individual decisions to compute the highest-likelihood total ordering of hypotheses. The construction of an optimal ordering from weighted pairwise preferences is an NP-hard problem (via reduction of CYCLIC-ORDERING; Barzilay and Elhadad, 2002), but a greedy search yields a close approximation (Cohen et al., 1999).

Alignment score(3)	Unaligned material (10)
Adjuncts (7)	Apposition (2)
Modality (5)	Factives (8)
Polarity (5)	Quantors (4)
Tense (2)	Dates (6)
Root (2)	Semantic Relations (4)
Semantic relatedness (7)	Structural Match (5)
Compatibility of locations and entities (4)	

Table 1: Entailment feature groups provided by the Stanford RTE system, with number of features

Both models can be used to predict system-level scores from sentence-level scores. Again, we have two method for doing this. The basic method (BASIC) predicts the quality of each system directly as the percentage of sentences for which its output was rated best among all systems. However, we noticed that the manual rankings for the WMT 2007 dataset show a tie for best system for almost 30% of sentences. BASIC is systematically unable to account for these ties. We therefore implemented a "tie-aware" prediction method (WITHTIES) that uses the same sentence-level output as BASIC, but computes system-level quality differently, as the percentage of sentences where the system's hypothesis was scored *better or at most ε worse than the best system*, for some global "tie interval" ε.

Features. We use the Stanford RTE system (MacCartney et al., 2006) to generate a set of entailment features (RTE) for each pair of MT hypothesis and reference translation. Features are generated in both directions to avoid biases towards short or long translations. The Stanford RTE system uses a three-stage architecture. It (a) constructs a robust, dependency-based linguistic analysis of the two sentences; (b) identifies the best alignment between the two dependency graphs given similarity scores from a range of lexical resources, using a Markov Chain Monte Carlo sampling strategy; and (c) computes roughly 75 features over the aligned pair of dependency graphs. The different feature groups are shown in Table 1. A small number features are real-valued, measuring different quality aspects of the alignment. The other features are binary, indicating matches and mismatches of different types (e.g., alignment between predicates embedded under compatible or incompatible modals, respectively).

To judge to what extent the entailment-based model delivers improvements that cannot be obtained with established methods, we also experiment with a feature set formed from a set of established MT evaluation metrics (TRADMT). We combine different parametrization of (smoothed) BLEU (Papineni et al., 2002), NIST (Doddington, 2002), and TER (Snover et al., 2006), to give a total of roughly 100 features. Finally, we consider a combination of both feature sets (COMB).

3 Experimental Evaluation

Setup. To assess and compare the performance of our models, we use corpora that were created by past instances of the WMT workshop. We optimize the feature weights for the ABS models on the WMT 2006 and 2007 absolute score annotations, and correspondingly for the PAIR models on the WMT 2007 absolute score and ranking annotations. All models are evaluated on WMT 2008 to compare against the published results.

Finally, we need to set the tie interval ε. Since we did not want to optimize ε, we simply assumed that the percentage of ties observed on WMT 2007 generalizes to test sets such as the 2008 dataset. We set ε so that there are ties for first place on 30% of the sentences, with good practical success (see below).

Results. Table 2 shows our results. The first results column (Cons) shows consistency, i.e., accuracy in predicting human pairwise preference judgments. Note that the performance of a random baseline is not at 50%, but substantially lower. This is due to (a) the presence of contradictions and ties in the human judgments, which cannot be predicted; and (b) WMT's requirement to compute a total ordering of all translations for a given sentence (rather than independent binary judgments), which introduces transitivity constraints. See Callison-Burch et al. (2008) for details. Among our models, PAIR shows a somewhat better consistency than ABS, as can be expected from a model directly optimized on pairwise judgments. Across feature sets, COMB works best with a consistency of 0.53, competitive with published WMT 2008 results.

The two final columns (BASIC and WITHTIES) show Spearman's ρ for the correlation between human judgments and the two types of system-level predictions.

For BASIC system-level predictions, we find that PAIR performs considerably worse than ABS, by a margin of up to $\rho = 0.1$. Recall that the system-level analysis considers only the top-ranked hypotheses; apparently, a model optimized on pairwise judgments has a harder time choosing the best among the top-ranked hypotheses. This interpretation is supported by the large benefit that PAIR derives from explicit tie modeling. ABS gains as well, although not as much, so that the correlation of the tie-aware predictions is similar for ABS and PAIR.

Comparing different feature sets, BASIC show a similar pattern to the consistency figures. There is no clear winner between RTE and TRADMT. The performance of TRADMT is considerably better than the performance of BLEU and TER in the WMT 2008 evaluation, where $\rho \leq 0.55$. RTE is able to match the performance of an ensemble of state-of-the-art metrics, which validates our hope that linguistically motivated entailment features are sufficiently robust to make a positive contribution in MT evaluation. Furthermore, the two individual feature sets are outperformed by the combined feature set COMB. We interpret this as support for our regression-based combination approach.

Model	Feature set	Cons (Acc.)	BASIC (ρ)	WITHTIES (ρ)
ABS	TRADMT	0.50	0.74	0.74
ABS	RTE	0.51	0.72	**0.78**
ABS	COMB	0.51	0.74	0.74
PAIR	TRADMT	0.52	0.63	0.73
PAIR	RTE	0.51	0.66	**0.77**
PAIR	COMB	0.53	0.70	**0.77**
WMT 2008 (worst)		0.44	0.37	
WMT 2008 (best)		0.56	0.83	

Table 2: Evaluation on the WMT 2008 dataset for our regression models, compared to results from WMT 2008

Moving to WITHTIES, we see the best results from the RTE model which improves by $\Delta\rho = 0.06$ for ABS and $\Delta\rho = 0.11$ for PAIR. There is less improvement for the other feature sets, in particular COMB. We submitted the two overall best models, ABS-RTE and PAIR-RTE with tie-aware prediction, to the WMT 2009 challenge.

Data Analysis. We analyzed at the models' predictions to gain a better understanding of the differences in the behavior of TRADMT-based and RTE-based models. As a first step, we computed consistency numbers for the set of "top" translations (hypotheses that were ranked highest for a given reference) and for the set of "bottom" translations (hypotheses that were ranked worst for a given reference). We found small but consistent differences between the models: RTE performs about 1.5 percent better on the top hypotheses than on the bottom translations. We found the inverse effect for the TRADMT model, which performs 2 points *worse* on the top hypotheses than on the bottom hypotheses. Revisiting our initial concern that the entailment features are too noisy for very bad translations, this finding indicates some ungrammaticality-induced degradation for the entailment features, but not much. Conversely, these numbers also provide support for our initial hypothesis that surface-based features are good at detecting very deviant translations, but can have trouble dealing with legitimate linguistic variation.

Next, we analyzed the average size of the score differences between the best and second-best hypotheses for correct and incorrect predictions. We found that the RTE-based model predicted on average almost twice the difference for correct predictions ($\Delta = 0.30$) than for incorrect predictions ($\Delta = 0.16$), while the difference was considerably smaller for the TRADMT-based model ($\Delta = 0.17$ for correct vs. $\Delta = 0.13$ for incorrect). We believe it is this better discrimination on the top hypothe-

Segment	TRADMT	RTE	COMB	Gold
REF: Scottish NHS boards need to improve criminal records checks for employees outside Europe, a watchdog has said. HYP: The Scottish health ministry should improve the controls on extra-community employees to check whether they have criminal precedents, said the monitoring committee. [1357, lium-systran]	Rank: 3	Rank: **1**	Rank: 2	Rank: 1
REF: Arguments, bullying and fights between the pupils have extended to the relations between their parents. HYP: Disputes, chicane and fights between the pupils transposed in relations between the parents. [686, rbmt4]	Rank: **5**	Rank: 2	Rank: 4	Rank: 5

Table 3: Examples of reference translations and MT output from the WMT 2008 French-English News dataset. Rank judgments are out of five (smaller is better).

ses that explains the increased benefit the RTE-based model obtains from tie-aware predictions: if the best hypothesis is wrong, chances are much better than for the TRADMT-based model that counting the second-best hypothesis as "best" is correct. Unfortunately, this property is not shared by COMB to the same degree, and it does not improve as much as RTE.

Table 3 illustrates the difference between RTE and TRADMT. In the first example, RTE makes a more accurate prediction than TRADMT. The human rater's favorite translation deviates considerably from the reference translation in lexical choice, syntactic structure, and word order, for which it is punished by TRADMT. In contrast, RTE determines correctly that the propositional content of the reference is almost completely preserved. The prediction of COMB is between the two extremes. The second example shows a sentence where RTE provides a worse prediction. This sentence was rated as bad by the judge, presumably due to the inappropriate translation of the main verb. This problem, together with the reformulation of the subject, leads TRADMT to correctly predict a low score (rank 5/5). RTE's deeper analysis comes up with a high score (rank 2/5), based on the existing semantic overlap. The combined model is closer to the truth, predicting rank 4.

Feature Weights. Finally, we assessed the importance of the different entailment feature groups in the RTE model.[1] Since the presence of correlated features makes the weights difficult to interpret, we restrict ourselves to two general observations.

First, we find high weights not only for the score of the alignment between hypothesis and reference, but also for a number of syntacto-semantic match and mismatch features. This means that we do get an additional benefit from the presence of these features. For example, features with a negative effect include dropping adjuncts, unaligned root nodes, incompatible modality between the main clauses, person and location mismatches (as opposed to general mismatches) and wrongly handled passives. Conversely, some factors that increase the prediction are good alignment, matching embeddings under factive verbs, and matches between appositions.

[1]The feature weights are similar for the COMB model.

Second, we find clear differences in the usefulness of feature groups between MT evaluation and the RTE task. Some of them, in particular structural features, can be linked to the generally lower grammaticality of MT hypotheses. A case in point is a feature that fires for mismatches between dependents of predicates and which is too unreliable on the SMT data. Other differences simply reflect that the two tasks have different profiles, as sketched in Section 2.1. RTE exhibits high feature weights for quantifier and polarity features, both of which have the potential to influence entailment decisions, but are relatively unimportant for MT evaluation, at least at the current state of the art.

4 Conclusion

In this paper, we have investigated an approach to MT evaluation that is inspired by the similarity between this task and textual entailment. Our two models – one predicting absolute scores and one predicting pairwise preference judgments – use entailment features to predict the quality of MT hypotheses, thus replacing surface matching with syntacto-semantic matching. Both models perform similarly, showing sufficient robustness and coverage to attain comparable performance to a committee of established MT evaluation metrics.

We have described two refinements: (1) combining the features into a superior joint model; and (2) adding a confidence interval around the best hypothesis to model ties for first place. Both strategies improve correlation; however, unfortunately the benefits do not currently combine. Our feature weight analysis indicates that syntacto-semantic features do play an important role in score prediction in the RTE model. We plan to assess the additional benefit of the full entailment feature set against the TRADMT feature set extended by a proper lexical similarity metric, such as METEOR.

The computation of entailment features is more heavyweight than traditional MT evaluation metrics. We found the speed (about 6 s per hypothesis on a current PC) to be sufficient for easily judging the quality of datasets of the size conventionally used for MT evaluation. However, this may still be too expensive as part of an MT model that directly optimizes some performance measure, e.g., minimum error rate training (Och, 2003).

References

Satanjeev Banerjee and Alon Lavie. 2005. METEOR: An automatic metric for MT evaluation with improved correlation with human judgments. In *Proceedings of the ACL Workshop on Intrinsic and Extrinsic Evaluation Measures for Machine Translation and Summarization*, pages 65–72, Ann Arbor, MI.

R. Barzilay and N. Elhadad. 2002. Inferring strategies for sentence ordering in multidocument news summarization. *Journal of Artificial Intelligence Research*, 17:35–55.

Chris Callison-Burch, Miles Osborne, and Philipp Koehn. 2006. Re-evaluating the role of BLEU in machine translation research. In *Proceedings of EACL*, pages 249–256, Trento, Italy.

Chris Callison-Burch, Cameron Fordyce, Philipp Koehn, Christof Monz, and Josh Schroeder. 2008. Further meta-evaluation of machine translation. In *Proceedings of the ACL Workshop on Statistical Machine Translation*, pages 70–106, Columbus, OH.

Yee Seng Chan and Hwee Tou Ng. 2008. MAXSIM: A maximum similarity metric for machine translation evaluation. In *Proceedings of ACL-08: HLT*, pages 55–62, Columbus, Ohio.

William W. Cohen, Robert E. Schapire, and Yoram Singer. 1999. Learning to order things. *Journal of Artificial Intelligence Research*, 10:243–270.

Ido Dagan, Oren Glickman, and Bernardo Magnini. 2005. The PASCAL recognising textual entailment challenge. In *Proceedings of the PASCAL Challenges Workshop on Recognising Textual Entailment*, Southampton, UK.

Ido Dagan, Oren Glickman, Alfio Gliozzo, Efrat Marmorshtein, and Carlo Strapparava. 2006. Direct word sense matching for lexical substitution. In *Proceedings of ACL*, Sydney, Australia.

George Doddington. 2002. Automatic evaluation of machine translation quality using n-gram cooccurrence statistics. In *Proceedings of HLT*, pages 128–132, San Diego, CA.

Jesús Giménez and Lluís Màrquez. 2008. A smorgasbord of features for automatic MT evaluation. In *Proceedings of the Third Workshop on Statistical Machine Translation*, pages 195–198, Columbus, Ohio.

Sanda Harabagiu and Andrew Hickl. 2006. Methods for using textual entailment in open-domain question answering. In *Proceedings of ACL*, pages 905–912, Sydney, Australia.

Bill MacCartney and Christopher D. Manning. 2008. Modeling semantic containment and exclusion in natural language inference. In *Proceedings of Coling*, pages 521–528, Manchester, UK.

Bill MacCartney, Trond Grenager, Marie-Catherine de Marneffe, Daniel Cer, and Christopher D. Manning. 2006. Learning to recognize features of valid textual entailments. In *Proceedings of NAACL*, pages 41–48, New York City, NY.

Franz Josef Och. 2003. Minimum error rate training in statistical machine translation. In *Proceedings of ACL*, pages 160–167, Sapporo, Japan.

Karolina Owczarzak, Josef van Genabith, and Andy Way. 2007. Dependency-based automatic evaluation for machine translation. In *Proceedings of the NAACL-HLT / AMTA Workshop on Syntax and Structure in Statistical Translation*, pages 80–87, Rochester, NY.

Kishore Papineni, Salim Roukos, Todd Ward, and Wei-Jing Zhu. 2002. BLEU: a method for automatic evaluation of machine translation. In *Proceedings of ACL*, pages 311–318, Philadelphia, PA.

Matthew Snover, Bonnie Dorr, Richard Schwartz, Linnea Micciulla, and John Makhoul. 2006. A study of translation edit rate with targeted human annotation. In *Proceedings of AMTA*, pages 223–231, Cambridge, MA.

Combining Multi-Engine Translations with Moses

Yu Chen[1], **Michael Jellinghaus**[1], **Andreas Eisele**[1,2], **Yi Zhang**[1,2], **Sabine Hunsicker**[1], **Silke Theison**[1], **Christian Federmann**[2], **Hans Uszkoreit**[1,2]
1: Universität des Saarlandes, Saarbrücken, Germany
2: Deutsches Forschungszentrum für Künstliche Intelligenz GmbH, Saarbrücken, Germany
{yuchen,micha,yzhang,sabineh,sith}@coli.uni-saarland.de
{eisele,cfedermann,uszkoreit}@dfki.de

Abstract

We present a simple method for generating translations with the Moses toolkit (Koehn et al., 2007) from existing hypotheses produced by other translation engines. As the structures underlying these translation engines are not known, an evaluation-based strategy is applied to select systems for combination. The experiments show promising improvements in terms of BLEU.

1 Introduction

With the wealth of machine translation systems available nowadays (many of them online and for free), it makes increasing sense to investigate clever ways of combining them. Obviously, the main objective lies in finding out how to integrate the respective advantages of different approaches: Statistical machine translation (SMT) and rule-based machine translation (RBMT) systems often have complementary characteristics. Previous work on building hybrid systems includes, among others, approaches using reranking, regeneration with an SMT decoder (Eisele et al., 2008; Chen et al., 2007), and confusion networks (Matusov et al., 2006; Rosti et al., 2007; He et al., 2008).

The approach by (Eisele et al., 2008) aimed specifically at filling lexical gaps in an SMT system with information from a number of RBMT systems. The output of the RBMT engines was word-aligned with the input, yielding a total of seven phrase tables which where simply concatenated to expand the phrase table constructed from the training corpus. This approach differs from the confusion network approaches mainly in that the final hypotheses do not necessarily follow any of the input translations as the skeleton. On the other hand, it emphasizes that the additional translations should be produced by RBMT systems with lexicons that cannot be learned from the data.

The present work continues on the same track as the paper mentioned above but implements a number of important changes, most prominently a relaxation of the restrictions on the number and type of input systems. These differences are described in more detail in Section 2. Section 3 explains the implementation of our system and Section 4 its application in a number of experiments. Finally, Section 5 concludes this paper with a summary and some thoughts on future work.

2 Integrating Multiple Systems of Unknown Type and Quality

When comparing (Eisele et al., 2008) to the present work, our proposal is more general in a way that the requirement for knowledge about the systems is minimum. The types and the identities of the participated systems are assumed unknown. Accordingly, we are not able to restrict ourselves to a certain class of systems as (Eisele et al., 2008) did. We rely on a standard phrase-based SMT framework to extract the valuable pieces from the system outputs. These extracted segments are also used to improve an existing SMT system that we have access to.

While (Eisele et al., 2008) included translations from all of a fixed number of RBMT systems and added one feature to the translation model for each system, integrating all given system outputs in this way in our case could expand the search space tremendously. Meanwhile, we cannot rely on the assumption that all candidate systems actually have the potential to improve our baseline. This implies the need for a first step of system selection where the best candidate systems are identified and a limited number of them is chosen to be included in the combination. Our approach would not work without a small set of tuning data being available so that we can evaluate the systems for later selection and adjust the weights of our systems. Such tuning data is included in this year's

Proceedings of the Fourth Workshop on Statistical Machine Translation , pages 42–46,
Athens, Greece, 30 March – 31 March 2009. ©2009 Association for Computational Linguistics

task.

In this paper, we use the Moses decoder to construct translations from the given system outputs. We mainly propose two slightly different ways: One is to construct translation models solely from the given translations and the other is to extend an existing translation model with these additional translations.

3 Implementation

Despite the fact that the output of current MT systems is usually not comparable in quality to human translations, the machine-generated translations are nevertheless "parallel" to the input so that it is straightforward to construct a translation model from data of this kind. This is the spirit behind our method for combining multiple translations.

3.1 Direct combination

Clearly, for the same source sentence, we expect to have different translations from different translation systems, just like we would expect from human translators. Also, every system may have its own advantages. We break these translations into smaller units and hope to be able to select the best ones and form them into a better translation.

One single translation of a few thousand sentences is normally inadequate for building a reliable general-purpose SMT system (data sparseness problem). However, in the system combination task, this is no longer an issue as the system only needs to translate sentences within the data set.

When more translation engines are available, the size of this set becomes larger. Hence, we collect translations from all available systems and pair them with the corresponding input text, thus forming a medium-sized "hypothesis" corpus. Our system starts processing this corpus with a standard phrase-based SMT setup, using the Moses toolkit (Koehn et al., 2007).

The hypothesis corpus is first tokenized and lowercased. Then, we run GIZA++ (Och and Ney, 2003) on the corpus to obtain word alignments in both directions. The phrases are extracted from the intersection of the alignments with the "grow" heuristics. In addition, we also generate a reordering model with the default configuration as included in the Moses toolkit. This "*hypothesis*" translation model can already be used by the Moses decoder together with a language model to perform translations over the corresponding sentence set.

3.2 Integration into existing SMT system

Sometimes, the goal of system combination is not only to produce a translation but also to improve one of the systems. In this paper, we aim at incorporating the additional system outputs to improve an out-of-domain SMT system trained on the Europarl corpus (Koehn, 2005). Our hope is that the additional translation hypotheses could bring in new phrases or, more generally, new information that was not contained in the Europarl model. In order to facilitate comparisons, we use in-domain LMs for all setups.

We investigate two alternative ways of integrating the additional phrases into the existing SMT system: One is to take the hypothesis translation model described in Section 3.1, the other is to construct system-specific models constructed with only translations from one system at a time.

Although the Moses decoder is able to work with two phrase tables at once (Koehn and Schroeder, 2007), it is difficult to use this method when there is more than one additional model. The method requires tuning on at least six more features, which expands the search space for the translation task unnecessarily. We instead integrate the translation models from multiple sources by extending the phrase table. In contrast to the prior approach presented in (Chen et al., 2007) and (Eisele et al., 2008) which concatenates the phrase tables and adds new features as system markers, our extension method avoids duplicate entries in the final combined table.

Given a set of hypothesis translation models (derived from an arbitrary number of system outputs) and an original large translation model to be improved, we first sort the models by quality (see Section 3.3), always assigning the highest priority to the original model. The additional phrase tables are appended to the large model in sorted order such that only phrase pairs that were never seen before are included. Lastly, we add new features (in the form of additional columns in the phrase table) to the translation model to indicate each pair's origin.

3.3 System evaluation

Since both the system translations and the reference translations are available for the tuning set, we first compare each output to the reference translation using BLEU (Papineni et al., 2001) and METEOR (Banerjee and Lavie, 2005) and a combined scoring scheme provided by the ULC toolkit (Gimenez and Marquez, 2008). In our experiments, we selected a subset of 5 systems for the combination, in most cases, based on BLEU.

On the other hand, some systems may be designed in a way that they deliver interesting unique translation segments. Therefore, we also measure the similarity among system outputs as shown in Table 2 in a given collection by calculating average similarity scores across every pair of outputs.

	de-en	fr-en	es-en	en-de	en-fr	en-es
Num.	20	23	28	15	16	9
Median	19.87	26.55	22.50	13.78	24.76	23.70
Range	16.37	17.06	9.74	4.75	11.05	13.94
Top 5	de-en	fr-en	es-en	en-de	en-fr	en-es
Median	22.26	27.93	26.43	15.21	26.62	26.61
Range	4.31	4.76	5.71	1.71	0.68	5.56

Table 1: Statistics of system outputs' BLEU scores

The range of BLEU scores cannot indicate the similarity of the systems. The direction with the most systems submitted is Spanish-English but their respective performances are very close to each other. As for the selected subset, the English-French systems have the most similar performance in terms of BLEU scores. The French-English translations have the largest range in BLEU but the similarity in this group is **not** the lowest.

	de-en	fr-en	es-en	en-de	en-fr	en-es
All	34.09	46.48	61.83	31.74	44.95	38.11
Selected	36.65	56.16	56.06	33.92	52.78	57.25

Table 2: Similarity of the system outputs

Ideally, we should select systems with highest quality scores and lowest similarity scores. For German-English, we selected the three with the highest METEOR scores and another two with high METEOR scores but low similarity scores to the first three. For the other language directions, we chose five systems from different institutions with the highest scores.

3.4 Language models

We use a standard n-gram language model for each target language using the monolingual training data provided in the translation task. These LMs are thus specific to the same domain as the input texts. Moreover, we also generate *"hypothesis"* LMs solely based on the given system outputs, that is, LMs that model how the candidate systems convey information in the target language. These LMs do not require any additional training data. Therefore, we do not require any training data other than the given system outputs by using the "hypothesis" language model and the "hypothesis" translation model.

3.5 Tuning

After building the models, it is essential to tune the SMT system to optimize the feature weights. We use Minimal Error Rate Training (Och, 2003) to maximize BLEU on the complete development data. Unlike the standard tuning procedure, we do not tune the final system directly. Instead, we obtain the weights using models built from the tuning portion of the system outputs.

For each combination variant, we first train models on the provided outputs corresponding to the tuning set. This system, called the *tuning system*, is also tuned on the tuning set. The initial weights of any additional features not included in the standard setting are set to 0. We then adapt the weights to the system built with translations corresponding to the test set. The procedure and the settings for building this system must be identical to that of the tuning system.

4 Experiments

The purpose of this exercise is to understand the nature of the system combination task in practice. Therefore, we restrict ourselves to the training data and system translations provided by the shared task. The types of the systems that produced the translations are assumed to be unknown. We report results for six translation directions between four languages.

4.1 Data and baseline

We build an SMT system from release v4 of the Europarl corpus (Koehn, 2005), following a standard routine using the Moses toolkit. The system also includes 5-gram language models trained on in-domain corpora of the respective target languages using SRILM (Stolcke, 2002).

The systems in this paper, including the baseline, are all tuned on the same 501-sentence tuning set. Note also that the provided n-best outputs are excluded in our experiments.

4.2 Results

The experiments include three different setups for direct system combination, involving only hypothesis translation models. System S_0, the baseline for this group, uses a hypothesis translation model built with all available system translations and a hypothesis LM (also from the machine-generated outputs). S_1 differs from S_0 in that the LM in S_1 is generated from a large news corpus. S_2 consists of translation models built with only the five selected systems. The BLEU scores of these systems are shown in Table 3.

	de-en	fr-en	es-en	en-de	en-fr	en-es
Top 1	21.16	30.91	28.54	14.96	26.55	27.84
Mean	17.29	23.78	21.39	12.76	22.96	21.43
S_0	20.46	27.50	23.35	13.95	27.29	25.59
S_1	21.76	28.05	25.49	15.16	27.70	26.09
S_2	21.71	24.98	27.26	15.62	24.28	25.22

Table 3: BLEU scores of direct system combination

When all outputs are included, the combined system can always produce translations better than most of the systems. When only a hypothesis LM is used, the BLEU scores are always higher than the average BLEU scores of the outputs. It even outperforms the top system for English-French. This simple setup (S_0) is certainly a feasible solution when no additional data is available and no system evaluation is possible. This approach appears to be more effective on typically difficult language pairs that involve German.

As for the systems with normal language models, neither of the systems ensure better translations. The translation quality is not completely determined by the number of included translations and their quality. On the other hand, the output set with higher diversity (Table 2) usually leads to better combination results. This observation is consistent with the results from the system integration experiments shown in Table 4.

	de-en	fr-en	es-en	en-de	en-fr	en-es
Bas	19.13	25.07	24.55	13.59	23.67	23.67
Med	17.99	24.56	20.70	13.19	24.19	22.12
All	21.40	28.00	27.75	15.21	27.20	26.41
Top5	21.70	26.01	28.53	15.52	27.87	27.92

Table 4: BLEU scores of integrated SMT systems (Bas: Baseline, Med: Median)

There are two variants in our experiments on system integration. *All* in Table 4 represents the system that integrates the complete hypothesis translation model with the Europarl model, while *Top 5* refers to the system that incorporates the five system-specific models separately. Both setups result in an improvement over the baseline Europarl-based SMT system. BLEU scores increase by up to 4.25 points. The integrated SMT system sometimes produces translations better than the best system (7 out of 12 cases).

5 Conclusion

This work uses the Moses toolkit to combine translations from multiple engines in a simple way. The experiments on six translation directions show interesting results: The final translations are always better than the majority of the given systems, while the combination performs better than the best system in half the cases. A similar approach was applied to improve an existing SMT system which was built in a domain different from the test task. We achieved improvements in all cases.

There are many possible future directions to continue this work. As we have shown, the quality of the combined system is more related to the diversity of the involved systems than to the number of the systems or their quality. Hand-picked systems lead to better combinations than those selected by BLEU scores. It would be interesting to develop a more comprehensive system selection strategy.

Acknowledgments

This work was supported by the EuroMatrix project (IST-034291) which is funded by the European Community under the Sixth Framework Programme for Research and Technological Development.

References

Satanjeev Banerjee and Alon Lavie. 2005. METEOR: An automatic metric for MT evaluation with improved correlation with human judgments. In *Proceedings of the ACL Workshop on Intrinsic and Extrinsic Evaluation Measures for Machine Translation and/or Summarization*, pages 65–72, Ann Arbor, Michigan, June. Association for Computational Linguistics.

Yu Chen, Andreas Eisele, Christian Federmann, Eva Hasler, Michael Jellinghaus, and Silke Theison. 2007. Multi-engine machine translation with an open-source SMT decoder. In *Proceedings of*

WMT07, pages 193–196, Prague, Czech Republic, June. Association for Computational Linguistics.

Andreas Eisele, Christian Federmann, Hervé Saint-Amand, Michael Jellinghaus, Teresa Herrmann, and Yu Chen. 2008. Using Moses to integrate multiple rule-based machine translation engines into a hybrid system. In *Proceedings of the Third Workshop on Statistical Machine Translation*, pages 179–182, Columbus, Ohio, June. Association for Computational Linguistics.

Jesus Gimenez and Lluis Marquez. 2008. A smorgasbord of features for automatic MT evaluation. In *Proceedings of the Third Workshop on Statistical Machine Translation*, pages 195–198, Columbus, Ohio, June. Association for Computational Linguistics.

Xiaodong He, Mei Yang, Jianfeng Gao, Patrick Nguyen, and Robert Moore. 2008. Indirect-HMM-based hypothesis alignment for combining outputs from machine translation systems. In *Proceedings of the 2008 Conference on Empirical Methods in Natural Language Processing*, pages 98–107, Honolulu, Hawaii, October. Association for Computational Linguistics.

Philipp Koehn and Josh Schroeder. 2007. Experiments in domain adaptation for statistical machine translation. In *Proceedings of the Second Workshop on Statistical Machine Translation*, pages 224–227, Prague, Czech Republic, June. Association for Computational Linguistics.

Philipp Koehn, Hieu Hoang, Alexandra Birch Mayne, Christopher Callison-Burch, Marcello Federico, Nicola Bertoldi, Brooke Cowan, Wade Shen, Christine Moran, Richard Zens, Chris Dyer, Ondrej Bojar, Alexandra Constantin, and Evan Herbs. 2007. Moses: Open source toolkit for statistical machine translation. In *Proceedings of Annual meeting of the Association for Computation Linguistics (acl), demonstration session*, pages 177–180, Prague, Czech, June.

Philipp Koehn. 2005. Europarl: A Parallel Corpus for Statistical Machine Translation. In *Proceedings of MT Summit 2005*.

Evgeny Matusov, Nicola Ueffing, and Hermann Ney. 2006. Computing consensus translation from multiple machine translation systems using enhanced hypotheses alignment. In *Conference of the European Chapter of the Association for Computational Linguistics*, pages 33–40, Trento, Italy, April.

Franz Josef Och and Hermann Ney. 2003. A systematic comparison of various statistical alignment models. *Computational Linguistics*, 29(1):19–51.

Franz Josef Och. 2003. Minimum error rate training in statistical machine translation. In *ACL '03: Proceedings of the 41st Annual Meeting on Association for Computational Linguistics*, pages 160–167, Morristown, NJ, USA. Association for Computational Linguistics.

Kishore Papineni, Salim Roukos, Todd Ward, and Wei-Jing Zhu. 2001. BLEU: a method for automatic evaluation of machine translation. In *Proceedings of the 40th Annual Meeting on Association for Computational Linguistics*, pages 311–318, Morristown, NJ, USA. Association for Computational Linguistics.

Antti-Veikko I. Rosti, Spyridon Matsoukas, and Richard M. Schwartz. 2007. Improved word-level system combination for machine translation. In *ACL*.

Andreas Stolcke. 2002. SRILM - an extensible language modeling toolkit. In *the 7th International Conference on Spoken Language Processing (ICSLP) 2002*, Denver, Colorado.

CMU System Combination for WMT'09

Almut Silja Hildebrand
Carnegie Mellon University
Pittsburgh, USA
silja@cs.cmu.edu

Stephan Vogel
Carnegie Mellon University
Pittsburgh, USA
vogel@cs.cmu.edu

Abstract

This paper describes the CMU entry for the system combination shared task at WMT'09. Our combination method is hypothesis selection, which uses information from n-best lists from several MT systems. The sentence level features are independent from the MT systems involved. To compensate for various n-best list sizes in the workshop shared task including first-best-only entries, we normalize one of our high-impact features for varying sub-list size. We combined restricted data track entries in French - English, German - English and Hungarian - English using provided data only.

1 Introduction

For the combination of machine translation systems there have been two main approaches described in recent publications. One uses confusion network decoding to combine translation systems as described in (Rosti et al., 2008) and (Karakos et al., 2008). The other approach selects whole hypotheses from a combined n-best list (Hildebrand and Vogel, 2008).

Our setup follows the approach described in (Hildebrand and Vogel, 2008). We combine the output from the available translation systems into one joint n-best list, then calculate a set of features consistently for all hypotheses. We use MER training on a development set to determine feature weights and re-rank the joint n-best list.

2 Features

For our entries to the WMT'09 we used the following feature groups:

- Language model score
- Word lexicon scores
- Sentence length features
- Rank feature
- Normalized n-gram agreement

The details on language model and word lexicon scores can be found in (Hildebrand and Vogel, 2008). We use two sentence length features, which are the ratio of the hypothesis length to the length of the source sentence and the difference between the hypothesis length and the average length of the hypotheses in the n-best list for the respective source sentence. We also use the rank of the hypothesis in the original system's n-best list as a feature.

2.1 Normalized N-gram Agreement

The participants of the WMT'09 shared translation task provided output from their translation systems in various sizes. Most submission were 1st-best translation only, some submitted 10-best up to 300-best lists.

In preliminary experiments we saw that adding a high scoring 1st-best translation to a joint n-best list composed of several larger n-best lists does not yield the desired improvement. This might be due to the fact, that hypotheses within an n-best list originating from one single system (sub-list) tend to be much more similar to each other than to hypotheses from another system. This leads to hypotheses from larger sub-lists scoring higher in the n-best list based features, e.g. because they collect more n-gram matches within their sub-list, which "supports" them the more the larger it is.

Previous experiments on Chinese-English showed, that the two feature groups with the highest impact on the combination result are the language model and the n-best list based n-gram agreement. Therefore we decided to focus on the n-best list n-gram agreement for exploring sub-list

Proceedings of the Fourth Workshop on Statistical Machine Translation, pages 47–50,
Athens, Greece, 30 March – 31 March 2009.

size normalization to adapt to the data situation with various n-best list sizes.

The n-gram agreement score of each n-gram in the target sentence is the relative frequency of target sentences in the n-best list for one source sentence that contain the n-gram e, independent of the position of the n-gram in the sentence. This feature represents the percentage of the translation hypotheses, which contain the respective n-gram. If a hypothesis contains an n-gram more than once, it is only counted once, hence the maximum for the agreement score $a(e)$ is 1.0 (100%). The agreement score $a(e)$ for each n-gram e is:

$$a(e) = \frac{C}{L} \tag{1}$$

where C is the count of the hypotheses containing the n-gram and L is the size of the n-best list for this source sentence.

To compensate for the various n-best list sizes provided to us we modified the n-best list n-gram agreement by normalizing the count of hypotheses that contain the n-gram by the size of the sub-list it came from. It can be viewed as either collecting fractional counts for each n-gram match, or as calculating the n-gram agreement percentage for each sub-list and then interpolating them. The normalized n-gram agreement score $a_{norm}(e)$ for each n-gram e is:

$$a_{norm}(e) = \frac{1}{P} \sum_{j=1}^{P} \frac{C_j}{L_j} \tag{2}$$

where P is the number of systems, C_j is the count of the hypotheses containing the n-gram e in the sublist p_j and L_j is the size of the sublist p_j.

For the extreme case of a sub-list size of one the fact of finding an n-gram in that hypothesis or not has a rather strong impact on the normalized agreement score. Therefore we introduce a smoothing factor λ in a way that it has an increasing influence the smaller the sub-list is:

$$a_{smooth}(e) = \frac{1}{P} \sum_{j=1}^{P} \left[\frac{C_j}{L_j} (1 - \frac{\lambda}{L_j}) \right] + \left[\frac{L_j - C_j}{L_j} \frac{\lambda}{L_j} \right] \tag{3}$$

where P is the number of systems, C_j is the count of the hypotheses containing the n-gram in the sublist p_j and L_j is the size of the sublist p_j. We used an initial value of $\lambda = 0.1$ for our experiments.

In all three cases the score for the whole hypothesis is the sum over the word scores normalized by the sentence length. We use n-gram lengths $n = 1..6$ as six separate features.

3 Preliminary Experiments Arabic-English

For the development of the modification on the n-best list n-gram agreement feature we used n-best lists from three large scale Arabic to English translation systems. We evaluate using the case insensitive BLEU score for the MT08 test set with four references, which was unseen data for the individual systems as well as the system combination. Table 1 shows the initial scores of the three input systems.

system	MT08
A	47.47
B	46.33
C	44.42

Table 1: Arabic-English Baselines: BLEU

To compare the behavior of the combination result for different n-best list sizes we combined the 100-best lists from systems A and C and then added three n-best list sizes from the middle system B into the combination: 1-best, 10-best and full 100-best. For each of these four combination options we ran the hypothesis selection using the plain version of the n-gram agreement feature a as well as the normalized version without a_{norm} and with smoothing a_{smooth}.

combination	a	a_{norm}	a_{smooth}
A & C	48.04	48.09	48.13
A & C & B_1	47.84	48.34	48.21
A & C & B_{10}	48.29	48.33	48.47
A & C & B_{100}	48.91	48.95	49.02

Table 2: Combination results: BLEU on MT08

The modified feature has as expected no impact on the combination of n-best lists of the same size (see Table 2), however it shows an improvement of BLEU +0.5 for the combination with the 1st-best from system B. The smoothing seems to have no significant impact for this dataset, but different smoothing factors will be investigated in the future.

4 Workshop Results

To train our language models and word lexica we only used provided data. Therefore we excluded systems from the combination, which were to our knowledge using unrestricted training data (google). We did not include any contrastive systems.

We trained the statistical word lexica on the parallel data provided for each language pair[1]. For each combination we used two language models, a 1.2 giga-word 3-gram language model, trained on the provided monolingual English data and a 4-gram language model trained on the English part of the parallel training data of the respective languages. We used the SRILM toolkit (Stolcke, 2002) for training.

For each of the three language pairs we submitted a combination that used the plain version of the n-gram agreement feature as well as one using the normalized smoothed version.

The provided system combination development set, which we used for tuning our feature weights, was the same for all language pairs, 502 sentences with only one reference.

For combination we tokenized and lowercased all data, because the n-best lists were submitted in various formats. Therefore we report the case insensitive scores here. The combination was optimized toward the BLEU metric, therefore results for TER and METEOR are not very meaningful here and only reported for completeness.

4.1 French-English

14 systems were submitted to the restricted data track for the French-English translation task. The scores on the combination development set range from BLEU 27.56 to 15.09 (case insensitive evaluation).

We received n-best lists from five systems, a 300-best, a 200-best two 100-best and one 10-best list. We included up to 100 hypotheses per system in our joint n-best list.

For our workshop submission we combined the top nine systems with the last system scoring 24.23 as well as all 14 systems. Comparing the results for the two combinations of all 14 systems (see Table 3), the one with the sub-list normalization for the n-gram agreement feature gains +0.8 BLEU on unseen data compared to the one without normalization.

system	dev	test	TER	Meteor
best single	27.56	26.88	56.32	52.68
top 9 a_{smooth}	29.85	28.07	55.23	53.90
all 14 a_{smooth}	30.39	28.46	55.12	54.35
all 14	29.49	27.65	55.41	53.74

Table 3: French-English Results: BLEU

Our system combination via hypothesis selection could improve the translation quality by +1.6 BLEU on the unseen test set compared to the best single system.

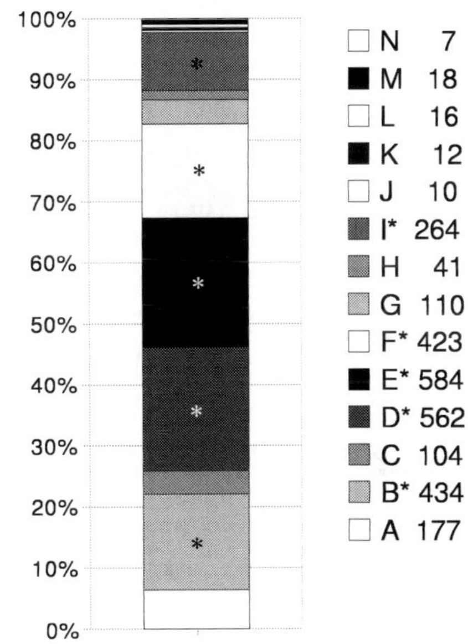

Figure 1: Contributions of the individual systems to the final translation.

Figure 1 shows, how many hypotheses were contributed by the individual systems to the final translation (unseen data). The systems A to N are ordered by their BLEU score on the development set. The systems which provided n-best lists, marked with a star in the diagram, clearly dominate the selection. The low scoring systems contribute very little as expected.

4.2 German-English

14 systems were submitted to the restricted data track for the German-English translation task. The scores on the combination development set range

[1] http://www.statmt.org/wmt09/translation-task.html#training

from BLEU 27.56 to 7 (case insensitive evaluation). The two lowest scoring systems at BLEU 11 and 7 were so far from the rest of the systems that we decided to exclude them, assuming an error had occurred.

Within the remaining 12 submissions were four n-best lists, three 100-best and one 10-best.

For our submissions we combined the top seven systems between BLEU 22.91 and 20.24 as well as the top 12 systems where the last one of those was scoring BLEU 16.00 on the development set. For this language pair the combination with the normalized n-gram agreement also outperforms the one without by +0.8 BLEU (see Table 4).

system	dev	test	TER	Meteor
best single	22.91	21.03	61.87	47.96
top 7 a_{smooth}	25.13	22.86	60.73	49.71
top 12 a_{smooth}	25.32	22.98	60.72	50.01
top 12	25.12	22.20	60.95	49.33

Table 4: German-English Results: BLEU

Our system combination via hypothesis selection could improve translation quality by +1.95 BLEU on the unseen test set over the best single system.

4.3 Hungarian-English

Only three systems were submitted for the Hungarian-English translation task. Scores on the combination development set ranged from BLEU 13.63 to 10.04 (case insensitive evaluation). Only the top system provided an n-best list. We used 100-best hypotheses.

system	dev	test	TER	Meteor
best single	13.63	12.73	68.75	36.76
3 sys a_{smooth}	14.98	13.74	72.34	38.20
3 sys	14.14	13.18	74.29	37.52

Table 5: Hungarian-English Results: BLEU

We submitted combinations of the three systems by using the modified smoothed n-gram agreement feature and the plain version of the n-gram agreement feature. Here also the normalized version of the feature gives an improvement of +0.56 BLEU with an overall improvement of +1.0 BLEU over the best single system (see Table 5).

5 Summary

It is beneficial to include more systems, even if they are more than 7 points BLEU behind the best system, as the comparison to the combinations with fewer systems shows.

In the mixed size data situation of the workshop the modified feature shows a clear improvement for all three language pairs. Different smoothing factors should be investigated for these data sets in the future.

Acknowledgments

We would like to thank the participants in the WMT'09 workshop shared translation task for providing their data, especially n-best lists.

References

Almut Silja Hildebrand and Stephan Vogel. 2008. Combination of machine translation systems via hypothesis selection from combined n-best lists. In *MT at work: Proceedings of the Eighth Conference of the Association for Machine Translation in the Americas*, pages 254–261, Waikiki, Hawaii, October. Association for Machine Translation in the Americas.

Damianos Karakos, Jason Eisner, Sanjeev Khudanpur, and Markus Dreyer. 2008. Machine translation system combination using itg-based alignments. In *Proceedings of ACL-08: HLT, Short Papers*, pages 81–84, Columbus, Ohio, June. Association for Computational Linguistics.

Antti-Veikko Rosti, Bing Zhang, Spyros Matsoukas, and Richard Schwartz. 2008. Incremental hypothesis alignment for building confusion networks with application to machine translation system combination. In *Proceedings of the Third Workshop on Statistical Machine Translation*, pages 183–186, Columbus, Ohio, June. Association for Computational Linguistics.

Andreas Stolcke. 2002. Srilm - an extensible language modeling toolkit. In *Proceedings International Conference for Spoken Language Processing*, Denver, Colorado, September.

The RWTH System Combination System for WMT 2009

Gregor Leusch, Evgeny Matusov, and Hermann Ney
RWTH Aachen University
Aachen, Germany

Abstract

RWTH participated in the System Combination task of the Fourth Workshop on Statistical Machine Translation (WMT 2009). Hypotheses from 9 German→English MT systems were combined into a consensus translation. This consensus translation scored 2.1% better in BLEU and 2.3% better in TER (abs.) than the best single system. In addition, cross-lingual output from 10 French, German, and Spanish→English systems was combined into a consensus translation, which gave an improvement of 2.0% in BLEU/3.5% in TER (abs.) over the best single system.

1 Introduction

The RWTH approach to MT system combination is a refined version of the ROVER approach in ASR (Fiscus, 1997), with additional steps to cope with reordering between different hypotheses, and to use true casing information from the input hypotheses. The basic concept of the approach has been described by Matusov et al. (2006). Several improvements have been added later (Matusov et al., 2008). This approach includes an enhanced alignment and reordering framework. In contrast to existing approaches (Jayaraman and Lavie, 2005; Rosti et al., 2007), the context of the whole corpus rather than a single sentence is considered in this iterative, unsupervised procedure, yielding a more reliable alignment. Majority voting on the generated lattice is performed using the prior probabilities for each system as well as other statistical models such as a special n-gram language model.

2 System Combination Algorithm

In this section we present the details of our system combination method. Figure 1 gives an overview of the system combination architecture described in this section. After preprocessing the MT hypotheses, pairwise alignments between the hypotheses are calculated. The hypotheses are then reordered to match the word order of a selected primary hypothesis. From this, we create a confusion network (CN), which we then rescore using system prior weights and a language model (LM). The single best path in this CN then constitutes the consensus translation.

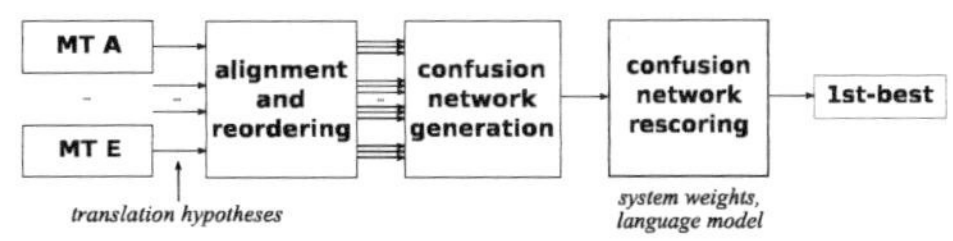

Figure 1: The system combination architecture.

2.1 Word Alignment

The proposed alignment approach is a statistical one. It takes advantage of multiple translations for a whole corpus to compute a consensus translation for each sentence in this corpus. It also takes advantage of the fact that the sentences to be aligned are in the same language.

For each source sentence F in the test corpus, we select one of its translations $E_n, n=1,\ldots,M$, as the *primary* hypothesis. Then we align the *secondary* hypotheses $E_m(m = 1,\ldots,M; n \neq m)$ with E_n to match the word order in E_n. Since it is not clear which hypothesis should be primary, i. e. has the "best" word order, we let every hypothesis play the role of the primary translation, and align all pairs of hypotheses (E_n, E_m); $n \neq m$.

The word alignment is *trained* in analogy to the alignment training procedure in statistical MT. The difference is that the two sentences that have to be aligned are in the same language. We use the IBM Model 1 (Brown et al., 1993) and the Hidden Markov Model (HMM, (Vogel et al., 1996)) to estimate the alignment model.

The alignment training corpus is created from a test corpus[1] of effectively $M \cdot (M-1) \cdot N$ sentences translated by the involved MT engines. The single-word based lexicon probabilities $p(e|e')$ are initialized from normalized lexicon counts collected over the sentence pairs (E_m, E_n) on this corpus. Since all of the hypotheses are in the same language, we count co-occurring identical words, i. e. whether $e_{m,j}$ is the same word as $e_{n,i}$ for some i and j. In addition, we add a fraction of a count for words with identical prefixes.

[1]A test corpus can be used directly because the alignment training is unsupervised and only automatically produced translations are considered.

Proceedings of the Fourth Workshop on Statistical Machine Translation, pages 51–55,
Athens, Greece, 30 March – 31 March 2009.

The model parameters are trained iteratively using the GIZA++ toolkit (Och and Ney, 2003). The training is performed in the directions $E_m \rightarrow E_n$ and $E_n \rightarrow E_m$. After each iteration, the updated lexicon tables from the two directions are interpolated. The final alignments are determined using a cost matrix C for each sentence pair (E_m, E_n). Elements of this matrix are the local costs $C(j, i)$ of aligning a word $e_{m,j}$ from E_m to a word $e_{n,i}$ from E_n. Following Matusov et al. (2004), we compute these local costs by interpolating the negated logarithms of the state occupation probabilities from the "source-to-target" and "target-to-source" training of the HMM model. Two different alignments are computed using the cost matrix C: the alignment $\tilde{a}$ used for reordering each secondary translation E_m, and the alignment $\bar{a}$ used to build the confusion network.

In addition to the GIZA++ alignments, we have also conducted preliminary experiments following He et al. (2008) to exploit character-based similarity, as well as estimating $p(e|e') := \sum_f p(e|f)p(f|e')$ directly from a bilingual lexicon. But we were not able to find improvements over the GIZA++ alignments so far.

2.2 Word Reordering and Confusion Network Generation

After reordering each secondary hypothesis E_m and the rows of the corresponding alignment cost matrix according to $\tilde{a}$, we determine $M - 1$ monotone *one-to-one* alignments between E_n as the primary translation and $E_m, m = 1, \ldots, M; m \neq n$. We then construct the confusion network. In case of many-to-one connections in $\tilde{a}$ of words in E_m to a single word from E_n, we only keep the connection with the lowest alignment costs.

The use of the one-to-one alignment $\bar{a}$ implies that some words in the secondary translation will not have a correspondence in the primary translation and vice versa. We consider these words to have a null alignment with the empty word ε. In the corresponding confusion network, the empty word will be transformed to an ε-arc.

$M - 1$ monotone one-to-one alignments can then be transformed into a confusion network. We follow the approach of Bangalore et al. (2001) with some extensions. Multiple insertions with regard to the primary hypothesis are sub-aligned to each other, as described by Matusov et al. (2008). Figure 2 gives an example for the alignment.

2.3 Voting in the confusion network

Instead of choosing a fixed sentence to define the word order for the consensus translation, we generate confusion networks for all hypotheses as primary, and unite them into a single lattice. In our experience, this approach is advantageous in terms of translation quality, e.g. by 0.7% in BLEU compared to a minimum Bayes risk primary (Rosti et al., 2007). Weighted majority voting on a single confusion network is straightforward and analogous to ROVER (Fiscus, 1997). We sum up the probabilities of the arcs which are labeled with the same word and have the same start state and the same end state. To exploit the true casing abilities of the input MT systems, we sum up the scores of arcs bearing the same word but in different cases. Here, we leave the decision about upper or lower case to the language model.

2.4 Language Models

The lattice representing a union of several confusion networks can then be directly rescored with an n-gram language model (LM). A transformation of the lattice is required, since LM history has to be memorized.

We train a trigram LM on the outputs of the systems involved in system combination. For LM training, we took the system hypotheses for the same test corpus for which the consensus translations are to be produced. Using this "adapted" LM for lattice rescoring thus gives bonus to n-grams from the original system hypotheses, in most cases from the original phrases. Presumably, many of these phrases have a correct word order, since they are extracted from the training data. Previous experimental results show that using this LM in rescoring together with a word penalty (to counteract any bias towards short sentences) notably improves translation quality. This even results in better translations than using a "classical" LM trained on a monolingual training corpus. We attribute this to the fact that most of the systems we combine are phrase-based systems, which already include such general LMs. Since we are using a true-cased LM trained on the hypotheses, we can exploit true casing information from the input systems by using this LM to disambiguate between the separate arcs generated for the variants (see Section 2.3).

After LM rescoring, we add the probabilities of identical partial paths to improve the estimation of the score for the best hypothesis. This is done through determinization of the lattice.

2.5 Extracting Consensus Translations

To generate our consensus translation, we extract the single-best path within the rescored confusion network. With our approach, we could also extract N-best hypotheses. In a subsequent step, these N-best lists could be rescored with additional statistical models (Matusov et al., 2008). But as we did not have the resources in the WMT 2009 evaluation, this step was dropped for our submission.

3 Tuning system weights

System weights, LM factor, and word penalty need to be tuned to produce good consensus translations. We optimize these parameters using the

<table>
<tr><td rowspan="4">system hypotheses</td><td colspan="9">0.25 would your like coffee or tea</td></tr>
<tr><td colspan="9">0.35 have you tea or Coffee</td></tr>
<tr><td colspan="9">0.10 would like your coffee or</td></tr>
<tr><td colspan="9">0.30 I have some coffee tea would you like</td></tr>
<tr><td rowspan="3">alignment and reordering</td><td colspan="9">have|would you|your $|like Coffee|coffee or|or tea|tea</td></tr>
<tr><td colspan="9">would|would your|your like|like coffee|coffee or|or $|tea</td></tr>
<tr><td colspan="9">I|$</b> would|<b>would</b> you|<b>your</b> like|<b>like</b> have|<b>$ some|$ coffee|coffee $|or tea|tea</td></tr>
<tr><td rowspan="4">confusion network</td><td>$</b></td><td><b>would</b></td><td><b>your</b></td><td><b>like</b></td><td><b>$</td><td>$</td><td>coffee</td><td>or</td><td>tea</td></tr>
<tr><td>$</td><td>have</td><td>you</td><td>$</td><td>$</td><td>$</td><td>Coffee</td><td>or</td><td>tea</td></tr>
<tr><td>$</td><td>would</td><td>your</td><td>like</td><td>$</td><td>$</td><td>coffee</td><td>or</td><td>$</td></tr>
<tr><td>I</td><td>would</td><td>you</td><td>like</td><td>have</td><td>some</td><td>coffee</td><td>$</td><td>tea</td></tr>
<tr><td rowspan="4">voting (normalized)</td><td>$</b></td><td><b>would</b></td><td><b>you</b></td><td>$</td><td>$</b></td><td><b>$</td><td>coffee</td><td>or</td><td>tea</td></tr>
<tr><td>0.7</td><td>0.65</td><td>0.65</td><td>0.35</td><td>0.7</td><td>0.7</td><td>0.5</td><td>0.7</td><td>0.9</td></tr>
<tr><td>I</td><td>have</td><td>your</td><td>like</td><td>have</td><td>some</td><td>Coffee</td><td>$</td><td>$</td></tr>
<tr><td>0.3</td><td>0.35</td><td>0.35</td><td>0.65</td><td>0.3</td><td>0.3</td><td>0.5</td><td>0.3</td><td>0.1</td></tr>
<tr><td>consensus translation</td><td colspan="9">would you like coffee or tea</td></tr>
</table>

Figure 2: Example of creating a confusion network from monotone one-to-one word alignments (denoted with symbol |). The words of the primary hypothesis are printed in bold. The symbol $ denotes a null alignment or an ε-arc in the corresponding part of the confusion network.

Table 1: Systems combined for the WMT 2009 task. Systems written in oblique were also used in the Cross Lingual task (`rbmt3` for FR→EN).

DE→EN	*`google`*, `liu`, *`rbmt3`*, `rwth`, `stuttgart`, `systran`, `uedin`, *`uka`*, `umd`
ES→EN	*`google`*, `nict`, *`rbmt4`*, *`rwth`*, `talp-upc`, `uedin`
FR→EN	`dcu`, *`google`*, `jhu`, `limsi`, *`lium-systran`*, *`rbmt4`*, `rwth`, *`uedin`*, `uka`

publicly available CONDOR optimization toolkit (Berghen and Bersini, 2005). For the WMT 2009 Workshop, we selected a linear combination of BLEU (Papineni et al., 2002) and TER (Snover et al., 2006) as optimization criterion, $\hat{\Theta} := \text{argmax}_{\Theta}\{(2 \cdot \text{BLEU}) - \text{TER}\}$, based on previous experience (Mauser et al., 2008). We used the whole dev set as a tuning set. For more stable results, we used the case-insensitive variants for both measures, despite the explicit use of case information in our approach.

4 Experimental results

Due to the large number of submissions (71 in total for the language pairs DE→EN, ES→EN, FR→EN), we had to select a reasonable number of systems to be able to tune the parameters in a reliable way. Based on previous experience, we manually selected the systems with the best BLEU/TER score, and tried different variations of this selection, e.g. by removing systems which had low weights after optimization, or by adding promising systems, like rule based systems.

Table 1 lists the systems which made it into our final submission. In our experience, if a large number of systems is available, using n-best translations does not give better results than using single best translations, but raises optimization time significantly. Consequently, we only used single best translations from all systems.

The results also confirm another observation: Even though rule-based systems by itself may have significantly lower automatic evaluation scores (e.g. by 2% or more in BLEU on DE→EN), they are often very important in system combination, and can improve the consensus translation e.g. by 0.5% in BLEU.

Having submitted our translations to the WMT workshop, we calculated scores on the WMT 2009 test set, to verify the results on the tuning data. Both the results on the tuning set and on the test set can be found in the following tables.

4.1 The Google Problem

One particular thing we noticed is that in the language pairs of FR→EN and ES→EN, the translations from one provided single system (Google) were much better in terms of BLEU and TER than those of all other systems – in the former case by more than 4% in BLEU. In our experience, our system combination approach requires at least three "comparably good" systems to be able to achieve significant improvements. This was confirmed in the WMT 2009 task as well: Neither in FR→EN nor in ES→EN we were able to achieve an improvement over the Google system. For this reason, we did not submit consensus translations for these two language pairs. On the other hand, we would have achieved significant improvements over all (remaining) systems leaving out Google.

4.2 German→English (DE→EN)

Table 2 lists the scores on the tuning and test set for the DE→EN task. We can see that the best systems are rather close to each other in terms of BLEU. Also, the rule-based translation system (RBMT), here SYSTRAN, scores rather well. As a consequence, we find a large improvement using system combination: 2.9%/2.7% abs. on the tuning set, and still 2.1%/2.3% on test, which means that system combination generalizes well here.

4.3 Spanish→English (ES→EN), French→English (FR→EN)

In Table 3, we see that on the ES→EN and FR→EN tasks, a single system – Google – scores significantly better on the TUNE set than any other

Table 2: German→English task: case-insensitive scores. Best single system was Google, second best UKA, best RBMT Systran. SC stands for system combination output.

German→English	TUNE BLEU	TUNE TER	TEST BLEU	TEST TER
Best single	23.2	59.5	21.3	61.3
Second best single	23.0	58.8	21.0	61.7
Best RBMT	21.3	61.3	18.9	63.7
SC (9 systems)	**26.1**	**56.8**	**23.4**	**59.0**
w/o RBMT	24.5	57.3	22.5	59.2
w/o Google	24.9	57.4	23.0	59.1

Table 3: Spanish→English and French→English task: scores on the tuning set after system combination weight tuning (case-insensitive). Best single system was Google, second best was Uedin (Spanish) and UKA (French). No results on TEST were generated.

Spanish→English	ES→EN BLEU	ES→EN TER	FR→EN BLEU	FR→EN TER
Best single	**29.5**	**53.6**	**32.2**	**50.1**
Second best single	26.9	56.1	28.0	54.6
SC (6/9 systems)	28.7	53.6	30.7	52.5
w/o Google	27.5	55.6	30.0	52.8

system, namely by 2.6%/4.2% resp. in BLEU. As a result, a combination of these systems scores better than any other system, even when leaving out the Google system. But it gives worse scores than the single best system. This is explainable, because system combination is trying to find a *consensus* translation. For example, in one case, the majority of the systems leave the French term *"wagon-lit"* untranslated; spurious translations include "baggage car", "sleeping car", and "alive". As a result, the consensus translation also contains "wagon-lit", not the correct translation "sleeper" which only the Google system provides. Even tuning all other system weights to zero would not result in pure Google translations, as these weights neither affect the LM nor the selection of the primary hypothesis in our approach.

4.4 Cross-Lingual→English (XX→EN)

Finally, we have conducted experiments on cross-lingual system combination, namely combining the output from DE→EN, ES→EN, and FR→EN systems to a single English consensus translation. Some interesting results can be found in Table 4. We see that this consensus translation scores 2.0%/3.5% better than the best single system, and 4.4%/5.6% better than the second best single system. While this is only 0.8%/2.5% better than the combination of only the three Google systems, the combination of the non-Google systems leads to translations that could compete with the FR→EN Google system. Again, we see that RBMT systems lead to a small improvement of 0.4% in BLEU, although their scores are significantly worse than those of the competing SMT systems.

Table 4: Cross-lingual task: combination of German→English, Spanish→English, and French→English. Case-insensitive scores. Best single system was Google for all language pairs.

Cross-lingual → English	TUNE BLEU	TUNE TER	TEST BLEU	TEST TER
Best single German	23.2	59.5	21.3	61.3
Best single Spanish	29.5	53.6	28.7	53.8
Best single French	32.2	50.1	31.1	51.7
SC (10 systems)	**35.5**	**46.4**	**33.1**	**48.2**
w/o RBMT	35.1	46.5	32.7	48.3
w/o Google	32.3	48.8	29.9	50.5
3 Google systems	34.2	48.0	32.3	49.2
w/o German	34.0	49.3	31.5	50.9
w/o Spanish	33.4	49.8	31.0	51.9
w/o French	30.5	51.4	28.6	52.3

Regarding languages, we see that despite the large differences in the quality of the systems (10 points between DE→EN and FR→EN), all languages seem to provide significant information to the consensus translation: While FR→EN certainly has the largest influence (−4.5% in BLEU when left out), even DE→EN "contributes" 1.6 BLEU points to the final submission.

5 Conclusions

We have shown that our system combination system can lead to significant improvements over single best MT output where a significant number of comparably good translations is available on a single language pair. For cross-lingual system combination, we observe even larger improvements, even if the quality in terms of BLEU or TER between the systems of different language pairs varies significantly. While the input of high-quality SMT systems has the largest weight for the consensus translation quality, we find that RBMT systems can give important additional information leading to better translations.

Acknowledgments

This work was partly realized as part of the Quaero Programme, funded by OSEO, French State agency for innovation. This work was partly supported by the Defense Advanced Research Projects Agency (DARPA) under Contract No. HR0011-06-C-0023.

References

S. Bangalore, G. Bordel, and G. Riccardi. 2001. Computing consensus translation from multiple machine translation systems. In *IEEE Automatic Speech Recognition and Understanding Workshop*, Madonna di Campiglio, Italy, December.

F. V. Berghen and H. Bersini. 2005. CONDOR, a new parallel, constrained extension of Powell's UOBYQA algorithm: Experimental results and comparison with the DFO algorithm. *Journal of Computational and Applied Mathematics*, 181:157–175.

P. F. Brown, S. A. Della Pietra, V. J. Della Pietra, and R. L. Mercer. 1993. The mathematics of statistical machine translation: parameter estimation. *Computational Linguistics*, 19(2):263–311, June.

J. Fiscus. 1997. A post-processing system to yield reduced word error rates: Recognizer output voting error reduction (ROVER). In *IEEE Workshop on Automatic Speech Recognition and Understanding*.

X. He, M. Yang, J. Gao, P. Nguyen, and R. Moore. 2008. Indirect-HMM-based hypothesis alignment for combining outputs from machine translation systems. In *Proceedings of the 2008 Conference on Empirical Methods in Natural Language Processing*, pages 98–107, Honolulu, Hawaii, October.

S. Jayaraman and A. Lavie. 2005. Multi-engine machine translation guided by explicit word matching. In *Proc. of the 10th Annual Conf. of the European Association for Machine Translation (EAMT)*, pages 143–152, Budapest, Hungary, May.

E. Matusov, R. Zens, and H. Ney. 2004. Symmetric word alignments for statistical machine translation. In *COLING '04: The 20th Int. Conf. on Computational Linguistics*, pages 219–225, Geneva, Switzerland, August.

E. Matusov, N. Ueffing, and H. Ney. 2006. Computing consensus translation from multiple machine translation systems using enhanced hypotheses alignment. In *Conference of the European Chapter of the Association for Computational Linguistics (EACL)*, pages 33–40, Trento, Italy, April.

E. Matusov, G. Leusch, R. E. Banchs, N. Bertoldi, D. Dechelotte, M. Federico, M. Kolss, Y. S. Lee, J. B. Marino, M. Paulik, S. Roukos, H. Schwenk, and H. Ney. 2008. System combination for machine translation of spoken and written language. *IEEE Transactions on Audio, Speech and Language Processing*, 16(7):1222–1237, September.

A. Mauser, S. Hasan, and H. Ney. 2008. Automatic evaluation measures for statistical machine translation system optimization. In *International Conference on Language Resources and Evaluation*, Marrakech, Morocco, May.

F. J. Och and H. Ney. 2003. A systematic comparison of various statistical alignment models. *Computational Linguistics*, 29(1):19–51, March.

K. Papineni, S. Roukos, T. Ward, and W. J. Zhu. 2002. BLEU: a Method for Automatic Evaluation of Machine Translation. In *Proc. of the 40th Annual Meeting of the Association for Computational Linguistics (ACL)*, pages 311–318, Philadelphia, PA, July.

A. V. Rosti, S. Matsoukas, and R. Schwartz. 2007. Improved word-level system combination for machine translation. In *Proceedings of the 45th Annual Meeting of the Association of Computational Linguistics (ACL)*, pages 312–319, Prague, Czech Republic, June.

M. Snover, B. Dorr, R. Schwartz, L. Micciulla, and J. Makhoul. 2006. A Study of Translation Error Rate with Targeted Human Annotation. In *Proc. of the 7th Conf. of the Association for Machine Translation in the Americas (AMTA)*, pages 223–231, Boston, MA, August.

S. Vogel, H. Ney, and C. Tillmann. 1996. HMM-based word alignment in statistical translation. In *COLING '96: The 16th Int. Conf. on Computational Linguistics*, pages 836–841, Copenhagen, Denmark, August.

Machine Translation System Combination with Flexible Word Ordering

Kenneth Heafield, Greg Hanneman, Alon Lavie
Language Technologies Institute, Carnegie Mellon University
5000 Forbes Avenue, Pittsburgh, PA 15213, USA
{kheafiel,ghannema,alavie}@cs.cmu.edu

Abstract

We describe a synthetic method for combining machine translations produced by different systems given the same input. One-best outputs are explicitly aligned to remove duplicate words. Hypotheses follow system outputs in sentence order, switching between systems mid-sentence to produce a combined output. Experiments with the WMT 2009 tuning data showed improvement of 2 BLEU and 1 METEOR point over the best Hungarian-English system. Constrained to data provided by the contest, our system was submitted to the WMT 2009 shared system combination task.

1 Introduction

Many systems for machine translation, with different underlying approaches, are of competitive quality. Nonetheless these approaches and systems have different strengths and weaknesses. By offsetting weaknesses with strengths of other systems, combination can produce higher quality than does any component system.

One approach to system combination uses confusion networks (Rosti et al., 2008; Karakos et al., 2008). In the most common form, a skeleton sentence is chosen from among the one-best system outputs. This skeleton determines the ordering of the final combined sentence. The remaining outputs are aligned with the skeleton, producing a list of alternatives for each word in the skeleton, which comprises a confusion network. A decoder chooses from the original skeleton word and its alternatives to produce a final output sentence. While there are a number of variations on this theme, our approach differs fundamentally in that the effective skeleton changes on a per-phrase basis.

Our system is an enhancement of our previous work (Jayaraman and Lavie, 2005). A hypothesis uses words from systems in order, switching between systems at phrase boundaries. Alignments and a synchronization method merge meaning-equivalent output from different systems. Hypotheses are scored based on system confidence, alignment support, and a language model.

We contribute a few enhancements to this process. First, we introduce an alignment-sensitive method for synchronizing available hypothesis extensions across systems. Second, we pack similar partial hypotheses, which allows greater diversity in our beam search while maintaining the accuracy of n-best output. Finally, we describe an improved model selection process that determined our submissions to the WMT 2009 shared system combination task.

The remainder of this paper is organized as follows. Section 2 describes the system with emphasis on our modifications. Tuning, our experimental setup, and submitted systems are described in Section 3. Section 4 concludes.

2 System

The system consists of alignment (Section 2.1) and phrase detection (Section 2.2) followed by decoding. The decoder constructs hypothesis sentences one word at a time, starting from the left. A partially constructed hypothesis comprises:

Word The most recently decoded word. Initially, this is the beginning of sentence marker.

Used The set of used words from each system. Initially empty.

Phrase The current phrase constraint from Section 2.2, if any. The initial hypothesis is not in a phrase.

Features Four feature values defined in Section 2.4 and used in Section 2.5 for beam search

Proceedings of the Fourth Workshop on Statistical Machine Translation , pages 56–60,
Athens, Greece, 30 March – 31 March 2009. ©2009 Association for Computational Linguistics

and hypothesis ranking. Initially, all features are 1.

Previous A set of preceding hypothesis pointers described in Section 2.5. Initially empty.

The leftmost unused word from each system corresponds to a continuation of the partial hypothesis. Therefore, for each system, we extend a partial hypothesis by appending that system's leftmost unused word, yielding several new hypotheses. The appended word, and those aligned with it, are marked as used in the new hypothesis. Since systems do not align perfectly, too few words may be marked as used, a problem addressed in Section 2.3. As described in Section 2.4, hypotheses are scored using four features based on alignment, system confidence, and a language model. Since the search space is quite large, we use these partial scores for a beam search, where the beam contains hypotheses of equal length. This space contains hypotheses that extend in precisely the same way, which we exploit in Section 2.5 to increase diversity. Finally, a hypothesis is complete when the end of sentence marker is appended.

2.1 Alignment

Sentences from different systems are aligned in pairs using a modified version of the METEOR (Banerjee and Lavie, 2005) matcher. This identifies alignments in three phases: exact matches up to case, WordNet (Fellbaum, 1998) morphology matches, and shared WordNet synsets. These sources of alignments are quite precise and unable to pick up on looser matches such as "mentioned" and "said" that legitimately appear in output from different systems. Artificial alignments are intended to fill gaps by using surrounding alignments as clues. If a word is not aligned to any word in some other sentence, we search left and right for words that are aligned into that sentence. If these alignments are sufficiently close to each other in the other sentence, words between them are considered for artificial alignment. An artificial alignment is added if a matching part of speech is found. The algorithm is described fully by Jayaraman and Lavie (2005).

2.2 Phrases

Switching between systems is permitted outside phrases or at phrase boundaries. We find phrases in two ways. Alignment phrases are maximally long sequences of words which align, in the same order and without interruption, to a word sequence from at least one other system. Punctuation phrases place punctuation in a phrase with the preceding word, if any. When the decoder extends a hypothesis, it considers the longest phrase in which no word is used. If a punctuation phrase is partially used, the decoder marks the entire phrase as used to avoid extraneous punctuation.

2.3 Synchronization

While phrases address near-equal pieces of translation output, we must also deal with equally meaningful output that does not align. The immediate effect of this issue is that too few words are marked as used by the decoder, leading to duplication in the combined output. In addition, partially aligned system output results in lingering unused words between used words. Often these are function words that, with language model scoring, make output unnecessarily verbose. To deal with this problem, we expire lingering words by marking them as used. Specifically, we consider the frontier of each system, which is the leftmost unused word. If a frontier lags behind, words as used to advance the frontier. Our two methods for synchronization differ in how frontiers are compared across systems and the tightness of the constraint.

Previously, we measured frontiers from the beginning of sentence. Based on this measurement, the synchronization constraint requires that the frontiers of each system differ by at most s. Equivalently, a frontier is lagging if it is more than s words behind the rightmost frontier. Lagging frontiers are advanced until the synchronization constraint becomes satisfied. We found this method can cause problems in the presence of variable length output. When the variability in output length exceeds s, proper synchronization requires distances between frontiers greater than s, which this constraint disallows.

Alignments indicate where words are synchronous. Words near an alignment are also likely to be synchronous even without an explicit alignment. For example, in the fragments "even more serious, you" and "even worse, you" from WMT 2008, "serious" and "worse" do not align but do share relative position from other alignments, suggesting these are synchronous. We formalize this by measuring the relative position of frontiers from alignments on each side. For example, if the frontier itself is aligned then relative position is zero. For each pair of systems, we check if these relative positions differ by at most s under an alignment on either side. Confidence in a system's frontier is the sum of the system's own confidence plus confidence in systems for which the pair-wise constraint is satisfied. If confidence in any frontier falls below 0.8, the least confident lagging frontier is advanced. The process repeats until the constraint becomes satisfied.

2.4 Scores

We score partial and complete hypotheses using system confidence, alignments, and a language model. Specifically, we have four features which operate at the word level:

Alignment Confidence in the system from which the word came plus confidence in systems to which the word aligns.

Language Model Score from a suffix array language model (Zhang and Vogel, 2006) trained on English from monolingual and French-English data provided by the contest.

N-Gram $\left(\frac{1}{3}\right)^{order-ngram}$ using language model $order$ and length of $ngram$ found.

Overlap $\frac{overlap}{order-1}$ where $overlap$ is the length of intersection between the preceding and current n-grams.

The N-Gram and Overlap features are intended to improve fluency across phrase boundaries. Features are combined using a log-linear model trained as discussed in Section 3. Hypotheses are scored using the geometric average score of each word in the hypothesis.

2.5 Search

Of note is that a word's score is impacted only by its alignments and the n-gram found by the language model. Therefore two partial hypotheses that differ only in words preceding the n-gram and in their average score are in some sense duplicates. With the same set of used words and same phrase constraint, they extend in precisely the same way. In particular, the highest scoring hypothesis will never use a lower scoring duplicate.

We use duplicate detecting beam search to explore our hypothesis space. A beam contains partial hypotheses of the same length. Duplicate hypotheses are detected on insertion and packed, with the combined hypothesis given the highest score of those packed. Once a beam contains the top scoring partial hypotheses of length l, these hypotheses are extended to length $l+1$ and placed in another beam. Those hypotheses reaching end of sentence are placed in a separate beam, which is equivalent to packing them into one final hypothesis. Once we remove partial hypothesis that did not extend to the final hypothesis, the hypotheses are a lattice connected by parent pointers.

While we submitted only one-best hypotheses, accurate n-best hypotheses are important for training as explained in Section 3. Unpacking the hypothesis lattice into n-best hypotheses is guided by scores stored in each hypothesis. For this task, we use an n-best beam of paths from the end of sentence hypothesis to a partial hypothesis. Paths are built by induction, starting with a zero-length path from the end of sentence hypothesis to itself. The top scoring path is removed and its terminal hypothesis is examined. If it is the beginning of sentence, the path is output as a complete hypothesis. Otherwise, we extend the path to each parent hypothesis, adjusting each path score as necessary, and insert into the beam. This process terminates with n complete hypotheses or an empty beam.

3 Tuning

Given the 502 sentences made available for tuning by WMT 2009, we selected feature weights for scoring, a set of systems to combine, confidence in each selected system, and the type and distance s of synchronization. Of these, only feature weights can be trained, for which we used minimum error rate training with version 1.04 of IBM-style BLEU (Papineni et al., 2002) in case-insensitive mode. We treated the remaining parameters as a model selection problem, using 402 randomly sampled sentences for training and 100 sentences for evaluation. This is clearly a small sample on which to evaluate, so we performed two folds of cross-validation to obtain average scores over 200 untrained sentences. We chose to do only two folds due to limited computational time and a desire to test many models.

We scored systems and our own output using case-insensitive IBM-style BLEU 1.04 (Papineni et al., 2002), METEOR 0.6 (Lavie and Agarwal, 2007) with all modules, and TER 5 (Snover et al., 2006). For each source language, we ex-

In	Sync s	BLEU	METE	TER	Systems and Confidences				
cz	length 8	.236	.507	59.1	google .46	cu-bojar .27	uedin .27		
cz	align 5	.226	.499	57.8	google .50	cu-bojar .25	uedin .25		
cz	align 7	.211	.508	65.9	cu-bojar .60	google .20	uedin .20		
cz		*.231*	*.504*	*57.8*	*google*				
de	length 7	.255	.531	54.2	google .40	uka .30	stuttgart .15	umd .15	
de	length 6	.260	.532	55.2	google .50	systran .25	umd .25		
de	align 9	.256	.533	55.5	google .40	uka .30	stuttgart .15	umd .15	
de	align 6	.200	.514	54.2	google .31	uedin .22	systran .18	umd .16	uka .14
de		*.244*	*.523*	*57.5*	*google*				
es	align 8	.297	.560	52.7	google .75	uedin .25			
es	length 5	.289	.548	52.1	google .50	talp-upc .17	uedin .17	rwth .17	
es		*.297*	*.558*	*52.7*	*google*				
fr	align 6	.329	.574	49.9	google .70	lium1 .30			
fr	align 8	.314	.596	48.6	google .50	lium1 .30	limsi1 .20		
fr	length 8	.323	.570	48.5	google .50	lium1 .25	limsi1 .25		
fr		*.324*	*.576*	*48.7*	*google*				
hu	length 5	.162	.403	69.2	umd .50	morpho .40	uedin .10		
hu	length 8	.158	.407	69.5	umd .50	morpho .40	uedin .10		
hu	align 7	.153	.392	68.0	umd .33	morpho .33	uedin .33		
hu		*.141*	*.391*	*66.1*	*umd*				
xx	length 5	.326	.584	49.6	google-fr .61	google-es .39			
xx	align 4	.328	.580	49.5	google-fr .80	google-es .20			
xx	align 5	.324	.576	48.6	google-fr .61	google-es .39			
xx	align 7	.319	.587	51.1	google-fr .50	google-es .50			
xx		*.324*	*.576*	*48.7*	*google-fr*				

Table 1: Combination models used for submission to WMT 2009. For each language, we list our primary combination, contrastive combinations, and a high-scoring system for comparison in italic. All translations are into English. The xx source language combines translations from different languages, in our case French and Spanish. Scores from BLEU, METEOR, and TER are the average of two cross-validation folds with 100 evaluation sentences each. Numbers following system names indicate contrastive systems. More evaluation, including human scores, will be published by WMT.

perimented with various sets of high-scoring systems to combine. We also tried confidence values proportional to various powers of BLEU and METEOR scores, as well as hand-picked values. Finally we tried both variants of synchronization with values of s ranging from 2 to 9. In total, 405 distinct models were evaluated. For each source source language, our primary system was chosen by performing well on all three metrics. Models that scored well on individual metrics were submitted as contrastive systems. In Table 1 we report the models underlying each submitted system.

4 Conclusion

We found our combinations are quite sensitive to presence of and confidence in the underlying systems. Further, we show the most improvement when these systems are close in quality, as is the case with our Hungarian-English system. The two methods of synchronization were surprisingly competitive, a factor we attribute to short sentence length compared with WMT 2008 Europarl sentences. Opportunities for further work include per-sentence system confidence, automatic training of more parameters, and different alignment models. We look forward to evaluation results from WMT 2009.

Acknowledgments

The authors wish to thank Jonathan Clark for training the language model and other assistance. This work was supported in part by the DARPA GALE program and by a NSF Graduate Research Fellowship.

References

Satanjeev Banerjee and Alon Lavie. 2005. METEOR: An automatic metric for MT evaluation with improved correlation with human judgments. In *Proc. ACL Workshop on Intrinsic and Extrinsic Evaluation Measures for Machine Translation and/or Summarization*, pages 65–72.

Christiane Fellbaum. 1998. *WordNet: An Electronic Lexical Database*. MIT Press.

Shyamsundar Jayaraman and Alon Lavie. 2005. Multi-engine machine translation guided by explicit word matching. In *Proc. EAMT*, pages 143–152.

Damianos Karakos, Jason Eisner, Sanjeev Khudanpur, and Markus Dreyer. 2008. Machine translation system combination using ITG-based alignments. In *Proc. ACL-08: HLT, Short Papers (Companion Volume)*, pages 81–84.

Alon Lavie and Abhaya Agarwal. 2007. METEOR: An automatic metric for MT evaluation with high levels of correlation with human judgments. In *Proc. Second Workshop on Statistical Machine Translation*, pages 228–231, Prague, Czech Republic, June.

Kishore Papineni, Salim Roukos, Todd Ward, and Wei-Jing Zhu. 2002. BLEU: A method for automatic evalution of machine translation. In *Proc. 40th Annual Meeting of the Association for Computational Linguistics*, pages 311–318, Philadelphia, PA, July.

Antti-Veikko I. Rosti, Bing Zhang, Spyros Matsoukas, and Richard Schwartz. 2008. Incremental hypothesis alignment for building confusion networks with application to machine translation system combination. In *Proc. Third Workshop on Statistical Machine Translation*, pages 183–186.

Matthew Snover, Bonnie Dorr, Richard Schwartz, Linnea Micciulla, and John Makhoul. 2006. A study of translation edit rate with targeted human annotation. In *Proc. Seventh Conference of the Association for Machine Translation in the Americas*, pages 223–231, Cambridge, MA, August.

Ying Zhang and Stephan Vogel. 2006. Suffix array and its applications in empirical natural language processing. Technical Report CMU-LTI-06-010, Language Technologies Institute, School of Computer Science, Carnegie Mellon University, Pittsburgh, PA, Dec.

Incremental Hypothesis Alignment with Flexible Matching for Building Confusion Networks: BBN System Description for WMT09 System Combination Task

Antti-Veikko I. Rosti and **Bing Zhang** and **Spyros Matsoukas** and **Richard Schwartz**
BBN Technologies, 10 Moulton Street, Cambridge, MA 02138
{arosti,bzhang,smatsouk,schwartz}@bbn.com

Abstract

This paper describes the incremental hypothesis alignment algorithm used in the BBN submissions to the WMT09 system combination task. The alignment algorithm used a sentence specific alignment order, flexible matching, and new shift heuristics. These refinements yield more compact confusion networks compared to using the pair-wise or incremental TER alignment algorithms. This should reduce the number of spurious insertions in the system combination output and the system combination weight tuning converges faster. System combination experiments on the WMT09 test sets from five source languages to English are presented. The best BLEU scores were achieved by combing the English outputs of three systems from all five source languages.

1 Introduction

Machine translation (MT) systems have different strengths and weaknesses which can be exploited by system combination methods resulting in an output with a better performance than any individual MT system output as measured by automatic evaluation metrics. Confusion network decoding has become the most popular approach to MT system combination. The first confusion network decoding method (Bangalore et al., 2001) was based on multiple string alignment (MSA) (Durbin et al., 1988) borrowed from biological sequence analysis. However, MSA does not allow re-ordering. The translation edit rate (TER) (Snover et al., 2006) produces an alignment between two strings and allows shifts of blocks of words. The availability of the TER software has made it easy to build a high performance system combination baseline (Rosti et al., 2007).

The pair-wise TER alignment originally described by Sim et al. (2007) has various limitations. First, the hypotheses are aligned independently against the skeleton which determines the word order of the output. The same word from two different hypotheses may be inserted in different positions w.r.t. the skeleton and multiple insertions require special handling. Rosti et al. (2008) described an incremental TER alignment to mitigate these problems. The incremental TER alignment used a global order in which the hypotheses were aligned. Second, the TER software matches words with identical surface strings. The pair-wise alignment methods proposed by Ayan et al. (2008), He et al. (2008), and Matusov et al. (2006) are able to match also synonyms and words with identical stems. Third, the TER software uses a set of heuristics which is not always optimal in determining the block shifts. Karakos et al. (2008) proposed using inversion transduction grammars to produce different pair-wise alignments.

This paper is organized as follows. A refined incremental alignment algorithm is described in Section 2. Experimental evaluation comparing the pair-wise and incremental TER alignment algorithms with the refined alignment algorithm on WMT09 system combination task is presented in Section 3. Conclusions and future work are presented in Section 4.

2 Incremental Hypothesis Alignment with Flexible Matching

2.1 Sentence Specific Alignment Order

Rosti et al. (2008) proposed incremental hypothesis alignment using a system specific order. This is not likely to be optimal since one MT system may have better output on one sentence and worse on another. More principled approach is similar to MSA where the order is determined by the edit distance of the hypothesis from the network for

Proceedings of the Fourth Workshop on Statistical Machine Translation , pages 61–65,
Athens, Greece, 30 March – 31 March 2009. ©2009 Association for Computational Linguistics

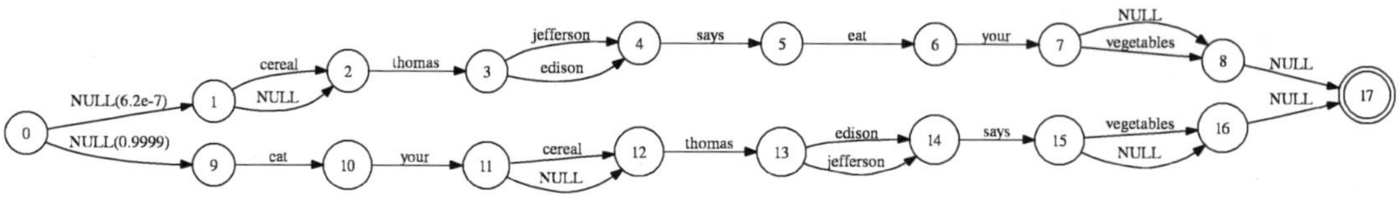

(a) Alignment using the standard TER shift heuristics.

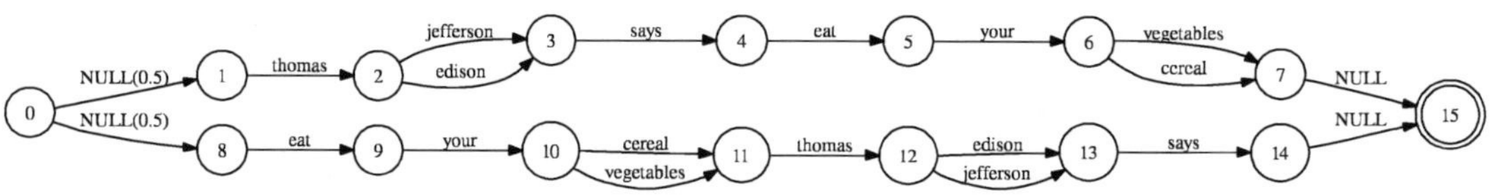

(b) Alignment using the modified shift heuristics.

Figure 1: Combined confusion networks using different shift heuristics. The initial NULL arcs include the prior probability estimates in parentheses.

each sentence. The TER scores of the remaining unaligned hypotheses using the current network as the reference are computed. The hypothesis with the lowest edit cost w.r.t. the network is aligned. Given N systems, this increases the number of alignments performed from N to $0.5(N^2 - N)$.

2.2 Flexible Matching

The TER software assigns a zero cost for matching tokens and a cost of one for all errors including insertions, deletions, substitutions, and block shifts. Ayan et al. (2008) modified the TER software to consider substitutions of synonyms with a reduced cost. Recently, Snover et al. (2009) extended the TER algorithm in a similar fashion to produce a new evaluation metric, TER plus (TERp), which allows tuning of the edit costs in order to maximize correlation with human judgment. The incremental alignment with flexible matching uses WordNet (Fellbaum, 1998) to find all possible synonyms and words with identical stems in a set of hypotheses. Substitutions involving synonyms and words with identical stems are considered with a reduced cost of 0.2.

2.3 Modified Shift Heuristics

The TER is computed by trying shifts of blocks of words that have an exact match somewhere else in the reference in order to find a re-ordering of the hypothesis with a lower edit distance to the reference. Karakos et al. (2008) showed that the shift heuristics in TER do not always yield an optimal alignment. Their example used the following two hypotheses:

1. thomas jefferson says eat your vegetables
2. eat your cereal thomas edison says

A system combination lattice using TER alignment is shown in Figure 1(a). The blocks "eat your" are shifted when building both confusion networks. Using the second hypothesis as the skeleton seems to give a better alignment. The lower number of edits also results in a higher skeleton prior shown between nodes 0 and 9. There are obviously some undesirable paths through the lattice but it is likely that a language model will give a higher score to the reasonable hypotheses.

Since the flexible matching allows substitutions with a reduced cost, the standard TER shift heuristics have to be modified. A block of words may have some words with identical matches and other words with synonym matches. In TERp, synonym and stem matches are considered as exact matches for the block shifts, otherwise the TER shift constraints are used. In the flexible matching, the shift heuristics were modified to allow any block shifts that do not increase the edit cost. A system combination lattice using the modified shift heuristics is shown in Figure 1(b). The optimal shifts of blocks "eat your cereal" and "eat your vegetables" were found and both networks received equal skeleton priors. TERp would yield this alignment only if these blocks appear in the paraphrase table or if "cereal" and "vegetables" are considered synonyms. This example is artificial and does not guarantee that optimal shifts are always found.

3 Experimental Evaluation

System combination experiments combining the English WMT09 translation task outputs were performed. A total of 96 English outputs were provided including primary, contrastive, and N-best outputs. Only the primary 1-best outputs were combined due to time constraints. The numbers of primary systems per source language were: 3 for Czech, 15 for German, 9 for Spanish, 15 for French, and 3 for Hungarian. The English bigram and 5-gram language models were interpolated from four LM components trained on the English monolingual Europarl (45M tokens) and News (510M tokens) corpora, and the English sides of the News Commentary (2M tokens) and Giga-FrEn (683M tokens) parallel corpora. The interpolation weights were tuned to minimize perplexity on `news-dev2009` set. The system combination weights – one for each system, LM weight, and word and NULL insertion penalties – were tuned to maximize the BLEU (Papineni et al., 2002) score on the tuning set (`newssyscomb2009`). Since the system combination was performed on tokenized and lower cased outputs, a trigram-based true caser was trained on all News training data. The tuning may be summarized as follows:

1. Tokenize and lower case the outputs;
2. Align hypotheses incrementally using each output as a skeleton;
3. Join the confusion networks into a lattice with skeleton specific prior estimates;
4. Extract a 300-best list from the lattice given the current weights;
5. Merge the 300-best list with the hypotheses from the previous iteration;
6. Tune new weights given the current merged N-best list;
7. Iterate 4-6 three times;
8. Extract a 300-best list from the lattice given the best decoding weights and re-score hypotheses with a 5-gram;
9. Tune re-scoring weights given the final 300-best list;
10. Extract 1-best hypotheses from the 300-best list given the best re-scoring weights, re-case, and detokenize.

After tuning the system combination weights, the outputs on a test set may be combined using the same steps excluding 4-7 and 9. The hypothesis scores and tuning are identical to the setup used in (Rosti et al., 2007).

Case insensitive TER and BLEU scores for the combination outputs using the pair-wise and incremental TER alignment as well as the flexible alignment on the tuning (dev) and test sets are shown in Table 1. Only case insensitive scores are reported since the re-casers used by different systems are very different and some are trained using larger resources than provided for WMT09. The scores of the worst and best individual system outputs are also shown. The best and worst TER and BLEU scores are not necessarily from the same system output. Both `incremental` and `flexible` alignments used sentence specific alignment order. Combinations using the incremental and flexible hypothesis alignment algorithms consistently outperform the ones using the pair-wise TER alignment. The flexible alignment is slightly better than the incremental alignment on Czech, Spanish, and Hungarian, and significantly better on French to English test set scores.

Since the test sets for each language pair consist of translations of the same documents, it is possible to combine outputs from many source languages to English. There were a total of 46 English primary 1-best system outputs. Using all 46 outputs would have required too much memory in tuning, so a subset of 11 outputs was chosen. The 11 outputs consist of `google`, `uedin`, and `uka` outputs on all languages. Case insensitive TER and BLEU scores for the `xx-en` combination are shown in Table 2. In addition to `incremental` and `flexible` alignment methods which used sentence specific alignment order, scores for incremental TER alignment with a fixed alignment order used in the BBN submissions to WMT08

dev	cz-en		de-en		es-en		fr-en		hu-en	
System	TER	BLEU	TER	BLEU	TER	BLEU	TER	BLEU	TER	BLEU
worst	67.30	17.63	82.01	6.83	65.64	19.74	69.19	15.21	78.70	10.33
best	58.16	23.12	57.24	23.20	53.02	29.48	49.78	32.27	66.77	13.59
pairwise	59.60	24.01	56.35	26.04	53.11	29.49	51.03	31.65	69.58	14.60
incremental	59.22	24.31	55.73	26.73	53.05	29.72	50.72	32.09	70.15	14.85
flexible	59.38	24.18	55.51	26.71	52.62	30.24	50.22	32.58	69.83	14.88

test	cz-en		de-en		es-en		fr-en		hu-en	
System	TER	BLEU	TER	BLEU	TER	BLEU	TER	BLEU	TER	BLEU
worst	67.74	16.37	82.39	6.81	65.44	19.04	71.44	14.49	81.21	9.90
best	59.53	21.18	59.41	21.30	53.34	28.69	51.33	31.14	68.32	12.75
pairwise	61.02	21.25	58.75	23.41	53.65	28.15	53.17	29.83	71.50	13.39
incremental	60.63	21.67	58.13	23.96	53.47	28.38	52.51	30.45	71.69	13.60
flexible	60.34	21.87	58.05	23.86	53.13	28.57	51.98	31.30	71.17	13.84

Table 1: Case insensitive TER and BLEU scores on `newssyscomb2009` (dev) and `newstest2009` (test) for five source languages.

(Rosti et al., 2008) are marked as `incr-wmt08`. The sentence specific alignment order yields about a half BLEU point gain on the tuning set and a one BLEU point gain on the test set. All system combination experiments yield very good BLEU gains on both sets. The scores are also significantly higher than any combination from a single source language. This shows that the outputs from different source languages are likely to be more diverse than outputs from different MT systems on a single language pair. The combination is not guaranteed to be the best possible as the set of outputs was chosen arbitrarily.

The compactness of the confusion networks may be measured by the average number of nodes and arcs per segment. All `xx-en` confusion networks for `newssyscomb2009` and `newstest2009` after the incremental TER alignment had on average 44.5 nodes and 112.7 arcs per segment. After the flexible hypothesis alignment, there were on average 41.1 nodes and 104.6 arcs per segment. The number of NULL word arcs may also be indicative of the alignment quality. The flexible hypothesis alignment reduced the average number of NULL word arcs from 29.0 to 24.8 per segment. The rate of convergence in the N-best list based iterative tuning may be monitored by the number of new hypotheses in the merged N-best lists from iteration to iteration. By the third tuning iteration, there were 10% fewer new hypotheses in the merged N-best list when using the flexible hypothesis alignment.

xx-en	dev		test	
System	TER	BLEU	TER	BLEU
worst	74.21	12.80	75.84	12.05
best	49.78	32.27	51.33	31.14
pairwise	46.10	35.95	47.77	33.53
incr-wmt08	44.58	36.84	46.60	33.61
incremental	44.59	37.30	46.42	34.61
flexible	44.54	37.38	45.82	34.48

Table 2: Case insensitive TER and BLEU scores on `newssyscomb2009` (dev) and `newstest2009` (test) for `xx-en` combination.

4 Conclusions

This paper described a refined incremental hypothesis alignment algorithm used in the BBN submissions to the WMT09 system combination task. The new features included sentence specific alignment order, flexible matching, and modified shift heuristics. The refinements yield more compact confusion networks which should allow fewer spurious insertions in the output and faster convergence in tuning. The future work will investigate tunable edit costs and methods to choose an optimal subset of outputs for combination.

Acknowledgments

This work was supported by DARPA/IPTO Contract No. HR0011-06-C-0022 under the GALE program.

References

Necip Fazil Ayan, Jing Zheng, and Wen Wang. 2008. Improving alignments for better confusion networks for combining machine translation systems. In *Proceedings of the 22nd International Conference on Computational Linguistics (Coling 2008)*, pages 33–40.

Srinivas Bangalore, German Bordel, and Giuseppe Riccardi. 2001. Computing consensus translation from multiple machine translation systems. In *Proceedings of the Automatic Speech Recognition and Understanding Workshop (ASRU)*, pages 351–354.

Richard Durbin, Sean R. Eddy, Anders Krogh, and Graeme Mitchison. 1988. *Biological Sequence Analysis: Probabilistic Models of Proteins and Nucleic Acids*. Cambridge University Press.

Christiane Fellbaum, editor. 1998. *WordNet: An Electronic Lexical Database*. MIT Press.

Xiaodong He, Mei Yang, Jianfeng Gao, Patrick Nguyen, and Robert Moore. 2008. Indirect-HMM-based hypothesis alignment for combining outputs from machine translation systems. In *Proceedings of the 2008 Conference on Empirical Methods in Natural Language Processing*, pages 98–107.

Damianos Karakos, Jason Eisner, Sanjeev Khudanpur, and Markus Dreyer. 2008. Machine translation system combination using ITG-based alignments. In *Proceedings of ACL-08: HLT*, pages 81–84.

Evgeny Matusov, Nicola Ueffing, and Hermann Ney. 2006. Computing consensus translation from multiple machine translation systems using enhanced hypotheses alignment. In *Proceedings of the 11th Conference of the European Chapter of the Association for Computational Linguistics*, pages 33–40.

Kishore Papineni, Salim Roukos, Todd Ward, and Wei-Jing Zhu. 2002. BLEU: a method for automatic evaluation of machine translation. In *Proceedings of the 40th Annual Meeting of the Association for Computational Linguistics*, pages 311–318.

Antti-Veikko I. Rosti, Spyros Matsoukas, and Richard Schwartz. 2007. Improved word-level system combination for machine translation. In *Proceedings of the 45th Annual Meeting of the Association of Computational Linguistics*, pages 312–319.

Antti-Veikko I. Rosti, Bing Zhang, Spyros Matsoukas, and Richard Schwartz. 2008. Incremental hypothesis alignment for building confusion networks with application to machine translation system combination. In *Proceedings of the Third Workshop on Statistical Machine Translation*, pages 183–186.

Khe Chai Sim, William J. Byrne, Mark J.F. Gales, Hichem Sahbi, and Phil C. Woodland. 2007. Consensus network decoding for statistical machine translation system combination. In *Proceedings of the 32nd IEEE International Conference on Acoustics, Speech, and Signal Processing*, pages 105–108.

Matthew Snover, Bonnie Dorr, Richard Schwartz, Linnea Micciula, and John Makhoul. 2006. A study of translation edit rate with targeted human annotation. In *Proceedings of the 7th Conference of the Association for Machine Translation in the Americas*, pages 223–231.

Matthew Snover, Nitin Madnani, Bonnie Dorr, and Richard Schwartz. 2009. Fluency, adequacy, or HTER? Exploring different human judgments with a tunable MT metric. In *Proceedings of the Fourth Workshop on Statistical Machine Translation*.

The RWTH Machine Translation System for WMT 2009

Maja Popović, David Vilar, Daniel Stein, Evgeny Matusov and Hermann Ney
RWTH Aachen University
Aachen, Germany

Abstract

RWTH participated in the shared translation task of the Fourth Workshop of Statistical Machine Translation (WMT 2009) with the German-English, French-English and Spanish-English pair in each translation direction. The submissions were generated using a phrase-based and a hierarchical statistical machine translation systems with appropriate morpho-syntactic enhancements. POS-based reorderings of the source language for the phrase-based systems and splitting of German compounds for both systems were applied. For some tasks, a system combination was used to generate a final hypothesis. An additional English hypothesis was produced by combining all three final systems for translation into English.

1 Introduction

For the WMT 2009 shared task, RWTH submitted translations for the German-English, French-English and Spanish-English language pair in both directions. A phrase-based translation system enhanced with appropriate morpho-syntactic transformations was used for all translation directions. Local POS-based word reorderings were applied for the Spanish-English and French-English pair, and long range reorderings for the German-English pair. For this language pair splitting of German compounds was also applied. Special efforts were made for the French-English and German-English translation, where a hierarchical system was also used and the final submissions are the result of a system combination. For translation into English, an additional hypothesis was produced as a result of combination of the final German-to-English, French-to-English and Spanish-to-English systems.

2 Translation models

2.1 Phrase-based model

We used a standard phrase-based system similar to the one described in (Zens et al., 2002). The pairs of source and corresponding target phrases are extracted from the word-aligned bilingual training corpus. Phrases are defined as non-empty contiguous sequences of words. The phrase translation probabilities are estimated using relative frequencies. In order to obtain a more symmetric model, the phrase-based model is used in both directions.

2.2 Hierarchical model

The hierarchical phrase-based approach can be considered as an extension of the standard phrase-based model. In this model we allow the phrases to have "gaps", i.e. we allow non-contiguous parts of the source sentence to be translated into possibly non-contiguous parts of the target sentence. The model can be formalized as a synchronous context-free grammar (Chiang, 2007). The model also included some additional heuristics which have shown to be helpful for improving translation quality, as proposed in (Vilar et al., 2008).

The first step in the hierarchical phrase extraction is the same as for the phrased-based model. Having a set of initial phrases, we search for phrases which contain other smaller sub-phrases and produce a new phrase with gaps. In our system, we restricted the number of non-terminals for each hierarchical phrase to a maximum of two, which were also not allowed to be adjacent. The scores of the phrases are again computed as relative frequencies.

2.3 Common models

For both translation models, phrase-based and hierarchical, additional common models were used: word-based lexicon model, phrase penalty, word penalty and target language model.

Proceedings of the Fourth Workshop on Statistical Machine Translation , pages 66–69,
Athens, Greece, 30 March – 31 March 2009. ©2009 Association for Computational Linguistics

The target language model was a standard n-gram language model trained by the SRI language modeling toolkit (Stolcke, 2002). The smoothing technique we apply was the modified Kneser-Ney discounting with interpolation. In our case we used a 4-gram language model.

3 Morpho-syntactic transformations

3.1 POS-based word reorderings

For the phrase-based systems, the local and long range POS-based reordering rules described in (Popović and Ney, 2006) were applied on the training and test corpora as a preprocessing step.

Local reorderings were used for the Spanish-English and French-English language pairs in order to handle differences between the positions of nouns and adjectives in the two languages. Adjectives in Spanish and French, as in most Romanic languages, are usually placed after the corresponding noun, whereas for English it is the other way round. Therefore, for these language pairs local reorderings of nouns and adjective groups in the source language were applied. The following sequences of words are considered to be an adjective group: a single adjective, two or more consecutive adjectives, a sequence of adjectives and coordinate conjunctions, as well as an adjective along with its corresponding adverb. If the source language is Spanish or French, each noun is moved behind the corresponding adjective group. If the source language is English, each adjective group is moved behind the corresponding noun.

Long range reorderings were applied on the verb groups for the German-English language pair. Verbs in the German language can often be placed at the end of a clause. This is mostly the case with infinitives and past participles, but there are many cases when other verb forms also occur at the clause end. For the translation from German into English, following verb types were moved towards the beginning of a clause: infinitives, infinitives+zu, finite verbs, past participles and negative particles. For the translation from English to German, infinitives and past participles were moved to the end of a clause, where punctuation marks, subordinate conjunctions and finite verbs are considered as the beginning of the next clause.

3.2 German compound words

For the translation from German into English, German compounds were split using the frequency-based method described in (Koehn and Knight, 2003). For the other translation direction, the English text was first translated into the modified German language with split compounds. The generated output was then postprocessed, i.e. the components were merged using the method described in (Popović et al., 2006): a list of compounds and a list of components are extracted from the original German training corpus. If the word in the generated output is in the component list, check if this word merged with the next word is in the compound list. If it is, merge the two words.

4 System combination

For system combination we used the approach described in (Matusov et al., 2006). The method is based on the generation of a consensus translation out of the output of different translation systems. The core of the method consists in building a confusion network for each sentence by aligning and combining the (single-best) translation hypothesis from one MT system with the translations produced by the other MT systems (and the other translations from the same system, if n-best lists are used in combination). For each sentence, each MT system is selected once as "primary" system, and the other hypotheses are aligned to this hypothesis. The resulting confusion networks are combined into a signle word graph, which is then weighted with system-specific factors, similar to the approach of (Rosti et al., 2007), and a trigram LM trained on the MT hypotheses. The translation with the best total score within this word graph is selected as consensus translation. The scaling factors of these models are optimized using the Condor toolkit (Berghen and Bersini, 2005) to achieve optimal BLEU score on the dev set.

5 Experimental results

5.1 Experimental settings

For all translation directions, we used the provided EuroParl and News parallel corpora to train the translation models and the News monolingual corpora to train the language models. All systems were optimised for the BLEU score on the development data (the "dev-a" part of the 2008 evaluation data). The other part of the 2008 evaluation set ("dev-b") is used as a blind test set. The results reported in the next section will be referring to this test set. For the tasks including a system combination, the parameters for the system combination were also trained on the "dev-b" set. The reported evaluation metrics are the BLEU score and two syntax-oriented metrics which have shown a high correlation with human evaluations: the PBLEU score (BLEU calculated on POS sequences) and the POS-F-score PF (similar to the BLEU score but based on the F-measure instead of precision and on arithmetic mean instead of geometric mean). The POS tags used for reorderings and for syntactic evaluation metrics for the English and the German corpora were generated using the statistical n-gram-based TnT-tagger (Brants, 2000). The Spanish corpora are annotated using the FreeLing analyser (Carreras et al., 2004), and the French texts using the TreeTagger[1].

5.2 Translation results

Table 1 presents the results for the German-English language pair. For translation from German into English, results for the phrase-based system with and without verb reordering and compound splitting are shown. The hierarchical system was trained with split German compounds. The final submission was produced by combining those five systems. The improvement obtained by system combination on the unseen test data 2009 is similar, i.e. from the systems with BLEU scores of 17.0%, 17.2%, 17.5%, 17.6% and 17.7% to the final system with 18.5%.

German→English	BLEU	PBLEU	PF
phrase-based	17.8	31.6	39.7
+reorder verbs	18.2	32.6	40.3
+split compounds	18.0	31.9	40.0
+reord+split	18.4	33.1	40.7
hierarchical+split	18.5	33.5	40.1
system combination	19.2	33.8	40.9

English→German	BLEU	PBLEU	PF
phrase-based	13.6	31.6	39.7
+reorder verbs	13.7	32.4	40.2
+split compounds	13.7	32.3	40.1
+reord+split	13.7	32.3	40.1
system combination	14.0	32.7	40.3

Table 1: Translation results [%] for the German-English language pair, News2008_dev-b.

The other translation direction is more difficult and improvements from morpho-syntactic transformations are smaller. No hierarchical system was trained for this translation direction. The combination of the four phrase-based systems leads to further improvements (on the unseen test set as well: contrastive hypotheses have the BLEU scores in the range from 12.7% to 13.0%, and the final BLEU score is 13.2%).

The results for the French-English language pair are shown in Table 2. For the French-to-English system, we submitted the result of the combination of three systems: a phrase-based with and without local reorderings and a hierarchical system. For the unseen test set, the BLEU score of the system combination output is 24.4%, whereas the contrastive hypotheses have 23.2%, 23.4% and 24.1%. For the other translation direction we did not use the system combination, the submission is produced by the phrase-based system with local adjective reorderings.

French→English	BLEU	PBLEU	PF
phrase-based	20.9	37.1	43.2
+reorder adjectives	21.3	38.2	43.6
hierarchical	20.3	36.7	42.6
system combination	21.7	38.5	43.8

English→French	BLEU	PBLEU	PF
phrase-based	20.2	39.5	45.9
+reorder adjectives	20.7	40.6	46.4

Table 2: Translation results [%] for the French-English language pair, News2008_dev-b.

Table 3 presents the results for the Spanish-English language pair. As in the English-to-French translation, the phrase-based system with adjective reorderings is used to produce the submitted hypothesis for both translation directions.

Spanish→English	BLEU	PBLEU	PF
phrase-based	22.1	38.5	44.1
+reorder adjectives	22.5	39.2	44.6

English→Spanish	BLEU	PBLEU	PF
phrase-based	20.6	29.3	35.7
+reorder adjectives	21.1	29.7	35.9

Table 3: Translation results [%] for the Spanish-English language pair, News2008_dev-b.

[1] http://www.ims.uni-stuttgart.de/projekte/corplex/TreeTagger/

The result of the additional experiment, i.e. for the multisource translation int English is presented in Table 4. The English hypothesis is produced by the combination of the three best systems for each language pair, and it can be seen that the translation performance increases in all measures. This suggests that each language pair poses different difficulties for the translation task, and the combination of all three can improve performance.

F+S+G→English	BLEU	PBLEU	PF
system combination	25.1	41.0	46.4

Table 4: Multisource translation results [%]: the English hypothesis is obtained as result of a system combination of all language pairs, News2008_dev-b.

6 Conclusions

The RWTH system submitted to the WMT 2009 shared translation task used a phrase-based system and a hierarchical system with appropriate morpho-syntactic extensions, i.e. POS based word reorderings and splitting of German compounds were used. System combination produced gains in BLEU score over phrasal-system baselines in the German-to-English, English-to-German and French-to-English tasks.

Acknowledgments

This work was realised as part of the Quaero Programme, funded by OSEO, French State agency for innovation.

References

Frank Vanden Berghen and Hugues Bersini. 2005. CONDOR, a new parallel, constrained extension of Powell's UOBYQA algorithm: Experimental results and comparison with the DFO algorithm. *Journal of Computational and Applied Mathematics*, 181:157–175.

Thorsten Brants. 2000. Tnt – a statistical part-of-speech tagger. In *Proceedings of the 6th Applied Natural Language Processing Conference (ANLP)*, pages 224–231, Seattle, WA.

Xavier Carreras, Isaac Chao, Lluís Padró, and Muntsa Padró. 2004. FreeLing: An Open-Source Suite of Language Analyzers. In *Proceedings 4th International Conference on Language Resources and Evaluation (LREC)*, pages 239–242, Lisbon, Portugal, May.

David Chiang. 2007. Hierarchical phrase-based translation. *Computational Linguistics*, (33):201–228.

Philipp Koehn and Kevin Knight. 2003. Empirical methods for compound splitting. In *Proceedings 10th Conference of the European Chapter of the Association for Computational Linguistics (EACL)*, pages 347–354, Budapest, Hungary, April.

Evgeny Matusov, Nicola Ueffing, and Hermann Ney. 2006. Computing Consensus Translation from Multiple Machine Translation Systems Using Enhanced Hypotheses Alignment. In *Proceedings of EACL 2006 (11th Conference of the European Chapter of the Association for Computational Linguistics)*, pages 33–40, Trento, Italy, April.

Maja Popović and Hermann Ney. 2006. POS-based Word Reorderings for Statistical Machine Translation. In *Proceedings of the Fifth International Conference on Language Resources and Evaluation (LREC)*, pages 1278–1283, Genoa, Italy, May.

Maja Popović, Daniel Stein, and Hermann Ney. 2006. Statistical machine translation of german compound words. In *Proceedings of the 5th International Conference on Natural Language Processing (FinTAL)*, pages 616–624, Turku, Finland, August. Lecture Notes in Computer Science, Springer Verlag.

Antti-Veikko Rosti, Necip Fazil Ayan, Bing Xiang, Spyros Matsoukas, Richard Schwartz, and Bonnie Dorr. 2007. Combining Outputs from Multiple Machine Translation Systems. In *Human Language Technologies 2007: The Conference of the North American Chapter of the Association for Computational Linguistics; Proceedings of the Main Conference*, pages 228–235, Rochester, New York, April. Association for Computational Linguistics.

Andreas Stolcke. 2002. SRILM – an extensible language modeling toolkit. In *Proceedings International Conference on Spoken Language Processing (ICSLP)*, volume 2, pages 901–904, Denver, CO.

David Vilar, Daniel Stein, and Hermann Ney. 2008. Analysing soft syntax features and heuristics for hierarchical phrase based machine translation. *International Workshop on Spoken Language Translation 2008*, pages 190–197, October.

Richard Zens, Franz Josef Och, and Hermann Ney. 2002. Phrase-based statistical machine translation. In M. Jarke, J. Koehler, and G. Lakemeyer, editors, *25th German Conference on Artificial Intelligence (KI2002)*, volume 2479 of *Lecture Notes in Artificial Intelligence (LNAI)*, pages 18–32, Aachen, Germany, September. Springer Verlag.

Translation Combination using Factored Word Substitution

Christian Federmann[1], Silke Theison[2], Andreas Eisele[1,2], Hans Uszkoreit[1,2], Yu Chen[2], Michael Jellinghaus[2], Sabine Hunsicker[2]
1: Deutsches Forschungszentrum für Künstliche Intelligenz GmbH, Saarbrücken, Germany
2: Universität des Saarlandes, Saarbrücken, Germany
{cfedermann,eisele,uszkoreit}@dfki.de, {sith,yuchen,micha,sabineh}@coli.uni-sb.de

Abstract

We present a word substitution approach to combine the output of different machine translation systems. Using part of speech information, candidate words are determined among possible translation options, which in turn are estimated through a precomputed word alignment. Automatic substitution is guided by several decision factors, including part of speech, local context, and language model probabilities. The combination of these factors is defined after careful manual analysis of their respective impact. The approach is tested for the language pair German-English, however the general technique itself is language independent.

1 Introduction

Despite remarkable progress in machine translation (MT) in the last decade, automatic translation is still far away from satisfactory quality. Even the most advanced MT technology as summarized by (Lopez, 2008), including the best statistical, rule-based and example-based systems, produces output rife with errors. Those systems may employ different algorithms or vary in the linguistic resources they use which in turn leads to different characteristic errors.

Besides continued research on improving MT techniques, one line of research is dedicated to better exploitation of existing methods for the combination of their respective advantages (Macherey and Och, 2007; Rosti et al., 2007a).

Current approaches for system combination involve post-editing methods (Dugast et al., 2007; Theison, 2007), re-ranking strategies, or shallow phrase substitution. The combination procedure applied for this pape tries to optimize word-level translations within a "trusted" sentence frame selected due to the high quality of its syntactic structure. The underlying idea of the approach is the improvement of a given (original) translation through the exploitation of additional translations of the same text. This can be seen as a simplified version of (Rosti et al., 2007b).

Considering our submission from the shared translation task as the "trusted" frame, we add translations from four additional MT systems that have been chosen based on their performance in terms of automatic evaluation metrics. In total, the combination system performs 1,691 substitutions, i.e., an average of 0.67 substitutions per sentence.

2 Architecture

Our system combination approach computes a combined translation from a given set of machine translations. Below, we present a short overview by describing the different steps in the derivation of a combined translation.

Compute POS tags for translations. We apply part-of-speech (POS) tagging to prepare the selection of possible substitution candidates. For the determination of POS tags we use the Stuttgart TreeTagger (Schmid, 1994).

Create word alignment. The alignment between source text and translations is needed to identify translation options within the different systems' translations. Word alignment is computed using the GIZA++ toolkit (Och and Ney, 2003), only one-to-one word alignments are employed.

Select substitution candidates. For the shared task, we decide to substitute nouns, verbs and adjectives based on the available POS tags. Initially, any such source word is considered as a possible substitution candidate. As we do not want to require substitution can-

Proceedings of the Fourth Workshop on Statistical Machine Translation, pages 70–74,
Athens, Greece, 30 March – 31 March 2009. ©2009 Association for Computational Linguistics

didates to have exactly the same POS tag as the source, we use groups of "similar" tags.

Compute decision factors for candidates. We define several decision factors to enable an automatic ranking of translation options. Details on these can be found in section 4.

Evaluate the decision factors and substitute. Using the available decision factors we compute the best translation and substitute.

The general combination approach is language independent as it only requires a (statistical) POS tagger and GIZA++ to compute the word alignments. More advanced linguistic resources are not required. The addition of lexical resources to improve the extracted word alignments has been considered, however the idea was then dropped as we did not expect any short-term improvements.

3 System selection

Our system combination engine takes any given number of translations and enables us to compute a combined translation out of these. One of the given system translations is chosen to provide the "sentence skeleton", i.e. the global structure of the translation, thus representing the *reference system.* All other systems can only contribute single words for substitution to the combined translation, hence serve as *substitution sources*.

3.1 Reference system

Following our research on hybrid translation trying to combine the strengths of rule-based MT with the virtues of statistical MT, we choose our own (usaar) submission from the shared task to provide the sentence frame for our combination system. As this translation is based upon a rule-based MT system, we expect the overall sentence structure to be of a sufficiently high quality.

3.2 Substitution sources

For the implementation of our combination system, we need resources of potential substitution candidates. As sources for possible substitution, we thus include the translation results of the following four systems:

- Google (google)[1]
- University of Karlsruhe (uka)
- University of Maryland (umd)
- University of Stuttgart (stuttgart)

[1] The Google submission was translated by the Google MT production system offered within the Google Language Tools as opposed to the qualitatively superior Google MT research system.

The decision to select the output of these particular MT systems is based on their performance in terms of different automatic evaluation metrics obtained with the IQMT Framework by (Giménez and Amigó, 2006). This includes BLEU, BLEU1, TER, NIST, METEOR, RG, MT06, and WMT08. The results, listing only the three best systems per metric, are given in table 1.

metric	best three systems		
BLEU1	google 0.599	uka 0.593	systran 0.582
BLEU	google 0.232	uka 0.231	umd 0.223
TER	umd 0.350	rwth.c3 0.335	uka 0.332
NIST	google 6.353	umd 6.302	uka 6.270
METEOR	google 0.558	uka 0.555	stuttgart 0.548
RG	umd 0.527	uka 0.525	google 0.520
MT06	umd 0.415	google 0.413	stuttgart 0.410
WMT08	stuttgart 0.344	rbmt3 0.341	google 0.336

Table 1: Automatic evaluation results.

On grounds of these results we anticipate the four above named translation engines to perform best when being combined with our hybrid machine translation system. We restrict the substitution sources to the four potentially best systems in order to omit bad substitutions and to reduce the computational complexity of the substitution problem. It is possible to choose any other number of substitution sources.

4 Substitution

As mentioned above, we consider nouns, verbs and adjectives as possible substitution candidates. In order to allow for automatic decision making amongst several translation options we define a set of factors, detailed in the following. Furthermore, we present some examples in order to illustrate the use of the factors within the decision process.

4.1 Decision factors

The set of factors underlying the decision procedure consists of the following:

A: Matching POS. This Boolean factor checks whether the target word POS tag matches the source word's POS category. The factor compares the source text to the reference translation as we want to preserve the sentential structure of the latter.

B: Majority vote. For this factor, we compute an ordered list of the different translation options, sorted by decreasing frequency. A consensus between several systems may help to identify the best translation.

Both the reference system and the Google submission receive a $+1$ bonus, as they appeared to offer better candidates in more cases within the small data sample of our manual analysis.

C: POS context. Further filtering is applied determining the words' POS context. This is especially important as we do not want to degrade the sentence structure maintained by the translation output of the reference system.

In order to optimize this factor, we conduct trials with the single word, the -1 left, and the $+1$ right context. To reduce complexity, we shorten POS tags to a single character, e.g. $NN \to N$ or $NPS \to N$.

D: Language Model. We use an English language model to score the different translation options. As the combination system only replaces single words within a bi-gram context, we employ the bi-gram portion of the English Gigaword language model.

The language model had been estimated using the SRILM toolkit (Stolcke, 2002).

4.2 Factor configurations

To determine the best possible combination of our different factors, we define four potential factor configurations and evaluate them manually on a small set of sentences. The configurations differ in the consideration of the *POS context* for factor C (*strict* including -1 left context versus *relaxed* including no context) and in the usage of factor A *Matching POS* (*+A*). Table 2 shows the settings of factors A and C for the different configurations.

configuration	Matching POS	POS context
strict	disabled	-1 left
strict+A	enabled	-1 left
relaxed	disabled	single word
relaxed+A	enabled	single word

Table 2: Factor configurations for combination.

Our manual evaluation of the respective substitution decisions taken by different factor combination is suggestive of the "relaxed+A" configuration to produce the best combination result. Thus, this configuration is utilized to produce sound combined translations for the complete data set.

4.3 Factored substitution

Having determined the configuration of the different factors, we compute those for the complete data set, in order to apply the final substitution step which will create the combined translation.

The factored substitution algorithm chooses among the different translation options in the following way:

(a) Matching POS? If factor A is activated for the current factor configuration (*+A*), substitution of the given translation options can only be possible if the factor evaluates to True. Otherwise the substitution candidate is skipped.

(b) Majority vote winner? If the majority vote yields a unique winner, this translation option is taken as the final translation.

Using the $+1$ bonuses for both the reference system and the Google submission we introduce a slight bias that was motivated by manual evaluation of the different systems' translation results.

(c) Language model. If several majority vote winners can be determined, the one with the best language model score is chosen.

Due to the nature of real numbers this step always chooses a winning translation option and thus the termination of the substitution algorithm is well-defined.

Please note that, while factors A, B, and D are explicitly used within the substitution algorithm, factor C *POS context* is implicitly used only when computing the possible translation options for a given substitution candidate.

configuration	substitutions	ratio
strict	1,690	5.714%
strict+A	1,347	4.554%
relaxed	2,228	7.532%
relaxed+A	1,691	5.717%

Table 3: Substitutions for 29,579 candidates.

Interestingly we are able to obtain best results without considering the -1 left POS context, i.e. only checking the POS tag of the single word translation option for factor C.

4.4 Combination results

We compute system combinations for each of the four factor configurations defined above. Table 3 displays how many substitutions are conducted within each of these configurations.

The following examples illustrate the performance of the substitution algorithm used to produce the combined translations.

"Einbruch": the reference translation for "Einbruch" is "collapse", the substitution sources propose "slump" and "drop", but also "collapse", all three, considering the context, forming good translations. The majority vote rules out the suggestions different to the reference translation due to the fact that 2 more systems recommend "collapse" as the correct translation.

"Rückgang": the reference system translates this word as "drop" while all of the substitution sources choose "decline" as the correct translation. Since factor A evaluates to True, i.e. the POS tags are of the same nature, "decline" is clearly selected as the best translation by factor B *Majority vote* and thus replaces "drop" in the final combined translation result.

"Tagesgeschäfte": our reference system translates "Tagesgeschäfte" with "requirements", while two of the substitution systems indicate "business" to be a better translation. Due to the $+1$ bonus for our reference translation a tie between the two possible translations emerges, leaving the decision to the language model score, which is higher for "business".

4.5 Evaluation results

Table 4 shows the results of the manual evaluation campaign carried out as part of the WMT09 shared task. Randomly chosen sentences are presented to the annotator, who then has to put them into relative order. Note that each annotator is shown a random subset of the sentences to be evaluated.

system	relative rank	data points
google	-2.74	174
uka	-3.00	217
umd	-3.03	170
stuttgart	-2.89	163
usaar	-2.78	186
usaar-combo	-2.91	164

Table 4: Relative ranking results from the WMT09 manual evalution campaign.

Interestingly, our combined system is not able to outperform the baseline, i.e., additional data did not improve translation results. However the evaluation is rather intransparent since it does not allow for a strict comparison between sentences.

5 Conclusion

Within the system described in this paper, we approach a hybrid translation technique combining the output of different MT systems. Substituting particular words within a well-structured translation frame equips us with considerably enhanced translation output. We obtain promising results providing substantiated proof that our approach is going in the right direction.

Further steps in the future will include machine learning methods to optimize the factor selection. This was, due to limited amount of time and data, not feasible thus far. We will also investigate the potential of phrase-based substitution taking into account multi-word alignments instead of just single word mappings. Additionally, we would like to continue work on the integration of lexical resources to post-correct the word alignments obtained by GIZA++ as this will directly improve the overall system performance.

Acknowledgments

This work was supported by the EuroMatrix project (IST-034291) which is funded by the European Community under the Sixth Framework Programme for Research and Technological Development.

References

Loïc Dugast, Jean Senellart, and Philipp Koehn. 2007. Statistical post-editing on SYSTRAN's rule-based translation system. In *Proceedings of the Second Workshop on Statistical Machine Translation*, pages 220–223, Prague, Czech Republic, June. Association for Computational Linguistics.

Jesús Giménez and Enrique Amigó. 2006. IQMT: A framework for automatic machine translation evaluation. In *Proceedings of the 5th International Conference on Language Resources and Evaluation (LREC'06)*.

Adam Lopez. 2008. Statistical machine translation. *ACM Computing Surveys*, 40(3):1–49.

Wolfgang Macherey and Franz J. Och. 2007. An empirical study on computing consensus translations from multiple machine translation systems. In *Proceedings of the 2007 Joint Conference on Empirical Methods in Natural Language Processing and Computational Natural Language Learning (EMNLP-CoNLL)*, pages 986–995, Prague, Czech Republic, June. Association for Computational Linguistics.

Franz Josef Och and Hermann Ney. 2003. A systematic comparison of various statistical alignment models. *Computational Linguistics*, 29(1):19–51.

Antti-Veikko Rosti, Necip Fazil Ayan, Bing Xiang, Spyros Matsoukas, Richard Schwartz, and Bonnie Dorr. 2007a. Combining outputs from multiple machine translation systems. In *Human Language Technologies 2007: The Conference of the North American Chapter of the Association for Computational Linguistics; Proceedings of the Main Conference*, pages 228–235, Rochester, New York, April. Association for Computational Linguistics.

Antti-Veikko Rosti, Spyros Matsoukas, and Richard Schwartz. 2007b. Improved word-level system combination for machine translation. In *Proceedings of the 45th Annual Meeting of the Association of Computational Linguistics*, pages 312–319, Prague, Czech Republic, June. Association for Computational Linguistics.

Helmut Schmid. 1994. Probabilistic part-of-speech tagging using decision trees. In *Proceedings of International Conference on New Methods in Language Processing*, September.

Andreas Stolcke. 2002. SRILM - an extensible language modeling toolkit. In *the 7th International Conference on Spoken Language Processing (ICSLP) 2002*, Denver, Colorado.

Silke Theison. 2007. Optimizing rule-based machine translation output with the help of statistical methods. Master's thesis, Saarland University, Computational Linguistics department.

NUS at WMT09: Domain Adaptation Experiments for English-Spanish Machine Translation of News Commentary Text

Preslav Nakov
Department of Computer Science
National University of Singapore
13 Computing Drive
Singapore 117417
nakov@comp.nus.edu.sg

Hwee Tou Ng
Department of Computer Science
National University of Singapore
13 Computing Drive
Singapore 117417
nght@comp.nus.edu.sg

Abstract

We describe the system developed by the team of the National University of Singapore for English to Spanish machine translation of News Commentary text for the WMT09 Shared Translation Task. Our approach is based on domain adaptation, combining a small in-domain *News Commentary* bi-text and a large out-of-domain one from the *Europarl* corpus, from which we built and combined two separate phrase tables. We further combined two language models (in-domain and out-of-domain), and we experimented with cognates, improved tokenization and recasing, achieving the highest lowercased NIST score of 6.963 and the second best lowercased Bleu score of 24.91% for training without using additional external data for English-to-Spanish translation at the shared task.

1 Introduction

Modern Statistical Machine Translation (SMT) systems are typically trained on sentence-aligned parallel texts (bi-texts) from a particular domain. When tested on text from that domain, they demonstrate state-of-the art performance, but on out-of-domain test data the results can deteriorate significantly. For example, on the WMT06 Shared Translation Task, the scores for French-to-English translation dropped from about 30 to about 20 Bleu points for nearly all systems when tested on *News Commentary* instead of the *Europarl*[1] text, which was used for training (Koehn and Monz, 2006).

Subsequently, in 2007 and 2008, the WMT Shared Translation Task organizers provided a limited amount of bilingual *News Commentary* training data (1-1.3M words) in addition to the large amount of *Europarl* data (30-32M words), and set up separate evaluations on *News Commentary* and on *Europarl* data, thus inviting interest in domain adaptation experiments for the *News* domain (Callison-Burch et al., 2007; Callison-Burch et al., 2008). This year, the evaluation is on *News Commentary* only, which makes domain adaptation the central focus of the Shared Translation Task.

The team of the National University of Singapore (NUS) participated in the WMT09 Shared Translation Task with an English-to-Spanish system.[2] Our approach is based on domain adaptation, combining the small in-domain *News Commentary* bi-text (1.8M words) and the large out-of-domain one from the Europarl corpus (40M words), from which we built and combined two separate phrase tables. We further used two language models (in-domain and out-of-domain), cognates, improved tokenization, and additional smart recasing as a post-processing step.

2 The NUS System

Below we describe separately the standard and the nonstandard settings of our system.

2.1 Standard Settings

In our baseline experiments, we used the following general setup: First, we tokenized the par-

[1]See (Koehn, 2005) for details about the *Europarl* corpus.

[2]The task organizers invited submissions translating forward and/or backward between English and five other European languages (French, Spanish, German, Czech and Hungarian), but we only participated in English→Spanish, due to time limitations.

Proceedings of the Fourth Workshop on Statistical Machine Translation, pages 75–79,
Athens, Greece, 30 March – 31 March 2009.

allel bi-text, converted it to lowercase, and filtered out the overly-long training sentences, which complicate word alignments (we tried maximum length limits of 40 and 100). We then built separate English-to-Spanish and Spanish-to-English directed word alignments using IBM model 4 (Brown et al., 1993), combined them using the *intersect+grow heuristic* (Och and Ney, 2003), and extracted phrase-level translation pairs of maximum length 7 using the *alignment template approach* (Och and Ney, 2004). We thus obtained a *phrase table* where each phrase translation pair is associated with the following five standard parameters: forward and reverse phrase translation probabilities, forward and reverse lexical translation probabilities, and phrase penalty.

We then trained a log-linear model using the standard feature functions: language model probability, word penalty, distortion costs (we tried distance based and lexicalized reordering models), and the parameters from the phrase table. We set all feature weights by optimizing Bleu (Papineni et al., 2002) directly using *minimum error rate training* (MERT) (Och, 2003) on the tuning part of the development set (`dev-test2009a`). We used these weights in a beam search decoder (Koehn et al., 2007) to translate the test sentences (the English part of `dev-test2009b`, tokenized and lowercased). We then recased the output using a monotone model that translates from lowercase to uppercase Spanish, we post-cased it using a simple heuristic, de-tokenized the result, and compared it to the gold standard (the Spanish part of `dev-test2009b`) using Bleu and NIST.

2.2 Nonstandard Settings

The nonstandard features of our system can be summarized as follows:

Two Language Models. Following Nakov and Hearst (2007), we used two language models (LM) – an in-domain one (trained on a concatenation of the provided monolingual Spanish *News Commentary* data and the Spanish side of the training *News Commentary* bi-text) and an out-of-domain one (trained on the provided monolingual Spanish *Europarl* data). For both LMs, we used 5-gram models with Kneser-Ney smoothing.

Merging Two Phrase Tables. Following Nakov (2008), we trained and merged two phrase-based SMT systems: a small in-domain one using the *News Commentary* bi-text, and a large out-of-domain one using the *Europarl* bi-text. As a result, we obtained two phrase tables, T_{news} and T_{euro}, and two lexicalized reordering models, R_{news} and R_{euro}. We merged the phrase table as follows. First, we kept all phrase pairs from T_{news}. Then we added those phrase pairs from T_{euro} which were not present in T_{news}. For each phrase pair added, we retained its associated features: forward and reverse phrase translation probabilities, forward and reverse lexical translation probabilities, and phrase penalty. We further added two new features, F_{news} and F_{euro}, which show the source of each phrase. Their values are 1 and 0.5 when the phrase was extracted from the *News Commentary* bi-text, 0.5 and 1 when it was extracted from the *Europarl* bi-text, and 1 and 1 when it was extracted from both. As a result, we ended up with seven parameters for each entry in the merged phrase table.

Merging Two Lexicalized Reordering Tables. When building the two phrase tables, we also built two lexicalized reordering tables (Koehn et al., 2005) for them, R_{news} and R_{euro}, which we merged as follows: We first kept all phrases from R_{news}, then we added those from R_{euro} which were not present in R_{news}. This resulting lexicalized reordering table was used together with the above-described merged phrase table.

Cognates. Previous research has shown that using cognates can yield better word alignments (Al-Onaizan et al., 1999; Kondrak et al., 2003), which in turn often means higher-quality phrase pairs and better SMT systems. Linguists define cognates as words derived from a common root (Bickford and Tuggy, 2002). Following previous researchers in *computational* linguistics (Bergsma and Kondrak, 2007; Mann and Yarowsky, 2001; Melamed, 1999), however, we adopted a simplified definition which ignores origin, defining cognates as words in different languages that are mutual translations and have a similar orthography. We extracted and used such potential cognates in order to bias the training of the IBM word alignment models. Following Melamed (1995), we measured the orthographic similarity using *longest common subsequence ratio* (LCSR), which is defined as follows:

$$\text{LCSR}(s_1, s_2) = \frac{|\text{LCS}(s_1,s_2)|}{\max(|s_1|,|s_2|)}$$

where $\text{LCS}(s_1, s_2)$ is the *longest common subsequence* of s_1 and s_2, and $|s|$ is the length of s.

Following Nakov et al. (2007), we combined the LCSR similarity measure with *competitive linking* (Melamed, 2000) in order to extract potential cognates from the training bi-text. Competitive linking assumes that, given a source English sentence and its Spanish translation, a source word is either translated with a single target word or is not translated at all. Given an English-Spanish sentence pair, we calculated LCSR for all cross-lingual word pairs (excluding stopwords and words of length 3 or less), which induced a fully-connected weighted bipartite graph. Then, we performed a greedy approximation to the maximum weighted bipartite matching in that graph (competitive linking) as follows: First, we aligned the most similar pair of unaligned words and we discarded these words from further consideration. Then, we aligned the next most similar pair of unaligned words, and so forth. The process was repeated until there were no words left or the maximal word pair similarity fell below a pre-specified threshold θ ($0 \leq \theta \leq 1$), which typically left some words unaligned.[3] As a result we ended up with a list C of potential cognate pairs. Following (Al-Onaizan et al., 1999; Kondrak et al., 2003; Nakov et al., 2007) we filtered out the duplicates in C, and we added the remaining cognate pairs as additional "sentence" pairs to the bi-text in order to bias the subsequent training of the IBM word alignment models.

Improved (De-)tokenization. The default tokenizer does not split on hyphenated compound words like *nation-building*, *well-rehearsed*, *self-assured*, *Arab-Israeli*, *domestically-oriented*, *etc.* While linguistically correct, this can be problematic for machine translation since it can cause data sparsity issues. For example, the system might know how to translate into Spanish both *well* and *rehearsed*, but not *well-rehearsed*, and thus at translation time it would be forced to handle it as an unknown word, *i.e.*, copy it to the output untranslated. A similar problem is related to double dashes, as illustrated by the following training sentence: "*So the question now is what can China do to freeze--and, if possible, to reverse--North Korea's nuclear program.*" We changed the tokenizer so that it splits on '-' and '--'; we altered the detokenizer accordingly.

Improved Recaser. The default recaser suggested by the WMT09 organizers was based on a monotone translation model. We trained such a recaser on the Spanish side of the *News Commentary* bi-text that translates from lowercase to uppercase Spanish. While being good overall, it had a problem with unknown words, leaving them in lowercase. In a *News Commentary* text, however, most unknown words are named entities – persons, organization, locations – which are spelled with a capitalized initial in Spanish. Therefore, we used an additional recasing script, which runs over the output of the default recaser and sets the casing of the unknown words to the original casing they had in the English input. It also makes sure all sentences start with a capitalized initial.

[3]For *News Commentary*, we used $\theta = 0.4$, which was found by optimizing on the development set; for *Europarl*, we set $\theta = 0.58$ as suggested by Kondrak et al. (2003).

Rule-based Post-editing. We did a quick study of the system errors on the development set, and we designed some heuristic post-editing rules, *e.g.*,

- **? or ! without ¿ or ¡ to the left:** if so, we insert ¿/¡ at the sentence beginning;
- **numbers:** we change English numbers like 1,185.32 to Spanish-style 1.185,32;
- **duplicate punctuation:** we remove duplicate sentence end markers, quotes, commas, parentheses, *etc.*

3 Experiments and Evaluation

Table 1 shows the performance of a simple baseline system and the impact of different cumulative modifications to that system when tuning on `dev-test2009a` and testing on `dev-test2009b`. The table report the Bleu and NIST scores measured on the detokenized output under three conditions: (1) without recasing ('*Lowercased*'), 2) using the default recaser ('*Recased (default)*'), and (3) using an improved recaser and post-editing rules *Post-cased & Post-edited*'). In the following discussion, we will discuss the Bleu results under condition (3).

System 1 uses sentences of length up to 40 tokens from the *News Commentary* bi-text, the default (de-)tokenizer, distance reordering, and a 3-gram language model trained on the Spanish side of the bi-text. Its performance is quite modest: 15.32% of Bleu with the default recaser, and 16.92% when the improved recaser and the post-editing rules are used.

System 2 increases to 100 the maximum length of the sentences in the bi-text, which yields 0.55% absolute improvement in Bleu.

System 3 uses the new (de-)tokenizer, but this turns out to make almost no difference.

#	Bitext	System	Lowercased Bleu	Lowercased NIST	Recased (default) Bleu	Recased (default) NIST	Post-cased & Post-edited Bleu	Post-cased & Post-edited NIST
1	news	*News Commentary* baseline	18.38	5.7837	15.32	5.2266	16.92	5.5091
2	news	+ max sentence length 100	18.91	5.8540	15.93	5.3119	17.47	5.5874
3	news	+ improved (de-)tokenizer	18.96	5.8706	15.97	5.3254	17.48	5.6020
4	news	+ lexicalized reordering	19.81	5.9422	16.64	5.3793	18.28	5.6696
5	news	+ LM: old+monol. *News*, 5-gram	22.29	6.2791	18.91	5.6901	20.55	5.9924
6	news	+ LM_2: *Europarl*, 5-gram	22.46	6.2438	19.10	5.6606	20.75	5.9570
7	news	+ cognates	23.14	6.3504	19.64	5.7478	21.32	6.0478
8	euro	*Europarl* (~ system 6)	23.73	6.4673	20.23	5.8707	21.89	6.1577
9	euro	+ cognates (~ system 7)	23.95	6.4709	20.44	5.8742	22.10	6.1607
10	both	Combining 7 & 9	**24.40**	**6.5723**	**20.74**	**5.9575**	**22.37**	**6.2506**

Table 1: **Impact of the combined modifications for English-to-Spanish machine translation on `dev-test2009b`.** We report the Bleu and NIST scores measured on the detokenized output under three conditions: (1) without recasing ('*Lowercased*'), (2) using the default recaser ('*Recased (default)*'), and (3) using an improved recaser and post-editing rules ('*Post-cased & Post-edited*'). The *News Commentary* baseline system uses sentences of length up to 40 tokens from the *News Commentary* bi-text, the default tokenizer and de-tokenizer, a distance-based reordering model, and a trigram language model trained on the Spanish side of the bi-text. The *Europarl* system is the same as system 6, except that it uses the *Europarl* bi-text instead of the *News Commentary* bi-text.

System 4 adds a lexicalized re-ordering model, which yields 0.8% absolute improvement.

System 5 improves the language model. It adds the additional monolingual Spanish *News Commentary* data provided by the organizers to the Spanish side of the bi-text, and uses a 5-gram language model instead of the 3-gram LM used by Systems 1-4. This yields a sizable absolute gain in Bleu: 2.27%.

System 6 adds a second 5-gram LM trained on the monolingual *Europarl* data, gaining 0.2%.

System 7 augments the training bi-text with cognate pairs, gaining another 0.57%.

System 8 is the same as *System 6*, except that it is trained on the out-of-domain *Europarl* bi-text instead of the in-domain *News Commentary* bi-text. Surprisingly, this turns out to work better than the in-domain *System 6* by 1.14% of Bleu. This is a quite surprising result since in both WMT07 and WMT08, for which comparable kinds and size of training data was provided, training on the out-of-domain *Europarl* was always worse than training on the in-domain *News Commentary*. We are not sure why it is different this year, but it could be due to the way the dev-train and dev-test was created for the 2009 data – by extracting alternating sentences from the original development set.

System 9 augments the *Europarl* bi-text with cognate pairs, gaining another 0.21%.

System 10 merges the phrase tables of systems 7 and 9, and is otherwise the same as them. This adds another 0.27%.

Our official submission to WMT09 is the post-edited *System 10*, re-tuned on the full development set: `dev-test2009a` + `dev-test2009b` (in order to produce more stable results with MERT).

4 Conclusion and Future Work

As we can see in Table 1, we have achieved not only a huge 'vertical' absolute improvement of 5.5-6% in Bleu from System 1 to System 10, but also a significant 'horizontal' one: our recased and post-edited result for *System 10* is better than that of the default recaser by 1.63% in Bleu (22.37% vs. 20.74%). Still, the lowercased Bleu of 24.40% suggests that there may be a lot of room for further improvement in recasing – we are still about 2% below it. While this is probably due primarily to the system choosing a different sentence-initial word, it certainly deserves further investigation in future work.

Acknowledgments

This research was supported by research grant POD0713875.

References

Yaser Al-Onaizan, Jan Curin, Michael Jahr, Kevin Knight, John Lafferty, Dan Melamed, Franz Joseph Och, David Purdy, Noah Smith, and David Yarowsky. 1999. Statistical machine translation. Technical report, CLSP, Johns Hopkins University, Baltimore, MD.

Shane Bergsma and Grzegorz Kondrak. 2007. Alignment-based discriminative string similarity. In *Proceedings of the Annual Meeting of the Association for Computational Linguistics (ACL'07)*, pages 656–663, Prague, Czech Republic.

Albert Bickford and David Tuggy. 2002. Electronic glossary of linguistic terms. http://www.sil.org/mexico/ling/glosario/E005ai-Glossary.htm.

Peter Brown, Vincent Della Pietra, Stephen Della Pietra, and Robert Mercer. 1993. The mathematics of statistical machine translation: parameter estimation. *Computational Linguistics*, 19(2):263–311.

Chris Callison-Burch, Cameron Fordyce, Philipp Koehn, Christof Monz, and Josh Schroeder. 2007. (Meta-) evaluation of machine translation. In *Proceedings of the Second Workshop on Statistical Machine Translation*, pages 136–158, Prague, Czech Republic.

Chris Callison-Burch, Cameron Fordyce, Philipp Koehn, Christof Monz, and Josh Schroeder. 2008. Further meta-evaluation of machine translation. In *Proceedings of the Third Workshop on Statistical Machine Translation*, pages 70–106, Columbus, OH, USA.

Philipp Koehn and Christof Monz. 2006. Manual and automatic evaluation of machine translation between European languages. In *Proceedings of the First Workshop on Statistical Machine Translation*, pages 102–121, New York, NY, USA.

Philipp Koehn, Amittai Axelrod, Alexandra Birch Mayne, Chris Callison-Burch, Miles Osborne, and David Talbot. 2005. Edinburgh system description for the 2005 IWSLT speech translation evaluation. In *Proceedings of the International Workshop on Spoken Language Translation (IWSLT'05)*, Pittsburgh, PA, USA.

Philipp Koehn, Hieu Hoang, Alexandra Birch, Chris Callison-Burch, Marcello Federico, Nicola Bertoldi, Brooke Cowan, Wade Shen, Christine Moran, Richard Zens, Chris Dyer, Ondrej Bojar, Alexandra Constantin, and Evan Herbst. 2007. Moses: Open source toolkit for statistical machine translation. In *Proceedings of the Annual Meeting of the Association for Computational Linguistics (ACL'07). Demonstration session*, pages 177–180, Prague, Czech Republic.

P. Koehn. 2005. Europarl: A parallel corpus for evaluation of machine translation. In *Proceedings of the X MT Summit*, pages 79–86, Phuket, Thailand.

Grzegorz Kondrak, Daniel Marcu, and Kevin Knight. 2003. Cognates can improve statistical translation models. In *Proceedings of the Annual Meeting of the North American Association for Computational Linguistics (NAACL'03)*, pages 46–48, Sapporo, Japan.

Gideon Mann and David Yarowsky. 2001. Multipath translation lexicon induction via bridge languages. In *Proceedings of the Annual Meeting of the North American Association for Computational Linguistics (NAACL'01)*, pages 1–8, Pittsburgh, PA, USA.

Dan Melamed. 1995. Automatic evaluation and uniform filter cascades for inducing N-best translation lexicons. In *Proceedings of the Third Workshop on Very Large Corpora*, pages 184–198, Cambridge, MA, USA.

Dan Melamed. 1999. Bitext maps and alignment via pattern recognition. *Computational Linguistics*, 25(1):107–130.

Dan Melamed. 2000. Models of translational equivalence among words. *Computational Linguistics*, 26(2):221–249.

Preslav Nakov and Marti Hearst. 2007. UCB system description for the WMT 2007 shared task. In *Proceedings of the Second Workshop on Statistical Machine Translation*, pages 212–215, Prague, Czech Republic.

Preslav Nakov, Svetlin Nakov, and Elena Paskaleva. 2007. Improved word alignments using the Web as a corpus. In *Proceedigs of Recent Advances in Natural Language Processing (RANLP'07)*, pages 400–405, Borovets, Bulgaria.

Preslav Nakov. 2008. Improving English-Spanish statistical machine translation: Experiments in domain adaptation, sentence paraphrasing, tokenization, and recasing. In *Proceedings of the Third Workshop on Statistical Machine Translation*, pages 147–150, Columbus, OH, USA.

Franz Josef Och and Hermann Ney. 2003. A systematic comparison of various statistical alignment models. *Computational Linguistics*, 29(1):19–51.

Franz Josef Och and Hermann Ney. 2004. The alignment template approach to statistical machine translation. *Computational Linguistics*, 30(4):417–449.

Franz Josef Och. 2003. Minimum error rate training in statistical machine translation. In *Proceedings of the Annual Meeting of the Association for Computational Linguistics (ACL'03)*, pages 160–167, Sapporo, Japan.

Kishore Papineni, Salim Roukos, Todd Ward, and Wei-Jing Zhu. 2002. Bleu: a method for automatic evaluation of machine translation. In *Proceedings of the Annual Meeting of the Association for Computational Linguistics (ACL'02)*, pages 311–318, Philadelphia, PA, USA.

The Universität Karlsruhe Translation System for the EACL-WMT 2009

Jan Niehues, Teresa Herrmann, Muntsin Kolss and Alex Waibel
Universität Karlsruhe (TH)
Karlsruhe, Germany
{jniehues,therrman,kolss,waibel}@ira.uka.de

Abstract

In this paper we describe the statistical machine translation system of the Universität Karlsruhe developed for the translation task of the Fourth Workshop on Statistical Machine Translation. The state-of-the-art phrase-based SMT system is augmented with alternative word reordering and alignment mechanisms as well as optional phrase table modifications. We participate in the constrained condition of German-English and English-German as well as in the constrained condition of French-English and English-French.

1 Introduction

This paper describes the statistical MT system used for our participation in the WMT'09 Shared Translation Task and the particular language-pair-dependent variations of the system. We use standard alignment and training tools and a phrase-based SMT decoder for creating state-of-the-art MT systems for our contribution in the translation directions English-German, German-English, English-French and French-English.

Depending on the language pair, the baseline system is augmented with part-of-speech (POS)-based short-range and long-range word reordering models, discriminative word alignment (DWA) and several modifications of the phrase table. Experiments with different system variants were conducted including some of those additional system components. Significantly better translation results could be achieved compared to the baseline results.

An overview of the system will follow in Section 2, which describes the baseline architecture, followed by descriptions of the additional system components. Translation results for the different languages and system variants are presented in Section 5.

2 Baseline System

The core of our system is the STTK decoder (Vogel, 2003), a phrase-based SMT decoder with a local reordering window of 2 words. The decoder generates a translation for the input text or word lattice by searching translation model and language model for the hypothesis that maximizes phrase translation probabilities and target language probabilities. The translation model, i.e. the SMT phrase table is created during the training phase by a modified version of the Moses Toolkit (Koehn et al., 2007) applying GIZA++ for word alignment. Language models are built using the SRILM Toolkit. The POS-tags for the reordering models were generated with the TreeTagger (Schmid, 1994) for all languages.

2.1 Training, Development and Test Data

We submitted translations for the English-German, German-English, English-French and French-English tasks. All systems were trained on the Europarl and News Commentary corpora using the Moses Toolkit and apply 4-gram language models created from the respective monolingual News corpora. All feature weights are automatically determined and optimized with respect to BLEU via MERT (Venugopal et al., 2005). For development and testing we used data provided by the WMT'09, news-dev2009a and news-dev2009b, consisting of 1026 sentences each.

3 Word Reordering Model

One part of our system that differs from the baseline system is the reordering model. To account for the different word orders in the languages, we used the POS-based reordering model presented in Rottmann and Vogel (2007). This model learns rules from a parallel text to reorder the source side. The aim is to generate a reordered source side that can be translated in a more monotone way.

Proceedings of the Fourth Workshop on Statistical Machine Translation, pages 80–84,
Athens, Greece, 30 March – 31 March 2009.

In this framework, first, reordering rules are extracted from an aligned parallel corpus and POS information is added to the source side. These rules are of the form *VVIMP VMFIN PPER* → *PPER VMFIN VVIMP* and describe how the source side has to be reordered to match the target side. Then the rules are scored according to their relative frequencies.

In a preprocessing step to the actual decoding different reorderings of the source sentences are encoded in a word lattice. Therefore, for all reordering rules that can be applied to a sentence the resulting reorderings are added to the lattice if the score is better than a given threshold. The decoding is then performed on the resulting word lattice.

This approach does model the reordering well if only short-range reorderings occur. But especially when translating from and to German, there are also long-range reorderings that require the verb to be shifted nearly across the whole sentence. During this shift of the verb, the rest of the sentence remains mainly unchanged. It does not matter which words are in between, since they are moved as a whole. Furthermore, rules including an explicit sequence of POS-tags spanning the whole sentence would be too specific. A lot more rules would be needed to cover long-range reorderings with each rule being applicable only very sparsely. Therefore, we model long-range reordering by generalizing over the unaffected sequences and introduce rules with gaps. (For more details see Niehues and Kolss (2009)). These are learned in a way similar to the other type of reordering rules described above, but contain a gap representing one or several arbitrary words. It is, for example, possible to have the following rule *VAFIN * VVPP* → *VAFIN VVPP **, which puts both parts of the German verb next to each other.

4 Translation Model

The translation models of all systems we submitted differ in some parts from the baseline system. The main changes done will be described in this section.

4.1 Word Alignment

The baseline method for creating the word alignment is to create the GIZA++ alignments in both directions and then to combine both alignments using a heuristic, e.g. grow-diag-final-and heuristic, as provided by the Moses Toolkit. In some of the submitted systems we used a discriminative word alignment model (*DWA*) to generate the alignments as described in Niehues and Vogel (2008) instead. This model is trained on a small amount of hand-aligned data and uses the lexical probability as well as the fertilities generated by the GIZA++ Toolkit and POS information. We used all local features, the GIZA and indicator fertility features as well as first order features for 6 directions. The model was trained in three steps, first using the maximum likelihood optimization and afterwards it was optimized towards the alignment error rate. For more details see Niehues and Vogel (2008).

4.2 Phrase Table Smoothing

The relative frequencies of the phrase pairs are a very important feature of the translation model, but they often overestimate rare phrase pairs. Therefore, the raw relative frequency estimates found in the phrase translation tables are smoothed by applying modified Kneser-Ney discounting as described in Foster et al. (2006).

4.3 Lattice Phrase Extraction

For the test sentences the POS-based reordering allows us to change the word order in the source sentence, so that the sentence can be translated more easily. But this approach does not reorder the training sentences. This may cause problems for phrase extraction, especially for long-range reorderings. For example, if the English verb is aligned to both parts of the German verb, this phrase can not be extracted, since it is not continuous on the German side. In the case of German as source language, the phrase could be extracted if we also reorder the training corpus.

Therefore, we build lattices that encode the different reorderings for every training sentence. Then we can not only extract phrase pairs from the monotone source path, but also from the reordered paths. So it would be possible to extract the example mentioned before, if both parts of the verb were put together by a reordering rule. To limit the number of extracted phrase pairs, we extract a source phrase only once per sentence even if it may be found on different paths. Furthermore, we do not use the weights in the lattice.

If we use the same rules as for the test sets, the lattice would be so big that the number of extracted phrase pairs would be still too high. As mentioned before, the word reordering is mainly a problem at the phrase extraction stage if one word is aligned to two words which are far away from each other in the sentence. Therefore, the short-range reordering rules do not help much in this case. So, only the long-range reordering rules were used to generate the lattice for the training corpus. This already leads to an increase of the number of source phrases in the filtered phrase table from 724K to 971K. The number of phrase pairs grows from 5.1M to 6.7M.

4.4 Phrase Table Adaption

For most of the different tasks there was a huge amount of parallel out-of-domain training data available, but only a much smaller amount of in-domain training data. Therefore, we tried to adapt our system to the in-domain data. We want to make use of the big out-of-domain data, but do not want to lose the information encoded in the in-domain data.

To achieve this, we built an additional phrase table trained only on the in-domain data. Since the word alignment does not depend heavily on the domain we used the same word alignment. Then we combined both phrase tables in the following way. A phrase pair with features θ from the first phrase table is added to the combined one with features $< \theta, 1 >$, where 1 is a vector of ones with length equal to the number of features in the other phrase table. The phrase pairs of the other phrase table were added with the features $< 1, \theta >$.

5 Results

We submitted system translations for the English-German, German-English, English-French and French-English task. Their performance is measured applying the BLEU metric. All BLEU scores are computed on the lower-cased translations.

5.1 English-German

The system translating from English to German was trained on the data described in Section 2.1. The first system already uses the POS-based reordering model for short-range reorderings. The results of the different systems are shown in Table 1.

We could improve the translation quality on the test set by using the smoothed relative frequencies in the phrase table as described before and by adapting the phrase table. Then we used the discriminative word alignment to generate a new word alignment. For the training of the model we used 500 hand-aligned sentences from the Europarl corpus. By training a translation model based on this word alignment we could improve the translation quality further. At last we added the model for long-range reorderings, which performs best on the test set.

The improvement achieved by smoothing is significant at a level of 5%, the remaining changes are not significant on their own. In all language pairs, the problem occurs that some features do not lead to an improvement on the development set, but on the test set. One reason for this may be that the development set is quite small.

Table 1: Translation results for English-German (BLEU Score)

System	Dev	Test
Short-range	13.96	14.99
+ Smoothing	14.36	15.38
+ Adaptation	13.96	15.44
+ Discrim. WA	14.45	15.61
+ Long-range reordering	14.58	**15.70**

5.2 German-English

The German-English system was trained on the same data as the English-German except that we perform compound splitting as an additional preprocessing step. The compound splitting was done with the frequency-based method described in Koehn et al. (2003). For this language direction, the initial system already uses phrase table smoothing, adaptation and discriminative word alignment, in addition to the techniques of the English-German baseline system. The results are shown in Table 2.

For this language pair, we could improve the translation quality, first, by adding the long-range reordering model. Further improvements could be achieved by using lattice phrase extraction as described before.

5.3 English-French

For creating the English-French translations, first, the baseline system as described in Section 2 was used. This baseline was then augmented with phrase table smoothing, short-range word reordering and phrase table adaptation as described above. In addition, the adapted phrase table was

Table 2: Translation results for German-English (BLEU Score)

System	Dev	Test
Initial System	20.52	22.01
+ Long-range reordering	21.04	22.36
+ Lattice phrase extraction	20.69	**22.64**

postprocessed such that phrase table entries include the same amount of punctuation marks, especially quotation marks, in both source and target phrase. In contrast to the English↔German language pairs, the word reordering required in English↔French translations are restricted to rather local word shifts which can be covered by the short-range reordering feature. Applying additional long-range reordering is scarcely expected to yield further improvements for these language pairs and was not applied specifically in this task. Table 3 shows the results of the system variants.

Table 3: Translation results for English-French (BLEU Score)

System	Dev	Test
Baseline	20.97	20.87
+ Smoothing	21.42	21.32
+ Short-range reordering	20.79	**22.26**
+ Adaptation	21.05	21.97
+ cleanPT	21.50	21.98

Both on development and test set, smoothing the probabilities in the phrase table resulted in an increase of nearly 0.5 BLEU points. Applying short-range word reordering did not lead to an improvement on the development set. However, the increase in BLEU on the test set is substantial. The opposite is the case when adapting the phrase table: While phrase table adaptation improves the translation quality on the development set, adaptation leads to lower scores on the test set.

Thus, the system configuration that performed best on the test set applies phrase table smoothing and short-range word reordering. For creating the translations for our submission, this configuration was used.

5.4 French-English

For the French-English task, similar experiments have been conducted. With respect to the baseline system, improvements in translation quality could be measured when applying phrase table smoothing. An increase of 0.43 BLEU points was achieved using short-range word reordering. Additional experiments with adapting the phrase table to the domain of the test set led to further improvement. Submissions for the shared task were created using the system including all mentioned features.

Table 4: Translation results for French-English (BLEU Score)

System	Dev	Test
Baseline	21.29	22.41
+ Smoothing	21.55	22.59
+ Short-range reordering	22.55	23.02
+ Adaptation	21.72	23.20
+ cleanPT	22.60	**23.21**

6 Conclusions

We have presented our system for the WMT'09 Shared Translation Task. The submissions for the language pairs English-German, German-English, English-French and French-English have been created by the STTK decoder applying different additional methods for each individual language pair to enhance translation quality.

Word reordering models covering short-range reordering for the English↔French and English↔German and long-range reordering for English↔German respectively proved to result in better translations.

Smoothing the phrase probabilities in the phrase table also increased the scores in all cases, while adapting the phrase table to the test domain only showed a positive influence on translation quality in some of our experiments. Further tuning of the adaptation procedure could help to clarify the benefit of this method.

Using discriminative word alignment as an alternative to performing word alignment with GIZA++ did also improve the systems translating between English and German. Future experiments will be conducted applying discriminative word alignment also in the English↔French systems.

Acknowledgments

This work was partly supported by Quaero Programme, funded by OSEO, French State agency for innovation.

References

George Foster, Roland Kuhn, and Howard Johnson. 2006. Phrasetable Smoothing for Statistical Machine Translation. In *Proc. of Empirical Methods in Natural Language Processing*. Sydney, Australia.

Philipp Koehn, Franz Josef Och and Daniel Marcu. 2003. Statistical Phrase-Based Translation. In *HLT/NAACL 2003*. Edmonton, Canada.

Philipp Koehn, Hieu Hoang, Alexandra Birch, Chris Callison-Burch, Marcello Federico, Nicola Bertoldi, Brooke Cowan, Wade Shen, Christine Moran, Richard Zens, Chris Dyer, Ondrej Bojar, Alexandra Constantin and Evan Herbst. 2007. Moses: Open Source Toolkit for Statistical Machine Translation. In *Proc. of Second ACL Workshop on Statistical Machine Translation*. Prague, Czech Republic.

Jan Niehues and Stephan Vogel. 2008. Discriminative Word Alignment via Alignment Matrix Modeling. In *Proc. of Third ACL Workshop on Statistical Machine Translation*. Columbus, OH, USA.

Jan Niehues and Muntsin Kolss. 2009. A POS-Based Model for Long-Range Reorderings in SMT. In *Proc. of Forth ACL Workshop on Statistical Machine Translation*. Athens, Greece.

Kay Rottmann and Stephan Vogel. 2007. Word Reordering in Statistical Machine Translation with a POS-Based Distortion Model. In *TMI*. Skövde, Sweden.

Helmut Schmid. 1994. Probabilistic Part-of-Speech Tagging Using Decision Trees. In *International Conference on New Methods in Language Processing*. Manchester, UK.

Ashish Venugopal, Andreas Zollman and Alex Waibel. 2005. Training and Evaluation Error Minimization Rules for Statistical Machine Translation. In *Proc. of ACL 2005, Workshop on Data-drive Machine Translation and Beyond (WPT-05)*. Ann Arbor, MI.

Stephan Vogel. 2003. SMT Decoder Dissected: Word Reordering. In *NLP-KE'03*. Beijing, China.

The TALP-UPC phrase-based translation system for EACL-WMT 2009

José A.R. Fonollosa and **Maxim Khalilov** and **Marta R. Costa-jussà** and
José B. Mariño and **Carlos A. Henríquez Q.** and **Adolfo Hernández H.** and
Rafael E. Banchs
TALP Research Center
Universitat Politècnica de Catalunya, Barcelona 08034
{adrian,khalilov,mruiz,canton,carloshq,adolfohh,rbanchs}@talp.upc.edu

Abstract

This study presents the TALP-UPC submission to the EACL Fourth Worskhop on Statistical Machine Translation 2009 evaluation campaign. It outlines the architecture and configuration of the 2009 phrase-based statistical machine translation (SMT) system, putting emphasis on the major novelty of this year: combination of SMT systems implementing different word reordering algorithms.

Traditionally, we have concentrated on the Spanish-to-English and English-to-Spanish *News Commentary* translation tasks.

1 Introduction

TALP-UPC (Center of Speech and Language Applications and Technology at the Universitat Politècnica de Catalunya) is a permanent participant of the ACL WMT shared translations tasks, traditionally concentrating on the Spanish-to-English and vice versa language pairs. In this paper, we describe the 2009 system's architecture and design describing individual components and distinguishing features of our model.

This year's system stands aside from the previous years' configurations which were performed following an N-gram-based (tuple-based) approach to SMT. By contrast to them, this year we investigate the translation models (TMs) interpolation for a state-of-the-art phrase-based translation system. Inspired by the work presented in (Schwenk and Estève, 2008), we attack this challenge using the coefficients obtained for the corresponding monolingual language models (LMs) for TMs interpolation.

On the second step, we have performed additional word reordering experiments, comparing the results obtained with a statistical method (R. Costa-jussà and R. Fonollosa, 2009) and syntax-based algorithm (Khalilov and R. Fonollosa, 2008). Further the outputs of the systems were combined selecting the translation with the Minimum Bayes Risk (MBR) algorithm (Kumar, 2004) that allowed significantly outperforming the baseline configuration.

The remainder of this paper is organized as follows: Section 2 presents the TALP-UPC'09 phrase-based system, along with the translation models interpolation procedure and other minor novelties of this year. Section 3 reports on the experimental setups and outlines the results of the participation in the EACL WMT 2009 evaluation campaign. Section 4 concludes the paper with discussions.

2 TALP-UPC phrase-based SMT

The system developed for this year's shared task is based on a state-of-the-art SMT system implemented within the open-source MOSES toolkit (Koehn et al., 2007). A phrase-based translation is considered as a three step algorithm: (1) the source sequence of words is segmented in phrases, (2) each phrase is translated into target language using translation table, (3) the target phrases are reordered to be inherent in the target language.

A bilingual phrase (which in the context of SMT do not necessarily coincide with their linguistic analogies) is any pair of m source words and n target words that satisfies two basic constraints: (1) words are consecutive along both sides of the bilingual phrase and (2) no word on either side of the phrase is aligned to a word outside the phrase. Given a sentence pair and a corresponding word-to-word alignment, phrases are extracted following the criterion in (Och and Ney, 2004). The probability of the phrases is estimated by relative frequencies of their appearance in the training corpus.

Proceedings of the Fourth Workshop on Statistical Machine Translation , pages 85–89,
Athens, Greece, 30 March – 31 March 2009. ©2009 Association for Computational Linguistics

Classically, a phrase-based translation system implements a log-linear model in which a foreign language sentence $f_1^J = f_1, f_2, ..., f_J$ is translated into another language $e_1^I = e_1, e_2, ..., e_I$ by searching for the translation hypothesis $\hat{e}_1^I$ maximizing a log-linear combination of several feature models (Brown et al., 1990):

$$\hat{e}_1^I = \arg\max_{e_1^I} \left\{ \sum_{m=1}^{M} \lambda_m h_m(e_1^I, f_1^J) \right\}$$

where the feature functions h_m refer to the system models and the set of λ_m refers to the weights corresponding to these models.

2.1 Translation models interpolation

We implemented a TM interpolation strategy following the ideas proposed in (Schwenk and Estève, 2008), where the authors present a promising technique of target LMs linear interpolation; in (Koehn and Schroeder, 2007) where a log-linear combination of TMs is performed; and specifically in (Foster and Kuhn, 2007) where the authors present various ways of TM combination and analyze in detail the TM domain adaptation.

In the framework of the evaluation campaign, there were two Spanish-to-English parallel training corpora available: *Europarl v.4* corpus (about 50M tokens) and *News Commentary* (NC) corpus (about 2M tokens). The test dataset provided by the organizers this year was from the news domain, so we considered the Europarl training corpus as "out-of-domain" data and the News Commentary as "in-domain" training material. Unfortunately, the in-domain corpus is much smaller in size, however the Europarl corpus can be also used to increase the final translation and reordering tables in spite of its different nature.

A straightforward approach to the TM interpolation would be an iterative TM reconstruction adjusting scale coefficients on each step of the loop with use of the highest BLEU score as a maximization criterion.

However, we did not expect a significant gain from this time-consumption strategy and we decided to follow a simpler approach. In the presented results, we obtained the best interpolation weight following the standard entropy-based optimization of the target-side LM. We adjust the weight coefficient $\lambda_{Europarl}$ ($\lambda_{NC} = 1 - \lambda_{Europarl}$) of the linear interpolation of the target-side LMs:

$$P(w) = \lambda_{Europarl} \cdot P^w_{Europarl} + \lambda_{NC} \cdot P^w_{NC} \quad (1)$$

where $P^w_{Europarl}$ and P^w_{NC} are probabilities assigned to the word sequence w by the LM estimated on Europarl and NC data, respectively.

The scale factor values are automatically optimized to obtain the lowest perplexity $ppl(w)$ produced by the interpolated LM $P(w)$. We used the standard script $compute - best - mix$ from the SRI LM package (Stolcke, 2002) for optimization.

On the next step, the optimized coefficients $\lambda_{Europarl}$ and λ_{NC} are generalized on the interpolated translation and reordering models. In other words, reordering and translation models are interpolated using the same weights which yield the lowest perplexity for LM interpolation.

The word-to-word alignment was obtained from the joint (merged) database (*Europarl + NC*). Then, we separately computed the translation and reordering tables corresponding to the in- and out-of-domain parts of the joint alignment. The final tables, as well as the final target LM were obtained using linear interpolation. The weights were selected using a minimum perplexity criterion estimated on the corresponding interpolated combination of the target-side LMs.

The optimized coefficient values are: for Spanish: NC weight = 0.526, Europarl weight = 0.474; for English: NC weight = 0.503, Europarl weight = 0.497. The perplexity results obtained using monolingual LMs and the 2009 development set (English and Spanish references) can be found in Table 1, while the corresponding improvement in BLEU score is presented in Section 3.3 and summary of the obtained results (Table 4).

	Europarl	NC	Interpolated
English	463.439	489.915	353.305
Spanish	308.802	347.092	246.573

Table 1: *Perplexity results obtained on the Dev 2009 corpus and the monolingual LMs.*

Note that the corresponding reordering models are interpolated with the same weights.

2.2 Statistical Machine Reordering

The idea of the Statistical Machine Reordering (SMR) stems from the idea of using the powerful techniques developed for SMT and to translate the source language (S) into a reordered source language (S'), which more closely matches the order of the target language. To infer more reorderings, it makes use of word classes. To correctly integrate the SMT and SMR systems, both are concatenated by using a word graph which offers weighted reordering hypotheses to the SMT system. The details are described in (?).

2.3 Syntax-based Reordering

Syntax-based Reordering (SBR) approach deals with the word reordering problem and is based on non-isomorphic parse subtree transfer as described in details in (Khalilov and R. Fonollosa, 2008).

Local and long-range word reorderings are driven by automatically extracted permutation patterns operating with source language constituents. Once the reordering patterns are extracted, they are further applied to monotonize the bilingual corpus in the same way as shown in the previous subsection. The target-side parse tree is considered as a filter constraining reordering rules to the set of patterns covered both by the source- and target-side subtrees.

2.4 System Combination

Over the past few years the MBR algorithm utilization to find the best consensus outputs of different translation systems has proved to improve the translation accuracy (Kumar, 2004). The system combination is performed on the 200-best lists which are generated by the three systems: (1) MOSES-based system without pre-translation monotonization (baseline), (2) MOSES-based SMT enhanced with SMR monotonization and (3) MOSES-based SMT augmented with SBR monotonization. The results presented in Table 4 show that the combined output significantly outperforms the baseline system configuration.

3 Experiments and results

We followed the evaluation baseline instructions [1] to train the MOSES-based translation system.

In some experiments we used MBR decoding (Kumar and Byrne, 2004) with the smoothed BLEU score as a similarity criteria, that allowed gaining 0.2 BLEU points comparing to the standard procedure of outputting the translation with the highest probability (HP). We applied the Moses implementation of this algorithm to the list of 200 best translations generated by the TALP-UPC system. The results obtained over the official 2009 Test dataset can be found in Table 2.

Task	HP	MBR
EsEn	24.48	24.62
EnEs	23.46	23.64

Table 2: *MBR versus MERT decoding.*

The *"recase"* script provided within the baseline was supplemented with and additional module, which restore the original case for unknown words (many of them are proper names and loosing of case information leads to a significant performance degradation).

3.1 Language models

The target-side language models were estimated using the SRILM toolkit (Stolcke, 2002). We tried to use all the available in-domain training material: apart from the corresponding portions of the bilingual NC corpora we involved the following monolingual corpora:

- News monolingual corpus (49M tokens for English and 49M for Spanish)
- Europarl monolingual corpus (about 504M tokens for English and 463M for Spanish)
- A collection of News development and test sets from previous evaluations (151K tokens for English and 175K for Spanish)
- A collection of Europarl development and test sets from previous evaluations (295K tokens for English and 311K for Spanish)

Five LMs per language were estimated on the corresponding datasets and interpolated following the maximum perplexity criteria. Hence, the larger LMs incorporating in- and out-of-domain data were used in decoding.

3.2 Spanish enclitics separation

For the Spanish portion of the corpus we implemented an enclitics separation procedure on the preprocessing step, i.e. the pronouns attached to the verb were separated and contractions as *del* or *al* were splitted into *de el* or *a el*. Consequently, training data sparseness due to Spanish morphology was reduced improving the performance of the overall translation system. As a

[1] http://www.statmt.org/wmt09/baseline.html

post-processing, the segmentation was recovered in the English-to-Spanish direction using target-side Part-of-Speech tags (de Gispert, 2006).

3.3 Results

The automatic scores provided by the WMT'09 organizers for TALP-UPC submissions calculated over the News 2009 dataset can be found in Table 3. BLEU and NIST case-insensitive (CI) and case-sensitive (CS) metrics are considered.

Task	Bleu CI	Bleu CS	NIST CI	NIST CS
EsEn	25.93	24.54	7.275	7.017
EnEs	24.85	23.37	6.963	6.689

Table 3: *BLEU and NIST scores for preliminary official test dataset 2009 (primary submission) with 500 sentences excluded.*

The TALP-UPC primary submission was ranked the 3rd among 28 presented translations for the Spanish-to-English task and the 4th for the English-to-Spanish task among 9 systems.

The following system configurations and the internal results obtained are reported:

- *Baseline*: Moses-based SMT, as proposed on the web-page of the evaluation campaign with Spanish enclitics separation and modified version of "recase" tool,
- *Baseline+TMI*: *Baseline* enhanced with TM interpolation as described in subsection 2.1,
- *Baseline+TMI+MBR*: the same as the latter but with MBR decoding,
- *Baseline+TMI+SMR*: the same as *Baseline+TMI* but with SMR technique applied to monotonize the source portion of the corpus, as described in subsection 2.2,
- *Baseline+SBR*: the same as *Baseline* but with SBR algorithm applied to monotonize the source portion of the corpus, as described in subsection 2.3,
- *System Combination*: a combined output of the 3 previous systems done with the MBR algorithm, as described in subsection 2.4.

Impact of TM interpolation and MBR decoding is more significant for the English-to-Spanish translation task, for which the target-side monolingual corpus is smaller than for the Spanish-to-English translation.

We did not have time to meet the evaluation deadline for providing the system combination output. Nevertheless, during the post-evaluation period we performed the experiments reported in the last three lines of Table 4 (*Baseline+TMI+SMR*, *Baseline+SBR* and *System combination*).

Note that the results presented in Table 4 differ from the ones which can be found the Table 3 due to selective conditions of preliminary evaluation done by the Shared Task organizers.

System	News 2009 Test CI	News 2009 Test CS
Spanish-to-English		
Baseline	25.82	24.37
Baseline+TMI	25.84	24.47
Baseline+TMI+MBR (Primary)	26.04	24.62
Baseline+SMR	24.95	23.62
Baseline+SBR	24.24	22.89
System combination	26.44	25.00
English-to-Spanish		
Baseline	24.56	23.05
Baseline+TMI	25.01	23.41
Baseline+TMI+MBR (Primary)	25.16	23.64
Baseline+SMR	24.09	22.65
Baseline+SBR	23.52	22.05
System combination	25.39	23.86

Table 4: Experiments summary.

4 Conclusions

In this paper, we present the TALP-UPC phrase-based translation system developed for the EACL-WMT 2009 evaluation campaign. The major novelties of this year are translation models interpolation done in linear way and combination of SMT systems implementing different word reordering algorithms. The system was ranked pretty well for both translation tasks in which our institution has participated.

Unfortunately, the promising reordering techniques and the combination of their outputs were not applied within the evaluation deadline, however we report the obtained results in the paper.

5 Acknowledgments

This work has been funded by the Spanish Government under grant TEC2006-13964-C03 (AVIVAVOZ project).

References

P. Brown, J. Cocke, S. Della Pietra, V. Della Pietra, F. Jelinek, J.D. Lafferty, R. Mercer, and P.S. Roossin. 1990. A statistical approach to machine translation. *Computational Linguistics*, 16(2):79–85.

A. de Gispert. 2006. *Introducing linguistic knowledge into Statistical Machine Translation*. Ph.D. thesis, Universitat Politècnica de Catalunya, December.

G. Foster and R. Kuhn. 2007. Mixture-model adaptation for SMT. In *In Annual Meeting of the Association for Computational Linguistics: Proc. of the Second Workshop on Statistical Machine Translation (WMT)*, pages 128–135, Prague, Czech Republic, June.

M. Khalilov and J. R. Fonollosa. 2008. A new subtree-transfer approach to syntax-based reordering for statistical machine translation. Technical report, Universitat Politècnica de Catalunya.

Ph. Koehn and J. Schroeder. 2007. Experiments in domain adaptation for statistical machine translation. In *In Annual Meeting of the Association for Computational Linguistics: Proc. of the Second Workshop on Statistical Machine Translation (WMT)*, pages 224–227, Prague, Czech Republic, June.

Ph. Koehn, H. Hoang, A. Birch, C. Callison-Burch, M. Federico, N. Bertoldi, B. Cowan, W. Shen, C. Moran, R. Zens, C. Dyer, O. Bojar, A. Constantin, and E. Herbst. 2007. Moses: open-source toolkit for statistical machine translation. In *Proceedings of the Association for Computational Linguistics (ACL) 2007*, pages 177–180.

Sh. Kumar and W. Byrne. 2004. Minimum bayes-risk decoding for statistical machine translation. In *In HLTNAACL'04*, pages 169–176.

Sh. Kumar. 2004. *Minimum Bayes-Risk Techniques in Automatic Speech Recognition and Statistical Machine Translation*. Ph.D. thesis, Johns Hopkins University.

F. Och and H. Ney. 2004. The alignment template approach to statistical machine translation. *Computational Linguistics*, 3(4):417–449, December.

M. R. Costa-jussà and J. R. Fonollosa. 2009. An Ngram reordering model. *Computer Speech and Language*. ISSN 0885-2308, accepted for publication.

H. Schwenk and Y. Estève. 2008. Data selection and smoothing in an open-source system for the 2008 nist machine translation evaluation. In *Proceedings of the Interspeech'08*, pages 2727–2730, Brisbane, Australia, September.

A. Stolcke. 2002. SRILM: an extensible language modeling toolkit. In *Proceedings of the Int. Conf. on Spoken Language Processing*, pages 901–904.

Deep Linguistic Multilingual Translation and Bilingual Dictionaries

Eric Wehrli, Luka Nerima & Yves Scherrer
LATL-Department of Linguistics
University of Geneva
{Eric.Wehrli, Luka.Nerima, Yves.Scherrer}@unige.ch

Abstract

This paper describes the MulTra project, aiming at the development of an efficient multilingual translation technology based on an abstract and generic linguistic model as well as on object-oriented software design. In particular, we will address the issue of the rapid growth both of the transfer modules and of the bilingual databases. For the latter, we will show that a significant part of bilingual lexical databases can be derived automatically through transitivity, with corpus validation.

1 Introduction

The goal of the MulTra project is to develop a grammar-based translation model capable of handling not just a couple of languages, but potentially a large number of languages. This is not an original goal, but as 50 years of work and investment have shown, the task is by no means an easy one, and although SMT has shown fast and impressive results towards it (e.g. EuroMatrix), we believe that a (principled) grammar-based approach is worth developing, taking advantage of the remarkable similarities displayed by languages at an abstract level of representation. In the first phase of this project (2007-2009), our work has focused on French, English, German, Italian and Spanish, with preliminary steps towards Greek, Romanian, Russian and Japanese.

To evaluate the quality of the (still under development) system, we decided to join the WMT09 translation evaluation with prototypes for the following language pairs: English to French, French to English and German to English. In this short paper, we will first give a rough description of the MulTra system architecture and then turn to the difficult issue of the bilingual dictionaries.

The MulTra project relies to a large extent on abstract linguistics, inspired from recent work in generative grammar (Chomsky, 1995, Culicover & Jackendoff, 2005, Bresnan, 2001). The grammar formalism developed for this project is both rich enough to express the structural diversity of all the languages taken into account, and abstract enough to capture the generalizations hidden behind obvious surface diversity. At the software level, an object-oriented design has been used, similar in many ways to the one adopted for the multilingual parser (cf. Wehrli, 2007).

The rapid growth of the number of transfer modules has often been viewed as a major flaw of the transfer model when applied to multilingual translation (cf. Arnold, 2000, Kay, 1997). This argument, which relies on the fact that the number of transfer modules and of the corresponding bilingual dictionaries increases as a quadratic function of the number of languages, is considerably weakened if one can show that transfer modules can be made relatively simple and light (cf. section 2), compared to the analysis and generation modules (whose numbers are a linear function of the number of languages). Likewise, section 3 will show how one can drastically reduce the amount of work by deriving bilingual dictionaries by transitivity.

2 The architecture of the MulTra system

To a large extent, this system can be viewed as an extension of the Multilingual Fips parsing project. For one thing, the availability of the "deep linguistic" Fips parser for the targeted languages is a crucial element for the MulTra project; second, the MulTra software design matches the one developed for the multilingual parser. In both cases, the goal is to set up a generic system which can be redefined (through type extension and method redefinition) to suit the specific needs of, respectively, a particular language or a particular language pair.

Proceedings of the Fourth Workshop on Statistical Machine Translation, pages 90–94,
Athens, Greece, 30 March – 31 March 2009. ©2009 Association for Computational Linguistics

2.1 Methodology

The translation algorithm follows the traditional pattern of a transfer system. First the input sentence is parsed by the Fips parser, producing an information-rich phrase-structure representation with associated predicate-argument representations. The parser also identifies multiword expressions such as idioms and collocations – crucial elements for a translation system (cf. Seretan & Wehrli, 2006). The transfer module maps the source-language abstract representation into the target-language representation. Given the abstract nature of this level of representation, the mapping operation is relatively simple and can be sketched as follows: recursively traverse the source-language phrase structure in the order: head, right subconstituents, left subconstituents. Lexical transfer (the mapping of a source-language lexical item with an equivalent target-language item) occurs at the head-transfer level (provided the head is not empty) and yields a target-language equivalent term often, but by no means always, of the same category. Following the projection principle used in the Fips parser, the target-language structure is projected on the basis of the lexical item which is its head. In other words, we assume that the lexical head determines a syntactic projection (or meta-projection).

Projections (ie. constituents) which have been analyzed as arguments of a predicate undergo a slightly different transfer process, since their precise target-language properties may be in part determined by the subcategorization features of the target-language predicate. To take a simple example, the direct object of the French verb *regarder* in (1a) will be transferred into English as a prepositional phrase headed by the preposition *at*, as illustrated in (2a). This information comes from the lexical database. More specifically, the French-English bilingual lexicon specifies a correspondence between the French lexeme [$_{VP}$ regarder NP] and the English lexeme [$_{VP}$ look [$_{PP}$ at NP]]. For both sentences, we also illustrate the syntactic structures as built, respectively, by the parser for the source sentence and by the translator for the target sentence.

(1)a. Paul a regardé la voiture.

b. [$_{TP}$ [$_{DP}$ Paul] a [$_{VP}$ regardé [$_{DP}$ la [$_{NP}$ voiture]]]]

(2)a. Paul looked at the car.

b. [$_{TP}$ [$_{DP}$ Paul] [$_{VP}$ looked [$_{PP}$ at [$_{DP}$ the [$_{NP}$ car]]]]]

2.2 Adding a language to the system

Given the general model as sketched above, the addition of a language to the system requires (i) a parser and (ii) a generator. Then for each language pair for which that language is concerned, the system needs (iii) a (potentially empty) language-pair specific transfer module, and (iv) a bilingual lexical database. The first three components are described below, while the fourth will be the topic of section 3.

Parser The Fips multilingual parser is assumed. Adding a new language requires the following tasks: (i) grammar description in the Fips formalism, (ii) redefinition of the language-specific parsing methods to suit particular properties of the language, and (iii) creation of an appropriate lexical database for the language.

Generator Target-language generation is done in a largely generic fashion (as described above with the transfer and projection mechanisms). What remains specific in the generation phase is the selection of the proper morphological form of a lexical item.

Language-pair-specific transfer Transfer from language A to language B requires no language-pair specification if the language structures of A and B are isomorphic. Simplifying a little bit, this happens among closely related languages, such as Spanish and Italian for instance. For languages which are typologically different, the transfer module must indicate how the precise mapping is to be done.

Consider, for instance, word-order differences such as adjectives which are prenominal in English and postnominal in French – *a* **red** *car* vs. *une voiture* **rouge**. The specific English-French transfer module specifies that French adjectives, which do not bear the [+prenominal] lexical feature, correspond to right subconstituents (vs. left subconstituents) of the head noun. Other cases are more complicated, such as the V2 phenomenon in German, pronominal cliticization in Romance languages, or even the use of the *do* auxiliary in English interrogative or negative sentences. Such cases are handled by means of specific procedures, which are in some ways reminiscent of transformation rules of the standard theory of generative grammar, ie. rules that can insert, move or even delete phrase-structure constituents (cf. Akmajian & Heny, 1975).

So far, the languages taken into account in the MulTra project are those for which the Fips parser has been well developed, that is English, French, German, Italian and Spanish. Of the 20 potential language pairs five are currently operational (English-French, French-English, German-French, German-English, Italian-French), while 6 other pairs are at various stages of development.

3 Multilingual lexical database

3.1 Overview of the lexical database

The lexical database is composed for each language of (i) a lexicon of words, containing all the inflected forms of the words of the language, (ii) a lexicon of lexemes, containing the syntactic/semantic information of the words (corresponding roughly to the entries of a classical dictionary) and (iii) a lexicon of collocations (in fact multi-word expressions including collocations and idioms). We call the lexemes and the collocations the *lexical items* of a language.

The bilingual lexical database contains the information necessary for the lexical transfer from one language to another. For storage purposes, we use a relational database management system. For each language pair, the bilingual dictionary is implemented as a relational table containing the associations between lexical items of language A and lexical items of language B. The bilingual dictionary is bi-directional, i.e. it also associates lexical items of language B with lexical items of language A. In addition to these links, the table contains transfer information such as translation context (eg. sport, finance, law, etc.), ranking of the pairs in a one-to-many correspondence, semantic descriptors (used for interactive disambiguation), argument matching for predicates (mostly for verbs). The table structures are identical for all pairs of languages.

Although the bilingual lexicon is bidirectional, it is not symmetrical. If a word v from language A has only one translation w in language B, it doesn't necessarily mean that w has only one translation v. For instance the word *tongue* corresponds to French *langue*, while in the opposite direction the word *langue* has two translations, *tongue* and *language*. In this case the descriptor attribute from French to English will mention respectively "body part" and "language". Another element of asymmetry is the ranking attribute used to mark the preferred correspondences in a one-to-many translation[1]. For instance the lexicographer can mark his preference to translate *lovely* into the French word *charmant* rather than *agréable*. Of course the opposite translation direction must be considered independently.

What is challenging in this project is that it necessitates as many bilingual tables as the number of language pairs considered, i.e. $n(n-1)/2$ tables. We consider that an appropriate bilingual coverage (for general purpose translation) requires well over 60'000 correspondences per language pair.

In the framework of this project we consider 5 languages (French, English, German, Italian, Spanish). Currently, our database contains 4 bilingual dictionaries (out of the 10 needed) with the number of entries given in figure 1:

language pair	Number of entries
English - French	77'569
German - French	47'797
French - Italian	38'188
Spanish - French	23'696

Figure 1: Number of correspondences in bilingual dictionaries

Note that these 4 bilingual dictionaries were manually created by lexicographers and the quality of the entries can be considered as good.

3.2 Automatic generation

The importance of multilingual lexical resources in MT and, unfortunately, the lack of available multilingual lexical resources has motivated many initiatives and research work to establish collaboratively made multilingual lexicons, e.g. the Papillon project (Boitet & al. 2002) or automatically generated multilingual lexicons (see for instance Aymerish & Camelo, 2007, Gamallo, 2007).

We plan to use semi-automatic generation to build the 6 remaining dictionaries. For this purpose we will derive a bilingual lexicon by transitivity, using two existing ones. For instance, if we have bilingual correspondences for language pair

[1]This attribute takes the form of an integer between 6 (preferred) and 0 (lowest).

A $\rightarrow$ B and B $\rightarrow$ C, we can obtain A $\rightarrow$ C. We will see below how the correspondences are validated.

The idea of using a pivot language for deriving bilingual lexicons from existing ones is not new. The reader can find related approaches in (Paik & al. 2004, Ahn & Frampton 2006, Zhang & al. 2007) . The specificity of our approach is that the initial resources are manually made, i.e. non noisy, lexicons.

The derivation process goes as follows:

1. Take two bilingual tables for language pairs (A, B) and (B, C) and perform a relational equi-join. Perform a filtering based on the preference attribute to avoid combinatory explosion of the number of generated correspondences.

2. Consider as valid all the unambiguous correspondences. We consider that a generated correspondence $a \rightarrow c$ is unambiguous if for the lexical item a there exists only one correspondence $a \rightarrow b$ in the bilingual lexicon (A, B) and for b there exists only one correspondence $b \rightarrow c$ in (B, C). As the lexicon is non symmetrical, this process is performed twice, once for each translation direction.

3. Consider as valid all the correspondences obtained by a pivot lexical item of type collocation. We consider as very improbable that a collocation is ambiguous.

4. All other correspondences are checked in a parallel corpus, i.e. only the correspondences actually used as translations in the corpus are kept. First, the parallel corpus is tagged by the Fips tagger (Wehrli, 2007) in order to lemmatize the words. This is especially valuable for languages with rich inflection, as well as for verbs with particles. In order to check the validity of the correspondences, we count the effective occurrences of a given correspondence in a sentence-aligned parallel corpus, as well as the occurrences of each of the lexical items of the correspondence. At the end of the process, we apply the *log likelihood ratio* test to decide whether to keep or discard the correspondence.

3.3 Results of automatic generation

The English-German lexicon that we used in the shared translation task was generated automatically. We derived it on the basis of English-French and German-French lexicons. For the checking of the validity of the correspondences (point 4 of the process) we used the parallel corpus of the debates of the European Parliament during the period 1996 to 2001 (Koehn, 2005). Figure 2 summarizes the results of the four steps of the derivation process:

Step	Type	Eng.-Ger.
1	Candidate corresp.	89'022
2	Unambiguous corresp.	67'012
3	Collocation pivot	2'642
4	Corpus checked	2'404
	Total validated corresp.	72'058

Figure 2: Number of derived entries for English-German

We obtained a number of entries comparable to those of the manually built bilingual lexicons. The number of the correspondences for which a validation is necessary is 19'368 (89'022-(67'012+2'642)), of which 2'404 (approximately 12%) have been validated based on the the EuroParl corpus, as explained above. The low figure, well below our expectations, is due to the fact that the corpus we used is not large enough and is probably not representative of the general language.

Up to now, the English-German dictionary required approximately 1'400 entries to be added manually, which is less than 2% of the entire lexicon.

4 Conclusion

Based on a deep linguistic transfer approach and an object-oriented design, the MulTra multilingual translation system aims at developing a large number of language pairs while significantly reducing the development cost as the number of pairs grows. We have argued that the use of an abstract and relatively generic linguistic level of representation, as well as the use of an object-oriented software design play a major role in the reduction of the complexity of language-pair transfer modules. With respect to the bilingual databases, (corpus-checked) automatic derivation by transitivity has been shown to drastically reduce the amount of work.

Acknowledgments

The research described in this paper has been supported in part by a grant from the Swiss national science foundation (no 100015-113864).

5 References

Ahn, K. and Frampton, M. 2006. "Automatic Generation of Translation Dictionaries Using Intermediary Languages´´ in Cross-Language knowledge Induction Workshop of the EACL 06, Trento, Italy, pp 41- 44.

Akmajian, A. and F. Heny, 1975. *An Introduction to the Principles of Generative Syntax*, MIT Press.

Arnold, D. 2000. "Why translation is difficult for computers" in H.L. Somers (ed.) *Computers and Translation : a handbook for translators*, John Benjamin.

Aymerich, J. and Camelo, H. 2007." Automatic extraction of entries for a machine translation dictionary using bitexts´´ in MT Summit XI, Copenhagen, pp. 21-27

Boitet, Ch. 2001. "Four technical and organizational keys to handle more languages and improve quality (on demand) in MT" in *Proceedings of MT-Summit VIII*, Santiago de Compostela, 18-22.

Boitet, Ch., Mangeot, M. and Sérasset, G. 2002. "The PAPILLON project: cooperatively building a multilingual lexical database to derive open source dictionaries & lexicons" in *Proceedings of the 2nd workshop on NLP and XML*, COLING 2002, Taipei, Taiwan.

Bresnan, J. 2001. *Lexical Functional Syntax*, Oxford, Blackwell.

Chomsky, N. 1995. *The Minimalist Program*, Cambridge, Mass., MIT Press.

Culicover, P. & R. Jackendoff, 2005. *Simpler Syntax*, Oxford, Oxford University Press.

Gamallo, P. 2007. "Learning Bilingual Lexicons from Comparable English and Spanish Corpora" in *Proceedings of MT Summit XI*, Copenhagen.

Hutchins, J. 2003. "Has machine translation improved?" in *Proceedings of MT-Summit IX*, New Orleans, 23-27.

Kay, M. 1997. "Machine Translation : the Disappointing Past and Present" in R.A. Cole, J. Mariani, H. Uskoreit, G. Varile, A. Zaenen and A. Zampoli *Survey of the State of the Art in Human Language Technology*, Giardini Editori.

Koehn, P. 2005. "Europarl: A Parallel Corpus for Statistical Machine Translation´´ in MT Summit 2005.

Ney, H. 2005. "One Decade of Statistical Machine Translation" in *Proceedings of MT-Summit X*, Pukhet, Thailand.

Paik, K., Shirai, S. and Nakaiwa, H. 2004. "Automatic Construction of a Transfer Dictionary Considering Directionality", in COLING 2004 Multilingual Linguistic Resources Workshop, Geneva, pp. 25-32.

Seretan, V. & E. Wehrli, 2006. "Accurate Collocation Extraction Using a Multilingual Parser" in *Proceedings of the ACL*, 953-960, Sydney, Australia.

Wehrli, E. 2007. "Fips, a "deep" linguistic multilingual parse" in *Proceedings of the ACL 2007 Workshop on Deep Linguistic processing*, 120-127, Prague, Czech Republic.

Zhang, Y., Ma, Q. and Isahara, H. 2007. "Building Japanese-Chinese Translation Dictionary Based on EDR Japanese-English Bilingual Dictionary" in *MT Summit XI*, Copenhagen, pp 551-557.

MATREX: The DCU MT System for WMT 2009

Jinhua Du, Yifan He, Sergio Penkale, Andy Way
Centre for Next Generation Localisation
Dublin City University
Dublin 9, Ireland
{jdu,yhe,spenkale,away}@computing.dcu.ie

Abstract

In this paper, we describe the machine translation system in the evaluation campaign of the Fourth Workshop on Statistical Machine Translation at EACL 2009.

We describe the modular design of our multi-engine MT system with particular focus on the components used in this participation.

We participated in the translation task for the following translation directions: French–English and English–French, in which we employed our multi-engine architecture to translate. We also participated in the system combination task which was carried out by the MBR decoder and Confusion Network decoder. We report results on the provided development and test sets.

1 Introduction

In this paper, we present a multi-engine MT system developed at DCU, MATREX (Machine Translation using Examples). This system exploits EBMT, SMT and system combination techniques to build a cascaded translation framework.

We participated in both the French–English and English-French News tasks. In these two tasks, we employ three individual MT system which are 1) Baseline: phrase-based system (PB); 2) EBMT: Monolingually chunking both source and target sides of the dataset using a marker-based chunker (Gough and Way, 2004). 3) HPB: a typical hierarchical phrase-based system (Chiang, 2005). Meanwhile, we also use a word-level combination framework (Rosti et al., 2007) to combine the multiple translation hypotheses and employ a new rescoring model to generate the final result.

For the system combination task, we first use the minimum Bayes-risk (MBR) (Kumar and Byrne, 2004) decoder to select the best hypothesis as the alignment reference for the Confusion Network (CN) (Mangu et al., 2000). We then build the CN using the TER metric (Snover et al., 2006), and finally search and generate the translation.

The remainder of this paper is organised as follows: Section 2 details the various components of our system, in particular the multi-engine strategies used for the shared task. In Section 3, we outline the complete system setup for the shared task and provide results on the development and test sets. Section 4 is our conclusion.

2 The MATREX System

2.1 System Architecture

The MATREX system is a combination-based multi-engine architecture, which exploits aspects of both the EBMT and SMT paradigms.

This architecture includes three individual systems which are phrase-based, example-based and hierarchical phrase-based.

The combination structure is the MBR decoder and CN decoder, which is based on the word-level combination strategy.

In the final stage, we use a new rescoring module to process the N-best list generated by the combination module. See Figure 1 as a detailed illustration.

2.2 Example-Based Machine Translation

EBMT obtains resources using the Marker Hypothesis (Green, 1979), a psycholinguistic constraint which posits that all languages are marked for surface syntax by a specific closed set of lexemes or morphemes which signify context. Given a set of closed-class words we segment each sentence into chunks, creating a chunk at each new occurrence of a marker word, with the restriction that each segment must contain at least one non-marker word (Gough and Way, 2004).

Proceedings of the Fourth Workshop on Statistical Machine Translation, pages 95–99,
Athens, Greece, 30 March – 31 March 2009. ©2009 Association for Computational Linguistics

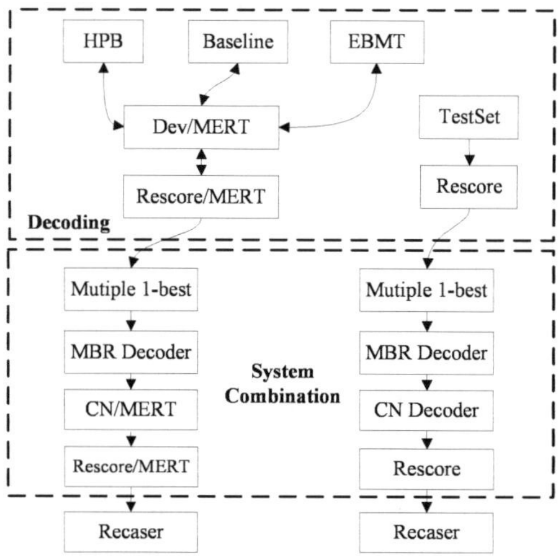

Figure 1: System Framework

We then align these segments using an edit-distance-style algorithm, in which the insertion and deletion probabilities depend on word-to-word translation probabilities and word-to-word cognates (Stroppa and Way, 2006).

We extracted phrases of at most 7 words on each side. We then merged these phrases with the phrases extracted by the baseline system adding word alignment information, and used this system seeded with this additional information.

2.3 Hierarchical Machine Translation

HPB translation system is a re-implementation of the hierarchical phrase translation model which is based on PSCFG (Chiang, 2005). We generate recursively PSCFG rules from the *initial rules* as

$$N \rightarrow f_1 \dots f_m / e_1 \dots e_n$$

where N is a rule which is initial or includes nonterminals.

$$M \rightarrow f_i \dots f_j / e_u \dots e_v$$

where $1 \leq i \leq j \leq m$ and $1 \leq u \leq v \leq n$, at which point a new rule can be obtained, named,

$$N \rightarrow f_1^{i-1} X_k f_{j+1}^m / e_1^{u-1} X_k e_{v+1}^n$$

where k is an index for the nonterminal X. The number of nonterminals permitted in a rule is no more than two.

When extracting hierarchical rules,we set some limitations that initial rules are of no more than 7 words in length and other rules should have no more than 5 terminals and nonterminals, and we disallow rules with adjacent source-side and target-side nonterminals.

The decoder is an enhanced CYK-style chart parser that maximizes the derivation probability and spans up to 12 source words. A 4-gram language model generated by SRI Language Modeling toolkit (SRILM) (Stolcke, 2002) is used in the cube-pruning process. The search space is pruned with a chart cell size limit of 50.

2.4 System Combination

For multiple system combination, we implement an MBR-CN framework as shown in Figure 1. Instead of using a single system output as the skeleton, we employ a minimum Bayes-risk decoder to select the best single system output from the merged N-best list by minimizing the BLEU (Papineni et al., 2002) loss.

The confusion network is built by the output of MBR as the backbone which determines the word order of the combination. The other hypotheses are aligned against the backbone based on the TER metric. NULL words are allowed in the alignment. Each arc in the CN represents an alternative word at that position in the sentence and the number of votes for each word is counted when constructing the network. The features we used are as follows:

- word posterior probability (Fiscus, 1997);
- 3, 4-gram target language model;
- word length penalty;
- Null word length penalty;

Also, we use MERT (Och, 2003) to tune the weights of confusion network.

2.5 Rescore

Rescore is a very important part in post-processing which can select a better hypothesis from the N-best list. We add some new global features in rescore model. The features we used are as follows:

- Direct and inverse IBM model;
- 3, 4-gram target language model;
- 3, 4, 5-gram POS language model (Ratnaparkhi, 1996; Schmid, 1994);

- Sentence length posterior probability (Zens and Ney, 2006);
- N-gram posterior probabilities within the N-Best list (Zens and Ney, 2006);
- Minimum Bayes Risk probability;
- Length ratio between source and target sentence;

The weights are optimized via MERT algorithm.

3 Experimental Setup

The following section describes the system and experimental setup for the French-English and English-French translation tasks.

3.1 Statistics of Data

Parallel Corpus

We used Europarl and Giga data for this evaluation. The statistics of parallel data are shown in Table 1.

Corpra	Sen	Token-En	Token-Fr	Len
Europarl	1.46M	39,240,672	42,252,067	80
Giga	2M	48,648,104	57,869,002	65

Table 1: Statistics of Parallel Data

In this table, *Sen* indicates the number of sentence pairs; *Len* denotes the maximum sentence length of each corpus. This year the translation task is only evaluated on *News Domain*. Experimental results showed that giga data is more correlated than Europarl and the BLEU score is significantly improved(See Table 4).

Monolingual Corpus

In this evaluation, we trained a small 4-gram language model using data in Table 1 and a large 4-gram language model using data in Table 2. We configured these two LMs for Baseline and EBMT systems while HPB only used the large one.

Language	Sen	Token	Source
English	9,966,838	240,849,221	E/N/NC
French	9,966,838	260,520,313	E/N/NC

Table 2: Statistics of Monolingual Data

In the above table, *E/N/NC* refers to Europarl/News/New_Commentary corpus.

3.2 Pre-Processing

We preprocessed both Europarl and Giga Release 1 corpus. For the Europarl corpus, we removed the reserved characters in GIZA++ and tokenized and lowercased the corpus with tools provided by WMT09. The Giga corpus was too large for our resource, so we performed sentence selection before cleaning, in the following steps.

- We split the Giga corpus into even segments, each segment consisting of 20 lines.
- We trained an SVM classifier on English side with positive examples from the monolingual news data and negative examples from noisy sentences (numbers, meaningless word combinations, and random segments) from the Giga corpus. We used "-ly" and "-ing" to approximate adverbs and present participles and did not use other POS-induced features, as in (Ferizis and Bailey, 2006). We added these features to remove noise: average length of sentences, frequency of capitalized characters, frequency of numerical characters and short word penalty (equals to 1 when average length of words < 4, and 0 otherwise). We used the classifier to remove 20% segments of lowest scores.
- We selected $1,600$ words having the highest mutual information scores with monolingual training data against the Giga corpus.
- We selected $100,000$ segments where these words occurred most frequently. However the sentence was dropped if the length ratio between English and French was larger than 1.5 or less than 0.67.

3.3 System Configuration

The two language models were done using the SRILM employing linear interpolation and modified K-N discounting (Chen and Goodman, 1996).

The configuration for the three systems is listed in Table 3.

System	P-Table	Length	LM	Features
Baseline-E	55.9M	7	2	15
Baseline-G	58.4M	7	2	15
EBMT	59.4M	7	2	15
HPB	122M	5	1	8

Table 3: Statistics of MT Systems

In this table, *E* indicates the Europarl corpus

which is used for all three systems, and G stands for the Giga corpus which is only used for the Baseline system. We can see from Table 3 that the size of the HPB phrase-table is more than 2 times as large as the other phrase tables. How to filter and process such a huge hierarchical table is a challenging problem.

We tuned our systems on the development set *devset2009-a* and *devset2009-b*, and performed the crossover experiment by these two devsets.

3.4 Experimental Results

The system output is evaluated with respect to BLEU score. In Table 4, we used *devset2009-b* to tune the various parameters in our three single systems and *devset2009-a* for testing. In terms of the Europarl data, we can see that the three systems we used achieved similar performance on the test set for both translation directions, with the Baseline-E system yielding slightly better results than the other two.

System	Fr-En	En-Fr
Baseline-E	22.24	22.68
Baseline-G	24.90	—[1]
EBMT	22.04	22.12
HPB	21.69	21.12
MBR	25.11	22.68
CN	25.24	22.76
Rescore	25.40	22.97

Table 4: Experimental Results on *Devset2009-a*

We then used the translations of the *devset2009-a* produced by each system to tune the parameters of our system combination module. From Table 4, we can see that using MBR and confusion network decoding leads to a slight improvement over the strongest single system, i.e. the baseline Phrase-Based SMT system. Rescoring the N-best lists yielded an increase of 0.5 (2.0 relative) absolute BLEU points over the baseline for French–English Translation and 0.29 (1.28 relative) absolute BLEU points for English–French Translation.

Table 5 is the results on 2009 *Test Data*. The scores with a slash in the last two rows are lowercased and cased respectively. From the table we can see that combination yielded 0.45 and 0.79 absolute BLEU points over the best single system for Fr-En and En-Fr direction respectively. However, 1.93 (7.2 relative) and 1.64 (6.58 relative) BLEU points are dropped between cased and lowercased results of both directions. Accordingly, training an effective recasing model is very important for our future work.

System	Fr-En	En-Fr
Baseline-E	25.64	24.47
Baseline-G	26.75	—
EBMT	25.67	24.43
HPB	25.20	24.19
Combination	27.20/25.14	25.26/22.28
Official-Auto[2]	26.86/24.93	23.78/22.14

Table 5: Summary of Results on *2009 Test Data*

[1]Not much time to do the experiments on English-French direction. EBMT and HPB just used the Europarl corpus.

[2]The official automatic result is scored on 2525 sentences out of the whole 3007 sentences in test set. The other 502 sentences are used as the development set for combination evaluation task.

4 Conclusion

This paper presents our machine translation system in WMT2009 shared task campaign. We developed a multi-engine framework which combined the output results of the three MT systems and generated a new N-best list after CN decoding. Then by using some global features the rescoring model generated the final translation output. The experimental result proved that the combination module and rescoring module are effective in our framework.

We also applied simple yet effective methods of genre and topical classification to remove noise and out-of-domain sentences in the Giga corpus, from which we built better translation models than from Europarl.

In future work, we will refine our system framework to investigate its effect on the tasks presented here, and we will develop more powerful post-processing tools such as recaser to reduce the BLEU loss.

Acknowledgments

This work is supported by Science Foundation Ireland (Grant No. 07/CE/I1142). Thanks also to the reviewers for their insightful comments and suggestions.

References

Chen, S. F. and Goodman, J. (1996). An Empirical Study of Smoothing Techniques for Language Modeling. In *Proceedings of the Thirty-Fourth Annual Meeting of the Association for Computational Linguistics*, pages 310–318, San Francisco, CA.

Chiang, D. (2005). A Hierarchical Phrase-Based Model for Statistical Machine Translation. In *Proceedings of the*

43rd Annual Meeting of the Association for Computational Linguistics (ACL'05), pages 263–270, Ann Arbor, MI.

Ferizis, G. and Bailey, P. (2006). Towards practical genre classification of web documents. In *Proceedings of the 15th international conference on World Wide Web (WWW '06)*, pages 1013–1014, New York, USA.

Fiscus, J. G. (1997). A post-processing system to yield reduced word error rates: Recognizer output voting error reduction (ROVER). In *Proceedings 1997 IEEE Workshop on Automatic Speech Recognition and Understanding (ASRU)*, pages 347–352, Santa Barbara, CA.

Gough, N. and Way, A. (2004). Robust Large-Scale EBMT with Marker-Based Segmentation. In *Proceedings of the 10th International Conference on Theoretical and Methodological Issues in Machine Translation (TMI-04)*, pages 95–104, Baltimore, MD.

Green, T. (1979). The Necessity of Syntax Markers. Two experiments with artificial languages. *Journal of Verbal Learning and Behavior*, 18:481–496.

Kumar, S. and Byrne, W. (2004). Minimum Bayes-Risk Decoding for Statistical Machine Translation. In *Proceedings of the Joint Meeting of the Human Language Technology Conference and the North American Chapter of the Association for Computational Linguistics (HLT-NAACL 2004)*, pages 169–176, Boston, MA.

Mangu, L., Brill, E., and Stolcke, A. (2000). Finding consensus in speech recognition: Word error minimization and other applications of confusion networks. *Computer Speech and Language*, 14(4):373–400.

Och, F. (2003). Minimum error rate training in statistical machine translation. In *Proceedings of the 41st Annual Meeting of the Association for Computational Linguistics (ACL)*, pages 160–167, Sapporo, Japan.

Papineni, K., Roukos, S., Ward, T., and Zhu, W.-J. (2002). BLEU: a Method for Automatic Evaluation of Machine Translation. In *Proceedings of the 40th Annual Meeting of the Association for Computational Linguistics (ACL-02)*, pages 311–318, Philadelphia, PA.

Ratnaparkhi, A. (1996). A Maximum Entropy Model for Part-Of-Speech Tagging. In *Proceedings of the Empirical Methods in Natural Language Processing Conference (EMNLP)*, pages 133–142, Philadelphia, PA.

Rosti, A.-V. I., Xiang, B., Matsoukas, S., Schwartz, R., Ayan, N. F., and Dorr, B. J. (2007). Combining outputs from multiple machine translation systems. In *Proceedings of the Joint Meeting of the Human Language Technology Conference and the North American Chapter of the Association for Computational Linguistics (HLT-NAACL 2007)*, pages 228–235, Rochester, NY.

Schmid, H. (1994). Probabilistic Part-of-Speech Tagging Using Decision Trees. In *Proceedings of International Conference on New Methods in Language Processing*, pages 44–49, Manchester, UK.

Snover, M., Dorr, B., Schwartz, R., Micciula, L., and Makhoul, J. (2006). A study of translation edit rate with targeted human annotation. In *Proceedings of the 7th Conference of the Association for Machine Translation in the Americas (AMTA 2006)*, pages 223–231, Cambridge, MA.

Stolcke, A. (2002). SRILM - An Extensible Language Modeling Toolkit. In *Proceedings of the International Conference Spoken Language Processing*, pages 901–904, Denver, CO.

Stroppa, N. and Way, A. (2006). MaTrEx: the DCU machine translation system for IWSLT 2006. In *Proceedings of the International Workshop on Spoken Language Translation*, pages 31–36, Kyoto, Japan.

Zens, R. and Ney, H. (2006). N-gram Posterior Probabilities for Statistical Machine Translation. In *Proceedings of the Joint Meeting of the Human Language Technology Conference and the North American Chapter of the Association for Computational Linguistics (HLT-NAACL 2006)*, pages 72–77, New York, USA.

LIMSI's statistical translation systems for WMT'09

Alexandre Allauzen, Josep Crego, Aurélien Max and François Yvon
LIMSI/CNRS and Université Paris-Sud 11, France
BP 133, 91403 Orsay Cédex
firstname.lastname@limsi.fr

Abstract

This paper describes our Statistical Machine Translation systems for the WMT09 (en:fr) shared task. For this evaluation, we have developed four systems, using two different MT Toolkits: our primary submission, in both directions, is based on Moses, boosted with contextual information on phrases, and is contrasted with a conventional Moses-based system. Additional contrasts are based on the Ncode toolkit, one of which uses (part of) the English/French GigaWord parallel corpus.

1 Introduction

This paper describes our Statistical Machine Translation systems for the WMT09 (en:fr) shared task. For this evaluation, we have developed four systems, using two different MT toolkits: our primary submission, in both direction, is based on Moses, boosted with contextual information on phrases; we also provided a contrast with a vanilla Moses-based system. Additional contrasts are based on the N-code decoder, one of which takes advantage of (part of) the English/French GigaWord parallel corpus.

2 System architecture and resources

In this section, we describe the main characteristics of the baseline phrase-based systems used in this evaluation and the resources that were used to train our models.

2.1 Pre- and post-processing tools

All the available textual corpora were processed and normalized using in-house text processing tools. Our last year experiments (Déchelotte et al., 2008) revealed that using better normalization tools provides a significant reward in BLEU, a fact that we could observe again this year. The downside is the need to post-process our outputs so as to "detokenize" them for scoring purposes, which is unfortunately an error-prone process.

Based again on last year's experiments, our systems are built in "true case": the first letter of each sentence is lowercased when it should be, and the remaining tokens are left as is.

Finally, the N-code (see 2.5) and the context-aware (see 3) systems require the source to be morpho-syntactically analysed. This was performed using the TreeTagger[1] for both languages.

2.2 Alignment and translation models

Our baseline translation models (see 2.4 and 2.5) use all the parallel corpora distributed for this evaluation: Europarl V4, news commentary (2006-2009) and the additional news data, totalling 1.5M sentences. Our preliminary attempts with larger translation models using the GigaWord corpus are reported in section 3.2. All these corpora were aligned with GIZA++[2] using default settings.

2.3 Language Models

To train our language models (LMs), we took advantage of the *a priori* information that the test set would be of newspaper/newswire genre. We

[1] http://www.ims.uni-stuttgart.de/projekte/corplex/TreeTagger.
[2] http://www.fjoch.com/GIZA++.html.

Proceedings of the Fourth Workshop on Statistical Machine Translation, pages 100–104,
Athens, Greece, 30 March – 31 March 2009. ©2009 Association for Computational Linguistics

	Source	Period	M. words
En	News texts	1994-06	3 317
	BN transcripts	2000-07	341
	WMT		86
Fr	Newswires	1994-07	723
	Newspapers	1987-06	486
	WEB	2008	23
	WMT		46
	News-train08		167

Table 1: Corpora used to train the target language models in English and French.

thus built much larger LMs for translating both to French and to English, and optimized their combination on the first part of the official development data (dev2009a).

Corpora and vocabulary Statistics regarding the training material are summarized in table 1 in terms of source, time period, and millions of occurrences. "WMT" stands for all text provided for the evaluation. Development sets and the large training corpora (news-train08 and the GigaWord corpus) were not included. Altogether, these data contain a total number of 3.7 billion tokens for English and 1.4 billion tokens for French.

To estimate such large LMs, a vocabulary was first defined for both languages by including all tokens in the WMT parallel data. This initial vocabulary of 130K words was then extended by adding the most frequent words observed in the additional training data. This procedure yielded a vocabulary of one million words in both languages.

Language model training The training data were divided into several sets based on dates on genres (resp. 7 and 9 sets for English and French). On each set, a standard 4-gram LM was estimated from the 1M word vocabulary with in-house tools using absolute discounting interpolated with lower order models. The resulting LMs were then linearly interpolated using interpolation coefficients chosen so as to minimise perplexity of the development set (dev2009a). Due to memory limitations, the final LMs were pruned using perplexity as pruning criterion.

Out of vocabulary word and perplexity To evaluate our vocabulary and LMs, we used the official devtest and test sets. The out-of-vocabulary (OOV) rate was drastically reduced by increasing the vocabulary size, the mean OOV rate decreasing from 2.5% to 0.7%, a trend observed in both languages.

For French, using a small LM trained on the "WMT" data only resulted in a perplexity of 301 on the devtest corpus and 299 on the test set. Using all additional data yielded a large decrease in perplexity (106 on the devtest and 108 on the test); again the same trend was observed for English.

2.4 A Moses baseline

Our baseline system was a vanilla phrase-based system built with Moses (Koehn et al., 2007) using default settings. Phrases were extracted using the 'grow-diag-final-and' heuristics, using a maximum phrase length of 7; non-contextual phrase scores contain the 4 translation model scores, plus a fixed phrase penalty; 6 additional scores parameterize the lexicalized reordering model. Default decoding options were used (20 alternatives per phrase, maximum distortion distance of 7, etc.)

2.5 A N-code baseline

N-code implements the n-gram-based approach to Statistical Machine Translation (Mariño et al., 2006). In a nutshell, the translation model is implemented as a stochastic finite-state transducer trained using a n-gram model of (source,target) pairs (Casacuberta and Vidal, 2004). Training such a model requires to reorder source sentences so as to match the target word order. This is also performed via a stochastic finite-state reordering model, which uses part-of-speech information to generalise reordering patterns beyond lexical regularities. The reordering model is trained on a version of the parallel corpora where the source sentences have been reordered via the unfold heuristics (Crego and Mariño, 2007). A conventional n-gram language model of the target language provides the third component of the system.

In all our experiments, we used 4-gram reordering models and bilingual tuple models built using Kneser-Ney backoff (Chen and Goodman, 1996). The maximum tuple size was also set to 7.

2.6 Tuning procedure

The Moses-based systems were tuned using the implementation of minimum error rate training (MERT) (Och, 2003) distributed with the Moses decoder, using the development corpus (dev2009a). For the context-less systems, tuning concerned the 14 usual weights; tuning the

22 weights of the context-aware systems (see 3.1) proved to be much more challenging, and the weights used in our submissions are probably far from optimal. The N-code systems only rely on 9 weights, since they dispense with the lexical reordering model; these weights were tuned on the same dataset, using an in-house implementation of the simplex algorithm.

3 Extensions

3.1 A context-aware system

In phrase-based translation, source phrases are translated irrespective of their (source) context. This is often not perceived as a limitation as (i) typical text domains usually contain only few senses for polysemous words, thus limiting the use of word sense disambiguation (WSD); and (ii) using long-span target language models (4-grams and more) often capture sufficient context to select the more appropriate translation for a source phrase based on the target context. In fact, attempts at using source contexts in phrase-based SMT have to date failed to show important gains on standard evaluation test sets (Carpuat and Wu, 2007; Stroppa et al., 2007; Gimpel and Smith, 2008; Max et al., 2008). Importantly, in all conditions where gains have been obtained, the target language was the "morphologically-poor" English.

Nonetheless, there seems to be a clear consensus on the importance of better exploiting source contexts in SMT, so as to improve *phrase disambiguation*. The following sentence extract from the devtest corpus is a typical example where the lack of context in our phrase-based system yields an incorrect translation:

Source: *the long weekend comes with a price ...*
Target: *Le long week-end vient avec un prix ...*
(the long weekend comes accompanied by a price)

While grammatically correct, the French translation sounds unnatural, and getting the correct meaning requires knowledge of the idiom in the source language. In such a situation, the right context of the phrase *comes with* can be successfully used to propose a better translation.[3]

From an engineering perspective, integrating context into phrase-based SMT systems can be performed by (i) transforming source words into unique tokens, so as to record the original context of each entry of the phrase table; and by (ii) adding one or several contextual scores to the phrase table. Using standard MERT, the corresponding weights can be optimized on development data.

A typical contextual score corresponds to $p(\mathbf{e}|\mathbf{f}, C(\mathbf{f}))$, where $C(\mathbf{f})$ is some contextual information about the source phrase $\mathbf{f}$. An external disambiguation system can be used to provide one global context score (Stroppa et al., 2007; Carpuat and Wu, 2007; Max et al., 2008)); alternatively, several scores based on single features can be estimated using relative frequencies (Gimpel and Smith, 2008):

$$p(\mathbf{e}|\mathbf{f}, C(\mathbf{f})) = \frac{count(\mathbf{e}, \mathbf{f}, C(\mathbf{f}))}{\sum_{\mathbf{e}'} count(\mathbf{e}', \mathbf{f}, C(\mathbf{f}))}$$

For these experiments, we followed the latter approach, restricting ourselves to features representing the local context up to a fixed distance d (using the values 1 and 2 in our experiments) from the source phrase $\mathbf{f}_{start}^{end}$:

- lexical context features:
  - left context: $p(\mathbf{e}|\mathbf{f}, \mathbf{f}_{start-d}^{start-1})$
  - right context: $p(\mathbf{e}|\mathbf{f}, \mathbf{f}_{end+1}^{end+d})$
- shallow syntactic features (denoting t_1^F the sequence of POS tags for the source sentence):
  - left context: $p(\mathbf{e}|\mathbf{f}, t_{start-d}^{start-1})$
  - right context: $p(\mathbf{e}|\mathbf{f}, t_{end+1}^{end+d})$

As in (Gimpel and Smith, 2008), we filtered out all translations for which $p(\mathbf{e}|\mathbf{f}) < 0.0002$. This was necessary to make score computation practical given our available hardware resources.

Results on the devtest corpus for English→French were similar for the context-aware phrase-based and the baseline phrase-based system; small gains were achieved in the reverse direction (see Table 2). The same trend was observed on the test data.

Manual inspection of the output of the baseline and context-aware systems on the devtest corpus for English→French translation confirmed two facts: (1) performing phrase translation disambiguation is only useful if a more appropriate translation has been seen during training ; and (2) phrase translation disambiguation can capture important source dependencies that the target language model can not recover. The following ex-

[3] Our context-aware phrase-based system indeed proposes the appropriate translation: *Le long week-end a un prix.*

ample, involving an unseen sense[4] (*ball* in the semantic field of *dance* rather than *sports*), illustrates our first remark:

Source: *about 500 people attended the* ***ball***.
Baseline : *Environ 500 personnes ont assisté à la* ***balle***.
+Context: *Environ 500 personnes ont participé à la* ***balle***.

The next example is a case where contextual information helped selecting an appropriate translation, in contrast to the baseline system.

Source: ... *the new method for calculating pensions* ***due to begin*** *next year* ...
Baseline : ... *le nouveau mode de calcul des pensions* ***due à commencer*** *l'année prochaine* ...
+Context: ... *la nouvelle méthode de calcul des pensions* ***qui va débuter*** *l'année prochaine* ...

3.2 Preliminary experiments with the GigaWord parallel corpus

One exciting novelty of this year's campaign was the availability of a very large parallel corpus for the en:fr pair, containing about 20M aligned sentences.

Our preliminary work consisted in selecting the most useful pairs of sentences, based on their average perplexity, as computed on our development language models. The top ranking sentences (about 8M sentences) were then fed into the usual system development procedure: alignment, reordering (for the N-code system), phrase pair extraction, model estimation. Given the unusual size of this corpus, each of these steps proved extremely resource intensive, and, for some systems, actually failed to complete. Contrarily, the N-code systems, conceptually simpler, proved to scale nicely.

Given the very late availability of this corpus, our experiments were very limited and we eventually failed to deliver the test submissions of our "GigaWord" system. Preliminary experiments using the N-code systems (see Table 2), however, showed a clear improvement of performance. There is no reason to doubt that similar gains would be observed with the Moses systems.

3.3 Experiments

The various systems presented above were all developed according to the same procedure: training used all the available parallel text; tuning was performed on dev2009a (1000 sentences), and our internal tests were performed on dev2009b (1000 sentences). Results are reported in table 2.

	en → fr		fr → en	
	Moses	Ncode	Moses	Ncode
small LM	20.06	18.98	21.14	20.41
Large LM	22.93	21.95	22.20	22.28
+context	23.06		22.69	
+giga		23.21		23.14

Table 2: Results on the devtest set

Our primary submission corresponds to the +context entry, our first contrast to Moses+LargeLM, and our second contrast to Ncode+largeLM. Due to lack of time, no official submission was submitted for the +giga variant. For the record, the score we eventually obtained on the test corpus was 26.81, slightly better than our primary submission which obtained a score of 25.74 (all these numbers were computed on the complete test set).

4 Conclusion

In this paper, we presented our statistical MT systems developed for the WMT'09 shared task. We used last year experiments to build competitive systems, which greatly benefited from in-house normalisation and language modeling tools.

One motivation for taking part in this campaign was to use the GigaWord corpus. Even if time did not allow us to submit a system based on this data, it was a interesting opportunity to confront ourselves with the technical challenge of scaling up our system development tools to very large parallel corpora. Our preliminary results indicate that this new resource can actually help improve our systems.

Naturally, future work includes adapting our systems so that they can use models learnt from corpora of the size of the GigaWord corpus. In parallel, we intend to keep on working on context-aware systems to study the impact of more types of scores, e.g. based on grammatical dependencies as in (Max et al., 2008). Given the difficulties we had tuning our systems, we feel that a preliminary task should be improving our tuning tools before addressing these developments.

[4] This was confirmed after careful inspection of the phrase tables of the baseline system.

Acknowledgments

This work was partly realised as part of the Quaero Program, funded by OSEO, the French agency for innovation.

References

M. Carpuat and D. Wu. 2007. Context-Dependent Phrasal Translation Lexicons for Statistical Machine Translation. In *Proceedings of Machine Translation Summit XI*, pages 73–80, Copenhagen, Denmark.

F. Casacuberta and E. Vidal. 2004. Machine translation with inferred stochastic finite-state transducers. *Computational Linguistics*, 30(3):205–225.

S. F. Chen and J. T. Goodman. 1996. An empirical study of smoothing techniques for language modeling. In *Proceedings of the 34th Annual Meeting of the Association for Computational Linguistics*, pages 310–318, Santa Cruz, NM.

J. M. Crego and J. B. Mariño. 2007. Improving SMT by coupling reordering and decoding. *Machine Translation*, 20(3):199–215.

D. Déchelotte, G. Adda, A. Allauzen, O. Galibert, J.-L. Gauvain, H. Meynard, and F. Yvon. 2008. Limsi's statistical translation systems for WMT'08. In *Proceedings of the NAACL-HTL Statistical Machine Translation Workshop*, pages 107-100, Columbus, Ohio.

K. Gimpel and N. A. Smith. 2008. Rich Source-Side Context for Statistical Machine Translation. In *Proceedings of the Third Workshop on Statistical Machine Translation*, pages 9–17, Columbus, Ohio.

P. Koehn, H. Hoang, A. Birch, C. Callison-Burch, M. Federico, N. Bertoldi, B. Cowan, W. Shen, C. Moran, R. Zens, C. Dyer, O. Bojar, A. Constantin, and E. Herbst. 2007. Moses: Open source toolkit for statistical machine translation. In *ACL, demonstration session*, Prague, Czech Republic.

A. Max, R. Makhloufi, and P. Langlais. 2008. Explorations in using grammatical dependencies for contextual phrase translation disambiguation. In *Proceedings of EAMT, poster session*, Hamburg, Germany.

J. B. Mariño, R. E. Banchs R, J.M. Crego, A. de Gispert, P. Lambert, J.A.R. Fonollosa, and M. R. Costa-Jussà. 2006. N-gram-based machine translation. *Computational Linguistics*, 32(4):527–549.

F. J. Och. 2003. Minimum error rate training in statistical machine translation. In *Proceedings of the 41st Annual Meeting of the Association for Computational Linguistics*, pages 160–167, Sapporo, Japan.

N. Stroppa, A. van den Bosch, and A. Way. 2007. Exploiting source similarity for SMT using context-informed features. In *Proceedings of the 11th International Conference on Theoretical and Methodological Issues in Machine Translation (TMI'07)*, pages 231–240, Skövde, Sweden.

NICT@WMT09: Model Adaptation and Transliteration for Spanish-English SMT

Michael Paul, Andrew Finch and Eiichiro Sumita
Language Translation Group
MASTAR Project
National Institute of Information and Communications Technology
Michael.Paul@nict.go.jp

Abstract

This paper describes the NICT statistical machine translation (SMT) system used for the WMT 2009 Shared Task (WMT09) evaluation. We participated in the *Spanish-English* translation task. The focus of this year's participation was to investigate model adaptation and transliteration techniques in order to improve the translation quality of the baseline phrase-based SMT system.

1 Introduction

This paper describes the NICT statistical machine translation (SMT) system used for the shared task of the Fourth Workshop on Statistical Machine Translation. We participated in the *Spanish-English* translation task under the *Constrained Condition*. For the training of the SMT engines, we used two parallel Spanish-English corpora provided by the organizers: the *Europarl* (*EP*) corpus (Koehn, 2005), which consists of 1.4M parallel sentences extracted from the proceedings of the European Parliament, and the *News Commentary* (*NC*) corpus (Callison-Burch et al., 2008), which consists of 74K parallel sentences taken from major news outlets like *BBC*, *Der Spiegel*, and *Le Monde*.

In order to adapt SMT systems to a specific domain, recent research focuses on model adaptation techniques that adjust their parameters based on information about the evaluation domain (Foster and Kuhn, 2007; Finch and Sumita, 2008a). Statistical models can be trained on *in-domain* and *out-of-domain* data sets and combined at run-time using probabilistic weighting between domain-specific statistical models. As the official WMT09 evaluation testset consists of documents taken from the news domain, we applied statistical model adaptation techniques to combine *translation models* (tm), *language models* (lm) and *distortion models* (dm) trained on (a) the in-domain *NC* corpus and (b) the out-of-domain *EP* corpus (cf. Section 2).

One major problem in the given translation task was the large amount of *out-of-vocabulary* (OOV) words, i.e., source language words that do not occur in the training corpus. For unknown words, no translation entry is available in the statistical translation model (*phrase-table*). As a result, these OOV words cannot be translated. Dealing with languages with a rich morphology like *Spanish* and having a limited amount of bilingual resources make this problem even more severe.

There have been several efforts in dealing with OOV words to improve translation quality. In addition to parallel text corpora, external bilingual dictionaries can be exploited to reduce the OOV problem (Okuma et al., 2007). However, these approaches depend on the coverage of the utilized external dictionaries.

Data sparseness problems due to inflectional variations were previously addressed by applying word transformations using stemming or lemmatization (Popovic and Ney, 2005; Gupta and Federico, 2006). A tight integration of morpho-syntactic information into the translation model was proposed by (Koehn and Hoang, 2007) where lemma and morphological information are translated separately, and this information is combined on the output side to generate the translation. However, these approaches still suffer from the data sparseness problem, since lemmata and inflectional forms never seen in the training corpus cannot be translated.

In order to generate translations for unknown words, previous approaches focused on *transliteration* methods, where a sequence of characters is mapped from one writing system into another. For example, in order to translate names and technical terms, (Knight and Graehl, 1997) introduced a probabilistic model that replaces Japanese

Proceedings of the Fourth Workshop on Statistical Machine Translation , pages 105–109,
Athens, Greece, 30 March – 31 March 2009.

katakana[1] words with phonetically equivalent English words. More recently, (Finch and Sumita, 2008b) proposed a transliteration method that is based directly on techniques developed for phrase-based SMT, and transforms a character sequence from one language into another in a subword-level, character-based manner. We extend this approach by exploiting the phrase-table of the baseline SMT system to train a phrase-based transliteration model that generates English translations of Spanish OOV words as described in Section 3. The effects of the proposed techniques are investigated in detail in Section 4.

2 Model Adaptation

Phrase-based statistical machine translation engines use multiple statistical models to generate a translation hypothesis in which (1) the *translation model* ensures that the source phrases and the selected target phrases are appropriate translations of each other, (2) the *language model* ensures that the target language is fluent, (3) the *distortion model* controls the reordering of the input sentence, and (4) the *word penalty* ensures that the translations do not become too long or too short. During decoding, all model scores are weighted and combined to find the most likely translation hypothesis for a given input sentence (Koehn et al., 2007).

In order to adapt SMT systems to a specific domain, separate statistical models can be trained on parallel text corpora taken from the respective domain (*in-domain*) and additional *out-of-domain* language resources. The models are then combined using mixture modeling (Hastie et al., 2001), i.e., each model is weighted according to its fit with in-domain development data sets and the linear combination of the respective scores is used to find the best translation hypothesis during the decoding of unseen input sentences.

In this paper, the above model adaptation technique is applied to combine the *NC* and the *EP* language resources provided by the organizers for the *Spanish-English* translation task. As the WMT09 evaluation testset consists of documents taken from the news domain, we used the *NC* corpus to train the in-domain models and the *EP* corpus to train the out-of-domain component models. Using mixture modeling, the above mentioned statistical models are combined where each component model is optimized separately. Weight optimization is carried out using a simple grid-search method. At each point on the grid of weight parameter values, the translation quality of the combined weighted component models is evaluated for development data sets taken from (a) the *NC* corpus and (b) from the *EP* corpus.

3 Transliteration

Source language input words that cannot be translated by the standard phrase-based SMT models are either left untranslated or simply removed from the translation output. Common examples are named entities such as *personal names* or *technical terms*, but also include content words like *common nouns* or *verbs* that are not covered by the training data. Such unknown occurrences could benefit from being transliterated into the MT system's output during translation of orthographically related languages like Spanish and English.

In this paper, we apply a phrase-based transliteration approach similar to the one proposed in (Finch and Sumita, 2008b). The transliteration method is based directly on techniques developed for phrase-based SMT and treats the task of transforming a character sequence from one language into another as a character-level translation process. In contrast to (Finch and Sumita, 2008b) where external dictionaries and inter-language links in Wikipedia[2] are utilized, the transliteration training examples used for the experiments in Section 4 are extracted directly from the phrase-table of the baseline SMT systems trained on the provided data sets. For each phrase-table entry, corresponding word pairs are identified according to a string similarity measure based on the *edit-distance* (Wagner, 1974) that is defined as the sum of the costs of *insertion*, *deletion*, and *substitution* operations required to map one character sequence into the other and can be calculated by a *dynamic programming* technique (Cormen et al., 1989). In order to reduce noise in the training data, only word pairs whose word length and similarity are above a pre-defined threshold are utilized for the training of the transliteration model.

The obtained transliteration model is applied as a post-process filter to the SMT decoding process, i.e.. all source language words that could not be translated using the SMT engine are replaced with the corresponding transliterated word forms in order to obtain the final translation output.

[1] A special syllabary alphabet used to write down foreign names or loan words.

[2] http://www.wikipedia.org

4 Experiments

The effects of *model adaptation* and *transliteration* techniques were evaluated using the Spanish-English language resources summarized in Table 1. In addition, the characteristics of this year's testset are given in Table 2. The sentence length is given as the average number of words per sentence. The OOV word figures give the percentage of words in the evaluation data set that do not appear in the *NC/EP* training data. In order to get an idea how difficult the translation task may be, we also calculated the language perplexity of the respective evaluation data sets according to 5-gram target language models trained on the *NC/EP* data sets.

Concerning the development sets, the *news-dev2009* data taken from the same news sources as the evaluation set of the shared task was used for the tuning of the SMT engines, and the *devtest2006* data taken from the *EP* corpus was used for system parameter optimization. For the evaluation of the proposed methods, we used the testsets of the Second Workshop on SMT (*nc-test2007* for *NC* and *test2007* for *EP*). All data sets were case-sensitive with punctuation marks tokenized.

The numbers in Table 1 indicate that the characteristics of this year's testset differ largely from testsets of previous evaluation campaigns. The *NC* devset (2,438/1,378 OOVs) contains twice as many untranslatable Spanish words as the *NC* evalset (1,168/73 OOVs) and the *EP* devset (912/63 OOVs). In addition, the high language perplexity figures for this year's testset show that the translation quality output for both baseline systems is expected to be much lower than those for the *EP* evaluation data sets. In this paper, translation quality is evaluated according to (1) the *BLEU* metrics which calculates the *geometric mean of n-gram precision* by the system output with respect to reference translations (Papineni et al., 2002), and (2) the *METEOR* metrics that calculates unigram overlaps between translations (Banerjee and Lavie, 2005). Scores of both metrics range between 0 (worst) and 1 (best) and are displayed in percent figures.

4.1 Baseline

Our baseline system is a fairly typical phrase-based machine translation system (Finch and Sumita, 2008a) built within the framework of a feature-based exponential model containing the following features:

Table 1: Language Resources

Corpus			Train	Dev	Eval
NC	Spanish	sentences	74K	2,001	2,007
		words	2,048K	49,116	56,081
		vocab	61K	9,047	8,638
		length	27.6	24.5	27.9
		OOV (%)	–	5.2 / 2.9	1.4 / 0.9
	English	sentences	74K	2,001	2,007
		words	1,795K	46,524	49,693
		vocab	47K	8,110	7,541
		length	24.2	23.2	24.8
		OOV (%)	–	5.2 / 2.9	1.2 / 0.9
		perplexity	–	349 / 381	348 / 458
EP	Spanish	sentences	1,404K	1,861	2,000
		words	41,003K	50,216	61,293
		vocab	170K	7,422	8,251
		length	29.2	27.0	30.6
		OOV (%)	–	2.4 / 0.1	2.4 / 0.2
	English	sentences	1,404K	1,861	2,000
		words	39,354K	48,663	59,145
		vocab	121K	5,869	6,428
		length	28.0	26.1	29.6
		OOV (%)	–	1.8 / 0.1	1.9 / 0.1
		perplexity	–	210 / 72	305 / 125

Table 2: Testset 2009

Corpus			Test
NC	Spanish	sentences	3,027
		words	80,591
		vocab	12,616
		length	26.6

- Source-target phrase translation probability
- Inverse phrase translation probability
- Source-target lexical weighting probability
- Inverse lexical weighting probability
- Phrase penalty
- Language model probability
- Lexical reordering probability
- Simple distance-based distortion model
- Word penalty

For the training of the statistical models, standard word alignment (GIZA++ (Och and Ney, 2003)) and language modeling (SRILM (Stolcke, 2002)) tools were used. We used 5-gram language models trained with modified Knesser-Ney smoothing. The language models were trained on the target side of the provided training corpora. Minimum error rate training (MERT) with respect to BLEU score was used to tune the decoder's parameters, and performed using the technique proposed in (Och, 2003). For the translation, the in-house multi-stack phrase-based decoder **CleopATRa** was used.

The automatic evaluation scores of the baseline systems trained on (a) only the *NC* corpus and (b) only on the *EP* corpus are summarized in Table 3.

Table 3: Baseline Performance

	NC Eval		*EP* Eval	
	BLEU	METEOR	BLEU	METEOR
baseline	17.56	40.52	33.00	56.50

4.2 Effects of Model Adaptation

In order to investigate the effect of model adaptation, each model component was optimized separately using the method described in Section 2. Table 4 summarizes the automatic evaluation results for various model combinations. The combination of *NC* and *EP* models using equal weights achieves only a slight improvement for the *NC* task (BLEU: +0.4%, METEOR: +0.4%), but a large improvement for the *EP* task (BLEU: +1.0%, METEOR: +1.7%). Weight optimization further improves all translation tasks where the highest evaluation scores are achieved when the optimized weights for all statistical models are used. In total, model adaptation gains 1.1% and 1.3% in BLEU and 0.8% and 1.8% in METEOR for the *NC* and *EP* translation tasks, respectively.

Table 4: Effects of Model Adaptation

weight	*NC* Eval		*EP* Eval	
optimization	BLEU	METEOR	BLEU	METEOR
–	17.92	40.72	34.00	58.20
tm	18.13	40.95	34.05	58.23
tm+lm	18.25	41.23	34.12	58.22
tm+dm	18.36	41.06	34.24	58.34
tm+lm+dm	**18.65**	**41.35**	**34.35**	**58.36**

4.3 Effects of Transliteration

In order to investigate the effects of transliteration, we trained three different transliteration using the phrase-table of the baseline systems trained on (a) only the *NC* corpus, (b) only the *EP* corpus, and (c) on the merged corpus (*NC+EP*). The performance of these phrase-based transliteration models is evaluated for 2000 randomly selected transliteration examples. Table 5 summarizes the haracter-based automatic evaluation scores for the *word error rate* (WER) metrics, i.e., the edit distance between the system output and the closest reference translation (Niessen et al., 2000), as well as the BLEU and METEOR metrics. The best performance is achieved when training examples from both domains are exploit to transliterate unknown Spanish words into English. Therefore, the *NC+EP* transliteration model was applied to the translation outputs of all mixture models described in Section 4.2.

The effects of the transliteration post-process are summarized in Table 6. Transliteration consistently improves the translation quality of all mixture models, although the gains obtained for the *NC* task (BLEU: +1.3%, METEOR: +1.3%) are much larger than those for the *EP* task (BLEU: +0.1%, METEOR: +0.2%) which is due to the larger amount of untranslatable words in the *NC* evaluation data set.

Table 5: Transliteration Performance

Training	character-based		
Data	WER	BLEU	METEOR
NC	13.10	83.62	86.74
EP	11.76	85.93	87.89
NC+EP	**11.72**	**86.08**	**87.89**

Table 6: Effects of Transliteration

weight	*NC* Eval		*EP* Eval	
optimization	BLEU	METEOR	BLEU	METEOR
tm	19.14	42.39	34.11	58.46
tm+lm	19.46	42.65	34.16	58.44
tm+dm	19.77	42.35	34.38	58.57
tm+lm+dm	**19.95**	**42.64**	**34.48**	**58.60**

4.4 WMT09 Testset Results

Based on the automatic evaluation results presented in the previous sections, we selected the SMT engine based on the *tm+lm+dm* weights optimized on the *NC* devset as the primary run for our testset run submission. All other model weight combinations were submitted as contrastive runs. The BLEU scores of these runs are listed in Table 7 and confirm the results obtained for the above experiments, i.e., the best performing system is the one based on the mixture models using separately optimized weights in combination with the transliteration of untranslatable Spanish words using the phrase-based transliteration model trained on all available language resources.

Table 7: Testset 2009 Performance

weight	*NC* Eval	*EP* Eval
optimization	BLEU	BLEU
tm	21.07	20.81
tm+lm	20.95	20.59
tm+dm	21.45	21.32
tm+lm+dm	**21.67***	21.27

5 Conclusion

The work for this year's shared task focused on the task of effectively utilizing out-of-domain language resources and handling OOV words to improve translation quality. Overall our experiments show that the incorporation of mixture models and phrase-based transliteration techniques largely out-performed standard phrase-based SMT engines gaining a total of 2.4% in BLEU and 2.1% in METEOR for the news domain.

References

S. Banerjee and A. Lavie. 2005. METEOR: An Automatic Metric for MT Evaluation with Improved Correlation with Human Judgments. In *Proceedings of the ACL Workshop on Intrinsic and Extrinsic Evaluation Measures for MT*, pages 65–72, Ann Arbor, Michigan.

C. Callison-Burch, C. Fordyce, P. Koehn, C. Monz, and J. Schroeder. 2008. Further Meta-Evaluation of Machine Translation. In *Proceedings of the 3rd Workshop on SMT*, pages 70–106, Columbus, Ohio.

H. Cormen, C. Leiserson, and L. Rivest. 1989. *Introduction to Algorithms*. MIT Press.

A. Finch and E. Sumita. 2008a. Dynamic Model Interpolation for Statistical Machine Translation. In *Proceedings of the 3rd Workshop on SMT*, pages 208–215, Columbus, Ohio.

A. Finch and E. Sumita. 2008b. Phrase-based Machine Transliteration. In *Proceedings of the IJCNLP*, pages 13–18, Hyderabad, India.

G. Foster and R. Kuhn. 2007. Mixture-Model Adaptation for SMT. In *Proceedings of the 2nd Workshop on SMT*, pages 128–135, Prague, Czech Republic.

D. Gupta and M. Federico. 2006. Exploiting Word Transformation in SMT from Spanish to English. In *Proceedings of the EAMT*, pages 75–80, Oslo, Norway.

T. Hastie, R. Tibshirani, and J. Friedman. 2001. *The Elements of Statistical Learning*. Springer, New York.

K. Knight and J. Graehl. 1997. Machine Transliteration. In *Proceedings of the 35th ACL*, pages 128–135, Madrid, Spain.

P. Koehn and H. Hoang. 2007. Factored Translation Models. In *Proceedings of the EMNLP-CoNLL*, pages 868–876, Prague, Czech Republic.

P. Koehn, F.J. Och, and D. Marcu. 2007. Statistical Phrase-Based Translation. In *Proceedings of the HLT-NAACL*, pages 127–133, Edmonton, Canada.

P. Koehn. 2005. Europarl: A Parallel Corpus for Statistical Machine Translation. In *Proceedings of the MT Summit X*, pages 79–86, Phuket, Thailand.

S. Niessen, F.J. Och, G. Leusch, and H. Ney. 2000. An Evaluation Tool for Machine Translation: Fast Evaluation for MT Research. In *Proc. of the 2nd LREC*, pages 39–45, Athens, Greece.

F.J. Och and H. Ney. 2003. A Systematic Comparison of Various Statistical Alignment Models. *Computational Linguistics*, 29(1):19–51.

F.J. Och. 2003. Minimum Error Rate Training in Statistical Machine Translation. In *Proceedings of the 41st ACL*, pages 160–167, Sapporo, Japan.

H. Okuma, H. Yamamoto, and E. Sumita. 2007. Introducing Translation Dictionary into phrase-based SMT. In *Proceedings of MT Summit XI*, pages 361–368, Copenhagen, Denmark.

K. Papineni, S. Roukos, T. Ward, and W. Zhu. 2002. BLEU: a Method for Automatic Evaluation of Machine Translation. In *Proceedings of the 40th ACL*, pages 311–318, Philadelphia, USA.

M. Popovic and H. Ney. 2005. Exploiting Phrasal Lexica and Additional Morpho-synatctic Language Resources for SMT with Scarce Training Data. In *Proceedings of the EAMT*, pages 212–218, Budapest, Hungary.

A. Stolcke. 2002. SRILM - an extensible language modeling toolkit. In *Proceedings of ICSLP*, pages 901–904, Denver.

R.W. Wagner. 1974. The string-to-string correction problem. *Journal of the ACM*, 21(1):169–173.

Statistical Post Editing and Dictionary Extraction: Systran/Edinburgh submissions for ACL-WMT2009

Loic Dugast[*,**] and **Jean Senellart**[*]
[*]SYSTRAN S.A.
La Grande Arche
1, Parvis de la Défense
92044 Paris
La Défense Cedex
France

Philipp Koehn[**]
[**]School of Informatics
University of Edinburgh
10 Crichton Street,
Edinburgh
United Kingdom

Abstract

We describe here the two Systran/University of Edinburgh submissions for WMT2009. They involve a statistical post-editing model with a particular handling of named entities (English to French and German to English) and the extraction of phrasal rules (English to French).

1 Introduction

Previous results had shown a rather satisfying performance for hybrid systems such as the Statistical Phrase-based Post-Editing (SPE) (Simard et al., 2007) combination in comparison with purely phrase-based statistical models, reaching similar BLEU scores and often receiving better human judgement (German to English at WMT2007) against the BLEU metric. This last result was in accordance with the previous acknowledgment (Callison-Burch et al., 2006) that systems of too differing structure could not be compared reliably with BLEU. We participated in the recent Workshop on Machine Translation (WMT'09) in the language pairs English to French and German to English. On the one hand we trained a Post-Editing system with an additional special treatment to avoid the loss of entities such as dates and numbers. On the other hand we trained an additional English-to-French system (as a secondary submission) that made use of automatically extracted linguistic entries. In this paper, we will present both approaches. The latter is part of ongoing work motivated by the desire to both make use of corpus statistics and keep the advantage of the often (relative to automatic metrics's scores) higher rank in human judgement given to rule-based systems on out-of-domain data, as seen on the WMT 2008 results for both English to French and German to English (Callison-Burch et al., 2008).

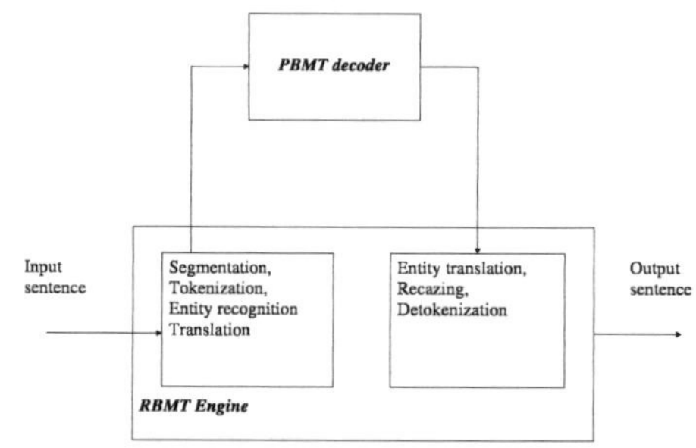

Figure 1: Translation with PBMT post-editing

2 Statistical Post Editing systems

2.1 Baseline

The basic setup is identical to the one described in (Dugast et al., 2007). A statistical translation model is trained between the rule-based translation of the source-side and the target-side of the parallel corpus. This is done separately for each parallel corpus. Language models are trained on each target half of the parallel corpora and also on additional in-domain corpora. Figure 1 shows the translation process.

Here are a few additional details which tend to improve training and limit unwanted statistical effects in translation:

- Named entities are replaced by special tokens on both sides. By reducing vocabulary and combined with the next item mentioned, this should help word alignment. Moreover, entity translation is handled more reliably by the rule-based engine.

- The intersection of both vocabularies (i.e. vo-

Proceedings of the Fourth Workshop on Statistical Machine Translation, pages 110–114,
Athens, Greece, 30 March – 31 March 2009. ©2009 Association for Computational Linguistics

cabularies of the rule-based output and the reference translation) is used to produce an additional parallel corpus (whose target is identical to source). This was added to the parallel text to improve the word alignment.

- Rule-based output and reference translations are lowercased before performing alignment, leaving the recasing job up to the rule-based engine.
- Singleton phrase pairs are deleted from the phrase table to avoid overfitting.
- Phrase pairs non cohesive regarding entities are also discarded. We make the hypothesis that entities are always passed to the target language and all entities in the target language originate from the source language. This point is discussed in section 2.2.

We will discuss some of these details further in the upcoming sections.

Due to time constraints, we did not use the Giga French-English Parallel corpus provided for the workshop. We only made use of the News Commentary and the Europarl corpora. We used additional in-domain news corpora to train 5 grams language models, according to the baseline recommendations. Weights for these separate models were tuned through the Mert algorithm provided in the Moses toolkit (Koehn et al., 2007), using the provided news tuning set.

2.2 Trimming

In a statistical translation model, trimming of the phrase table had been shown to be beneficial (Johnson et al., 2007). For our post-editing model, we can afford to perform an even more aggressive trimming of the phrase table, since the rule-based system already provides us with a translation and we only aim at correcting the most frequent errors. Therefore, we suppress all unique phrase pairs before calculating the probabilities for the final phrase table.

2.3 Avoiding the loss of entities

Deleted and spurious content is a well known problem for statistical models (Chiang et al., 2008). Though we do not know of any study proving it, it seems obvious that Named Entities that would be either deleted or added to the output out of nowhere is an especially problematic kind of error for the translation quality. The rule-based translation engine benefits from an entity recognition layer for numbers, dates and hours, addresses, company names and URIs. We therefore "trim" (delete) from the extracted phrase pairs any item that would not translate all entities from the source (i.e. the RBMT output) to the target or add spurious entities which were not present in the source side of the phrase pair. Table 1 illustrates the kind of phrase pairs that are excluded from the model. For example, the first phrase pair, when applied, would simply erase the date entity which was expressed in the source sentence, which we of course do not want.

Rule-Based French	Reference French
__ent_date	et
__ent_date	__ent_numeric et
__ent_numeric de golfe .	du golfe __ent_date .
décennie	__ent_numeric ans
et __ent_numeric .	.

Table 1: Examples of problematic phrase pairs

3 Rule Extraction

The baseline Systran rule-based system is more or less a linguistic-oriented system that makes use of a dependency analysis, general transfer rules and dictionary entries, and finally a synthesis/reordering stage. The dictionary entries have long been the main entry point for customization of the system. Such lexical translation rules are fully linguistically coded dictionary entries, with the following features attached: part-of-speech, inflection category, headword and possibly some semantic tags. Table 2 displays a sample of manually-entered entries. These entries may both match any inflected form of the source and generate the appropriate (according to general agreement rules and depending on the source analysis) target inflection.

Motivations for adding phrasal dictionary entries (compound words) are twofold: first, just as for statistical translation models which went from word-based to phrase-based models, it helps solve disambiguation and non-literal translations. Second, as the rule-based engine makes use of a syntactic analysis of a source sentence, adding unambiguous phrasal chunks as entries will reduce the overall syntactic ambiguity and lead to a better source analysis.

POS	English	French	headword_English	headword_French
Noun	college level	niveau d'études universitaires	level	niveau
Adverb	on bail	sous caution	on	sous
Verb	badmouth	médire de	badmouth	médire

Table 2: Example dictionary entries

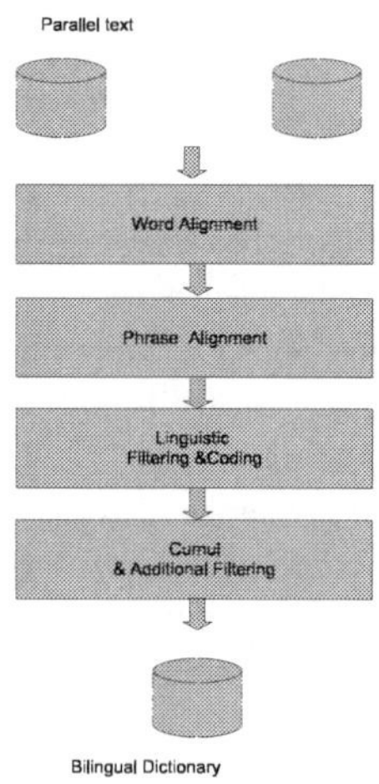

Figure 2: Extraction pipeline: from parallel texts to bilingual dictionary

3.1 Manual customization through dictionary entries

The Systran system provides a dictionary coding tool (Senellart et al., 2003). This tool allows the manual task of coding entries to be partially automated with the use of monolingual dictionaries and probabilistic context-free grammars, while allowing the user to fine-tune it by correcting the automatic coding and/or add more features. However, this remains first of all a time-consuming task. Moreover, it is not easy for humans to select the best translation among a set of alternatives, let alone assign them probabilities. Last but not least, the beneficial effect on translation is not guaranteed (especially, the effect on the rule-based dependency analysis).

3.2 Automatic extraction of dictionary entries

The problem consists of selecting relevant phrase pairs from a set, coding them linguistically and assign them probabilities. The extraction setup as depicted in figure 2) starts from a parallel corpus dataset. The baseline procedure is followed (word alignment using GIZA++ and use of common heuristics to extract phrase pairs (Koehn et al., 2007)) to extract phrase pairs. At this stage the "phrases" are plain word sequences, not necessarily linguistically motivated. Some statistical information is attached to each phrase pair: frequency of the pair and lexical weights in both directions. Each unique phrase pair is then processed by our dictionary coding tool which tries to map both word sequences to a given category. If both sides are mapped to the same category, the phrase pair, now lemmatized, is retained as a bilingual entry. Otherwise, the candidate is excluded. Given that a bilingual entry with a same lemma may have various inflectional forms in corpus, we then sum the lemma counts. Finally, in the current setup, we only keep the most frequent translation for each source.

For our secondary submission for English-French, we extracted such entries from both the News Commentary and the Europarl corpus.

3.3 Validation of dictionary entries

The coding procedure, when applied to phrase pairs extracted from the corpus instead of manually entered entries, may generate rules that do not lead to an improved translation. Recall that we start from an existing system and only want to learn additional rules to adapt to the domain of the bilingual corpus we have at our disposal.

Now the problem consists of building the optimal subset from the set of candidate entries, according to a translation evaluation metric (here, BLEU). Unlike the Mert procedure, we would like to do more than assign global weights for the whole set of translation rules, but instead make a decision for each individual phrasal rule.

As an approximate response to this problem, we test each extracted entry individually, starting from the lower n-grams to the longer (source) chunks, following algorithm 1. This results in dictionaries of 5k and 170k entries for the News Commentary and the Europarl parallel corpora, respectively.

System	BLEU
RBMT English-French	20.48
RBMT+SPE English-French	21.90
RBMT+Extracted dictionary English-French	20.82
RBMT German-English	15.13
RBMT+SPE German-English	17.50

Table 3: Compared results of original RBMT system,post-editing and dictionary extraction: real-cased, untokenized NIST Bleu scores on the full newstest2009 set(%)

System	**nc-test2007** (news commentary)	**test2007** (europarl)	**newstest2009** (news)
RBMT	24.88	22.75	20.48
RBMT +Dictionary extracted from News Commentary	26.54	-	20.57
RBMT +Dictionary extracted from Europarl	-	25.55	-
RBMT +Dictionary extracted from NC and Europarl, priority on NC	26.65	-	20.82

Table 4: Results of dictionary extraction for English-French: real-cased, untokenized NIST Bleu scores (%)

Algorithm 1 Dictionary Validation Algorithm

n=1
for n=1 to Nmax **do**
    map all n-gram entries to parallel sentences
    translate training corpus with current dictionary
    for each entry **do**
        translate all relevant sentences with current dictionary, plus this entry
        compute BLEU scores without and with the entry
    end for
    Select entries with better/worse sentences ratio above threshold
    add these entries to current dictionary
end for

4 Results

BLEU scores of the dictionary extraction experiments for the English-French language pair and three types of corpora are displayed in table 4. Table 3 shows results on the news test set. Post-editing setups were tuned on the news tuning set.

5 Conclusion and future work

We presented a few improvements to the Statistical Post Editing setup. They are part of an effort to better integrate a linguistic, rule-based system and the statistical correcting layer also illustrated in (Ueffing et al., 2008). Moreover, we presented a dictionary extraction setup which resulted in an improvement of 2 to 3 BLEU points over the baseline rule-based system when in-domain,as can be seen in table 4. This however improved translation very little on the "news" domain which was used for evaluation. We think that is a different issue, namely of domain adaptation. In order to push further this rule-extraction approach and according to our previous work (Dugast et al., 2007) (Dugast et al., 2008), the most promising would probably be the use of alternative meanings and a language model to decode the best translation in such a lattice. Another path for improvement would be to try and extract rules with more features, such as constraints of lexical subcategorization as they already exist in the manually entered entries. Finally, we would like to try combining the dictionary extraction setup with a Statistical Post-Editing layer to see if the latter supersedes the former.

Acknowledgement

We would like to thank the anonymous reviewers for their comments and corrections.

References

C. Callison-Burch, M. Osborne, and P. Koehn. 2006. Re-evaluating the role of bleu in machine translation research. In *In proceedings of EACL 2006.*

Chris Callison-Burch, Cameron Fordyce, Philipp Koehn, Christof Monz, and Josh Schroeder. 2008. Further meta-evaluation of machine translation. In *Proceedings of the Third Workshop on Statistical Machine Translation*, pages 70–106, Columbus, Ohio, June. Association for Computational Linguistics.

David Chiang, Steve Deneefe, Yee S. Chan, and Hwee T. Ng. 2008. Decomposability of translation metrics for improved evaluation and efficient algorithms. In *Proceedings of the 2008 Conference on Empirical Methods in Natural Language Processing*, pages 610–619, Honolulu, Hawaii, October. Association for Computational Linguistics.

Loïc Dugast, Jean Senellart, and Philipp Koehn. 2007. Statistical post-editing on SYSTRAN's rule-based translation system. In *Proceedings of the Second Workshop on Statistical Machine Translation*, pages 220–223, Prague, Czech Republic, June. Association for Computational Linguistics.

Loïc Dugast, Jean Senellart, and Philipp Koehn. 2008. Can we relearn an rbmt system? In *Proceedings of the Third Workshop on Statistical Machine Translation*, Columbus, Ohio, U.S.A., June. Association for Computational Linguistics.

Howard Johnson, Joel Martin, George Foster, and Roland Kuhn. 2007. Improving translation quality by discarding most of the phrasetable. In *Proceedings of the 2007 Joint Conference on Empirical Methods in Natural Language Processing and Computational Natural Language Learning (EMNLP-CoNLL)*, pages 967–975, Prague, Czech Republic, June. Association for Computational Linguistics.

Philipp Koehn, Hieu Hoang, Alexandra Birch, Chris Callison-Burch, Marcello Federico, Nicola Bertoldi, Brooke Cowan, Wade Shen, Christine Moran, Richard Zens, Chris Dyer, Ondrej Bojar, Alexandra Constantin, and Evan Herbst. 2007. Moses: Open source toolkit for statistical machine translation. In *ACL 2007, demonstration session.*

Jean Senellart, Jin Yang, and Anabel Rebollo. 2003. Technologie systran intuitive coding. In *in Proceedings of MT Summit IX.*

M. Simard, C. Goutte, and P. Isabelle. 2007. Statistical phrase-based post-editing. In *proceedings of the NAACL-HLT. 2007. NRC 49288.*

Nicola Ueffing, Jens Stephan, Evgeny Matusov, Loïc Dugast, George Foster, Roland Kuhn, Jean Senellart, and Jin Yang. 2008. Tighter integration of rule-based and statistical MT in serial system combination. In *Proceedings of the 22nd International Conference on Computational Linguistics (Coling 2008)*, pages 913–920, Manchester, UK, August. Coling 2008 Organizing Committee.

Experiments in morphosyntactic processing for translating to and from German

Alexander Fraser
Institute for Natural Language Processing
University of Stuttgart
fraser@ims.uni-stuttgart.de

Abstract

We describe two shared task systems and associated experiments. The German to English system used reordering rules applied to parses and morphological splitting and stemming. The English to German system used an additional translation step which recreated compound words and generated morphological inflection.

1 Introduction

The Institute for Natural Language Processing (IfNLP), Stuttgart, participated in the WMT-2009 shared tasks for German to English and English to German translation with constrained systems which employed morphological and syntactic processing techniques. The systems were based on the open source Moses docoder (Koehn et al., 2007). We combined IfNLP tools for syntactic and morphological analysis (which are publicly available and widely used) with preprocessing techniques that were successfully used by other groups in WMT-2008, and extended these. For English to German translation, we additionally performed a step which recreated compound words and generated morphological inflection.

1.1 Baseline

The baseline is the standard system supplied for the shared task. We used the default parameters of the Moses toolkit, except for a small difference in the generation of the word alignments, see section 3.

2 Improvements

2.1 Character Normalization

We normalize both the English and German by converting all characters to their nearest equivalent in Latin-1 (ISO 8859-1) encoding[1], except for the euro sign, which is handled specially. We did not modify the SGML files used for calculating BLEU and METEOR scores in any way.

2.2 German Writing Reform

German underwent a writing reform from the *alte Rechtschreibung* (old spelling rules/orthography) to the *neue Rechtschreibung* (gloss: new spelling rules/orthography) recently. Early Europarl data are written using the *alte Rechtschreibung* and hence need to be converted to the *neue Rechtschreibung* in order to match the news data, which is in the new form.

We began the process by mapping all cased variants of a particular word to a single class (such as by mapping two words which are written with *ue* and *ü*, but are otherwise identical, to a single class). We then tried to automatically identify the correct variant under the writing reform for each class. Initially we tried the linux tool *aspell* but found that its coverage (the recall of its lexicon) was poor.

We used a simple technique for finding the best variant. We separated the Europarl corpus into portions written using the old and new forms. We used the incidence of the word *dass* (the complementizer meaning *that*) and its old rules variant *daß*. We used a chunk size of 70 sentences to segment Europarl into old and new by counting whether there were more instances of *daß* or *dass*, respectively, in each chunk. We added the news corpora to the new portion. For each variant we counted the number of times it occurred in the new data and subtracted the number of times it occurred in the old data; the variant with the highest adjusted count was selected.

[1]Latin-1 is an 8-bit encoding which has the common accented characters used in Western European languages. A reviewer pointed out that ISO 8859-15 has superseded ISO 8859-1.

Proceedings of the Fourth Workshop on Statistical Machine Translation, pages 115–119,
Athens, Greece, 30 March – 31 March 2009. ©2009 Association for Computational Linguistics

2.3 Reordering German

German word order differs from English substantially. Preprocessing approaches involving the use of a syntactic parse of the source sentence to change the word order to more closely match the word order of the target language have been studied by Niessen and Ney (2004), Xia and McCord (2004), Drábek and Yarowsky (2004), Collins et al. (2005), Popović and Ney (2006), Wang et al. (2007) and many others.

To obtain a parse of each German sentence in the training, dev and test corpora, we employed the IfNLP BitPar probabilistic parser (Schmid, 2004), using models learned from the Tiger Treebank for German.

Dealing with morphological productivity is important in the syntactic parsing of German. BitPar has been designed with this in mind. IfNLP's SMOR analyzer is used for morphological analysis (Schmid et al., 2004). SMOR is run over a list of types in each German sentence, and outputs a list of analyses for each type, each of which corresponds to a POS tag. BitPar is limited to choosing one of these POS tags for this type. Words which SMOR fails to analyze are allowed to occur with any POS tag.

We reimplemented the syntactic preprocessing approach of Collins et al. (2005), with modifications. Reordering rules are applied to a German parse tree (generated by BitPar), and focus on reordering the words in the German clause structure to more closely resemble English clause structure. The rules are applied to both the training data for the SMT system, and the input (the dev and test sets). We previously performed an error analysis of this approach and for the work described here we addressed some of the shortcomings identified through the analysis. The analysis was performed on the Europarl dev2006 set.

The first error that we noticed occurring frequently was that some large clausal units which were labeled as subjects were being moved forward in the sentence. We modified the rule moving subjects forward to not apply to the constituents *S*, *CS*, *VP* and *CVP*. See the first part of table 3 for an example. The phrase "dass der Balkan ist kein Gebiet" is moved under the original rules, and with the modification is no longer moved[2].

[2]Note that there is an unrelated reordering error at the end of the sentence for both BEFORE and AFTER, *gibt* (gloss: gives) should have moved to follow *das* (gloss: that).

System	BLEU	METEOR	LR
no processing	18.91	49.50	1.0097
c+w	19.37	49.69	1.0067
c+w, s/s	19.18	51.13	1.0035
c+w, old reordering	19.61	50.44	1.0092
c+w, new reordering	19.91	50.84	1.0059
c+w, new reordering, s/s (submitted, bug)	19.65	51.57	1.0093
* c+w, new reordering, s/s	19.73	51.59	1.0062
as * IRSTLM quantized	19.52	51.33	1.0003
as * IRSTLM	19.75	51.61	1.0013
as * IRSTLM 21.2 quantized	19.52	51.51	1.0095
as * RANDLM	19.67	51.73	1.0067
as * RANDLM 21.2	21.03	51.96	1.0111

Table 1: German to English, dev-2009b (case sensitive), c+w = char+word normalization, s/s = splitting/stemming, 21.2 = larger LM

System	BLEU	METEOR	LR
no processing	13.55	38.31	0.9910
c+w (no second step)	14.11	38.27	0.9991
c+w, s/s, second step (submitted, bug)	12.34	37.89	1.0338
c+w, s/s, second step	13.05	37.94	1.0157

Table 2: English to German, dev-2009b (case sensitive), c+w = char+word normalization, s/s = splitting/stemming

The second error that we handled was that *S-RC* constituents which do not have a complementizer are reordered incorrectly. We modified the original verb 2nd rule, so that if there is no complementizer in a *S-RC* constituent, then the head is moved to the second position, see the second part of table 3 for an example. Using the original rules, the verb 2nd rule fails to fire, incorrectly leaving *haben* (gloss: have) at the end of the clause.

2.4 Morphological Decomposition

We implemented the frequency-based word splitting approach of Koehn and Knight (2003), and made modifications, including some similar to those described by Stymne et al. (2008). This well-known technique splits compound words. In addition, we performed simple suffix elimination, aimed at removing inflection marking features such as gender and case that are not necessary for translation to English. We took the stem combination with the highest geometric mean of the frequencies of the stems, but following Stymne et al. (2008), we restricted stems to minimum length 4, and we allowed an extended list of infixes: *s*, *n*, *en*, *nen*, *es*, *er* and *ien*. For suffixes, we allowed: *e*, *en*, *n*, *es*, *s*, *em* and *er*, which is more aggressive

INPUT	Mir ist bewusst , dass der Balkan kein Gebiet ist , das Anlass zu Optimismus gibt .
gloss	me is clear , that the Balkans not area is , that opportunity for optimism gives .
BEFORE	Mir dass der Balkan ist kein Gebiet ist bewusst , , das Anlass zu Optimismus gibt .
gloss	me that the Balkans is not area is clear , that opportunity for optimism gives .
AFTER	Mir ist bewusst , dass der Balkan ist kein Gebiet , das Anlass zu Optimismus gibt .
gloss	me is clear , that the Balkans is not area , that opportunity for optimism gives .
REF	I am aware that the Balkans are not the most promising area for optimism .
INPUT	Am 23. November 1999 hat ein Partnerschaftstag stattgefunden , an dem viele von uns teilgenommen haben .
gloss	on 23 November 1999 have a partnership-day took-place , in which many of us participated have .
BEFORE	Am 23. November 1999 ein Partnerschaftstag hat stattgefunden , an dem teilgenommen viele von uns haben .
gloss	on 23 November 1999 a partnership-day have took-place , in which participated many of us have .
AFTER	Am 23. November 1999 ein Partnerschaftstag hat stattgefunden , an dem viele von uns haben teilgenommen .
gloss	on 23 November 1999 a partnership-day have took-place , in which many of us have participated .
REF	A partnership day was held on 23 November 1999 , in which many of us participated .

Table 3: Differences in reordering: BEFORE is reordering using rules in (Collins et al., 2005), AFTER is our modified reordering

than used in previous work (and therefore generalizes more but at the same time causes some erroneous conflation). We stripped *e*, *en* and *n* from all stems (but remembered the most frequent variant, so that applying the procedure to *Kirchturm* results in *Kirche Turm* (gloss: church tower)). We store an alignment from the original German to the simplified German which we will use in the next section.

2.5 Morphological Generation

For translation from English to German, we first translated from English to the simplified German presented in the previous section, and then performed an independent translation step from simplified German to fully inflected German.

Two processes are handled by this step. First, series of stems corresponding to compound words are recomposed (along with infixes which are not present in the simplified German form) into compound words. Second, inflection is added (e.g., case and gender agreement is handled). Both of these processes are implemented using a Moses system trained on a parallel corpus where the source language is simplified German and the target language is fully inflected German. The alignment is error-free as it was generated as a side effect of the splitting and stemming process described in the previous section. In translation, reordering is not allowed, but we otherwise use standard Moses settings.

3 Experiments

3.1 German to English

We trained our German to English system on the constrained parallel data. The English data was processed using character normalization. The German data was first processed using character and word (writing reform) normalization. We then parsed the German data using BitPar and applied the modified reordering rules. After this the splitting and stemming process was applied. Finally, we lowercased the data.

Word alignments were generated using Model 4 (Brown et al., 1993) using the multi-threaded implementation of GIZA++ (Och and Ney, 2003; Gao and Vogel, 2008). We first trained Model 4 with English as the source language, and then with German as the source language, resulting in two Viterbi alignments[3]. The resulting Viterbi alignments were combined using the *Grow Diag Final And* symmetrization heuristic (Koehn et al., 2003). We estimated a standard Moses system using default settings. MERT was run until convergence using dev-2009a (separately for each experiment).

One limitation of our German to English system is that we were unable to scale to the full language modeling data using SRILM (Stolcke, 2002), 5-grams and modified Kneser-Ney with no singleton deletion[4]. The language model in our submitted system is based on all of the available English data, but news-train08 is truncated to the first 10193376 lines, meaning that we did not train on the remaining 11038787 lines, so we used a little less than half of the data. We converted the lan-

[3]We used 5 iterations of Model 1, 4 iterations of HMM (Vogel et al., 1996) and 4 iterations of Model 4.

[4]SRILM failed when trained on the full data, even when a machine with 32 GB RAM and 48 GB swap was used.

guage model trained using SRILM to the binary format using IRSTLM.

Experiments are presented in table 1, using BLEU (Papineni et al., 2001) and METEOR[5] (Banerjee and Lavie, 2005), and we also show the length ratio (ratio of hypothesized tokens to reference tokens). For translation into English METEOR had superior correlation with human rankings to BLEU at WMT 2008 (Callison-Burch et al., 2008). Our submitted system had a bug where the environment variable *LC_ALL* was set to *en_US* when creating the binarized filtered lexicalized reordering table for the test set (and for the blindtest set, but not for the dev set used for MERT). This caused minor degradation, see the system marked (*) for the system with the bug corrected.

Each system increases in both BLEU and METEOR as improvements are added. An exception is that splitting/stemming decreases BLEU somewhat. However, we trust the METEOR results more due to their better correlation with human judgements.

We also compared using a different language model instead of the SRILM model (the bottom half of table 1). These used either the reduced English language modeling data or the full data (21.2 M segments, marked *21.2* in the results). RANDLM (Talbot and Osborne, 2007) performs well and scaled to the full data with improvement (resulting in our best overall system). IRSTLM (Federico and Cettolo, 2007) also performs well, but the quantized model on the 21.2 data did not improve over the smaller quantized model[6]. IRSTLM uses an approximation of Witten-Bell smoothing, our results support that this is competitive.

3.2 English to German

We trained our English to German system on the constrained parallel data. The first SMT system translates from lowercased English to lowercased simplified German, which is then recased. The syntactic reordering process is not used, but otherwise the German data is processed identically. The alignment from simplified German to English is generated as described in the previous section. We used all of the German data to train the language model on simplified German. The second SMT system translates mixed case simplified German to mixed case unsimplified German. The translation model is built only on the simplified German from the parallel text, and the language model is trained on all German data.

We present the results in table 2. METEOR[7] did not correlate as well as BLEU for translation out of English in WMT 2008. The BLEU score of our final system is worse than the baseline. We had chosen to submit this system as we found it more interesting than submitting a vanilla system. In addition, the system of Stymne et al. (2008) received a good human evaluation despite having a relatively low BLEU score, and we hoped we were performing similar morphological generalization. We expect to be able to improve this system through error analysis. In an initial inspection we found case mismatching problems between step one and step two.

4 Conclusion

We presented our German to English system which employed character normalization, compensated for problems caused by the German writing reform, used modified syntactic reordering rules (in combination with morphologically aware parsing), and employed substring-based morphological analysis. Our best system improves by 2.46 METEOR and 1.12 BLEU over a standard Moses system. Our English to German system used the same two normalizations and the substring-based morphological analysis, and additionally implemented a second translation step for recreating compound words and generating case and gender inflection. We will improve this system in future work.

References

Satanjeev Banerjee and Alon Lavie. 2005. METEOR: An automatic metric for MT evaluation with improved correlation with human judgments. In *Proceedings of Workshop on Intrinsic and Extrinsic Evaluation Measures for MT and/or Summarization at the 43th Annual Meeting of the Association of Computational Linguistics (ACL-2005)*, Ann Arbor, Michigan.

Peter F. Brown, Stephen A. Della Pietra, Vincent J. Della Pietra, and R. L. Mercer. 1993. The mathematics of statistical machine translation: parameter

[5]METEOR used default weights, stemming and Wordnet synsets.

[6]After speaking with the authors, we plan to try IRSTLM on the full data using memory mapping for binarization.

[7]METEOR for this task is calculated using default weights but no Wordnet synsets.

estimation. *Computational Linguistics*, 19(2):263–311.

Chris Callison-Burch, Cameron Fordyce, Philipp Koehn, Christof Monz, and Josh Schroeder. 2008. Further meta-evaluation of machine translation. In *ACL Third Workshop on Statistical Machine Translation*, Columbus, Ohio.

Michael Collins, Philipp Koehn, and Ivona Kučerová. 2005. Clause restructuring for statistical machine translation. In *ACL*, pages 531–540, Ann Arbor, MI.

Elliott F. Drábek and David Yarowsky. 2004. Improving bitext word alignments via syntax-based reordering of English. In *The Companion Volume to the Proceedings of the 42nd Annual Meeting of the Association for Computational Linguistics*, pages 146–149, Barcelona, Spain.

Marcello Federico and Mauro Cettolo. 2007. Efficient handling of n-gram language models for statistical machine translation. In *Proceedings of the Second Workshop on Statistical Machine Translation*, pages 88–95, Prague, Czech Republic.

Qin Gao and Stephan Vogel. 2008. Parallel implementations of word alignment tool. In *Software Engineering, Testing, and Quality Assurance for Natural Language Processing*, pages 49–57.

Philipp Koehn and Kevin Knight. 2003. Empirical methods for compound splitting. In *EACL*, pages 187–193, Morristown, NJ.

Philipp Koehn, Franz J. Och, and Daniel Marcu. 2003. Statistical phrase-based translation. In *HLT-NAACL*, pages 127–133, Edmonton, Canada.

Philipp Koehn, Hieu Hoang, Alexandra Birch, Chris Callison-Burch, Marcello Federico, Nicola Bertoldi, Brooke Cowan, Wade Shen, Christine Moran, Richard Zens, Chris Dyer, Ondrej Bojar, Alexandra Constantin, and Evan Herbst. 2007. Moses: Open source toolkit for statistical machine translation. In *ACL, Demonstration Program*, Prague, Czech Republic.

Sonja Niessen and Hermann Ney. 2004. Statistical machine translation with scarce resources using morpho-syntactic information. *Computational Linguistics*, 30(2):181–204.

Franz J. Och and Hermann Ney. 2003. A systematic comparison of various statistical alignment models. *Computational Linguistics*, 29(1):19–51.

Kishore A. Papineni, Salim Roukos, Todd Ward, and Wei-Jing Zhu. 2001. BLEU: a method for automatic evaluation of machine translation. Technical Report RC22176 (W0109-022), IBM Research Division, Thomas J. Watson Research Center, Yorktown Heights, NY.

Maja Popović and Hermann Ney. 2006. POS-based word reorderings for statistical machine translation. In *LREC*, pages 1278–1283, Genoa, Italy.

Helmut Schmid, Arne Fitschen, and Ulrich Heid. 2004. SMOR: a German computational morphology covering derivation, composition, and inflection. In *LREC*, pages 1263–1266, Lisbon, Portugal.

Helmut Schmid. 2004. Efficient parsing of highly ambiguous context-free grammars with bit vectors. In *COLING*, Geneva, Switzerland.

Andreas Stolcke. 2002. SRILM - an extensible language modeling toolkit. In *Intl. Conf. Spoken Language Processing*, Denver, Colorado.

Sara Stymne, Maria Holmqvist, and Lars Ahrenberg. 2008. Effects of morphological analysis in translation between German and English. In *Proceedings of the Third Workshop on Statistical Machine Translation*, pages 135–138, Columbus, Ohio.

David Talbot and Miles Osborne. 2007. Randomised language modelling for statistical machine translation. In *ACL*, pages 512–519, Prague, Czech Republic.

Stephan Vogel, Hermann Ney, and Christoph Tillmann. 1996. HMM-based word alignment in statistical translation. In *COLING*, pages 836–841, Copenhagen, Denmark.

Chao Wang, Michael Collins, and Philipp Koehn. 2007. Chinese syntactic reordering for statistical machine translation. In *EMNLP-CONLL*, pages 737–745.

Fei Xia and Michael McCord. 2004. Improving a statistical MT system with automatically learned rewrite patterns. In *COLING*.

Improving alignment for SMT by reordering and augmenting the training corpus

Maria Holmqvist, Sara Stymne, Jody Foo and Lars Ahrenberg
Department of Computer and Information Science
Linköping University, Sweden
{marho,sarst,jodfo,lah}@ida.liu.se

Abstract

We describe the LIU systems for English-German and German-English translation in the WMT09 shared task. We focus on two methods to improve the word alignment: (i) by applying Giza++ in a second phase to a reordered training corpus, where reordering is based on the alignments from the first phase, and (ii) by adding lexical data obtained as high-precision alignments from a different word aligner. These methods were studied in the context of a system that uses compound processing, a morphological sequence model for German, and a part-of-speech sequence model for English. Both methods gave some improvements to translation quality as measured by Bleu and Meteor scores, though not consistently. All systems used both out-of-domain and in-domain data as the mixed corpus had better scores in the baseline configuration.

1 Introduction

It is an open question whether improved word alignment actually improves statistical MT. Fraser and Marcu (2007) found that improved alignments as measured by AER will not necessarily improve translation quality, whereas Ganchev et al. (2008) did improve translation quality on several language pairs by extending the alignment algorithm.

For this year's shared task we therefore studied the effects of improving word alignment in the context of our system for the WMT09 shared task. Two methods were tried: (i) applying Giza++ in a second phase to a reordered training corpus, where reordering is based on the alignments from the first phase, and (ii) adding lexical data obtained as high-precision alignments from a different word aligner. The submitted system includes the first method in addition to the processing of compounds and additional sequence models used by Stymne et al. (2008). Heuristics were used to generate true-cased versions of the translations that were submitted, as reported in section 6.

In this paper we report case-insensitive Bleu scores (Papineni et al., 2002), unless otherwise stated, calculated with the NIST tool, and case-insensitive Meteor-ranking scores, without WordNet (Agarwal and Lavie, 2008).

2 Baseline system

Our baseline system uses compound splitting, compound merging and part-of-speech/morphological sequence models (Stymne et al., 2008). Except for these additions it is similar to the baseline system of the workshop[1].

The translation system is a factored phrase-based translation system that uses the Moses toolkit (Koehn et al., 2007) for decoding and training, GIZA++ for word alignment (Och and Ney, 2003), and SRILM (Stolcke, 2002) for language models. Minimum error rate training was used to tune the model feature weights (Och, 2003).

Tuning was performed on the news-dev2009a set with 1025 sentences. All development testing was performed on the news-dev2009b set with 1026 sentences.

2.1 Sequence model based on part-of-speech and morphology

The translation models were factored with one additional output factor. For English we used part-of-speech tags obtained with TreeTagger (Schmid, 1994). For German we enriched the tags from TreeTagger with morphological information, such as case or tense, that we get from a commercial

[1] http://www.statmt.org/wmt09/baseline.html

Proceedings of the Fourth Workshop on Statistical Machine Translation, pages 120–124,
Athens, Greece, 30 March – 31 March 2009.

dependency parser[2].

We used the extra factor in an additional sequence model which can improve agreement between words, and word order. For German this factor was also used for compound merging.

2.2 Compound processing

Prior to training and translation, compound processing was performed using an empirical method based on (Koehn and Knight, 2003; Stymne, 2008). Words were split if they could be split into parts that occur in a monolingual corpus. We chose the split with the highest arithmetic mean of the corpus frequencies of compound parts. We split nouns, adjectives and verbs into parts that were content words or particles. A part had to be at least 3 characters in length and a stop list was used to avoid parts that often lead to errors, such as *arische* (*Aryan*) in *konsularische* (*consular*). Compound parts sometimes have special compound suffixes, which could be additions or truncations of letters, or combinations of these. We used the top 10 suffixes from a corpus study of Langer (1998), and we also treated hyphens as suffixes of compound parts. Compound parts were given a special part-of-speech tag that matched the head word.

For translation into German, compound parts were merged to form compounds, both during test and tuning. The merging is based on the special part-of-speech tag used for compound parts (Stymne, 2009). A token with this POS-tag is merged with the next token, either if the POS-tags match, or if it results in a known word.

3 Domain adaptation

This year three training corpora were available, a small bilingual news commentary corpus, a reasonably large Europarl corpus, and a very large monolingual news corpus, see Table 1 for details. The bilingual data was filtered to remove sentences longer than 60 words. Because the German news training corpus contained a number of English sentences, this corpus was cleaned by removing sentences containing a number of common English words.

Based on Koehn and Schroeder (2007) we adapted our system from last year, which was focused on Europarl, to perform well on test data from the news domain. We used the possibility to include several translation models in the Moses decoder by using multiple alternative decoding paths. We first trained systems on either bilingual news data or Europarl. Then we trained a mixed system, with two translation models one from each corpus, a language model from the bilingual news data, and a Europarl reordering model. The mixed system was slightly better than the Europarl only system. All sequence models used 5-grams for surface form and 7-grams for part-of-speech. All scores are shown in Table 2.

We wanted to train sequence models on the large monolingual corpora, but due to limited computer resources, we had to use a lower order for this, than on the small corpus. Thus our sequence models on this data has lower order than those trained on bilingual news or Europarl, with 4-grams for surface form and 6-grams for part-of-speech. We also used the entropy-based pruning included in the SRILM toolkit, with 10^{-8} as a threshold. Using these sequence models in the mixed model, called mixed+, improved the results drastically, as shown in Table 2.

The other experiments reported in this paper are based on the mixed+ system.

Corpus	German	English
news-commentary09	81,141	
Europarl	1,331,262	
news-train08	9,619,406	21,215,311

Table 1: Number of sentences in the corpora (after filtering)

Corpus	En⇒De		De⇒En	
	Bleu	Meteor	Bleu	Meteor
News com.	12.13	47.01	17.21	36.08
Europarl	12.92	47.27	18.53	37.65
Mixed	12.91	47.96	18.76	37.69
Mixed+	**14.62**	**49.48**	**19.92**	**38.18**

Table 2: Results of domain adaptation

4 Improved alignment by reordering

Word alignment with Giza++ has been shown to improve from making the source and target language more similar, e.g., in terms of segmentation (Ma et al., 2007) or word order.

We used the following simple procedure to improve alignment of the training corpus by reordering the words in one of the texts according to the

[2]Machinese syntax, from Connexor Oy `http://www.connexor.eu`

Corpus	En⇒De		De⇒En	
	Bleu	Meteor	Bleu	Meteor
Mixed+	14.62	49.48	19.92	38.18
Re-Src	**14.63**	**49.80**	**20.54**	**38.86**
Re-Trg	14.51	48.62	20.48	38.73

Table 3: Results of reordering experiments

word order in the other language:

1. Word align the corpus with Giza++.

2. Reorder the German words according to the order of the English words they are aligned to. (This is a common step in approaches that extract reordering rules for translation. However, this is not what we use it for here.)

3. Word align the reordered German and original English corpus with Giza++.

4. Put the reordered German words back into their original position and adjust the alignments so that the improved alignment is preserved.

After this step we will have a possibly improved alignment compared to the original Giza++ alignment. A phrase table was extracted from the alignment and training was performed as usual. The reordering procedure was carried out on both source (Re-Src) and target data (Re-Trg) and the results of translating devtest data using these alignments are shown in Table 3.

Compared with our baseline (mixed+), Bleu and Meteor increased for the translation direction German–English. Both source reordering and target reordering resulted in a 0.6 increase in Bleu.

For translation into German, source reordering resulted in a somewhat higher Meteor score, but overall did not seem to improve translation. Target reordering in this direction resulted in lower scores.

It is not clear why reordering improved translation for German–English and not for English–German. In all experiments, the heuristic symmetrization of directed Giza++ alignments was performed in the intended translation direction [3].

[3] Our experiments show that symmetrization in the wrong translation direction will result in lower translation quality scores.

5 Augmenting the corpus with an extracted dictionary

Previous research (Callison-Burch et al., 2004; Fraser and Marcu, 2006) has shown that including word aligned data during training can improve translation results. In our case we included a dictionary extracted from the news-commentary corpus during the word alignment.

Using a method originally developed for term extraction (Merkel and Foo, 2007), the news-commentary09 corpus was grammatically annotated and aligned using a heuristic word aligner. Candidate dictionary entries were extracted from the alignments. In order to optimize the quality of the dictionary, dictionary entry candidates were ranked according to their Q-value, a metric specifically designed for aligned data (Merkel and Foo, 2007). The Q-value is based on the following statistics:

- Type Pair Frequencies (TPF), i.e. the number of times where the source and target types are aligned.

- Target types per Source type (TpS), i.e. the number of target types a specific source type has been aligned to.

- Source types per Target type (SpT), i.e. the number of source types a specific target type has been aligned to.

The Q-value is calculated as $Q\text{-}value = \frac{TPF}{TpS+SpT}$. A high Q-value indicates a dictionary candidate pair with a relatively low number of translation variations. The candidates were filtered using a Q-value threshold of 0.333, resulting in a dictionary containing 67287 entries.

For the experiments, the extracted dictionary was inserted 200 times into the corpus used during word alignment. The added dictionary entries were removed before phrase extraction. Experiments using the extracted dictionary as an additional phrase table were also run, but did not result in any improvement of translation quality.

The results can be seen in Table 4. There was no evident pattern how the inclusion of the dictionary during alignment (DictAl) affected the translation quality. The inclusion of the dictionary produced both higher and lower Bleu scores than the

Corpus	En⇒De		De⇒En	
	Bleu	Meteor	Bleu	Meteor
Mixed+	14.62	49.48	19.92	38.18
DictAl	14.73	49.39	18.93	37.71

Table 4: Results of domain adaptation

Corpus	En⇒De	De⇒En
Mixed+	13.31	17.47
with OOV	13.74	17.96

Table 5: Case-sensitive Bleu scores

baseline system depending on the translation direction. Meteor scores were however consistently lower than the baseline system.

6 Post processing of out-of-vocabulary words

In the standard systems all out-of-vocabulary words are transferred as is from the translation input to the translation output. Many of these words are proper names, which do not get capitalized properly, or numbers, which have different formatting in German and English. We used post-processing to improve this.

For all unknown words we capitalized either the first letter, or all letters, if they occur in that form in the translation input. For unknown numbers we switched between the German decimal comma and the English decimal point for decimal numbers. For large numbers, English has a comma to separate thousands, and German has a period. These were also switched. This improved case-sensitive Bleu scores in both translation directions, see Table 5.

7 Submitted system

For both translation directions De-En and En-De we submitted a system with two translation models trained on bilingual news and Europarl. The alignment was improved by using the reordering techniques described in section 4. The systems also use all features described in this paper except for the lexical augmentation (section 5) which did not result in significant improvement. The results of the submitted systems on devtest data are bold-faced in Table 3.

Corpus	En⇒De	De⇒En
All	14.63	20.54
En-De orig.	19.93	26.82
Other set	11.66	16.17

Table 6: Bleu scores for the reordered systems on two sections of development set news-dev2009b. NIST scores show the same distribution.

8 Results on two sections of devtest data

Comparisons of translation output with reference translations on devtest data showed some surprising differences, which could be attributed to corresponding differences between source and reference data. The differences were not evenly distributed but especially frequent in those sections where the original language was something other than English or German. To check the homogeneity of the devtest data we divided it into two sections, one for documents of English or German origin, and the other for the remainder. It turned out that scores were dramatically different for the two sections, as shown in Table 6.

The reason for the difference is likely to be that only the En-De set contains source texts and translations, while the other section contains parallel translations from the same source. This suggests that it would be interesting to study the effects of splitting the training corpus in the same way before training.

9 Conclusion

The results of augmenting the training corpus with an extracted lexicon were inconclusive. However, the alignment reordering improved translation quality, especially in the De–En direction. The result of these reordering experiments indicates that better word alignment quality will improve SMT. The reordering method described in this paper also has the advantage of only requiring two runs of Giza++, no additional resources or training is necessary to get an improved alignment.

References

Abhaya Agarwal and Alon Lavie. 2008. Meteor, M-BLEU and M-TER: Evaluation metrics for high-correlation with human rankings of machine translation output. In *Proceedings of the Third Workshop on Statistical Machine Translation*, pages 115–118, Columbus, Ohio.

Chris Callison-Burch, David Talbot, and Miles Osborne. 2004. Statistical machine translation with word- and sentence-aligned parallel corpora. In *Proceedings of the 42nd Annual Meeting of ACL*, pages 175–182, Barcelona, Spain.

Alexander Fraser and Daniel Marcu. 2006. Semi-supervised training for statistical word alignment. In *Proceedings of the 21st International Conference on Computational Linguistics and 44th Annual Meeting of ACL*, pages 769–776, Sydney, Australia.

Alexander Fraser and Daniel Marcu. 2007. Measuring word alignment quality for statistical machine translation. *Computational Linguistics*, 33(3):293–303.

Kuzman Ganchev, João de Almeida Varelas Graça, and Ben Taskar. 2008. Better alignments = better translations? In *Proceedings of the 46th Annual Meeting of ACL*, pages 986–993, Columbus, Ohio.

Philipp Koehn and Kevin Knight. 2003. Empirical methods for compound splitting. In *Proceedings of the tenth conference of EACL*, pages 187–193, Budapest, Hungary.

Philipp Koehn and Josh Schroeder. 2007. Experiments in domain adaptation for statistical machine translation. In *Proceedings of the Second Workshop on Statistical Machine Translation*, pages 224–227, Prague, Czech Republic.

Philipp Koehn, Hieu Hoang, Alexandra Birch, Chris Callison-Burch, Marcello Federico, Nicola Bertoldi, Brooke Cowan, Wade Shen, Christine Moran, Richard Zens, Chris Dyer, Ondrej Bojar, Alexandra Constantin, and Evan Herbst. 2007. Moses: Open source toolkit for statistical machine translation. In *Proceedings of the 45th Annual Meeting of ACL, demonstration session*, Prague, Czech Republic.

Stefan Langer. 1998. Zur Morphologie und Semantik von Nominalkomposita. In *Tagungsband der 4. Konferenz zur Verarbeitung natürlicher Sprache (KONVENS)*, pages 83–97.

Yanjun Ma, Nicolas Stroppa, and Andy Way. 2007. Boostrapping word alignment via word packing. In *Proceedings of the 45th Annual Meeting of ACL*, pages 304–311, Prague, Czech Republic.

Magnus Merkel and Jody Foo. 2007. Terminology extraction and term ranking for standardizing term banks. In *Proceedings of the 16th Nordic Conference of Computational Linguistics (NODALIDA-2007)*, pages 349–354, Tartu, Estonia.

Franz Josef Och and Hermann Ney. 2003. A systematic comparison of various statistical alignment models. *Computational Linguistics*, 29(1):19–51.

Franz Josef Och. 2003. Minimum error rate training in statistical machine translation. In *Proceedings of the 41st Annual Meeting of ACL*, pages 160–167, Sapporo, Japan.

Kishore Papineni, Salim Roukos, Todd Ward, and Wei-Jing Zhu. 2002. BLEU: a method for automatic evaluation of machine translation. In *Proceedings of the 40th Annual Meeting of ACL*, pages 311–318, Philadelphia, Pennsylvania.

Helmut Schmid. 1994. Probabilistic part-of-speech tagging using decision trees. In *International Conference on New Methods in Language Processing*, pages 44–49, Manchester, UK.

Andreas Stolcke. 2002. SRILM - an extensible language modeling toolkit. In *Proceedings of the Seventh International Conference on Spoken Language Processing (ICSLP)*, pages 901–904, Denver, Colorado.

Sara Stymne, Maria Holmqvist, and Lars Ahrenberg. 2008. Effects of morphological analysis in translation between German and English. In *Proceedings of the Third Workshop on Statistical Machine Translation*, pages 135–138, Columbus, Ohio.

Sara Stymne. 2008. German compounds in factored statistical machine translation. In Aarne Ranta and Bengt Nordström, editors, *Proceedings of GoTAL, 6th International Conference on Natural Language Processing*, LNCS/LNAI Volume 5221, pages 464–475.

Sara Stymne. 2009. A comparison of merging strategies for translation of German compounds. In *Proceedings of the EACL09 Student Research Workshop*, Athens, Greece.

English-Czech MT in 2008 *

Ondřej Bojar, David Mareček, Václav Novák, Martin Popel, Jan Ptáček, Jan Rouš, Zdeněk Žabokrtský
Charles University, Institute of Formal and Applied Linguistics
Malostranské nám. 25, Praha 1, CZ-118 00, Czech Republic
{bojar,marecek,novak,ptacek,zabokrtsky}@ufal.mff.cuni.cz
{popel,jan.rous}@matfyz.cz

Abstract

We describe two systems for English-to-Czech machine translation that took part in the WMT09 translation task. One of the systems is a tuned phrase-based system and the other one is based on a linguistically motivated analysis-transfer-synthesis approach.

1 Introduction

We participated in WMT09 with two very different systems: (1) a phrase-based MT based on Moses (Koehn et al., 2007) and tuned for English→Czech translation, and (2) a complex system in the TectoMT platform (Žabokrtský et al., 2008).

2 Data

2.1 Monolingual Data

Our Czech monolingual data consist of (1) the Czech National Corpus (CNC, versions SYN200[056], 72.6%, Kocek et al. (2000)), (2) a collection of web pages downloaded by Pavel Pecina (Web, 17.1%), and (3) the Czech monolingual data provided by WMT09 organizers (10.3%). Table 1 lists sentence and token counts (see Section 2.3 for the explanation of a- and t-layer).

Sentences	52 M
with nonempty t-layer	51 M
a-nodes (i.e. tokens)	0.9 G
t-nodes	0.6 G

Table 1: Czech monolingual training data.

2.2 Parallel Data

As the source of parallel data we use an internal release of Czech-English parallel corpus CzEng (Bojar et al., 2008) extended with some additional texts. One of the added sections was gathered from two major websites containing Czech subtitles to movies and TV series[1]. The matching of the Czech and English movies is rather straightforward thanks to the naming conventions. However, we were unable to reliably determine the series number and the episode number from the file names. We employed a two-step procedure to automatically pair the TV series subtitle files. For every TV series:

1. We clustered the files on both sides to remove duplicates
2. We found the best matching using a provisional translation dictionary. This proved to be a successful technique on a small sample of manually paired test data. The process was facilitated by the fact that the correct pairs of episodes usually share some named entities which the human translator chose to keep in the original English form.

Table 2 lists parallel corpus sizes and the distribution of text domains.

	English	Czech
Sentences	6.91 M	
with nonempty t-layer	6.89 M	
a-nodes (i.e. tokens)	61 M	50 M
t-nodes	41 M	33 M

Distribution:	[%]		[%]
Subtitles	68.2	Novels	3.3
Software Docs	17.0	Commentaries/News	1.5
EU (Legal) Texts	9.5	Volunteer-supplied	0.4

Table 2: Czech-English data sizes and sources.

* The work on this project was supported by the grants MSM0021620838, 1ET201120505, 1ET101120503, GAUK 52408/2008, MŠMT ČR LC536 and FP6-IST-5-034291-STP (EuroMatrix).

[1] www.opensubtitles.org and titulky.com

Proceedings of the Fourth Workshop on Statistical Machine Translation, pages 125–129,
Athens, Greece, 30 March – 31 March 2009. ©2009 Association for Computational Linguistics

2.3 Data Preprocessing using TectoMT platform: Analysis and Alignment

As we believe that various kinds of linguistically relevant information might be helpful in MT, we performed automatic analysis of the data. The data were analyzed using the layered annotation scheme of the Prague Dependency Treebank 2.0 (PDT 2.0, Hajič and others (2006)), i.e. we used three layers of sentence representation: morphological layer, surface-syntax layer (called analytical (a-) layer), and deep-syntax layer (called tectogrammatical (t-) layer).

The analysis was implemented using TectoMT, (Žabokrtský et al., 2008). TectoMT is a highly modular software framework aimed at creating MT systems (focused, but by far not limited to translation using tectogrammatical transfer) and other NLP applications. Numerous existing NLP tools such as taggers, parsers, and named entity recognizers are already integrated in TectoMT, especially for (but again, not limited to) English and Czech.

During the analysis of the large Czech monolingual data, we used Jan Hajič's Czech tagger shipped with PDT 2.0, Maximum Spanning Tree parser (McDonald et al., 2005) with optimized set of features as described in Novák and Žabokrtský (2007), and a tool for assigning functors (semantic roles) from Klimeš (2006), and numerous other components of our own (e.g. for conversion of analytical trees into tectogrammatical ones).

In the parallel data, we analyzed the Czech side using more or less the same scenario as used for the monolingual data. English sentences were analyzed using (among other tools) Morce tagger Spoustová et al. (2007) and Maximum Spanning Tree parser.[2]

The resulting deep syntactic (tectogrammatical) Czech and English trees are then aligned using T-aligner—a feature based greedy algorithm implemented for this purpose (Mareček et al., 2008). T-aligner finds corresponding nodes between the two given trees and links them. For deciding whether to link two nodes or not, T-aligner makes use of a bilingual lexicon of tectogrammatical lemmas, morphosyntactic similarities between the two candidate nodes, their positions in the trees and other similarities between their parent/child nodes. It also uses word alignment generated from surface shapes of sentences by GIZA++ tool, Och and Ney (2003). We use acquired aligned tectogrammatical trees for training some models for the transfer.

As analysis of such amounts of data is obviously computationally very demanding, we run it in parallel using Sun Grid Engine[3] cluster of 40 4-CPU computers. For this purpose, we implemented a rather generic tool that submits any TectoMT pipeline to the cluster.

3 Factored Phrase-Based MT

We essentially repeat our experiments from last year (Bojar and Hajič, 2008): GIZA++ alignments[4] on a-layer lemmas (a-layer nodes correspond 1-1 to surface tokens), symmetrized using grow-diag-final (no -and) heuristic[5].

Probably due to the domain difference (the test set is news), including Subtitles in the parallel data and Web in the monolingual data did not bring any improvement that would justify the additional performance costs. For most of the phrase-based experiments, we thus used only 2.2M parallel sentences (27M Czech and 32M English tokens) and 43M Czech sentences (694 M tokens).

In Table 3 below, we report the scores for the following setups selected from about 50 experiments we ran in total:

Moses T is a simple phrase-based translation (T) with no additional factors. The translation is performed on truecased word forms (i.e. sentence capitalization removed unless the first word seems to be a name). The 4-gram language model is based on the 43M sentences.

Moses T+C is a factored setup with form-to-form translation (T) and target-side morphological coherence check following Bojar and Hajič (2008). The setup uses two language models: 4-grams of word forms and 7-grams of morphological tags.

Moses T+C+C&T+T+G 84k is a setup desirable from the linguistic point of view. Two independent translation paths are used: (1) form→form translation with two target-side checks (lemma and tag generated from the target-side form) as a fine-grained baseline

[2] In some previous experiments (e.g.Žabokrtský et al. (2008)), we used phrase-structure parser Collins (1999) with subsequent constituency-dependency conversion.

[3] `http://gridengine.sunsource.net/`

[4] Default settings, IBM models and iterations: $1^5 3^3 4^3$.

[5] Later, we found out that the grow-diag-final-and heuristic provides insignificantly superior results.

with the option to resort to (2) an independent translation of lemma→lemma and tag→tag finished by a generation step that combines target-side lemma and tag to produce the final target-side form.

We use three language models in this setup (3-grams of forms, 3-grams of lemmas, and 10-grams of tags).

Due to the increased complexity of the setup, we were able to train this model on 84k parallel sentences only (the Commentaries section) and we use the target-side of this small training data for language models, too.

For all the setups we perform standard MERT training on the provided development set.[6]

4 Translation Setup Based on Tectogrammatical Transfer

In this translation experiment, we follow the traditional analysis-transfer-synthesis approach, using the set of PDT 2.0 layers: we analyze the input English sentence up to the tectogrammatical layer (through the morphological and analytical ones), then perform the tectogrammatical transfer, and then synthesize the target Czech sentence from its tectogrammatical representation. The whole procedure consists of about 80 steps, so the following description is necessarily very high level.

4.1 Analysis

Each sentence is tokenized (roughly according to the Penn Treebank conventions), tagged by the English version of the Morce tagger Spoustová et al. (2007), and lemmatized by our lemmatizer. Then the dependency parser (McDonald et al., 2005) is applied. Then the analytical trees resulting from the parser are converted to the tectogrammatical ones (i.e. functional words are removed, only morphologically indispensable categories are left with the nodes using a sequence of heuristic procedures). Unlike in PDT 2.0, the information about the original syntactic form is stored with each t-node (values such as `v:inf` for an infinitive verb form, `v:since+fin` for the head of a subordinate clause of a certain type, `adj:attr` for an adjective in attribute position, `n:for+X` for a given prepositional group are distinguished).

[6]We used the full development set of 2k sentences for "Moses T" and a subset of 1k sentences for the other two setups due to time constraints.

One of the steps in the analysis of English is named entity recognition using Stanford Named Entity Recognizer (Finkel et al., 2005). The nodes in the English t-layer are grouped according to the detected named entities and they are assigned the type of entity (location, person, or organization). This information is preserved in the transfer of the deep English trees to the deep Czech trees to allow for the appropriate capitalization of the Czech translation.

4.2 Transfer

The transfer phase consists of the following steps:

- Initiate the target-side (Czech) t-trees simply by "cloning" the source-side (English) t-trees. Subsequent steps usually iterate over all t-nodes. In the following, we denote a source-side t-node as *S* and the corresponding target-side node as *T*.

- Translate formemes using two probabilistic dictionaries ($p(T.formeme|S.formeme, S.parent.lemma)$ and $p(T.formeme|S.formeme)$) and a few manual rules. The formeme translation probability estimates were extracted from a part of the parallel data mentioned above.

- Translate lemmas using a probabilistic dictionary ($p(T.lemma|S.lemma)$) and a few rules that ensure compatibility with the previously chosen formeme. Again, this probabilistic dictionary was obtained using the aligned tectogrammatical trees from the parallel corpus.

- Fill the grammatemes (deep-syntactic equivalent of morphological categories) *gender* (for denotative nouns) and *aspect* (for verbs) according to the chosen lemma. We also fix grammateme values where the English-Czech grammateme correspondence is non-trivial (e.g. if an English gerund expression is translated to Czech as a subordinating clause, the *tense* grammateme has to be filled). However, the transfer of grammatemes is definitely much easier task than the transfer of formemes and lemmas.

4.3 Synthesis

The transfer step yields an abstract deep syntactico-semantical tree structure. Firstly, we derive surface morphological categories from their deep counterparts taking care of their agreement where appropriate and we also remove personal pronouns in subject positions (because Czech is a pro-drop language).

To arrive at the surface tree structure, auxiliary nodes of several types are added, including (1) reflexive particles, (2) prepositions, (3) subordinating conjunctions, (4) modal verbs, (5) verbal auxiliaries, and (6) punctuation nodes. Also, grammar-based node ordering changes (implemented by rules) are performed: e.g. if an English possessive attribute is translated using Czech genitive, it is shifted into post-modification position.

After finishing the inflection of nouns, verbs, adjectives and adverbs (according to the values of morphological categories derived from agreement etc.), prepositions may need to be vocalized: the vowel *-e* or *-u* is attached to the preposition if the pronunciation of prepositional group would be difficult otherwise.

After the capitalization of the beginning of each sentence (and each named entity instance), we obtain the final translation by flattening the surface tree.

4.4 Preliminary Error Analysis

According to our observations most errors happen during the transfer of lemmas and formemes. Usually, there are acceptable translations of lemma and formeme in respective n-best lists but we fail to choose the best one. The scenario described in Section 4.2 uses quite a primitive transfer algorithm where formemes and lemmas are translated separately in two steps. We hope that big improvements could be achieved with more sophisticated algorithms (optimizing the probability of the whole tree) and smoothed probabilistic models (such as $p(T.lemma|S.lemma, T.parent.lemma)$ and $p(T.formeme|S.formeme, T.lemma, T.parent.lemma)$).

Other common errors include:

- Analysis: parsing (especially coordinations are problematic with McDonald's parser).
- Transfer: the translation of idioms and collocations, including named entities. In these cases, the classical transfer at the t-layer is not appropriate and utilization of some phrase-based MT would help.
- Synthesis: reflexive particles, word order.

5 Experimental Results and Discussion

Table 3 reports lowercase BLEU and NIST scores and preliminary manual ranks of our submissions in contrast with other systems participating in English→Czech translation, as evaluated on the official WMT09 unseen test set. Note that automatic metrics are known to correlate quite poorly with human judgements, see the best ranking but "lower scoring" PC Translator this year and also in Callison-Burch et al. (2008).

System	BLEU	NIST	Rank
Moses T	**14.24**	**5.175**	-3.02 (4)
Moses T+C	13.86	5.110	–
Google	13.59	4.964	-2.82 (3)
U. of Edinburgh	13.55	5.039	-3.24 (5)
Moses T+C+C&T+T+G 84k	10.01	4.360	-
Eurotran XP	09.51	4.381	-2.81 (2)
PC Translator	09.42	4.335	**-2.77 (1)**
TectoMT	07.29	4.173	-3.35 (6)

Table 3: Automatic scores and preliminary human rank for English→Czech translation. Systems in italics are provided for comparison only. Best results in bold.

Unfortunately, this preliminary evaluation suggests that simpler models perform better, partly because it is easier to tune them properly both from computational point of view (e.g. MERT not stable and prone to overfitting with more features[7]), as well as from software engineering point of view (debugging of complex pipelines of tools is demanding). Moreover, simpler models run faster: "Moses T" with 12 sents/minute is 4.6 times faster than "Moses T+C". (Note that we have not tuned either of the models for speed.)

While "Moses T" is probably nearly identical setup as Google and Univ. of Edinburgh use, the knowledge of correct language-dependent tokenization and the use of relatively high quality large language model data seems to bring moderate improvements.

6 Conclusion

We described our experiments with a complex linguistically motivated translation system and various (again linguistically-motivated) setups of factored phrase-based translation. An automatic evaluation seems to suggest that simpler is better, but we are well aware that a reliable judgement comes only from human annotators.

[7]For "Moses T+C+C&T+T+G", we observed BLEU scores on the test set varying by up to five points absolute for various weight settings yielding nearly identical dev set scores.

References

Ondřej Bojar and Jan Hajič. 2008. Phrase-Based and Deep Syntactic English-to-Czech Statistical Machine Translation. In *Proceedings of the Third Workshop on Statistical Machine Translation*, pages 143–146, Columbus, Ohio, June. Association for Computational Linguistics.

Ondřej Bojar, Miroslav Janíček, Zdeněk Žabokrtský, Pavel Češka, and Peter Beňa. 2008. CzEng 0.7: Parallel Corpus with Community-Supplied Translations. In *Proceedings of the Sixth International Language Resources and Evaluation (LREC'08)*, Marrakech, Morocco, May. ELRA.

Chris Callison-Burch, Cameron Fordyce, Philipp Koehn, Christof Monz, and Josh Schroeder. 2008. Further meta-evaluation of machine translation. In *Proceedings of the Third Workshop on Statistical Machine Translation*, pages 70–106, Columbus, Ohio, June. Association for Computational Linguistics.

Michael Collins. 1999. *Head-driven Statistical Models for Natural Language Parsing*. Ph.D. thesis, University of Pennsylvania, Philadelphia.

Jenny Rose Finkel, Trond Grenager, and Christopher Manning. 2005. Incorporating non-local information into information extraction systems by gibbs sampling. In *ACL '05: Proceedings of the 43rd Annual Meeting on Association for Computational Linguistics*, pages 363–370, Morristown, NJ, USA. Association for Computational Linguistics.

Jan Hajič et al. 2006. Prague Dependency Treebank 2.0. CD-ROM, Linguistic Data Consortium, LDC Catalog No.: LDC2006T0 1, Philadelphia.

Václav Klimeš. 2006. *Analytical and Tectogrammatical Analysis of a Natural Language*. Ph.D. thesis, Faculty of Mathematics and Physics, Charles University, Prague, Czech Rep.

Jan Kocek, Marie Kopřivová, and Karel Kučera, editors. 2000. *Český národní korpus - úvod a příručka uživatele*. FF UK - ÚČNK, Praha.

Philipp Koehn, Hieu Hoang, Alexandra Birch, Chris Callison-Burch, Marcello Federico, Nicola Bertoldi, Brooke Cowan, Wade Shen, Christine Moran, Richard Zens, Chris Dyer, Ondřej Bojar, Alexandra Constantin, and Evan Herbst. 2007. Moses: Open Source Toolkit for Statistical Machine Translation. In *ACL 2007, Proceedings of the 45th Annual Meeting of the Association for Computational Linguistics Companion Volume Proceedings of the Demo and Poster Sessions*, pages 177–180, Prague, Czech Republic, June. Association for Computational Linguistics.

David Mareček, Zdeněk Žabokrtský, and Václav Novák. 2008. Automatic Alignment of Czech and English Deep Syntactic Dependency Trees. In *Proceedings of European Machine Translation Conference (EAMT 08)*, pages 102–111, Hamburg, Germany.

Ryan McDonald, Fernando Pereira, Kiril Ribarov, and Jan Hajič. 2005. Non-projective dependency parsing using spanning tree algorithms. In *HLT '05: Proceedings of the conference on Human Language Technology and Empirical Methods in Natural Language Processing*, pages 523–530, Vancouver, British Columbia, Canada.

Václav Novák and Zdeněk Žabokrtský. 2007. Feature engineering in maximum spanning tree dependency parser. In Václav Matoušek and Pavel Mautner, editors, ***Lecture Notes in Artificial Intelligence**, Proceedings of the 10th I nternational Conference on Text, Speech and Dialogue*, Lecture Notes in Computer Science, pages 92–98, Pilsen, Czech Republic. Springer Science+Business Media Deutschland GmbH.

Franz Josef Och and Hermann Ney. 2003. A Systematic Comparison of Various Statistical Alignment Models. *Computational Linguistics*, 29(1):19–51.

Drahomíra Spoustová, Jan Hajič, Jan Votrubec, Pavel Krbec, and Pavel Květoň. 2007. The best of two worlds: Cooperation of statistical and rule-based taggers for czech. In *Proceedings of the Workshop on Balto-Slavonic Natural Language Processing, ACL 2007*, pages 67–74, Praha.

Zdeněk Žabokrtský, Jan Ptáček, and Petr Pajas. 2008. TectoMT: Highly Modular Hybrid MT System with Tectogrammatics Used as Transfer Layer. In *Proc. of the ACL Workshop on Statistical Machine Translation*, pages 167–170, Columbus, Ohio, USA.

SMT and SPE Machine Translation Systems for WMT'09

Holger Schwenk and **Sadaf Abdul-Rauf** and **Loïc Barrault**
LIUM, University of Le Mans
72085 Le Mans cedex 9, FRANCE
schwenk,abdul,barrault@lium.univ-lemans.fr

Jean Senellart
SYSTRAN SA
92044 Paris La Défense cedex, FRANCE
senellart@systran.fr

Abstract

This paper describes the development of several machine translation systems for the 2009 WMT shared task evaluation. We only consider the translation between French and English. We describe a statistical system based on the Moses decoder and a statistical post-editing system using SYSTRAN's rule-based system. We also investigated techniques to automatically extract additional bilingual texts from comparable corpora.

1 Introduction

This paper describes the machine translation systems developed by the Computer Science laboratory at the University of Le Mans (LIUM) for the 2009 WMT shared task evaluation. This work was performed in cooperation with the company SYSTRAN. We only consider the translation between French and English (in both directions). The main differences to the previous year's system (Schwenk et al., 2008) are as follows: better usage of SYSTRAN's bilingual dictionary in the statistical system, less bilingual training data, additional language model training data (*news-train08* as distributed by the organizers), usage of comparable corpora to improve the translation model, and development of a statistical post-editing system (SPE). These different components are described in the following.

2 Used Resources

In the frame work of the 2009 WMT shared translation task many resources were made available. The following sections describe how they were used to train the translation and language models of the systems.

2.1 Bilingual data

The latest version of the French/English Europarl and news-commentary corpus were used. We realized that the first corpus contains parts with foreign languages. About 1200 such lines were excluded.[1] Additional bilingual corpora were available, namely the Canadian Hansard corpus (about 68M English words) and an UN corpus (about 198M English words). In several initial experiments, we found no evidence that adding this data improves the overall system and they were not used in the final system, in order to keep the phrase-table small. We also performed experiments with the provided so-called bilingual French/English Gigaword corpus (575M English words in release 3). Again, we were not able to achieve any improvement by adding this data to the training material of the translation model. These findings are somehow surprising since it was eventually believed by the community that adding large amounts of bitexts should improve the translation model, as it is usually observed for the language model (Brants et al., 2007).

In addition to these human generated bitexts, we also integrated a high quality bilingual dictionary from SYSTRAN. The entries of the dictionary were directly added to the bitexts. This technique has the potential advantage that the dictionary words could improve the alignments of these words when they also appear in the other bitexts. However, it is not guaranteed that multi-word expressions will be correctly aligned by GIZA++ and that only meaningful translations will actually appear in the phrase-table. A typical example is *fire engine – camion de pompiers*, for which the individual constituent words are not good translations of each other. The use of a dictionary to improve an SMT system was also investigated by

[1] Lines 580934–581316 and 599839–600662.

Proceedings of the Fourth Workshop on Statistical Machine Translation , pages 130–134,
Athens, Greece, 30 March – 31 March 2009.

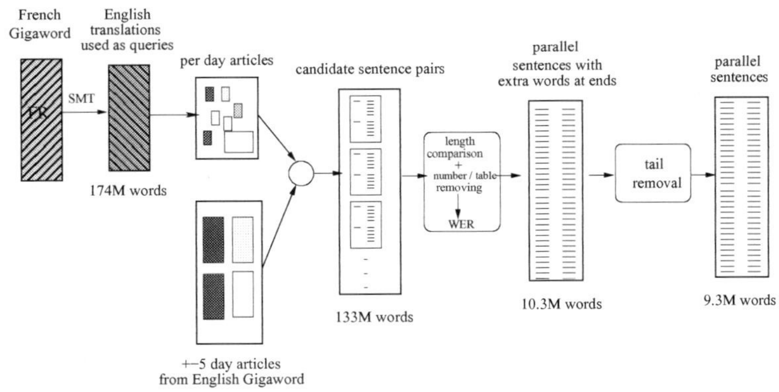

Figure 1: Architecture of the parallel sentence extraction system (Rauf and Schwenk, 2009).

(Brown et al., 1993).

In comparison to our previous work (Schwenk et al., 2008), we also included all verbs in the French *subjonctif* and *passé simple* tense. In fact, those tenses seem to be frequently used in news material. In total about 10,000 verbs, 1,500 adjectives/adverbs and more than 100,000 noun forms were added.

2.2 Use of Comparable corpora

Available human translated bitexts such as the UN and the Hansard corpus seem to be out-of domain for this task, as mentioned above. Therefore, we investigated a new method to automatically extract and align parallel sentences from comparable in-domain corpora. In this work we used the AFP news texts since there are available in the French and English LDC Gigaword corpora.

The general architecture of our parallel sentence extraction system is shown in figure 1. We first translate 174M words from French into English using an SMT system. These English sentences are then used to search for translations in the English AFP texts of the Gigaword corpus using information retrieval techniques. The Lemur toolkit (Ogilvie and Callan, 2001) was used for this purpose. Search was limited to a window of ± 5 days of the date of the French news text. The retrieved candidate sentences were then filtered using the word error rate with respect to the automatic translations. In this study, sentences with an error rate below 32% were kept. Sentences with a large length difference (French versus English) or containing a large fraction of numbers were also discarded. By these means, about 9M words of additional bitexts were obtained. An improved version of this algorithm using TER instead of the word error rate is described in detail in (Rauf and Schwenk, 2009).

2.3 Monolingual data

The French and English target language models were trained on all provided monolingual data. We realized that the *news-train08* corpora contained some foreign texts, in particular in German. We tried to filter those lines using simple regular expressions. We also discarded lines with a large fraction of numerical expressions. In addition, LDC's Gigaword collection, the Hansard corpus and the UN corpus were used for both languages. Finally, about 30M words crawled from the WEB were used for the French LM. All this data predated the evaluation period.

2.4 Development data

All development was done on *news-dev2009a* and *news-dev2009b* was used as internal test set. The default Moses tokenization was used. All our models are case sensitive and include punctuation. The BLEU scores reported in this paper were calculated with the NIST tool and are case sensitive.

3 Language Modeling

Language modeling plays an important role in SMT systems. 4-gram back-off language models (LM) were used in all our systems. The word list contains all the words of the bitext used to train the translation model and all words that appear at least ten times in the *news-train08* corpus. Separate LMs were build on each data source with the SRI LM toolkit (Stolcke, 2002) and then linearly interpolated, optimizing the coefficients with an EM procedure. The perplexities of these LMs

Corpus	# Fr words	Dev09a	Dev09b	Test09
SMT system				
Eparl+NC	46.5M	22.44	22.38	25.60
Eparl+NC+dict	48.5M	22.60	22.55	26.01
Eparl+NC+dict+AFP	57.8M	22.82	**22.63***	26.18
SPE system				
SYSTRAN	-	17.76	18.13	19.98
Eparl+NC	45.5M	22.84	**22.59**#	25.59
Eparl+NC+AFP	54.4M	22.72	21.96	25.40

Table 1: Case sensitive NIST BLEU scores for the French-English systems. "NC" denotes the news-commentary bitexts, "dict" SYSTRAN's bilingual dictionary and "AFP" the automatically aligned news texts (*=primary, #=contrastive system)

are given in Table 2. Adding the new *news-train08* monolingual data had an important impact on the quality of the LM, even when the Gigaword data is already included.

Data	French	English
Vocabulary size	407k	299k
Eparl+news	248.8	416.7
+ LDC Gigaword	142.2	194.9
+ Hansard and UN	137.5	187.5
news-train08 alone	165.0	245.9
all	120.6	174.8

Table 2: Perplexities on the development data of various language models.

4 Architecture of the SMT system

The goal of statistical machine translation (SMT) is to produce a target sentence e from a source sentence f. It is today common practice to use phrases as translation units (Koehn et al., 2003; Och and Ney, 2003) and a log linear framework in order to introduce several models explaining the translation process:

$$\begin{aligned} e^* &= \arg\max p(e|f) \\ &= \arg\max_e \{exp(\sum_i \lambda_i h_i(e,f))\} \quad (1) \end{aligned}$$

The feature functions h_i are the system models and the λ_i weights are typically optimized to maximize a scoring function on a development set (Och and Ney, 2002). In our system fourteen features functions were used, namely phrase and lexical translation probabilities in both directions, seven features for the lexicalized distortion model, a word and a phrase penalty and a target language model (LM).

The system is based on the Moses SMT toolkit (Koehn et al., 2007) and constructed as follows. First, word alignments in both directions are calculated. We used a multi-threaded version of the GIZA++ tool (Gao and Vogel, 2008).[2] This speeds up the process and corrects an error of GIZA++ that can appear with rare words. This previously caused problems when adding the entries of the bilingual dictionary to the bitexts.

Phrases and lexical reorderings are extracted using the default settings of the Moses toolkit. The parameters of Moses are tuned on *news-dev2009a*, using the cmert tool. The basic architecture of the system is identical to the one used in the 2008 WMT evaluation (Schwenk et al., 2008), but we did not use two pass decoding and n-best list rescoring with a continuous space language model.

The results of the SMT systems are summarized in the upper part of Table 1 and 3. The dictionary and the additional automatically produced AFP bitexts achieved small improvements when translating from French to English. In the opposite translation direction, the systems that include the additional AFP texts exhibit a bad generalisation behavior. We provide also the performance of the different systems on the official test set, calculated after the evaluation. In most of the cases, the observed improvements carry over on the test set.

5 Architecture of the SPE system

During the last years statistical post-editing systems have shown to achieve very competitive performance (Simard et al., 2007; Dugast et al., 2007). The main idea of this techniques is to use

[2]The source is available at `http://www.cs.cmu.edu/~qing/`

Corpus	# En words	Dev09a	Dev09b	Test09
SMT system				
Eparl+NC	41.6M	21.89	21.78	23.80
Eparl+NC+dict	44.0M	22.28	**22.35**$^{\#}$	24.13
Eparl+NC+dict+AFP	51.7M	22.21	21.43	23.88
SPE system				
SYSTRAN	-	18.68	18.84	20.29
Eparl+NC	44.2M	23.03	23.15	24.36
Eparl+NC+AFP	53.3M	22.95	**23.15***	24.62

Table 3: Case sensitive NIST BLEU scores for the English-French systems. "NC" denotes the news-commentary bitexts, "dict" denotes SYSTRAN's bilingual dictionary and "AFP" the automatically aligned news texts (*=primary, $^{\#}$=contrastive system)

an SMT system to correct the errors of a rule-based translation system. In this work, SYSTRAN server version 6, followed by an SMT system based on Moses were used. The post-editing systems uses exactly the same language models than the above described stand-alone SMT systems. The translation model was trained on the Europarl, the news-commentary and the extracted AFP bitexts. The results of these SPE systems are summarized in the lower part of Table 1 and 3. SYSTRAN's rule-based system alone already achieves remarkable BLEU scores although it was not optimized or adapted to this task. This could be significantly improved using statistical post-editing. The additional AFP texts were not useful when translating form French to English, but helped to improve the generalisation behavior for the English/French systems.

When translating from English to French (Table 3), the SPE system is clearly better than the carefully optimized SMT system. Consequently, it was submitted as primary system and the SMT system as contrastive one.

6 Conclusion and discussion

We described the development of two complementary machine translation systems for the 2009 WMT shared translation task: an SMT and an SPE system. The last one is based on SYSTRAN's rule-based system. Interesting findings of this research include the fact that the SPE system outperforms the SMT system when translating into French. This system has also obtained the best scores in the human evaluation.

With respect to the SMT system, we were not able to improve the translation model by adding large amounts of bitexts, although different sources were available (Canadian Hansard, UN or WEB data). Eventually these corpora are too noisy or out-of-domain. On the other hand, the integration of a high quality bilingual dictionary was helpful, as well as the automatic alignment of news texts from comparable corpora.

Future work will concentrate on the integration of previously successful techniques, in particular continuous space language models and lightly-supervised training (Schwenk, 2008). We also believe that the tokenization could be improved, in particular for the French sources texts. Numbers, dates and other numerical expressions could be translated by a rule-based system.

System combination has recently shown to provide important improvements of translation quality. We are currently working on a combination of the SMT and SPE system. It may be also interesting to add a third (hierarchical) MT system.

7 Acknowledgments

This work has been partially funded by the French Government under the project INSTAR (ANR JCJC06_143038) and the by the Higher Education Commission, Pakistan through the HEC Overseas Scholarship 2005.

References

Thorsten Brants, Ashok C. Popat, Peng Xu, Franz J. Och, and Jeffrey Dean. 2007. Large language models in machine translation. In *EMNLP*, pages 858–867.

Peter F. Brown, Stephen A. Della Pietra, Vincent J. Della Pietra, Meredith J. Goldsmith, Jan Hajic, Robert L. Mercer, and Surya Mohanty. 1993. But dictionaries are data too. In *Proceedings of the workshop on Human Language Technology*, pages 202–205, Princeton, New Jersey.

Loïc Dugast, Jean Senellart, and Philipp Koehn. 2007. Statistical post-editing on SYSTRAN's rule-based translation system. In *Second Workshop on SMT*, pages 179–182.

Qin Gao and Stephan Vogel. 2008. Parallel implementations of word alignment tool. In *Software Engineering, Testing, and Quality Assurance for Natural Language Processing*, pages 49–57, Columbus, Ohio, June. Association for Computational Linguistics.

Philipp Koehn, Franz Josef Och, and Daniel Marcu. 2003. Statistical phrased-based machine translation. In *HLT/NACL*, pages 127–133.

Philipp Koehn et al. 2007. Moses: Open source toolkit for statistical machine translation. In *ACL, demonstration session.*

Franz Josef Och and Hermann Ney. 2002. Discriminative training and maximum entropy models for statistical machine translation. In *ACL*, pages 295–302.

Franz Josef Och and Hermann Ney. 2003. A systematic comparison of various statistical alignement models. *Computational Linguistics*, 29(1):19–51.

Paul Ogilvie and Jamie Callan. 2001. Experiments using the Lemur toolkit. In *In Proceedings of the Tenth Text Retrieval Conference (TREC-10)*, pages 103–108.

Sadaf Abdul Rauf and Holger Schwenk. 2009. On the use of comparable corpora to improve SMT performance. In *EACL*, page to be published.

Holger Schwenk, Jean-Baptiste Fouet, and Jean Senellart. 2008. First steps towards a general purpose French/English statistical machine translation system. In *Third Workshop on SMT*, pages 119–122.

Holger Schwenk. 2008. Investigations on large-scale lightly-supervised training for statistical machine translation. In *IWSLT*, pages 182–189.

Michel Simard, Nicola Ueffing, Pierre Isabelle, and Roland Kuhn. 2007. Rule-based translation with statistical phrase-based post-editing. In *Second Workshop on SMT*, pages 203–206.

Andreas Stolcke. 2002. SRILM - an extensible language modeling toolkit. In *ICSLP*, pages II: 901–904.

Joshua: An Open Source Toolkit for Parsing-based Machine Translation

Zhifei Li, Chris Callison-Burch, Chris Dyer,[†] **Juri Ganitkevitch,**[+] **Sanjeev Khudanpur, Lane Schwartz,**[⋆] **Wren N. G. Thornton, Jonathan Weese** and **Omar F. Zaidan**
Center for Language and Speech Processing, Johns Hopkins University, Baltimore, MD
† Computational Linguistics and Information Processing Lab, University of Maryland, College Park, MD
+ Human Language Technology and Pattern Recognition Group, RWTH Aachen University, Germany
⋆ Natural Language Processing Lab, University of Minnesota, Minneapolis, MN

Abstract

We describe **Joshua**, an open source toolkit for statistical machine translation. Joshua implements all of the algorithms required for synchronous context free grammars (SCFGs): chart-parsing, n-gram language model integration, beam- and cube-pruning, and k-best extraction. The toolkit also implements suffix-array grammar extraction and minimum error rate training. It uses parallel and distributed computing techniques for scalability. We demonstrate that the toolkit achieves state of the art translation performance on the WMT09 French-English translation task.

1 Introduction

Large scale parsing-based statistical machine translation (e.g., Chiang (2007), Quirk et al. (2005), Galley et al. (2006), and Liu et al. (2006)) has made remarkable progress in the last few years. However, most of the systems mentioned above employ tailor-made, dedicated software that is not open source. This results in a high barrier to entry for other researchers, and makes experiments difficult to duplicate and compare. In this paper, we describe **Joshua**, a general-purpose open source toolkit for parsing-based machine translation, serving the same role as Moses (Koehn et al., 2007) does for regular phrase-based machine translation.

Our toolkit is written in Java and implements all the essential algorithms described in Chiang (2007): chart-parsing, n-gram language model integration, beam- and cube-pruning, and k-best extraction. The toolkit also implements suffix-array grammar extraction (Lopez, 2007) and minimum error rate training (Och, 2003). Additionally, parallel and distributed computing techniques are exploited to make it scalable (Li and Khudanpur, 2008b). We have also made great effort to ensure that our toolkit is easy to use and to extend.

The toolkit has been used to translate roughly a million sentences in a parallel corpus for large-scale discriminative training experiments (Li and Khudanpur, 2008a). We hope the release of the toolkit will greatly contribute the progress of the syntax-based machine translation research.[1]

2 Joshua Toolkit

When designing our toolkit, we applied general principles of software engineering to achieve three major goals: *Extensibility*, *end-to-end coherence*, and *scalability*.

Extensibility: The Joshua code is organized into separate *packages* for each major aspect of functionality. In this way it is clear which files contribute to a given functionality and researchers can focus on a single package without worrying about the rest of the system. Moreover, to minimize the problems of unintended interactions and unseen dependencies, which is common hinderance to extensibility in large projects, all extensible components are defined by Java *interfaces*. Where there is a clear point of departure for research, a basic implementation of each interface is provided as an *abstract class* to minimize the work necessary for new extensions.

End-to-end Cohesion: There are many components to a machine translation pipeline. One of the great difficulties with current MT pipelines is that these diverse components are often designed by separate groups and have different file format and interaction requirements. This leads to a large investment in scripts to convert formats and connect the different components, and often leads to untenable and non-portable projects as well as hinder-

[1]The toolkit can be downloaded at `http://www.sourceforge.net/projects/joshua`, and the instructions in using the toolkit are at `http://cs.jhu.edu/~ccb/joshua`.

Proceedings of the Fourth Workshop on Statistical Machine Translation, pages 135–139,
Athens, Greece, 30 March – 31 March 2009. ©2009 Association for Computational Linguistics

ing repeatability of experiments. To combat these issues, the Joshua toolkit integrates most critical components of the machine translation pipeline. Moreover, each component can be treated as a stand-alone tool and does not rely on the rest of the toolkit we provide.

Scalability: Our third design goal was to ensure that the decoder is scalable to large models and data sets. The parsing and pruning algorithms are carefully implemented with dynamic programming strategies, and efficient data structures are used to minimize overhead. Other techniques contributing to scalability includes suffix-array grammar extraction, parallel and distributed decoding, and bloom filter language models.

Below we give a short description about the main functions implemented in our Joshua toolkit.

2.1 Training Corpus Sub-sampling

Rather than inducing a grammar from the full parallel training data, we made use of a method proposed by Kishore Papineni (personal communication) to select the subset of the training data consisting of sentences useful for inducing a grammar to translate a particular test set. This method works as follows: for the development and test sets that will be translated, every n-gram (up to length 10) is gathered into a map $\mathcal{W}$ and associated with an initial count of zero. Proceeding in order through the training data, for each sentence pair whose source-to-target length ratio is within one standard deviation of the average, if any n-gram found in the *source sentence* is also found in $\mathcal{W}$ with a count of less than k, the sentence is selected. When a sentence is selected, the count of every n-gram in $\mathcal{W}$ that is found in the source sentence is incremented by the number of its occurrences in the source sentence. For our submission, we used $k = 20$, which resulted in 1.5 million (out of 23 million) sentence pairs being selected for use as training data. There were 30,037,600 English words and 30,083,927 French words in the subsampled training corpus.

2.2 Suffix-array Grammar Extraction

Hierarchical phrase-based translation requires a translation grammar extracted from a parallel corpus, where grammar rules include associated feature values. In real translation tasks, the grammars extracted from large training corpora are often far too large to fit into available memory.

In such tasks, feature calculation is also very expensive in terms of time required; huge sets of extracted rules must be sorted in two directions for relative frequency calculation of such features as the translation probability $p(f|e)$ and reverse translation probability $p(e|f)$ (Koehn et al., 2003). Since the extraction steps must be re-run if any change is made to the input training data, the time required can be a major hindrance to researchers, especially those investigating the effects of tokenization or word segmentation.

To alleviate these issues, we extract only a subset of all available rules. Specifically, we follow Callison-Burch et al. (2005; Lopez (2007) and use a source language suffix array to extract only those rules which will actually be used in translating a particular set of test sentences. This results in a vastly smaller rule set than techniques which extract all rules from the training set.

The current code requires suffix array rule extraction to be run as a pre-processing step to extract the rules needed to translate a particular test set. However, we are currently extending the decoder to directly access the suffix array. This will allow the decoder at runtime to efficiently extract exactly those rules needed to translate a particular sentence, without the need for a rule extraction pre-processing step.

2.3 Decoding Algorithms[2]

Grammar formalism: Our decoder assumes a probabilistic synchronous context-free grammar (SCFG). Currently, it only handles SCFGs of the kind extracted by Heiro (Chiang, 2007), but is easily extensible to more general SCFGs (e.g., (Galley et al., 2006)) and closely related formalisms like synchronous tree substitution grammars (Eisner, 2003).

Chart parsing: Given a source sentence to decode, the decoder generates a one-best or k-best translations using a CKY algorithm. Specifically, the decoding algorithm maintains a *chart*, which contains an array of *cells*. Each cell in turn maintains a list of proven *items*. The parsing process starts with the axioms, and proceeds by applying the inference rules repeatedly to prove new items until proving a goal item. Whenever the parser proves a new item, it adds the item to the appropriate chart cell. The item also maintains back-

[2]More details on the decoding algorithms are provided in (Li et al., 2009a).

pointers to antecedent items, which are used for k-best extraction.

Pruning: Severe pruning is needed in order to make the decoding computationally feasible for SCFGs with large target-language vocabularies. In our decoder, we incorporate two pruning techniques: beam and cube pruning (Chiang, 2007).

Hypergraphs and k-best extraction: For each source-language sentence, the chart-parsing algorithm produces a *hypergraph*, which represents an exponential set of likely derivation hypotheses. Using the k-best extraction algorithm (Huang and Chiang, 2005), we extract the k most likely derivations from the hypergraph.

Parallel and distributed decoding: We also implement *parallel decoding* and a *distributed language model* by exploiting multi-core and multi-processor architectures and distributed computing techniques. More details on these two features are provided by Li and Khudanpur (2008b).

2.4 Language Models

In addition to the distributed LM mentioned above, we implement three local n-gram language models. Specifically, we first provide a straightforward implementation of the n-gram scoring function in Java. This Java implementation is able to read the standard ARPA backoff n-gram models, and thus the decoder can be used independently from the SRILM toolkit.[3] We also provide a native code bridge that allows the decoder to use the SRILM toolkit to read and score n-grams. This native implementation is more scalable than the basic Java LM implementation. We have also implemented a Bloom Filter LM in Joshua, following Talbot and Osborne (2007).

2.5 Minimum Error Rate Training

Johsua's MERT module optimizes parameter weights so as to maximize performance on a development set as measuered by an automatic evaluation metric, such as Bleu. The optimization consists of a series of line-optimizations along the dimensions corresponding to the parameters. The search across a dimension uses the efficient method of Och (2003). Each iteration of our MERT implementation consists of multiple weight updates, each reflecting a greedy selection of the dimension giving the most gain. Each iteration also optimizes several random "intermediate initial" points in addition to the one surviving from the previous iteration, as an approximation to performing multiple random restarts. More details on the MERT method and the implementation can be found in Zaidan (2009).[4]

3 WMT-09 Translation Task Results

3.1 Training and Development Data

We assembled a very large French-English training corpus (Callison-Burch, 2009) by conducting a web crawl that targted bilingual web sites from the Canadian government, the European Union, and various international organizations like the Amnesty International and the Olympic Committee. The crawl gathered approximately 40 million files, consisting of over 1TB of data. We converted pdf, doc, html, asp, php, etc. files into text, and preserved the directory structure of the web crawl. We wrote set of simple heuristics to transform French URLs onto English URLs, and considered matching documents to be translations of each other. This yielded 2 million French documents paired with their English equivalents. We split the sentences and paragraphs in these documents, performed sentence-aligned them using software that IBM Model 1 probabilities into account (Moore, 2002). We filtered and de-duplcated the resulting parallel corpus. After discarding 630 thousand sentence pairs which had more than 100 words, our final corpus had 21.9 million sentence pairs with 587,867,024 English words and 714,137,609 French words.

We distributed the corpus to the other WMT09 participants to use in addition to the Europarl v4 French-English parallel corpus (Koehn, 2005), which consists of approximately 1.4 million sentence pairs with 39 million English words and 44 million French words. Our translation model was trained on these corpora using the subsampling descried in Section 2.1.

For language model training, we used the monolingual news and blog data that was assembled by the University of Edinburgh and distributed as part of WMT09. This data consisted

[3]This feature allows users to easily try the Joshua toolkit without installing the SRILM toolkit and compiling the native bridge code. However, users should note that the basic Java LM implementation is not as scalable as the native bridge code.

[4]The module is also available as a standalone application, *Z-MERT*, that can be used with other MT systems. (Software and documentation at: `http://cs.jhu.edu/~ozaidan/zmert`.)

of 21.2 million English sentences with half a billion words. We used SRILM to train a 5-gram language model using a vocabulary containing the 500,000 most frequent words in this corpus. Note that we did not use the English side of the parallel corpus as language model training data.

To tune the system parameters we used News Test Set from WMT08 (Callison-Burch et al., 2008), which consists of 2,051 sentence pairs with 43 thousand English words and 46 thousand French words. This is in-domain data that was gathered from the same news sources as the WMT09 test set.

3.2 Translation Scores

The translation scores for four different systems are reported in Table 1.[5]

Baseline: In this system, we use the GIZA++ toolkit (Och and Ney, 2003), a suffix-array architecture (Lopez, 2007), the SRILM toolkit (Stolcke, 2002), and minimum error rate training (Och, 2003) to obtain word-alignments, a translation model, language models, and the optimal weights for combining these models, respectively.

Minimum Bayes Risk Rescoring: In this system, we re-ranked the n-best output of our baseline system using Minimum Bayes Risk (Kumar and Byrne, 2004). We re-score the top 300 translations to minimize expected loss under the Bleu metric.

Deterministic Annealing: In this system, instead of using the regular MERT (Och, 2003) whose training objective is to minimize the one-best error, we use the deterministic annealing training procedure described in Smith and Eisner (2006), whose objective is to minimize the *expected* error (together with the entropy regularization technique).

Variational Decoding: Statistical models in machine translation exhibit *spurious ambiguity*. That is, the probability of an output string is split among many distinct derivations (e.g., trees or segmentations). In principle, the goodness of a string is measured by the total probability of its many derivations. However, finding the best string (e.g., during decoding) is then computationally intractable. Therefore, most systems use a simple Viterbi approximation that measures the goodness of a string using only its most probable derivation. Instead, we develop a variational approximation, which considers all the derivations but still allows tractable decoding. More details will be provided in Li et al. (2009b). In this system, we have used both deterministic annealing (for training) and variational decoding (for decoding).

[5]Note that the implementation of the novel techniques used to produce the non-baseline results is not part of the current Joshua release, though we plan to incorporate it in the next release.

System	BLEU-4
Joshua Baseline	25.92
Minimum Bayes Risk Rescoring	26.16
Deterministic Annealing	25.98
Variational Decoding	**26.52**

Table 1: The uncased BLEU scores on WMT-09 French-English Task. The test set consists of 2525 segments, each with one reference translation.

4 Conclusions

We have described a scalable toolkit for parsing-based machine translation. It is written in Java and implements all the essential algorithms described in Chiang (2007) and Li and Khudanpur (2008b): chart-parsing, n-gram language model integration, beam- and cube-pruning, and k-best extraction. The toolkit also implements suffix-array grammar extraction (Callison-Burch et al., 2005; Lopez, 2007) and minimum error rate training (Och, 2003). Additionally, parallel and distributed computing techniques are exploited to make it scalable. The decoder achieves state of the art translation performance.

Acknowledgments

This research was supported in part by the Defense Advanced Research Projects Agency's GALE program under Contract No. HR0011-06-2-0001 and the National Science Foundation under grants No. 0713448 and 0840112. The views and findings are the authors' alone.

References

Chris Callison-Burch, Colin Bannard, and Josh Schroeder. 2005. Scaling phrase-based statistical machine translation to larger corpora and longer phrases. In *Proceedings of ACL*.

Chris Callison-Burch, Cameron Fordyce, Philipp Koehn, Christof Monz, and Josh Schroeder. 2008. Further meta-evaluation of machine translation. In *Proceedings of the Third Workshop on Statistical Machine Translation (WMT08)*.

Chris Callison-Burch. 2009. A 10^9 word parallel corpus. In preparation.

David Chiang. 2007. Hierarchical phrase-based translation. *Computational Linguistics*, 33(2):201–228.

Jason Eisner. 2003. Learning non-isomorphic tree mappings for machine translation. In *Proceedings of ACL*.

Michel Galley, Jonathan Graehl, Kevin Knight, Daniel Marcu, Steve DeNeefe, Wei Wang, and Ignacio Thayer. 2006. Scalable inference and training of context-rich syntactic translation models. In *Proceedings of the ACL/Coling*.

Liang Huang and David Chiang. 2005. Better k-best parsing. In *Proceedings of the International Workshop on Parsing Technologies*.

Philipp Koehn, Franz Josef Och, and Daniel Marcu. 2003. Statistical phrase-based translation. In *Proceedings of HLT/NAACL*.

Philipp Koehn, Hieu Hoang, Alexandra Birch, Chris Callison-Burch, Marcello Federico, Nicola Bertoldi, Brooke Cowan, Wade Shen, Christine Moran, Richard Zens, Chris Dyer, Ondrej Bojar, Alexandra Constantin, , and Evan Herbst. 2007. Moses: Open source toolkit for statistical machine translation. In *Proceedings of the ACL-2007 Demo and Poster Sessions*.

Philipp Koehn. 2005. A parallel corpus for statistical machine translation. In *Proceedings of MT-Summit*, Phuket, Thailand.

Shankar Kumar and William Byrne. 2004. Minimum bayes-risk decoding for statistical machine translation. In *Proceedings of HLT/NAACL*.

Zhifei Li and Sanjeev Khudanpur. 2008a. Large-scale discriminative n-gram language models for statistical machine translation. In *Proceedings of AMTA*.

Zhifei Li and Sanjeev Khudanpur. 2008b. A scalable decoder for parsing-based machine translation with equivalent language model state maintenance. In *In Proceedings Workshop on Syntax and Structure in Statistical Translation*.

Zhifei Li, Chris Callison-Burch, Sanjeev Khudanpur, and Wren Thornton. 2009a. Decoding in joshua: Open source, parsing-based machine translation. *The Prague Bulletin of Mathematical Linguistics*, 91:47–56.

Zhifei Li, Jason Eisner, and Sanjeev Khudanpur. 2009b. Variational decoding for statistical machine translation. In preparation.

Yang Liu, Qun Liu, and Shouxun Lin. 2006. Tree-to-string alignment templates for statistical machine translation. In *Proceedings of the ACL/Coling*.

Adam Lopez. 2007. Hierarchical phrase-based translation with suffix arrays. In *Proceedings of EMNLP-CoLing*.

Robert C. Moore. 2002. Fast and accurate sentence alignment of bilingual corpora. In *Proceedings of AMTA*.

Franz Josef Och and Hermann Ney. 2003. A systematic comparison of various statistical alignment models. *Computational Linguistics*, 29(1):19–51.

Franz Josef Och. 2003. Minimum error rate training for statistical machine translation. In *Proceedings of ACL*.

Chris Quirk, Arul Menezes, and Colin Cherry. 2005. Dependency treelet translation: Syntactically informed phrasal smt. In *Proceedings of ACL*.

David A. Smith and Jason Eisner. 2006. Minimum risk annealing for training log-linear models. In *Proceedings of the ACL/Coling*.

Andreas Stolcke. 2002. SRILM - an extensible language modeling toolkit. In *Proceedings of the International Conference on Spoken Language Processing*, Denver, Colorado, September.

David Talbot and Miles Osborne. 2007. Randomised language modelling for statistical machine translation. In *Proceedings of ACL*.

Omar F. Zaidan. 2009. Z-MERT: A fully configurable open source tool for minimum error rate training of machine translation systems. *The Prague Bulletin of Mathematical Linguistics*, 91:79–88.

An Improved Statistical Transfer System for French–English Machine Translation

Greg Hanneman, Vamshi Ambati, Jonathan H. Clark, Alok Parlikar, Alon Lavie
Language Technologies Institute
Carnegie Mellon University
Pittsburgh, PA 15213 USA
{ghannema, vamshi, jhclark, aup, alavie}@cs.cmu.edu

Abstract

This paper presents the Carnegie Mellon University statistical transfer MT system submitted to the 2009 WMT shared task in French-to-English translation. We describe a syntax-based approach that incorporates both syntactic and non-syntactic phrase pairs in addition to a syntactic grammar. After reporting development test results, we conduct a preliminary analysis of the coverage and effectiveness of the system's components.

1 Introduction

The statistical transfer machine translation group at Carnegie Mellon University has been developing a hybrid approach combining a traditional rule-based MT system and its linguistically expressive formalism with more modern techniques of statistical data processing and search-based decoding. The Stat-XFER framework (Lavie, 2008) provides a general environment for building new MT systems of this kind. For a given language pair or data condition, the framework depends on two main resources extracted from parallel data: a probabilistic bilingual lexicon, and a grammar of probabilistic synchronous context-free grammar rules. Additional monolingual data, in the form of an n-gram language model in the target language, is also used. The statistical transfer framework operates in two stages. First, the lexicon and grammar are applied to synchronously parse and translate an input sentence; all reordering is applied during this stage, driven by the syntactic grammar. Second, a monotonic decoder runs over the lattice of scored translation pieces produced during parsing and assembles the highest-scoring overall translation according to a log-linear feature model.

Since our submission to last year's Workshop on Machine Translation shared translation task (Hanneman et al., 2008), we have made numerous improvements and extensions to our resource extraction and processing methods, resulting in significantly improved translation scores. In Section 2 of this paper, we trace our current methods for data resource management for the Stat-XFER submission to the 2009 WMT shared French–English translation task. Section 3 explains our tuning procedure, and Section 4 gives our experimental results on various development sets and offers some preliminary analysis.

2 System Construction

Because of the additional data resources provided for the 2009 French–English task, our system this year is trained on nearly eight times as much data as last year's. We used three officially provided data sets to make up a parallel corpus for system training: version 4 of the Europarl corpus (1.43 million sentence pairs), the News Commentary corpus (0.06 million sentence pairs), and the pre-release version of the new Giga-FrEn corpus (8.60 million sentence pairs)[1]. The combined corpus of 10.09 million sentence pairs was preprocessed to remove blank lines, sentences of 80 words or more, and sentence pairs where the ratio between the number of English and French words was larger than 5 to 1 in either direction. These steps removed approximately 3% of the corpus. Given the filtered corpus, our data preparation pipeline proceeded according to the descriptions below.

[1] Because of data processing time, we were unable to use the larger verions 1 or 2 of Giga-FrEn released later in the evaluation period.

Proceedings of the Fourth Workshop on Statistical Machine Translation , pages 140–144,
Athens, Greece, 30 March – 31 March 2009.

2.1 Parsing and Word Alignment

We parsed both sides of our parallel corpus with independent automatic constituency parsers. We used the Berkeley parser (Petrov and Klein, 2007) for both English and French, although we obtained better results for French by tokenizing the data with our own script as a preprocessing step and not allowing the parser to change it. There were approximately 220,000 English sentences that did not return a parse, which further reduced the size of our training corpus by 2%.

After parsing, we re-extracted the leaf nodes of the parse trees and statistically word-aligned the corpus using a multi-threaded implementation (Gao and Vogel, 2008) of the GIZA++ program (Och and Ney, 2003). Unidirectional alignments were symmetrized with the "grow-diag-final" heuristic (Koehn et al., 2005).

2.2 Phrase Extraction and Combination

Phrase extraction for last year's statistical transfer system used automatically generated parse trees on both sides of the corpus as absolute constraints: a syntactic phrase pair was extracted from a given sentence only when a contiguous sequence of English words exactly made up a syntactic constituent in the English parse tree and could also be traced though symmetric word alignments to a constituent in the French parse tree. While this "tree-to-tree" extraction method is precise, it suffers from low recall and results in a low-coverage syntactic phrase table. Our 2009 system uses an extended "tree-to-tree-string" extraction process (Ambati and Lavie, 2008) in which, if no suitable equivalent is found in the French parse tree for an English node, a copy of the English node is projected into the French tree, where it spans the French words aligned to the yield of the English node. This method can result in a 50% increase in the number of extracted syntactic phrase pairs. Each extracted phrase pair retains a syntactic category label; in our current system, the node label in the English parse tree is used as the category for both sides of the bilingual phrase pair, although we subsequently map the full set of labels used by the Berkeley parser down to a more general set of 19 syntactic categories.

We also ran "standard" phrase extraction on the same corpus using Steps 4 and 5 of the Moses statistical machine translation training script (Koehn et al., 2007). The two types of phrases were then merged in a syntax-prioritized combination that removes all Moses-extracted phrase pairs that have source sides already covered by the tree-to-tree-string syntactic phrase extraction. The syntax prioritization has the advantage of still including a selection of non-syntactic phrases while producing a much smaller phrase table than a direct combination of all phrase pairs of both types. Previous experiments we conducted indicated that this comes with only a minor drop in automatic metric scores.

In our current submission, we modify the procedure slightly by removing singleton phrase pairs from the syntactic table before the combination with Moses phrases. The coverage of the combined table is not affected — our syntactic phrase extraction algorithm produces a subset of the non-syntactic phrase pairs extracted from Moses, up to phrase length constraints — but the removal allows Moses-extracted versions of some phrases to survive syntax prioritization. In effect, we are limiting the set of category-labeled syntactic translations we trust to those that have been seen more than once in our training data. For a given syntactic phrase pair, we also remove all but the most frequent syntactic category label for the pair; this removes a small number of entries from our lexicon in order to limit label ambiguity, but does not affect coverage.

From our training data, we extracted 27.6 million unique syntactic phrase pairs after singleton removal, reducing this set to 27.0 million entries after filtering for category label ambiguity. Some 488.7 million unique phrase pairs extracted from Moses were reduced to 424.0 million after syntax prioritization. (The remaining 64.7 million phrase pairs had source sides already covered by the 27.0 million syntactically extracted phrase pairs, so they were thrown out.) This means non-syntactic phrases outnumber syntactic phrases by nearly 16 to 1. However, when filtering the phrase table to a particular development or test set, we find the syntactic phrases play a larger role, as this ratio drops to approximately 3 to 1.

Sample phrase pairs from our system are shown in Figure 1. Each pair includes two rule scores, which we calculate from the source-side syntactic category (c_s), source-side text (w_s), target-side category (c_t), and target-side text (w_t). In the case of Moses-extracted phrase pairs, we use the "dummy" syntactic category PHR. Rule score $r_{t|s}$ is a maximum likelihood estimate of the distri-

c_s	c_t	w_s	w_t	$r_{t\|s}$	$r_{s\|t}$
ADJ	ADJ	espagnols	Spanish	0.8278	0.1141
N	N	représentants	officials	0.0653	0.1919
NP	NP	représentants de la Commission	Commission officials	0.0312	0.0345
PHR	PHR	haute importance à	very important to	0.0357	0.0008
PHR	PHR	est chargé de	has responsibility for	0.0094	0.0760

Figure 1: Sample lexical entries, including non-syntactic phrases, with rule scores (Equations 1 and 2).

bution of target-language translations and source- and target-language syntactic categories given the source string (Equation 1). The $r_{s|t}$ score is similar, but calculated in the reverse direction to give a source-given-target probability (Equation 2).

$$r_{t|s} = \frac{\#(w_t, c_t, w_s, c_s)}{\#(w_s) + 1} \quad (1)$$

$$r_{s|t} = \frac{\#(w_t, c_t, w_s, c_s)}{\#(w_t) + 1} \quad (2)$$

Add-one smoothing in the denominators counteracts overestimation of the rule scores of lexical entries with very infrequent source or target sides.

2.3 Syntactic Grammar

Syntactic phrase extraction specifies a node-to-node alignment across parallel parse trees. If these aligned nodes are used as decomposition points, a set of synchronous context-free rules that produced the trees can be collected. This is our process of syntactic grammar extraction (Lavie et al., 2008). For our 2009 WMT submission, we extracted 11.0 million unique grammar rules, 9.1 million of which were singletons, from our parallel parsed corpus. These rules operate on our syntactically extracted phrase pairs, which have category labels, but they may also be partially lexicalized with explicit source or target word strings. Each extracted grammar rule is scored according to Equations 1 and 2, where now the right-hand sides of the rule are used as w_s and w_t.

As yet, we have made only minimal use of the Stat-XFER framework's grammar capabilities, especially for large-scale MT systems. For the current submission, the syntactic grammar consisted of 26 manually chosen high-frequency grammar rules that carry out some reordering between English and French. Since rules for high-level reordering (near the top of the parse tree) are unlikely to be useful unless a large amount of parse structure can first be built, we concentrate our rules on low-level reorderings taking place within or around small constituents. Our focus for this selection is the well-known repositioning of adjectives and adjective phrases when translating from French to English, such as from *le Parlement européen* to *the European Parliament* or from *l' intervention forte et substantielle* to *the strong and substantial intervention*. Our grammar thus consists of 23 rules for building noun phrases, two rules for building adjective phrases, and one rule for building verb phrases.

2.4 English Language Model

We built a suffix-array language model (Zhang and Vogel, 2006) on approximately 700 million words of monolingual data: the unfiltered English side of our parallel training corpus, plus the 438 million words of English monolingual news data provided for the WMT 2009 shared task. With the relatively large amount of data available, we made the somewhat unusual decision of building our language model (and all other data resources for our system) in mixed case, which adds approximately 12.3% to our vocabulary size. This saves us the need to build and run a recaser as a postprocessing step on our output. Our mixed-case decision may also be validated by preliminary test set results, which show that our submission has the smallest drop in BLEU score (0.0074) between uncased and cased evaluation of any system in the French–English translation task.

3 System Tuning

Stat-XFER uses a log-linear combination of seven features in its scoring of translation fragments: language model probability, source-given-target and target-given-source rule probabilities, source-given-target and target-given-source lexical probabilities, a length score, and a fragmentation score based on the number of parsed translation fragments that make up the output sentence. We tune the weights for these features with several rounds of minimum error rate training, optimizing to-

Data Set	Primary			Contrastive		
	METEOR	BLEU	TER	METEOR	BLEU	TER
news-dev2009a-425	0.5437	0.2299	60.45	—	—	—
news-dev2009a-600	—	—	—	0.5134	0.2055	63.46
news-dev2009b	0.5263	0.2073	61.96	0.5303	0.2104	61.74
nc-test2007	0.6194	0.3282	51.17	0.6195	0.3226	51.49

Figure 2: Primary and contrastive system results on tuning and development test sets.

wards the BLEU metric. For each tuning iteration, we save the n-best lists output by the system from previous iterations and concatenate them onto the current n-best list in order to present the optimizer with a larger variety of translation outputs and score values.

From the provided "news-dev2009a" development set we create two tuning sets: one using the first 600 sentences of the data, and a second using the remaining 425 sentences. We tuned our system separately on each set, saving the additional "news-dev2009b" set as a final development test to choose our primary and contrastive submissions[2]. At run time, our full system takes on average between four and seven seconds to translate each input sentence, depending on the size of the final bilingual lexicon.

4 Evaluation and Analysis

Figure 2 shows the results of our primary and contrastive systems on four data sets. First, we report final (tuned) performance on our two tuning sets — the last 425 sentences of news-dev2009a for the primary system, and the first 600 sentences of the same set for the contrastive. We also include our development test (news-dev2009b) and, for additional comparison, the "nc-test2007" news commentary test set from the 2007 WMT shared task. For each, we give case-insensitive scores on version 0.6 of METEOR (Lavie and Agarwal, 2007) with all modules enabled, version 1.04 of IBM-style BLEU (Papineni et al., 2002), and version 5 of TER (Snover et al., 2006).

From these results, we highlight two interesting areas of analysis. First, the low tuning and development test set scores bring up questions about system coverage, given that the news domain was not strongly represented in our system's training data. We indeed find a significantly larger proportion of out-of-vocabulary (OOV) words in news-domain sets: the news-dev2009b set is translated by our primary submission with 402 of 6263 word types (6.42%) or 601 of 27,821 word tokens (2.16%) unknown. The same system running on the 2007 WMT "test2007" set of Europarl-derived data records an OOV rate of only 87 of 7514 word types (1.16%) or 105 of 63,741 word tokens (0.16%).

Second, we turn our attention to the usefulness of the syntactic grammar. Though small, we find it to be both beneficial and precise. In the 1026-sentence news-dev2009b set, for example, we find 351 rule applications — the vast majority of them (337) building noun phrases. The three most frequently occurring rules are those for reordering the sequence [DET N ADJ] to [DET ADJ N] (52 occurrences), the sequence [N ADJ] to [ADJ N] (51 occurrences), and the sequence [N^1 *de* N^2] to [N^2 N^1] (45 occurrences). We checked precision by manually reviewing the 52 rule applications in the first 150 sentences of news-dev2009b. There, 41 of the occurrences (79%) were judged to be correct and beneficial to translation output. Of the remainder, seven were judged incorrect or detrimental and four were judged either neutral or of unclear benefit.

We expect to continue to analyze the output and effectiveness of our system in the coming months. In particular, we would like to learn more about the usefulness of our 26-rule grammar with the view of using significantly larger grammars in future versions of our system.

Acknowledgments

This research was supported in part by NSF grants IIS-0121631 (AVENUE) and IIS-0534217 (LETRAS), and by the DARPA GALE program. We thank Yahoo! for the use of the M45 research computing cluster, where we ran the parsing stage of our data processing.

[2]Due to a data processing error, the choice of the primary submission was based on incorrectly computed scores. In fact, the contrastive system has better performance on our development test set.

References

Vamshi Ambati and Alon Lavie. 2008. Improving syntax driven translation models by re-structuring divergent and non-isomorphic parse tree structures. In *Proceedings of the Eighth Conference of the Association for Machine Translation in the Americas*, pages 235–244, Waikiki, HI, October.

Qin Gao and Stephan Vogel. 2008. Parallel implementations of word alignment tool. In *Software Engineering, Testing, and Quality Assurance for Natural Language Processing*, pages 49–57, Columbus, OH, June.

Greg Hanneman, Edmund Huber, Abhaya Agarwal, Vamshi Ambati, Alok Parlikar, Erik Peterson, and Alon Lavie. 2008. Statistical transfer systems for French–English and German–English machine translation. In *Proceedings of the Third Workshop on Statistical Machine Translation*, pages 163–166, Columbus, OH, June.

Philipp Koehn, Amittai Axelrod, Alexandra Birch Mayne, Chris Callison-Burch, Miles Osborne, and David Talbot. 2005. Edinburgh system description for the 2005 IWSLT speech translation evaluation. In *Proceedings of IWSLT 2005*, Pittsburgh, PA, October.

Philipp Koehn, Hieu Hoang, Alexandra Birch, Chris Callison-Burch, Marcello Federico, Nicola Bertoldi, Brooke Cowan, Wade Shen, Christine Moran, Richard Zens, Chris Dyer, Ondrej Bojar, Alexandra Constantin, and Evan Herbst. 2007. Moses: Open source toolkit for statistical machine translation. In *Proceedings of the ACL 2007 Demo and Poster Sessions*, pages 177–180, Prague, Czech Republic, June.

Alon Lavie and Abhaya Agarwal. 2007. METEOR: An automatic metric for MT evaluation with high levels of correlation with human judgments. In *Proceedings of the Second Workshop on Statistical Machine Translation*, pages 228–231, Prague, Czech Republic, June.

Alon Lavie, Alok Parlikar, and Vamshi Ambati. 2008. Syntax-driven learning of sub-sentential translation equivalents and translation rules from parsed parallel corpora. In *Proceedings of the Second ACL Workshop on Syntax and Structure in Statistical Translation*, pages 87–95, Columbus, OH, June.

Alon Lavie. 2008. Stat-XFER: A general search-based syntax-driven framework for machine translation. In *Computational Linguistics and Intelligent Text Processing*, Lecture Notes in Computer Science, pages 362–375. Springer.

Franz Josef Och and Hermann Ney. 2003. A systematic comparison of various statistical alignment models. *Computational Linguistics*, 29(1):19–51.

Kishore Papineni, Salim Roukos, Todd Ward, and Wei-Jing Zhu. 2002. BLEU: A method for automatic evalution of machine translation. In *Proceedings of the 40th Annual Meeting of the Association for Computational Linguistics*, pages 311–318, Philadelphia, PA, July.

Slav Petrov and Dan Klein. 2007. Improved inference for unlexicalized parsing. In *Proceedings of NAACL HLT 2007*, pages 404–411, Rochester, NY, April.

Matthew Snover, Bonnie Dorr, Richard Schwartz, Linnea Micciulla, and John Makhoul. 2006. A study of translation edit rate with targeted human annotation. In *Proceedings of the Seventh Conference of the Association for Machine Translation in the Americas*, pages 223–231, Cambridge, MA, August.

Ying Zhang and Stephan Vogel. 2006. Suffix array and its applications in empirical natural language processing. Technical Report CMU-LTI-06-010, Carnegie Mellon University, Pittsburgh, PA, December.

The University of Maryland Statistical Machine Translation System for the Fourth Workshop on Machine Translation

Chris Dyer[*†], **Hendra Setiawan**[†], **Yuval Marton**[*†], **and Philip Resnik**[*†]
[†]UMIACS Laboratory for Computational Linguistics and Information Processing
[*]Department of Linguistics
University of Maryland, College Park, MD 20742, USA
{redpony, hendra, ymarton, resnik} AT umd.edu

Abstract

This paper describes the techniques we explored to improve the translation of news text in the German-English and Hungarian-English tracks of the WMT09 shared translation task. Beginning with a convention hierarchical phrase-based system, we found benefits for using word segmentation lattices as input, explicit generation of beginning and end of sentence markers, minimum Bayes risk decoding, and incorporation of a feature scoring the alignment of function words in the hypothesized translation. We also explored the use of monolingual paraphrases to improve coverage, as well as co-training to improve the quality of the segmentation lattices used, but these did not lead to improvements.

1 Introduction

For the shared translation task of the Fourth Workshop on Machine Translation (WMT09), we focused on two tasks: German to English and Hungarian to English translation. Despite belonging to different language families, German and Hungarian have three features in common that complicate translation into English:

1. productive compounding (especially of nouns),

2. rich inflectional morphology,

3. widespread mid- to long-range word order differences with respect to English.

Since these phenomena are poorly addressed with conventional approaches to statistical machine translation, we chose to work primarily toward mitigating their negative effects when constructing our systems. This paper is structured as follows. In Section 2 we describe the baseline model, Section 3 describes the various strategies we employed to address the challenges just listed, and Section 4 summarizes the final translation system.

2 Baseline system

Our translation system makes use of a hierarchical phrase-based translation model (Chiang, 2007), which we argue is a strong baseline for these language pairs. First, such a system makes use of lexical information when modeling reordering (Lopez, 2008), which has previously been shown to be useful in German-to-English translation (Koehn et al., 2008). Additionally, since the decoder is based on a CKY parser, it can consider all licensed reorderings of the input in polynomial time, and German and Hungarian may require quite substantial reordering. Although such decoders and models have been common for several years, there have been no published results for these language pairs.

The baseline system translates lowercased and tokenized source sentences into lowercased target sentences. The features used were the rule translation relative frequency $P(\bar{e}|\bar{f})$, the "lexical" translation probabilities $P_{lex}(\bar{e}|\bar{f})$ and $P_{lex}(\bar{f}|\bar{e})$, a rule count, a target language word count, the target (English) language model $P(e_1^I)$, and a "pass-through" penalty for passing a source language word to the target side.[1] The rule feature values were computed online during decoding using the suffix array method described by Lopez (2007).

[1]The "pass-through" penalty was necessary since the English language modeling data contained a large amount of source-language text.

Proceedings of the Fourth Workshop on Statistical Machine Translation , pages 145–149,
Athens, Greece, 30 March – 31 March 2009.

2.1 Training and development data

To construct the translation suffix arrays used to compute the translation grammar, we used the parallel training data provided. The preprocessed training data was filtered for length and aligned using the GIZA++ implementation of IBM Model 4 (Och and Ney, 2003) in both directions and symmetrized using the `grow-diag-final-and` heuristic. We trained a 5-gram language model from the provided English monolingual training data and the non-Europarl portions of the parallel training data using modified Kneser-Ney smoothing as implemented in the SRI language modeling toolkit (Kneser and Ney, 1995; Stolcke, 2002). We divided the 2008 workshop "news test" sets into two halves of approximately 1000 sentences each and designated one the dev set and the other the dev-test set.

2.2 Automatic evaluation metric

Since the official evaluation criterion for WMT09 is human sentence ranking, we chose to minimize a linear combination of two common evaluation metrics, BLEU and TER (Papineni et al., 2002; Snover et al., 2006), during system development and tuning:

$$\frac{\text{TER} - \text{BLEU}}{2}$$

Although we are not aware of any work demonstrating that this combination of metrics correlates better than either individually in sentence ranking, Yaser Al-Onaizan (personal communication) reports that it correlates well with the human evaluation metric HTER. In this paper, we report uncased TER and BLEU individually.

2.3 Forest minimum error training

To tune the feature weights of our system, we used a variant of the minimum error training algorithm (Och, 2003) that computes the error statistics from the target sentences from the translation search space (represented by a *packed forest*) that are exactly those that are minimally discriminable by changing the feature weights along a single vector in the dimensions of the feature space (Macherey et al., 2008). The loss function we used was the linear combination of TER and BLEU described in the previous section.

3 Experimental variations

This section describes the experimental variants explored.

3.1 Word segmentation lattices

Both German and Hungarian have a large number of compound words that are created by concatenating several morphemes to form a single orthographic token. To deal with productive compounding, we employ *word segmentation lattices*, which are word lattices that encode alternative possible segmentations of compound words. Doing so enables us to use possibly inaccurate approaches to guess the segmentation of compound words, allowing the decoder to decide which to use during translation. This is a further development of our general source-lattice approach to decoding (Dyer et al., 2008).

To construct the segmentation lattices, we define a log-linear model of compound word segmentation inspired by Koehn and Knight (2003), making use of features including number of morphemes hypothesized, frequency of the segments as free-standing morphemes in a training corpus, and letters in each segment. To tune the model parameters, we selected a set of compound words from a subset of the German development set, manually created a linguistically plausible segmentation of these words, and used this to select the parameters of the log-linear model using a lattice minimum error training algorithm to minimize WER (Macherey et al., 2008). We reused the same features and weights to create the Hungarian lattices. For the test data, we created a lattice of every possible segmentation of any word 6 characters or longer and used forward-backward pruning to prune out low-probability segmentation paths (Sixtus and Ortmanns, 1999). We then concatenated the lattices in each sentence.

Source	Condition	BLEU	TER
German	baseline	20.8	60.7
	lattice	**21.3**	**59.9**
Hungarian	baseline	11.0	71.1
	lattice	**12.3**	**70.4**

Table 1: Impact of compound segmentation lattices.

To build the translation model for lattice system, we segmented the training data using the one-best split predicted by the segmentation model, and word aligned this with the English side. This variant version of the training data was then concatenated with the baseline system's training data.

3.1.1 Co-training of segmentation model

To avoid the necessity of manually creating segmentation examples to train the segmentation model, we attempted to generate sets of training examples by selecting the compound splits that were found along the path chosen by the decoder's one-best translation. Unfortunately, the segmentation system generated in this way performed slightly worse than the one-best baseline and so we continued to use the parameter settings derived from the manual segmentation.

3.2 Modeling sentence boundaries

Incorporating an n-gram language model probability into a CKY-based decoder is challenging. When a partial hypothesis (also called an "item") has been completed, it has not yet been determined what strings will eventually occur to the left of its first word, meaning that the exact computation must deferred, which makes pruning a challenge. In typical CKY decoders, the beginning and ends of the sentence (which often have special characteristics) are not conclusively determined until the whole sentence has been translated and the probabilities for the beginning and end sentence probabilities can be added. However, by this point it is often the case that a possibly better sentence beginning has been pruned away. To address this, we explicitly generate beginning and end sentence markers as part of the translation process, as suggested by Xiong et al. (2008). The results of doing this are shown in Table 2.

Source	Condition	BLEU	TER
German	baseline	21.3	**59.9**
	+boundary	**21.6**	60.1
Hungarian	baseline	12.3	70.4
	+boundary	**12.8**	**70.4**

Table 2: Impact of modeling sentence boundaries.

3.3 Source language paraphrases

In order to deal with the sparsity associated with a rich source language morphology and limited-size parallel corpora (bitexts), we experimented with a novel approach to paraphrasing out-of-vocabulary (OOV) source language phrases in our Hungarian-English system, using monolingual contextual similarity rather than phrase-table pivoting (Callison-Burch et al., 2006) or monolingual bitexts (Barzilay and McKeown, 2001; Dolan et al., 2004). Distributional profiles for source phrases were represented as context vectors over a sliding window of size 6, with vectors defined using log-likelihood ratios (cf. Rapp (1999), Dunning (1993)) but using cosine rather than city-block distance to measure profile similarity.

The 20 distributionally most similar source phrases were treated as paraphrases, considering candidate phrases up to a width of 6 tokens and filtering out paraphrase candidates with cosine similarity to the original of less than 0.6. The two most likely translations for each paraphrase were added to the grammar in order to provide mappings to English for OOV Hungarian phrases.

This attempt at monolingually-derived source-side paraphrasing did not yield improvements over baseline. Preliminary analysis suggests that the approach does well at identifying many content words in translating extracted paraphrases of OOV phrases (e.g., *a kommunista part vezetaje* $\Rightarrow$, *leader of the communist party* or *a ra tervezett* $\Rightarrow$ *until the planned to*), but at the cost of more frequently omitting target words in the output.

3.4 Dominance feature

Although our baseline hierarchical system permits long-range reordering, it lacks a mechanism to identify the most appropriate reordering for a specific sentence translation. For example, when the most appropriate reordering is a long-range one, our baseline system often also has to consider shorter-range reorderings as well. In the worst case, a shorter-range reordering has a high probability, causing the wrong reordering to be chosen. Our baseline system lacks the capacity to address such cases because all the features it employs are independent of the phrases being moved; these are modeled only as an unlexicalized generic nonterminal symbol.

To address this challenge, we included what we call a *dominance feature* in the scoring of hypothesis translations. Briefly, the premise of this feature is that the function words in the sentence hold the key reordering information, and therefore function words are used to model the phrases being moved. The feature assesses the quality of a reordering by looking at the phrase alignment between pairs of function words. In our experiments, we treated the 128 most frequent words in the corpus as function words, similar to Setiawan et al. (2007). Due to space constraints, we will discuss the details in another publication. As Table 3 reports, the use of this feature yields positive results.

Source	Condition	BLEU	TER
German	baseline	21.6	60.1
	+dom	**22.2**	**59.8**
Hungarian	baseline	**12.8**	70.4
	+dom	12.6	**70.0**

Table 3: Impact of alignment dominance feature.

3.5 Minimum Bayes risk decoding

Although during minimum error training we assume a decoder that uses the maximum derivation decision rule, we find benefits to translating using a *minimum risk* decision rule on a test set (Kumar and Byrne, 2004). This seeks the translation E of the input lattice $\mathcal{F}$ that has the least *expected loss*, measured by some loss function L:

$$\hat{E} = \arg\min_{E'} \mathbb{E}_{P(E|\mathcal{F})}[L(E, E')] \quad (1)$$

$$= \arg\min_{E'} \sum_{E} P(E|\mathcal{F}) L(E, E') \quad (2)$$

We approximate the posterior distribution $P(E|\mathcal{F})$ and the set of possible candidate translations using the unique 500-best translations of a source lattice $\mathcal{F}$. If $H(E, \mathcal{F})$ is the decoder's path weight, this is:

$$P(E|\mathcal{F}) \propto \exp \alpha H(E, \mathcal{F})$$

The optimal value for the free parameter α must be experimentally determined and depends on the ranges of the feature functions and weights used in the model, as well as the amount and kind of pruning using during decoding.[2] For our submission, we used $\alpha = 1$. Since our goal is to minimize $\frac{\text{TER}-\text{BLEU}}{2}$ we used this as the loss function in (2). Table 4 shows the results on the dev-test set for MBR decoding.

[2]If the free parameter α lies in $(1, \infty)$ the distribution is sharpened, if it lies in $[0, 1)$, the distribution is flattened.

Source	Decoder	BLEU	TER
German	Max-D	22.2	59.8
	MBR	**22.6**	**59.4**
Hungarian	Max-D	12.6	70.0
	MBR	**12.8**	**69.8**

Table 4: Performance of maximum derivation vs. MBR decoders.

4 Conclusion

Table 5 summarizes the impact on the dev-test set of all features included in the University of Maryland system submission.

Condition	German		Hungarian	
	BLEU	TER	BLEU	TER
baseline	20.8	60.7	11.0	71.1
+lattices	21.3	59.9	12.3	70.4
+boundary	21.6	60.1	12.8	70.4
+dom	22.2	59.8	12.6	70.0
+MBR	22.6	59.4	12.8	69.8

Table 5: Summary of all features

Acknowledgments

This research was supported in part by the GALE program of the Defense Advanced Research Projects Agency, Contract No. HR0011-06-2-001, and the Army Research Laboratory. Any opinions, findings, conclusions or recommendations expressed in this paper are those of the authors and do not necessarily reflect the view of the sponsors. Discussions with Chris Callison-Burch were helpful in carrying out the monolingual paraphrase work.

References

Regina Barzilay and Kathleen McKeown. 2001. Extracting paraphrases from a parallel corpus. In *In Proceedings of ACL-2001*.

Chris Callison-Burch, Philipp Koehn, and Miles Osborne. 2006. Improved statistical machine translation using paraphrases. In *Proceedings NAACL-2006*.

D. Chiang. 2007. Hierarchical phrase-based translation. *Computational Linguistics*, 33(2):201–228.

B. Dolan, C. Quirk, and C. Brockett. 2004. Unsupervised construction of large paraphrase corpora:

exploiting massively parallel news sources. In *Proceedings of the 20th International Conference on Computational Linguistics of the Association for Computational Linguistics*, Geneva, Switzerland.

T. Dunning. 1993. Accurate methods for the statistics of surprise and coincidence. *Computational Linguistics*, 19(1):61–74.

Chris Dyer, Smaranda Muresan, and Philip Resnik. 2008. Generalizing word lattice translation. In *Proceedings of ACL-08: HLT*. Association for Computational Linguistics, June.

R. Kneser and H. Ney. 1995. Improved backing-off for m-gram language modeling. In *Proceedings of IEEE Internation Conference on Acoustics, Speech, and Signal Processing*, pages 181–184.

P. Koehn and K. Knight. 2003. Empirical methods for compound splitting. In *Proceedings of the EACL 2003*.

Philipp Koehn, Abhishek Arun, and Hieu Hoang. 2008. Towards better machine translation quality for the German-English language pairs. In *ACL Workshop on Statistical Machine Translation*.

S. Kumar and W. Byrne. 2004. Minimum Bayes-risk decoding for statistical machine translation. In *Processings of HLT-NAACL*.

Adam Lopez. 2007. Hierarchical phrase-based translation with suffix arrays. In *Proceedings of the 2007 Joint Conference on Empirical Methods in Natural Language Processing and Computational Natural Language Learning (EMNLP-CoNLL)*, pages 976–985.

Adam Lopez. 2008. Tera-scale translation models via pattern matching. In *Proceedings of COLING*, Manchester, UK.

Wolfgang Macherey, Franz Josef Och, Ignacio Thayer, and Jakob Uszkoreit. 2008. Lattice-based minimum error rate training for statistical machine translation. In *Proceedings of EMNLP*, Honolulu, HI.

F. Och and H. Ney. 2003. A systematic comparison of various statistical alignment models. *Computational Linguistics*, 29(1):19–51.

F. Och. 2003. Minimum error rate training in statistical machine translation. In *Proceedings of the 41st Annual Meeting of the Association for Computational Linguistics (ACL)*, pages 160–167, Sapporo, Japan, July.

K. Papineni, S. Roukos, T. Ward, and W.-J. Zhu. 2002. BLEU: a method for automatic evaluation of machine translation. In *Proceedings of the 40th Annual Meeting of the ACL*, pages 311–318.

Reinhard Rapp. 1999. Automatic identification of word translations from unrelated English and German corpora. In *Proceedings of the 37th Annual Conference of the Association for Computational Linguistics.*, pages 519–525.

Hendra Setiawan, Min-Yen Kan, and Haizhao Li. 2007. Ordering phrases with function words. In *Proceedings of ACL*.

S. Sixtus and S. Ortmanns. 1999. High quality word graphs using forward-backward pruning. In *Proceedings of ICASSP*, Phoenix, AZ.

Matthew Snover, Bonnie J. Dorr, Richard Schwartz, Linnea Micciulla, and John Makhoul. 2006. A study of translation edit rate with targeted human annotation. In *Proceedings of Association for Machine Translation in the Americas*.

A. Stolcke. 2002. SRILM – an extensible language modeling toolkit. In *Intl. Conf. on Spoken Language Processing*.

Deyi Xiong, Min Zhang, Ai Ti Aw, Haitao Mi, Qun Liu, and Shouxun Lin. 2008. Refinements in BTG-based statistical machine translation. In *Proceedings of IJCNLP 2008*.

Toward Using Morphology in French-English Phrase-based SMT

Marine Carpuat
Center for Computational Learning Systems
Columbia University
475 Riverside Drive, New York, NY 10115
marine@ccls.columbia.edu

Abstract

We describe the system used in our submission to the WMT-2009 French-English translation task. We use the Moses phrase-based Statistical Machine Translation system with two simple modications of the decoding input and word-alignment strategy based on morphology, and analyze their impact on translation quality.

1 Introduction

In this first participation to the French-English translation task at WMT, our goal was to build a standard phrase-based statistical machine translation system and study the impact of French morphological variations at different stages of training and decoding.

Many strategies have been proposed to integrate morphology information in SMT, including factored translation models (Koehn and Hoang, 2007), adding a translation dictionary containing inflected forms to the training data (Schwenk *et al.*, 2008), entirely replacing surface forms by representations built on lemmas and POS tags (Popović and Ney, 2004), morphemes learned in an unsupervised manner (Virpojia *et al.*, 2007), and using Porter stems and even 4-letter prefixes for word alignment (Watanabe *et al.*, 2006). In non-European languages, such as Arabic, heavy effort has been put in identifying appropriate input representations to improve SMT quality (e.g., Sadat and Habash (2006))

As a first step toward using morphology information in our French-English SMT system, this submission focused on studying the impact of different input representations for French based on the POS and lemmatization provided by the Treetagger tool (Schmid, 1994). In the WMT09 French-English data sets, we observe that more than half of the words that are unknown in the translation lexicon actually occur in the training data under different inflected forms. We show that combining a lemma backoff strategy at decoding time and improving alignments by generalizing across verb surface forms improves OOV rates and translation quality.

*The author was partially funded by GALE DARPA Contract No. HR0011-06-C-0023. Any opinions, findings and conclusions or recommendations expressed in this material are those of the authors and do not necessarily reflect the views of the Defense Advanced Research Projects Agency.

2 Translation system

2.1 Data sets

We use a subset of the data made available for the official French to English translation task. The evaluation test set consists of French news data from September to October 2008, however the bulk of the training data is not from the same domain. The translation model was trained on the Europarl corpus (europarl-v4) and the small news commentary corpus (news-commentary09). Following Déchelotte *et al.* (2008), we learn a single phrase table and reordering model rather than one for each domain, as it was found to yield better performance in a very similar setting. The language model was trained on the English side of these parallel corpora augmented with non-parallel English news data (news-train08.en). Parameter tuning was performed on the designated development data, which is also in the news domain: news-dev2009a was used as the development set and news-dev2009b as the test set.

Using those data sets, there is therefore a mismatch between the training and evaluation domains, as in the domain adaptation tasks of the previous WMT evaluations. A large automatically extracted parallel corpus was made available, but we were not able to use it due to time constraints. Additional use of this in-domain data would im-

Proceedings of the Fourth Workshop on Statistical Machine Translation , pages 150–154,
Athens, Greece, 30 March – 31 March 2009. ©2009 Association for Computational Linguistics

prove coverage and translation quality.

2.2 Preprocessing

French and English corpora processing followed the same three steps:

First, long sentences are resegmented using simple punctuation-based heuristics.

Second, tokenization, POS tagging and lemmatization are performed with Treetagger (Schmid, 1994) using the standard French and English parameter files[1]. Treetagger is based on Hidden Markov Models where transition probabilities are estimated with decision trees. The POS tag set consists of 33 tags which capture tense information for verbs, but not gender and number.

Third, sentence-initial capitalized words are normalized to their most frequent form as reported by Zollmann *et al.* (2006).

2.3 Core system

We use the Moses phrase-based statistical machine translation system (Koehn *et al.*, 2007) and follow standard training, tuning and decoding strategies.

The translation model consists of a standard Moses phrase-table with lexicalized reordering. Bidirectional word alignments obtained with GIZA++ are intersected using the grow-diag-final heuristic. Translations of phrases of up to 7 words long are collected and scored with translation probilities and lexical weighting.

The English language model is a 4-gram model with Kneser-Ney smoothing, built with the SRI language modeling toolkit (Stolcke, 2002).

The loglinear model feature weights were learned using minimum error rate training (MERT) (Och, 2003) with BLEU score (Papineni *et al.*, 2002) as the objective function.

Other decoding parameters were selected manually on an earlier version of the system trained and evaluated on the single-domain Europarl data. While the configuration achieved competitive results on the previous, it is not be optimal for this domain adaptation task.

We will first conduct an analysis of this core SMT system, and experiment with two modifications of input representation for decoding and alignment respectively.

[1] www.ims.uni-stuttgart.de/projekte/corplex/TreeTagger/

OOV verbs	**w/ surface form in training corpus**	**w/ lemma+ POS in training corpus**
dev2009a	21 (28%)	48 (63%)
dev2009b	16 (24%)	33 (49%)

Table 1: Unknown verbs statistics

3 Many unknown words are (almost) seen in training

Our baseline system is set up to copy unknown words to the output. This is a helpful strategy to translate unknown names and cognates, but is far from optimal. In this section, we take a closer look at those unknown words.

About 25% of the dev and test set sentences contain at least one unknown token. After eliminating number expressions, which can be handled with translation rules, the majority of unknown words are content words, nouns, verbs and adjectives. As reported in Table 1, we find that many of the verbs that are not in the phrase-table vocabulary were actually seen in the training data in the exact same form: they are therefore out of vocabulary due to alignment errors. In addition, for more than half of the unknown verb occurrences, another inflexion form for the same lemma and POS tag are observed in the training corpus.

Using only the surface form of words therefore leads us to ignore potentially useful information available in our training corpus. Additional training data would naturally improve coverage, but will not cover all possible morphological variations of all verbs, especially for tenses and persons that are not used frequently in news coverage. It is therefore necessary to generalize beyond word surface forms.

4 Using morphological information in decoding

A simple strategy for handling unknown words at decoding time consists in replacing their occurrences in the test set with their lemma, when it is part of the translation lexicon vocabulary. Unlike with factored models (Koehn and Hoang, 2007) or additional translation lexicons (Schwenk *et al.*, 2008), we do not generate the surface form back from the lemma translation, which means that tense, gender and number information are

news-dev2009a	representation	OOV %	METEOR	BLEU	NIST
baseline	surface form only	*2.24*	*49.05*	*20.45*	*6.135*
decoding	lemma backoff	2.13	49.12	20.44	6.143
word alignment	lemma+POS for all	2.24	48.87	20.36	6.145
	lemma+POS for adj	2.25	48.94	20.46	6.131
	lemma+POS for verbs	2.21	49.05	20.47	6.137
decoding + alignment	backoff + all	2.10	48.97	20.36	6.147
	backoff + adj	2.12	49.05	20.48	6.140
	backoff + verbs	**2.08**	**49.15**	**20.50**	**6.148**
news-dev2009b	**representation**	**OOV %**	**METEOR**	**BLEU**	**NIST**
baseline	surface form only	*2.52*	*49.60*	**21.10**	*6.211*
decoding	lemma backoff	2.43	49.66	21.02	6.210
word alignment	lemma+POS for all	2.53	49.56	21.03	6.199
	lemma+POS for adj	2.52	49.74	21.00	6.213
	lemma+POS for verbs	2.47	49.73	**21.10**	**6.217**
decoding+alignment	backoff + all	2.44	49.59	20.92	6.194
	backoff + adj	2.43	49.80	21.03	**6.217**
	backoff + verbs	**2.39**	**49.80**	21.03	**6.217**

Table 2: Evaluation of the decoding backoff strategy, the modified word alignment strategy and their combination

Input	Même s'il démissionnait, la situation ne changerait pas.
Baseline	even if it *démissionnait*, the situation will not change.
Lemma backoff	even if it **resign**, the situation will not change.
Reference	even if he resigned, the situation would remain the same.
Input	Tant que tu gagnes, on te laisse en paix
Baseline	As you *gagnes*, it leaves you in peace
Lemma backoff	As you **win**, it leaves you in peace
Reference	As Long as You Gain, We Let You
Input	Le groupe a réagi comme il faut, il a sorti un nouveau et meilleur disque.
Baseline	The group has reacted properly, it has *emerged* a new and better records.
Lemma+POS for verbs	The group has reacted properly, it has **produced** a new and better records.
Reference	The group responded with a new and even better CD.
Input	Un trader qui ne prend pas de vacances est un trader qui ne veut pas laisser son book à un autre", conclut Kerviel.
Baseline	A senior trader which does not take holiday is a senior trader which does not *allow* his book to another, " concludes Kerviel.
Lemma+POS for verbs	A senior trader which does not take holiday is a senior trader who do not wish to **leave** his book to another, " concludes Kerviel.
Reference	A broker who does not take vacations is a broker who does not want anybody to look into his records," Kerviel concluded.

Table 3: Examples of improved translations by morphological analysis

Input	54 pour cent ne font pas du tout confiance au premier ministre et 27 pour cent au président du Fidesz.
Baseline	54% are not all confidence to Prime Minister and the President of Fidesz 1.27%.
Backoff + verbs	54% do not all confidence to Prime Minister and 27% to the President of Fidesz.
Reference	Fifty-four percent said they did not trust the PM, while 27 percent said they mistrusted the Fidesz chairman.
Input	Le prsident Václav Klaus s'est nouveau prononc sur la problématique du rchauffement plantaire.
Baseline	President Václav Klaus has once again voted on the problem of global warming.
Backoff+verbs	President Václav Klaus has again pronounced on the problem of global warming.
Reference	President Václav Klaus has again commented on the problem of global warming.
Input	Mais les supérieurs étaient au courant de tout, ou plutôt, ils s'en doutaient.
Baseline	But superiors were aware of everything, or rather, they knew.
Backoff+verbs	But superiors were aware of everything, or rather, they doubted.
Reference	But his superiors are said to have known, or rather suspected the whole thing.

Table 4: Examples of translations that are not improved morphological analysis

lost. However, imperfect lemma translations can be more useful to understand the meaning of the input sentence than copying the unknown word to the output.

We report the impact of this strategy on automatic evaluation scores in the decoding section of Table 2. Since only a small subset of the test sentences are affected by the change, the score variation is small, but the OOV rate decreases and translation quality is not degraded. In addition to the BLEU and NIST n-gram precision metrics which only count exact matches between system output and reference, we report METEOR scores which take into account matches after lemmatization using both the Porter stemmer and the WordNet lemmas (Banerjee and Lavie, 2005). The improvement in METEOR scores results from more matches with the references, yielding both improved precision and recall.

Manual inspection of the output sentences shows that the translations are better to the human eye and potentially more useful to subsequent text understanding applications (Table 3).

5 Using morphological information in word-alignment

In this experiment, we would like to use morphological analysis to alleviate the alignment errors because of which some words from the parallel corpus are not in the phrase-table. We adopt a two-step approach: (1) before word alignment, replace surface forms by lemma and POS tags. In our experiments, this replacement is performed for 3 categories of words: verbs only, adjectives only and all words. (2) the phrase-table and reordering models are learned as usual using word surface forms, but with the alignment links from step 1.

In constrast with Watanabe *et al.* (2006), we attempt to generalize for specific word categories only, rather than use lemmas across all surface forms, as we found in earlier experiments that this approach did not help translation quality in our particular setting.

Unlike other approaches which use morphological analysis to change the representation of the input (e.g., Popović and Ney (2004), Sadat and Habash (2006), Virpojia *et al.* (2007)), our system still uses word surface forms as input during decoding. This is a constraint imposed by the relatively coarse analysis given by the default Treetagger lemmas and POS tags. Since they do not capture information that is crucial in translation such as number and gender, we need to keep surface forms as the input for translation.

The impact of this strategy on automatic evaluation metrics is reported in the word alignment section of Table 2. Note that all experiments were performed using the parameters learned by MERT on news-dev2009a using the baseline configuration. Again the impact in numbers is small, but does not degrade translation quality. The METEOR score is slightly improved on the real test set. As expected given our POS tag set, it seems better to restrict the modifications of the input for word alignment to verbs or adjectives.

This simple modification of the training procedure improves the coverage of the phrase-table, but the OOV rate remains higher than with the lemma backoff strategy. For the news-dev2009b test set, 1186 additional phrases are available in the phrase-table after replacing verb surface forms by their lemma and POS combination. About half of the test sentences are changed. As reflected by the scores, most of the changes are small and do not yield significantly different sentences. However, some translations are improved as can be seen in Table 3.

The impact of both strategies combined is reported in the decoding + alignment section of Table 2. Tables 3 and 4 show positive and negative examples of translations using the best combination.

6 Conclusion

We have described the system used for our submission, which is based on Moses with two simple modifications of the decoding input and word-alignment strategy in order to improve coverage without using additional training data. While the improvements on automatic metrics are small, manual inspection suggests that better morphological analysis for the French side has potential to improve translation quality. In future work, we plan to improve the core model by including the new large in-domain parallel corpus in training, and to further experiment with French input representations at different stages of training and decoding using more expressive POS tags such as the MULTITAG tag set (Allauzen and Bonneau-Maynard, 2008).

References

Alexandre Allauzen and Hélène Bonneau-Maynard. Training and evaluation of pos taggers on the french multitag corpus. In European Language Resources Association (ELRA), editor, *Proceedings of the Sixth International Language Resources and Evaluation (LREC'08)*, Marrakech, Morocco, may 2008.

Satanjeev Banerjee and Alon Lavie. METEOR: An automatic metric for MT evaluation with improved correlation with human judgement. In *Proceedings of Workshop on Intrinsic and Extrinsic Evaluation Measures for MT and/or Summarization at the 43th Annual Meeting of the Association of Computational Linguistics (ACL-2005)*, Ann Arbor, Michigan, June 2005.

Daniel Déchelotte, Gilles Adda, Alexandre Allauzen, Hélène Bonneau-Maynard, Olivier Galibert, Jean-Luc Gauvain, Philippe Langlais, and François Yvon. LIMSIs statistical translation systems for WMT08. In *Proceedings of the Third Workshop on Statistical Machine Translation*, pages 107–110, Columbus, Ohio, 2008.

Philipp Koehn and Hieu Hoang. Factored translation models. In *Proceedings of the 2007 Joint Conference on Empirical Methods in Natural Language Processing and Computational Natural Language Learning (EMNLP-CoNLL)*, pages 868–876, 2007.

Philipp Koehn, Hieu Hoang, Alexandra Birch, Chris Callison-Burch, Marcello Federico, Nicola Bertoldi, Brooke Cowan, Wade Shen, Christine Moran, Richard Zens, Chris Dyer, Ondrej Bojar, Alexandra Constantin, and Evan Herbst. Moses: Open source toolkit for statistical machine translation. In *Annual Meeting of the Association for Computational Linguistics (ACL), demonstration session*, Prague, Czech Republic, June 2007.

Franz Josef Och. Minimum error rate training in statistical machine translation. In *Proceedings of the 41st Annual Meeting of the Association for Computational Linguistics*, pages 160–167, 2003.

Kishore Papineni, Salim Roukos, Todd Ward, and Wei-Jing Zhu. BLEU: a method for automatic evaluation of machine translation. In *Proceedings of the 40th Annual Meeting of the Association for Computational Linguistics*, 2002.

Maja Popović and Hermann Ney. Towards the use of word stems and suffixes for statistical machine translation. In *Proceedings of the 4th International Conference on Language Resources and Evaluation (LREC-2004)*, 2004.

Fatiha Sadat and Nizar Habash. Combination of arabic preprocessing schemes for statistical machine translation. In *ACL-44: Proceedings of the 21st International Conference on Computational Linguistics and the 44th annual meeting of the Association for Computational Linguistics*, pages 1–8, Morristown, NJ, USA, 2006. Association for Computational Linguistics.

Helmut Schmid. Probabilistic part–of–speech tagging using decision trees. In *Proceedings of the Conference on New Methods in Language Processin*, pages 44–49, Manchester, UK, 1994.

Holger Schwenk, Jean-Baptiste Fouet, and Jean Senellart. First steps towards a general purpose French/English statistical machine translation system. In *Proceedings of the Third Workshop on Statistical Machine Translation*, pages 119–122, Columbus, Ohio, June 2008. Association for Computational Linguistics.

Andreas Stolcke. SRILM—an extensible language modeling toolkit. In *International Conference on Spoken Language Processing*, Denver, Colorado, September 2002.

Sami Virpojia, Jaako J. Väyrynen, Mathias Creutz, and Markus Sadeniemi. Morphology-aware statistical machine translation based on morphs induced in an unsupervised manner. In *Machine Translation Summit XI*, pages 491–498, Copenhagen, Denmark, September 2007.

Taro Watanabe, Hajime Tsukada, and Hideki Isozaki. Ntt system description for the wmt2006 shared task. In *Proceedings on the Workshop on Statistical Machine Translation*, pages 122–125, New York City, June 2006. Association for Computational Linguistics.

Andreas Zollmann, Ashish Venugopal, Stephan Vogel, and Alex Waibel. The CMU-UKA Syntax Augmented Machine Translation System for IWSLT-06. In *Proceedings of the International Workshop on Spoken Language Translation*, pages 138–144, Kyoto, Japan, 2006.

MorphoLogic's submission for the WMT 2009 Shared Task

Attila Novák
MorphoLogic
Kardhegy utca 5, Budapest 1116, Hungary
novak@morphologic.hu

Abstract

In this article, we describe the machine translation systems we used to create MorphoLogic's submissions to the WMT09 shared Hungarian to English and English to Hungarian shared translation tasks. We used our rule based MetaMorpho system to generate our primary submission. In addition, we created a hybrid system where the Moses decoder is used to rank translations or assemble partial translations created by MetaMorpho. Our third system was a purely statistical morpheme based system for the Hungarian to English task.

1 Introduction

This year, MorphoLogic submitted translations for the WMT09 shared Hungarian to English and English to Hungarian translation tasks. Our primary submissions were translated by MetaMorpho, a purely rule based machine translation system (Prószéky and Tihanyi, 2002). Since last year's workshop we improved the Hungarian to English grammar of MetaMorpho by making more efficient the handling of certain structural ambiguities and making the way the system handles long sentences more robust.

The way Metamorpho selects the translation to output is not optimal whether or not a full parse for the source sentence could be obtained by its parser.[1] Thus we decided to experiment with a hybrid system where translations and partial translations produced by MetaMorpho are ranked or assembled by the Moses decoder (Koehn et al., 2007) using a target language model.

In addition, we created a purely statistical morpheme based system (also using Moses) for the Hungarian to English task. However, results obtained with the latter setup have been clearly inferior in quality to those produced by the rule based system both in terms of BLEU score and subjective human judgment.

2 The MetaMorpho translation system

MetaMorpho is a rule based system the architecture of which differs from that of most well-known rule based systems: it does not contain a separate transfer component. Its grammar operates with pairs of patterns (context-free rules enriched with features) that consist of one source pattern used during bottom-up parsing and one or more target patterns that are applied during top-down generation of the translation. The architecture of the grammar is completely homogeneous: the same formalism is used to represent general rules of grammar, more-or-less idiomatic phrases and fully lexicalized items, these differ only in the degree of underspecification.

The translation of the parsed structures is already determined during parsing the source language input. The actual generation of the target language representations does not involve any additional transfer operations: target language structures corresponding to substructures of the source language parse tree are combined and the leaves of the resulting tree are interpreted by a morphological generator.
MetaMorpho processes input by first segmenting it into sentences, then tokenizing them and performing morphological analysis on tokens, assigning morphosyntactic attribute vectors to them. This is followed by parsing the network of ambiguous token sequences using the source side of the grammar. Features are used in the grammar to express constraints on the applicability of rules and to store morphosyntactic, valence and lexical information concerning the parsed input.

When no applicable rules remain, translation is generated in a top-down fashion by combining the target structures corresponding to the source

[1] In the first case, simply the first translation is output instead of considering all possible translations and selecting the best, while in the second case, the algorithm that combines the partial translations does not check how well the target language side of the pieces fit together.

Proceedings of the Fourth Workshop on Statistical Machine Translation, pages 155–159,
Athens, Greece, 30 March – 31 March 2009.

patterns constituting the source language parse tree. A source language rule may have more than one associated target rule. The selection of the target structure to apply relies on constraints on the actual values of features in the source rule.

Unlike in classical transfer-based systems, word order rearrangement is already determined during parsing the source language input by the applied rules and the values of the features. During generation, the already determined rearranged structures are simply spelled out. The morphosyntactic feature vectors on the terminal level of the generated tree are interpreted by a morphological generator that synthesizes the corresponding target language word forms.

Handling ambiguity is always a difficult problem in a rule based system. MetaMorpho gets rid of alternatives either by using high level heuristics or by specific rules explicitly overriding some more general alternatives. Generally MetaMorpho only generates the first possible translation corresponding to the first parse it produces. In the case of long sentences however, MetaMorpho still may run into the problem of generating too many hypotheses. The solution to this problem originally was simply to abort the parser when it had spent too much time on analyzing a sentence. This resulted in a sequence of words at the end of the sentence remaining untranslated. We managed to alleviate this problem by introducing subsentential segmentation that partitions the input sentence into chunks at presumably safe places (usually clause boundaries).

3 Using a target language model to combine partial parses

During parsing, a hierarchy of partial structures is built by the parser. If the parser fails to produce full parse of the sentence, MetaMorpho reverts to using a heuristic process that constructs an output by combining the output of a selected set of these partial structures covering the whole sentence. These assembled translations are usually suboptimal, because in the absence of a full parse some structural information such as agreement is often lost.

3.1 Pronoun dropping

In the case of Hungarian to English translation, pronoun dropping in Hungarian is a further problem when trying to assemble a translation from partial structures. Since the number and person of the subject and the definiteness of the object (in the case of transitive verbs) is exactly expressed by Hungarian verbal agreement suffixes, explicit subject and object pronouns may be (and usually are) dropped (unless they are focused or otherwise stressed). The problem is that the same verb forms are used when the subject or object is a full NP. In these cases, however no pronoun is incorporated in the verbal suffix:

Hallja.	*He/she/it hears him/her/it.*
Fred hallja a doktort.	*Fred hears the doctor.*

For single verb forms the MetaMorpho parser only generates English phrases that contain subject pronouns (and in the case of a transitive definite verb like *hallja* also an object pronoun: *he hears it*), because the verb is only represented in the grammar by structures that inherently contain its possible argument structures. This results in extra pronouns appearing in the assembled output translation if there is in fact an overt subject and/or object in the sentence. The same thing applies to 3rd person singular possessive constructions:

háza	*his house*
Fred háza.	*Fred's house.*

3.2 Utilizing the Moses decoder

The original partial structure combination algorithm in MetaMorpho does not utilize a statistical model of the target language. In our experiments, we replaced the original phrase combination algorithm with a statistical model using the Moses decoder hoping that this would improve the translations produced in these cases. We created an interface to the parser that can output all partial parses generated during parsing the input sentence along with their translations.

We directly constructed a phrase table from the partial translations and used the Moses decoder to select the best translation using a surface target language model. We assumed a uniform distribution on the translations in the phrase table (for lack of a better estimation of the translation probabilities) and assigned a zero weight to the phrase model in the Moses configuration. Neither did we use a lexicalized distortion table. The decoder thus selects the best translation based on the language model score assigned to it. In our experiments we used 5-gram language models created from the WMT09 bilingual training data. We could not use language models created from the larger monolingual corpora: the RAM installed in our test machine was not enough for that.[2]

We experimented with various parameter settings and ways of building the phrase table. While including partial translations in the phrase table for sentences that had a full parse definitely hurt performance, adding all alternative full translations (if the parser managed to parse the whole sentence) to the phrase table and letting the language model select the best one (instead of MetaMorpho defaulting to the first successful parse) improved performance as could be expected. We needed to increase the maximum allowed phrase length parameter from the default to allow the decoder to use the full sentence translations (failing to do so resulted in a serious degradation of performance).

Adding alternative versions of phrases containing possibly spurious pronouns to the phrase table with the pronouns removed or properly modified also had a beneficial effect as this reduced the frequency of extra inserted pronouns in the translations.

While our original phrase assembly algorithm never attempts to reorder the chunks it selects, we did experiment with different distortion parameter settings in the statistical approach since reordering comes for free with the Moses decoder. (Well, there is in fact a price to pay for distortion: a sharp fall in decoding speed.) We found that not penalizing word order changes by the decoder clearly had a detrimental effect on the accuracy of translations. The default distortion limit and penalty (distortion limit was of six words (d=6) in this setting; distortion penalty weight was identical with the language model weight) often resulted in translations with completely out-of-place chunks at the end of the sentence. We got the best results (also in terms of BLEU score) when disallowing distortion altogether even though this results in somewhat disfluent output, especially if the target language is English and the original Hungarian sentence was verb final. Disallowing distortion also made decoding more than ten times faster.

[2] Building lower-order LMs, cutting off singletons, and/or limiting the LM's vocabulary to the most frequent phrases could be possible solutions to that problem as the reviewer of the paper pointed out. We are going to try to solve the memory problem using a combination these techniques in our follow-up experiments.

3.3 Results

Unfortunately, even with the best parameter settings that we have found, we managed to achieve only a slight improvement in BLEU scores compared to the original heuristics used in MetaMorpho. The following table lists the (case insensitive) BLEU scores achieved by the original purely rule based system and various versions of the hybrid system on the WMT09 test set.[3]

Hungarian to English	
MetaMorpho	9.96
d=6, no distortion penalty, reassembling full parses	9.62
d=6, distortion penalty, no partial analyses for full parse sentences	9.70
d=0, no distortion, no partial analyses for full parse sentences, pronoun dropping	10.10
English to Hungarian	
MetaMorpho	8.13
d=6, distortion penalty, no partial analyses for full parse sentences	8.22
d=0, no distortion, no partial analyses for full parse sentences	8.44

Although we got slightly better results using the hybrid system, we submitted the output of the original fully rule based MetaMorpho system as our primary submission.

4 A morpheme based Hungarian to English statistical translation system

In addition to the hybrid system above, we also experimented with a statistical system using the Moses toolkit that we used to build a Hungarian to English translation system. The model that we implemented is based on a morpheme based representation of both languages instead of a word form based or factored representation.

4.1 The architecture of the system

The Hungarian side of the WMT09 parallel training corpus was analyzed and stemmed using the *Humor* morphological analyzer (Prószéky and Kis, 1999; Prószéky and Novák, 2005) and we used the *Hunpos* tagger (Halácsy, Kornai and Oravecz, 2007) for disambiguating the morpho-

[3] We first used a cleaned-up version of the WMT08 test set (with typos and badly converted characters fixed) in our experiments. Then we rerun some of the test configurations on the WMT09 test set and got similarly improving results, which we report here.

logical tagging. For English tagging, we used *CRFTagger* (Phan, 2006), a Java-based conditional random fields POS tagger, while stemming was performed by *morpha* (Minnen, Carroll and Pearce, 2001). We used the corresponding *morphg* word form generator to generate the output surface word forms. Unfortunately, morpha neutralizes some present and past forms of the copula, we needed to fix this to get the proper forms in the output.

We segmented both sides of the corpus into morphemes based on the analyses, so the tokens in our system were morphemes instead of word forms. The following is a lowercased example sentence pair from the training corpus:

a[det] 137[szn] apró[mn] csillag[fn] [ela] álló[mn] spirál[fn] meg+[ik] duplázódik[ige] [me3] .[punct]

the_dt spiral_nn of_in 137_cd tiny_jj star_nn s_nns double_vb ed_vbd itself_prp ._.

The motivation for this approach was that Hungarian has a very rich morphology with thousands of possible inflected forms for each word in the open word classes. In addition, many English function words, such as prepositions, possessive and other pronouns etc. correspond to bound morphemes in Hungarian, which makes already the word alignment part of the Moses training procedure a difficult task. It is difficult capture generalizations like the ones above using a word form based representation. There are also systematic morpheme order differences between these corresponding morphemes: the inflectional suffixes (or postpositions) corresponding to English prepositions follow noun phrases rather than preceding them and the same applies to possessive pronouns and subject pronouns (the latter corresponding to verb agreement suffixes). We hoped that these difficulties could be addressed by a morpheme based solution adequately.

The phrase table was built using the default *grow-diag-final* heuristic from *Giza++* alignments that we acquired from the morpheme based representation of the corpus. We used the default settings for Giza++. We also used a lexicalized reordering table. The distortion parameter was left at the default value. We also analyzed and tried to use a 5-gram language model built from the monolingual English corpus that was published as part of the WMT09 shared translation task training material but the resulting model was too big to be loaded into the 3GB RAM of the machine that we used in our experiments. We tried to use IRSTLM instead of SRILM but we did not manage to solve the memory overload problem. So in the end we used a 5-gram morpheme based language model that was built from the English side of the bilingual training corpus only.

We run the MERT parameter optimization procedure using a morpheme based BLEU score computed on the morpheme segmented version of the WMT09 Hungarian to English tuning set. MERT took several days to run.

4.2 Results

We used the parameter settings suggested by the (morpheme BLEU score based) MERT optimization and generated English surface word forms using *morphg*. We expected that the morpheme based solution would pose a new problem: that of misplaced morphemes in the output that do not correspond to any valid surface word form. In such cases we resorted to skipping the misplaced morpheme, although this is obviously not an optimal solution.

The BLEU score we obtained on the detokenized output was not very encouraging, to put it mildly: 7.82. When we rerun the decoder with the parameter settings obtained from a previous broken down MERT session, we obtained somewhat better results: 7.95. But this is still very far from the 9.96/10.10 points achieved by MetaMorpho and the hybrid solution. Inspection of the translation results confirmed that the translations generated by the morpheme based setup are far inferior to those generated by our rule based system.

Inspecting Giza++ alignments revealed that, contrary to our hopes, segmenting the training corpus into morphemes did not in itself solve the word alignment quality problem: the alignments look even worse than those achieved on the plain text version of the corpus. On the other hand, all the drawbacks of the approach that we predicted: reduced span of local dependencies in the language models and the phase table due to the increased number of tokens spanning the same span of input, misplaced morphemes, etc. seem to have hit us.

5 Conclusion

In this article, we described the rule based, hybrid and statistical systems that we implemented and used in the WMT09 shared translation task.

Although we only managed to slightly improve the performance of our rule based machine translation system in our hybrid experiment and with our first attempt at a morpheme based statistical system we obtained more modest results than we hoped, we think that it is still worth to make further attempts to build better translation systems for the Hungarian English language pair along these lines.

Acknowledgments

This research has been supported by the European Commission in the FP6-IST project EuroMatrix. We also would like to thank László Laki and Borbála Siklósi for the work they have put into the statistical system that we built.

References

Péter Halácsy, András Kornai, and Csaba Oravecz. 2007. HunPos – an open source trigram tagger In: *Proceedings of the 45th Annual Meeting of the Association for Computational Linguistics Companion Volume Proceedings of the Demo and Poster Sessions,* Association for Computational Linguistics, Prague, Czech Republic, 209–212.

Philipp Koehn, Hieu Hoang, Alexandra Birch, Chris Callison-Burch, Marcello Federico, Nicola Bertoldi, Brooke Cowan, Wade Shen, Christine Moran, Richard Zens, Chris Dyer, Ondrej Bojar, Alexandra Constantin, Evan Herbst. 2007. Moses: Open Source Toolkit for Statistical Machine Translation In: *Proceedings of the 45th Annual Meeting of the Association for Computational Linguistics Companion Volume Proceedings of the Demo and Poster Sessions,* Association for Computational Linguistics, Prague, Czech Republic, 177–180.

Guido Minnen, John Carroll and Darren Pearce. 2001. *Applied morphological processing of English,* Natural Language Engineering, 7(3). 207–223.

Xuan-Hieu Phan. 2006. *CRFTagger: CRF English POS Tagger,* http://crftagger.sourceforge.net/

Gábor Prószéky and Attila Novák. 2005. Computational Morphologies for Small Uralic Languages. In: A. Arppe, L. Carlson, K. Lindén, J. Piitulainen, M. Suominen, M. Vainio, H. Westerlund, A. Yli-Jyrä (eds.): *Inquiries into Words, Constraints and Contexts Festschrift in the Honour of Kimmo Koskenniemi on his 60th Birthday,* 116–125. Gummerus Printing, Saarijärvi/CSLI Publications, Stanford.

Gábor Prószéky and László Tihanyi. 2002. MetaMorpho: A Pattern-Based Machine Translation System. In: *Proceedings of the 24th 'Translating and the Computer' Conference,* 19–24. ASLIB, London, United Kingdom.

Edinburgh's Submission to all Tracks of the WMT2009 Shared Task with Reordering and Speed Improvements to Moses

Philipp Koehn and Barry Haddow
School of Informatics
University of Edinburgh
pkoehn@inf.ed.ac.uk bhaddow@inf.ed.ac.uk

Abstract

Edinburgh University participated in the WMT 2009 shared task using the Moses phrase-based statistical machine translation decoder, building systems for all language pairs. The system configuration was identical for all language pairs (with a few additional components for the German-English language pairs). This paper describes the configuration of the systems, plus novel contributions to Moses including truecasing, more efficient decoding methods, and a framework to specify reordering constraints.

1 Introduction

The commitment of the University of Edinburgh to the WMT shared tasks is to provide a strong statistical machine translation baseline with our open source tools for all language pairs. We are again the only institution that participated in all tracks.

The shared task is also an opportunity to incorporate novel contributions and test them against the best machine translation systems for these language pairs. In this paper we describe the speed improvements to the Moses decoder (Koehn et al., 2007), as well as a novel framework to specify reordering constraints with XML markup, which we tested with punctuation-based constraints.

2 System Configuration

We trained a default Moses system with the following non-default settings:

- maximum sentence length 80
- grow-diag-final-and symmetrization of GIZA++ alignments
- interpolated Kneser-Ney discounted 5-gram language model
- msd-bidrectional-fe lexicalized reordering

Language	ep	nc	news	intpl.
English	449	486	216	192
French	264	311	147	131
German	785	821	449	402
Spanish	341	392	219	190
Czech	*:1475	1615	752	690
Hungarian	hung:2148		815	786

Table 1: Perplexity (ppl) of the domain-trained (ep = Europarl (CzEng for Czech), nc = News Commentary, news = News) and interpolated language models.

2.1 Domain Adaptation

In contrast to last year's task, where news translation was presented as a true out-of-domain problem, this year large monolingual news corpora and a tuning set (last year's test set) were provided. While still no in-domain news parallel corpora were made available, the monolingual corpora could be exploited for domain adaption.

For all language pairs, we built a 5-gram language model, by first training separate language models for the different training corpora (the parallel Europarl and News Commentary and new monolingual news), and then interpolated them by optimizing perplexity on the provided tuning set. Perplexity numbers are shown in Table 1.

2.2 Truecasing

Our traditional method to handle case is to lowercase all training data, and then have a separate recasing (or recapitalization) step. Last year, we used truecasing: all words are normalized to their natural case, e.g. *the, John, eBay*, meaning that only sentence-leading words may be changed to their most frequent form.

To refine last year's approach, we record the seen truecased instances and truecase words in test sentences (even in the middle of sentences) to seen forms, if possible.

Truecasing leads to small degradation in case-

Proceedings of the Fourth Workshop on Statistical Machine Translation , pages 160–164,
Athens, Greece, 30 March – 31 March 2009. ©2009 Association for Computational Linguistics

language pair		baseline	w/ news	mbr/mp	truecased	big beam	ued'08	best'08
French-English	uncased	21.2	23.1	23.3	22.7	22.9	19.2	21.9
	cased			21.7	21.6	21.8		
English-French	uncased	17.8	19.4	19.6	19.6	19.7	18.2	21.4
	cased			18.1	18.7	18.8		
Spanish-English	uncased	22.5	24.4	24.7	24.5	24.7	20.1	22.9
	cased			23.0	23.3	23.4		
English-Spanish	uncased	22.4	23.9	24.2	23.8	24.4	20.7	22.7
	cased			22.1	22.8	23.1		
Czech-English	uncased	16.9	18.9	18.9	18.6	18.6	14.5	14.7
	cased			17.3	17.4	17.4		
English-Czech	uncased	11.4	13.5	13.6	13.6	13.8	9.6	11.9
	cased			12.2	13.0	13.2		
Hungarian-English	uncased	-	11.3	11.4	10.9	11.0	8.8	
	cased			8.3	10.1	10.2		
English-Hungarian	uncased	-	9.0	9.3	9.2	9.5	6.5	
	cased			8.1	8.4	8.7		

Table 2: Results overview for news-dev2009b sets: We see significant BLEU score increases with the addition of news data to the language model and using truecasing. As a comparison our results and the best systems from last year on the full news-dev2009 set are shown.

insensitive BLEU, but to a significant gain in case-sensitive BLEU. Note that we still do not properly address all-caps portions or headlines with our approach.

2.3 Results

Results on the development sets are summarized in Table 2. We see significant gains with the addition of news data to the language model (about 2 BLEU points) and using truecasing (about 0.5–1.0 BLEU points), and minor if any gains using minimum Bayes risk decoding (mbr), the monotone-at-punctuation reordering constraint (mp, see Section 3.2), and bigger beam sizes.

2.4 German–English

For German–English, we additionally incorporated

rule-based reordering — We parse the input using the Collins parser (Collins, 1997) and apply a set of reordering rules to re-arrange the German sentence so that it corresponds more closely English word order (Collins et al., 2005).

compound splitting — We split German compound words (mostly nouns), based on the frequency of the words in the potential decompositions (Koehn and Knight, 2003a).

part-of-speech language model — We use factored translation models (Koehn and Hoang, 2007) to also output part-of-speech tags with each word in a single phrase mapping and run a second n-gram model over them. The English part-of-speech tags are obtained using MXPOST (Ratnaparkhi, 1996).

German–English (ued'08: 17.1, best'08: 19.7)	**BLEU (uncased)**
baseline	16.6
+ interpolated news LM	20.6
+ minimum Bayes risk decoding	20.6
+ monotone at punctuation	20.9
+ truecasing	20.9
+ rule-based reordering	21.7
+ compound splitting	22.0
+ part-of-speech LM	22.1
+ big beam	22.3

Table 3: Results for German–English with the incremental addition of methods beyond a baseline trained on the parallel corpus

English–German (ued'08: 12.1, best'08: 14.2)	**BLEU (uncased)**
baseline	13.5
+ interpolated news LM	15.2
+ minimum Bayes risk decoding	15.2
+ monotone at punctuation	15.2
+ truecasing	15.2
+ morphological LM	15.2
+ big beam	15.7

Table 4: Results for English–German with the incremental addition of methods beyiond a baseline trained on the parallel corpus

2.5 English-German

For English–German, we additionally incorporated a morphological language model the same way we incorporated a part-of-speech language model in the other translation direction. The morphological tags were obtained using LoPar (Schmidt and Schulte im Walde, 2000).

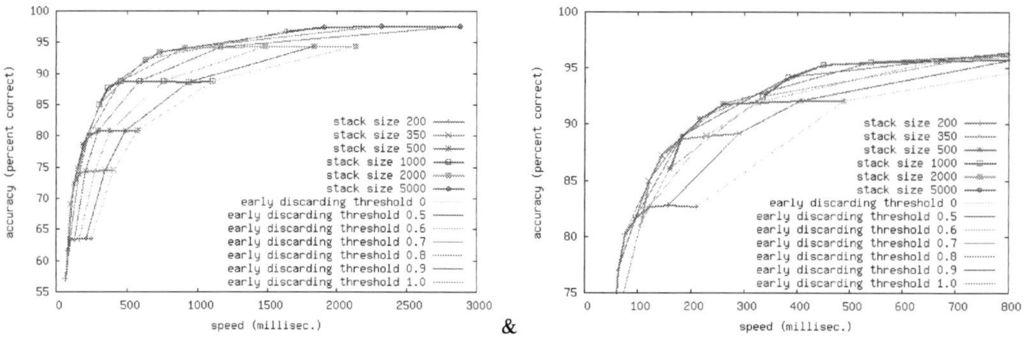

German-English & French-English

Figure 1: Early discarding results in speedier but still accurate search, compared to reducing stack size.

3 Recent Improvements

In this section, we describe recent improvements to the Moses decoder for the WMT 2009 shared task.

3.1 Early Discarding

We implemented in Moses a more efficient beam search, following suggestions by Moore and Quirk (2007). In short, the guiding principle of this work is not to build a hypothesis and not to compute its language model scores, if it is likely to be too bad anyway.

Before a hypothesis is generated, the following checks are employed:

1. the **minimum allowed score** for a hypothesis is the worst score on the stack (if full) or the threshold for the stack (if higher or stack not full) *plus* an early discarding threshold cushion
2. if (a) new hypothesis future score, (b) the current hypothesis actual score, and (c) the future cost of the translation option are worse than the allowed score, do not generate the hypothesis
3. if adding all real costs except for the language model costs (i.e., reordering costs) makes the score worse than the allowed score, do not generate the hypothesis.
4. complete generation of the hypothesis and add it to the stack

Note that check 1 and 2 mostly consists of adding and comparing already computed values. In our implementation, step 3 implies the somewhat costly construction of the hypothesis data structure, while step 4 performs the expensive language model calculation. Without these optimizations, the decoder spends about 60-70% of the search time computing language model scores. With these optimization, the vast majority of potential hypotheses are not built.

See Figure 1 for the time/search-accuracy trade-offs using this early discarding strategy. Given a stack size, we can vary the threshold cushion mentioned in step 1 above. A tighter threshold (the factor 1.0 implies no cushion at all), results in speedier but worse search. Note, however, that the degradation in quality for a given time point is less severe than the alternative — reducing the stack size (and also tightening the beam threshold, not shown in the figure). To mention just two data points in the German-English setting: Stack size of 500 and early discarding threshold of 1.0 results in faster search (150ms/word) and better quality (73.5% search accuracy) than the default search setting of a stack size 200 and no early discarding (252ms/word for 62.5% seach accuracy). Accuracy is measured against the best translations found under any setting.

Note that this early discarding is related to ideas behind cube pruning (Huang and Chiang, 2007), which generates the top n most promising hypotheses, but in our method the decision not to generate hypotheses is guided by the quality of hypotheses on the result stack.

3.2 Framework to Specify Reordering Constraints

Commonly in statistical machine translation, punctuation tokens are treated just like words. For tokens such as commas, many possible translations are collected and they may be translated into any of these choices or reordered if the language model sees gains. In fact, since the comma is one

Requiring the translation of quoted material as a block:
```
He said <zone> " yes " </zone> .
```
Hard reordering constraint:
```
Number 1 :  <wall/> the beginning .
```
Local hard reordering constraint within zone:
```
A new idea <zone> ( <wall/> maybe not new <wall/> ) </zone> has come forward .
```
Nesting:
```
The <zone> " new <zone> ( old ) </zone> " </zone> proposal .
```

Figure 2: Framework to specify reordering constraints with zones and walls. Words within zones have to be translated without reordering with outside material. Walls form hard reordering constraints, over which words may not be reordered (limited to zones, if defined within them).

the most frequent tokens in a corpus and not very consistently translated across languages, it has a very noisy translation table, often with 10,000s if not 100,000s of translations.

Punctuation has a meaningful role in structuring a sentence, and we see some gains exploiting this in the systems we built last year. By disallowing reordering over commas and sentence-ending punctuation, we avoid mixing words from different clauses, and typically see gains of 0.1–0.2 BLEU.

But also other punctuation tokens imply reordering constraints. Parentheses, brackets, and quotation marks typically define units that should be translated as blocks, meaning that words should not be moved in or out of sequences in quotes and alike.

To handle such reordering constraints, we introduced a framework that uses what we call **zones** and **walls**. A zone is a sequence of words that should be translated as block. This does not mean that the sequence cannot be reordered as a whole, but that once we start to translate words in a zone, we have to finish all its words before moving outside again. To put it another way: words may not reordered into or out of zones.

A wall is a hard reordering constraint that requires that all words preceeding it have to be translated before words after may be translated. If we specify walls within zones, then we consider them **local walls** where the before-mentioned constraint only applies within the zone.

Walls and zones may be specified with XML markup to the Moses decoder. See Figure 2 for a few examples. We use the extended XML framework to

1. limit reordering of clause-ending punctuation (walls)
2. define zones for quoted and parenthetical word sequences
3. limit reordering of quotes and parentheses (local walls within zones)
4. specify translations for punctuation (not comma).

Only (1) leads to any noticable change in BLEU in the WMT 2009 shared task, a slight gain 0.1–0.2.

Note that this framework may be used in other ways. For instance, we may want to revisit our work on noun phrase translation (Koehn and Knight, 2003b), and check if enforcing the translation of noun phrases as blocks is beneficial or harmful to overall machine translation performance.

Acknowledgements

This work was supported by the EuroMatrix project funded by the European Commission (6th Framework Programme) and made use of the resources provided by the Edinburgh Compute and Data Facility (`http://www.ecdf.ed.ac.uk/`). The ECDF is partially supported by the eDIKT initiative (`http://www.edikt.org.uk/`).

References

Collins, M. (1997). Three generative, lexicalized models for statistical parsing. In *Proceedings of the 35th Annual Meeting of the Association of Computational Linguistics (ACL)*.

Collins, M., Koehn, P., and Kucerova, I. (2005). Clause restructuring for statistical machine translation. In *Proceedings of the 43rd Annual*

Meeting of the Association for Computational Linguistics (ACL'05), pages 531–540, Ann Arbor, Michigan. Association for Computational Linguistics.

Huang, L. and Chiang, D. (2007). Forest rescoring: Faster decoding with integrated language models. In *Proceedings of the 45th Annual Meeting of the Association of Computational Linguistics*, pages 144–151, Prague, Czech Republic. Association for Computational Linguistics.

Koehn, P. and Hoang, H. (2007). Factored translation models. In *Proceedings of the 2007 Joint Conference on Empirical Methods in Natural Language Processing and Computational Natural Language Learning (EMNLP-CoNLL)*, pages 868–876.

Koehn, P., Hoang, H., Birch, A., Callison-Burch, C., Federico, M., Bertoldi, N., Cowan, B., Shen, W., Moran, C., Zens, R., Dyer, C. J., Bojar, O., Constantin, A., and Herbst, E. (2007). Moses: Open source toolkit for statistical machine translation. In *Proceedings of the 45th Annual Meeting of the Association for Computational Linguistics Companion Volume Proceedings of the Demo and Poster Sessions*, pages 177–180, Prague, Czech Republic. Association for Computational Linguistics.

Koehn, P. and Knight, K. (2003a). Empirical methods for compound splitting. In *Proceedings of Meeting of the European Chapter of the Association of Computational Linguistics (EACL)*.

Koehn, P. and Knight, K. (2003b). Feature-rich translation of noun phrases. In *41st Annual Meeting of the Association of Computational Linguistics (ACL)*.

Moore, R. C. and Quirk, C. (2007). Faster beam-search decoding for phrasal statistical machine translation. In *Proceedings of the MT Summit XI*.

Ratnaparkhi, A. (1996). A maximum entropy part-of-speech tagger. In *Proceedings of the Empirical Methods in Natural Language Processing Conference*.

Schmidt, H. and Schulte im Walde, S. (2000). Robust German noun chunking with a probabilistic context-free grammar. In *Proceedings of the International Conference on Computational Linguistics (COLING)*.

Mining a comparable text corpus for a Vietnamese - French statistical machine translation system

Thi-Ngoc-Diep Do *,, Viet-Bac Le *, Brigitte Bigi*, Laurent Besacier*, Eric Castelli****
*LIG Laboratory, CNRS/UMR-5217, Grenoble, France
** MICA Center, CNRS/UMI-2954, Hanoi, Vietnam
thi-ngoc-diep.do@imag.fr

Abstract

This paper presents our first attempt at constructing a Vietnamese-French statistical machine translation system. Since Vietnamese is an under-resourced language, we concentrate on building a large Vietnamese-French parallel corpus. A document alignment method based on publication date, special words and sentence alignment result is proposed. The paper also presents an application of the obtained parallel corpus to the construction of a Vietnamese-French statistical machine translation system, where the use of different units for Vietnamese (syllables, words, or their combinations) is discussed.

1 Introduction

Over the past fifty years of development, machine translation (MT) has obtained good results when applied to several pairs of languages such as English, French, German, Japanese, etc. However, for under-resourced languages, it still remains a big gap. For instance, although Vietnamese is the 14th widely-used language in the world, research on MT for Vietnamese is very rare.

The earliest MT system for Vietnamese is the system from the *Logos Corporation*, developed as an English-Vietnamese system for translating aircraft manuals during the 1970s (Hutchins, 2001). Until now, in Vietnam, there are only four research groups working on MT for Vietnamese-English (Ho, 2005). However the results are still modest.

MT research on Vietnamese-French occurs even more rarely. Doan (2001) proposed a translation module for Vietnamese within ITS3, a multilingual MT system based on the classical analysis-transfer-generation approach. Nguyen (2006) worked on Vietnamese language and Vietnamese-French text alignment. But no complete MT system for this pair of languages has been published so far.

There are many approaches for MT: rule-based (direct translation, interlingua-based, transfer-based), corpus-based (statistical, example-based) as well as hybrid approaches. We focus on building a Vietnamese-French statistical machine translation (SMT) system. Such an approach requires a parallel bilingual corpus for source and target languages. Using this corpus, we build a statistical translation model for source/target languages and a statistical language model for target language. Then the two models and a search module are used to decode the best translation (Brown et al., 1993; Koehn et al., 2003).

Thus, the first task is to build a large parallel bilingual text corpus. This corpus can be described as a set of bilingual sentence pairs. At the moment, such a large parallel corpus for Vietnamese-French is unavailable. (Nguyen, 2006) presents a Vietnamese-French parallel corpus of law and economics documents. Our SMT system was trained using Vietnamese-French news corpus created by mining a comparable bilingual text corpus from the Web.

Section 2 presents the general methodology of mining a comparable text corpus. We present an overview of document alignment methods and sentence alignment methods, and discuss the document alignment method we utilized, which is based on publishing date, special words, and sentence alignment results. Section 3 describes our experiments in automatically mining a multilingual news website to create a Vietnamese-French parallel text corpus. Section 4 presents

Proceedings of the Fourth Workshop on Statistical Machine Translation , pages 165–172,
Athens, Greece, 30 March – 31 March 2009.

our application to rapidly build Vietnamese-French SMT systems using the obtained parallel corpus, where the use of different units for Vietnamese (syllables, words, or their combination) is discussed. Section 5 concludes and discusses future work.

2 Mining a comparable text corpus

In (Munteanu and Daniel Marcu, 2006), the authors present a method for extracting parallel sub-sentential fragments from comparable bilingual corpora. However this method is in need of an initial parallel bilingual corpus, which is not available for the pair of language Vietnamese-French (in the news domain).

The overall process of mining a bilingual text corpus which is used in a SMT system typically takes five following steps (Koehn, 2005): raw data collection, document alignment, sentence splitting, tokenization and sentence alignment. This section presents the two main steps: document alignment and sentence alignment. We also discuss the proposed document alignment method.

2.1 Document alignment

Let *S1* be set of documents in language *L1*; let *S2* be set of documents in language *L2*. Extracting parallel documents or aligning documents from the two sets *S1, S2* can be seen as finding the translation document *D2* (in the set *S2*) of a document *D1* (in the set *S1*). We call this pair of documents *D1-D2* a *parallel document pair (PDP).*

For collecting bilingual text data for the two sets *S1, S2*, the Web is an ideal source as it is large, free and available (Kilgarriff and Grefenstette, 2003). For this kind of data, various methods to align documents have been proposed. Documents can be simply aligned based on the anchor link, the clue in URL (Kraaij et al., 2003) or the web page structure (Resnik and Smith, 2003). However, this information is not always available or trustworthy. The titles of documents *D1, D2* can also be used (Yang and Li, 2002), but sometimes they are completely different.

Another useful source of information is invariant words, such as named entities, dates, and numbers, which are often common in news data. We call these words *special words*. (Patry and Langlais, 2005) used numbers, punctuation, and entity names to measure the parallelism between two documents. The order of this information in document is used as an important criterion. However, this order is not always respected in a PDP (see an example in Table 1).

French document	Vietnamese document
*Selon l'Administration nationale du tourisme, les voyageurs en provenance de l'Asie du Nord-Est (Japon, République de Corée,...) représentent **33%**, de l'Europe, **16%**, de l'Amérique du Nord, **13%**, d'Australie et de Nouvelle-Zélande, **6%**.* *En outre, depuis le début de cette année, environ **2,8** millions de touristes étrangers ont fait le tour du Vietnam, **78%** d'eux sont venus par avion.* *Cela témoigne d'un afflux des touristes riches au Vietnam....*	*Trong số gần **2,8** triệu lượt khách quốc tế đến Việt Nam từ đầu năm đến nay, lượng khách đến bằng đường hàng không vẫn chiếm chủ đạo với khoảng **78%**.* *Điều này cho thấy, dòng khách du lịch chất lượng cao đến Việt Nam tăng nhanh.* *Theo thống kê thị khách quốc tế vào Việt Nam cho thấy khách Đông Bắc Á (Nhật Bản, Hàn Quốc) chiếm tới **33%**, châu Âu chiếm **16%**, Bắc Mỹ **13%**, Ôxtrâylia và Niu Dilân chiếm **6%**....*

Table 1. An example of a French-Vietnamese parallel document pair in our corpus.

2.2 Sentence alignment

From a PDP *D1-D2*, the sentence alignment process identifies parallel sentence pairs (PSPs) between two documents *D1* and *D2*. For each *D1-D2*, we have a set SenAlignmentD1-D2 of PSPs.

$SenAlignment_{D1-D2}$ = *{"sen1-sen2"| sen1 is zero/one/many sentence(s) in document D1, sen2 is zero/one/many sentence(s) in document D2, sen1-sen2 is considered as a PSP}.*

We call a PSP *sen1-sen2* alignment type *m:n* when *sen1* contains *m* consecutive sentences and *sen2* contains *n* consecutive sentences.

Several automatic sentence alignment approaches have been proposed based on sentence length (Brown et al., 1991) and lexical information (Kay and Roscheisen, 1993). A hybrid approach is presented in (Gale and Church, 1993) whose basic hypothesis is that "longer sentences in one language tend to be translated into longer sentences in the other language, and shorter sentences tend to be translated into shorter sentences". Some toolkits such as Hunalign[1] and Vanilla[2] implement these approaches. However, they tend to work best when documents *D1, D2* contain few sentence deletions and insertions, and mainly contain PSPs of type 1:1.

[1] http://mokk.bme.hu/resources/hunalign

[2] http://nl.ijs.si/telri/Vanilla/

Ma (2006) provides an open source software called Champollion[1] to solve this limitation. Champollion permits alignment type *m:n* (*m, n = 0,1,2,3,4*), so the length of sentence does not play an important role. Champollion uses also lexical information (lexemes, stop words, bilingual dictionary, etc.) to align sentences. Champollion can easily be adapted to new pairs of languages. Available language pairs in Champollion are English-Arabic and English-Chinese (Ma, 2006).

2.3 Our document alignment method

Figure 1 describes our methodology for document alignment. For each document *D1* in the set *S1*, we find the aligned document *D2* in the set *S2*.

We propose to use publishing date, special words, and the results of sentence alignment to discover PDPs. First, the publishing date is used to reduce the number of possible documents *D2*. Then we use a filter based on special words contained in the documents to determine the candidate documents *D2*. Finally, we eliminate candidates in *D2* based on the combination of document length information and lexical information, which are extracted from the results of sentence alignment.

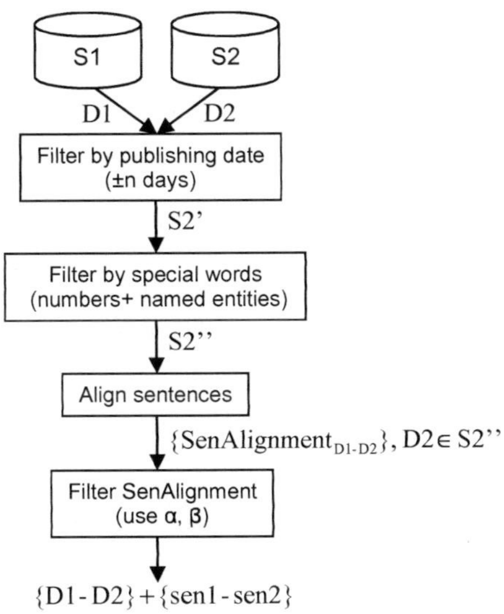

Figure 1. Our document alignment scheme.

2.3.1 The first filter: publishing date

We assume that the document *D2* is translated and published at most *n* days after the publishing date of the original document. We do not know whether *D1* or *D2* is the original document, so we assume that *D2* is published *n* days before or after *D1*. After filtering by publishing date criterion, we obtain a subset *S2'* containing possible documents *D2*.

2.3.2 The second filter: special words

In our case, the special words are *numbers* and *named entities*. Not only numbers (*0-9*) but also attached symbols (*'$', '%', '‰', ';', '.'...*) are extracted from documents, for example: *"12.000$"; "13,45"; "50%";...* Named entities are specified by one or several words in which the first letter of each word is upper case, e.g. "*Paris*", "*Nations Unies*" in French.

While named entities in language *L1* are usually translated into the corresponding names in language *L2,* in some cases the named entities in *L1* (such as personal names or organization names) do not change in *L2*. In particular, many Vietnamese personal names are translated into other languages by removal of diacritical marks (see examples in Table 2).

	French	**Vietnamese**	**Vietnamese -Removed diacritic**
Changed	*Nations Unies*	*Liên Hợp Quốc*	*Lien Hop Quoc*
	France	*Pháp*	*Phap*
Not changed	*ASEAN*	*ASEAN*	*ASEAN*
	Nong Duc Manh	*Nông Đức Mạnh*	*Nong Duc Manh*
	Dien Bien	*Điện Biên*	*Dien Bien*

Table 2. Some examples of named entities in French-Vietnamese.

All special words are extracted from document *D1*. This gives a list of special words $w_1, w_2, \ldots w_n$. For each special word, we search in the set *S2'* documents *D2* which contain this special word. For each word, we obtain a list of documents *D2*. The document *D2* which has the biggest number of appearance in all lists is chosen. It is the document containing the highest number of special words. We can find zero, one or several documents which are satisfactory. We call this set of documents set *S2''* (see in Figure 2).

The way that we use special words is different from the way used in (Patry and Langlais, 2005). We do not use punctuation as special words. We use the attached symbols ('$', '%', '‰', ...) with the number. Furthermore, in our method, the order of special words in documents is not important, and if a special word appears several times in a document, it does not affect the result.

[1] http://champollion.sourceforge.net

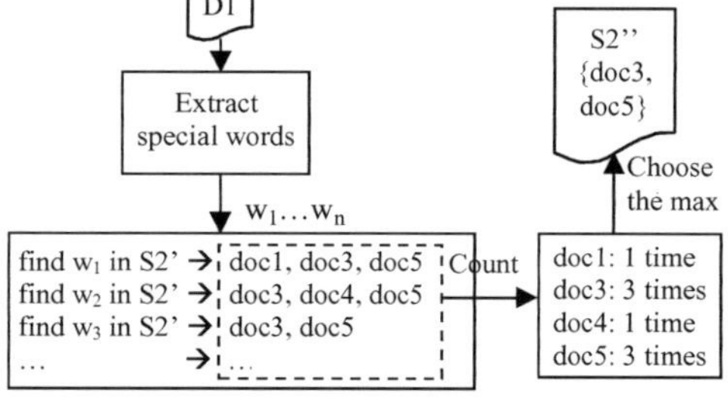

Figure 2. Using special words to filter documents *D2*.

2.3.3 The third filter: sentence alignments

As mentioned in section 2.3.2, for each document *D1*, we discover a set *S2''*, which contains zero, one or several documents *D2*. When we continue to align sentences for each PDP *D1-D2*, we get a lot of low quality PSPs. The results of sentence alignment allow us to further filter the documents *D2*.

After aligning sentences, we have a set of PSPs, $SenAlignment_{D1\text{-}D2}$, for each PDP *D1-D2*. We add two rules to filter documents *D2*.

When *D1-D2* is not a true PDP, it is hard to find out PSPs. So we note the number of PSPs in the set $SenAlignment_{D1\text{-}D2}$ by $card(SenAlignment_{D1\text{-}D2})$. The number of sentence pairs which can not find their alignment partner (when *sen1* or *sen2* is "null") is noted by $nbr\_omitted(SenAlignment_{D1\text{-}D2})$.

When $\frac{\text{nbr\_omitted}(\text{SenAlignment}_{\text{D1-D2}})}{\text{card}(\text{SenAlignment}_{\text{D1-D2}})} > \alpha$, this PDP *D1-D2* will be eliminated.

This first rule also deals with the problem of document length, sentence deletions and sentence insertions.

The second rule makes use of lexical information. For each PSP, we add two scores x_{L1} and x_{L2} for *sen1* and *sen2*.

$$x_{Li} = \frac{number-of-translated-words-in-sen_i}{number-of-words-in-sen_i}$$

Translated words are words having translation equivalents in the other sentence. In this rule, we do not take into account the stop words. Table 3 shows an example for calculating two scores x_{L1} and x_{L2} for a PSP.

In the second rule, when all PSPs in $SenAlignment_{D1\text{-}D2}$ have two scores x_{L1} and x_{L2} that are both smaller than β, this PDP *D1-D2* will be eliminated. This rule removes the low quality PDP which creates a set of low quality PSPs.

<table>
<tr><td colspan="2">sen1 (in French) : ils ont échangé leurs opinions pour parvenir à la signature de documents constituant la base du développement et de l' intensification de la coopération en économie en commerce et en investissement ainsi que celles dans la culture le sport et le tourisme entre les deux pays
sen2 (in Vietnamese) : hai bên đã tiến_hành trao_đổi để ký_kết các văn_bản làm cơ_sở cho việc mở_rộng và tăng_cường quan_hệ hợp_tác kinh_tế thương_mại đầu_tư văn_hoá thể_thao và du_lịch giữa hai nước
Translated words :
"échanger:trao_đổi" ;"base:cơ_sở","intensification:tăng_cường" ;"coopération:hợp_tác","économie:kinh_tế" ; investissement:đầu_tư","sport:thể_thao" ; "tourisme :du_lịch" ; "pays:nước"</td></tr>
<tr><td>Number of non-stop words in sen1</td><td>19</td></tr>
<tr><td>Number of non-stop words in sen2</td><td>21</td></tr>
<tr><td>Number of translated words</td><td>9</td></tr>
<tr><td colspan="2">x_{L1} = 9/19=0.47 ; x_{L2} = 9/21=0.43</td></tr>
</table>

Table 3. Example for calculating two scores x_{L1} and x_{L2}.

After using three filters based on information of publishing date, special words, and the results of sentence alignment, we have a corpus of PDPs, and also a corpus of corresponding PSPs. To ensure the quality of output PSPs, we can continue to filter PSPs. For example, we can keep only the PSPs whose scores (x_{L1} and x_{L2}) are higher than a threshold.

3 Experiments

3.1 Characteristics of Vietnamese

The basic unit of the Vietnamese language is syllable. In writing, syllables are separated by a white space. One word corresponds to one or more syllables (Nguyen, 2006). Table 4 presents an example of a Vietnamese sentence segmented into syllables and words.

<table>
<tr><td><u>Vietnamese sentence</u>: Thành phố hy vọng sẽ đón nhận khoảng 3 triệu khách du lịch nước ngoài trong năm nay
<u>Segmentation in syllables</u>: Thành | phố | hy | vọng | sẽ | đón | nhận | khoảng | 3 | triệu | khách | du | lịch | nước | ngoài | trong | năm | nay
<u>Segmentation in words</u>: Thành_phố | hy_vọng | sẽ | đón_nhận | khoảng | 3 | triệu | khách_du_lịch | nước_ngoài | trong | năm | nay</td></tr>
<tr><td><u>Corresponding English sentence</u>: The city is expected to receive 3 million foreign tourists this year</td></tr>
</table>

Table 4. An example of a Vietnamese sentence segmented into syllables and words.

In Vietnamese, words do not change their form. Instead of conjugation for verb, noun or adjective, Vietnamese language uses additional words, such as "*những*", "*các*" to express the plural; "*đã*", "*sẽ*" to express the past tense and the future. The syntactic functions are also determined by the order of words in the sentence (Nguyen, 2006).

3.2 Data collecting

In order to build a Vietnamese-French parallel text corpus, we applied our proposed methodology to mine a comparable text corpus from a Vietnamese daily news website, the *Vietnam News Agency*[1] (VNA). This website contains news articles written in four languages (Vietnamese, English, French, and Spanish) and divided in 9 categories including "Politics - Diplomacy", "Society - Education", "Business - Finance", "Culture - Sports", "Science - Technology", "Health", "Environment", "Asian corner" and "World". However, not all of the Vietnamese articles have been translated into the other three languages. The distribution of the amount of data in four languages is shown in figure 3.

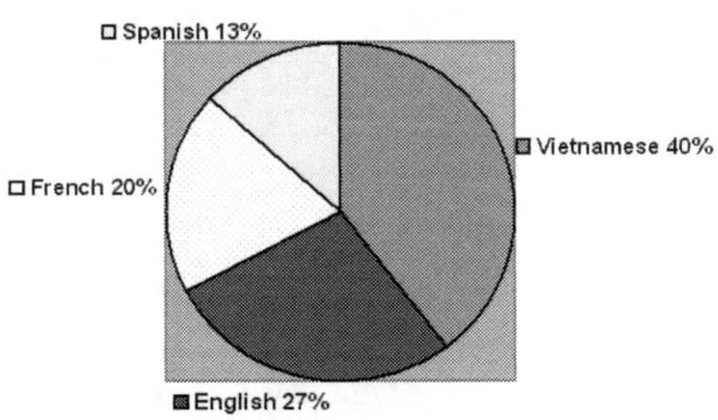

Figure 3. Distribution of the amount of data for each language on VNA website.

Each document (i.e., article) can be obtained via a permanent URL link from VNA. To date, we have obtained about 121,000 documents in four languages, which are gathered from 12 April 2006 to 14 August 2008; each document contains, on average, 10 sentences, with around 30 words per sentence.

3.3 Data pre-processing

We splitted the collected data into 2 sets. The development set, designated S_{DEV}, contained 1000 documents, was used to tune the mining system parameters. The rest of data, designated S_{TRAIN}, was used as a training set, where the estimated parameters were applied to build the entire corpus. We applied the following pre-process to each set S_{DEV} and S_{TRAIN}:

1. Extract contents from documents.
2. Classify documents by language (using TextCat[2], an n-gram based language identification).
3. Process and clean both Vietnamese and French documents by using the CLIPS-Text-Tk toolkit (LE et al., 2003): convert html to text file, convert character code, segment sentence, segment word. The resulting clean corpora are *S1* (for French) and *S2* (for Vietnamese).

3.4 Parameters estimation

Our proposed document alignment method was applied to the sets *S1* and *S2* extracted from the set S_{DEV}. To filter by publishing date, we assumed that n=2.

The second filter was implemented on the set *S1* and the new set *S2** which was created by removing diacritical marks from the set *S2* (in the case of Vietnamese).

The sentence alignment process was implemented by using data from sets *S1, S2* and the Champollion toolkit. We adapted Champollion to Vietnamese-French by changing some parameters: the ratio of French word to Vietnamese translation word is set to 1.2, penalty for alignment type 1-1 is set to 1, for type 0-1 to 0.8, for type 2-1, 1-2 and 2-2 to 0.75, and we did not use the other types (see more in (Ma, 2006)). After using two filters, the result data is shown in Table 5. The true PDPs were manually extracted.

S_{DEV}	- Number of documents: 1000 - Number of French documents: 173 - Number of Vietnamese documents: 348 - Number of true PDPs: 129
S2''	- Number of found PDPs: 379 - Number of hits PDPs: 129 - Precision = 34.04% , Recall = 100%

Table 5. Result data after using two filters.

The third filter was applied in which α was set to (*0.4, 0.5, 0.6, 0.7*) and β was set to (*0.1, 0.15, 0.2, 0.25, 0.3, 0.35, 0.4*). The precision and recall were calculated according to our true PDPs and the F-measure (F1 score) was estimated.

F-measure

β \ α	0.1	0.15	0.2	0.25	0.3	0.35	0.4
0.4	0.69	0.71	0.71	0.60	0.48	0.36	0.21
0.5	0.76	0.79	0.77	0.65	0.52	0.39	0.23
0.6	0.77	0.83	0.82	0.70	0.56	0.41	0.26
0.7	0.75	0.84	0.83	0.73	0.59	0.44	0.27

Table 6. Filter result with different values of α and β on the S_{DEV}.

[1] http://www.vnagency.com.vn/

[2] http://www.let.rug.nl/~vannoord/TextCat/

From the results mentioned in Table 6, we chose α=*0.7* and β=*0.15*.

3.5 Mining the entire corpus

We applied the same methodology with the parameters estimated in section 3.4 to the set S_{TRAIN}. The obtained corpus is presented in Table 7.

S_{TRAIN}	- Number of documents: 120,218 - Number of French documents: 20,884 - Number of Vietnamese documents: 54,406
Entire corpus	- Number of PDPs: 12,108 - Number of PSPs: 50,322

Table 7. The obtained corpus from S_{TRAIN}.

4 Application: a Vietnamese - French statistical machine translation system

With the obtained parallel corpus, we attempted to rapidly build a SMT system for Vietnamese-French. The system was built using the Moses toolkit[1]. The Moses toolkit contains all of the components needed to train both the translation model and the language model. It also contains tools for tuning these models using minimum error rate training and for evaluating the translation result using the BLEU score (Koehn et al., 2007).

4.1 Preparing data

From the entire corpus, we chose 50 PDPs (351 PSPs) for developing (Dev), 50 PDPs (384 PSPs) for testing (Tst), with the rest PDPs (49,587 PSPs) reserved for training (Trn).

Concerning the developing and testing PSPs, we manually verified and eliminated low quality PSPs, which produced 198 good quality PSPs for developing and 210 good quality PSPs for testing. The data used to create the language model were extracted from 49,587 PSPs of the training set.

4.2 Baseline system

We built translation systems in two translation directions: French to Vietnamese (F→V) and Vietnamese to French (V→F). The Vietnamese data were segmented into either words or syllables. So we first have four translation systems. We removed sentences longer than 100 words/syllables from the training and development sets according to the Moses condition (so the number of PSPs used in the training set differs slightly between systems). All words found are implicitly added to the vocabulary.

System	Direction	Vietnamese is segmented into	Nbr of PSPs
S1FV	F→V	Syllable	Training: 47,081 Developing: 198 Testing: 210
S1VF	V→F		
S2FV	F→V	Word	Training: 48,864 Developing: 198 Testing: 210
S2VF	V→F		

System	Set - Language		Nbr. of vocab (K)	Nbr. of running words/syllables (K)
S1FV S1VF	Trn	Fr	38.6	1783.6
		Vn	21.9	2190.2
	Dev	Fr	1.8	6.3
		Vn	1.2	6.9
	Tst	Fr	1.9	6.4
		Vn	1.3	7.1
S2FV S2VF	Trn	Fr	39.7	1893
		Vn	33.4	1629
	Dev	Fr	1.8	6.3
		Vn	1.5	4.8
	Tst	Fr	1.9	6.3
		Vn	1.6	4.9

Table 8. Our four translation systems.

We obtained the performance results for those systems in Table 9. In the case of the systems where Vietnamese was segmented into words, the Vietnamese sentences were changed back to syllable representation before calculating the BLEU scores, so that all the BLEU scores evaluated can be compared to each other.

	S1FV	S1VF	S2FV	S2VF
BLEU	*0.40*	*0.31*	*0.40*	*0.30*

Table 9. Evaluation of SMTs on the Tst set.

The BLEU scores for *French to Vietnamese* translation direction are around 0.40 and the BLEU scores for *Vietnamese to French* translation direction are around 0.31, which is encouraging as a first result. Moreover, only one reference was used to estimate BLEU scores in our experiments. It is also interesting to note that segmenting Vietnamese sentences into words or syllables does not significantly change the performance for both translation directions. An example of translation from four systems is presented in Table 10.

[1] http://www.statmt.org/moses/

Given a pair of parallel sentences FR: selon le département de gestion des travailleurs à l' étranger le qatar est un marché prometteur et nécessite une grande quantité de travailleurs étrangers VNsyl : theo cục quản lý lao động ngoài nước cata là thị trường đầy tiềm năng và có nhu cầu lớn lao động nước ngoài VNword : theo cục quản_lý lao_động ngoài nước cata là thị_trường đầy tiềm_năng và có nhu_cầu lớn lao_động nước_ngoài	
S1FV	Input: FR Reference: VNsyl Output: theo cục quản lý lao động ở nước ngoài phía cata là một thị trường đầy tiềm năng và cần một lượng lớn lao động nước ngoài
S2FR	Input: FR Reference: VNword Output: theo thống_kê của cục quản_lý lao_động ngoài nước cata là một thị_trường đầy tiềm_năng và cần có sự lớn lượng lao_động nước_ngoài
S1VF	Input: VNsyl Reference: FR Output: selon le département de gestion des travailleurs étrangers cata était un marché plein de potentialités et aux besoins importants travailleurs étrangers
S2VF	Input: VNword Reference: FR Output : selon le département de gestion des travailleurs étrangers cata marché plein de potentialités et la grande travailleurs étrangers

Table 10 : Example of translation from systems.

4.3 Combining word- and syllable-based systems

We performed another experiment on combining syllable and word units on the Vietnamese side. We carried out the experiment on the *Vietnamese to French* translation direction only. In fact, the Moses toolkit supports the combination of phrase-tables. The phrase-tables of the system S1VF (T_{syl}) and system S2VF (T_{word}) were used. Another phrase-table (T_{word*}) was created from the T_{word}, in which all words in the phrase table were changed back into syllable representation (in this latter case, the word segmentation information was used during the alignment process and the phrase table construction, while the unit kept at the end remains the syllable). The combinations of these three phrase-tables were also created (by simple concatenation of the phrase tables). The Vietnamese input for this experiment was either in word or in syllable representation. As usual, the developing set was used for tuning the log-linear weights and the testing set was used to estimate the BLEU score. The obtained results are presented in Table 11. Some performances are marked as X since those combinations of input and phrase table do not make sense (for instance the combination of input in words and syllable-based phrase table).

Phrase-tables used	Input in syllable		Input in word	
	Dev	Tst	Dev	Tst
T_{syl}	**0.35**	**0.31**	X	X
T_{word}	X	X	0.35	0.30
T_{word*}	0.37	0.31	X	X
$T_{syl} + T_{word}$	0.35	0.31	0.36	0.30
$T_{syl} + T_{word*}$	**0.38**	**0.32**	X	X
$T_{word} + T_{word*}$	0.37	0.30	0.36	0.30

Table 11: The BLEU scores obtained from combination of phrase-tables on Dev set and Tst set (Vietnamese to French machine translation).

These results show that the performance can be improved by combining information from word and syllable representations of Vietnamese. (BLEU improvement from 0.35 to 0.38 on the Dev set and from 0.31 to 0.32 on the Tst set). In the future, we will analyze more the combination of syllable and word units for Vietnamese MT and we will investigate the use of confusion networks as an MT input, which have the advantage to keep both segmentations (word, syllable) into a same structure.

4.4 Comparing with Google Translate[1]

Google Translate system has recently supported Vietnamese. In most cases, it uses English as an intermediary language. For the first comparative evaluation, some simple tests were carried out. Two sets of data were used: *in domain data set* (the Tst set in section 4.2) and *out of domain data set*. The latter was obtained from a Vietnamese-French bilingual website[2] which is not a news website. After pre-processing and aligning manually, we obtained 100 PSPs in the out of domain data set. In these tests, the Vietnamese data were segmented into syllables. Both data sets were inputted to our translation systems (S1FV, S1VF) and the Google Translate system. The outputs of Google Translate system were post-processed (lowercased) and then the BLEU scores were estimated. Table 12 presents the results of these tests. While our system is logically better for in domain data set, it is also slightly better than Google for out of domain data set.

[1] http://translate.google.com
[2] http://www.ambafrance-vn.org

	Direction	BLEU score	
		Our system	Google
In domain (210 PSPs)	F→V	0.40	0.25
	V→F	0.31	0.16
Out of domain (100 PSPs)	F→V	0.25	0.24
	V→F	0.20	0.16

Table 12: Comparing with Google Translate.

5 Conclusions and perspectives

In this paper, we have presented our work on mining a comparable Vietnamese-French corpus and our first attempts at Vietnamese-French SMT. The paper has presented our document alignment method, which is based on publication date, special words and sentence alignment result. The proposed method is applied to Vietnamese and French news data collected from VNA. For Vietnamese and French data, we obtained around 12,100 parallel document pairs and 50,300 parallel sentence pairs. This is our first Vietnamese-French parallel bilingual corpus. We have built SMT systems using Moses. The BLEU scores for *French to Vietnamese* translation systems and *Vietnamese to French* translation systems were 0.40 and 0.31 in turn. Moreover, combining information from word and syllable representations of Vietnamese can be useful to improve the performance of Vietnamese MT system.

In the future, we will attempt to increase the corpus size (by using unsupervised SMT for instance) and investigate further the use of different Vietnamese lexical units (syllable, word) in a MT system.

References

Brown, Peter F., Jennifer C. Lai and Robert L. Mercer. 1991. *Aligning sentences in parallel corpora.* Proceedings of 47th Annual Meeting of the Association for Computational Linguistics.

Brown, Peter F., Stephen A. Della Pietra, Vincent J. Della Pietra and Robert L. Mercer. 1993. *The Mathematics of Statistical Machine Translation: Parameter Estimation.* Computational Linguistics. Vol. 19, no. 2.

Doan, Nguyen Hai. 2001. *Generation of Vietnamese for French-Vietnamese and English-Vietnamese Machine Translation.* ACL, Proceedings of the 8th European workshop on Natural Language Generation.

Gale, William A. and Kenneth W. Church. 1993. *A program for aligning sentences in bilingual corpora.* Proceedings of the 29th annual meeting on Association for Computational Linguistics.

Ho, Tu Bao. 2005. *Current Status of Machine Translation Research in Vietnam Towards Asian wide multi language machine translation project.* Vietnamese Language and Speech Processing Workshop.

Hutchins, W.John. 2001. *Machine translation over fifty years.* Histoire, epistemologie, langage: HEL, ISSN 0750-8069, Vol. 23, N° 1, 2001 , pages. 7-32.

Kay, Martin and Martin Roscheisen. 1993. *Text - translation alignment.* Association for Computational Linguistics.

Kilgarriff, Adam and Gregory Grefenstette. 2003. *Introduction to the Special Issue on the Web as Corpus.* Computational Linguistics, volume 29.

Koehn, Philipp, Franz Josef Och and Daniel Marcu. 2003. *Statistical phrase-based translation.* Conference of the North American Chapter of the Association for Computational Linguistics on Human Language Technology - Volume 1.

Koehn, Philipp. 2005. *Europarl: A Parallel Corpus for Statistical Machine Translation.* Machine Translation Summit.

Koehn, Philipp, Hieu Hoang, Alexandra Birch, Chris Callison-Burch, Richard Zens, Marcello Federico, Nicola Bertoldi, Brooke Cowan, Wade Shen and Christine Moran. 2007. *Moses: Open Source Toolkit for Statistical Machine Translation.* Proceedings of the ACL.

Kraaij, Wessel, Jian-Yun Nie and Michel Simard. 2003. *Embedding web-based statistical translation models in cross-language information retrieval.* Computational Linguistics, Volume 29 , Issue 3.

LE, Viet Bac, Brigitte Bigi, Laurent Besacier and Eric Castelli. 2003. *Using the Web for fast language model construction in minority languages.* Eurospeech'03.

Ma, Xiaoyi. 2006. *Champollion: A Robust Parallel Text Sentence Aligner.* LREC: Fifth International Conference on Language Resources and Evaluation.

Munteanu, Dragos Stefan and Daniel Marcu. 2006. *Extracting parallel sub-sentential fragments from non-parallel corpora* . 44th annual meeting of the Association for Computational Linguistics

Nguyen, Thi Minh Huyen. 2006. *Outils et ressources linguistiques pour l'alignement de textes multilingues français-vietnamiens.* Thèse présentée pour l'obtention du titre de Docteur de l'Université Henri Poincaré, Nancy 1 en Informatique.

Patry, Alexandre and Philippe Langlais. 2005. *Paradocs: un système d'identification automatique de documents parallèles.* 12e Conference sur le Traitement Automatique des Langues Naturelles. Dourdan, France.

Resnik, Philip and Noah A. Smith. 2003. *The Web as a Parallel Corpus.* Computational Linguistics.

Yang, Christopher C. and Kar Wing Li. 2002. *Mining English/Chinese Parallel Documents from the World Wide Web.* Proceedings of the 11th International World Wide Web Conference, Honolulu, USA.

Improving Arabic-Chinese Statistical Machine Translation using English as Pivot Language

Nizar Habash
Center for Computational Learning Systems
Columbia University
New York, NY 10115, USA
habash@ccls.columbia.edu

Jun Hu
Computer Science Department
Columbia University
New York, NY 10115, USA
jh2740@columbia.edu

Abstract

We present a comparison of two approaches for Arabic-Chinese machine translation using English as a pivot language: sentence pivoting and phrase-table pivoting. Our results show that using English as a pivot in either approach outperforms direct translation from Arabic to Chinese. Our best result is the phrase-pivot system which scores higher than direct translation by 1.1 BLEU points. An error analysis of our best system shows that we successfully handle many complex Arabic-Chinese syntactic variations.

1 Introduction

Arabic and Chinese are two languages with a very large global presence; however, there has not been, to our knowledge, any work on MT for this pair. Given the cost involved in creating parallel corpora for Arabic and Chinese and given that there are lots of available resources (in particular parallel corpora) for Arabic and English and for Chinese and English, we are interested in exploring the role English might serve as a pivot (or bridge) language. In this paper we explore different ways of pivoting through English to translate Arabic to Chinese. Our work is similar to previous research on pivot languages except in that our three languages (source, pivot and target) are very different and from completely unrelated families. We focus our experiments on a trilingual parallel corpus to keep all conditions experimentally clean. Our results show that using English as a pivot language for translating Arabic to Chinese actually outperforms direct translation. We believe this may be a result of English being a sort of middle ground between Arabic and Chinese in terms of different linguistic features and, in particular, word order.

Section 2 describes previous work. Section 3 discusses relevant linguistic issues of Arabic, Chinese and English. Section 4 describes our system and different pivoting techniques. And Section 5 presents our experimental results.

2 Previous Work

There has been a lot of work on translation from Chinese to English (Wang et al., 2007; Crego and Mariño, 2007; Carpuat and Wu, 2007; among others) and from Arabic to English (Sadat and Habash, 2006, Al-Onaizan and Papineni, 2006; among others). There is also a fair amount of work on translation into Chinese from Japanese, Korean and English (Isahara et al., 2007; Kim et al., 2002; Ye et al., 2007; among others). In 2008, the National Institute of Standards and Technology (NIST) MT Evaluation competition introduced English-Chinese as a new evaluation track.[1]

Much work has been done on exploiting multilingual corpora for MT or related tasks such as lexical induction or word alignment. Schafer and Yarowsky (2002) induced translation lexicons for languages without common parallel corpora using a bridge language that is related to the target languages. Simard (1999) described a sentence aligner that makes simultaneous decisions in a trilingual parallel text. Kumar et al. (2007) improved Arabic-English MT by using available parallel data in other languages. Callison-Burch et al (2006) exploited the existence of multiple parallel corpora to learn paraphrases for Phrase-based MT. Filali and Bilmes (2005) improved word alignment by leveraging multilingual parallel translations.

Most related to our work on pivoting are the following: Utiyama and Isahara (2007) studied

[1] http://www.nist.gov/speech/tests/mt/2008/doc/

Proceedings of the Fourth Workshop on Statistical Machine Translation, pages 173–181,
Athens, Greece, 30 March – 31 March 2009. ©2009 Association for Computational Linguistics

sentence and phrase pivoting strategies using three European languages (Spanish, French and German). Their results showed that pivoting does not work as well as direct translation. Wu and Wang (2007) focused on phrase pivoting. They proposed an interpolated scheme that employs two phrase tables: one extracted from a small amount of direct parallel data; and the other extracted from large amounts of indirect data with a third pivoting language. They compared results for different European language as well as Chinese-Japanese translation using English as a pivoting language. Their results show that simple pivoting does not improve over direct MT; however, extending the direct MT system with phrases learned through pivoting helps. Babych et al. (2007) compared two methods for translating into English from Ukrainian: direct Ukrainian-English MT versus translation via a cognate language, Russian. Their comparison showed that it is possible to achieve better translation quality via pivoting.

In this paper we use a standard phrase-based MT approach (Koehn, 2004) that is in the same spirit of most statistical MT nowadays. We believe that we are the first to explore the Arabic-Chinese language pair in MT. We differ from previous pivoting research in showing that pivoting can outperform direct translation even when the source, target and pivot languages are all linguistically unrelated.

3 Linguistic Issues

In this section we discuss different linguistic phenomena in which Arabic, English and Chinese are divergent. We consider orthography, morphology and syntax. We also present a new metric for quantifying linguistic differences.

3.1 Orthography

Arabic is written from right-to-left using an alphabet of 36 letters and eight *optional* diacritical marks. Arabic is written in a cursive mostly word-internal connected form, but words are separated by white spaces. The absence of Arabic diacritics adds a lot of ambiguity.

Chinese uses a complex orthography that includes around 10,000 characters in common use. Characters convey semantic rather than phonological information. Chinese is written from left-to-right or top-down. Chinese words can be made out of one, two or more characters. However, words are written without separating spaces. Word segmentation is a major challenge for processing Chinese (Wu, 1998).

English uses the Roman alphabet and its words are written with separating white spaces. English orthography is much closer to Arabic than it is to Chinese.

3.2 Morphology

Arabic is a morphologically rich language with a large set of morphological features such person, number, gender, voice, aspect, mood, case, and state. Arabic features are realized using both concatenative (affixes and stems) and templatic (root and patterns) morphology with a variety of morphological, phonological and orthographic adjustments. In addition, Arabic has a set of very common clitics that are written attached to the word, e.g., the conjunction +و *w+* 'and', the preposition +ب *b+*[2] 'with/in', the definite article +ال *Al+* 'the' and a range of pronominal clitics that can attach to nouns (as possessives) or verbs and prepositions (as objects).

In stark contrast to Arabic, Chinese is an isolating language with no morphology to talk of. However, what Chinese lacks in morphology it replaces with a complex system of nominal quantifiers and verbal aspects. For example, in Figure 1 (at the end of this paper), Chinese marks the definiteness and humanness of the word 学生 *Xue Sheng* 'student' using the two characters 这位 *Zhe Wei* 'this person', while the indefiniteness and book-*ness* of the word 书 *Shu* 'book' are indicated through the characters 一本 *Yi Ben* 'one book-type'.

English has a simple limited morphology primarily indicating number and tense. English stands in the middle between Arabic and Chinese in terms of morphological complexity.

3.3 Syntax

Arabic is morpho-syntactically complex with many differences from Chinese and English. We describe here three prominent syntactic issues in which Arabic, Chinese and English vary widely: subject-verb order, verb-

[2] Arabic transliteration is in the Habash-Soudi-Buckwalter scheme (Habash et al. 2007).

prepositional phrase order and nominal modification.

First, Arabic verb subjects may be: (a.) pro-dropped (verb conjugated), (b.) pre-verbal, or (c.) post-verbal. The morphology of the Arabic verb varies in the three cases. By contrast English and Chinese are both generally subject-verb languages. When translating from Arabic, the challenge is to determine whether there is an explicit subject and, if there is, whether it is pre- or post-verbal. Since Arabic objects also follow the verb, a sequence of *Verb NounPhrase* may be a *verb subject* or a *pro-drop-verb object*. In the example in Figure 1, the subject (*student*) appears after the sentence initial verb in Arabic, but at the beginning of the sentence in Chinese and English.

Secondly, as for the word order of prepositional phrases (PP), Arabic and English are similar in that PPs generally appear at the end of the sentence (after all the verbal arguments) and to a lesser extent at its beginning. In Chinese, however, some PPs (in particular locatives and temporals) must appear between subject and verb. Other PPs may appear at end of sentence. In the example in Figure 1, the location of the *reading*, 'in the classroom' appears at the end of the Arabic and English sentences; however, it is between subject and verb in Chinese.

Finally, we distinguish three types of nominal modification: adjectival (as in 'red book'), possessive (as in 'John's book') and relative (as in 'the book [which] John gave me'). All of these modification types are handled in a similar manner in Chinese: using the particle 的 *De* to connect modifier with modified. Modifiers always precede the modified. For example, in Figure 1, 'a book about China' appears as 关于中国 的书 *Guan Yu Zhong Guo De Shu 'about China De book'*. Similarly, 'the student's book' would be translated as 学生 的 书 *Xue Sheng De Shu 'student DE book'*. Like Chinese, English adjectival modifiers precede what they modify. However, relative modifiers follow. Possessive modifiers in English can appear before or after: 'the student's book' or 'the book of the student'. Unlike English and Chinese, Arabic adjectival modifiers typically follow their nouns (with a small exception of some superlative adjectives). However, similar to English but not Chinese, Arabic relative modifiers follow what they modify. As for possessive modifiers, Arabic has a special construction called *Idafa*, in which modifiers immediately follow what they modify without connecting particles. For example, 'the student's book' can only be translated in Arabic as كتاب الطالب ***ktAb*** *AlTAlb 'book the-student'*.[3]

These different phenomena are summarized in Table 1. It is interesting to point out that English phenomena are a middle ground for Arabic and Chinese: in some cases English is closer to Arabic and in others to Chinese.

	Arabic	**English**	**Chinese**
Orthography	reduced alphabet	alphabet	Characters
Morphology	Rich	Poor	Very Poor
Subject-Verb	V Subj Subj V V_{subj}	Subj V	Subj … V
Verb-PP	V…PP	V…PP	PP V V PP
Adjectival Modifier	N Adj	Adj N	Adj DE N
Possessive Modifier	N Poss	N of Poss Poss 's N	Poss DE N
Relative Modifier	N Rel	N Rel	Rel DE N

Table 1: Comparing different linguistic phenomena in Arabic, English and Chinese

3.4 Quantifying Linguistic Differences

The previous section described specific types of linguistic phenomena without distinguishing them in terms of frequency or effect distance. For example, Arabic nominals (nouns, adjectives and adverbs) are seven times as frequent as verbs; and nominal modification phenomena are more likely local than long distance compared to verb-subject order. A proper quantification of these different phenomena requires trilingual parallel treebanks, which are not available. As such, we propose a simple metric to quantify linguistic differences by measuring the translation complexity of different language pairs. The metric is Average Relative Alignment Length (ARAL):

$$ARAL = \frac{1}{|L|} \sum_{l_{ab} \in L} \left| \frac{p_a}{S_a} - \frac{p_b}{S_b} \right|$$

[3] Arabic dialects allow an additional construction. We focus here on Modern Standard Arabic.

We define L as the set of all alignment links linking words in a parallel corpus of languages A and B. For each alignment link, l_{ab}, linking words a and b, we define p_a and p_b as the position of words a and b in their respective sentences. We also define S_a and S_b as the lengths of the sentences in which a and b appear, respectively. ARAL is the mean of the absolute difference in relative word position (p_i/S_i) of the words of every alignment link. The larger ARAL is, the more reordering and insertions/deletions we expect, and the more complexity and difference. ARAL is a harsh metric since it ignores syntactic structure facts that explain how clusters of words move together.

A-C	A-E	E-C
0.1679	0.0846	0.1531

Table 2: Average Relative Alignment Length for pairs of Arabic (A), English (E) and Chinese (C)

Table 2 presents the ARAL scores for each language pair. These scores are computed over the *grow-diag-final* symmetrized alignment we use in our system (Koehn, 2004). $ARAL_{AC}$ is the highest and $ARAL_{AE}$ is the lowest. The average length of sentences is generally close among these languages (given the segmentation we use): Arabic is ~32 words, English is ~31 and Chinese is ~29. Arabic and English are much closer to each other than either to Chinese. This may be the result of Arabic tokenization and Chinese segmentation technologies which have been developed for translation into English. We address this issue in section 4.1. The ARAL scores agree with our assessment that English is closer to Arabic and to Chinese than Arabic is to Chinese. As a result, we believe it may serve as a good pivot language for translating Arabic to Chinese.

4 System Description

In this section, we describe the different systems we compare.

4.1 Data

Our data collection is the United Nations (UN) multilingual corpus, provided by the LDC [4] (catalog no. LDC2004E12). The UN corpus has in principle parallel sentences for Arabic, English and Chinese. However, the Arabic-English (A-E) data and Chinese-English (C-E) data sets were not in synch. The A-E data set has 3.2M lines while the C-E data set has 5.0M lines. We used the document ID provided in the data to match sentences from A-E against those in C-E to generate a three-way parallel corpus with 2.6M lines.

We tokenized the Arabic data in the Arabic Treebank scheme (Sadat and Habash, 2006). Chinese was segmented into words using a segmenter developed by Howard Johnson for the Portage Chinese-English MT system.[5] So a sentence consists of multiple words with spaces between them and each word is comprised of one or more characters. English was simply processed to split punctuation and "'s". The same preprocessing was used in all systems compared.

We are aware of two potentially biased aspects of our experimental setting. First, the Arabic and Chinese portions of our data collection, the UN corpus, are known to be generated from English originals. And secondly, the preprocessing techniques we used on Arabic and Chinese were developed for translation from these languages into English. These two aspects make English potentially more central to our experiments than if the data collection and preprocessing were done on Arabic and Chinese independent of English. Of course, it must be noted that the data bias is not unique to our work but rather a challenge for any bilingual corpus, in which translation is done from one language to another. Additionally, we can argue that the English bias in data and preprocessing does not only affect the Arabic-English and English-Chinese pipelines, but it also makes the Arabic and Chinese data potentially closer. Finally, given the expense involved in creating direct Arabic-Chinese parallel text and given the large amounts of Arabic-English and English-Chinese data, we think our results (with English bias) are still valid and interesting. That said, we leave the question of Arabic-Chinese optimization to future work.

4.2 Direct A-C MT System

In our baseline direct A-C system, we used the Arabic and Chinese portions of our parallel corpus to train a direct phrase-based MT system. We use GIZA++ (Och and Ney, 2003) for

[4] http://www.ldc.upenn.edu

[5] http://iit-iti.nrc-cnrc.gc.ca/projects-projets/portage_e.html

word alignment, and the Pharaoh system suite to build the phrase table and decode (Koehn, 2004). The Chinese language model (LM) used 200M words from the UN corpus segmented in a manner consistent with our training. The trigram LM was built using the SRILM toolkit (Stolcke, 2002).

4.3 Sentence Pivoting MT System

The sentence pivoting system (A-s-C) used English as an interface between two separate pharse-based MT systems: an Arabic-English direct system and an English-Chinese direct system. When translating Arabic to Chinese, the English top-1 output of the Arabic-English system was passed as input to the English-Chinese system. The English LM used to train the Arabic-English system is built from the counterpart of the Chinese data used to build the Chinese LM in our parallel corpus. We use 210M English words in total.

4.4 Phrase Pivoting MT System

The phrase pivoting system (A-p-C) extracts a new Arabic to Chinese phrase table using the Arabic-English phrase table and the English-Chinese phrase table. We consider a Chinese phrase a translation of an Arabic phrase only if some English phrase can bridge the two. We use the following formulae to compute the lexical and phrase probabilities in the new phrase table in a similar manner to Utiyama and Isahara (2007). Here, ϕ is the lexical probability and p_w is the phrase probability.

$$\phi'(a \mid c) = \sum_e \phi(a \mid e)\phi(e \mid c)$$

$$\phi'(c \mid a) = \sum_e \phi(c \mid e)\phi(e \mid a)$$

$$p_w'(a \mid c) = \sum_e p_w(a \mid e) p_w(e \mid c)$$

$$p_w'(c \mid a) = \sum_e p_w(c \mid e) p_w(e \mid a)$$

The left hand side of the formulae represents the four required probabilities in a Pharaoh Arabic-Chinese phrase table.

5 Evaluation

For each of the direct system, the sentence-pivoting system and the phrase-pivoting system, we conduct four sets of experiments with different data sizes. Table 3 illustrates the training data size for each experiment. The training data is collected from the beginning of the same parallel corpus, so the larger training sets include the smaller ones.

	Lines	Words (Arabic)
S	32500	1 Million
M	65000	2 Million
L	130000	4 Million
XL	260000	8 Million

Table 3: Training Data Size

We use two other data sets (1K lines each) for tuning and testing. Each sentence in these sets has only one reference. Tuning and testing data sets are the same across all experiments and systems. In all our experiments, we decode using Pharaoh (Koehn, 2004) with a distortion limit of 4 and a maximum phrase length of 7. Tuning is done for each experimental condition using Och's Minimum Error Training (Och, 2003).

Note that for each set of experiments with the same data size, we draw Chinese, Arabic and English from the same chunk of three way parallel corpus. For example, in S size experiments, the two phrase tables used to build a new table in the phrase-pivoting approach are extracted respectively from the A-E and E-C systems built in the sentence-pivoting approach with size S corpora.

5.1 Direct System Results

Table 4 shows the results of the direct translation system A-C. It also includes the result for A-E and E-C direct translation. As expected, as we double the size of the data, the BLEU score (Papineni et al., 2002) increases. However, the rate of increase is not always consistent. In particular, the M and L conditions vary highly in A-E compared to A-C. This is odd especially given that we are comparing the same set of data from the three parallel corpora. We speculate that this may have to do with an oddity in that portion of the data set that may have a different quality than the rest. We see the effect of this drop in A-E in the next section. BLEU is measured on English case-insensitively. BLEU is measured on Chinese using segmented words not characters.

	A-C	A-E	E-C
S	11.17	21.89	19.29
M	13.43 (+20.2%)	23.86 (+9.0%)	20.85 (+8.1%)
L	14.62 (+8.9%)	24.86 (+4.2%)	22.42 (+7.5%)
XL	16.17 (+10.6%)	27.96 (+12.5%)	24.11 (+7.5%)

Table 4: BLEU-4 scores comparing performance of direct translation of Arabic-Chinese (A-C), Arabic-English (A-E) and English-Chinese (E-C) for four training data sizes. The percentage increases are against the immediately lower data size.

5.2 Pivoting System Results

In Table 5, we present the results of the sentence pivoting system (A-s-C) and the phrase pivoting system (A-p-C). Under all conditions, A-s-C and A-p-C outperform A-C. A-p-C generally outperforms A-s-C except in the M data condition. The effect in the S conditions is bigger than the XL condition. In our best result (XL), we increase the BLEU score by over 1.12 points. Furthermore, the relative BLEU score increase from the L condition for A-p-C is 15.5% as opposed to A-C's 10.6%. The A-s-C relative increase from L to XL is 12.8%. This suggests that we are making better use of the available resources. The differences between A-s-C and A-C and between A-p-C and A-C are statistically significant at the 95% confidence level (Zhang et al., 2004). The differences between the two pivoting systems are not statistically significant. Examples from our best performing system are shown in Figure 2.

	A-C	A-s-C		A-p-C	
S	11.17	12.24	9.6%	13.12	17.5%
M	13.43	14.10	5.0%	13.75	2.4%
L	14.62	14.96	2.3%	14.97	2.4%
XL	16.17	16.88	4.4%	17.29	6.9%

Table 5: Word-based BLEU-4 scores. A-C is direct translation. A-s-C is indirect translation through sentence pivoting and A-p-C is indirect translation through phrase pivoting. The percentages indicate relative improvement over A-C.

Our results are consistent with (Utiyama and Isahara, 2007) in that phrase-pivoting generally does better than sentence pivoting. However, we disagree with them in that, for us, direct translation is not the best system to use. We believe that this effect is caused by the combination of the very different languages we use. English is truly bridging between Arabic and Chinese in many linguistic dimensions. We think it's English's middle-ground-ness that makes these results possible.

		A-C	A-s-C		A-p-C	
BLEU-1	**S**	53.75	54.38	1.2%	54.64	1.7%
	M	56.65	57.00	0.6%	55.88	-1.4%
	L	58.37	57.69	-1.2%	58.79	0.7%
	XL	**59.90**	**60.34**	**0.7%**	**60.28**	**0.6%**
BLEU-4	**S**	21.32	21.80	2.3%	22.88	7.3%
	M	23.84	24.22	1.6%	23.76	-0.3%
	L	24.98	25.14	0.6%	25.87	3.6%
	XL	**25.95**	**27.11**	**4.5%**	**27.70**	**6.7%**
BLEU-7	**S**	9.82	10.02	2.0%	11.42	16.3%
	M	11.56	11.84	2.4%	11.64	0.7%
	L	12.23	12.52	2.4%	13.09	7.0%
	XL	**12.69**	**13.52**	**6.5%**	**14.57**	**14.8%**

Table 6: Character-based BLEU scores for n-grams of maximum size 1, 4, and 7. The percentages are relative to the direct system.

In Table 6, we present additional scores using BLEU-1, BLEU-4 and BLEU-7 measured at the character level as opposed to the harsher measure at word level. Ignoring the odd behavior in M and L conditions, the sentence-pivot and phrase-pivot approaches improve over the direct translation baseline in terms of fluency (BLEU-7) and accuracy (BLEU-1). Under the small data condition, the phrase-pivot approach increases the BLEU-4 score three times the increase of the sentence-pivot approach. That ratio reduces to 1.5 times in the XL condition. The relative improvements of the pivoting systems over the direct system are small at BLEU-1 and much bigger at higher BLEU scores. This suggests that differences between the pivoting systems and the direct system are not in terms of lexical coverage but rather in terms of better reordering.

The lengths of the outputs of all the systems (direct and pivoting) are larger than the reference length which means no brevity penalty was applied in BLEU calculation. Also, no BLEU-gaming was done by OOV deletion: all OOV words were left in the output.

5.3 Error Analysis

We conducted an error analysis of our best performing system (Phrase Pivot XL) to understand what issues need to be addressed in the future. We took a sample of 50 sentences restricted in length to be between 15 and 35 Chinese words. A Chinese native speaker compared our output to the reference translation and judged its quality in terms of two categories: syntax and lexical choice.

In terms of syntax, our judge identified all the occurrences of (a) subjects and verbs, (b) prepositional phrases and verbs and (c) modified nouns. Each case was judged as *acceptable* or *wrong*. Placing a verb before its subject, a preverbal prepositional phrase after its verb, or a modifier after the noun it modifies are all considered *wrong*. We correctly produce subject-verb order 73% of the time; and we produce nominal modification order correctly 64% of the time. Our biggest weakness in terms of syntax is prepositional phrase order. It is worth noting that the two phenomena we do better on are addressed in translation from Arabic to English, unlike prepositional phrase order which is where Chinese is different from both Arabic and English.

In terms of lexical choice our judge considered the translation quality of three classes of words: Nominals (nouns, pronouns, adjectives and adverbs), Verbs, and other particles (prepositions, conjunctions and quantifiers). An incorrectly translated or deleted word is considered *wrong*. We perform on nominals and particles at about the same level of 90%. Verbs are our biggest challenge with accuracy below 80%. The ratio of deleted words among all wrong words is rather high at about 30% (for nominals and for verbs). The detailed results of the error analysis are shown in Table 7.

Finally, there are 27 instances of Arabic Out-of-Vocabulary (OOV) words (1.93% of all words) that are not handled. Ten (37%) of these are proper nouns. The rest belong to mostly nouns and adjectives. Orthogonally, 19 (70%) of all OOV words belong to the genre of science reports, which is quite different from the data we train on. The OOVs include complex terms like السيبروفلوكساسين *AlsybrwflwksAsyn* 'ciprofloxacin' and رجاجات مدارية *rjAjAt mdAryħ* '[chemical] orbital shakers'. Other less frequent OOV cases involve bad tokenization and less common morphological constructions.

		Total	Acceptable	Wrong
Syntax	Subj-Verb	48	35(73%)	13 (27%)
	Verb-PP	46	17 (37%)	29 (63%)
	Noun-Mod	97	62 (64%)	35 (36%)
Lexical Choice	Nominal	408	368 (90%)	40 (10%)
	Verb	124	98 (79%)	26 (21%)
	Particle	116	106 (91%)	10 (9%)

Table 7: Results of human error analysis on a sample from the A-p-C system (XL)

6 Conclusion and Future Work

We presented a comparison of two approaches for Arabic-Chinese MT using English as a pivot language against direct MT. Our results show that using English as a pivot in either approach outperforms direct translation from Arabic to Chinese. We believe that this is a result of English being a sort of middle ground between Arabic and Chinese in terms of different linguistic features (in particular word order). Our best result is the phrase-pivot system which scores higher than direct translation by 1.1 BLEU points. An error analysis of our system shows that we successfully handle many complex Arabic-Chinese syntactic variations although there is a large space for improvement still.

In the future, we plan on exploring tighter coupling of Arabic and Chinese through comparing different methods of preprocessing Arabic for Arabic-Chinese MT, in a similar manner to Sadat and Habash (2006). We also plan to study how well these results carry on to different corpora (bilingual Arabic-English and English-Chinese) as opposed to the trilingual corpus used in this paper. We also plan to investigate whether our findings in Arabic-English-Chinese can be used for other different language triples.

Acknowledgements

We would like to thank Roland Kuhn, George Foster and Howard Johnson of the National Research Council Canada for helpful advice and discussions and for providing us with the Chinese preprocessing tools.

Figure 1: An example highlighting Arabic-English-Chinese syntactic differences

يقرأ$_1$ الطالب$_2$ المجتهد$_3$ كتابا$_4$ عن$_5$ الصين$_6$ في$_7$ الصف$_8$.

yqrÂ$_1$ AlTAlb$_2$ Almjthd$_3$ ktAbA$_4$ çn$_5$ AlSyn$_6$ fy$_7$ AlSf$_8$.

read$_1$ the-student$_2$ the-diligent$_3$ a-book$_4$ about$_5$ china$_6$ in$_7$ the-classroom$_8$.

这$_1$位$_2$勤奋$_3$ 的$_4$学生$_5$ 在$_6$教室$_7$ 读$_8$ 一$_9$本$_{10}$ 关于$_{11}$ 中国$_{12}$ 的$_{13}$书$_{14}$。

this$_1$ quant$_2$ diligent$_3$ de$_4$ student$_5$ in$_6$ classroom$_7$ read$_8$ one$_9$ quant$_{10}$ about$_{11}$ china$_{12}$ de$_{13}$ book$_{14}$

Zhe$_1$ Wei$_2$ Qin Fen$_3$ De$_4$ Xue Sheng$_5$ Zai$_6$ Jiao Shi$_7$ Du$_8$ Yi$_9$ Ben$_{10}$ Guan Yu$_{11}$ Zhong Guo$_{12}$ De$_{13}$ Shu$_{14}$

The diligent student is reading a book about China in the classroom.

Figure 2: Examples of Arabic-Chinese MT output. English references and English glosses for Arabic and Chinese are provided to ease readability.

Arabic	وبناء على ذلك ، فان هذه البيئة معرضة للفساد وانعدام الكفاءة الى حد بعيد . and-building upon this , therefore this environment susceptible to-corruption and-lack qualification to extent big .
Eng-Ref	Consequently , this environment lends itself to significant degrees of corruption and inefficiency .
Chn-Ref	因此,这种环境导致了高度腐败和效率低下。 Therefore, this kind environment caused have high-degree corruption and efficiency low.
Chn-Out	因此,这种环境中的腐败和缺乏 效率在很大程度上 。 Therefore , this kind environment inside DE corruption and lack efficiency on big degree top.

Arabic	واذا لم ترد المعلومات المطلوبة في غضون 90 يوما اخرى ، يسقط الطلب . and-if did-not arrive information requested in period 90 day other , lapse application .
Eng-Ref	If the requested information is not received within a further 90 days , the application will lapse.
Chn-Ref	如果再过 90 天仍未收到所 要求的资料,则申请失效。 If again pass 90 day yet not received requested DE information , then application loose validity.
Chn-Out	如果没有收到所 要求的资料 90 天内提供更多的要求。 If not receive requested DE information 90 day within provide more DE request.

Arabic	... تيسير تبادل المعلومات والتشارك في الموارد بين الاجهزة الحكومية . … facilitation exchanging the-information and-the-sharing in the-resources between the-agencies the-governmental .
Eng-Ref	… to facilitate the sharing of information and resources between government agencies .
Chn-Ref	…为各政府机构之间交流信息和资源提供便利 。 …for all government agencies among exchanging information and resource offer convenience.
Chn-Out	…旨在促进信息交流和分享资源政府间机构。 ...purpose in facilitate information exchanging and sharing resource governments among agency .

Arabic	وينبغي للحكومات ان تنظر في استحداث تدابير مناسبة وفعالة للتقليل الى الحد الادنى من احتمالات الفساد . and-should to-government that look in introducing measures appropriate and-effective to-reduce to extent least from possibilities the-corruption
Eng-Ref	Governments should consider introducing appropriate and effective measures to minimize the potential for corruption.
Chn-Ref	各国政府应考虑采取适当的有效措施,最大 限度地 减少产生腐败的可能性 。 all countries governments should consider adopt appropriate DE effective methods , to-biggest-extent DE reduce producing corruption DE possibility.
Chn-Out	各 国政府应考虑建立适当的有效措施,最大限度地减少腐败的可能性 。 all countries governments should consider build appropriate DE effective methods , to-biggest-extent DE reduce corruption DE possibility.

References

Yaser Al-Onaizan and Kishore Papineni. 2006 Distortion models for statistical machine translation. *In Proceedings of* Coling-ACL'06. Sydney, Australia.

Bogdan Babych, Anthony Hartley, and Serge Sharoff. 2007. Translating from under-resourced languages: comparing direct transfer against pivot translation. *In Proceedings of* MT Summit XI, Copenhagen, Denmark.

Tim Buckwalter. 2002. Buckwalter Arabic morphological analyzer version 1.0.

Chris Callison-Burch, Philipp Koehn, and Miles Osborne. 2006. Improved statistical machine translation using paraphrases. *In Proceedings of HLT-NAACL'06.* New York, NY, USA.

Marine Carpuat and Dekai Wu. 2007. Context-dependent phrasal translation lexicons for statistical machine translation. *In Proceedings of* MT Summit XI, Copenhagen, Denmark.

Josep M. Crego and José B. Mariño. 2007. Syntax-enhanced n-gram-based SMT. *In Proceedings of* MT Summit XI, Copenhagen, Denmark.

Karim Filali and Jeff Bilmes. Leveraging Multiple Languages to Improve Statistical MT Word Alignments. *In Proceedings of* ASRU'05, Cancun, Mexico.

Nizar Habash. 2007. Syntactic preprocessing for statistical machine translation. *In Proceedings of* MT Summit XI, Copenhagen, Denmark.

Nizar Habash, Abdelhadi Soudi, and Tim Buckwalter. 2007. On Arabic Transliteration. In A. van den Bosch and A. Soudi, editors, Arabic Computational Morphology: Knowledge-based and Empirical Methods. Springer.

Hitoshi Isahara, Sadao Kurohashi, Jun'ichi Tsujii, Kiyotaka Uchimoto, Hiroshi Nakagawa, Hiroyuki Kaji, and Shun'ichi Kikuchi. 2007. Development of a Japanese-Chinese machine translation system. *In Proceedings of* MT Summit XI, Copenhagen, Denmark.

Philipp Koehn. 2004. Pharaoh: a Beam Search Decoder for Phrase-based Statistical Machine Translation Models. *In Proceedings of* AMTA'04, Washington, DC, USA.

Shankar Kumar, Franz Och, and Wolfgang Macherey. 2007. Improving word alignment with bridge languages. *In Proceedings of* EMNLP-CoNLL'07, Prague, Czech Republic.

Young-Suk Lee. 2004. Morphological Analysis for Statistical Machine Translation. *In Proceedings of* HLT-NAACL'04, Boston, MA, USA.

Franz Josef Och and Hermann Ney. 2003. A Systematic Comparison of Various Statistical Alignment Models. *Computational Linguistics*, 29 (1):19–52.

Franz Josef Och. 2003. Minimum Error Rate Training for Statistical Machine Translation. *In Proceedings of* ACL'03, Sapporo, Japan.

Fatiha Sadat and Nizar Habash. 2006. Combination of Arabic preprocessing schemes for statistical machine translation. *In Proceedings of* Coling-ACL'06. Sydney, Australia.

Kishore Papineni, Salim Roukos, Todd Ward, and Wei-Jing Zhu. 2002. BLEU: a Method for Automatic Evaluation of Machine Translation. *In Proceedings of* ACL'02, Philadelphia, PA, USA.

Charles Schafer & David Yarowsky. 2002. Inducing translation lexicons via diverse similarity measures and bridge languages. *In Proceedings of* CoNLL'02, Taipei, Taiwan.

Micheal. Simard. 1999. Text translation alignment: Three languages are better than two. *In Proceedings of EMNLP-VLC'99, College Park, MD, USA.*

Michel Simard, Nicola Ueffing, Pierre Isabelle, and Roland Kuhn. 2007. Rule-based translation with statistical phrase-based post-editing. *In Proceedings* of the workshop on Statistical Machine Translation, ACL'07, Prague, Czech Republic.

Andreas Stolcke. 2002. SRILM - an Extensible Language Modeling Toolkit. I*n Proceedings of* ICSLP'02, Denver, CO, USA.

Masao Utiyama and Hitoshi Isahara. 2007. A comparison of pivot methods for phrase-based statistical machine translation. *In Proceedings of* NAACL-HLT'07, Rochester, NY, USA.

Chao Wang, Michael Collins, and Philipp Koehn. 2007. Chinese syntactic reordering for statistical machine translation. *In Proceedings of* EMNLP-CoNLL'07, Prague, Czech Republic.

Dekai Wu. 1998. A Position Statement on Chinese Segmentation. *Presented at the Chinese Language Processing Workshop.* http://www.cs.ust.hk/~dekai/papers/segmentation.html.

Hua Wu and Haifeng Wang. 2007. Pivot language aproach for phrase-based statistical machine translation. *In Proceedings of* ACL'07, Prague, Czech Republic.

Yang Ye, Karl-Michael Schneider, and Steven Abney. 2007. Aspect marker generation in English-to-Chinese machine translation. *In Proceedings of* MT Summit XI, Copenhagen, Denmark.

Ying Zhang, Stephan Vogel and Alex Waibel, Interpreting Bleu/NIST scores: How much improvement do we need to have a better system?, *In Proceedings of* LREC'04, Lisbon, Portugal.

Domain Adaptation for Statistical Machine Translation with Monolingual Resources

Nicola Bertoldi **Marcello Federico**
FBK-irst - Ricerca Scientifica e Tecnologica
Via Sommarive 18, Povo (TN), Italy
{bertoldi, federico}@fbk.eu

Abstract

Domain adaptation has recently gained interest in statistical machine translation to cope with the performance drop observed when testing conditions deviate from training conditions. The basic idea is that in-domain training data can be exploited to adapt all components of an already developed system. Previous work showed small performance gains by adapting from limited in-domain bilingual data. Here, we aim instead at significant performance gains by exploiting large but cheap monolingual in-domain data, either in the source or in the target language. We propose to synthesize a bilingual corpus by translating the monolingual adaptation data into the counterpart language. Investigations were conducted on a state-of-the-art phrase-based system trained on the Spanish–English part of the UN corpus, and adapted on the corresponding Europarl data. Translation, re-ordering, and language models were estimated after translating in-domain texts with the baseline. By optimizing the interpolation of these models on a development set the BLEU score was improved from 22.60% to 28.10% on a test set.

1 Introduction

A well-known problem of Statistical Machine Translation (SMT) is that performance quickly degrades as soon as testing conditions deviate from training conditions. The very simple reason is that the underlying statistical models always tend to closely approximate the empirical distributions of the training data, which typically consist of bilingual texts and monolingual target-language texts. The former provide a means to learn likely translations pairs, the latter to form correct sentences with translated words. Besides the general difficulties of language translation, which we do not consider here, there are two aspects that make machine learning of this task particularly hard. First, human language has intrinsically very sparse statistics at the surface level, hence gaining complete knowledge on translation phrase pairs or target language n-grams is almost impractical. Second, language is highly variable with respect to several dimensions, style, genre, domain, topics, etc. Even apparently small differences in domain might result in significant deviations in the underlying statistical models. While data sparseness corroborates the need of large language samples in SMT, linguistic variability would indeed suggest to consider many alternative data sources as well. By rephrasing a famous saying we could say that "no data is better than more *and assorted* data".

The availability of language resources for SMT has dramatically increased over the last decade, at least for a subset of relevant languages and especially for what concerns monolingual corpora. Unfortunately, the increase in quantity has not gone in parallel with an increase in assortment, especially for what concerns the most valuable resource, that is bilingual corpora. Large parallel data available to the research community are for the moment limited to texts produced by international organizations (European Parliament, United Nations, Canadian Hansard), press agencies, and technical manuals.

The limited availability of parallel data poses challenging questions regarding the portability of SMT across different application domains and language pairs, and its adaptability with respect to language variability within the same application domain.

This work focused on the second issue, namely the adaptation of a Spanish-to-English phrase-based SMT system across two apparently close domains: the United Nation corpus and the Euro-

Proceedings of the Fourth Workshop on Statistical Machine Translation, pages 182–189,
Athens, Greece, 30 March – 31 March 2009.

pean Parliament corpus. Cross-domain adaptation is faced under the assumption that only monolingual texts are available, either in the source language or in the target language.

The paper is organized as follows. Section 2 presents previous work on the problem of adaptation in SMT; Section 3 introduces the exemplar task and research questions we addressed; Section 4 describes the SMT system and the adaptation techniques that were investigated; Section 5 presents and discusses experimental results; and Section 6 provides conclusions.

2 Previous Work

Domain adaptation in SMT has been investigated only recently. In (Eck et al., 2004) adaptation is limited to the target language model (LM). The background LM is combined with one estimated on documents retrieved from the WEB by using the input sentence as query and applying cross-language information retrieval techniques. Refinements of this approach are described in (Zhao et al., 2004).

In (Hildebrand et al., 2005) information retrieval techniques are applied to retrieve sentence pairs from the training corpus that are relevant to the test sentences. Both the language and the translation models are retrained on the extracted data.

In (Foster and Kuhn, 2007) two basic settings are investigated: cross-domain adaptation, in which a small sample of parallel in-domain text is assumed, and dynamic adaptation, in which only the current input source text is considered. Adaptation relies on mixture models estimated on the training data through some unsupervised clustering method. Given available adaptation data, mixture weights are re-estimated ad-hoc. A variation of this approach was also recently proposed in (Finch and Sumita, 2008). In (Civera and Juan, 2007) mixture models are instead employed to adapt a word alignment model to in-domain parallel data.

In (Koehn and Schroeder, 2007) cross-domain adaptation techniques were applied on a phrase-based SMT trained on the Europarl task, in order to translate news commentaries, from French to English. In particular, a small portion of in-domain bilingual data was exploited to adapt the Europarl language model and translation models by means of linear interpolation techniques. Ueffing et al. (2007) proposed several elaborate adaptation methods relying on additional bilingual data synthesized from the development or test set.

Our work is mostly related to (Koehn and Schroeder, 2007) but explores different assumptions about available adaptation data: i.e. only monolingual in-domain texts are available. The adaptation of the translation and re-ordering models is performed by generating synthetic bilingual data from monolingual texts, similarly to what proposed in (Schwenk, 2008). Interpolation of multiple phrase tables is applied in a more principled way than in (Koehn and Schroeder, 2007): all entries are merged into one single table, corresponding feature functions are concatenated and smoothing is applied when observations are missing. The approach proposed in this paper has many similarities with the simplest technique in (Ueffing et al., 2007), but it is applied to a much larger monolingual corpus.

Finally, with respect to previous work we also investigate the behavior of the minimum error training procedure to optimize the combination of feature functions on a small in-domain bilingual sample.

3 Task description

This paper addresses the issue of adapting an already developed phrase-based translation system in order to work properly on a different domain, for which almost no parallel data are available but only monolingual texts.[1]

The main components of the SMT system are the translation model, which aims at porting the content from the source to the target language, and the language model, which aims at building fluent sentences in the target language. While the former is trained with bilingual data, the latter just needs monolingual target texts. In this work, a lexicalized re-ordering model is also exploited to control re-ordering of target words. This model is also learnable from parallel data.

Assuming some large monolingual in-domain texts are available, two basic adaptation approaches are pursued here: (i) generating synthetic bilingual data with an available SMT system and use this data to adapt its translation and re-ordering models; (ii) using synthetic or provided target texts to also, or only, adapt its language model. The following research questions

[1] We assume only availability of a development set and an evaluation set.

summarize our basic interest in this work:

- Is automatic generation of bilingual data effective to tackle the lack of parallel data?
- Is it more effective to use source language adaptation data or target language adaptation data?
- Is it convenient to combine models learned from adaptation data with models learned from training data?
- How can interpolation of models be effectively learned from small amounts of in-domain parallel data?

4 System description

The investigation presented in this paper was carried out with the Moses toolkit (Koehn et al., 2007), a state-of-the-art open-source phrase-based SMT system. We trained Moses in a standard configuration, including a 4-feature translation model, a 7-feature lexicalized re-ordering model, one LM, word and phrase penalties.

The translation and the re-ordering model relied on "grow-diag-final" symmetrized word-to-word alignments built using GIZA++ (Och and Ney, 2003) and the training script of Moses. A 5-gram language model was trained on the target side of the training parallel corpus using the IRSTLM toolkit (Federico et al., 2008), exploiting Modified Kneser-Ney smoothing, and quantizing both probabilities and backoff weights. Decoding was performed applying cube-pruning with a pop-limit of 6000 hypotheses.

Log-linear interpolations of feature functions were estimated with the parallel version of minimum error rate training procedure distributed with Moses.

4.1 Fast Training from Synthetic Data

The standard procedure of Moses for the estimation of the translation and re-ordering models from a bilingual corpus consists in three main steps:

1. A word-to-word alignment is generated with GIZA++.
2. Phrase pairs are extracted from the word-to-word alignment using the method proposed by (Och and Ney, 2003); countings and re-ordering statistics of all pairs are stored. A word-to-word lexicon is built as well.
3. Frequency-based and lexicon-based direct and inverted probabilities, and re-ordering probabilities are computed using statistics from step 2.

Recently, we enhanced Moses decoder to also output the word-to-word alignment between the input sentence and its translation, given that they have been added to the phrase table at training time. Notice that the additional information introduces an overhead in disk usage of about 70%, but practically no overhead at decoding time. However, when training translation and re-ordering models from synthetic data generated by the decoder, this feature allows to completely skip the time-expensive step 1.[2]

We tested the efficiency of this solution for training a translation model on a synthesized corpus of about 300K Spanish sentences and 8.8M running words, extracted from the EuroParl corpus. With respect to the standard procedure, the total training time was reduced by almost 50%, phrase extraction produced 10% more phrase pairs, and the final translation system showed a loss in translation performance (BLEU score) below 1% relative. Given this outcome we decided to apply the faster procedure in all experiments.

4.2 Model combination

Once monolingual adaptation data is automatically translated, we can use the synthetic parallel corpus to estimate new language, translation, and re-ordering models. Such models can either replace or be combined with the original models of the SMT system. There is another simple option which is to concatenate the synthetic parallel data with the original training data and re-build the system. We did not investigate this approach because it does not allow to properly balance the contribution of different data sources, and also showed to underperform in preliminary work.

Concerning the combination of models, in the following we explain how Moses was extended to manage multiple translation models (TMs) and multiple re-ordering models (RMs).

4.3 Using multiple models in Moses

In Moses, a TM is provided as a phrase table, which is a set $\mathcal{S} = \{(\tilde{f}, \tilde{e})\}$ of phrase pairs associated with a given number of features values

[2]Authors are aware of an enhanced version of GIZA++, which allows parallel computation, but it was not taken into account in this work.

$h(\tilde{f}, \tilde{e}; \mathcal{S})$. In our configuration, 5 features for the TM (the phrase penalty is included) are taken into account.

In the first phase of the decoding process, Moses generates translation options for all possible input phrases $\tilde{f}$ through a lookup into $\mathcal{S}$; it simply extracts alternative phrase pairs $(\tilde{f}, \tilde{e})$ for a specific $\tilde{f}$ and optionally applies pruning (based on the feature values and weights) to limit the number of such pairs. In the second phase of decoding, it creates translation hypotheses of the full input sentence by combining in all possible ways (satisfying given re-ordering constraints) the pre-fetched translation options. In this phase the hypotheses are scored, according to all features functions, ranked, and possibly pruned.

When more TMs $\mathcal{S}_j$ are available, Moses can behave in two different ways in pre-fetching the translation options. It searches a given $\tilde{f}$ in all sets and keeps a phrase pair $(\tilde{f}, \tilde{e})$ if it belongs to either i) their intersection or ii) their union. The former method corresponds to building one new TM $\mathcal{S}_I$, whose set is the intersection of all given sets:

$$\mathcal{S}_I = \{(\tilde{f}, \tilde{e}) \mid \forall j \; (\tilde{f}, \tilde{e}) \in \mathcal{S}_j\}$$

The set of features of the new TM is the union of the features of all single TMs. Straightforwardly, all feature values are well-defined.

The second method corresponds to building one new TM $\mathcal{S}_U$, whose set is the union of all given sets:

$$\mathcal{S}_U = \{(\tilde{f}, \tilde{e}) \mid \exists j \; (\tilde{f}, \tilde{e}) \in \mathcal{S}_j\}$$

Again, the set of features of the new TM is the union of the features of all single TMs; but for a phrase pair $(\tilde{f}, \tilde{e})$ belonging to $\mathcal{S}_U \setminus \mathcal{S}_j$, the feature values $h(\tilde{f}, \tilde{e}; \mathcal{S}_j)$ are undefined. In these undefined situations, Moses provides a default value of 0, which is the highest available score, as the feature values come from probabilistic distributions and are expressed as logarithms. Henceforth, a phrase pair belonging to all original sets is penalized with respect to phrase pairs belonging to few of them only.

To address this drawback, we proposed a new method[3] to compute a more reliable and smoothed score in the undefined case, based on the IBM model 1 (Brown et al., 1993). If $(\tilde{f} = f_1, \ldots, f_l, \tilde{e} = e_1, \ldots, e_l) \in \mathcal{S}_U \setminus \mathcal{S}_j$ for any j the phrase-based and lexical-based direct features are defined as follows:

$$h(\tilde{f}, \tilde{e}; \mathcal{S}_j) = \frac{\epsilon}{(l+1)^m} \prod_{k=1}^{m} \sum_{h=0}^{l} \phi(e_k \mid f_h)$$

Here, $\phi(e_k \mid f_h)$ is the probability of e_k given f_h provided by the word-to-word lexicon computed on $\mathcal{S}_j$. The inverted features are defined similarly. The phrase penalty is trivially set to 1. The same approach has been applied to build the union of re-ordering models. In this case, however, the smoothing value is constant and set to 0.001.

As concerns as the use of multiple LMs, Moses has a very easy policy, consisting of querying each of them to get the likelihood of a translation hypotheses, and uses all these scores as features.

It is worth noting that the exploitation of multiple models increases the number of features of the whole system, because each model adds its set of features. Furthermore, the first approach of Moses for model combination shrinks the size of the phrase table, while the second one enlarges it.

5 Evaluation

5.1 Data Description

In this work, the background domain is given by the Spanish-English portion of the UN parallel corpus,[4] composed by documents coming from the Office of Conference Services at the UN in New York spanning the period between 1988 and 1993. The adaptation data come from the European Parliament corpus (Koehn, 2002) (EP) as provided for the shared translation task of the 2008 Workshop on Statistical Machine Translation.[5] Development and test sets for this task, namely dev2006 and test2008, are supplied as well, and belong to the European Parliament domain.

We use the symbol S̄ (Ē) to denote synthetic Spanish (English) data. Spanish-to-English and English-to-Spanish systems trained on UN data were exploited to generate English and Spanish synthetic portions of the original EP corpus, respectively. In this way, we created two synthetic versions of the EP corpus, named SĒ-EP and S̄E-EP, respectively. All presented translation systems were optimized on the dev2006 set with respect to

[3] Authors are not aware of any work addressing this issue.

[4] Distributed by the Linguistic Data Consortium, catalogue # LDC94T4A.

[5] http://www.statmt.org/wmt08

the BLEU score (Papineni et al., 2002), and tested on test2008. (Notice that one reference translation is available for both sets.) Table 1 reports statistics of original and synthetic parallel corpora, as well of the employed development and evaluation data sets. All the texts were just tokenized and mixed case was kept. Hence, all systems were developed to produce case-sensitive translations.

corpus	sent	Spanish		English	
		word	dict	word	dict
UN	2.5M	50.5M	253K	45.2M	224K
EP	1.3M	36.4M	164K	35.0M	109K
SĒ-EP	1.3M	36.4M	164K	35.4M	133K
S̄E-EP	1.3M	36.2M	120K	35.0M	109K
dev	2,000	60,438	8,173	58,653	6,548
test	2,000	61,756	8,331	60,058	6,497

Table 1: Statistics of bilingual training corpora, development and test data (after tokenization).

5.2 Baseline systems

Three Spanish-to-English baseline systems were trained by exploiting different parallel or monolingual corpora summarized in the first three lines in Table 2. For each system, the table reports the perplexity and out-of-vocabulary (OOV) percentage of their LM, and its translation performance achieved on the test set in terms of BLEU score, NIST score, WER (word error rate) and PER (position independent error rate).

The distance in style, genre, jargon, etc. between the UN and the EP corpora is made evident by the gap in perplexity (Federico and De Mori, 1998) and OOV percentage between their English LMs: 286 vs 74 and 1.12% vs 0.15%, respectively.

Performance of the system trained on the EP corpus (third row) can be taken as an upper bound for any adaptation strategy trying to exploit parts of the EP corpus, while those of the first line clearly provide the corresponding lower-bound. The system in the second row can instead be consider as the lower bound when only monolingual English adaptation data are assumed.

The synthesis of the SĒ-EP corpus was performed with the system trained just on the UN training data (first row of Table 2), because we had assumed that the in-domain data were only monolingual Spanish and thus not useful for neither the TM, RM nor target LM estimation.

Similarly, the system in the last row of Table 2 was developed on the UN corpus to translate the English part of the EP data to generate the synthetic S̄E-EP corpus. Again, any in-domain data were exploited to train this sytem. Of course, this system cannot be compared with any other because of the different translation direction.

In order to compare reported performance with the state-of-the-art, Table 2 also reports results of the best system published in the EuroMatrix project website[6] and of the Google online translation engine.[7]

5.3 Analysis of the tuning process

It is well-known that tuning the SMT system is fundamental to achieve good performance. The standard tuning procedure consists of a minimum error rate training (mert) (Och and Ney, 2003) which relies on the availability of a development data set. On the other hand, the most important assumption we make is that almost no parallel in-domain data are available.

conf	sent	n-best	time (min)	BLEU (Δ)
–	–	–	–	22.28
a	2000	1000	2034	23.68 (1.40)
b	2000	200	391	23.67 (1.39)
c	200	1000	866	23.13 (0.85)
d	200	200	551	23.54 (1.26)

Table 3: Global time, not including decoding, of the tuning process and BLEU score achieved on the test set by the uniform interpolation weights (first row), and by the optimal weights with different configurations of the tuning parameters.

In a preliminary phase, we investigated different settings of the tuning process in order to understand how much development data is required to perform a reliable weight optimization. Our models were trained on the SĒ-EP parallel corpus and by using uniform interpolation weights the system achieved a BLEU score of 22.28% on the test set (see Table 3).

We assumed to dispose of either a regular in-domain development set of 2,000 sentences (dev2006), or a small portion of it of just 200 sen-

[6]http://www.euromatrix.net. Translations of the best system were downloaded on November 7th, 2008. Published results differ because we performed a case-sensitive evaluation.

[7]Google was queried on November 3rd, 2008.

language pair	training data		PP	OOV (%)	BLEU	NIST	WER	PER
	TM/RM	LM						
Spanish-English	UN	UN	286	1.12	22.60	6.51	64.60	48.52
"	UN	EP	74	0.15	27.83	7.12	60.93	45.19
"	EP	EP	"	"	32.80	7.84	56.47	41.15
"	UN	SĒ-EP	89	0.21	23.52	6.64	63.86	47.68
"	SĒ-EP	SĒ-EP	"	"	23.68	6.65	63.64	47.56
"	S̄E-EP	EP	74	0.15	28.10	7.18	60.86	44.85
"	Google		na	na	28.60	7.55	57.38	57.38
"	Euromatrix		na	na	32.99	7.86	56.36	41.12
English-Spanish	UN	UN	281	1.39	23.24	6.44	65.81	49.61

Table 2: Description and performance on the test set of compared systems in terms of perplexity, out-of-vocabulary percentage of their language model, and four translation scores: BLEU, NIST, word-error-rate, and position-independent error rate. Systems were optimized on the dev2006 development set.

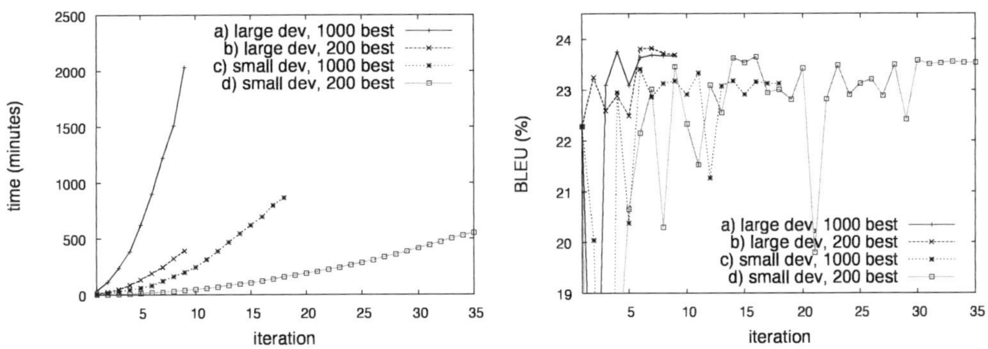

Figure 1: Incremental time of the tuning process (not including decoding phase) (left) and BLEU score on the test set using weights produced at each iteration of the tuning process. Four different configurations of the tuning parameters are considered.

tences. Moreover, we tried to employ either 1,000-best or 200-best translation candidates during the mert process.

From a theoretical point of view, computational effort of the tuning process is proportional to the square of the number of translation alternatives generated at each iteration times the number of iterations until convergence.

Figure 1 reports incremental tuning time and translation performance on the test set at each iteration. Notice that the four tuning configurations are ranked in order of complexity. Table 3 summaries the final performance of each tuning process, after convergence was reached.

Notice that decoding time is not included in this plot, as Moses allows to perform this step in parallel on a computer cluster. Hence, to our view the real bottleneck of the tuning process is actually related to the strictly serial part of the mert implementation of Moses.

As already observed in previous literature (Macherey et al., 2008), first iterations of the tuning process produces very bad weights (even close to 0); this exceptional performance drop is attributed to an over-fitting on the candidate repository.

Configurations exploiting the small development set (c,d) show a slower and more unstable convergence; however, their final performance in Table 3 result only slightly lower than that obtained with the standard dev sets (a, b). Due to the larger number of iterations they needed, both configurations are indeed more time consuming than the intermediate configuration (b), which seems the best one. In conclusion, we found that the size of the n-best list has essentially no effect on the quality of the final weights, but it impacts significantly on the computational time. Moreover, using the regular development set with few translation alternatives ends up to be the most efficient configuration in terms of computational effort, robustness, and performance.

Our analysis suggests that it is important to dispose of a sufficiently large development set although reasonably good weights can be obtained even if such data are very few.

5.4 LM adaptation

A set of experiments was devoted to the adaptation of the LM only. We trained three different LMs on increasing portions of the EP and we employed them either alone or in combination with the background LM trained on the UN corpus.

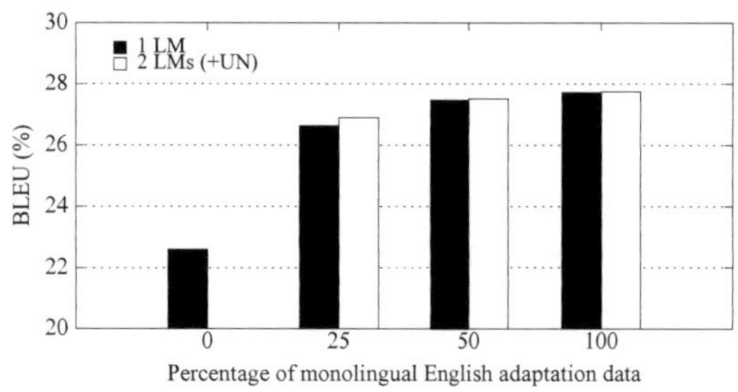

Figure 2: BLEU scores achieved by systems exploiting one or two LMs trained on increasing percentages of English in-domain data.

Figure 2 reports BLEU score achieved by these systems. The absolute gain with respect to the baseline is fairly high, even with the smallest amount of adaptation data (+4.02). The benefit of using the background data together with in-domain data is very small, and rapidly vanishes as the amount of such data increases.

If English synthetic texts are employed to adapt the LM component, the increase in performance is significantly lower but still remarkable (see Table 2). By employing all the available data, the gain in BLEU% score was of 4% relative, that is from 22.60 to 23.52.

5.5 TM and RM adaptation

Another set of experiments relates to the adaptation of the TM and the RM. In-domain TMs and RMs were estimated on three different versions of the full parallel EP corpus, namely EP, S$\bar{E}$-EP, and $\bar{S}$E-EP. In-domain LMs were trained on the corresponding English side. All in-domain models were either used alone or combined with the baseline models according to multiple-model paradigm explained in Section 4.3. Tuning of the interpolation weights was performed on the standard development set as usual. Results of these experiments are reported in Figure 3.

Results suggest that regardless of the used bilingual corpora the in-domain TMs and RMs work better alone than combined with the original models. We think that this behavior can be explained by a limited discriminative power of the resulting combined model. The background translation model could contain phrases which either do or do not fit the adaptation domain. As the weights are optimized to balance the contribution of all phrases, the system is not able to well separate the positive examples from the negative ones. In addition to it, system tuning is much more complex because the number of features increases from 14 to 26.

Finally, TMs and RMs estimated from synthetic data show to provide smaller, but consistent, contributions than the corresponding LMs. When English in-domain data is provided, BLEU% score increases from 22.60 to 28.10; TM and RM contribute by about 5% relative, by covering the gap from 27.83 to 28.10. When Spanish in-domain data is provided BLEU% score increases from 22.60 to 23.68; TM and RM contribute by about 15% relative, by covering the gap from 23.52 to 23.68 .

Summarizing, the most important role in the domain adaptation is played by the LM; nevertheless the adaptation of the TM and RM gives a small further improvement..

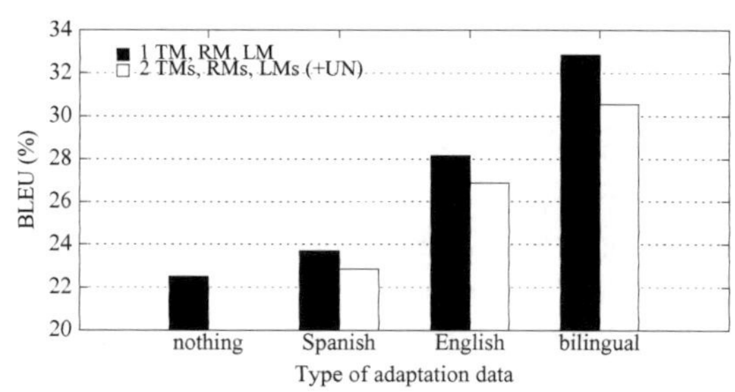

Figure 3: BLEU scores achieved by system exploiting both TM, RM and LM trained on different corpora.

6 Conclusion

This paper investigated cross-domain adaptation of a state-of-the-art SMT system (Moses), by exploiting large but cheap monolingual data. We proposed to generate synthetic parallel data by translating monolingual adaptation data with a background system and to train statistical models from the synthetic corpus.

We found that the largest gain (25% relative) is achieved when in-domain data are available for the target language. A smaller performance improvement is still observed (5% relative) if source adaptation data are available. We also observed that the most important role is played by the LM adaptation, while the adaptation of the TM and RM gives consistent but small improvement.

We also showed that a very tiny development set of only 200 parallel sentences is adequate enough to get comparable performance as a 2000-sentence set.

Finally, we described how to reduce the time for training models from a synthetic corpus generated through Moses by 50% at least, by exploiting word-alignment information provided during decoding.

References

Peter F. Brown, Stephen A. Della Pietra, Vincent J. Della Pietra, and Robert L. Mercer. 1993. The mathematics of statistical machine translation: Parameter estimation. *Computational Linguistics*, 19(2):263–312.

Jorge Civera and Alfons Juan. 2007. Domain adaptation in statistical machine translation with mixture modelling. In *Proceedings of the Second Workshop on Statistical Machine Translation*, pages 177–180, Prague, Czech Republic.

Matthias Eck, Stephan Vogel, and Alex Waibel. 2004. Language model adaptation for statistical machine translation based on information retrieval. In *Proceedings of the International Conference on Language Resources and Evaluation (LREC)*, pages 327–330, Lisbon, Portugal.

Marcello Federico and Renato De Mori. 1998. Language modelling. In Renato De Mori, editor, *Spoken Dialogues with Computers*, chapter 7, pages 199–230. Academy Press, London, UK.

Marcello Federico, Nicola Bertoldi, and Mauro Cettolo. 2008. Irstlm: an open source toolkit for handling large scale language models. In *Proceedings of Interspeech*, pages 1618–1621, Melbourne, Australia.

Andrew Finch and Eiichiro Sumita. 2008. Dynamic model interpolation for statistical machine translation. In *Proceedings of the Third Workshop on Statistical Machine Translation*, pages 208–215, Columbus, Ohio.

George Foster and Roland Kuhn. 2007. Mixture-model adaptation for SMT. In *Proceedings of the Second Workshop on Statistical Machine Translation*, pages 128–135, Prague, Czech Republic.

Almut Silja Hildebrand, Matthias Eck, Stephan Vogel, and Alex Waibel. 2005. Adaptation of the translation model for statistical machine translation based on information retrieval. In *Proceedings of the 10th Conference of the European Association for Machine Translation (EAMT)*, pages 133–142, Budapest.

Philipp Koehn and Josh Schroeder. 2007. Experiments in domain adaptation for statistical machine translation. In *Proceedings of the Second Workshop on Statistical Machine Translation*, pages 224–227, Prague, Czech Republic.

P. Koehn, H. Hoang, A. Birch, C. Callison-Burch, M. Federico, N. Bertoldi, B. Cowan, W. Shen, C. Moran, R. Zens, C. Dyer, O. Bojar, A. Constantin, and E. Herbst. 2007. Moses: Open source toolkit for statistical machine translation. In *Proceedings of the 45th Annual Meeting of the Association for Computational Linguistics Companion Volume Proceedings of the Demo and Poster Sessions*, pages 177–180, Prague, Czech Republic.

Philipp Koehn. 2002. Europarl: A multilingual corpus for evaluation of machine translation. Unpublished, `http://www.isi.edu/~koehn/europarl/`.

Wolfgang Macherey, Franz Och, Ignacio Thayer, and Jakob Uszkoreit. 2008. Lattice-based minimum error rate training for statistical machine translation. In *Proceedings of the 2008 Conference on Empirical Methods in Natural Language Processing*, pages 725–734, Honolulu, Hawaii.

Franz Josef Och and Hermann Ney. 2003. A systematic comparison of various statistical alignment models. *Computational Linguistics*, 29(1):19–51.

Kishore Papineni, Salim Roukos, Todd Ward, and Wei-Jing Zhu. 2002. BLEU: a method for automatic evaluation of machine translation. In *Proceedings of the 40th Annual Meeting of the Association of Computational Linguistics (ACL)*, pages 311–318, Philadelphia, PA.

Holger Schwenk. 2008. Investigations on Large-Scale Lightly-Supervised Training for Statistical Machine Translation. In *Proc. of the International Workshop on Spoken Language Translation*, pages 182–189, Hawaii, USA.

Nicola Ueffing, Gholamreza Haffari, and Anoop Sarkar. 2007. Semi-supervised model adaptation for statistical machine translation. *Machine Translation*, 21(2):77–94.

Bing Zhao, Matthias Eck, and Stephan Vogel. 2004. Language model adaptation for statistical machine translation via structured query models. In *Proceedings of Coling 2004*, pages 411–417, Geneva, Switzerland.

Chinese Syntactic Reordering for Adequate Generation of Korean Verbal Phrases in Chinese-to-Korean SMT

Jin-Ji Li, Jungi Kim, Dong-Il Kim[*], and Jong-Hyeok Lee
Department of Computer Science and Engineering,
Electrical and Computer Engineering Division,
Pohang University of Science and Technology (POSTECH),
San 31 Hyoja Dong, Pohang, 790-784, R. of Korea
E-mail: {ljj, yangpa, jhlee}@postech.ac.kr

*Language Engineering Institute,
Department of Computer, Electron and Telecommunication Engineering,
Yanbian University of Science and Technology (YUST),
Yanji, Jilin, 133-000, P.R. of China
E-mail: {dongil}@ybust.edu.cn

Abstract

Chinese and Korean belong to different language families in terms of word-order and morphological typology. Chinese is an SVO and morphologically poor language while Korean is an SOV and morphologically rich one. In Chinese-to-Korean SMT systems, systematic differences between the verbal systems of the two languages make the generation of Korean verbal phrases difficult. To resolve the difficulties, we address two issues in this paper. The first issue is that the verb position is different from the viewpoint of word-order typology. The second is the difficulty of complex morphology generation of Korean verbs from the viewpoint of morphological typology. We propose a Chinese syntactic reordering that is better at generating Korean verbal phrases in Chinese-to-Korean SMT. Specifically, we consider reordering rules targeting Chinese verb phrases (VPs), preposition phrases (PPs), and modality-bearing words that are closely related to Korean verbal phrases. We verify our system with two corpora of different domains. Our proposed approach significantly improves the performance of our system over a baseline phrased-based SMT system. The relative improvements in the two corpora are +9.32% and +5.43%, respectively.

1 Introduction

Recently, there has been a lot of research on encoding syntactic information into statistical machine translation (SMT) systems in various forms and in different stages of translation processes.

During preprocessing source language sentences undergo reordering and morpho-syntactic reconstruction phases to generate more target language-like sentences. Also, fixing erroneous words, generating complex morphology, and re-ranking translation results in post-processing phases may utilize syntactic information of both source and target languages. A syntax-based SMT system encodes the syntactic information in its translation model of the decoding step.

A number of researchers have proposed syntactic reordering as a preprocessing step (Xia and McCord, 2004; Collins *et al.*, 2005; Wang *et al.*, 2007). In these syntactic reordering approaches, source sentences are first parsed and a series of reordering rules are applied to the parsed trees to reorder the source sentences into target language-like word orders. Such an approach is an effective method for a phrase-based SMT system that employs a relatively simple distortion model in the decoding phase.

This paper concentrates upon reordering source sentences in the preprocessing step of a Chinese-to-Korean phrase-based SMT system using syntactic information. Chinese-to-Korean SMT has more difficulties than the language pairs studied in previous research (French-English, German-English, and Chinese-English). From the viewpoint of language typology, these language pairs are all SVO languages and they have relatively simpler morphological inflections. On the other hand, Korean is an SOV and agglutinative language with relatively free word order and with complex and rich inflections.

For the Chinese-to-Korean SMT, these systematic differences of the two languages make the generation of Korean verbal phrases very difficult. Firstly, the difference in the verb position of the two languages may not be reflected in the simple distortion model of a phrase-based SMT system. Secondly, Morphology generation of

Proceedings of the Fourth Workshop on Statistical Machine Translation, pages 190–196,
Athens, Greece, 30 March – 31 March 2009.

Korean verbs is difficult because of its complexity and the translation direction from a low-inflection language to a high-inflection language.

In the following sections, we describe the characteristics of Korean verbal phrases and their corresponding Chinese verbal phrases, and present a set of hand-written syntactic reordering rules including Chinese verb phrases (VPs), preposition phrases (PPs), and modality-bearing words. In the latter sections, we empirically verify that our reordering rules effectively reposition source words to target language-like order and improve the translation results.

2 Contrastive analysis of Chinese and Korean with a focus on Korean verbal phrase generations

In the Chinese-to-Korean SMT, the basic translation units are morphemes. For Chinese, sentences are segmented into words. As a typical isolating language, each segmented Chinese word is a morpheme. Korean is a highly agglutinative language and an *eojeol* refers to a fully inflected lexical form separated by a space in a sentence. Each *eojeol* in Korean consists of one or more base forms (stem morphemes or content morphemes) and their inflections (function morphemes). Inflections usually include postpositions and verb endings (verb affixes) of verbs and adjectives. These base forms and inflections are grammatical units in Korean, and they are defined as morphemes. As for the translation unit, *eojeol* cause data sparseness problems hence we consider a morpheme as a translation unit for Korean.

As briefly mentioned in the previous section, Chinese and Korean belong to different word-order typologies. The difference of verb position causes the difficulty in generating correct Korean verbal phrases. Also, the complexity of verb affixes in Korean verbs is problematic in SMT systems targeting Korean, especially if the source language is isolated.

In the Dong-A newspaper corpus on which we carry out our experiments in Section 4, Korean function morphemes occupy 41.3% of all Korean morphemes. Verb endings consist of 40.3% of all Korean function words, and the average number of function morphemes inflected by a verb or an adjective is 1.94 while that of other content morphemes is only 0.7.

These statistics indicate that the morphological form of Korean verbal phrases (Korean verbs)[1] are significantly complex. A verbal phrase in Korean consists of a series of verb affixes along with a verb stem. A verb stem cannot be used by itself but should take at least one affix to form a verbal complex. Verb affixes in Korean are ordered in a relative sequence within a verbal complex (Lee, 1991) and express different modality information[2]: tense, aspect, mood, negation, and voice (Figure 1). These five grammatical categories are the major constituents of modal expression in Korean.

K1: 먹**(stem)** + 고_ 있(aspect prt.) + 었(aspect prt.) + 었(tense prt.) + 다(*mood* prt.)
E1: had been **eating**

K2. 잡**(stem)** + 히(passive prt.) + 었(aspect prt.) + 을_ 수_있(*modality* prt.) + 다(*mood* prt.)
E2: might have been **caught**

Figure 1. Verbal phrases in Korean. Bold-faced content morphemes followed by functional ones with "+" symbols. Prt. is an acronym for particle.

The modality of Korean is expressed intensively by verb affixes. However, Chinese expresses modality using discontinuous morphemes scattered throughout a sentence (Figure 2). Also, the prominence of grammatical categories expressing modality information is different from language to language, and correlations of such categories in a language are also different. The differences between the two languages lead to difficulties in alignment and cause linking obscurities.

C3: 小偷(thief)/可能(might)/被(passive prt.)/警察(police)/**抓(catch)/**了(aspect prt.)/。

K3: 도둑(thief)+은 경찰(police)+에게 **잡(catch)**+히(passive prt.)+었(aspect prt.)+을_수_있(*modality* prt.)+다(*mood* prt.)+./

E3: The thief might have been **caught** by the police.

Figure 2. Underlined morphemes are modality-bearing morphemes in Chinese and Korean sentences. Chinese words are separated by a "/" symbol and Korean *eojeols* by a space.

[1] 'Korean verbal phrase' or 'Korean verbs' in this paper refer to Korean predicates (verbs or adjectives) in a sentence.

[2] Modality system refers to five grammatical categories: tense, aspect, mood (*modality & mood*), negation, and voice. The definition of these categories is described in detail in (Li *et al.*, 2005).

We consider two issues for generating adequate Korean verbal phrases. First is the correct position of verbal phrases, and the second is the generation of verb affixes which convey modality information.

3 Chinese syntactic reordering rules

In this section, we describe a set of manually constructed Chinese syntactic reordering rules.

Chinese sentences are first parsed by Stanford PCFG parser which uses Penn Chinese Treebank as the training corpus (Levy and Manning, 2003). Penn Chinese Treebank adopts 23 tags for phrases (Appendix A). We identified three categories in Chinese that need to be reordered: verb phrases (VPs), preposition phrases (PPs), and modality-bearing words.

3.1 Verb phrases

Korean is a verb-final language, and verb phrase modifiers and complements occur in the pre-verbal positions. However, in Chinese, verb phrase modifiers occur in the pre-verbal or post-verbal positions, and complements mostly occur in post-verbal positions.

We move the verb phrase modifiers and complements located before the verbal heads to the post-verbal position as demonstrated in the following examples. A verbal head consists of a verb (including verb compound) and an aspect sequence (Xue and Xia, 2000). Therefore, aspect markers such as "了 (perfective prt.)", "着 (durative prt.)", "过(experiential prt.)" positioned immediately after a verb should remain in the relatively same position with the preceding verb. The third one in the example reordering rules shows this case. Mid-sentence punctuations are also considered when constructing the reordering rules.

Examples of reordering rules of VPs[3]:

$VV_0\ NP_1 \rightarrow NP_1\ VV_0$
$VV_0\ IP_1 \rightarrow IP_1\ VV_0$
$VV_0\ AS_1\ NP_2 \rightarrow NP_2\ VV_0\ AS_1$
$VV_0\ PU_1\ IP_2 \rightarrow IP_2\ PU_1\ VV_0$

Original parse tree:

VP
  PP (P 按)
    NP (NN 需要)
  PP (P 对)
    NP (PN 它们)
  VP (VV 进行)
    NP (NN 配置)

Reordered parse tree:

VP
  PP (P 按)
    NP (NN 需要)
  PP (P 对)
    NP (PN 它们)
  NP (NN 配置)
    VP (VV 进行)

3.2 Preposition phrases

Chinese prepositions originate from verbs, and they preserve the characteristics of verbs. Chinese prepositions are translated into Korean verbs, other content words, or particles. We only consider the Chinese prepositions that translate into verbs and other content words. We swap the prepositions with their objects as demonstrated in the following examples.

Examples of reordering rules of PPs:

Case 1: translate into Korean verbs

$P(按)_0\ NP_1 \rightarrow NP_1\ P(按)_0$
$P(通过)_0\ IP_1 \rightarrow IP_1\ P(通过)_0$
$P(除了)_0\ LCP_1 \rightarrow LCP_1\ P(除了)_0$

Case 2: translate into other content words

$P(由于)_0\ IP_1 \rightarrow IP_1\ P(由于)_0$
$P(因为)_0\ NP_1 \rightarrow NP_1\ P(因为)_0$

Original parse tree:

VP
  PP (P 按)
    NP (NN 需要)
  PP (P 对)
    NP (PN 它们)
  VP (VV 进行)
    NP (NN 配置)

Reordered parse tree:

VP
  NP (NN 需要)
    PP (P 按)
  PP (P 对)
    NP (PN 它们)
  VP (VV 进行)
    NP (NN 配置)

[3] VV: common verb; AS: aspect marker; P: preposition; PU: punctuation; PN: pronoun;

3.3 Modality-bearing words

Verb affixes in Korean verbal phrases indicate modality information such as tense, aspect, mood, negation, and voice. The corresponding modality information is implicitly or explicitly expressed in Chinese. It is important to figure out what features are used to represent modality information. Li *et al.* (2008) describes in detail the features in Chinese that express modality information. However, since only lexical features can be reordered, we consider explicit modality features only.

Modality-bearing words are scattered over an entire sentence. We move them near their verbal heads because their correspondences in Korean sentences are always placed right after their verbs.

When constructing reordering rules, we consider temporal adverbs, auxiliary verbs, negation particles, and aspect particles only. The following example sentences show the results of a few of our reordering rules for modality-bearing words.

Examples of reordering rules of modality-bearing words:

Original parse tree:

```
VP
  ADVP (AD 将)              ← Temporal adverb
    PP (P 在)
      LCP
        NP (NN 法律) (NN 许可) (NN 范围)
        (LC 内)
    VP (VV 受到)
      NP (NN 起诉)
```

Reordered parse tree:

```
VP
  PP (P 在)
    LCP
      NP (NN 法律) (NN 许可) (NN 范围)
      (LC 内)
  ADVP (AD 将)
  VP (VV 受到)
    NP (NN 起诉)
```

Original parse tree:

```
VP (VV 要)                   ← Auxiliary verb
  VP
    PP (P 从)
      LCP
        NP (NN 文件) (NN 组)
        (LC 中)
    VP (VV 排除)
```

Reordered parse tree:

```
VP
  PP (P 从)
    LCP
      NP (NN 文件) (NN 组)
      (LC 中)
  VP (VV 要)
  VP (VV 排除)
```

Original parse tree:

```
VP
  ADVP (AD 不)              ← Negation particle
  VP (VV 应该)               ← Auxiliary verb
  VP
    PP (P 以)
      NP (NN 管理员) (NN 身份)
    VP (VV 运行)
```

Reordered parse tree:

```
VP
  PP (P 以)
    NP (NN 管理员) (NN 身份)
  ADVP (AD 不)
  VP (VV 应该)
  VP (VV 运行)
```

Generally speaking, Chinese does not have grammatical forms for voice. Although, voice is also a grammatical category expressing modality information, we have left it out of the current phase of our experiment since voice detection is another research issue and reordering rules for voice are unavoidably complicated.

4 Experiment

Our baseline system is a popular phrase-based SMT system, Moses (Koehn *et al.*, 2007), with 5-gram SRILM language model (Stolcke, 2002), tuned with *Minimum Error Training* (Och, 2003). We adopt NIST (NIST, 2002) and BLEU (Papineni *et al.*, 2001) as our evaluation metrics.

Chinese sentences in training and test corpora are first parsed and are applied a series of syntactic reordering rules. To evaluate the contribution of the three categories of syntactic reordering rules, we perform the experiments applying each category independently. Experiments of various combinations are also carried out.

4.1 Corpus profile

We automatically collected and constructed a sentence-aligned parallel corpus from the online

Dong-A newspaper[4]. Strictly speaking, it is a non-literally translated Korean-to-Chinese corpus. The other corpus is provided by MSRA (Microsoft Research Asia). It is a Chinese-Korean-English trilingual corpus of technical manuals and a literally translated corpus.

Chinese sentences are segmented by Stanford Chinese word segmenter (Tseng *et al.*, 2005), and parsed by Stanford Chinese parser (Levy and Manning, 2003). Korean sentences are segmented into morphemes by an in-house morphological analyzer.

The detailed corpus profiles are displayed in Table 1 and 2. The Dong-A newspaper corpus is much longer than the MSRA technical manual corpus. In Korean, we report the length of content and function words.

	Training (99,226 sentences)		
	Chinese	Korean	
		Content	Function
# of words	2,692,474	1,859,105	1,277,756
# of singletons	78,326	67,070	514
avg. sen. length	27.13	18.74	12.88
	Development (500 sentences)		
	Chinese	Korean	
		Content	Function
# of words	14,485	9,863	6,875
# of singletons	4,029	4,166	163
avg. sen. length	28.97	19.73	13.75
	Test (500 sentences)		
	Chinese	Korean	
		Content	Function
# of words	14,657	10,049	6,980
# of singletons	4,027	4,217	164
avg. sen. length	29.31	20.10	13.96

Table 1. Corpus profile of Dong-A newspaper.

	Training (29,754 sentences)		
	Chinese	Korean	
		Content	Function
# of words	425,023	316,289	207,909
# of singletons	5,746	4,689	197
avg. sen. length	14.29	10.63	6.99
	Development (500 sentences)		
	Chinese	Korean	
		Content	Function
# of words	6,380	4,853	3,214
# of singletons	1,174	975	93
avg. sen. length	12.76	9.71	6.43
	Test (500 sentences)		
	Chinese	Korean	
		Content	Function
# of words	7,451	5,336	3,548
# of singletons	1,182	964	99
avg. sen. length	14.90	10.67	7.10

Table 2. Corpus profile of MSRA technical manual.

4.2 Result and discussion

The experimental results are displayed in Table 3 and 4. Besides assessing the effectiveness of each reordering category, we test various combinations of the three categories.

Method	**NIST**	**BLEU**
Baseline	5.7801	20.49
Reorder.VP	5.8402	22.12 (+7.96%)
Reorder.PP	5.7773	20.10 (-1.90%)
Reorder.Modality	5.7682	20.93 (+2.15%)
Reorder.VP+PP	5.8176	21.96 (+7.17%)
Reorder.VP+Modality	5.9198	22.24 (+8.54%)
Reorder.All	*5.9361*	*22.40 (+9.32%)*

Table 3. Experimental results on the Dong-A newspaper corpus.

Method	**NIST**	**BLEU**
Baseline	7.2596	44.03
Reorder.VP	7.2238	44.57 (+1.23%)
Reorder.PP	7.2793	44.22 (+0.43%)
Reorder.Modality	7.3110	44.25 (+0.50%)
Reorder.VP+PP	7.3401	45.28 (+2.84%)
Reorder.VP+Modality	*7.4246*	*46.42 (+5.43%)*
Reorder.All	7.3849	46.33 (+5.22%)

Table 4. Experimental results on the MSRA technical manual corpus.

From the experimental result of the Dong-A newspaper corpus, we find that the most effective category is the reordering rules of VPs. When the VP reordering rules are combined with the modality ones, the performance is even better. The gain of BLEU is not significant, but the gain of NIST is significant from 5.8402 to 5.9198. The PP reordering rules do not contribute to the performance when they are singly applied. However, when combined with the other two categories, they contribute to the performance. The best performance is achieved when all three categories' reordering rules are applied and the relative improvement is +9.32% over the baseline system.

In the MSRA corpus, the performance of various combinations of the three categories is better than those of the individual categories. The PP category shows improvement when it is combined with the VP category. The combination of VP and modality category improves the performance by +5.43% over the baseline.

[4] http://www.donga.com/news/ (Korean) and http://chinese.donga.com/gb/index.html (Chinese)

These results agree with our expectations: resolving the word order and modality expression differences of verbal phrases between Chinese and Korean is an effective approach.

4.3 Error Analysis

We adopt an error analysis method proposed by Vilar *et al.* (2006). They presented a framework for classifying error types of SMT systems. (Appendix B.)

Since our approach focuses on verbal phrase differences between Chinese and Korean, we carry out the error analysis only on the verbal heads. Three types of errors are considered: word order, missing words, and incorrect words. We further classify the incorrect words category into two sub-categories: wrong lexical choice/extra word, and incorrect form of modality information. 50 sentences are selected from each test corpus on which to perform the error analysis. For each corpus, we choose the best system: Reorder.All for the Dong-A corpus and Reorder.VP+modality for the MSRA corpus.

The most frequent error type is wrong word order in both corpora. When a verb without any modality information appears in a wrong position, we only count it as a wrong word order but not as a wrong modality. Therefore, the number of wrong modalities is not as frequent as it should be.

Table 5 and 6 indicate that our proposed method helps improve the SMT system to reduce the number of error types related to verbal phrases.

Error type	Frequency	
	Baseline	Reorder.All
wrong word order	34	7
missing content word	18	5
wrong lexical choice/ extra word	6	1
wrong modality	10	6

Table 5. Error analysis of the Dong-A newspaper corpus.

Error type	Frequency	
	Baseline	Reorder. VP+Modality
wrong word order	19	11
missing content word	4	2
wrong lexical choice/ extra word	8	3
wrong modality	11	6

Table 6. Error analysis of the MSRA technical manual corpus.

5 Conclusion and future work

In this paper, we proposed a Chinese syntactic reordering more suitable to adequately generate Korean verbal phrases in Chinese-to-Korean SMT. Specifically, we considered reordering rules targeting Chinese VPs, PPs, and modality-bearing words that are closely related to Korean verbal phrases.

Through a contrastive analysis between the two languages, we first showed the difficulty of generating Korean verbal phrases when translating from a morphologically poor language, Chinese. Then, we proposed a set of syntactic reordering rules to reorder Chinese sentences into a more Korean like word order.

We conducted several experiments to assess the contributions of our method. The reordering of VPs is the most effective, and improves the performance even more when combined with the reordering rules of modality-bearing words. Applied to the Dong-A newspaper corpus and the MSRA technical manual corpus, our proposed approach improved the baseline systems by 9.32% and 5.43%, respectively. We also performed error analysis with a focus on verbal phrases. Our approach effectively decreased the size of all errors.

There remain several issues as possible future work. We only considered the explicit modality features and relocated them near the verbal heads. In the future, we may improve our system by extracting implicit modality features.

In addition to generating verbal phrases, there is the more general issue of generating complex morphology in SMT systems targeting Korean, such as generating Korean case markers. There are several previous studies on this topic (Minkov *et al.*, 2007; Toutanova *et al.*, 2008). This issue will also be the focus of our future work in both the phrase- and syntax-based SMT frameworks.

Acknowledgments

This work was supported in part by MKE & IITA through the IT Leading R&D Support Project and also in part by the BK 21 Project in 2009.

References

Charles N. Li, and Sandra A. Thompson 1996. *Mandarin Chinese: A functional reference grammar*, University of California Press, USA.

David Vilar, Jia Xu, Luis Fernando D'Haro, and Hermann Ney. 2006. *Error Analysis of Statistical*

Machine Translation Output. In Proceedings of LREC.

Einat Minkov, Kristina Toutanova, and Hisami Suzuki. 2007. *Generating Complex Morphology for Machine Translation*. In Proceedings of ACL.

Fei Xia and Michael McCord. 2004. *Improving a statistical MT system with automatically learned rewrite patterns*. In Proceedings of COLING.

Huihsin Tseng, Pichuan Chang, Galen Andrew, Daniel Jurafsky and Christopher Manning. 2005. *A Conditional Random Field Word Segmenter*. In Fourth SIGHAN Workshop on Chinese Language Processing.

HyoSang Lee 1991. *Tense, aspect, and modality: A discourse-pragmatic analysis of verbal affixes in Korean from a typological perspective*, PhD thesis, Univ. of California, Los Angeles.

Jin-Ji Li, Ji-Eun Roh, Dong-Il Kimand Jong-Hyeok Lee. 2005. *Contrastive Analysis and Feature Selection for Korean Modal Expression in Chinese-Korean Machine Translation System*. International Journal of Computer Processing of Oriental Languages, 18(3), 227--242.

Jin-Ji Li, Dong-Il Kim and Jong-Hyeok Lee. 2008. *Annotation Guidelines for Chinese-Korean Word Alignment*. In Proceedings of LREC.

Kristina Toutanova, Hisami Suzuki, and Achim Puopp. 2008. *Applying Morphology Generation Models to Machine Translation*. In Proceedings of ACL.

Nianwen Xue, and Fei Xia. 2000. *The bracketing guidelines for the Penn Chinese Treebank (3.0)*. IRCS technical report, University of Pennsylvania.

Nianwen Xue, Fei Xia, Fu-Dong Chiou, and Martha Palmer. 2005. *The Penn Chinese Treebank: Phrase structure annotation of a large corpus*. Natural Language Engineering, 11(2):207–238.

Michael Collins, Philipp Koehn, and Ivona Ku˘cerov´a. 2005. *Clause restructuring for statistical machine translation*. In Proceedings of ACL, pages 531–540.

NIST. 2002. *Automatic evaluation of machine translation quality using n-gram co-occurrence statistics*.

Och, F. J. 2003. *Minimum error rate training in statistical machine translation*. In Proceedings of ACL.

Philipp Koehn, Hieu Hoang, Alexandra Birch, Chris-Callison-Burch, Marcello Federico, Nicola Bertoldi, Brooke Cowan, Wade Shen, Christine Moran, Richard Zens, Chris Dyer, Ondrej Bojar, Alexandra Constrantin, and Evan Herbst. 2007. *Moses: Open source toolkit for statistical machine translation*. In Proceedings of ACL, Demonstration Session.

Roger Levy and Christopher D. Manning. 2003. *Is it harder to parse Chinese, or the Chinese Treebank?* In Proceedings of ACL.

Stolcke, A. 2002. *SRILM - an extensible language modeling toolkit*. In Proceedings of ICSLP, 2:901-904.

Appendix A. Tag for phrases in Penn Chinese Treebank.

ADJP	adjective phrase
ADVP	adverbial phrase headed by AD (adverb)
CLP	classifier phrase
CP	clause headed by C (complementizer)
DNP	phrase formed by "XP+DEG"
DP	determiner phrase
DVP	phrase formed by "XP+DEV"
FRAG	fragment
IP	simple clause headed by I (INFL)
LCP	phrase formed by "XP+LC"
LST	list marker
NP	noun phrase
PP	preposition phrase
PRN	parenthetical
QP	quantifier phrase
UCP	unidentical coordination phrase
VP	verb phrase

Appendix B. Classification of translation errors proposed by Vilar *et al.* (2006).

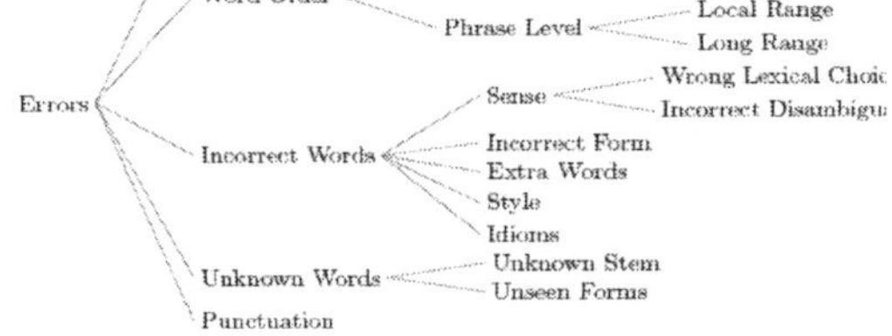

A Quantitative Analysis of Reordering Phenomena

Alexandra Birch a.c.birch-mayne@sms.ed.ac.uk
Phil Blunsom pblunsom@inf.ed.ac.uk
Miles Osborne miles@inf.ed.ac.uk
University of Edinburgh
10 Crichton Street
Edinburgh, EH8 9AB, UK

Abstract

Reordering is a serious challenge in statistical machine translation. We propose a method for analysing syntactic reordering in parallel corpora and apply it to understanding the differences in the performance of SMT systems. Results at recent large-scale evaluation campaigns show that synchronous grammar-based statistical machine translation models produce superior results for language pairs such as Chinese to English. However, for language pairs such as Arabic to English, phrase-based approaches continue to be competitive. Until now, our understanding of these results has been limited to differences in BLEU scores. Our analysis shows that current state-of-the-art systems fail to capture the majority of reorderings found in real data.

1 Introduction

Reordering is a major challenge in statistical machine translation. Reordering involves permuting the relative word order from source sentence to translation in order to account for systematic differences between languages. Correct word order is important not only for the fluency of output, it also affects word choice and the overall quality of the translations.

In this paper we present an automatic method for characterising syntactic reordering found in a parallel corpus. This approach allows us to analyse reorderings quantitatively, based on their number and span, and qualitatively, based on their relationship to the parse tree of one sentence. The methods we introduce are generally applicable, only requiring an aligned parallel corpus with a parse over the source or the target side, and can be extended to allow for more than one reference sentence and derivations on both source and target sentences. Using this method, we are able to compare the reordering capabilities of two important translation systems: a phrase-based model and a hierarchical model.

Phrase-based models (Och and Ney, 2004; Koehn et al., 2003) have been a major paradigm in statistical machine translation in the last few years, showing state-of-the-art performance for many language pairs. They search all possible reorderings within a restricted window, and their output is guided by the language model and a lexicalised reordering model (Och et al., 2004), both of which are local in scope. However, the lack of structure in phrase-based models makes it very difficult to model long distance movement of words between languages.

Synchronous grammar models can encode structural mappings between languages which allow complex, long distance reordering. Some grammar-based models such as the hierarchical model (Chiang, 2005) and the syntactified target language phrases model (Marcu et al., 2006) have shown better performance than phrase-based models on certain language pairs.

To date our understanding of the variation in reordering performance between phrase-based and synchronous grammar models has been limited to relative BLEU scores. However, Callison-Burch et al. (2006) showed that BLEU score alone is insufficient for comparing reordering as it only measures a partial ordering on n-grams. There has been little direct research on empirically evaluating reordering.

We evaluate the reordering characteristics of these two paradigms on Chinese-English and Arabic-English translation. Our main findings are as follows: (1) Chinese-English parallel sentences exhibit many medium and long-range reorderings, but less short range ones than Arabic-English, (2) phrase-based models account for short-range reorderings better than hierarchical models do, (3)

Proceedings of the Fourth Workshop on Statistical Machine Translation , pages 197–205,
Athens, Greece, 30 March – 31 March 2009. ©2009 Association for Computational Linguistics

by contrast, hierarchical models clearly outperform phrase-based models when there is significant medium-range reordering, and (4) none of these systems adequately deal with longer range reordering.

Our analysis provides a deeper understanding of why hierarchical models demonstrate better performance for Chinese-English translation, and also why phrase-based approaches do well at Arabic-English.

We begin by reviewing related work in Section 2. Section 3 describes our method for extracting and measuring reorderings in aligned and parsed parallel corpora. We apply our techniques to human aligned parallel treebank sentences in Section 4, and to machine translation outputs in Section 5. We summarise our findings in Section 6.

2 Related Work

There are few empirical studies of reordering behaviour in the statistical machine translation literature. Fox (2002) showed that many common reorderings fall outside the scope of synchronous grammars that only allow the reordering of child nodes. This study was performed manually and did not compare different language pairs or translation paradigms. There are some comparative studies of the reordering restrictions that can be imposed on the phrase-based or grammar-based models (Zens and Ney, 2003; Wellington et al., 2006), however these do not look at the reordering performance of the systems. Chiang et al. (2005) proposed a more fine-grained method of comparing the output of two translation systems by using the frequency of POS sequences in the output. This method is a first step towards a better understanding of comparative reordering performance, but neglects the question of what kind of reordering is occurring in corpora and in translation output.

Zollmann et al. (2008) performed an empirical comparison of the BLEU score performance of hierarchical models with phrase-based models. They tried to ascertain which is the stronger model under different reordering scenarios by varying distortion limits the strength of language models. They show that the hierarchical models do slightly better for Chinese-English systems, but worse for Arabic-English. However, there was no analysis of the reorderings existing in their parallel corpora, or on what kinds of reorderings were produced in their output. We perform a focused evaluation of these issues.

Birch et al. (2008) proposed a method for extracting reorderings from aligned parallel sentences. We extend this method in order to constrain the reorderings to a derivation over the source sentence where possible.

3 Measuring Reordering

Reordering is largely driven by syntactic differences between languages and can involve complex rearrangements between nodes in synchronous trees. Modeling reordering exactly would be sparse and heterogeneous and thus we make an important simplifying assumption in order for the detection and extraction of reordering data to be tractable and useful. We assume that reordering is a binary process occurring between two blocks that are adjacent in the source. We extend the methods proposed by Birch et al. (2008) to identify and measure reordering. Modeling reordering as the inversion in order of two adjacent blocks is similar to the approach taken by the Inverse Transduction Model (ITG) (Wu, 1997), except that here we are not limited to a binary tree. We also detect and include non-syntactic reorderings as they constitute a significant proportion of the reorderings.

Birch et al. (2008) defined the extraction process for a sentence pair that has been word aligned. This method is simple, efficient and applicable to all aligned sentence pairs. However, if we have access to the syntax tree, we can more accurately determine the groupings of embedded reorderings, and we can also access interesting information about the reordering such as the type of constituents that get reordered. Figure 1 shows the advantage of using syntax to guide the extraction process. Embedded reorderings that are extracted without syntax assume a right branching structure. Reorderings that are extracted using the syntactic extraction algorithm reflect the correct sentence structure. We thus extend the algorithm to extracting syntactic reorderings. We require that syntactic reorderings consist of blocks of whole sibling nodes in a syntactic tree over the source sentence.

In Figure 2 we can see a sentence pair with an alignment and a parse tree over the source. We perform a depth first recursion through the tree, extracting the reorderings that occur between whole sibling nodes. Initially a reordering is detected between the leaf nodes P and NN. The block growing algorithm described in Birch et al. (2008) is then used to grow block A to include NT and NN, and block B to include P and NR. The source and target spans of these nodes do not overlap the spans

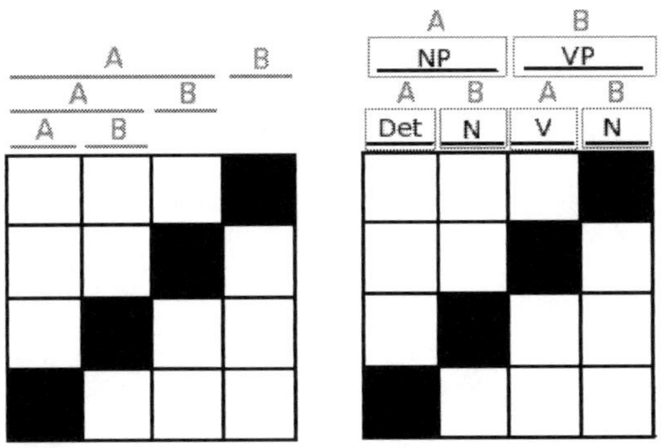

Figure 1. An aligned sentence pair which shows two different sets of reorderings for the case without and with a syntax tree.

of any other nodes, and so the reordering is accepted. The same happens for the higher level reordering where block A covers NP-TMP and PP-DIR, and block B covers the VP. In cases where the spans do overlap spans of nodes that are not siblings, these reorderings are then extracted using the algorithm described in Birch et al. (2008) without constraining them to the parse tree. These non-syntactic reorderings constitute about 10% of the total reorderings and they are a particular challenge to models which can only handle isomorphic structures.

RQuantity

The reordering extraction technique allows us to analyse reorderings in corpora according to the distribution of reordering widths and syntactic types. In order to facilitate the comparison of different corpora, we combine statistics about individual reorderings into a sentence level metric which is then averaged over a corpus. This metric is defined using reordering widths over the target side to allow experiments with multiple language pairs to be comparable when the common language is the target.

We use the average RQuantity (Birch et al., 2008) as our measure of the amount of reordering in a parallel corpus. It is defined as follows:

$$RQuantity = \frac{\sum_{r \in R} |r_{A_{\bar{t}}}| + |r_{B_{\bar{t}}}|}{I}$$

where R is the set of reorderings for a sentence, I is the target sentence length, A and B are the two blocks involved in the reordering, and $|r_{A_{\bar{s}}}|$ is the size or span of block A on the target side. RQuantity is thus the sum of the spans of all the reordering blocks on the target side, normalised

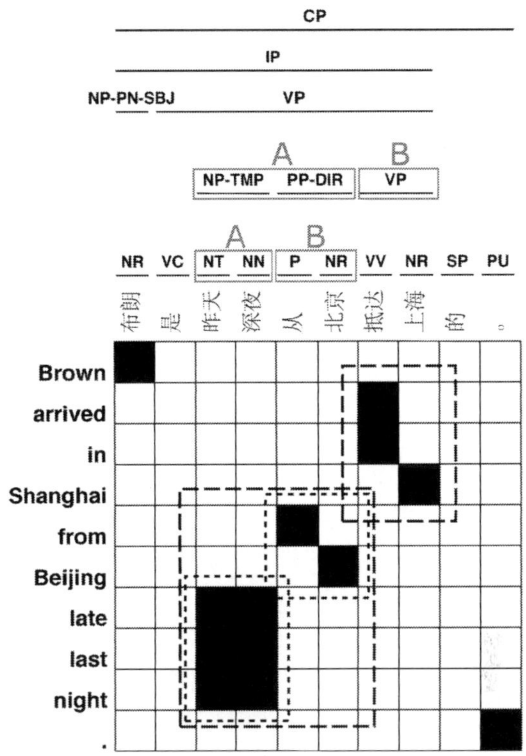

Figure 2. A sentence pair from the test corpus, with its alignment and parse tree. Two reorderings are shown with two different dash styles.

by the length of the target sentence. The minimum RQuantity for a sentence would be 0. The maximum RQuantity occurs where the order of the sentence is completely inverted and the RQuantity is $\sum_{i=2}^{I} i$. See, for example, Figure 1 where the RQuantity is $\frac{9}{4}$.

4 Analysis of Reordering in Parallel Corpora

Characterising the reordering present in different human generated parallel corpora is crucial to understanding the kinds of reordering we must model in our translations. We first need to extract reorderings for which we need alignments and derivations. We could use automatically generated annotations, however these contain errors and could be biased towards the models which created them. The GALE project has provided gold standard word alignments for Arabic-English (AR-EN) and Chinese-English (CH-EN) sentences.[1] A subset of these sentences come from the Arabic and Chinese treebanks, which provide gold standard parse trees. The subsets of parallel data for which we have both alignments and parse trees consist of

[1] see LDC corpus LDC2006E93 version GALE-Y1Q4

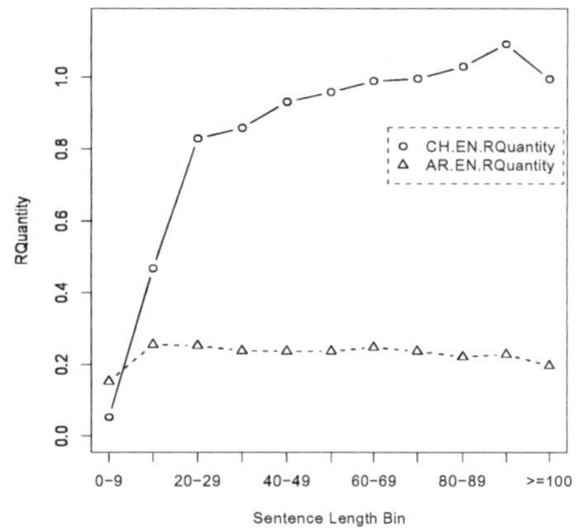

Figure 3. Sentence level measures of RQuantity for the CH-EN and AR-EN corpora for different English sentence lengths.

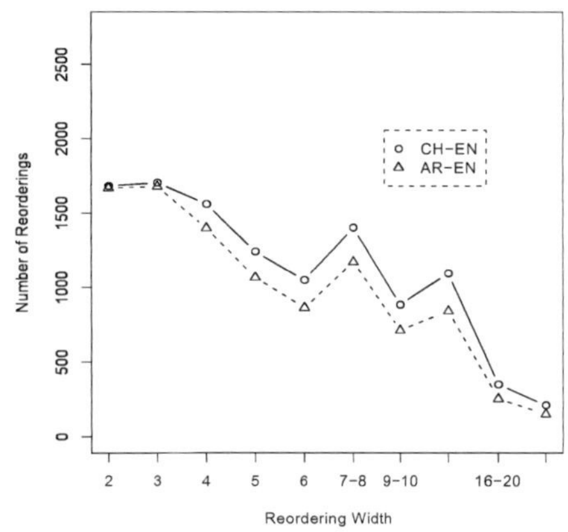

Figure 4. Comparison of reorderings of different widths for the CH-EN and AR-EN corpora.

3,380 CH-EN sentences and 4,337 AR-EN sentences.

Figure 3 shows that the different corpora have very different reordering characteristics. The CH-EN corpus displays about three times the amount of reordering (RQuantity) than the AR-EN corpus. For CH-EN, the RQuantity increases with sentence length and for AR-EN, it remains constant. This seems to indicate that for longer CH-EN sentences there are larger reorderings, but this is not the case for AR-EN. RQuantity is low for very short sentences, which indicates that these sentences are not representative of the reordering characteristics of a corpus. The measures seem to stabilise for sentences with lengths of over 20 words.

The average amount of reordering is interesting, but it is also important to look at the distribution of reorderings involved. Figure 4 shows the reorderings in the CH-EN and AR-EN corpora broken down by the total width of the source span of the reorderings. The figure clearly shows how different the two language pairs are in terms of reordering widths. Compared to the CH-EN language pair, the distribution of reorderings in AR-EN has many more reorderings over short distances, but many fewer medium or long distance reorderings. We define *short*, *medium* or *long distance* reorderings to mean that they have a reordering of width of between 2 to 4 words, 5 to 8 and more than 8 words respectively.

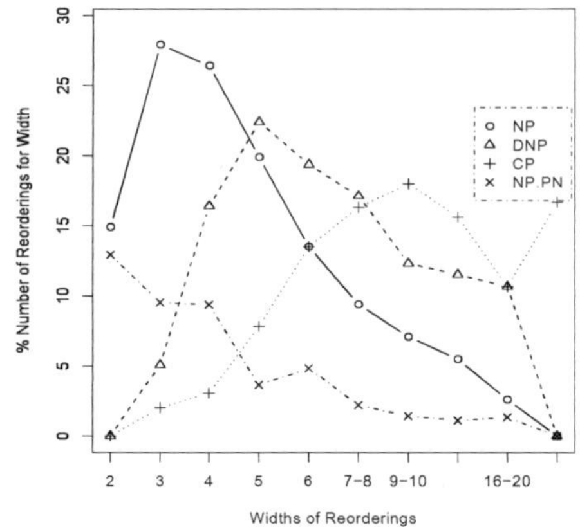

Figure 5. The four most common syntactic types being reordered forward in target plotted as % of total syntactic reorderings against reordering width (CH-EN).

Syntactic reorderings can reveal very rich language-specific reordering behaviour. Figure 5 is an example of the kinds of data that can be used to improve reordering models. In this graph we selected the four syntactic types that were involved in the largest number of reorderings. They covered the block that was moved forward in the target (block A). We can see that different syntactic types display quite different behaviour at different reordering widths and this could be important to model.

Having now characterised the space of reordering actually found in parallel data, we now turn to the question of how well our translation models account for them. As both the translation models investigated in this work do not use syntax, in the following sections we focus on non-syntactic analysis.

5 Evaluating Reordering in Translation

We are interested in knowing how current translation models perform specifically with regard to reordering. To evaluate this, we compare the reorderings in the parallel corpora with the reorderings that exist in the translated sentences. We com-

	None	Low	Medium	High
Average RQuantity				
CH-EN	0	0.39	0.82	1.51
AR-EN	0	0.10	0.25	0.57
Number of Sentences				
CH-EN	105	367	367	367
AR-EN	293	379	379	379

Table 1. The RQuantity and the number of sentences for each reordering test set.

pare two state-of-the-art models: the phrase-based system Moses (Koehn et al., 2007) (with lexicalised reordering), and the hierarchical model Hiero (Chiang, 2007). We use default settings for both models: a distortion limit of seven for Moses, and a maximum source span limit of 10 words for Hiero. We trained both models on subsets of the NIST 2008 data sets, consisting mainly of news data, totalling 547,420 CH-EN and 1,069,658 AR-EN sentence pairs. We used a trigram language model on the entire English side (211M words) of the NIST 2008 Chinese-English training corpus. Minimum error rate training was performed on the 2002 NIST test for CH-EN, and the 2004 NIST test set for AR-EN.

5.1 Reordering Test Corpus

In order to determine what effect reordering has on translation, we extract a test corpus with specific reordering characteristics from the manually aligned and parsed sentences described in Section 4. To minimise the impact of sentence length, we select sentences with target lengths from 20 to 39 words inclusive. In this range RQuantity is stable. From these sentences we first remove those with no detected reorderings, and we then divide up the remaining sentences into three sets of equal sizes based on the RQuantity of each sentence. We label these test sets: "none", "low", "medium" and "high".

All test sentences have only one reference English sentence. MT evaluations using one reference cannot make strong claims about any particular test sentence, but are still valid when used to compare large numbers of hypotheses.

Table 1 and Figure 6 show the reordering characteristics of the test sets. As expected, we see more reordering for Chinese-English than for Arabic to English.

It is important to note that although we might name a set "low" or "high", this is only relative to the other groups for the same language pair. The "high" AR-EN set, has a lower RQuantity than the "medium" CH-EN set. Figure 6 shows

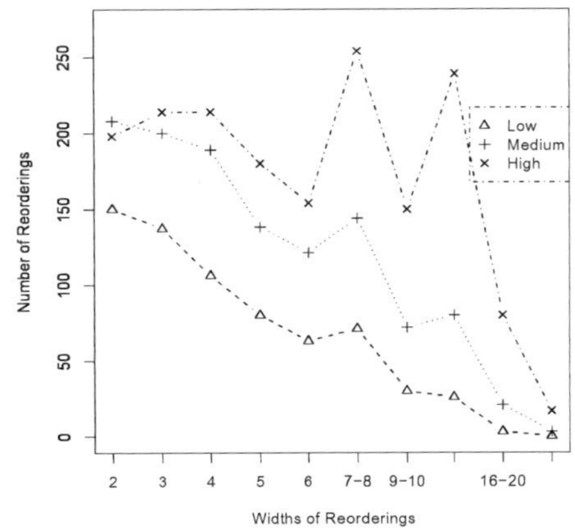

Figure 6. Number of reorderings in the CH-EN test set plotted against the total width of the reorderings.

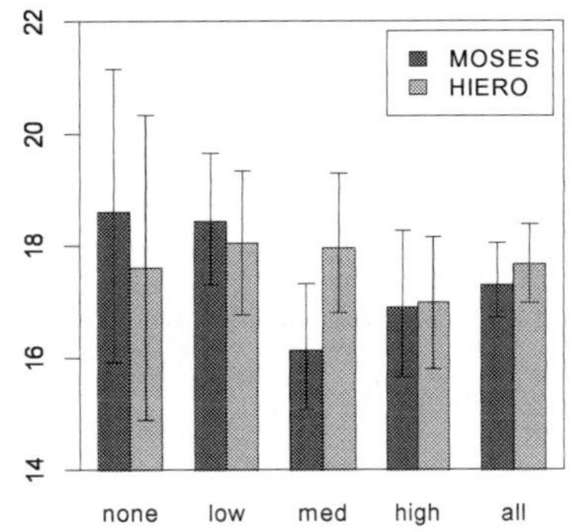

Figure 7. BLEU scores for the different CH-EN reordering test sets and the combination of all the groups for the two translation models.The 95% confidence levels as measured by bootstrap resampling are shown for each bar.

that the CH-EN reorderings in the higher RQuantity groups have more and longer reorderings. The AR-EN sets show similar differences in reordering behaviour.

5.2 Performance on Test Sets

In this section we compare the translation output for the phrase-based and the hierarchical system for different reordering scenarios. We use the test sets created in Section 5.1 to explicitly isolate the effect reordering has on the performance of two translation systems.

Figure 7 and Figure 8 show the BLEU score results of the phrase-based model and the hierarchical model on the different reordering test sets. The 95% confidence intervals as calculated by bootstrap resampling (Koehn, 2004) are shown for each of the results. We can see that the models show quite different behaviour for the different test sets and for the different language pairs. This demonstrates that reordering greatly influences the

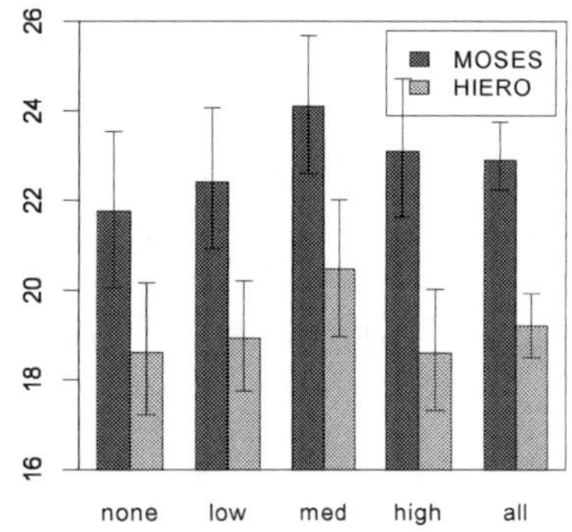

Figure 8. BLEU scores for the different AR-EN reordering test sets and the combination of all the groups for the two translation models. The 95% confidence levels as measured by bootstrap resampling are shown for each bar.

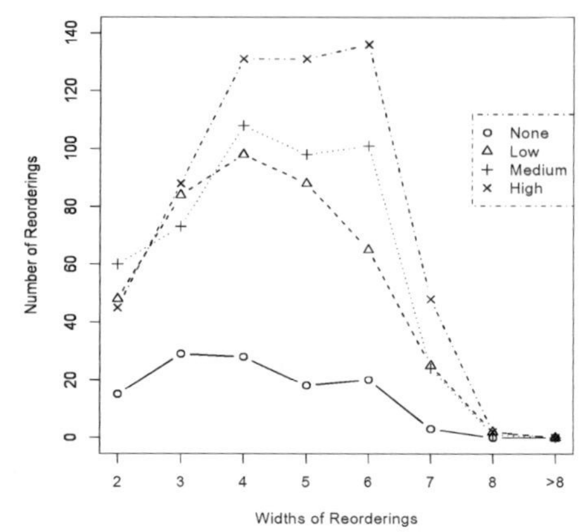

Figure 9. Reorderings in the CH-EN MOSES translation of the reordering test set, plotted against the total width of the reorderings.

BLEU score performance of the systems.

In Figure 7 we see that the hierarchical model performs considerably better than Moses on the "medium" CH-EN set, although the confidence interval for these results overlap somewhat. This supports the claim that Hiero is better able to capture longer distance reorderings than Moses.

Hiero performs significantly worse than Moses on the "none" and "low" sets for CH-EN, and for all the AR-EN sets, other than "none". All these sets have a relatively low amount of reordering, and in particular a low number of medium and long distance reorderings. The phrase-based model could be performing better because it searches all possible permutations within a certain window whereas the hierarchical model will only permit reorderings for which there is lexical evidence in the training corpus. Within a small window, this exhaustive search could discover the best reorderings, but within a bigger window, the more constrained search of the hierarchical model produces better results. It is interesting that Hiero is not always the best choice for translation performance, and depending on the amount of reordering and the distribution of reorderings, the simpler phrase-based approach is better.

The fact that both models show equally poor performance on the "high" RQuantity test set suggests that the hierarchical model has no advantage over the phrase-based model when the reorderings are long enough and frequent enough. Neither Moses nor Hiero can perform long distance reorderings, due to the local constraints placed on their search which allows performance to be linear with respect to sentence length. Increasing the window in which these models are able to perform reorderings does not necessarily improve performance, due to the number of hypotheses the models must discriminate amongst.

The performance of both systems on the "high" test set could be much worse than the BLEU score would suggest. A long distance reordering that has been missed, would only be penalised by BLEU once at the join of the two blocks, even though it might have a serious impact on the comprehension of the translation. This flaw seriously limits the conclusions that we can draw from BLEU score, and motivates analysing translations specifically for reordering as we do in this paper.

Reorderings in Translation

At best, BLEU can only partially reflect the reordering performance of the systems. We therefore perform an analysis of the distribution of reorderings that are present in the systems' outputs, in order to compare them with each other and with the source-reference distribution.

For each hypothesis translation, we record which source words and phrase pairs or rules were used to produce which target words. From this we create an alignment matrix from which reorderings are extracted in the same manner as previously done for the manually aligned corpora.

Figure 9 shows the distribution of reorderings that occur between the source sentence and the translations from the phrase-based model. This graph is interesting when compared with Figure 6, which shows the reorderings that exist in the original reference sentence pair. The two distributions are quite different. Firstly, as the models use phrases which are treated as blocks, reorderings which occur within a phrase are not recorded. This reduces the number of shorter distance reorderings in the distribution in Figure 6, as mainly short

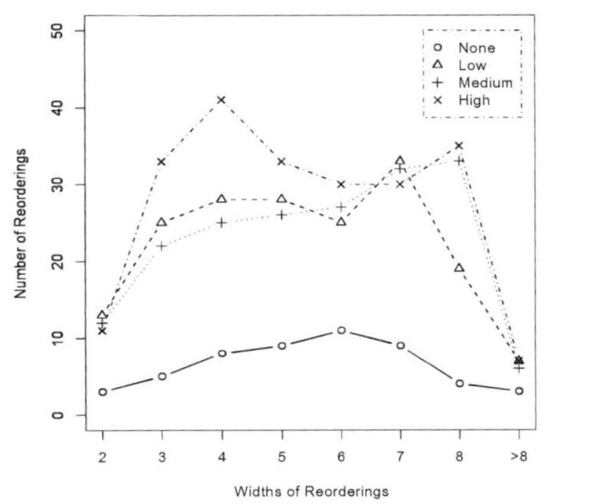

Figure 10. Reorderings in the CH-EN Hiero translation of the reordering test set, plotted against the total width of the reorderings.

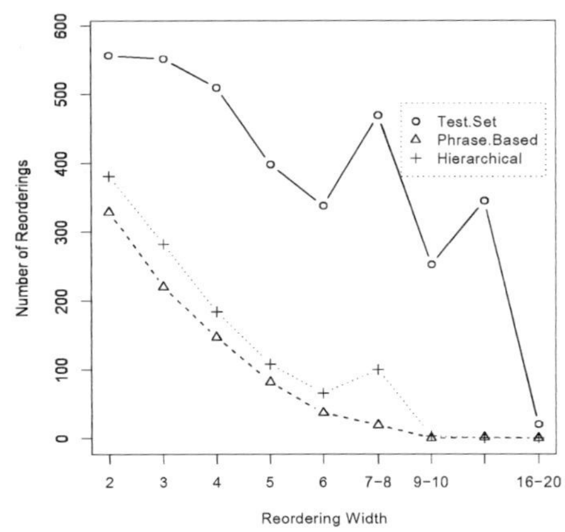

Figure 11. Number of reorderings in the original CH-EN test set, compared to the reorderings retained by the phrase-based and hierarchical models. The data is shown relative to the length of the total source width of the reordering.

phrases pairs are used in the hypothesis. However, even taking reorderings within phrase pairs into account, there are many fewer reorderings in the translations than in the references, and there are no long distance reorderings.

It is interesting that the phrase-based model is able to capture the fact that reordering increases with the RQuantity of the test set. Looking at the equivalent data for the AR-EN language pair, a similar pattern emerges: there are many fewer reorderings in the translations than in the references.

Figure 10 shows the reorderings from the output of the hierarchical model. The results are very different to both the phrase-based model output (Figure 9) and to the original reference reordering distribution (Figure 6). There are fewer reorderings here than even in the phrase-based output. However, the Hiero output has a slightly higher BLEU score than the Moses output. The number of reorderings is clearly not the whole story. Part of the reason why the output seems to have few reorderings and yet scores well, is that the output of hierarchical models does not lend itself to the analysis that we have performed successfully on the reference or phrase-based translation sentence pairs. This is because the output has a large number of non-contiguous phrases which prevent the extraction of reorderings from within their span. Only 4.6% of phrase-based words were blocked off due to non-contiguous phrases but 47.5% of the hierarchical words were. This problem can be ameliorated with the detection and unaligning of words which are obviously dependent on other words in the non-contiguous phrase.

Even taking blocked off phrases into account, however, the number of reorderings in the hierarchical output is still low, especially for the medium and long distance reorderings, as compared to the reference sentences. The hierarchical model's reordering behaviour is very different to human reordering. Even if human translations are freer and contain more reordering than is strictly necessary, many important reorderings are surely being lost.

Targeted Automatic Evaluation

Comparing distributions of reorderings is interesting, but it cannot approach the question of how many reorderings the system performed correctly. In this section we identify individual reorderings in the source and reference sentences and detect whether or not they have been reproduced in the translation.

Each reordering in the original test set is extracted. Then the source-translation alignment is inspected to determine whether the blocks involved in the original reorderings are in the reverse order in the translation. If so, we say that these reorderings have been retained from the reference to the translation.

If a reordering has been translated by one phrase pair, we assume that the reordering has been retained, because the reordering could exist inside the phrase. If the segmentation is slightly different, but a reordering of the correct size occurred at the right place, it is also considered to be retained.

Figure 11 shows that the hierarchical model retains more reorderings of all widths than the phrase-based system. Both systems retain few reorderings, with the phrase-based model missing almost all the medium distance reorderings, and both models failing on all the long distance re-

	Correct	Incorrect	NA
Retained	61	4	10
Not Retained	32	31	12

Table 2. Correlation between retaining reordering and it being correct - for humans and for system

orderings. This is possibly the most direct evidence of reordering performance so far, and again shows how Hiero has a slight advantage over the phrase-based system with regard to reordering performance.

Targeted Manual Analysis

The relationship between targeted evaluation and the correct reordering of the translation still needs to be established. The translation system can compensate for not retaining a reordering by using different lexical items. To judge the relevance of the targeted evaluation we need to perform a manual evaluation. We present evaluators with the reference and the translation sentences. We mark the target ranges of the blocks that are involved in the particular reordering we are analysing, and ask the evaluator if the reordering in the translation is correct, incorrect or not applicable. The not applicable case is chosen when the translated words are so different from the reference that their ordering is irrelevant. There were three evaluators who each judged 25 CH-EN reorderings which were retained and 25 CH-EN reorderings which were not retained by the Moses translation model.

The results in Table 2 show that the retained reorderings are generally judged to be correct. If the reordering is not retained, then the evaluators divided their judgements evenly between the reordering being correct or incorrect. It seems that the fact that a reordering is not retained does indicate that its ordering is more likely to be incorrect. We used Fleiss' Kappa to measure the correlation between annotators. It expresses the extent to which the amount of agreement between raters is greater than what would be expected if all raters made their judgements randomly. In this case Fleiss' kappa is 0.357 which is considered to be a fair correlation.

6 Conclusion

In this paper we have introduced a general and extensible automatic method for the quantitative analyse of syntactic reordering phenomena in parallel corpora.

We have applied our method to a systematic analysis of reordering both in the training corpus, and in the output, of two state-of-the-art translation models. We show that the hierarchical model performs better than the phrase-based model in situations where there are many medium distance reorderings. In addition, we find that the choice of translation model must be guided by the type of reorderings in the language pair, as the phrase-based model outperforms the hierarchical model when there is a predominance of short distance reorderings. However, neither model is able to capture the reordering behaviour of the reference corpora adequately. These result indicate that there is still much research to be done if statistical machine translation systems are to capture the full range of reordering phenomena present in translation.

References

Alexandra Birch, Miles Osborne, and Philipp Koehn. 2008. Predicting success in machine translation. In *Proceedings of the Empirical Methods in Natural Language Processing*.

Chris Callison-Burch, Miles Osborne, and Philipp Koehn. 2006. Re-evaluating the role of Bleu in machine translation research. In *Proceedings of the European Chapter of the Association for Computational Linguistics*, Trento, Italy.

David Chiang, Adam Lopez, Nitin Madnani, Christof Monz, Philip Resnik, and Michael Subotin. 2005. The Hiero machine translation system: Extensions, evaluation, and analysis. In *Proceedings of the Human Language Technology Conference and Conference on Empirical Methods in Natural Language Processing*, pages 779–786, Vancouver, Canada.

David Chiang. 2005. A hierarchical phrase-based model for statistical machine translation. In *Proceedings of the Association for Computational Linguistics*, pages 263–270, Ann Arbor, Michigan.

David Chiang. 2007. Hierarchical phrase-based translation. *Computational Linguistics (to appear)*, 33(2).

Heidi J. Fox. 2002. Phrasal cohesion and statistical machine translation. In *Proceedings of the Conference on Empirical Methods in Natural Language Processing*, pages 304–311, Philadelphia, USA.

Philipp Koehn, Franz Och, and Daniel Marcu. 2003. Statistical phrase-based translation. In *Proceedings of the Human Language Technology and North American Association for Computational Linguistics Conference*, pages 127–133, Edmonton, Canada. Association for Computational Linguistics.

Philipp Koehn, Hieu Hoang, Alexandra Birch, Chris Callison-Burch, Marcello Federico, Nicola Bertoldi, Brooke Cowan, Wade Shen, Christine Moran, Richard Zens, Chris Dyer, Ondrej Bojar, Alexandra Constantin, and Evan Herbst. 2007. Moses: Open source toolkit for statistical machine translation. In *Proceedings of the Association for Computational Linguistics Companion Demo and Poster Sessions*, pages 177–180, Prague, Czech Republic. Association for Computational Linguistics.

Philipp Koehn. 2004. Statistical significance tests for machine translation evaluation. In Dekang Lin and Dekai Wu, editors, *Proceedings of EMNLP 2004*, pages 388–395, Barcelona, Spain, July. Association for Computational Linguistics.

Daniel Marcu, Wei Wang, Abdessamad Echihabi, and Kevin Knight. 2006. SPMT: Statistical machine translation with syntactified target language phrases. In *Proceedings of the Conference on Empirical Methods in Natural Language Processing*, pages 44–52, Sydney, Australia.

Franz Josef Och and Hermann Ney. 2004. The alignment template approach to statistical machine translation. *Computational Linguistics*, 30(4):417–450.

Franz Josef Och, Daniel Gildea, Sanjeev Khudanpur, Anoop Sarkar, Kenji Yamada, Alex Fraser, Shankar Kumar, Libin Shen, David Smith, Katherine Eng, Viren Jain, Zhen Jin, and Dragomir Radev. 2004. A smorgasbord of features for statistical machine translation. In *Proceedings of Human Language Technology Conference and Conference on Empirical Methods in Natural Language Processing*, pages 161–168, Boston, USA. Association for Computational Linguistics.

Benjamin Wellington, Sonjia Waxmonsky, and I. Dan Melamed. 2006. Empirical lower bounds on the complexity of translational equivalence. In *Proceedings of the International Conference on Computational Linguistics and of the Association for Computational Linguistics*, pages 977–984, Sydney, Australia.

Dekai Wu. 1997. Stochastic inversion transduction grammars and bilingual parsing of parallel corpora. *Computational Linguistics*, 23(3):377–403.

Richard Zens and Hermann Ney. 2003. A comparative study on reordering constraints in statistical machine translation. In *Proceedings of the Association for Computational Linguistics*, pages 144–151, Sapporo, Japan.

Andreas Zollmann, Ashish Venugopal, Franz Och, and Jay Ponte. 2008. A systematic comparison of phrase-based, hierarchical and syntax-augmented statistical mt. In *Proceedings of International Conference On Computational Linguistics*.

A POS-Based Model for Long-Range Reorderings in SMT

Jan Niehues and Muntsin Kolss
Universität Karlsruhe
Karlsruhe, Germany
{jniehues,kolss}@ira.uka.de

Abstract

In this paper we describe a new approach to model long-range word reorderings in statistical machine translation (SMT). Until now, most SMT approaches are only able to model local reorderings. But even the word order of related languages like German and English can be very different. In recent years approaches that reorder the source sentence in a preprocessing step to better match target sentences according to POS(Part-of-Speech)-based rules have been applied successfully. We enhance this approach to model long-range reorderings by introducing discontinuous rules.

We tested this new approach on a German-English translation task and could significantly improve the translation quality, by up to 0.8 BLEU points, compared to a system which already uses continuous POS-based rules to model short-range reorderings.

1 Introduction

Statistical machine translation (SMT) is currently the most promising approach to machine translation of large vocabulary tasks. The approach was first presented by Brown et al. (1993) and has since been used in many translation systems (Wang and Waibel, 1998), (Och and Ney, 2000), (Yamada and Knight, 2000), (Vogel et al., 2003). State-of-the-art SMT systems often use translation models based on phrases to describe translation correspondences and word reordering between two languages. The reordering of words is one of the main difficulties in machine translation.

Phrase-based translation models by themselves have only limited capability to model different word orders in the source and target language, by capturing local reorderings within phrase pairs. In addition, the decoder can reorder phrases, subject to constraints such as confining reorderings to a relatively small window. In combination with a distance-based distortion model, some short-range reorderings can be handled. But for many language pairs this is not sufficient, and several authors have proposed additional reordering models as described in Section 2. In this work we present a new method that explicitly handles long-range word reorderings by applying discontinuous, POS-based reordering rules.

The paper is structured as follows: In the next section we present related work that was carried out in this area. Afterwards, we describe the problem of long-range reordering. In Section 4 the existing framework for reordering will be introduced. Section 5 describes the extraction of rules modeling long-range reorderings, and in the following section the integration into the framework will be explained. Finally, the model will be evaluated in Section 7, and a conclusion is given in Section 8.

2 Related Work

Several approaches have been proposed to address the problem of word reordering in SMT. Wu (1996) and Berger et al. (1996), for example, restrict the possible reorderings either during decoding time or during the alignment, but do not use any additional linguistic knowledge. A comparison of both methods can be found in Zens and Ney (2003).

Furthermore, techniques to use additional linguistic knowledge to improve the word order have been developed. Shen et al. (2004) and Och et al. (2004) presented approaches to re-rank the output of the decoder using syntactic information. Furthermore, lexical block-oriented reordering models have been developed in Tillmann and Zhang (2005) and Koehn et al. (2005). These models decide during decoding time for a given phrase, if

Proceedings of the Fourth Workshop on Statistical Machine Translation , pages 206–214,
Athens, Greece, 30 March – 31 March 2009. ©2009 Association for Computational Linguistics

the next phrase should be aligned to the left or to the right.

In recent years several approaches using reordering rules on the source side have been applied successfully in different systems. These rules can be used in rescoring as in Chen et al. (2006) or can be used in a preprocessing step. The aim of this step is to monotonize the source and target sentence. In Collins et al. (2005) and Popović and Ney (2006) hand-made rules were used to reorder the source side depending on information from a syntax tree or based on POS information. These rules had to be created manually, but only a few rules were needed and they were able to model long-range reorderings. Consequently, for every language pair these rules have to be created anew.

In contrast, other authors propose data-driven methods. In Costa-jussà and Fonollosa (2006) the source sentence is first translated into an auxiliary sentence, whose word order is similar to the one of the target sentences. Thereby statistical word classes were used. Rottmann and Vogel (2007),Zhang et al. (2007) and Crego and Habash (2008) used rules to reorder the source side and store different possible reorderings in a word lattice. They use POS tags and in the latter two cases also chunk tags to generalize the rules. The different reorderings are assigned weights depending on their relative frequencies (Rottmann and Vogel, 2007) or depending on a source side language model (Zhang et al., 2007).

In the presented work we will use discontinuous rules in addition to the rules used in Rottmann and Vogel (2007). This enables us to model long-range reorderings although we only need POS information and no chunk tags.

3 Long-Range Reorderings

One of the main problems when translating from German to English is the different word order in both languages. Although both languages are closely related, the word order is very different in some cases. Especially when translating the verb long-range reorderings have to be performed, since the position of the German verb is different from the one in the English sentence in many cases.

The finite verbs in the English language are always located at the second position, in the main clauses as well as in subordinate clauses. In German this is only true for the main clause. In contrast to that, in German subordinate clauses the verb (*glauben*) is at the final position as shown in Example 1.

Example 1: *..., die an den Markt und an die Gleichbehandlung aller glauben.*

... who believe in markets and equal treatment for all.

Example 2: *Das wird mit derart unterschiedlichen Mitgliedern unmöglich sein .*

That will be impossible with such disparate members.

A second difference in both languages is the position of the infinitive verb (*sein/be*) as shown in Example 2. In contrast to the English language, where it directly follows the finite verb, it is at the final position of the sentence in the German language.

The two examples show that in order to be able to handle the reorderings between German and English, the model has to allow some words to be shifted across the whole sentence. If this is not handled correctly, phrase-based systems sometimes generate translations that omit words, as will be shown in Section 7. This is especially problematic in the German-English case because the verb may be omitted, which carries the most important information of the sentence.

4 POS-Based Reordering

We will first briefly introduce the framework presented in Rottmann and Vogel (2007) since we extended it to also use discontinuous rules.

In this framework, the first step is to extract reordering rules. Therefore, an aligned parallel corpus and the POS tags of the source side are needed. For every sequence of source words where the target words are in a different order, a rule is extracted that describes how the source side has to be reordered to match the target side. A rule may for example look like this: *VVIMP VMFIN PPER → PPER VMFIN VVIMP*. The framework can handle rules that only depend on POS tags as well as rules that depend on POS tags and words. We will refer to these rules as short-range reordering rules.

The next step is to calculate the relative frequencies which are used as a score in the word lattice. The relative frequencies are calculated as the number of times the source side is reordered this way divided by the number of times the source side occurred in the corpus.

In a preprocessing step to the actual decoding,

different reorderings of the source sentences are encoded in a word lattice. For all reordering rules that can be applied to the sentence, the resulting edge is added to the lattice if the score is better than a given threshold. If a reordering is generated by different rules, only the path of the reordering with the highest score is added to the lattice. Then, decoding is performed on the resulting word lattice.

5 Rule Extraction

To be able to handle long-range reorderings, we extract discontinuous reordering rules in addition to the continuous ones. The extracted rules should look, for example, like this: *VAFIN * VVPP* → *VAFIN VVPP **, where the placeholder "*" represents one or more arbitrary POS tags.

Compared to the continuous, short-range reordering rules described in the previous section, extracting such discontinuous rules presents an additional difficulty. Not only do we need to find reorderings and extract the corresponding rules, but we also have to decide which parts of the rule should be replaced by the placeholder. Since it is not always clear what is the best part to be replaced, we extract four different types of discontinuous rules. Then we decide during decoding which type of rules to use.

In a first step the reordering rule has to be found. Since this is done in a different way than for the continuous one, we will first describe it in detail. Like the continuous rules, the discontinuous ones are extracted from a word aligned corpus, whose source side is annotated with POS tags. Then the source side is scanned for reorderings. This is done by comparing the alignment points a_i and a_{i+1} of two consecutive words. We found a reordering if the target words aligned to f_i and f_{i+1} are in a different order than the source words. In our case the target word $e_{a_{i+1}}$ has to precede the target word e_{a_i}. More formally said, we check the following condition:

$$a_i > a_{i+1} \tag{1}$$

In Figure 1 an example with an automatically generated alignment is given. There, for example, a reordering can be found at the position of the word "*Kenntnis*".

Since we only check the links of consecutive words, we may miss some reorderings where there is an unaligned word between the words with a

Figure 1: Example training sentence used to extract reordering rules

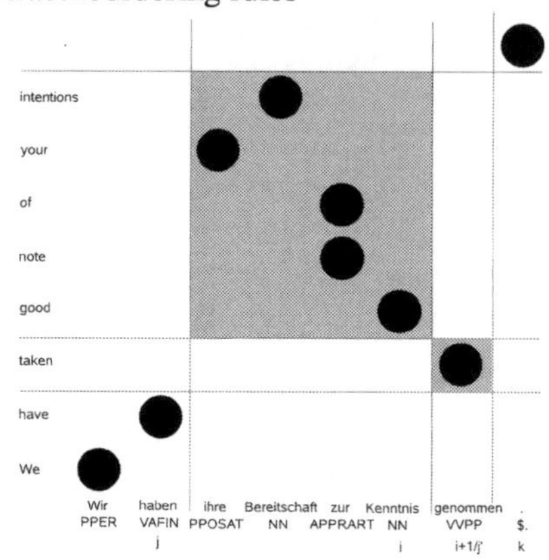

crossing link. However, in this case it is not clear where to place the unaligned word, so we do not extract rules from such a reordering.

So now we have found a reordering and also the border between the left and right part of the reordering. To be able to extract a rule for this reordering we need to find the beginning of the left and the end of the right part. This is done by searching for the last word before and the first word after the reordering. In the given example, the left part is "*ihre Bereitschaft zur Kenntnis*" and the right part would be "*genommen*". As shown in the figure, the words of the first part have to be aligned to target words that follow the target word aligned to the first word of the right part. Otherwise, they would not be part of the reordering. Consequently, to find the first word that is not part of the reordering, we search for the first word before the word f_{i+1} that is aligned to the word $e_{a_{i+1}}$ or to a target word before this word. More formally, we search for the word f_j that satisfies the following condition:

$$j = argmax_{l<i}\ a_l \leq a_{i+1} \tag{2}$$

The first word after the reordering is found in the same way. Formally, we search for the word f_k satisfying the condition:

$$k = argmax_{l>i+1}\ a_l \geq a_i \tag{3}$$

In our example, we now can extract the following reordering rule: *ihre Bereitschaft zur Kenntnis genommen* → *genommen ihre Bereitschaft zur Kenntnis*. In general, we will extract the rule: $f_{j+1} \ldots f_i f_{i+1} \ldots f_{k-1} \rightarrow f_{i+1} \ldots f_{k-1} f_{j+1} \ldots f_i$

An additional problem are unaligned words after f_j and before f_k. For these words it is not clear if they are part of the reordering or not. Therefore, we will include or exclude them depending on the type of rule we extract. To be able to write the rules in a easier way let $f_{j'}$ be the first word following f_j that is aligned and $f_{k'}$ the last word before f_k.

After extracting the reordering rule, we need to replace some parts of the rule by a placeholder to obtain more general rules. As described before, it is not directly clear which part of the rule should be replaced and therefore, we extract four different types of rules.

In the reordering, there is always a left part, in our example *ihre Bereitschaft zur Kenntnis*, and a right part (*genommen*). So we can either replace the left or the right part of the reordering by a placeholder. One could argue that always the longer sequence should be replaced, since that is more intuitive, but to lose no information we just extract both types of rules. Later we will see that depending on the language pair, one or the other type will generalize better. In the evaluation part the different types will be referred to as *Left* and *Right* rules.

Furthermore, not the whole part has to be replaced. It can be argued that the first or last word of the part is important to characterize the reordering and should therefore not be replaced. For each of the types described before, we extract two different sub-types of rules, which leads altogether to four different types of rules.

Let us first have a look at the types where we replace the left part. If we replace the whole part, in the example we would get the following rule: * *VVPP* $\rightarrow$ *VVPP* *. This would lead to problems during rule application. Since the rule begins with a placeholder, it is not clear where the matching should start. Therefore, we also include the last word before the reordering into the rule and can now extract the following rule from the sentence: *VAFIN* * *VVPP* $\rightarrow$ *VAFIN VVPP* *. In general, we extract the following rule to which we will refer as *Left All*:

$$f_j * f_{i+1} \dots f_{k'} \quad \rightarrow \quad f_j f_{i+1} \dots f_{k'} *$$

As mentioned in the beginning, we extracted a second sub-type of rule. This time, the first word of the left part is not replaced. The reason can be seen by looking at the reordered sequence. There, the second part of the reordering is moved between the last word before the reordering (f_j) and the first word of the first part (f_{j+1}). In our example this results in the following rule: *VAFIN PPOSAT* * *VVPP* $\rightarrow$ *VAFIN VVPP PPOSAT* * and in general, we extract the rule (*Left Part*):

$$f_j f_{j+1} * f_{i+1} \dots f_{k'} \quad \rightarrow \quad f_j f_{i+1} \dots f_{k'} f_{j+1} *$$

If we replace the right part by a star, we similarly get the following rule (*Right All*): *PPOSAT NN APPART NN* * $\rightarrow$ * *PPOSAT NN APPART NN*. The other rule (*Right Part*) can not be extracted from this example, since the right part has length one. But in general we get the two rules:

$$f_{j'} \dots f_i * f_{k-1} f_k \quad \rightarrow \quad * f_{k-1} f_{j+1} \dots f_i f_k$$
$$f_{j'} \dots f_i * f_k \quad \rightarrow \quad * f_{j'} \dots f_i f_k$$

Here we already see that the rules where the first part is replaced result in typical reordering between the German and English language. The second part of the verb is at the end of the sentence in German, but in an English sentence it directly follows the first part.

6 Rule Application

During the training of the system all reordering rules are extracted from the parallel corpus in the way described in the last section. The rules are only used if they occur more often than a given threshold value. In the experiments a threshold of 5 is used.

The rules are scored in the same way as the continuous rules were. The relative frequencies are calculated as the number of times the rule was extracted divided by the number of times both parts occur in one sentence.

Then, in the preprocessing step, continuous rules as described in Section 4 and discontinuous rules are applied to the source sentence. As in the framework presented before, the rules are applied only to the source sentence and not to the lattice. Thus the rules cannot be applied recursively. For the discontinuous rules the "*" could match any sequence of POS tags, but it has to consist of at least one tag. If more than one rule can be applied to a sequence of POS tags and they generate different output, all edges are added to the lattice. If they generate the same sequence, only the rule with the highest probability is applied.

In initial experiments we observed that some rules can be applied very often to a sentence and therefore the lattice gets quite big. Therefore, we first check how often a rule can be applied to a sentence. If this exceeds a given threshold, we do not use this rule for this sentence. In these cases, the rule will most likely not find a good reordering, but randomly shuffle the words. In the experiments we use 5 as threshold, since this reduces the lattices to a decent size.

These restrictions limit the number of reorderings that have to be tested during decoding. But if all reorderings that can be generated by the remaining rules would be inserted into the lattice, the size of the lattice would still be too big to be able to do efficient decoding. Therefore, only rules with a probability greater than a given threshold are used to reorder the source sentence. Since the probabilities of the long-range reorderings are quite small compared to those of the short-range reorderings, we used two different thresholds.

7 Evaluation

We performed the experiments on the translation task of the WMT'08 evaluation. Most of the experiments were done on the German-English task, but in the end also some results on German-French and English-German are shown. The systems were trained on the European Parliament Proceedings (EPPS) and the News Commentary corpus. For the German-French task we used the intersection of the parallel corpora from the German-English and English-French task. The data was preprocessed and we applied compound splitting to the German corpus for the tasks translating from German. Afterwards, the word alignment was generated with the GIZA++-Toolkit and the alignments of the two directions were combined using the *grow-diag-final-and* heuristic. Then the phrase tables were created where we performed additional smoothing of the relative frequencies (Foster et al., 2006). Furthermore, the phrase table applied in the news task was adapted to this domain. In addition, a 4-gram language model was trained on both corpora. The rules were extracted using the POS tags generated by the TreeTagger (Schmid, 1994). In the end a beam-search decoder as described in Vogel (2003) was used to optimize the weights using the MER-training on the development sets provided for the different task by the workshop. The systems were tested on the test2007 set for the EPPS task and on the nc-test2007 testset for the news task. For test set translations the statistical significance of the results was tested using the bootstrap technique as described in Zhang and Vogel (2004).

Table 1: Evaluation of different Lattice sizes generated by changing the short-range threshold θ_{short} and long-range threshold θ_{long}

θ_{short}	θ_{long}	#Edges	Dev	Test
0.2	1	112K	24.57	27.25
0.1	1	203K	24.71	27.48
0.2	0.2	113K	24.70	27.51
0.2	0.1	121K	24.97	27.56
0.2	0.05	152K	25.28	27.80
0.1	0.1	212K	24.97	27.49
0.1	0.05	243K	25.12	27.81

7.1 Lattice Creation

In a first group of experiments we analyzed the influence of the two thresholds that determine the minimal probability of a rule that is used to insert the reordering into the lattice. The experiments were performed on the news task and used only the long-range rules generated by the *Part All* rules. The results are shown in Table 1 where θ_{short} is the threshold for the short-range reorderings and θ_{long} for the long-range reorderings. Consequently, only paths were added that are generated by a short-range reordering rule that has a probability greater than θ_{short} or paths generated by a long-range reordering rule with a minimum probability of θ_{long}. We used different thresholds for both groups of rules since the probabilities of long-range reorderings are in general lower.

The first two systems use no long-range reorderings. Adding the long-range reorderings does improve the translation quality and it makes sense to add even all edges generated by rules with a probability of at least 0.05. Using this system, less short-range reorderings are needed. The system using the thresholds of 0.2 and 0.05 has a performance nearly as good as the one using the thresholds 0.1 and 0.05, but it needs fewer edges. If long-range reordering is applied, fewer edges are needed than in the case of using only short-range reordering even though the translation quality is better. Therefore, we used the thresholds 0.2 and 0.05 in the following experiments.

Figure 2: Most common long-range reordering rules of type *Left Part*

NN ADV * VAFIN	→	NN VAFIN ADV *
VAFIN ART * VVPP	→	VAFIN VVPP ART *
^ ADV * PPER	→	^ PPER ADV *
$, ART * VVINF PTKZU	→	$, VVINF PTKZU ART *
PRELS ART * VVFIN	→	PRELS VVFIN ART *

Figure 3: Most common long-range reordering rules of type *Left All*

PRELS * VAFIN	→	PRELS VAFIN *
PRELS * VAFIN VVPP	→	PRELS VAFIN VVPP *
PPER * VMFIN	→	PPER VMFIN *
PRELS * VMFIN	→	PRELS VMFIN *
VMFIN * VAINF	→	VMFIN VAINF *

Table 2: Number of long-range reordering rules of different types used to create the lattices

Type	Left	Right
Part	8079	1127
All	2470	509
Both	9223	1405

7.2 Rule Usage

We analyzed which long-range reordering rules were used to build the lattices. First, we compared the usage of the different types of rules. Therefore, we counted the number of rules that were applied to the development set of 2000 sentences if the thresholds 0.2 and 0.05 were used. The resulting numbers are shown in Table 2.

As it can be seen, the *Left* rules are more often used than the *Right* ones. This is what we expected, since when translating from German to English, the most important rules move the verb to the left. And these rules should be more general and therefore have a higher probability than the rules that move the words preceding the verb to the end of the sentence.

Next we analyzed which rules of the *Left Part* ones are used most frequently. The five most frequent rules are shown in Figure 2. The first, fourth and fifth rule moves the verb more to the front, as is often needed in English subordinate clauses. The second one moves both parts of the verb together.

The third most frequent rule moves personal pronouns to the front. In the English language the subject has to be always at the front. In contrast, in German the word order is not that strict and the subject can appear later.

We have done the same for the *Left All* rules. The rules are shown in Figure 3. In this type of rule the five most frequent rules all try to move the verb more to the front of the sentence. In the last case both parts of the verb are put together.

Table 3: Translation results for the German-English task using different rule types (BLEU)

Type	EPPS		NEWS	
	Dev	Test	Dev	Test
Left Part	26.99	29.16	25.12	27.88
Right Part	26.69	28.73	24.76	27.28
Right/Left Part	26.99	28.96	25.06	27.69
Left All	26.77	28.76	24.37	26.56
Left Part/All	26.99	29.32	25.38	27.86
All	27.02	29.14	25.20	27.63

7.3 Rule Types

In a next group of experiments we evaluated the performance of the different rule types. In Table 3 the translation performance of systems using different rule types is shown. The experiments were carried out on the EPPS task as well as on the NEWS task.

First it can be seen that the *Left* rules perform better than the *Right* rules. This is not surprising, since they better describe how to reorder from German to English and because they are more often used in the lattice. If both types are used this

Table 4: Summary of translation results for the German-English tasks (BLEU)

System	EPPS		NEWS	
	Dev	Test	Dev	Test
Baseline	25.47	27.24	23.40	25.90
Short	26.77	28.54	24.73	27.48
Long	26.99	29.32	25.38	27.86

Table 5: Translation results for the German-French translation task (BLEU)

System	EPPS		NEWS	
	Dev	Test	Dev	Test
Baseline	25.86	27.05	17.90	18.52
Short	27.02	28.06	18.59	19.99
Long	27.27	28.61	19.10	20.11

lowers the performance a little. So if it is clear which type explains the reordering better, only this type should be used, but if that is not possible using both types can still help.

If both types of rules are compared, it can be seen that *Part* rules seem to have a more positive influence than *All* ones. The reason for this may be that the *Part* rules can also be applied more often than the rules of the other type. Using the combination of both types of rules, the performance is better on one task and equally good on the other task. Consequently, we used the combination of both types in the remaining experiments.

7.4 German-English

The results on the German-English task are summarized in Table 4. The long-range reorderings could improve the performance by 0.8 and 0.4 BLEU points on the different tasks compared to a system applying only short-range reorderings. These improvements are significant at a level of 5%.

We also analyzed the influence of tagging errors. Therefore, we tagged every word of the test sentence with the tag that this word is mostly assigned to in the training corpus. If the word does not occur in the training corpus, it was tagged as a noun. This results in different tags for 5% of the words and a BLEU score of 27.68 on the NEWS test set using long-range reorderings. So the translation quality drops by about 0.2 BLEU points, but it is still better than the system using only short-range reorderings.

In Figure 4 example translations of the baseline system, the system modeling only short-range reorderings and the system using also long-range reorderings rules are shown. The part of the sentences that needs long-range reorderings is always underlined.

In the first two examples the verbal phrase consists of two parts and the German one is splitted. In these cases, it was impossible for the short-range reordering model to move the second part of the verb to the front so that it could be translated correctly. In one case this leads to a selection of a phrase pair that removes the verb from the translation. Thus it is hard to understand the meaning of the sentence.

In the other two examples the verb of the subordinate clause has to be moved from the last position in the German sentence to the second position in the English one. This is again only possible using the long-range reordering rules. Furthermore, if these rules are not used, it is possible that the verb will be not translated at all as in the last example.

7.5 German-French

We also performed similar experiments on the German-French task. Since the type of reordering needed for this language pair is similar to the one used in the German-English task, we used also the *Left* rules in the long-range reorderings. As it can be seen in Table 5, the long-range reordering rules could also help to improve the translation performance for this language pair. The improvement on the EPPS task is significant at a level of 5%.

7.6 English-German

In a last group of experiments we applied the same approach also to the English-German translation task. In this case the verb has to be moved to the right, so that we used the *Right* rules for the long-range reorderings. Looking at the rule usage of the different type of rules, the picture was quite promising. This time the *Right* rules could be applied more often and the *Left* ones only a few times. But if we look at the results as shown in Table 6, the long-range reorderings do not improve the performance. We will investigate the reasons for this in future work.

Figure 4: Example translation from German to English using different type of rules

Source:	Diese Maßnahmen werden als eine Art Wiedergutmachung für früher begangenes Unrecht angesehen .
Baseline:	these measures will as a kind of compensation for once injustice done .
Short:	these measures will as a kind of compensation for once injustice done .
Long:	these measures will be seen as a kind of compensation for once injustice done .
Source:	Das wird mit derart unterschiedlichen Mitgliedern unmöglich sein .
Baseline:	this will with such different impossible .
Short:	this will with such different impossible .
Long:	this will be impossible to such different members .
Source:	Er braucht die Unterstützung derer , die an den Markt und an die Gleichbehandlung aller glauben .
Baseline:	he needs the support of those who market and the equal treatment of all believe .
Short:	it needs the support of those who in the market and the equal treatment of all believe .
Long:	it needs the support of those who believe in the market and the equal treatment of all .
Source:	.., daß sie das Einwanderungsproblem als politischen Hebel benutzen .
Baseline:	.. that they the immigration problem as a political lever .
Short:	.. that the problem of immigration as a political lever .
Long:	.. that they use the immigration problem as a political lever .

Table 6: Translation results for the English-German translation task (BLEU)

System	EPPS		NEWS	
	Dev	Test	Dev	Test
Baseline	18.93	2072	16.31	17.91
Short	19.49	21.56	17.13	18.31
Long	19.56	21.33	16.93	18.15

8 Conclusion

We have presented a new method to model long-range reorderings in statistical machine translation. This method extends a framework based on extracting POS-based reordering rules from an aligned parallel corpus by adding discontinuous reordering rules. Allowing rules with gaps captures very long-range reorderings while avoiding the data sparseness problem of very long continuous reordering rules.

The extracted rules are used to generate a word lattice with different possible reorderings of the source sentence in a preprocessing step prior to decoding. Placing various restrictions on the application of the rules keeps the lattice small enough for efficient decoding. Compared to a baseline system that only uses continuous reordering rules, applying additional discontinuous rules improved the translation performance on a German-English translation task significantly by up to 0.8 BLEU points.

In contrast to approaches like Collins et al. (2005) and Popović and Ney (2006), the rules are created in a data-driven way and not manually. It was therefore easily possible to transfer this approach to the German-French translation task, and we showed that we could improve the translation quality for this language pair as well. Furthermore, this approach needs only the POS information and no syntax tree. Thus, if we use the approximation for the tags as described before, the approach could also easily be integrated into a real-time translation system.

An unsolved problem is still why this approach does not improve the results of the English-German translation task. An explanation might be that here the reordering problem is even more difficult, since the German word order is very free.

Acknowledgments

This work was partly supported by Quaero Programme, funded by OSEO, French State agency for innovation.

References

Adam L. Berger, Vincent J. Della Pietra, and Stephen A. Della Pietra. 1996. A Maximum Entropy Approach to Natural Language Processing. *Computational Linguistics*, 22(1):39–71.

Peter F. Brown, Stephen A. Della Pietra, Vincent J. Della Pietra, and Robert L. Mercer. 1993. The Mathematics of Statistical Machine Translation: Parameter Estimation. *Computational Linguistics*, 19(2):263–311.

Boxing Chen, Mauro Cettolo, and Marcello Federico. 2006. Reordering Rules for Phrase-based Statistical Machine Translation. In *International Workshop on Spoken Language Translation (IWSLT 2006)*, Kyoto, Japan.

Michael Collins, Philipp Koehn, and Ivona Kučerová. 2005. Clause Restructuring for Statistical Machine Translation. In *Proc. of the 43rd Annual Meeting on Association for Computational Linguistics (ACL)*, pages 531–540.

Marta R. Costa-jussà and José A. R. Fonollosa. 2006. Statistical Machine Reordering. In *Conference on Empirical Methods on Natural Language Processing (EMNLP 2006)*, Sydney, Australia.

Nizar Crego and Nizar Habash. 2008. Using Shallow Syntax Information to Improve Word Alignment and Reordering for SMT. In *46th Annual Meeting of the Association for Computational Linguistics: Human Language Technologies (ACL-08: HLT)*, Columbus, Ohio, USA.

George Foster, Roland Kuhn, and Howard Johnson. 2006. Phrasetable Smoothing for Statistical Machine Translation. In *Conference on Empirical Methods in Natural Language Processing (EMNLP 2006)*, Sydney, Australia.

Philipp Koehn, Amittai Axelrod, Alexandra B. Mayne, Chris Callison-Burch, Miles Osborne, and David Talbot. 2005. Edinburgh System Description for the 2005 IWSLT Speech Translation Evaluation. In *IWSLT*, Pittsburgh, PA, USA.

Franz Josef Och and Herman Ney. 2000. Improved Statistical Alignment Models. In *38th Annual Meeting of the Association for Computational Linguistics (ACL 2000)*, Hong Kong.

Franz J. Och, Daniel Gildea, Sanjeev P. Khudanpur, Anoop Sarkar, Kenji Yamada, Alexander Fraser, Shankar Kumar, Libin Shen, David A. Smith, Katherine Eng, Viren Jain, Zhen Jin, and Dragomir R. Radev. 2004. A Smorgasboard of Features for Statistical Machine Translation. In *Human Language Technology Conference and the 5th Meeting of the North American Association for Computational Linguistics (HLT-NAACL 2004)*, Boston, USA.

Maja Popović and Hermann Ney. 2006. POS-based Word Reorderings for Statistical Machine Translation. In *International Conference on Language Resources and Evaluation (LREC 2006)*, Genoa, Italy.

Kay Rottmann and Stephan Vogel. 2007. Word Reordering in Statistical Machine Translation with a POS-Based Distortion Model. In *TMI*, Skövde, Sweden.

Helmut Schmid. 1994. Probabilistic Part-of-Speech Tagging Using Decision Trees. In *International Conference on New Methods in Language Processing*, Manchester, UK.

Libin Shen, Anoop Sarkar, and Franz Och. 2004. Discriminative Reranking for Machine Translation. In *Human Language Technology Conference and the 5th Meeting of the North American Association for Computational Linguistics (HLT-NAACL 2004)*, Boston, USA.

Christoph Tillmann and Tong Zhang. 2005. A Localized Prediction Model for Statistical Machine Translation. In *43rd Annual Meeting of the Association for Computational Linguistics (ACL 2005)*, Ann Arbor, Michigan, USA.

Stephan Vogel, Ying Zhang, Fei Huang, Alicia Tribble, Ashish Venogupal, Bing Zhao, and Alex Waibel. 2003. The CMU Statistical Translation System. In *MT Summit IX*, New Orleans, LA, USA.

Stephan Vogel. 2003. SMT Decoder Dissected: Word Reordering. In *Int. Conf. on Natural Language Processing and Knowledge Engineering*, Beijing, China.

Yeyi Wang and Alex Waibel. 1998. Fast Decoding for Statistical Machine Translation. In *ICSLP'98*, Sydney, Australia.

Dekai Wu. 1996. A Polynomial-time Algorithm for Statistical Machine Translation. In *ACL-96: 34th Annual Meeting of the Assoc. for Computational Linguistics*, Santa Cruz, CA, USA, June.

Kenji Yamada and Kevin Knight. 2000. A Syntax-based Statistical Translation Model. In *38th Annual Meeting of the Association for Computational Linguistics (ACL 2000)*, Hong Kong.

Richard Zens and Hermann Ney. 2003. A Comparative Study on Reordering Constraints in Statistical Machine Translation. In *41st Annual Meeting of the Association for Computational Linguistics (ACL)*, pages 192–202, Sapporo, Japan.

Ying Zhang and Stephan Vogel. 2004. Measuring Confidence Intervals for mt Evaluation Metrics. In *TMI 2004*, Baltimore, MD, USA.

Yuqi Zhang, Richard Zens, and Hermann Ney. 2007. Chunk-Level Reordering of Source Language Sentences with Automatically Learned Rules for Statistical Machine Translation. In *HLT-NAACL Workshop on Syntax and Structure in Statistical Translation*, Rochester, NY, USA.

Disambiguating "DE" for Chinese-English Machine Translation

Pi-Chuan Chang, **Dan Jurafsky**, and **Christopher D. Manning**
Computer Science Department, Stanford University
Stanford, CA 94305
pichuan,jurafsky,manning@stanford.edu

Abstract

Linking constructions involving 的 (DE) are ubiquitous in Chinese, and can be translated into English in many different ways. This is a major source of machine translation error, even when syntax-sensitive translation models are used. This paper explores how getting more information about the syntactic, semantic, and discourse context of uses of 的 (DE) can facilitate producing an appropriate English translation strategy. We describe a finer-grained classification of 的 (DE) constructions in Chinese NPs, construct a corpus of annotated examples, and then train a log-linear classifier, which contains linguistically inspired features. We use the DE classifier to preprocess MT data by explicitly labeling 的 (DE) constructions, as well as reordering phrases, and show that our approach provides significant BLEU point gains on MT02 (+1.24), MT03 (+0.88) and MT05 (+1.49) on a phrased-based system. The improvement persists when a hierarchical reordering model is applied.

1 Introduction

Machine translation (MT) from Chinese to English has been a difficult problem: structural differences between Chinese and English, such as the different orderings of head nouns and relative clauses, cause BLEU scores to be consistently lower than for other difficult language pairs like Arabic-English. Many of these structural differences are related to the ubiquitous Chinese 的(DE) construction, used for a wide range of noun modification constructions (both single word and clausal) and other uses. Part of the solution to dealing with these ordering issues is hierarchical decoding, such as the Hiero system (Chiang, 2005), a method motivated by 的(DE) examples like the one in Figure 1. In this case, the translation goal is to rotate the noun head and the preceding relative clause around 的(DE), so that we can translate to "[one of few countries] 的 [have diplomatic relations with North Korea]". Hiero can learn this kind of lexicalized synchronous grammar rule.

But use of hierarchical decoders has not solved the DE construction translation problem. We analyzed the errors of three state-of-the-art systems (the 3 DARPA GALE phase 2 teams' systems), and even though all three use some kind of hierarchical system, we found many remaining errors related to reordering. One is shown here:

当地	一所	名声不佳	的	中学
local	a	bad reputation	DE	middle school

Reference: 'a local middle school with a bad reputation'
Team 1: 'a bad reputation of the local secondary school'
Team 2: 'the local a bad reputation secondary school'
Team 3: 'a local stigma secondary schools'

None of the teams reordered "bad reputation" and "middle school" around the 的. We argue that this is because it is not sufficient to have a formalism which *supports* phrasal reordering, but it is also necessary to have sufficient linguistic modeling that the system *knows when and how much to rearrange*.

An alternative way of dealing with structural differences is to reorder source language sentences to minimize structural divergence with the target language, (Xia and McCord, 2004; Collins et al., 2005; Wang et al., 2007). For example Wang et al. (2007) introduced a set of rules to decide if a 的(DE) construction should be reordered or not before translating to English:

- For DNPs (consisting of"XP+DEG"):
  - Reorder if XP is PP or LCP;
  - Reorder if XP is a non-pronominal NP
- For CPs (typically formed by "IP+DEC"):
  - Reorder to align with the "that+clause" structure of English.

Although this and previous reordering work has led to significant improvements, errors still remain. Indeed, Wang et al. (2007) found that the precision of their NP rules is only about 54.6% on a small human-judged set.

One possible reason the 的(DE) construction remains unsolved is that previous work has paid insufficient attention to the many ways the 的(DE) construction can be translated and the rich structural cues to the translation. Wang et al. (2007), for example, characterized 的(DE) into only two

Proceedings of the Fourth Workshop on Statistical Machine Translation, pages 215–223,
Athens, Greece, 30 March – 31 March 2009. ©2009 Association for Computational Linguistics

澳洲	是	与	北韩	有	邦交	的	少数	国家	之一	。
Aozhou	shi	yu	Beihan	you	bangjiao	DE	shaoshu	guojia	zhiyi	.
Australia	is	with	North Korea	have	diplomatic relations	that	few	countries	one of	.

'Australia is one of the few countries that have diplomatic relations with North Korea.'

Figure 1: An example of the DE construction from (Chiang, 2005)

classes. But our investigation shows that there are many strategies for translating Chinese [A 的 B] phrases into English, including the patterns in Table 1, only some involving reversal.

Notice that the presence of reordering is only one part of the rich structure of these examples. Some reorderings are relative clauses, while others involve prepositional phrases, but not all prepositional phrase uses involve reorderings. These examples suggest that capturing finer-grained translation patterns could help achieve higher accuracy both in reordering and in lexical choice.

In this work, we propose to use a statistical classifier trained on various features to predict for a given Chinese 的(DE) construction both whether it will reorder in English and which construction it will translate to in English. We suggest that the necessary classificatory features can be extracted from Chinese, rather than English. The 的(DE) in Chinese has a unified meaning of 'noun modification', and the choice of reordering and construction realization are mainly a consequence of facts of English noun modification. Nevertheless, most of the features that determine the choice of a felicitous translation are available in the Chinese source. Noun modification realization has been widely studied in English (e.g., (Rosenbach, 2003)), and many of the important determinative properties (e.g., topicality, animacy, prototypicality) can be detected working in the source language.

We first present some corpus analysis characterizing different DE constructions based on how they get translated into English (Section 2). We then train a classifier to label DEs into the 5 different categories that we define (Section 3). The fine-grained DEs, together with reordering, are then used as input to a statistical MT system (Section 4). We find that classifying DEs into finer-grained tokens helps MT performance, usually at least twice as much as just doing phrasal reordering.

2 DE classification

The Chinese character DE serves many different purposes. According to the Chinese Treebank tagging guidelines (Xia, 2000), the character can be tagged as DEC, DEG, DEV, SP, DER, or AS. Similar to (Wang et al., 2007), we only consider the majority case when the phrase with 的(DE) is a noun phrase modifier. The DEs in NPs have a part-of-speech tag of DEC (a complementizer or a nominalizer) or DEG (a genitive marker or an associative marker).

2.1 Class Definition

The way we categorize the DEs is based on their behavior when translated into English. This is implicitly done in the work of Wang et al. (2007) where they use rules to decide if a certain DE and the words next to it will need to be reordered. In this work, we categorize DEs into finer-grained categories. For a Chinese noun phrase [A 的 B], we categorize it into one of these five classes:

1. A B
   In this category, A in the Chinese side is translated as a pre-modifier of B. In most of the cases A is an adjective form, like Example 1.1 in Table 1 or the possessive adjective example in Example 1.2. Compound nouns where A becomes a pre-modifier of B also fit in this category (Example 1.3).
2. B *preposition* A
   There are several cases that get translated into the form B *preposition* A. For example, the *of*-genitive in Example 2.1 in Table 1.
   Example 2.2 shows cases where the Chinese A gets translated into a prepositional phrase that expresses location.
   When A becomes a gerund phrase and an object of a preposition, it is also categorized in the B *preposition* A category (Example 2.3).
3. A 's B
   In this class, the English translation is an explicit *s*-genitive case, as in Example 3.1. This class occurs much less often but is still interesting because of the difference from the *of*-genitive.
4. *relative clause*
   We include the obvious relative clause cases like Example 4.1 where a relative clause is

introduced by a relative pronoun. We also include reduced relative clauses like Example 4.2 in this class.

5. A *preposition* B
   This class is another small one. The English translations that fall into this class usually have some number, percentage or level word in the Chinese A.

Some NPs are translated into a hybrid of these categories, or just don't fit into one of the five categories, for instance, involving an adjectival premodifier and a relative clause. In those cases, they are put into an "other" category.[1]

2.2 Data annotation of DE classes

In order to train a classifier and test its performance, we use the Chinese Treebank 6.0 (LDC2007T36) and the English Chinese Translation Treebank 1.0 (LDC2007T02). The word alignment data (LDC2006E93) is also used to align the English and Chinese words between LDC2007T36 and LDC2007T02. The overlapping part of the three datasets are a subset of CTB6 files 1 to 325. After preprocessing those three sets of data, we have 3253 pairs of Chinese sentences and their translations. In those sentences, we use the gold-standard Chinese tree structure to get 3412 Chinese DEs in noun phrases that we want to annotate. Among the 3412 DEs, 530 of them are in the "other" category and are not used in the classifier training and evaluation. The statistics of the five classes are:

1. A B: 693 (24.05%)
2. B *preposition* A: 1381 (47.92%)
3. A 's B: 91 (3.16%)
4. *relative clause*: 669 (23.21%)
5. A *preposition* B: 48 (1.66%)

3 Log-linear DE classifier

In order to see how well we can categorize DEs in noun phrases into one of the five classes, we train a log-linear classifier to classify each DE according to features extracted from its surrounding context. Since we want the training and testing conditions to match, when we extract features for the classifier, we don't use gold-standard parses. Instead, we use a parser trained on CTB6 excluding files 1-325. We then use this parser to parse the 3253 Chinese sentences with the DE annotation and extract parse-related features from there.

[1]The "other" category contains many mixed cases that could be difficult Chinese patterns to translate. We will leave this for future work.

	5-class Acc. (%)	2-class Acc. (%)
baseline	-	76.0
DEPOS	54.8	71.0
+A-pattern	67.9	83.7
+POS-ngram	72.1	84.9
+Lexical	74.9	86.5
+SemClass	75.1	86.7
+Topicality	75.4	86.9

Table 2: 5-class and 2-class classification accuracy. "baseline" is the heuristic rules in (Wang et al., 2007). Others are various features added to the log-linear classifier.

3.1 Experimental setting

For the classification experiment, we exclude the "other" class and only use the 2882 examples that fall into the five pre-defined classes. To evaluate the classification performance and understand what features are useful, we compute the accuracy by averaging five 10-fold cross-validations.[2]

As a baseline, we use the rules introduced in Wang et al. (2007) to decide if the DEs require reordering or not. However, since their rules only decide if there is reordering in an NP with DE, their classification result only has two classes. So, in order to compare our classifier's performance with the rules in Wang et al. (2007), we have to map our five-class results into two classes. We mapped our five-class results into two classes. So we mapped *B preposition A* and *relative clause* into the class "*reordered*", and the other three classes into "*not-reordered*".

3.2 Feature Engineering

To understand which features are useful for DE classification, we list our feature engineering steps and results in Table 2. In Table 2, the 5-class accuracy is defined by:

$$\frac{\text{(number of correctly labeled DEs)}}{\text{(number of all DEs)}} \times 100$$

The 2-class accuracy is defined similarly, but it is evaluated on the 2-class "*reordered*" and "*not-reordered*" after mapping from the 5 classes.

The DEs we are classifying are within an NP; we refer to them as $[\text{A 的 B}]_{\text{NP}}$. A includes all the words in the NP before 的; B includes all the words in the NP after 的. To illustrate, we will use the following NP:

$$[[\text{韩国 最 大}]_{\text{A}} \text{ 的 } [\text{投资 对象国}]_{\text{B}}]_{\text{NP}}$$

[2]We evaluate the classifier performance using cross-validations to get the best setting for the classifier. The proof of efficacy of the DE classifier is MT performance on independent data in Section 4.

1.	`A B`
1.1.	优越(*excellent*)/的(*DE*)/地理(*geographical*)/条件(*qualification*) → "excellent geographical qualifications"
1.2.	我们(*our*)/的(*DE*)/金融(*financial*)/风险(*risks*) → "our financial risks"
1.3.	贸易(*trade*)/的(*DE*)/互补性(*complement*) → "trade complement"
2.	`B` ***preposition*** `A`
2.1.	投资(*investment*)/环境(*environment*)/的(*DE*)/改善(*improvement*) → "the improvement of the investment environment"
2.2.	崇明县(*Chongming county*)/内(*inside*)/的(*DE*)/单位(*organization*) → "organizations inside Chongming county"
2.3.	一(*one*)/个(*measure word*)/观察(*observe*)/中国(*China*)/市场(*market*)/的(*DE*)/小小(*small*)/窗口(*window*) → "a small window for watching over Chinese markets"
3.	`A` **'s** `B`
3.1.	国家(*nation*)/的(*DE*)/宏观(*macro*)/管理(*management*) → "the nation 's macro management"
4.	***relative clause***
4.1.	中国(*China*)/不能(*cannot*)/生产(produce)/而(*and*)/又(*but*)/很(*very*)/需要(*need*)/的(*DE*)/药品(*medicine*) → "medicine that cannot be produced by China but is urgently needed"
4.2.	外商(*foreign business*)/投资(*invest*)/企业(*enterprise*)/获得(*acquire*)/的(*DE*)/人民币(*RMB*)/贷款(*loan*) → "the loans in RMB acquired by foreign-invested enterprises"
5.	`A` ***preposition*** `B`
5.1.	四千多万(*more than 40 million*)/美元(*US dollar*)/的(*DE*)/产品(*product*) → more than 40 million US dollars in products

Table 1: Examples for the 5 DE classes

to show examples of each feature. The parse structure of the NP is listed in Figure 2.

```
(NP
  (NP (NR 韩国))
  (CP
    (IP
      (VP
        (ADVP (AD 最))
        (VP (VA 大))))
    (DEC 的))
  (NP (NN 投资) (NN 对象国)))))
```

Figure 2: The parse tree of the Chinese NP.

DEPOS: part-of-speech tag of DE

Since the part-of-speech tag of DE indicates its syntactic function, it is the first obvious feature to add. The NP in Figure 2 will have the feature "DEC". This basic feature will be referred to as DEPOS. Note that since we are only classifying DEs in NPs, ideally the part-of-speech tag of DE will either be DEC or DEG as described in Section 2. However, since we are using automatic parses instead of gold-standard ones, the DEPOS feature might have other values than just DEC and DEG. From Table 2, we can see that with this simple feature, the 5-class accuracy is low but at least better than simply guessing the majority class (47.92%). The 2-class accuracy is still lower than using the heuristic rules in (Wang et al., 2007), which is reasonable because their rules encode more information than just the POS tags of DEs.

A-pattern: Chinese syntactic patterns appearing before 的

Secondly, we want to incorporate the rules in (Wang et al., 2007) as features in the log-linear classifier. We added features for certain indicative patterns in the parse tree (listed in Table 3).

1. **A is ADJP**: true if A+DE is a DNP which is in the form of "ADJP+DEG".
2. **A is QP**: true if A+DE is a DNP which is in the form of "QP+DEG".
3. **A is pronoun**: true if A+DE is a DNP which is in the form of "NP+DEG", and the NP is a pronoun.
4. **A ends with VA**: true if A+DE is a CP which is in the form of "IP+DEC", and the IP ends with a VP that's either just a VA or a VP preceded by a ADVP.

Table 3: A-pattern features

Features 1–3 are inspired by the rules in (Wang et al., 2007), and the fourth rule is based on the observation that even though the predicative adjective VA acts as a verb, it actually corresponds to adjectives in English as described in (Xia, 2000).[3] We call these four features A-pattern. Our example NP in Figure 2 will have the fourth feature "A ends with VA" in Table 3, but not the other three features. In Table 2 we can see that after adding A-pattern, the 2-class accuracy is already much higher than the baseline. We attribute this to the fourth rule and also to the fact that the classifier can learn weights for each feature.[4]

[3] Quote from (Xia, 2000): "VA roughly corresponds to adjectives in English and stative verbs in the literature on Chinese grammar."

[4] We also tried extending a rule-based 2-class classifier with the fourth rule. The accuracy is 83.48%, only slightly lower than using the same features in a log-linear classifier.

POS-ngram: unigrams and bigrams of POS tags

The POS-ngram feature adds all unigrams and bigrams in A and B. Since A and B have different influences on the choice of DE class, we distinguish their ngrams into two sets of features. We also include the bigram pair across DE which gets another feature name for itself. The example NP in Figure 2 will have these features (we use b to indicate boundaries):

- POS unigrams in A: "NR", "AD", "VA"
- POS bigrams in A: "b-NR", "NR-AD", "AD-VA", "VA-b"
- cross-DE POS bigram: "VA-NN"
- POS unigram in B: "NN"
- POS bigrams in B: "b-NN", "NN-NN", "NN-b"

The part-of-speech ngram features add 4.24% accuracy to the 5-class classifier.

Lexical: lexical features

In addition to part-of-speech features, we also tried to use features from the words themselves. But since using full word identity resulted in a sparsity issue,[5] we take the one-character suffix of each word and extract suffix unigram and bigram features from them. The argument for using suffixes is that it often captures the larger category of the word (Tseng et al., 2005). For example, 中国 (China) and 韩国 (Korea) share the same suffix 国, which means "country". These suffix ngram features will result in these features for the NP in Figure 2:

- suffix unigrams: "国", "最", "大", "的", "资", "国"
- suffix bigrams: "b-国", "国-最", "最-大", "大-的", "的-资", "资-国", "国-b"

Other than the suffix ngram, we also add three other lexical features: first, if the word before DE is a noun, we add a feature that is the conjunction of POS and suffix unigram. Secondly, an "NR only" feature will fire when A only consists of one or more NRs. Thirdly, we normalize different forms of "percentage" representation, and add a feature if they exist. This includes words that start with "百分之" or ends with the percentage sign "%". The first two features are inspired by the fact that a noun and its type can help decide "B prep A" versus "A B". Here we use the suffix of the noun and the NR (proper noun) tag to help capture its animacy, which is useful in choosing between the *s*-genitive (*the boy's mother*) and the *of*-genitive (*the mother of the boy*) in English (Rosenbach, 2003). The third feature is added because many of the cases in the "A *preposition* B" class have a percentage number in A. We call these sets of features Lexical. Together they provide 2.73% accuracy improvement over the previous setting.

SemClass: semantic class of words

We also use a Chinese thesaurus, CiLin, to look up the semantic classes of the words in [A 的 B] and use them as features. CiLin is a Chinese thesaurus published in 1984 (Mei et al., 1984). CiLin is organized in a conceptual hierarchy with five levels. We use the level-1 tags which includes 12 categories.[6] This feature fires when a word we look up has one level-1 tag in CiLin. This kind of feature is referred to as SemClass in Table 2. For the example in Figure 2, two words have a single level-1 tag: "最"(most) has a level-1 tag K[7] and "投资"(investment) has a level-1 tag H[8]. "韩国" and "对象国" are not listed in CiLin, and "大" has multiple entries. Therefore, the SemClass features are: (*i*) before DE: "K"; (*ii*) after DE: "H"

Topicality: re-occurrence of nouns

The last feature we add is a Topicality feature, which is also useful for disambiguating *s*-genitive and *of*-genitive. We approximate the feature by caching the nouns in the previous two sentences, and fire a topicality feature when the noun appears in the cache. Take this NP in MT06 as an example:

"南韩 与 北韩 的 奥运 代表队"

For this NP, all words before DE and after DE appeared in the previous sentence. Therefore the topicality features "cache-before-DE" and "cache-after-DE" both fire.

After all the feature engineering above, the best accuracy on the 5-class classifier we have is 75.4%, which maps into a 2-class accuracy of 86.9%. Comparing the 2-class accuracy to the (Wang et al., 2007) baseline, we have a 10.9% absolute improvement. The 5-class accuracy and confusion matrix is listed in Table 4.

"A *preposition* B" is a small category and is the most confusing. "A 's B" also has lower accuracy, and is mostly confused with "B *preposition* A".

[5] The accuracy is worse when we tried using the word identity instead of the suffix.

[6] We also tried adding more levels but it did not help.

[7] K is the category 助语 (auxiliary) in CiLin.

[8] H is the category 活动 (activities) in CiLin.

real →	A 's B	AB	A *prep.* B	B *prep.* A	*rel. clause*
A 's B	168	36	0	110	0
AB	48	2473	73	227	216
A *prep.* B	0	18	46	23	11
B *prep.* A	239	691	95	5915	852
rel. clause	0	247	26	630	2266
Total	455	3465	240	6905	3345
Accuracy(%)	36.92	71.37	19.17	85.66	67.74

Table 4: The confusion matrix for 5-class DE classification

This could be due to the fact that there are some cases where the translation is correct both ways, but also could be because the features we added have not captured the difference well enough.

4 Machine Translation Experiments

4.1 Experimental Setting

For our MT experiments, we used a re-implementation of Moses (Koehn et al., 2003), a state-of-the-art phrase-based system. The alignment is done by the Berkeley word aligner (Liang et al., 2006) and then we symmetrized the word alignment using the grow-diag heuristic. For features, we incorporate Moses' standard eight features as well as the lexicalized reordering model. Parameter tuning is done with Minimum Error Rate Training (MERT) (Och, 2003). The tuning set for MERT is the NIST MT06 data set, which includes 1664 sentences. We evaluate the result with MT02 (878 sentences), MT03 (919 sentences), and MT05 (1082 sentences).

Our MT training corpus contains 1,560,071 sentence pairs from various parallel corpora from LDC.[9] There are 12,259,997 words on the English side. Chinese word segmentation is done by the Stanford Chinese segmenter (Chang et al., 2008). After segmentation, there are 11,061,792 words on the Chinese side. We use a 5-gram language model trained on the Xinhua and AFP sections of the Gigaword corpus (LDC2007T40) and also the English side of all the LDC parallel data permissible under the NIST08 rules. Documents of Gigaword released during the epochs of MT02, MT03, MT05, and MT06 were removed.

To run the DE classifier, we also need to parse the Chinese texts. We use the Stanford Chinese parser (Levy and Manning, 2003) to parse the Chinese side of the MT training data and the tuning and test sets.

[9]LDC2003E07, LDC2003E14, LDC2005E83, LDC2005T06, LDC2006E26, LDC2006E85, LDC2006E85, LDC2005T34, and LDC2005T34

4.2 Baseline Experiments

We have two different settings as baseline experiments. The first is without reordering or DE annotation on the Chinese side; we simply align the parallel texts, extract phrases and tune parameters. This experiment is referred to as BASELINE. Also, we reorder the training data, the tuning and the test sets with the NP rules in (Wang et al., 2007) and compare our results with this second baseline (WANG-NP).

The NP reordering preprocessing (WANG-NP) showed consistent improvement in Table 5 on all test sets, with BLEU point gains ranging from 0.15 to 0.40. This confirms that having reordering around DEs in NP helps Chinese-English MT.

4.3 Experiments with 5-class DE annotation

We use the best setting of the DE classifier described in Section 3 to annotate DEs in NPs in the MT training data as well as the NIST tuning and test sets.[10] If a DE is in an NP, we use the annotation of 的$_{AB}$, 的$_{AsB}$, 的$_{BprepA}$, 的$_{relc}$, or 的$_{AprepB}$ to replace the original DE character. Once we have the DEs labeled, we preprocess the Chinese sentences by reordering them.[11] Note that not all DEs in the Chinese data are in NPs, therefore not all DEs are annotated with the extra labels. Table 6 lists the statistics of the DE classes in the MT training data.

class of 的(DE)	counts	percentage
的$_{AB}$	112,099	23.55%
的$_{AprepB}$	2,426	0.51%
的$_{AsB}$	3,430	0.72%
的$_{BprepA}$	248,862	52.28%
的$_{relc}$	95,134	19.99%
的 (unlabeled)	14,056	2.95%
total number of 的	476,007	100%

Table 6: The number of different DE classes labeled for the MT training data.

After this preprocessing, we restart the whole MT pipeline – align the preprocessed data, extract phrases, run MERT and evaluate. This setting is referred to as DE-Annotated in Table 5.

4.4 Hierarchical Phrase Reordering Model

To demonstrate that the technique presented here is effective even with a hierarchical decoder, we

[10]The DE classifier used to annotate the MT experiment was trained on all the available data described in Section 2.2.

[11]Reordering is applied on DNP and CP for reasons described in Wang et al. (2007). We reorder only when the 的 is labeled as 的$_{BprepA}$ or 的$_{relc}$.

BLEU				
	MT06(tune)	MT02	MT03	MT05
BASELINE	32.39	32.51	32.75	31.42
WANG-NP	32.75(+0.36)	32.66(+0.15)	33.15(+0.40)	31.68(+0.26)
DE-Annotated	**33.39**(+1.00)	**33.75**(+1.24)	**33.63**(+0.88)	**32.91**(+1.49)
BASELINE+Hier	32.96	33.10	32.93	32.23
DE-Annotated+Hier	**33.96**(+1.00)	**34.33**(+1.23)	**33.88**(+0.95)	**33.01**(+0.77)
Translation Error Rate (TER)				
	MT06(tune)	MT02	MT03	MT05
BASELINE	61.10	63.11	62.09	64.06
WANG-NP	59.78(−1.32)	62.58(−0.53)	61.36(−0.73)	62.35(−1.71)
DE-Annotated	**58.21**(−2.89)	**61.17**(−1.94)	**60.27**(−1.82)	**60.78**(−3.28)

Table 5: MT experiments of different settings on various NIST MT evaluation datasets. We used both the BLEU and TER metrics for evaluation. All differences between DE-Annotated and BASELINE are significant at the level of 0.05 with the approximate randomization test in (Riezler and Maxwell, 2005)

conduct additional experiments with a hierarchical phrase reordering model introduced by Galley and Manning (2008). The hierarchical phrase reordering model can handle the key examples often used to motivated syntax-based systems; therefore we think it is valuable to see if the DE annotation can still improve on top of that. In Table 5, BASELINE+Hier gives consistent BLEU improvement over BASELINE. Using DE annotation on top of the hierarchical phrase reordering models (DE-Annotated+Hier) provides extra gain over BASELINE+Hier. This shows the DE annotation can help a hierarchical system. We think similar improvements are likely to occur with other hierarchical systems.

5 Analysis

5.1 Statistics on the Preprocessed Data

Since our approach DE-Annotated and one of the baselines (WANG-NP) are both preprocessing Chinese sentences, knowing what percentage of the sentences are altered will be one useful indicator of how different the systems are from the baseline. In our test sets, MT02 has 591 out of 878 sentences (67.3%) that have DEs under NPs; for MT03 it is 619 out of 919 sentences (67.4%); for MT05 it is 746 out of 1082 sentences (68.9%). This shows that our preprocessing affects the majority of the sentences and thus it is not surprising that preprocessing based on the DE construction can make a significant difference.

5.2 Example: how DE annotation affects translation

Our approach DE-Annotated reorders the Chinese sentence, which is similar to the approach proposed by Wang et al. (2007) (WANG-NP). However, our focus is on the annotation on DEs and how this can improve translation quality. Table 7 shows an example that contains a DE construction that translates into a relative clause in English.[12] The automatic parse tree of the sentence is listed in Figure 3. The reordered sentences of WANG-NP and DE-Annotated appear on the top and bottom in Figure 4. For this example, both systems decide to reorder, but DE-Annotated had the extra information that this 的 is a 的$_{\text{relc}}$. In Figure 4 we can see that in WANG-NP, "的" is being translated as "for", and the translation afterwards is not grammatically correct. On the other hand, the bottom of Figure 4 shows that with the DE-Annotated preprocessing, now "的$_{\text{relc}}$" is translated into "which was" and well connected with the later translation. This shows that disambiguating 的 helps in choosing a better English translation.

```
(IP
 (NP (NN 比亚吉))
 (VP
   (ADVP (AD 曾))
   (VP (VV 协助)
     (IP
       (VP (VV 草拟)
         (NP
           (QP (CD 一)
             (CLP (M 份)))
           (CP
             (IP
               (VP (VV 遭)
                 (NP
                   (NP (NN 工会)
                     (CC 和)
                     (NN 左翼) (NN 分子))
                   (ADJP (JJ 强烈))
                   (NP (NN 反对)))))
             (DEC 的))
           (NP (NN 就业) (NN 改革) (NN 方案)))))))
  (PU 。))
```

Figure 3: The parse tree of the Chinese sentence in Table 7.

[12]In this example, all four references agreed on the relative clause translation. Sometimes DE constructions have multiple appropriate translations, which is one of the reasons why certain classes are more confusable in Table 4.

Chinese	比亚吉 曾 协助 草拟 [一 份 遭 工会 和 左翼 分子 强烈 反对]$_A$ 的 [就业 改革 方案]$_B$ 。
Ref 1	biagi had assisted in drafting [an employment reform plan]$_B$ [that was strongly opposed by the labor union and the leftists]$_A$.
Ref 2	biagi had helped in drafting [a labor reform proposal]$_B$ [that provoked strong protests from labor unions and the leftists]$_A$.
Ref 3	biagi once helped drafting [an employment reform scheme]$_B$ [that was been strongly opposed by the trade unions and the left - wing]$_A$.
Ref 4	biagi used to assisted to draft [an employment reform plan]$_B$ [which is violently opposed by the trade union and leftest]$_A$.

Table 7: A Chinese example from MT02 that contains a DE construction that translates into a relative clause in English. The $[]_A$ $[]_B$ is hand-labeled to indicate the approximate translation alignment between the Chinese sentence and English references.

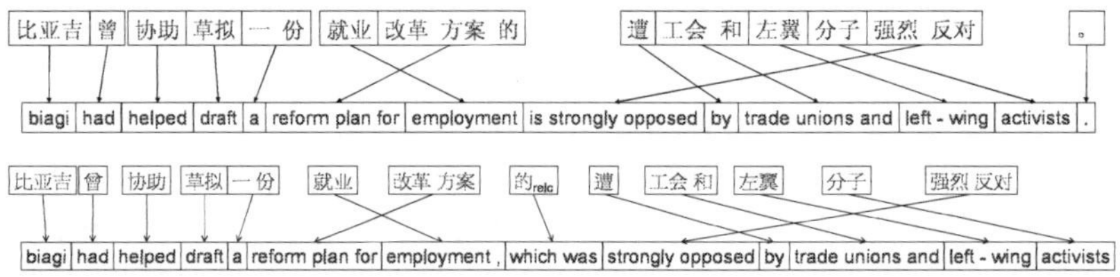

Figure 4: The top translation is from WANG-NP of the Chinese sentence in Table 7. The bottom one is from DE-Annotated. In this example, both systems reordered the NP, but DE-Annotated has an annotation on the 的.

6 Conclusion

In this paper, we presented a classification of Chinese 的(DE) constructions in NPs according to how they are translated into English. We applied this DE classifier to the Chinese sentences of MT data, and we also reordered the constructions that required reordering to better match their English translations. The MT experiments showed our preprocessing gave significant BLEU and TER score gains over the baselines. Based on our classification and MT experiments, we found that not only do we have better rules for deciding what to reorder, but the syntactic, semantic, and discourse information that we capture in the Chinese sentence allows us to give hints to the MT system which allows better translations to be chosen.

Acknowledgments

The authors would like to thank Michel Galley and Daniel Cer for useful discussions and technical help, and Spence Green for his comments on an earlier draft of the paper. This work is funded by a Stanford Graduate Fellowship to the first author and gift funding from Google for the project "Translating Chinese Correctly".

References

Pi-Chuan Chang, Michel Galley, and Christopher D. Manning. 2008. Optimizing Chinese word segmentation for machine translation performance. In *Proceedings of the Third Workshop on Statistical Machine Translation*, pages 224–232, Columbus, Ohio, June. Association for Computational Linguistics.

David Chiang. 2005. A hierarchical phrase-based model for statistical machine translation. In *Proceedings of ACL*, pages 263–270, Ann Arbor, Michigan, June. Association for Computational Linguistics.

Michael Collins, Philipp Koehn, and Ivona Kučerová. 2005. Clause restructuring for statistical machine translation. In *ACL '05: Proceedings of ACL*, pages 531–540, Morristown, NJ, USA. Association for Computational Linguistics.

Michel Galley and Christopher D. Manning. 2008. A simple and effective hierarchical phrase reordering model. In *Proceedings of EMNLP*, pages 847–855, Honolulu, Hawaii, October. Association for Computational Linguistics.

Philipp Koehn, Franz Josef Och, and Daniel Marcu. 2003. Statistical phrase-based translation. In *Proc. of NAACL-HLT*.

Roger Levy and Christopher Manning. 2003. Is it harder to parse Chinese, or the Chinese treebank? In *Proceedings of ACL*, pages 439–446, Morristown, NJ, USA. Association for Computational Linguistics.

Percy Liang, Ben Taskar, and Dan Klein. 2006. Alignment by agreement. In *Proceedings of HLT-NAACL*, pages 104–111, New York City, USA, June. Association for Computational Linguistics.

Jia-ju Mei, Yi-Ming Zheng, Yun-Qi Gao, and Hung-Xiang Yin. 1984. *TongYiCi CiLin*. Shanghai: the Commercial Press.

Franz Josef Och. 2003. Minimum error rate training for statistical machine translation. In *ACL*.

Stefan Riezler and John T. Maxwell. 2005. On some pitfalls in automatic evaluation and significance testing for MT. In *Proceedings of the ACL Workshop on Intrinsic and Extrinsic Evaluation Measures for Machine Translation and/or Summarization*, pages 57–64, Ann Arbor, Michigan, June. Association for Computational Linguistics.

Anette Rosenbach. 2003. Aspects of iconicity and economy in the choice between the s-genitive and the of-genitive in English. *Topics in English Linguistics*, 43:379–412.

Huihsin Tseng, Dan Jurafsky, and Christopher D. Manning. 2005. Morphological features help pos tagging of unknown words across language varieties. In *Proc. of the Fourth SIGHAN Workshop on Chinese Language Processing*.

Chao Wang, Michael Collins, and Philipp Koehn. 2007. Chinese syntactic reordering for statistical machine translation. In *Proceedings of EMNLP-CoNLL*, pages 737–745, Prague, Czech Republic, June. Association for Computational Linguistics.

Fei Xia and Michael McCord. 2004. Improving a statistical MT system with automatically learned rewrite patterns. In *Proceedings of Coling 2004*, pages 508–514, Geneva, Switzerland, Aug 23–Aug 27. COLING.

Fei Xia. 2000. The part-of-speech tagging guidelines for the Penn Chinese Treebank (3.0).

A Systematic Analysis of Translation Model Search Spaces

Michael Auli, Adam Lopez, Hieu Hoang and **Philipp Koehn**
University of Edinburgh
10 Crichton Street
Edinburgh, EH8 9AB
United Kingdom
m.auli@sms.ed.ac.uk, alopez@inf.ed.ac.uk, h.hoang@sms.ed.ac.uk, pkoehn@inf.ed.ac.uk

Abstract

Translation systems are complex, and most metrics do little to pinpoint causes of error or isolate system differences. We use a simple technique to discover induction errors, which occur when good translations are absent from model search spaces. Our results show that a common pruning heuristic drastically increases induction error, and also strongly suggest that the search spaces of phrase-based and hierarchical phrase-based models are highly overlapping despite the well known structural differences.

1 Introduction

Most empirical work in translation analyzes models and algorithms using BLEU (Papineni et al., 2002) and related metrics. Though such metrics are useful as sanity checks in iterative system development, they are less useful as analytical tools. The performance of a translation system depends on the complex interaction of several different components. Since metrics assess only output, they fail to inform us about the consequences of these interactions, and thus provide no insight into the errors made by a system, or into the design tradeoffs of competing systems.

In this work, we show that it is possible to obtain such insights by analyzing translation system components in isolation. We focus on model search spaces (§2), posing a very simple question: *Given a model and a sentence pair, does the search space contain the sentence pair?* Applying this method to the analysis and comparison of French-English translation using both phrase-based and hierarchical phrase-based systems yields surprising results, which we analyze quantitatively and qualitatively.

- First, we analyze the **induction error** of a model, a measure on the completeness of the search space. We find that low weight phrase translations typically discarded by heuristic pruning nearly triples the number of reference sentences that can be exactly reconstructed by either model (§3).
- Second, we find that the high-probability regions in the search spaces of phrase-based and hierarchical systems are nearly identical (§4). This means that reported differences between the models are due to their rankings of competing hypotheses, rather than structural differences of the derivations they produce.

2 Models, Search Spaces, and Errors

A translation model consists of two distinct elements: an unweighted ruleset, and a parameterization (Lopez, 2008a; 2009). A **ruleset** licenses the steps by which a source string $f_1...f_I$ may be rewritten as a target string $e_1...e_J$. A **parameterization** defines a weight function over every sequence of rule applications.

In a phrase-based model, the ruleset is simply the unweighted phrase table, where each phrase pair $f_i...f_{i'}/e_j...e_{j'}$ states that phrase $f_i...f_{i'}$ in the source can be rewritten as $e_j...e_{j'}$ in the target. The model operates by iteratively applying rewrites to the source sentence until each source word has been consumed by exactly one rule. There are two additional heuristic rules: The distortion limit *dl* constrains distances over which phrases can be reordered, and the translation option limit *tol* constrains the number of target phrases that may be considered for any given source phrase. Together, these rules completely determine the finite set of all possible target sentences for a given source sentence. We call this set of target sentences the **model search space**.

The parameterization of the model includes all information needed to score any particular se-

Proceedings of the Fourth Workshop on Statistical Machine Translation , pages 224–232,
Athens, Greece, 30 March – 31 March 2009. ©2009 Association for Computational Linguistics

quence of rule applications. In our phrase-based model, it typically includes phrase translation probabilities, lexical translation probabilities, language model probabilities, word counts, and coefficients on the linear combination of these. The combination of large rulesets and complex parameterizations typically makes search intractable, requiring the use of **approximate search**. It is important to note that, regardless of the parameterization or search used, the set of all possible output sentences is still a function of *only* the ruleset.

Germann et al. (2004) identify two types of translation system error: **model error** and **search error**.[1] Model error occurs when the optimal path through the search space leads to an incorrect translation. Search error occurs when the approximate search technique causes the decoder to select a translation other than the optimum.

Given the decomposition outlined above, it seems clear that model error depends on parameterization, while search error depends on approximate search. However, there is no error type that clearly depends on the ruleset (Table 1). We therefore identify a new type of error on the ruleset: **induction error**. Induction error occurs when the search space does not contain the correct target sentence at all, and is thus a more fundamental defect than model error. This is difficult to measure, since there could be many correct translations and there is no way to see whether they are all absent from the search space.[2] However, if we assume that a given reference sentence is ground truth, then as a proxy we can simply ask whether or not the model search space contains the reference. This assumption is of course too strong, but over a sufficiently large test set, it should correlate with metrics which depend on the reference, since under most metrics, exactly reproducing the reference results in a perfect score. More loosely, it should correlate with translation accuracy—even if there are many good translations, a model which is systematically unable to produce any reference sentences from a sufficiently large test sample is almost certainly deficient in some way.

3 Does Ruleset Pruning Matter?

The heuristic translation option limit *tol* controls the number of translation rules considered per source span. It plays a major role in keeping the search space manageable. Ignoring reordering, the complexity of the search in a phrase-based model is $O(n^{tol})$, where n is the number of French spans. Therefore tol has a major effect on efficiency. Tight pruning with tol is often assumed without question to be a worthwhile tradeoff. However, we wish to examine this assumption more closely.

ruleset	**induction error**
parameterization	model error
search	search error

Table 1: Translation system components and their associated error types.

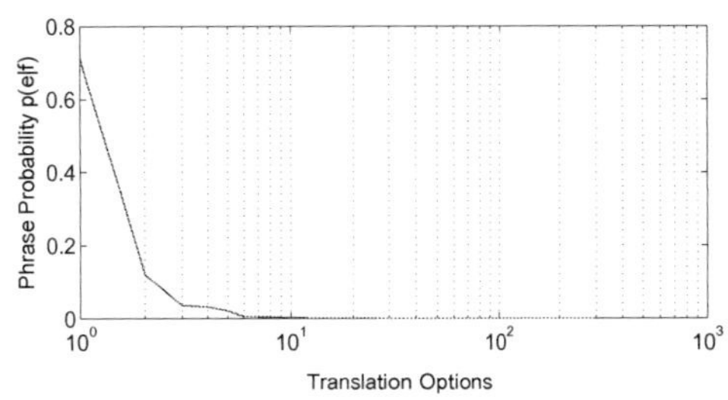

Figure 1: Distribution $p(f|e)$ of the English translation options for the French word *problème*.

Consider the French word *problème*. It has 288 different translation options in the phrase table of our French-English phrase-based system. The phrase translation probability $p(e|f)$ over these options is a familiar Zipf distribution (Figure 1). The most likely candidate translation for the word is *problem* with a probability of 0.71, followed by *issue* with a much smaller probability of 0.12. Further down, we find *challenge* at rank 25, *obstacle* at 44 and *dilemma* at rank 105. Depending on the context, these might be perfectly good translations. However, with a typical *tol* of 20, most of these options are not considered during decoding.

Table 2 shows that 93.8% of rules are available during decoding with the standard *tol* setting and only about 0.1% of French spans of the entire ruleset have more than 20 translation options. It seems as if already most of the information is available when using the default limit. However, a *tol* of 20 can clearly exclude good translations as illustrated by our example. Therefore we hypothesize the following: *Increasing the translation option limit gives the decoder a larger vocabulary which in turn will decrease the induction error.* We sup-

[1] They also identify variants within these types.

[2] It can also be gamed by using a model that can generate any English word from any French word. However, this is not a problem for the real models we investigate here.

tol	Ruleset Size	French Spans
20	93.8	99.9
50	96.8	100.0
100	98.3	100.0
200	99.2	100.0
400	99.7	100.0
800	99.9	100.0
All	100.0	100.0

Table 2: Ruleset size expressed as percentage of available rules when varying the limit of translation options *tol* per English span and percentage of French spans with up to *tol* translations.

port this hypothesis experimentally in §5.4.

4 How Similar are Model Search Spaces?

Most work on hierarchical phrase-based translation focuses quite intently on its structural differences from phrase-based translation.

- A hierarchical model can translate discontiguous groups of words as a unit. A phrase-based model cannot. Lopez (2008b) gives indirect experimental evidence that this difference affects performance.
- A standard phrase-based model can reorder phrases arbitrarily within the distortion limit, while the hierarchical model requires some lexical evidence for movement, resorting to monotone translation otherwise.
- While both models can indirectly model word deletion in the context of phrases, the hierarchical model can delete words using non-local context due to its use of discontiguous phrases.

The underlying assumption in most discussions of these models is that these differences in their generative stories are responsible for differences in performance. We believe that this assumption should be investigated empirically.

In an interesting analysis of phrase-based and hierarchical translation, Zollmann et al. (2008) forced a phrase-based system to produce the translations generated by a hierarchical system. Unfortunately, their analysis is incomplete; they do not perform the analysis in both directions. In §5.5 we extend their work by requiring each system to generate the 1-best output of the other. This allows us to see how their search spaces differ.

5 Experiments

We analyse rulesets in isolation, removing the influence of the parametrization and heuristics as much as possible for each system as follows: First, we disabled beam search to avoid pruning based on parametrization weights. Second, we require our decoders to generate the reference via disallowing reference-incompatible hypothesis or chart entries. This leaves only some search restrictions such as the distortion limit for the phrase-based system for which we controlled, or the maximum number of source words involved in a rule application for the hierarchical system.

5.1 Experimental Systems

Our phrase-based system is Moses (Koehn et al., 2007). We set its stack size to 10^5, disabled the beam threshold, and varied the translation option limit *tol*. Forced translation was implemented by Schwartz (2008) who ensures that hypothesis are a prefix of the reference to be generated.

Our hierarchical system is Hiero (Chiang, 2007), modified to construct rules from a small sample of occurrences of each source phrase in training as described by Lopez (2008b). The search parameters restricting the number of rules or chart entries as well as the minimum threshold were set to very high values (10^{50}) to prevent pruning. Forced translation was implemented by discarding rules and chart entries which do not match the reference.

5.2 Experimental Data

We conducted experiments in French-English translation, attempting to make the experimental conditions for both systems as equal as possible. Each system was trained on French-English Europarl (Koehn, 2005), version 3 (40M words). The corpus was aligned with GIZA++ (Och and Ney, 2003) and symmetrized with the grow-diag-final-and heuristic (Koehn et al., 2003). A trigram language model with modified Kneser-Ney discounting and interpolation was used as produced by the SRILM toolkit (Stolcke, 2002). Systems were optimized on the WMT08 French-English development data (2000 sentences) using minimum error rate training (Och, 2003) and tested on the WMT08 test data (2000 sentences). Rules based on unaligned words at the edges of foreign and source spans were not allowed unless otherwise stated, this is denoted as the *tightness con-*

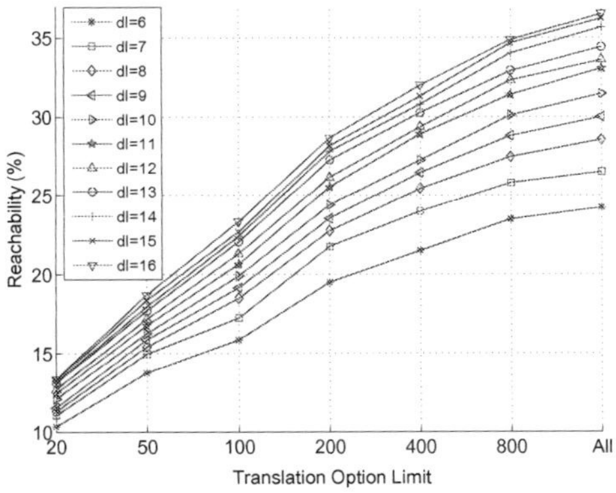

Figure 2: Coverage for phrase-based reference aligned translation on test data when varying the translation option and the distortion limits (dl).

French Spans	Number of Translations
des	3006
les	2464
la	1582
de	1557
en	1428
de la	1332
fait	1308
une	1303
à	1291
le	1273
d'	1271
faire	1263
l'	1111
c' est	1109
à la	1053
,	1035

Table 3: French spans with more than 1000 translation options.

straint. Ayan and Dorr (2006) showed that under certain conditions, this constraint could have significant impact on system performance. The maximum phrase lengths for both the hierarchical and phrase-based system were set to 7. The distortion limit (*dl*) for the phrase-based system was set to 6 unless otherwise mentioned. All other settings were left at their default values as described by Chiang (2007) and Koehn et al. (2007).

5.3 Metric: Reference Reachability

We measure system performance in terms of **reference reachability**, which is the inverse of induction error: A system is required to be able to exactly reproduce the reference, otherwise we regard the result as an error.

5.4 Analysis of Ruleset Pruning

In §3 we outlined the hypothesis that increasing the number of English translation options per French span can increase performance. Here we present results for both phrase-based and hierarchical systems to support this claim.

5.4.1 Quantitative Results

Figure 2 shows the experimental results when forcing our phrase-based system to generate unseen test data. We observe more than 30% increase in reachability from $tol = 20$ to $tol = 50$ for all $dl \geq 6$ which supports our hypothesis that increasing *tol* by a small multiple can have a significant impact on performance. With no limit on *tol*, reachability nearly triples.

Notably, the increase stems from the small fraction of French spans (0.1%) which have more than 20 translation options (Table 2). There are only 16 French spans (Table 3) which have more than 1000 translation options, however, utilising these can still achieve an increase in reachability of up to 5%. The list shown in Table 3 includes common articles, interpuncutation, conjunctions, prepositions but also verbs which have unreliable alignment points and therefore a very long tail of low probability translation options. Yet, the largest increase does not stem from using such unreliable translation options, but rather when increasing *tol* by a relatively small amount.

The increases we see in reachability are proportional to the size of the ruleset: The highest increases in ruleset size can be seen between $tol = 20$ and $tol = 200$ (Table 2), similarly, reachability performance has then the largest increase. For higher *tol* settings both the increases of ruleset size and reachability are smaller.

Figure 3 plots the average number of words per sentence for the reachable sentences. The average sentence length increases by up to six words when using all translation options. The black line represents the average number of words per sentence of the reference set. This shows that longer and more complex sentences can be generated when using more translation options.

Similarly, for our hierarchical system (see Fig-

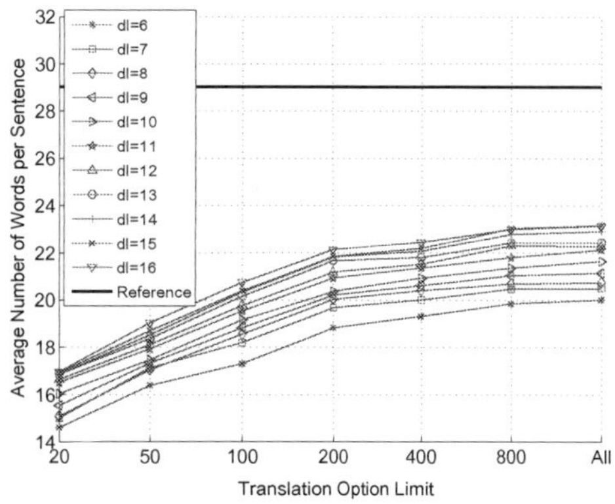

Figure 3: Average number of words per sentence for the reachable test data translations of the phrase-based system (as shown in Figure 2).

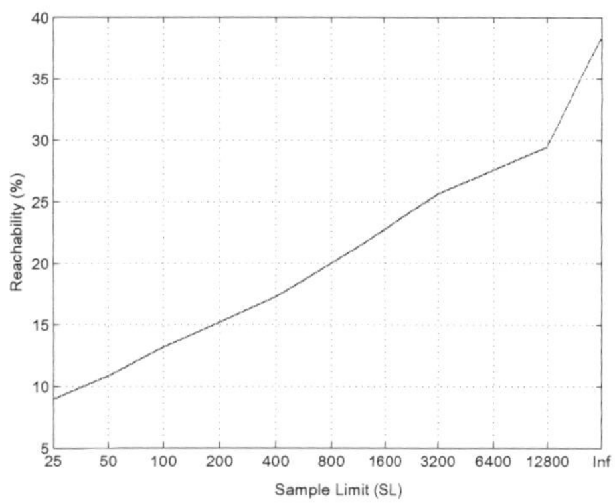

Figure 4: Coverage for hierarchical reference aligned translation on test data when varying the number of matching French samples (sl) drawn from the training data. The baseline setting is $sl = 300$.

ure 4) we find that reachability can be more than doubled when drawing a richer ruleset sample than in the baseline setting. Those results are not directly comparable to the phrase-based system due to the slightly different nature of the parameters which were varied: In the phrase-based case we have tol different English spans per French span. In the hierarchical system it is very likely to have duplicate French spans in the sample drawn from training data. Yet, the trend is the same and thus supports our claim.

5.4.2 Qualitative Results

We were interested how the performance increase could be achieved and therefore looked into which kind of translation options were involved when a translation was generable with a higher tol setting. One possibility is that the long tail of translation options includes all kinds of English spans that match some part of the reference but are simply an artifact of unreliable alignment points.

We looked at the first twenty translations produced by our phrase-based system under $dl = 10$ which could not be generated with $tol = 20$ but with $tol = 50$. The aim was to find out which translation options made it possible to reach the reference under $tol = 50$.

We found that nearly half (9) involved translation options which used a common or less common translation of the foreign span. The first four translations in Table 4 are examples for that. When allowing unaligned words at the rule edges it turns out that even 13 out of 20 translations are based on sound translation options.

The remaining sentences involved translation options which were an artifact of unreliable alignment points. An example rule is *la / their*, which erroneously translates a common determiner into an equally common adjective. The last translation in Figure 4 involves such a translation option.

This analysis demonstrates that the performance increase between $tol = 20$ to $tol = 50$ is to a considerable extent based on translation options which are meaningful.

5.5 Analysis of Mutual Reachability

The aim of this analysis was to find out by how much the high-probability search spaces of the phrase-based and hierarchical models differ. The necessary data was obtained via forcing each system to produce the 1-best translation of the other system denoted as the *unconstrained translation*. This unconstrained translation used the standard setting for the number of translation options.

We controlled for the way unaligned words were handled during rule extraction: The phrase-based system allowed unaligned words at the edges of phrases while the hierarchical system did not. We varied this condition for the phrase-based system. The distortion limit of the phrase-based system was set to 10. This is equal to the maximum span a rule can be applied within the hierarchical system.

We carried out the same experiment for German-English and English-German translation which serve as examples for translating into a mor-

S:	je voterai en **faveur** du projet de règlement .
R:	i will vote to **approve** the draft regulation .
O:	i shall be voting in favour of the draft regulation .
S:	... il npeut y avoir de délai transitoire **en matière de** respect des règles démocratiques .
R:	... there can be no transitional period **for** complying with democratic rules .
O:	... there can be no transitional period in the field of democratic rules .
S:	je souhaite aux négociateurs la **poursuite du** succès de leur travail dans ce domaine important .
R:	i wish the negotiators **continued** success with their work in this important area .
O:	i wish the negotiators the continuation of the success of their work on this important area .
S:	mais commencons par les **points positifs** .
R:	but let us begin with the **good news** .
O:	but let us begin with the positive points .
S:	... partage la plupart des conclusions que tire **le rapporteur** .
R:	... share the majority of conclusions that **he** draws .
O:	... share most of the conclusions that is the rapporteur .

Table 4: Example translations which could be generated with $tol = 50$ but not with $tol = 20$. For each translation the source (S), reference (R) and the unconstrained output (O) are shown. Bold phrases mark translation options which were not available under $tol = 20$.

phologically simpler and more complex language respectively. The test and training sets for these languages are similarly sized and are from the WMT08 shared task.

5.5.1 Quantitative Results

Table 5 shows the mutual reachability performance for our phrase-based and hierarchical system. The hierarchical system can generate almost all of the 1-best phrase-based translations, particularly when unaligned words at rule edges are disallowed which is the most equal condition we experimented with. The phrase-based reachability for English-German using tight rulesets is remarkably low. We found that this is because the hierarchical model allows unaligned words around gaps under the tight constraint. This makes it very hard for the phrase-based system to reach the hierarchical translation. However, the phrase-based system can overcome this problem when the tightness constraint is loosened (last row in Table 5).

Table 6 shows the translation performance measured in BLEU for both systems for normal unconstrained translation. It can be seen that the difference is rather marginal which is in line with our reachability results.

We were interested why certain translations of one system were not reachable by the other system. The following two subsections describe our analysis of these translations for the French-English language pair.

Translation Direction	fr-en	de-en	en-de
$H_t \rightarrow P_t$	99.40	97.65	98.50
$H_t \rightarrow P_{nt}$	95.95	93.95	94.30
$P_t \rightarrow H_t$	93.75	92.30	82.95
$P_{nt} \rightarrow H_t$	97.55	97.55	96.30

Table 5: Mutual reachability performance for French-English (fr-en), German-English (de-en) and Enlgish-German (en-de). P $\rightarrow$ H denotes how many hierarchical (H) high scoring outputs can be reached by the phrase-based (P) system. The subscripts nt (non-tight) and t (tight) denote the use of rules with unaligned words or not.

5.5.2 Qualitative Analysis of Unreachable Hierarchical Translations

We analysed the first twenty translations within the set of unreachable hierarchical translations when disallowing unaligned words at rule edges to find out why the phrase-based system fails to reach them. Two aspects were considered in this analysis: First, the successful hierarchical derivation and second, the relevant part of the phrase-based ruleset which was involved in the failed forced translation i.e. how much of the input and the reference could be covered by the raw phrase-pairs available to the phrase-based system.

Within the examined subset, the majority of sentences (14) involved hierarchical rules which could not be replicated by the phrase-based sys-

System	fr-en	de-en	en-de
Phrase-based	31.96	26.94	19.96
Hierarchical	31.62	27.18	20.20
Difference absolute	0.34	0.24	0.24
Difference (%)	1.06	0.90	1.20

Table 6: Performance for phrase-based and hierarchical systems in BLEU for French-English (fr-en), German-English (de-en) and English-German (en-de).

tem. We described this as the first structural difference in §4. Almost all of these translations (12 out of 14) could not be generated because of the third structural difference which involved rule that omits the translation of a word within the French span. An example is the rule $X \rightarrow estX_{\boxed{1}}ordinaireX_{\boxed{2}}/isX_{\boxed{1}}X_{\boxed{2}}$ which omits a translation for the French word *ordinaire* in the English span. For this particular subset the capability of the hierarchical system to capture long-distance reorderings did not make the difference, but rather the ability to drop words within a translation rule.

The phrase-based system cannot learn many rules which omit the translation of words because we disallowed unaligned words at phrase edges. The hierarchical system has the same restriction, but the constraint does not prohibit rules which have unaligned words *within* the rule. This allows the hierarchical system to learn rules such as the one presented above. The phrase-based system can learn similar knowledge, although less general, if it is allowed to have unaligned words at the phrase edges. In fact, without this constraint 13 out of the 20 analysed rules can be generated by the phrase-based system.

Figure 5 shows a seemingly simple hierarchical translation which fails to be constructed by the phrase-based system: The second rule application involves both the reordering of the translation of *postaux* and the omittance of a translation for *concurrence*. This translation could be easily captured by a phrase-pair, however, it requires that the training data contains exactly such an example which was not the case. The closest rule the phrase-based rulestore contains is *des services postaux / postal services* which fails since it does not cover all of the input. This is an example for when the generalisation of the hierarchical model is superior to the phrase-based approach.

5.5.3 Qualitative Analysis of Unreachable Phrase-based Translations

The size of the set of unreachable phrase-based translations is only 0.6% or 12 sentences. This means that almost all of the 1-best outputs of the phrase-based translations can be reached by the hierarchical system. Similarly to above, we analysed which words of the input as well as which words of the phrase-based translation can be covered by the available hierarchical translation rules.

We found that all of the translations were not generable because of the second structural difference we identified in §4. The hierarchical ruleset did not contain a rule with the necessary lexical evidence to perform the same *reordering* as the phrase-based model. Figure 6 shows a phrase-based translation which could not be reached by the hierarchical system because a rule of the form $X \rightarrow électoralesX_{\boxed{1}}/X_{\boxed{1}}electoral$ would be required to move the translation of *électorales* (electoral) just before the translation of *réunions* (meetings). Inspection of the hierarchical ruleset reveals that such a rule is not available and so the translation cannot be generated.

The small size of the set of unreachable phrase-based translations shows that the lexically informed reordering mechanism of the hierarchical model is not a large obstacle in generating most of the phrase-based outputs.

In summary, each system can reproduce nearly all of the highest-scoring outputs of the other system. This shows that the 1-best regions of both systems are nearly identical despite the differences discussed in §4. This means that differences in observed system performance are probably attributable to the degree of model error and search error in each system.

6 Related Work and Open Questions

Zhang et al. (2008) and Wellington et al. (2006) answer the question: what is the minimal grammar that can be induced to completely describe a training set? We look at the related question of what a heuristically induced ruleset can translate in an unseen test set, considering both phrase- and grammar-based models. We also extend the work of Zollmann et al. (2008) on Chinese-English, performing the analysis in both directions and providing a detailed qualitative explanation.

Our focus has been on the induction error of models, a previously unstudied cause of transla-

```
Source:        concurrence des services postaux
Reference:     competition between postal services
Hierarchical:  postal services
Deviation:
( [0-4: @S  ->  @X^1  |  @X^1 ]
     ( [0-4: @X  ->  concurrence @X^1 postaux  |  postal @X^1 ]        postal
          ( [1-3: @X  ->  des services  |  services ]       services
          )
     )
)
```

Figure 5: Derivation of a hierarchical translation which cannot be generated by the phrase-based system, in the format of Zollmann et al. (2008). The parse tree contains the outputs (shaded) at its leaves in infix order and each non-leaf node denotes a rule, in the form: [Source-span: LHS →RHS].

```
Source:        ceux qui me disaient cela faisaient par exemple rèfèrence à certaines des
               réunions électorales auxquelles ils avaient assisté .
Phrase-based:  those who said to me that were for example refer to some of  which
               they had been electoral meetings .
Reference:     they referred to some of the election meetings , for example , that
               they had gone to .
```

Figure 6: Phrase-based translation which cannot be reached by the hierarchical system because no rule to perform the necessary reordering is available. Marked sections are source and reference spans involved in the largest possible partial hierarchical derivation.

tion errors. Although the results described here are striking, our exact match criterion for reachability is surely too strict—for example, we report an error if even a single comma is missing. One solution is to use a more tolerant criterion such as WER and measure the amount of deviation from the reference. We could also maximize BLEU with respect to the reference as in Dreyer et al. (2007), but it is less interpretable.

7 Conclusion and Future Work

Sparse distributions are common in natural language processing, and machine translation is no exception. We showed that utilizing more of the entire distribution can dramatically improve the coverage of translation models, and possibly their accuracy. Accounting for sparsity explicitly has achieved significant improvements in other areas such as in part of speech tagging (Goldwater and Griffiths, 2007). Considering the entire tail is challenging, since the search space grows exponentially with the number of translation options. A first step might be to use features that facilitate more variety in the top 20 translation options. A more elaborate aim is to look into alternatives to maximum likelihood hood estimation such as in Blunsom and Osborne (2008).

Additionally, our expressiveness analysis shows clearly that the 1-best region of hierarchical and phrase-based models is nearly identical. Discounting cases in which systems handle unaligned words differently, we observe an overlap of between 96% and 99% across three language pairs. This implies that the main difference between the models is in their parameterization, rather than in the structural differences in the types of translations they can produce. Our results also suggest that the search spaces of both models are highly overlapping: The results for the 1-best region allow the conjecture that also other parts of the search space are behaving similarly since it appears rather unlikely that spaces are nearly disjoint with only the 1-best region being nearly identical. In future work we aim to use n-best lists or lattices to more precisely measure search space overlap. We also aim to analyse the effects of the model and search errors for these systems.

Acknowledgements

This research was supported by the Euromatrix Project funded by the European Commission (6th Framework Programme). The experiments were conducted using the resources provided by the Edinburgh Compute and Data Facility (ECDF). Many thanks to the three anonymous reviewers for very helpful comments on earlier drafts.

References

N. F. Ayan and B. Dorr. 2006. Going beyond AER: An extensive analysis of word alignments and their impact on MT. In *Proc. of ACL-COLING*, pages 9–16, Jul.

P. Blunsom and M. Osborne. 2008. Probabilistic inference for machine translation. In *Proc. of EMNLP*.

D. Chiang. 2007. Hierarchical phrase-based translation. *Computational Linguistics*, 33(2):201–228.

M. Dreyer, K. B. Hall, and S. P. Khudanpur. 2007. Comparing reordering constraints for SMT using efficient BLEU oracle computation. In *Proc. of Workshop on Syntax and Structure in Statistical Translation*, pages 103–110, Apr.

U. Germann, M. Jahr, K. Knight, D. Marcu, and K. Yamada. 2004. Fast and optimal decoding for machine translation. *Artificial Intelligence*, 154(1–2):127–143, Apr.

S. Goldwater and T. Griffiths. 2007. A fully Bayesian approach to unsupervised part-of-speech tagging. In *Proc. of ACL*, pages 744–751, Prague, Czech Republic, June.

P. Koehn, F. J. Och, and D. Marcu. 2003. Statistical phrase-based translation. In *Proc. of HLT-NAACL*, pages 48–54, Morristown, NJ, USA.

P. Koehn, H. Hoang, A. B. Mayne, C. Callison-Burch, M. Federico, N. Bertoldi, B. Cowan, W. Shen, C. Moran, R. Zens, C. Dyer, O. Bojar, A. Constantin, and E. Herbst. 2007. Moses: Open source toolkit for statistical machine translation. In *Proc. of ACL Demonstration Session*, pages 177–180, Jun.

P. Koehn. 2005. Europarl: A parallel corpus for statistical machine translation. In *MT Summit*.

A. Lopez. 2008a. Statistical machine translation. *ACM Computing Surveys*, 40(3).

A. Lopez. 2008b. Tera-scale translation models via pattern matching. In *Proc. of COLING*, pages 505–512, Aug.

A. Lopez. 2009. Translation as weighted deduction. In *Proc. of EACL*.

F. J. Och and H. Ney. 2003. A systematic comparison of various statistical alignment models. *Computational Linguistics*, 29(1):19–51.

F. J. Och. 2003. Minimum error rate training in statistical machine translation. In *Proc. of ACL*, pages 160–167, Morristown, NJ, USA.

K. Papineni, S. Roukos, T. Ward, and W. jing Zhu. 2002. BLEU: A method for automatic evaluation of machine translation. In *Proc. of ACL*, pages 311–318.

L. Schwartz. 2008. Multi-source translation methods. In *Proc. of AMTA*, October.

A. Stolcke. 2002. SRILM – an extensible language modeling toolkit. In *Proc. Int. Conf. Spoken Language Processing (ICSLP 2002)*.

B. Wellington, S. Waxmonsky, and I. D. Melamed. 2006. Empirical lower bounds on the complexity of translational equivalence. In *Proc. of ACL*, pages 977–984, Morristown, NJ, USA.

H. Zhang, D. Gildea, and D. Chiang. 2008. Extracting synchronous grammar rules from word-level alignments in linear time. In *Proc. of COLING*, pages 1081–1088, Manchester, UK.

A. Zollmann, A. Venugopal, F. Och, and J. Ponte. 2008. A systematic comparison of phrase-based, hierarchical and syntax-augmented statistical MT. In *Proc. of COLING*.

A Deep Learning Approach to Machine Transliteration

Thomas Deselaers and **Saša Hasan** and **Oliver Bender** and **Hermann Ney**
Human Language Technology and Pattern Recognition Group – RWTH Aachen University
`<surname>@cs.rwth-aachen.de`

Abstract

In this paper we present a novel transliteration technique which is based on deep belief networks. Common approaches use finite state machines or other methods similar to conventional machine translation. Instead of using conventional NLP techniques, the approach presented here builds on deep belief networks, a technique which was shown to work well for other machine learning problems. We show that deep belief networks have certain properties which are very interesting for transliteration and possibly also for translation and that a combination with conventional techniques leads to an improvement over both components on an Arabic-English transliteration task.

1 Introduction

Transliteration, i.e. the transcription of words such as proper nouns from one language into another or, more commonly from one alphabet into another, is an important subtask of machine translation (MT) in order to obtain high quality output.

We present a new technique for transliteration which is based on deep belief networks (DBNs), a well studied approach in machine learning. Transliteration can in principle be considered to be a small-scale translation problem and, thus, some ideas presented here can be transferred to the machine translation domain as well.

Transliteration has been in use in machine translation systems, e.g. Russian-English, since the existence of the field of machine translation. However, to our knowledge it was first studied as a machine learning problem by Knight and Graehl (1998) using probabilistic finite-state transducers. Subsequently, the performance of this system was greatly improved by combining different spelling and phonetic models (Al-Onaizan and Knight, 2002). Huang et al. (2004) construct a probabilistic Chinese-English edit model as part of a larger alignment solution using a heuristic bootstrapped procedure. Freitag and Khadivi (2007) propose a technique which combines conventional MT methods with a single layer perceptron.

In contrast to these methods which strongly build on top of well-established natural language processing (NLP) techniques, we propose an alternative model. Our new model is based on deep belief networks which have been shown to work well in other machine learning and pattern recognition areas (cf. Section 2). Since translation and transliteration are closely related and transliteration can be considered a translation problem on the character level, we discuss various methods from both domains which are related to the proposed approach in the following.

Neural networks have been used in NLP in the past, e.g. for machine translation (Asunción Castaño et al., 1997) and constituent parsing (Titov and Henderson, 2007). However, it might not be straight-forward to obtain good results using neural networks in this domain. In general, when training a neural network, one has to choose the structure of the neural network which involves certain trade-offs. If a small network with no hidden layer is chosen, it can be efficiently trained but has very limited representational power, and may be unable to learn the relationships between the source and the target language. The DBN approach alleviates some of the problems that commonly occur when working with neural networks: 1. they allow for efficient training due to a good initialisation of the individual layers. 2. Overfitting problems are addressed by creating generative models which are later refined discriminatively. 3. The network structure is clearly defined and only a few structure parameters have to be set. 4. DBNs can be interpreted as Bayesian probabilistic generative models.

Recently, Collobert and Weston (2008) proposed a technique which applies a convolutional DBN to a multi-task learning NLP problem. Their approach is able to address POS tagging, chunking, named entity tagging, semantic role and similar word identification in one model. Our model is similar to this approach in that it uses the same machine learning techniques but the encoding and the

Proceedings of the Fourth Workshop on Statistical Machine Translation, pages 233–241,
Athens, Greece, 30 March – 31 March 2009. ©2009 Association for Computational Linguistics

processing is done differently. First, we learn two independent generative models, one for the source input and one for the target output. Then, these two models are combined into a source-to-target encoding/decoding system (cf. Section 2).

Regarding that the target is generated and not searched in a space of hypotheses (e.g. in a word graph), our approach is similar to the approach presented by Bangalore et al. (2007) who present an MT system where the set of words of the target sentence is generated based on the full source sentence and then a finite-state approach is used to reorder the words. Opposed to this approach we do not only generate the letters/words in the target sentence but we generate the full sentence with ordering.

We evaluate the proposed methods on an Arabic-English transliteration task where Arabic city names have to be transcribed into the equivalent English spelling.

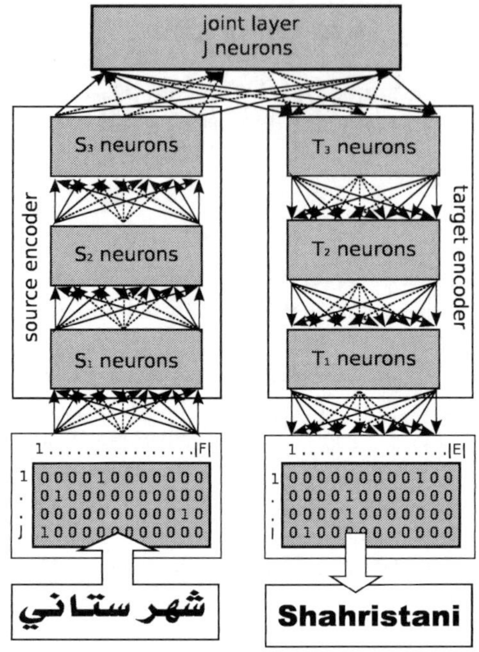

Figure 1: A schematic representation of our DBN for transliteration.

2 Deep Belief Networks for Transliteration

Although DBNs are thoroughly described in the literature, e.g. (Hinton et al., 2006), we give a short overview on the ideas and techniques and introduce our notation.

Deep architectures in machine learning and artificial intelligence are becoming more and more popular after an efficient training algorithm has been proposed (Hinton et al., 2006), although the idea is known for some years (Ackley et al., 1985). Deep belief networks consist of multiple layers of restricted Boltzmann machines (RBMs). It was shown that DBNs can be used for dimensionality reduction of images and text documents (Hinton and Salakhutdinow, 2006) and for language modelling (Mnih and Hinton, 2007). Recently, DBNs were also used successfully in image retrieval to create very compact but meaningful representations of a huge set of images (nearly 13 million) for retrieval (Torralba et al., 2008).

DBNs are built from RBMs by first training an RBM on the input data. A second RBM is built on the output of the first one and so on until a sufficiently deep architecture is created. RBMs are stochastic generative artificial neural networks with restricted connectivity. From a theoretical viewpoint, RBMs are interesting because they are able to discover complex regularities and find notable features in data (Ackley et al., 1985).

Hinton and Salakhutdinow (2006) present a deep belief network to learn a tiny representation of its inputs and to reconstruct the input with high accuracy which is demonstrated for images and textual documents. Here, we use DBNs similarly: first, we learn encoders for the source and target words respectively and then connect these two through a joint layer to map between the two languages. This joint layer is trained in the same way as the top-level neurons in the deep belief classifier from (Hinton et al., 2006).

In Figure 1, a schematic view of our DBN for transliteration is shown. On the left and on the right are encoders for the source and target words respectively. To transliterate a source word, it is passed through the layers of the network. First, it traverses through the source encoder on the left, then it passes into the joint layer, finally traversing down through the target encoder. Each layer consists of a set of neurons receiving the output of the preceding layer as input. The first layers in the source and target encoders consist of S_1 and T_1 neurons, respectively; the second layers have S_2 and T_2 nodes, and the third layers have S_3 and T_3 nodes, respectively. A joint layer with J nodes connects the source and the target encoders.

Here, the number of nodes in the individual layers are the most important parameters. The more nodes a layer has, the more information can be conveyed through it, but the harder the training: the amount of data needed for training and thus the computation time required is exponential in the size of the network (Ackley et al., 1985).

To transliterate a source word, it is first encoded as a D_F-dimensional binary vector S_F (cf. Section 2.1) and then fed into the first layer of the source encoder. The S_1-dimensional output vector O_{S1} of the first layer is computed as

$$O_{S1} \leftarrow 1/\exp\left(1 + w_{S1}S_F + b_{S1}\right), \quad (1)$$

where w_{S1} is a $S_1 \times D_F$-dimensional weight matrix and b_{S1} is an S_1-dimensional bias vector.

The output of each layer is used as input to the next layer as follows:

$$O_{S2} \leftarrow 1/\exp\left(1 + w_{S2}O_{S1} + b_{S2}\right), \quad (2)$$
$$O_{S3} \leftarrow 1/\exp\left(1 + w_{S3}O_{S2} + b_{S3}\right). \quad (3)$$

After the source encoder has been traversed, the joint layer is reached which processes the data twice: once using the input from the source encoder to get a state of the hidden neurons O_{SJ} and then to infer an output state O_{JT} as input to the topmost level of the output encoder

$$O_{SJ} \leftarrow 1/\exp\left(1 + w_{SJ}O_{S3} + b_{SJ}\right), \quad (4)$$
$$O_{JT} \leftarrow 1/\exp\left(1 + w_{JT}O_{SJ} + b_{JT}\right). \quad (5)$$

This output vector is decoded by traversing downwards through the output encoder:

$$O_{T3} \leftarrow 1/\exp\left(1 + w_{T3}O_{JT} + b_{T3}\right), \quad (6)$$
$$O_{T2} \leftarrow 1/\exp\left(1 + w_{T2}O_{T3} + b_{T2}\right), \quad (7)$$
$$O_{T1} \leftarrow w_{T1}O_{T2} + b_{T1}, \quad (8)$$

where O_{T1} is a vector encoding a word in the target language.

Note that this model is intrinsically bidirectional since the individual RBMs are bidirectional models and thus it is possible to transliterate from source to target and vice versa.

2.1 Source and Target Encoding

A problem with DBNs and transliteration is the data representation. The input and output data are commonly sequences of varying length but a DBN expects input data of constant length. To represent a source or target language word, it is converted into a sparse binary vector of dimensionality $D_F = |F| \cdot J$ or $D_E = |E| \cdot I$, respectively, where $|F|$ and $|E|$ are the sizes of the alphabets and I and J are the lengths of the longest words. If a word is shorter than this, a *padding letter* w_0 is used to fill the spaces. This encoding is depicted in the bottom part of Figure 1.

Since the output vector of the DBN is not binary, we infer the maximum a posterior hypothesis by selecting the letter with the highest output value for each position.

2.2 Training Method

For the training, we follow the method proposed in (Hinton et al., 2006). To find a good starting point for backpropagation on the whole network, each of the RBMs is trained individually. First, we learn the generative encoders for the source and target words, i.e. the weights w_{S1} and w_{T1}, respectively. Therefore, each of the layers is trained as a restricted Boltzmann machine, such that it learns to generate the input vectors with high probability, i.e. the weights are learned such that the data values have low values of the trained cost function.

After learning a layer, the activity vectors of the hidden units, as obtained from the real training data, are used as input data for the next layer. This can be repeated to learn as many hidden layers as desired. After learning multiple hidden layers in this way, the whole network can be viewed as a single, multi-layer generative model and each additional hidden layer improves a lower bound on the probability that the multi-layer model would generate the training data (Hinton et al., 2006).

For each language, the output of the first layer is used as input to learn the weights of the next layers w_{S2} and w_{T2}. The same procedure is repeated to learn w_{S3} and w_{T3}. Note that so far no connection between the individual letters in the two alphabets is created but each encoder only learns feature functions to represent the space of possible source and target words. Then, the weights for the joined layer are learned using concatenated outputs of the top layers of the source and target encoders to find an initial set of weights w_{SJ} and w_{JT}.

After each of the layers has been trained individually, backpropagation is performed on the whole network to tune the weights and to learn the connections between both languages. We use the average squared error over the output vectors between reference and inferred words as the training criterion. For the training, we split the training data into batches of 100 randomly selected words and allow for 10 training iterations of the individual layers and up to 200 training iterations for the backpropagation. Currently, we only optimise the parameters for the source to target direction and thus do not retain the bidirectionality[1].

Thus, the whole training procedure consists of 4 phases. First, an autoencoder for the source words is learnt. Second, an autoencoder for the target words is learnt. Third, these autoencoders are connected by a top connecting layer, and finally backpropagation is performed over the whole network for fine-tuning of the weights.

2.3 Creation of *n*-Best Lists

N-best lists are a common means for combination of several systems in natural language processing and for rescoring. In this section, we describe how a set of hypotheses can be created for a given input. Although these hypotheses are not n-best lists because they have not been obtained from a search process, they can be used similarly and can better be compared to randomly sampled '*good*' hypotheses from a full word-graph.

Since the values of the nodes in the individual layers are probabilities for this particular node to be activated, it is possible to sample a set of states from the distribution for the individual layers, which is called Gibbs sampling (Geman and Geman, 1984). This sampling can be used to create several hypotheses for a given input sentence, and this set of hypotheses can be used similar to an n-best list.

The layer in which the Gibbs sampling is done can in principle be chosen arbitrarily. However, we believe it is natural to sample in either the first layer, the joint layer, or the last layer. Sampling in the first layer leads to different features traversing the full network. Sampling in the joint layer only affects the generation of the target sentence, and sampling in the last layer is equal to directly sampling from the distribution of target hypotheses.

Conventional Gibbs sampling has a very strong impact on the outcome of the network because the smoothness of the distributions and the encoding of similar matches is entirely lost. Therefore, we use a weak variant of Gibbs sampling. Instead of replacing the states' probabilities with fully discretely sampled states, we keep the probabilities and add a fraction of a sampled state, effectively modifying the probabilities to give a slightly better score to the last sampled state. Let p be the D-dimensional vector of probabilities for D nodes in an RBM to be *on*. Normal Gibbs sampling would sample a D-dimensional vector S containing a state for each node from this distribution. Instead of replacing the vector p with S, we use $p' \leftarrow p + \varepsilon S$, leading to smoother changes than conventional Gibbs sampling. This process can easily be repeated to obtain multiple hypotheses.

[1]Note that it is easily possible to extend the backpropagation to include both directions, but to keep the computational demands lower we decided to start with only one direction.

3 Experimental Evaluation

In this section we present experimental results for an Arabic-English transliteration task. For evaluation we use the character error rate (CER) which is the commonly used word error rate (WER) on character level.

We use a corpus of 10,084 personal names in Arabic and their transliterated English ASCII representation (LDC corpus LDC2005G02). The Arabic names are written in the usual way, i.e. lacking vowels and diacritics. 1,000 names were randomly sampled for development and evaluation, respectively (Freitag and Khadivi, 2007). The vocabulary of the source language is 33 and the target language has 30 different characters (including the padding character). The longest word on both sides consists of 14 characters, thus the feature vector on the source side is 462-dimensional and the feature vector on the target side is 420-dimensional.

3.1 Network Structure

First, we evaluate how the structure of the network should be chosen. For these experiments, we fixed the numbers of layers and the size of the bottom layers in the target and source encoder and evaluate different network structures and the size of the joint layer.

The experiments we performed are described in Table 1. The top part of the table gives the results for different network structures. We compare networks with increasing layer sizes, identical layer sizes, and decreasing layer sizes. It can be seen that decreasing layer sizes leads to the best results. In these experiments, we choose the number of nodes in the joint layer to be three times as large as the topmost encoder layers.

In the bottom part, we kept most of the network structure fixed and only vary the number of nodes

Table 1: Transliteration experiments using different network structures.

number of nodes				CER [%]		
S_1,T_1	S_2,T_2	S_3,T_3	J	train	dev	eval
400	500	600	1800	0.3	27.2	28.1
400	400	400	1200	0.7	26.1	25.2
400	350	300	900	1.8	25.1	24.3
400	350	300	1000	1.7	24.8	24.0
400	**350**	**300**	**1500**	**1.3**	**24.1**	**22.7**
400	350	300	2000	0.2	24.2	23.5

in the joint layer. Here, a small number of nodes leads to suboptimal performance and a very high number of nodes leads to overfitting which can be seen in nearly perfect performance on the training data and an increasing CER on the development and eval data.

3.2 Network Size

Next, we evaluate systems with different numbers of nodes. Therefore, we start from the best parameters (400-350-300-1500) from the previous section and scale the number of nodes in the individual layers by a certain factor, i.e. factor 1.5 leads to (600-525-450-2250).

In Figure 2 and Table 2, the results from the experimental evaluation on the transliteration task are given. The network size denotes the number of nodes in the bottom layers of the source and the target encoder (i.e. S_1 and T_1) and the other layers are chosen according to the results from the experiments presented in the previous section.

The results show that small networks perform badly, the optimal performance is reached with medium sized networks of 400-600 nodes in the bottom layers, and larger networks perform worse, which is probably due to overfitting.

For comparison, we give results for a state-of-the-art phrase-based MT system applied on the character level with default system parameters (labelled as 'PBT untuned'), and the same system, where all scaling factors were tuned on dev data (labelled as 'PBT tuned'). The tuned phrase-based MT system clearly outperforms our approach.

Additionally, we perform an experiment with a standard multi-layer perceptron. Therefore, we choose the network structure with 400-350-300-1500 nodes, initialised these randomly and trained the entire network with backpropagation training.

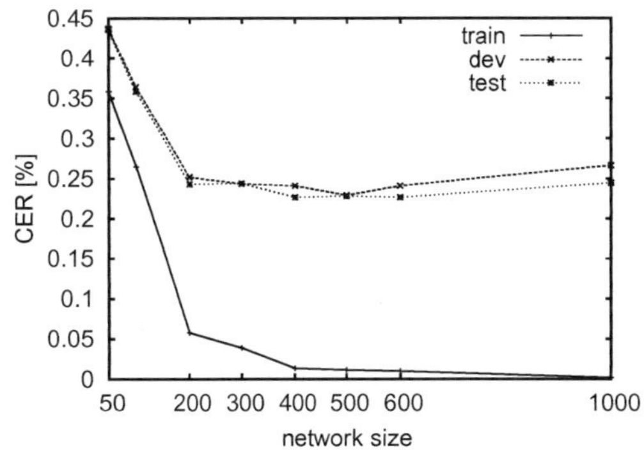

Figure 2: Results for the Arabic-English transliteration task depending on the network size.

The results (line 'MLP-400' in Table 2) of this experiment are far worse than any of the other results, which shows that, apart from the convenient theoretical interpretation, the creation of the DBN as described is a suitable method to train the system. The reason for the large difference is likely the bad initialisation of the network and the fact that the backpropagation algorithm gets stuck in a local optimum at this point.

3.3 Reordering capabilities

Although reordering is not an issue in transliteration, the proposed model has certain properties which we investigated and where interesting properties can be observed.

To investigate the performance under adverse reordering conditions, we also perform an experiment with reversed ordering of the target letters (i.e. a word $w = c_1, c_2, \ldots, c_J$ is now written $c_J, c_{J-1}, \ldots, c_1$). Since the DBN is fully symmetric, i.e. each input node is connected with each output node in the same way and vice versa, the DBN result is not changed except for some minor numerical differences due to random initialisation. Indeed, the DBN obtained is nearly identical except for a changed ordering of the weights in the joint layer, and if desired it is possible to construct a DBN for reverse-order target language from a fully trained DBN by permuting the weights.

On the same setup an experiment with our phrase-based decoder has been performed and here the performance is strongly decreased (bottom line of Table 2). The phrase-based MT system for this experiment used a reordering with IBM block-limit constraints with distortion limits and all default parameters were reasonably tuned. We observed that the position-independent

Table 2: Results for the Arabic-English transliteration task depending on the network size and a comparison with state of the art results using conventional phrase-based machine translation techniques

network size	CER [%] train	dev	eval
50	35.8	43.7	43.6
100	26.4	36.3	35.8
200	5.8	25.2	24.3
300	3.9	24.3	24.4
400	1.3	24.1	22.7
500	1.2	22.9	22.8
600	1.0	24.1	22.6
1000	0.2	26.6	24.4
MLP-400	22.0	64.1	63.2
untuned PBT	4.9	23.3	23.6
tuned PBT	2.2	12.9	13.3
(Freitag and Khadivi, 2007)	n/a	11.1	11.1
reversed task: PBT	13.0	35.2	35.7

error rate of the phrase-based MT system is hardly changed which also underlines that, in principle, the phrase-based MT system is currently better but that under adverse reordering conditions the DBN system has some advantages.

3.4 *N*-Best Lists

As described above, different possibilities to create n-best lists exists. Starting from the system with 400-350-300-1500 nodes, we evaluate the creation of n-best lists in the first source layer, the joint layer, and the last target layer. Therefore, we create n best lists with up to 10 hypotheses (sometimes, we have less due to duplicates after sampling, on the average we have 8.3 hypotheses per sequence), and evaluate the oracle error rate. In Table 3 it can be observed that sampling in the first layer leads to the best oracle error rates. The baseline performance (first best) for this system is 24.1% CER on the development data, and 22.7% CER on the eval data, which can be improved by nearly 10% absolute using the oracle from a 10-best list.

3.5 Rescoring

Using the n-best list sampled in the first source layer, we also perform rescoring experiments. Therefore, we rescore the transliteration hypotheses (after truncating the padding letters w_0) with additional models, which are commonly used in MT, and which we have trained on the training data:

Table 3: Oracle character error rates on 10-best lists.

sampling layer	oracle CER [%] dev	eval
S_1	15.8	14.8
joint layer	17.5	16.4
T_1	18.7	18.2

System		CER [%] dev	eval
DBN	w/o rescoring	24.1	22.7
	w/ rescoring	21.3	20.1

Table 4: Results from the rescoring experiments and fusion with the phrase-based MT system.

- IBM model 1 lexical probabilities modelling the probability for a target sequence given a source sequence

$$h_{\text{IBM1}}(f_1^J, e_1^I) = -\log\left(\frac{1}{(I+1)^J}\prod_{j=1}^{J}\sum_{i=0}^{I} p(f_j|e_i)\right)$$

- m-gram language model over the letter sequences

$$h_{\text{LM}}(e_1^I) = -\log\prod_{i=1}^{I} p(e_i|e_{i-m+1}^{i-1}),$$

  with m being the size of the m-gram, we choose $m = 9$.

- sequence length model (commonly referred to as word penalty).

Then, these models are fused in a log-linear model (Och and Ney, 2002), and we tune the model scaling factors discriminatively on the development n-best list using the downhill simplex algorithm. Results from the rescoring experiments are given in Table 4.

The performance of the DBN system is improved on the dev data from 24.1% to 21.3% CER and on the eval data from 22.7% to 20.1% CER.

3.6 Application Within a System Combination Framework

Although being clearly outperformed by the phrase-based MT system, we applied the transliteration candidates generated by the DBN approach within a system combination framework. Motivated by the fact that the DBN approach differs decisively from the other statistical approaches we applied to the machine transliteration task, we wanted to investigate the potential benefit of the diverse nature of the DBN transliterations. Taking the transliteration candidates obtained from another study which was intended to perform a comparison of various statistical approaches to the transliteration task, we performed the system combination as is customary in speech recognition, i.e. following the Recognizer Output Voting Error Reduction (ROVER) approach (Fiscus, 1997).

The following methods were investigated:

(Monotone) Phrase-based MT on character level: A state-of-the-art phrase-based SMT system (Zens and Ney, 2004) was used for name transliteration, i.e. translation of characters instead of words. No reordering model was employed due to the monotonicity of the transliteration task, and the model scaling factors were tuned on maximum transliteration accuracy.

Data-driven grapheme-to-phoneme conversion: In Grapheme-to-Phoneme conversion (G2P), or phonetic transcription, we seek the most likely pronunciation (phoneme sequence) for a given orthographic form (sequence of letters). Then, a grapheme-phoneme joint multi-gram, or *graphone* for short, is a pair of a letter sequence and a phoneme sequence of possibly different length (Bisani and Ney, 2008). The model training is done in two steps: First, maximum likelihood is used to infer the graphones. Second, the input is segmented into a stream of graphones and absolute discounting with leaving-one-out is applied to estimate the actual M-gram model. Interpreting the characters of the English target names as phonemes, we used the G2P toolkit of (Bisani and Ney, 2008) to transliterate the Arabic names.

Position-wise maximum entropy models / CRFs: The segmentation as provided by the G2P model is used and "null words" are inserted such that the transliteration task can be interpreted as a classical tagging task (e.g. POS, conceptual tagging, etc.). This means that we seek for a one-to-one mapping and define feature functions to model the posterior probability. Maximum entropy (ME) models are defined position-wise, whereas conditional random fields (CRFs) consider full sequences. Both models were trained according to the maximum class posterior criterion. We used an ME tagger (Bender et al., 2003) and the freely available CRF++ toolkit.[2]

Results for each of the individual systems and different combinations are given in Table 5. As expected, the DBN transliterations cannot keep up with the other approaches. The additional models (G2P, CRF and ME) perform slightly better than the PBT method. If we look at combinations of systems without the DBN approach, we observe only marginal improvements of around 0.1-0.2% CER. Interestingly, a combination of all 4 models (PBT, G2P, ME, CRF) works as good as individual 3-way combinations (the same 11.9% on dev are obtained). This can be interpreted as a potential "similarity" of the approaches. Adding e.g. ME to a combination of PBT, G2P and CRF does not improve results because the transliteration hypotheses are too similar. If we simply put together all 5 systems including DBN with equal weights, we have a similar trend. Since all systems are equally weighted and at least 3 of the systems are similar in individual performance (G2P, ME, CRF have all around 12% CER on the tested data sets), the DBN approach does not get a large impact on overall performance.

If we drop similar systems and tune for 3-way combinations, we observe a large reduction in CER if DBN comes into play. Compared to the best individual system of 12% CER, we now arrive at a CER of 10.9% for a combination of PBT, CRF and DBN which is significantly better than each of the individual methods. Our interpretation of this is that the DBN system has different hypotheses compared to all other systems and that the hypotheses from the other systems are too similar to be apt for combination. So, although DBN is much worse than the other approaches, it obviously helps in the system combination. Using the rescored variant of the DBN transliterations from

[2] `http://crfpp.sourceforge.net/`

System	CER [%] dev	eval
DBN	24.1	22.7
PBT	12.9	13.3
G2P	12.2	12.1
ME	12.3	12.4
CRF	12.0	12.0
ROVER		
best setting w/o DBN	11.9	11.8
5-way equal weights	11.7	11.9
best setting w/ DBN	**10.9**	**10.9**

Table 5: Results from the individual methods investigated versus ROVER combination.

Section 3.5, performance is similar to the one obtained for the DBN baseline.

4 Discussion and Conclusion

We have presented a novel method for machine transliteration based on DBNs, which despite not having competitive results can be an important additional cue for system combination setups. The DBN model has some immediate advantages: the model is in principle fully bidirectional and is based on sound and valid theories from machine learning. Instead of common techniques which are based on finite-state machines or phrase-based machine translation, the proposed system does not rely on word alignments and beam-search decoding and has interesting properties regarding the reordering of sequences. We have experimentally evaluated the network structure and size, reordering capabilities, the creation of multiple hypotheses, and rescoring and combination with other transliteration approaches. It was shown that, albeit the approach cannot compete with the current state of the art, deep belief networks might be a learning framework with some potential for transliteration. It was also shown that the proposed method is suited for combination with different state-of-the-art systems and that improvements over the single models can be obtained in a ROVER-like setting. Furthermore, adding DBN-based transliterations, although individually far behind the other approaches, significantly improves the overall results by 1% absolute.

Outlook

In the future we plan to investigate several details of the proposed model: we will exploit the inherent bidirectionality, further investigate the structure of the model, such as the number of layers and the numbers of nodes in the individual layers. Also, it is important to improve the efficiency of our implementation to allow for working on larger datasets and obtain more competitive results. Furthermore, we are planning to investigate convolutional input layers for transliteration and use a translation approach analogous to the one proposed by Collobert and Weston (2008) in order to allow for the incorporation of reorderings, language models, and to be able to work on larger tasks.

Acknowledgement. We would like to thank Geoffrey Hinton for providing the Matlab Code accompanying (Hinton and Salakhutdinow, 2006).

References

D. Ackley, G. Hinton, and T. Sejnowski. 1985. A learning algorithm for Boltzmann machines. *Cognitive Science*, 9(1):147–169.

Y. Al-Onaizan and K. Knight. 2002. Machine transliteration of names in Arabic text. In *ACL 2002 Workshop on Computationaal Approaches to Semitic Languages*.

M. Asunción Castaño, F. Casacuberta, and E. Vidal. 1997. Machine translation using neural networks and finite-state models. In *Theoretical and Methodological Issues in Machine Translation (TMI)*, pages 160–167, Santa Fe, NM, USA, July.

S. Bangalore, P. Haffner, and S. Kanthak. 2007. Statistical machine translation through global lexical selection and sentence reconstruction. In *Annual Meeting of the Association for Computational Lingustic (ACL)*, pages 152–159, Prague, Czech Republic.

O. Bender, F. J. Och, and H. Ney. 2003. Maximum entropy models for named entity recognition. In *Proc. 7th Conf. on Computational Natural Language Learning (CoNLL)*, pages 148–151, Edmonton, Canada, May.

M. Bisani and H. Ney. 2008. Joint-sequence models for grapheme-to-phoneme conversion. *Speech Communication*, 50(5):434–451, May.

R. Collobert and J. Weston. 2008. A unified architecture for natural language processing: Deep neural networks with multitask learning. In *International Conference on Machine Learning*, Helsinki, Finnland, July.

J. Fiscus. 1997. A post-processing system to yield reduced word error rates: Recognizer output voting error reduction (ROVER). In *IEEE Automatic Speech Recognition and Understanding Workshop (ASRU)*, pages 347–354, Santa Barbara, CA, USA, December.

D. Freitag and S. Khadivi. 2007. A sequence alignment model based on the averaged perceptron. In *Conference on Empirical methods in Natural Language Processing*, pages 238–247, Prague, Czech Republic, June.

S. Geman and D. Geman. 1984. Stochastic relaxation, Gibbs distributions, and the Bayesian restoration of images. *IEEE Transaction on Pattern Analysis and Machine Intelligence*, 6(6):721–741, November.

G. Hinton and R. R. Salakhutdinow. 2006. Reducing the dimensionality of data with neural networks. *Science*, 313:504–507, July.

G. Hinton, S. Osindero, and Y.-W. Teh. 2006. A fast learning algorithm for deep belief nets. *Neural Computation*, 18:1527–1554.

F. Huang, S. Vogel, and A. Waibel. 2004. Improving named entity translation combining phonetic and semantic similarities. In *HLT-NAACL*.

K. Knight and J. Graehl. 1998. Machine transliteration. *Computational Linguistics*, 24(2).

A. Mnih and G. Hinton. 2007. Three new graphical models for statistical language modelling. In *ICML '07: International Conference on Machine Learning*, pages 641–648, New York, NY, USA. ACM.

F. Och and H. Ney. 2002. Discriminative training and maximum entropy models for statistical machine translation. In *Annual Meeting of the Assoc. for Computational Linguistics*, pages 295–302, Philadelphia, PA, USA, July.

I. Titov and J. Henderson. 2007. Constituent parsing with incremental sigmoid belief networks. In *Proceedings of the 45th Annual Meeting of the Association of Computational Linguistics*, pages 632–639, Prague, Czech Republic, June.

A. Torralba, R. Fergus, and Y. Weiss. 2008. Small codes and large image databases for recognition. In *IEEE Conference on Computer Vision and Pattern Recognition*, Anchorage, AK, USA, June.

R. Zens and H. Ney. 2004. Improvements in phrase-based statistical machine translation. In *Proceedings of the Human Language Technology Conference of the North American Chapter of the Association for Computational Linguistics: HLT-NAACL 2004*, pages 257–264, Boston, MA, May.

Stabilizing Minimum Error Rate Training

George Foster and **Roland Kuhn**
National Research Council Canada
first.last@nrc.gc.ca

Abstract

The most commonly used method for training feature weights in statistical machine translation (SMT) systems is Och's minimum error rate training (MERT) procedure. A well-known problem with Och's procedure is that it tends to be sensitive to small changes in the system, particularly when the number of features is large. In this paper, we quantify the stability of Och's procedure by supplying different random seeds to a core component of the procedure (Powell's algorithm). We show that for systems with many features, there is extensive variation in outcomes, both on the development data and on the test data. We analyze the causes of this variation and propose modifications to the MERT procedure that improve stability while helping performance on test data.

1 Introduction

Most recent approaches in SMT, eg (Koehn et al., 2003; Chiang, 2005), use a log-linear model to combine probabilistic features. Minimum Error-Rate Training (MERT) aims to find the set of log-linear weights that yields the best translation performance on a development corpus according to some metric such as BLEU. This is an essential step in SMT training that can significantly improve performance on a test corpus compared to setting weights by hand. MERT is a difficult problem, however, because calculating BLEU as a function of log-linear weights requires decoding, which is an expensive operation. Moreover, because this function is not differentiable, efficient gradient-based optimization algorithms cannot be used.

Och's procedure is the most widely-used version of MERT for SMT (Och, 2003). To reduce computational cost, it relies on the key technique of optimizing weights over n-best lists of translation hypotheses rather than over all possible hypotheses. This allows the most probable hypothesis under a given set of weights—and the corresponding BLEU score—to be found by enumerating n-best entries rather than decoding. Some variant on Powell's algorithm (Press et al., 2002) is typically used to maximize BLEU in this setting. The n-best lists are constructed by alternating decoding and BLEU maximization operations: decoding adds new hypotheses to the current lists, then BLEU is maximized over the lists to find new best weights for the subsequent decoding step, etc. This process continues until no new hypotheses are found.

Och's procedure works well in practice, usually converging after 10–20 calls to the decoder, far fewer than would be required to maximize BLEU directly with a general-purpose optimization algorithm. However, it tends to be sensitive to small changes in the system, particularly for large feature sets. This is a well-known problem with Och's procedure (Och et al., 2004). It makes it difficult to assess the contribution of features, because the measured gain in performance due to a new feature can depend heavily on the setting of some apparently unrelated parameter such as the size of n-best list used. Features with the potential for statistically significant gains may be rejected because Och's procedure failed to find good weights for them.

In this paper we attempt to quantify the stability of Och's procedure under different conditions by measuring the variation in test-set scores across different random seeds used with Powell's algorithm. We show that there is extensive variation for large feature sets, and that it is due to two main factors: the occasional failure of Och's procedure to find a good maximum on the development set, and the failure of some maxima to generalize to

Proceedings of the Fourth Workshop on Statistical Machine Translation , pages 242–249,
Athens, Greece, 30 March – 31 March 2009.

the test set. We analyze the causes of each of these problems, and propose solutions for improving the stability of the overall procedure.

2 Previous Work

One possible approach to estimating log-linear weights on features is to dispense with the n-best lists employed by Och's procedure and, instead, to optimize weights by directly accessing the decoder. The disadvantage of this approach is that far more iterations of decoding of the full development set are required. In (Zens and Ney, 2004) the downhill simplex method is used to estimate the weights; around 200 iterations are required for convergence to occur. However, each iteration is unusually fast, because only monotone decoding is permitted (i.e., the order of phrases in the target language mirrors that in the source language). Similarly, Cettolo and Federico (2004) apply the simplex method to optimize weights directly using the decoder. In their experiments on NIST 2003 Chinese-English data, they found about 100 iterations of decoding were required. Although they obtained consistent and stable performance gains for MT, these were inferior to the gains yielded by Och's procedure in (Och, 2003). Taking Och's MERT procedure as a baseline, (Zens et al., 2007) experiment with different training criteria for SMT and obtain the best results for a criterion they call "expected BLEU score".

Moore and Quirk (2008) share the goal underlying our own research: improving, rather than replacing, Och's MERT procedure. They focus on the step in the procedure where the set of feature weights optimizing BLEU (or some other MT metric) for an n-best list is estimated. Typically, several different starting points are tried for this set of weights; often, one of the starting points is the best set of weights found for the previous set of n-best hypotheses. The other starting points are often chosen randomly. In this paper, Moore and Quirk look at the best way of generating the random starting points; they find that starting points generated by a random walk from previous maxima are superior to those generated from a uniform distribution. The criterion used throughout the paper to judge the performance of MERT is the BLEU score on the development test set (rather than, for instance, the variance of that score, or the BLEU score on held-out test data). Another contribution of the paper is ingenious methods for pruning the set of n-best hypotheses at each iteration.

Cer et al (2008) also aim at improving Och's MERT. They focus on the search for the best set of weights for an n-best list that follows choice of a starting point. They propose a modified version of Powell's in which "diagonal" directions are chosen at random. They also modify the objective function used by Powell's to reflect the width of the optima found. They are able to show that their modified version of MERT outperforms both a version using Powell's, and a more heuristic search algorithm devised by Philipp Koehn that they call Koehn Coordinate Descent, as measured on the development set and two test data sets. (Duh and Kirchhoff, 2008) ingeniously uses MERT as a weak learner in a boosting algorithm that is applied to the n-best reranking task, with good results (a gain of about 0.8 BLEU on the test set).

Recently, some interesting work has been done on what might be considered a generalization of Och's procedure (Macherey et al., 2008). In this generalization, candidate hypotheses in each iteration of the procedure are represented as lattices, rather than as n-best lists. This makes it possible for a far greater proportion of the search space to be represented: a graph density of 40 arcs per phrase was used, which corresponds to an n-best size of more than two octillion ($2 * 10^{27}$) entries. Experimental results for three NIST 2008 tasks were very encouraging: though BLEU scores for the lattice variant of Och's procedure did not typically exceed those for the n-best variant on development data, on test data the lattice variant outperformed the n-best approach by between 0.6 and 2.5 BLEU points. The convergence behaviour of the lattice variant was also much smoother than that of the n-best variant. It would be interesting to apply some of the insights of the current paper to the lattice variant of Och's procedure.

3 Och's MERT Procedure

Och's procedure works as follows. First the decoder is run using an initial set of weights to generate n best translations (usually around 100) for each source sentence. These are added to existing n-best lists (initially empty). Next, Powell's algorithm is used to find the weights that maximize BLEU score when used to choose the best hypotheses from the n-best lists. These weights are plugged back into the decoder, and the process repeats, nominally until the n-best lists stop growing, but often in practice until some criterion of convergence such as minimum weight change is attained. The weights that give the best BLEU score when used with the decoder are output.

The point of this procedure is to bypass direct search for the weights that result in maximum BLEU score, which would involve decoding using many different sets of weights in order to find which ones gave the best translations. Och's procedure typically runs the decoder only 10–20 times, which is probably at least one order of magnitude fewer than a direct approach. The main trick is to build up n-best lists that are representative of the search space, in the sense that a given set of weights will give approximately the same BLEU score when used to choose the best hypotheses from the n-best lists as it would when decoding. By iterating, the algorithm avoids weights that give good scores on the n-best lists but bad ones with the decoder, since the bad hypotheses that are scored highly by such weights will get added to the n-best lists, thereby preventing the choice of these weights in future iterations. Unfortunately, there is no corresponding guarantee that weights which give good scores with the decoder but bad ones on the nbest lists will get chosen.

Finding the set of weights that maximizes BLEU score over n-best lists is a relatively easy problem because candidate weight sets can be evaluated in time proportional to n (simply calculate the score of each hypothesis according to the current weight set, then measure BLEU on the highest scoring hypothesis for each source sentence). Powell's algorithm basically loops over each feature in turn, setting its weight to an optimum value before moving on.[1] Och's *linemax* algorithm is used to perform this optimization efficiently and exactly. However this does not guarantee that Powell's algorithm will find a global maximum, and so Powell's is typically run with many different randomly-chosen initial weights in order to try to find a good maximum.

4 Experimental Setup

The experiments described here were carried out with a standard phrase-based SMT system (Koehn et al., 2003) employing a log-linear combination of feature functions. HMM and IBM2 models were used to perform separate word alignments, which were symmetrized by the usual "diag-and" algorithm prior to phrase extraction. Decoding used beam search with the cube pruning algorithm (Huang and Chiang, 2007).

corpus	num sents	num Chinese toks
dev1	1506	38,312
dev2	2080	55,159
nist04	1788	53,446
nist06	1664	41,798

Table 1: Development and test corpora.

We used two separate log-linear models for MERT:

- *large*: 16 phrase-table features, 2 4-gram language model features, 1 distortion feature, and 1 word-count feature (20 features in total).
- *small*: 2 phrase-table features, 1 4-gram language model feature, 1 distortion feature, and 1 word-count feature (5 features in total).

The phrase-table features for the large model were derived as follows. Globally-trained HMM and IBM2 models were each used to extract phrases from UN and non-UN portions of the training corpora (see below). This produced four separate phrase tables, each of which was used to generate both relative-frequency and "lexical" conditional phrase-pair probabilities in both directions (target given source and vice versa). The two language model features in the large log-linear model were trained on the UN and non-UN corpora. Phrase-table features for the small model were derived by taking the union of the four individual tables, summing joint counts, then calculating relative frequencies.

All experiments were run using the Chinese/English data made available for NIST's 2008 MT evaluation. This included approximately 5M sentence pairs of data from the UN corpus, and approximatel 4M sentence pairs of other material. The English Gigaword corpus was not used for language model training. Two separate development corpora were derived from a mix of the NIST 2005 evaluation set and some webtext drawn from the training material (disjoint from the training set used). The evaluation sets for NIST 2004

[1] It can also choose to optimize linear combinations of weights in order to avoid ridges that are not aligned with the original coordinates, which can be done just as easily.

cfg	nist04			nist06		
	avg	Δ	S	avg	Δ	S
S1	31.17	1.09	0.28	26.95	0.90	0.27
S2	31.44	0.22	0.07	27.38	0.71	0.19
L1	33.03	1.09	0.37	29.22	0.97	0.34
L2	33.37	1.49	0.49	29.61	2.14	0.66

Table 2: Test-set BLEU score variation with 10 different random seeds, for small (S) and large (L) models on dev sets 1 and 2. The *avg* column gives the average BLEU score over the 10 runs; Δ gives the difference between the maximum and minimum scores, and S is the standard deviation.

and NIST 2005 corpora were used for testing. Table 1 summarizes the sizes of the devtest corpora, all of which have four reference translations.

5 Measuring the Stability of Och's Algorithm

To gauge the response of Och's algorithm to small changes in system configuration, we varied the seed value for initializing the random number generator used to produce random starting points for Powell's algorithm. For each of 10 different seed values, Och's algorithm was run for a maximum of 30 iterations[2] using 100-best lists. Table 2 shows the results for the two different log-linear models described in the previous section.

The two development sets exhibit a similar pattern: the small models appear to be somewhat more stable, but all models show considerable variation in test-set BLEU scores. For the large models, the average difference between best and worst BLEU scores is almost 1.5% absolute, with an average standard deviation of almost 0.5%. Differences of as little as 0.35% are significant at a 95% confidence level according to paired bootstrap resampling tests on this data, so these variations are much too large to be ignored.

The variation in table 2 might result from Och's algorithm failing to maximize development-set BLEU properly on certain runs. Alternatively, it could be finding different maxima that vary in the extent to which they generalize to the test sets. Both of these factors appear to play a role. The ranges of BLEU scores on the two development corpora with the large models are 0.86 and 1.3 respectively; the corresponding standard deviations are 0.27 and 0.38. Different runs clearly have significantly different degrees of success in maximizing BLEU.

[2]Sufficient for effective convergence in all cases we tested.

dev	nist04		nist06		inter
	ρ	r	ρ	r	ρ
dev1	0.18	0.42	-0.27	0.07	0.73
dev2	0.55	0.60	0.73	0.85	0.94

Table 3: Pearson (ρ) and Spearman rank (r) correlation between dev-set and test-set BLEU scores for the large log-linear model. The final column shows nist04/nist06 correlation.

To test whether the variation in development-set BLEU scores accounts completely for the variation in test-set scores, we measured the correlation between them. The results in table 3 show that this varies considerably across the two development and test corpora. Although the rank correlation is always positive and is in some cases quite high, there are many examples where higher development-set scores lead to lower test-set scores. Interestingly, the correlation between the two test-set scores (shown in the last column of the table) is much higher than that between the development and test sets. Since the test sets are not particularly similar to each other, this suggests that some sets of log-linear weights are in fact overfitting the development corpus.

5.1 Bootstrapping with Random Seeds

The results above indicate that the stability problems with Och's MERT can be quite severe, especially when tuning weights for a fairly large number of features. However, they also constitute a baseline solution to these problems: run MERT some number of times with different random seeds, then choose the run that achieves the highest BLEU score on a test set. Since test-set scores are highly correlated, these weights are likely to generalize well to new data. Applying this procedure using the nist04 corpus to choose weights yields a BLEU increase of 0.69 on nist06 compared to the average value over the 10 runs in table 2; operating in the reverse direction gives an increase of 0.37 on nist04.[3]

[3]These increases are averages over the increases on each development set. This comparison is not strictly fair to the baseline single-MERT procedure, since it relies on a test set for model selection (using the development set would have yielded gains of 0.25 for nist06 and 0.27 for nist04). However, it is fairly typical to select models (involving different feature sets, etc) using a test set, for later evaluation on a

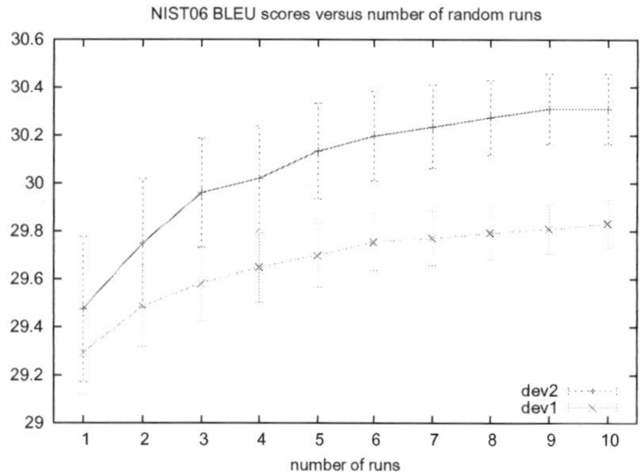

Figure 1: Results on the nist06 test corpus, using nist04 to choose best weights from varying numbers of MERT runs, averaged over 1000 random draws. The error bars indicate the magnitude of the standard deviation.

An obvious drawback to this technique is that it requires the expensive MERT procedure to be run many times. To measure the potential gain from using fewer runs, and to estimate the stability of the procedure, we used a bootstrap simulation. For each development set and each n from 1 to 10, we randomly drew 1000 sets of n runs from the data used for table 2, then recorded the behaviour of the nist06 scores that corresponded to the best nist04 score. The results are plotted in figure 1. There is no obvious optimal point on the curves, although 7 runs would be required to reduce the standard deviation on dev2 (the set with the higher variance) below 0.35. In the following sections we evaluate some alternatives that are less computationally expensive. The large model setting is assumed throughout.

6 Improving Maximization

In this section we address the problem of improving the maximization procedure over the development corpus. In general, we expect that being able to consistently find higher maxima will lead to lower variance in test-set scores. Previous work, eg (Moore and Quirk, 2008; Cer et al., 2008), has focused on improving the performance of Powell's algorithm. The degree to which this is effective depends on how good an approximation the current n-best lists are to the true search space. As illustrated in figure 2, it is possible for the true space to contain maxima that are absent from the approximate (n-best) space. Figure 3 gives some evidence that this happens in practice. It shows the evolution of decoder BLEU scores with iteration for the best and worst runs for dev2. Although the worst run explores a somewhat promising area at iteration 7, it converges soon afterwards in a region that gives lower true BLEU scores. This is not due to a failure of Powell's algorithm, since the scores on the n-best lists rise monotonically in this range.

second, blind, test set. A multi-MERT strategy could be naturally incorporated into such a regime, and seems unlikely to give rise to substantial bias.

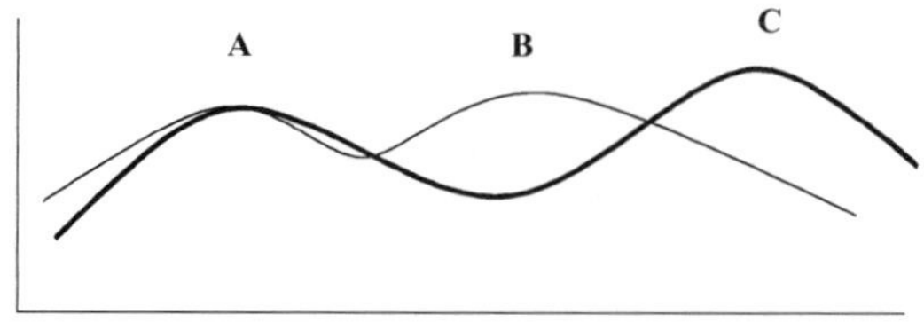

Figure 2: True objective function (bold curve) compared to n-best approximation (light curve). Och's algorithm can correct for false maxima like B by adding hypotheses to n-best lists, but may not find the true global maximum (C), converging to local peaks like A instead.

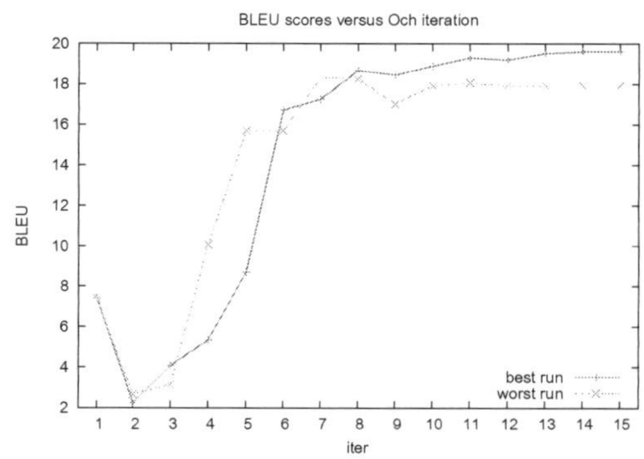

Figure 3: Development-set BLEU scores after each Och iteration for two different training runs on the dev2 corpus.

We explored various simple strategies for avoiding the kind of local-maximum behaviour exhibited in figure 3. These are orthogonal to improvements to Powell's algorithm, which was used in its standard form. Our baseline implementation of Och's algorithm calls Powell's three times starting with each of the three best weight sets from the previous iteration, then a certain number of times with randomly-generated weights. The total number of Powell's calls is determined by an algorithm that tries to minimize the probability of a new starting point producing a better maximum.[4]

The first strategy was simply to re-seed the random number generator (based on a given global seed value) for each iteration of Och's algorithm. Our implementation had previously re-used the same "random" starting points for Powell's across different Och iterations. This is arguably justifiable on the grounds that the function to be optimized is different each time.

The second strategy was motivated by the observation that after the first several iterations of Och's algorithm, the starting point that leads to the best Powell's result is nearly always one of the three previous best weight sets rather than a randomly-generated set. To encourage the algorithm to consider other alternatives, we used the three best results from *all* previous Och's iterations. That is, on iteration n, Powell's is started with the three best results from iteration $n-1$, then the three best from $n-2$, and so forth. If more than $3(n-1)$ points are required by the stopping algorithm described above, then they are generated randomly.

The final strategy is more explicitly aimed at forcing the algorithm to cover a broader portion of the search space. Rather than choosing the maximum-BLEU results from Powell's algorithm for the subsequent decoding step, we choose weight vectors that yield high BLEU scores *and* are dissimilar from previous decoding weights. Formally:

$$\hat{\alpha} = \underset{\alpha \in \mathcal{P}}{\operatorname{argmax}}\ w\,\mathrm{rbleu}(\alpha) + (1-w)\,\mathrm{rdist}(\alpha),$$

where $\mathcal{P}$ is the set of all weight vectors returned by Powell's on the current iteration, $\mathrm{rbleu}(\alpha)$ is α's BLEU score divided by the highest score for any vector in $\mathcal{P}$, and $\mathrm{rdist}(\alpha)$ is α's distance to previous weights divided by the largest distance for any vector in $\mathcal{P}$. Distance to previous weights is measured by taking the minimum L2 distance from α to any of the decoding weight vectors used during the previous m Och iterations.

Intuitively, the weight w that controls the importance of BLEU score relative to novelty should increase gradually as Och's algorithm progresses in order to focus the search on the best maximum found (roughly similar to simulated annealing search). To accomplish this, w is defined as:

$$w = 1 - a/(\mathrm{iter} + b),$$

where $b \geq 0$ and $a \leq b+1$ are parameters that control w's decay, and iter is the current Och iteration.

Each of the three strategies outlined above was run using 10 random seeds with both development corpora. The weight selection strategy was run with two different sets of values for the a and b parameters: $a = 1, b = 1$ and $a = 5, b = 9$. Each assigns equal weight to BLEU score and novelty on the first iteration, but under the first parameterization the weight on novelty decays more swiftly, to 0.03 by the final iteration compared to to 0.13.

The results are shown in table 4. The best strategy overall appears to be a combination of all three techniques outlined above. Under the $a = 5$, $b = 9$, $m = 3$ parametrization for the final (weight selection) strategy, this improves the development set scores by an average of approximately 0.4% BLEU compared to the baseline, while significantly reducing the variation across different runs. Performance of weight selection appears to be quite insensitive to its parameters: there is no significant difference between the $a = 1$, $b = 1$ and $a = 5$, $b = 9$ settings. It is possible that further tuning of these parameters would yield better results, but this is an expensive procedure; we were also wary of overfitting. A good fallback is the first two strategies, which together achieve results that are almost equivalent to the final gains due to weight selection.

7 Generalization

As demonstrated in section 5, better performance on the development set does not necessarily lead to better performance on the test set: two weight vectors that give approximately the same dev-set BLEU score can give very different test-set scores. We investigated several vectors with this characteristic from the experiments described above, but were unable to find any intrinsic property that was a good predictor of test-set performance, perhaps due to the fact that the weights are scale invariant. We also tried averaging BLEU over bootstrapped samples of the development corpora, but this was also not convincingly correlated with test-set BLEU.

[4] Whenever a new maximum is encountered, at least the current number of new starting points must be tried before stopping, with a minimum of 10 points in total. Experiments where the total number of starts was fixed at 30 did not produce significantly different results.

strategy	dev	avg	Δ	S
baseline	1	22.64	0.87	0.27
	2	19.11	1.31	0.38
re-seed	1	22.87	0.65	0.21
	2	19.37	0.60	0.17
+history	1	22.99	0.43	0.15
	2	19.44	0.35	0.11
+sel 1,1,3	1	23.12	0.59	0.19
	2	19.53	0.38	0.13
+sel 5,9,3	1	23.11	0.42	0.13
	2	19.46	0.44	0.14

Table 4: Performance of various strategies for improving maximization on the dev corpora: *baseline* is the baseline used in section 5; *re-seed* is random generator re-seeding; *history* is accumulation of previous best weights as starting point; and *sel a,b,m* is the final, weight selection, strategy described in section 6, parameterized by a, b, and m. Strategies are applied cumulatively, as indicated by the $+$ signs.

An alternate approach was inspired by the regularization method described in (Cer et al., 2008). In essence, this uses the average BLEU score from the points close to a given maximum as a surrogate for the BLEU at the maximum, in order to penalize maxima that are "narrow" and therefore more likely to be spurious. While Cer et al use this technique while maximizing along a single dimension within Powell's algorithm, we apply it over all dimensions with the vectors output from Powell's. Each individual weight is perturbed according to a normal distribution (with variance 1e-03), then the resulting vector is used to calculate BLEU over the n-best lists. The average score over 10 such perturbed vectors is used to calculate *rbleu* in the weight-selection method from the previous section.

The results from regularized weight selection are compared to standard weight selection and to the baseline MERT algorithm in table 5. Regularization appears to have very little effect on the weight selection approach. This does not necessarily contradict the results of Cer et al, since it is applied in a very different setting. The standard weight selection technique (in combination with the re-seeding and history accumulation strategies) gives a systematic improvement in average test-set BLEU score over the baseline, although it does not substantially reduce variance.

strategy	dev	test	avg	Δ	S
baseline	1	04	33.03	1.09	0.37
		06	29.22	0.97	0.34
	2	04	33.37	1.49	0.49
		06	29.61	2.14	0.66
(+) sel 5,9,3	1	04	33.43	1.23	0.41
		06	29.62	0.98	0.31
	2	04	33.95	1.03	0.37
		06	30.32	0.88	0.30
+ reg 10	1	04	33.36	1.45	0.49
		06	29.56	1.25	0.39
	2	04	33.81	0.94	0.28
		06	30.17	1.21	0.35

Table 5: Performance of various MERT techniques on the test corpora. *(+) sel 5,9,3* is the same configuration as *+sel 5,9,3* in table 4; *+ reg 10* uses regularized BLEU within this procedure.

8 Conclusion

In this paper, we have investigated the stability of Och's MERT algorithm using different random seeds within Powell's algorithm to simulate the effect of small changes to a system. We found that test-set BLEU scores can vary by 1 percent or more across 10 runs of Och's algorithm with different random seeds. Using a bootstrap analysis, we demonstrate that an effective, though expensive, way to stabilize MERT would be to run it many times (at least 7), then choose the weights that give best results on a held-out corpus. We propose less expensive simple strategies for avoiding local maxima that systematically improve test-set BLEU scores averaged over 10 MERT runs, as well as reducing their variance in some cases. An attempt to improve on these strategies by regularizing BLEU was not effective.

In future work, we plan to integrate improved variants on Powell's algorithm, which are orthogonal to the investigations reported here.

9 Acknowlegement

This material is partly based upon work supported by the Defense Advanced Research Projects Agency (DARPA) under Contract No. HR0011-06-C-0023. Any opinions, findings and conclusions or recommendations expressed in this material are those of the authors and do not necessarily reflect the views of the Defense Advanced Research Projects Agency (DARPA).

References

Daniel Cer, Daniel Jurafsky, and Christopher D. Manning. 2008. Regularization and search for minimum error rate training. In *Proceedings of the ACL Workshop on Statistical Machine Translation*, Columbus, June. WMT.

Mauro Cettolo and Marcello Federico. 2004. Minimum error training of log-linear translation models. In *International Workshop on Spoken Language Translation*, Kyoto, September.

David Chiang. 2005. A hierarchical phrase-based model for statistical machine translation. In *Proceedings of the 43th Annual Meeting of the Association for Computational Linguistics (ACL)*, Ann Arbor, Michigan, July.

Kevin Duh and Katrin Kirchhoff. 2008. Beyond log-linear models: Boosted minimum error rate training for n-best re-ranking. In *Proceedings of the 46th Annual Meeting of the Association for Computational Linguistics (ACL)*, Columbus, Ohio, June.

Liang Huang and David Chiang. 2007. Forest rescoring: Faster decoding with integrated language models. In *Proceedings of the 45th Annual Meeting of the Association for Computational Linguistics (ACL)*, Prague, Czech Republic, June.

Philipp Koehn, Franz Josef Och, and Daniel Marcu. 2003. Statistical phrase-based translation. In Eduard Hovy, editor, *Proceedings of the Human Language Technology Conference of the North American Chapter of the Association for Computational Linguistics*, pages 127–133, Edmonton, Alberta, Canada, May. NAACL.

Wolfgang Macherey, Franz Josef Och, Ignacio Thayer, and Jakob Uszkoreit. 2008. Lattice-based minimum error rate training for statistical machine translation. In *Proceedings of the 2008 Conference on Empirical Methods in Natural Language Processing (EMNLP)*, Honolulu.

Robert C. Moore and Chris Quirk. 2008. Random restarts in minimum error rate training for statistical machine translation. In *Proceedings of the International Conference on Computational Linguistics (COLING) 2008*, Manchester, August.

Franz Josef Och, Daniel Gildea, and Sanjeev Khudanpur et al. 2004. Final report of johns hopkins 2003 summer workshop on syntax for statistical machine translation (revised version). Technical report, February 25.

Franz Josef Och. 2003. Minimum error rate training for statistical machine translation. In *Proceedings of the 41th Annual Meeting of the Association for Computational Linguistics (ACL)*, Sapporo, July.

William H. Press, Saul A. Teukolsky, William T. Vetterling, and Brian P. Flannery. 2002. *Numerical Recipes in C++*. Cambridge University Press, Cambridge, UK.

Richard Zens and Hermann Ney. 2004. Improvements in phrase-based statistical machine translation. In *Proceedings of Human Language Technology Conference / North American Chapter of the ACL*, Boston, May.

Richard Zens, Sasa Hasan, and Hermann Ney. 2007. A systematic comparison of training criteria for statistical machine translation. In *Proceedings of the 2007 Conference on Empirical Methods in Natural Language Processing (EMNLP)*, Prague, Czech Republic.

On the Robustness of Syntactic and Semantic Features for Automatic MT Evaluation

Jesús Giménez and **Lluís Màrquez**
TALP Research Center, LSI Department
Universitat Politècnica de Catalunya
Jordi Girona Salgado 1–3, E-08034, Barcelona
{jgimenez,lluism}@lsi.upc.edu

Abstract

Linguistic metrics based on syntactic and semantic information have proven very effective for Automatic MT Evaluation. However, no results have been presented so far on their performance when applied to heavily ill-formed low quality translations. In order to glean some light into this issue, in this work we present an empirical study on the behavior of a heterogeneous set of metrics based on linguistic analysis in the paradigmatic case of speech translation between non-related languages. Corroborating previous findings, we have verified that metrics based on deep linguistic analysis exhibit a very robust and stable behavior at the system level. However, these metrics suffer a significant decrease at the sentence level. This is in many cases attributable to a loss of recall, due to parsing errors or to a lack of parsing at all, which may be partially ameliorated by backing off to lexical similarity.

1 Introduction

Recently, there is a growing interest in the development of automatic evaluation metrics which exploit linguistic knowledge at the syntactic and semantic levels. For instance, we may find metrics which compute similarities over shallow syntactic structures/sequences (Giménez and Màrquez, 2007; Popovic and Ney, 2007), constituency trees (Liu and Gildea, 2005) and dependency trees (Liu and Gildea, 2005; Amigó et al., 2006; Mehay and Brew, 2007; Owczarzak et al., 2007). We may also find metrics operating over shallow semantic structures, such as named entities and semantic roles (Giménez and Màrquez, 2007).

Linguistic metrics have been proven to produce more reliable system rankings than metrics limiting their scope to the lexical dimension, in particular when applied to test beds with a rich system typology, i.e., test beds in which there are automatic outputs produced by systems based on different paradigms, e.g., statistical, rule-based and human-aided (Giménez and Màrquez, 2007). The reason is that they are able to capture deep MT quality distinctions which occur beyond the shallow level of lexical similarities.

However, these metrics have the limitation of relying on automatic linguistic processors, tools which are not equally available for all languages and whose performance may vary depending on the type of analysis conducted and the application domain. Thus, it could be argued that linguistic metrics should suffer a significant quality drop when applied to a different translation domain, or to ill-formed sentences. Clearly, metric scores computed on partial or wrong syntactic/semantic structures will be less informed. But, should this necessarily lead to less reliable evaluations? In this work, we have analyzed this issue by conducting a contrastive empirical study on the behavior of a heterogeneous set of metrics over several evaluation scenarios of decreasing translation quality. In particular, we have studied the case of Chinese-to-English speech translation, which is a paradigmatic example of low quality and heavily ill-formed output.

The rest of the paper is organized as follows. In Section 2, prior to presenting experimental work, we describe the set of metrics employed in our experiments. We also introduce a novel family of metrics which operate at the properly semantic level by analyzing similarities over discourse representations. Experimental work is then presented in Section 3. Metrics are evaluated both in terms of human likeness and human acceptability (Amigó et al., 2006). Finally, in Section 4, main conclusions are summarized and future work is outlined.

Proceedings of the Fourth Workshop on Statistical Machine Translation , pages 250–258,
Athens, Greece, 30 March – 31 March 2009. ©2009 Association for Computational Linguistics

2 A Heterogeneous Metric Set

We have used a heterogeneous set of metrics selected out from the metric repository provided with the IQ$_{MT}$ evaluation package (Giménez and Màrquez, 2007)[1]. We have considered several metric representatives from different linguistic levels (lexical, syntactic and semantic). A brief description of the metric set is available in Appendix A.

In addition, taking advantage of newly available semantic processors, we have designed a novel family of metrics based on the Discourse Representation Theory, a theoretical framework offering a representation language for the examination of contextually dependent meaning in discourse (Kamp, 1981). A discourse is represented in a discourse representation structure (DRS), which is essentially a variation of first-order predicate calculus —its forms are pairs of first-order formulae and the free variables that occur in them.

2.1 Exploiting Semantic Similarity for Automatic MT Evaluation

'DR' metrics analyze similarities between automatic and reference translations by comparing their respective DRSs. These are automatically obtained using the C&C Tools (Clark and Curran, 2004)[2]. Sentences are first parsed on the basis of a combinatory categorial grammar (Bos et al., 2004). Then, the BOXER component (Bos, 2005) extracts DRSs. As an illustration, Figure 1 shows the DRS representation for the sentence *"Every man loves Mary."*. The reader may find the output of the BOXER component (top) together with the equivalent first-order formula (bottom).

DRS may be viewed as semantic trees, which are built through the application of two types of DRS conditions:

basic conditions: one-place properties (predicates), two-place properties (relations), named entities, time-expressions, cardinal expressions and equalities.

complex conditions: disjunction, implication, negation, question, and propositional attitude operations.

Three kinds of metrics have been defined:

DR-STM-*l* (Semantic Tree Matching) These metrics are similar to the *Syntactic Tree Matching* metric defined by Liu and Gildea (2005), in this case applied to DRSs instead of constituency trees. All semantic subpaths in the candidate and the reference trees are retrieved. The fraction of matching subpaths of a given length, $l \in [1..9]$, is computed. Then, average accumulated scores up to a given length are retrieved. For instance, 'DR-STM-4' corresponds to the average accumulated proportion of matching subpaths up to length-4.

DR-O_r-*t* These metrics compute lexical overlapping[3] between discourse representation structures (i.e., discourse referents and discourse conditions) according to their type 't'. For instance, 'DR-O_r-pred' roughly reflects lexical overlapping between the referents associated to predicates (i.e., one-place properties), whereas 'DR-O_r-imp' reflects lexical overlapping between referents associated to implication conditions. We also introduce the 'DR-O_r-$\star$' metric, which computes average lexical overlapping over all DRS types.

DR-O_{rp}-*t* These metrics compute morphosyntactic overlapping (i.e., between parts of speech associated to lexical items) between discourse representation structures of the same type t. We also define the 'DR-O_{rp}-$\star$' metric, which computes average morphosyntactic overlapping over all DRS types.

Note that in the case of some complex conditions, such as implication or question, the respective order of the associated referents in the tree is important. We take this aspect into account by making order information explicit in the construction of the semantic tree. We also make explicit the type, symbol, value and date of conditions when these are applicable (e.g., predicates, relations, named entities, time expressions, cardinal expressions, or anaphoric conditions).

Finally, the extension to the evaluation setting based on multiple references is computed by assigning the maximum score attained against each individual reference.

[1] `http://www.lsi.upc.edu/~nlp/IQMT`

[2] `http://svn.ask.it.usyd.edu.au/trac/candc`

[3] Overlapping is measured following the formulae and definitions by Giménez and Màrquez (2007). A short definition may be found in Appendix A.

```
drs([[4]:Y],
    [[4]:named(Y, mary, per, 0),
     [1]:imp(drs([[1]:X], [[2]:pred(X, man, n, 1)]),
             drs([[3]:E], [[3]:pred(E, love, v, 0), [3]:rel(E, X, agent, 0), [3]:rel(E, Y, patient, 0)]))])
```

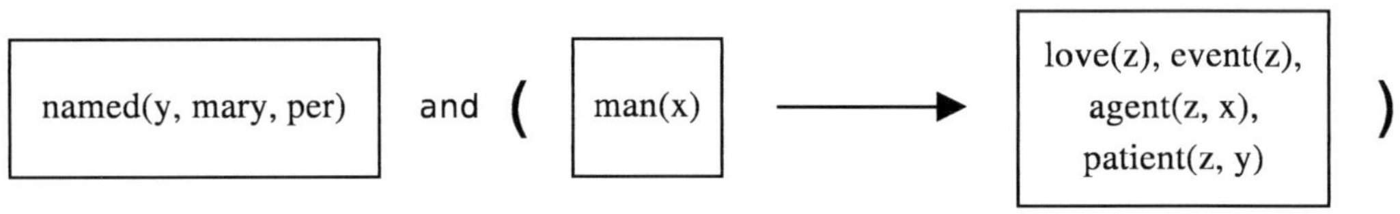

Formally:

$$\exists y\ named(y, mary, per) \wedge (\forall x\ man(x) \rightarrow \exists z\ love(z) \wedge event(z) \wedge agent(z, x) \wedge patient(z, y))$$

Figure 1: DRS representation for *"Every man loves Mary."*

3 Experimental Work

In this section, we present an empirical study on the behavior of a heterogeneous set of metrics based on linguistic analysis in the case of speech translation between non-related languages.

3.1 Evaluation Scenarios

We have used the test bed from the Chinese-to-English translation task at the *"2006 Evaluation Campaign on Spoken Language Translation"* (Paul, 2006)[4]. The test set comprises 500 translation test cases corresponding to simple conversations (question/answer scenario) in the travel domain. In addition, there are 3 different evaluation subscenarios of increasing translation difficulty, according to the translation source:

CRR: Translation of correct recognition results (as produced by human transcribers).

ASR read: Translation of automatic read speech recognition results.

ASR spont: Translation of automatic spontaneous speech recognition results.

For the purpose of automatic evaluation, 7 human reference translations and automatic outputs by 14 different MT systems for each evaluation subscenario are available. In addition, we count on the results of a process of manual evaluation. For each subscenario, 400 test cases from 6 different system outputs were evaluated, by three human assessors each, in terms of adequacy and fluency on a 1-5 scale (LDC, 2005). A brief numerical description of these test beds is available in Table 1. It includes the number of human references and system outputs available, as well as the number of sentences per output, and the number of system outputs and sentences per system assessed. For the sake of completeness, we report the performance of the Automatic Speech Recognition (ASR) system, in terms of accuracy, over the source Chinese utterances, both at the word and sentence levels. Also, in order to give an idea of the translation quality exhibited by automatic systems, average adequacy and fluency scores are also provided.

[4]`http://www.slc.atr.jp/IWSLT2006/`

3.2 Meta-Evaluation

Our experiment requires a mechanism for evaluating the quality of evaluation metrics, i.e., a meta-evaluation criterion. The two most prominent are:

- *Human Acceptability:* Metrics are evaluated in terms of their ability to capture the degree of acceptability to humans of automatic translations, i.e., their ability to emulate human assessors. The underlying assumption is that *good* translations should be acceptable to human evaluators. Human acceptability is usually measured on the basis of *correlation* between automatic metric scores and human assessments of translation quality.

	CRR	ASR read	ASR spont
#human-references	7	7	7
#system-outputs	14	14	13
#sentences	500	500	500
#outputs$_{\text{assessed}}$	6	6	6
#sentences$_{\text{assessed}}$	400	400	400
Word Recognition Accuracy	—	0.74	0.68
Sentence Recognition Accuracy	—	0.23	0.17
Average Adequacy	1.40	1.02	0.93
Average Fluency	1.16	0.98	0.98

Table 1: IWSLT 2006 MT Evaluation Campaign. Chinese-to-English test bed description

- *Human Likeness:* Metrics are evaluated in terms of their ability to capture the features which distinguish human from automatic translations. The underlying assumption is that *good* translations should resemble human translations. Human likeness is usually measured on the basis of *discriminative power* (Lin and Och, 2004b; Amigó et al., 2005).

In this work, metrics are evaluated both in terms of human acceptability and human likeness. In the case of human acceptability, metric quality is measured on the basis of correlation with human assessments both at the sentence and document (i.e., system) levels. We compute Pearson correlation coefficients. The sum of adequacy and fluency is used as a global measure of quality. Assessments from different judges have been averaged.

In the case of human likeness, we use the probabilistic KING measure defined inside the QARLA Framework (Amigó et al., 2005). KING represents the probability, estimated over the set of test cases, that the score attained by a human reference is equal or greater than the score attained by *any* automatic translation. Although KING computations do not require human assessments, for the sake of comparison, we have limited to the set of test cases counting on human assessments.

3.3 Results

Table 2 presents meta-evaluation results for a set of metric representatives from different linguistic levels over the three subscenarios defined ('CRR', 'ASR read' and 'ASR spont'). Highest scores in each column have been highlighted. Lowest scores appear in italics.

System-level Behavior

At the system level (R_{sys}, columns 7-9), the highest quality is in general attained by metrics based on deep linguistic analysis, either syntactic or semantic. Among lexical metrics, the highest correlation is attained by BLEU and the variant of GTM rewarding longer matchings ($e = 2$).

As to the impact of sentence ill-formedness, while most metrics at the lexical level suffer a significant variation across the three subscenarios, the performance of metrics at deeper linguistic levels is in general quite stable. However, in the case of the translation of automatically recognized spontaneous speech (ASR spont) we have found that the 'SR-O_r-$\star$' and 'SR-M_r-$\star$' metrics, respectively based on lexical overlapping and matching over semantic roles, suffer a very significant decrease far below the performance of most lexical metrics. Although 'SR-O_r-$\star$' has performed well on other test beds (Giménez and Màrquez, 2007), its low performance over the BTEC data suggests that it is not fully portable across all kind of evaluation scenarios.

Finally, it is highly remarkable the degree of robustness exhibited by semantic metrics introduced in Section 2.1. In particular, the metric variants based on lexical and morphosyntactic overlapping over discourse representations ('DR-O_r-$\star$' and 'DR-O_{rp}-$\star$', respectively), obtain a high system-level correlation with human assessments across the three subscenarios.

Sentence-level Behavior

At the sentence level (KING and R_{snt}, columns 1-6), highest quality is attained in most cases by metrics based on lexical matching. This result was expected since all MT systems are statistical and the test set is in-domain, that is it belongs to the

		Human Likeness			Human Acceptability					
		KING			R_{snt}			R_{sys}		
Level	Metric	CRR	ASR read	ASR spont	CRR	ASR read	ASR spont	CRR	ASR read	ASR spont
Lexical	**1-WER**	0.63	0.69	0.71	0.47	0.50	0.48	0.50	*0.32*	0.52
	1-PER	0.71	0.79	0.79	0.44	0.48	0.45	0.67	*0.39*	0.60
	1-TER	0.69	0.75	0.77	0.49	0.52	0.50	0.66	*0.36*	0.62
	BLEU	0.69	0.72	0.73	0.54	0.53	0.52	0.79	0.74	0.62
	NIST	0.79	0.84	0.85	0.53	0.54	0.53	*0.12*	*0.26*	*-0.02*
	GTM ($e = 1$)	0.75	0.81	0.83	0.50	0.52	0.52	*0.35*	*0.10*	*-0.09*
	GTM ($e = 2$)	0.72	0.78	0.79	**0.62**	**0.64**	**0.61**	0.78	0.65	0.62
	METEOR$_{wnsyn}$	**0.81**	**0.86**	**0.86**	0.44	0.50	0.48	0.55	*0.39*	*0.08*
	ROUGE$_{W_1.2}$	0.74	0.79	0.81	0.58	0.60	0.58	0.53	0.69	0.43
	O_l	0.74	0.81	0.82	0.57	0.62	0.58	0.77	0.51	0.34
Shallow Syntactic	**SP-O_p-⋆**	0.75	0.80	0.82	0.54	0.59	0.56	0.77	0.54	0.48
	SP-O_c-⋆	0.74	0.81	0.82	0.54	0.59	0.55	0.82	0.52	0.49
	SP-NIST$_l$	0.79	0.84	0.85	0.52	0.53	0.52	*0.10*	*0.25*	*-0.03*
	SP-NIST$_p$	0.74	0.78	0.80	0.44	0.42	0.43	*-0.02*	*0.24*	*0.04*
	SP-NIST$_{iob}$	0.65	0.69	0.70	*0.33*	*0.32*	*0.35*	*-0.09*	*0.17*	*-0.09*
	SP-NIST$_c$	*0.55*	*0.59*	*0.59*	*0.24*	*0.22*	*0.25*	*-0.07*	*0.19*	*0.08*
Syntactic	**CP-O_p-⋆**	0.75	0.81	0.82	0.57	0.63	0.59	**0.84**	0.67	0.52
	CP-O_c-⋆	0.74	0.80	0.82	**0.60**	**0.64**	**0.61**	0.71	0.53	0.43
	DP-O_l-⋆	0.68	0.75	0.76	0.48	0.50	0.50	**0.84**	0.77	0.67
	DP-O_c-⋆	0.71	0.76	0.77	0.41	0.46	0.43	0.76	0.65	0.71
	DP-O_r-⋆	0.75	0.80	0.81	0.51	0.53	0.51	0.81	0.75	0.62
	DP-HWC$_w$	*0.54*	*0.57*	*0.57*	*0.29*	*0.32*	*0.28*	0.73	0.74	0.37
	DP-HWC$_c$	*0.48*	*0.51*	*0.52*	*0.17*	*0.18*	*0.22*	0.73	0.64	0.67
	DP-HWC$_r$	*0.44*	*0.49*	*0.48*	*0.20*	*0.21*	*0.25*	0.71	0.58	0.56
	CP-STM	0.71	0.77	0.80	0.53	0.56	0.54	0.65	0.58	0.47
Shallow Semantic	**SR-M_r-⋆**	*0.40*	*0.43*	*0.45*	*0.29*	*0.28*	*0.29*	0.52	0.60	*0.20*
	SR-O_r-⋆	*0.45*	*0.49*	*0.51*	*0.35*	*0.35*	*0.36*	0.56	0.58	*0.14*
	SR-O_r	*0.31*	*0.33*	*0.35*	*0.16*	*0.15*	*0.18*	0.68	0.73	0.53
	SR-M_{rv}-⋆	*0.38*	*0.41*	*0.42*	*0.33*	*0.34*	*0.34*	0.79	**0.81**	0.42
	SR-O_{rv}-⋆	*0.40*	*0.44*	*0.45*	*0.36*	*0.38*	*0.38*	0.64	0.72	0.72
	SR-O_{rv}	*0.36*	*0.40*	*0.40*	*0.27*	*0.31*	*0.29*	*0.34*	0.78	0.38
Semantic	**DR-O_r-⋆**	0.67	0.73	0.75	0.48	0.53	0.50	**0.86**	0.74	0.77
	DR-O_{rp}-⋆	0.59	0.64	0.65	0.34	0.35	0.33	**0.84**	0.78	**0.95**
	DR-STM	0.58	0.63	0.65	*0.23*	*0.26*	*0.26*	0.75	0.62	0.67

Table 2: Meta-evaluation results for a set of metric representatives from different linguistic levels

same domain in which systems have been trained. Therefore, translation outputs have a strong tendency to share the sublanguage (i.e., word selection and word ordering) represented by the predefined set of human reference translations.

Metrics based on lexical overlapping and matching over shallow syntactic categories and syntactic structures ('SP-O_p-⋆', 'SP-O_c-⋆', 'CP-O_p-⋆', 'CP-O_c-⋆', 'DP-O_l-⋆', 'DP-O_c-⋆', and 'DP-O_r-⋆') perform similarly to lexical metrics. However, computing NIST scores over base phrase chunk sequences ('SP-NIST$_{iob}$', 'SP-NIST$_c$') is not as effective. Metrics based on head-word chain matching ('DP-HWC$_w$', 'DP-HWC$_c$', 'DP-HWC$_r$') suffer also a significant decrease. Interestingly, the metric based on syntactic tree matching ('CP-STM') performed well in all scenarios.

Metrics at the shallow semantic level suffer also a severe drop in performance. Particularly significant is the case case of the 'SR-O_r' metric, which does not consider any lexical information. Interestingly, the 'SR-O_{rv}' variant, which only differs in that it distinguishes between SRs associated to different verbs, performs slightly better.

At the semantic level, metrics based on lexical and morphosyntactic overlapping over discourse representations ('DR-O_r-⋆' and 'DR-O_{rp}-⋆') suffer only a minor decrease, whereas semantic tree matching ('DR-STM') reports as a specially bad predictor of human acceptability (R_{snt}).

However, the most remarkable result, in relation to the goal of this work, is that the behavior of syntactic and semantic metrics across the three evaluation subscenarios is, in general, quite stable —the three values in each subrow are in a very similar range. Therefore, answering the question posed in the introduction, *sentence ill-formedness is not a limiting factor in the performance of linguistic metrics*.

		Human Likeness			Human Acceptability					
		KING			R_{snt}			R_{sys}		
Level	Metric	CRR	ASR read	ASR spont	CRR	ASR read	ASR spont	CRR	ASR read	ASR spont
Lexical	NIST	0.79	0.84	0.85	0.53	0.54	0.53	*0.12*	*0.26*	*-0.02*
	GTM ($e = 2$)	0.72	0.78	0.79	**0.62**	**0.64**	**0.61**	0.78	0.65	0.62
	METEOR$_{wnsyn}$	0.81	**0.86**	**0.86**	0.44	0.50	0.48	0.55	*0.39*	*0.08*
	O_l	0.74	0.81	0.82	0.57	0.62	0.58	0.77	0.51	0.34
Syntactic	CP-O_p-$\star$	0.75	0.81	0.82	0.57	0.63	0.59	0.84	0.67	0.52
	CP-O_c-$\star$	0.74	0.80	0.82	**0.60**	**0.64**	**0.61**	0.71	0.53	0.43
	DP-O_l-$\star$	0.68	0.75	0.76	0.48	0.50	0.50	0.84	0.77	0.67
Shallow Semantic	SR-M_r-$\star$	*0.40*	*0.43*	*0.45*	*0.29*	*0.28*	*0.29*	0.52	0.60	*0.20*
	SR-M_r-$\star_b$	0.68	0.72	0.73	0.31	0.30	0.31	0.52	0.60	0.20
	SR-M_r-$\star_i$	**0.84**	**0.86**	**0.88**	0.34	0.34	0.34	0.56	0.63	0.25
	SR-O_r-$\star$	*0.45*	*0.49*	*0.51*	*0.35*	*0.35*	*0.36*	0.56	0.58	*0.14*
	SR-O_r-$\star_b$	0.71	0.75	0.78	0.38	0.38	0.38	0.56	0.58	0.14
	SR-O_r-$\star_i$	**0.84**	**0.88**	**0.89**	0.41	0.41	0.41	0.62	0.60	0.22
	SR-O_r	*0.31*	*0.33*	*0.35*	*0.16*	*0.15*	*0.18*	0.68	0.73	0.53
	SR-O_{rb}	0.54	0.58	0.60	0.19	0.18	0.20	0.68	0.73	0.53
	SR-O_{ri}	0.72	0.77	0.79	0.26	0.26	0.27	0.80	0.73	0.67
	SR-M_{rv}-$\star$	*0.38*	*0.41*	*0.42*	*0.33*	*0.34*	*0.34*	0.79	0.81	0.42
	SR-M_{rv}-$\star_b$	0.70	0.73	0.74	0.34	0.35	0.34	0.79	0.81	0.42
	SR-M_{rv}-$\star_i$	**0.88**	**0.90**	**0.92**	0.36	0.38	0.37	0.81	**0.82**	0.45
	SR-O_{rv}-$\star$	*0.40*	*0.44*	*0.45*	*0.36*	*0.38*	*0.38*	0.64	0.72	0.72
	SR-O_{rv}-$\star_b$	0.72	0.76	0.77	0.38	0.40	0.39	0.64	0.72	0.72
	SR-O_{rv}-$\star_i$	**0.88**	**0.90**	**0.91**	0.40	0.42	0.41	0.69	0.74	0.74
	SR-O_{rv}	*0.36*	*0.40*	*0.40*	*0.27*	*0.31*	*0.29*	*0.34*	0.78	0.38
	SR-O_{rvb}	0.66	0.70	0.71	0.29	0.32	0.30	0.34	0.78	0.38
	SR-O_{rvi}	**0.83**	**0.86**	**0.88**	0.33	0.36	0.33	0.49	**0.82**	0.56
Semantic	DR-O_r-$\star$	0.67	0.73	0.75	0.48	0.53	0.50	0.86	0.74	0.77
	DR-O_r-$\star_b$	0.69	0.75	0.77	0.50	0.53	0.50	**0.90**	0.69	0.56
	DR-O_r-$\star_i$	**0.83**	**0.87**	**0.89**	0.53	0.57	0.53	**0.88**	0.70	0.61
	DR-O_{rp}-$\star$	0.59	0.64	0.65	0.34	0.35	0.33	0.84	0.78	**0.95**
	DR-O_{rp}-$\star_b$	0.61	0.65	0.67	0.35	0.36	0.34	0.86	0.71	0.57
	DR-O_{rp}-$\star_i$	**0.80**	**0.84**	**0.85**	0.43	0.46	0.43	**0.90**	0.75	0.70
	DR-STM	0.58	0.63	0.65	0.23	0.26	0.26	0.75	0.62	0.67
	DR-STM-b	0.64	0.68	0.71	0.23	0.26	0.27	0.75	0.62	0.67
	DR-STM-i	**0.83**	**0.87**	**0.87**	0.33	0.36	0.36	0.84	0.63	0.66

Table 3: Meta-evaluation results. Improved sentence-level evaluation of SR and DR metrics

Improved Sentence-level Behavior

By inspecting particular instances, we have found that linguistic metrics are, in many cases, unable to produce any evaluation result. The number of unscored sentences is particularly significant in the case of SR metrics. For instance, the 'SR-O_r-$\star$' metric is unable to confer an evaluation score in 57% of the cases. Several reasons explain this fact. The first and most important is that linguistic metrics rely on automatic processors trained on out-of-domain data, which are, thus, prone to error. Second, we argue that the test bed itself does not allow for fully exploiting the capabilities of these metrics. Apart from being based on a reduced vocabulary (2,346 distinct words), test cases consist mostly of very short segments (14.64 words on average), which in their turn consist of even shorter sentences (8.55 words on average)[5].

A possible solution could be to back off to a measure of lexical similarity in those cases in which linguistic processors are unable to produce any linguistic analysis. This should significantly increase their recall. With that purpose, we have designed two new variants for each of these metrics. Given a linguistic metric x, we define:

- $\boldsymbol{x_b}$ $\rightarrow$ by backing off to lexical overlapping, O_l, only when the linguistic processor was not able to produce a parsing. Lexical scores are conveniently scaled so that they are in a similar range to x scores. Specifically, we multiply them by the average x score attained over all other test cases for which the parser succeeded. Formally, given a test case t belonging to a set of test cases T:

$$x_b(t) = \begin{cases} x(t) & \text{if t} \in ok(T) \\ O_l(t)\frac{\sum_{j \in ok(T)} x(j)}{|ok(T)|} & \text{otherwise} \end{cases}$$

[5] Vocabulary size and segment/sentence average lengths have been computed over the set of reference translations.

where $ok(T)$ is the subset of test cases in T which were successfully parsed.

- $\boldsymbol{x_i}$ $\longrightarrow$ by linearly interpolating x and O_l scores for all test cases, via arithmetic mean:

$$x_i(t) = \frac{x(t) + O_l(t)}{2}$$

In both cases, system-level scores are calculated by averaging over all sentence-level scores.

Table 3 shows meta-evaluation results on the performance of these variants for several representatives from the SR and DR families. For the sake of comparison, we also show the scores attained by the base versions, and by some of the top-scoring metrics from other linguistic levels.

The first observation is that in all cases the new variants outperform their respective base metric, being linear interpolation the best alternative. The increase is particularly significant in terms of human likeness. New variants even outperform lexical metrics, including the O_l metric, which suggests that, in spite of its simplicity, this is a valid combination scheme. However, in terms of human acceptability, the gain is only moderate, and still their performance is far from top-scoring metrics.

Sentence-level improvements are also reflected at the system level, although to a lesser extent. Interestingly, in the case of the translation of automatically recognized spontaneous speech (ASR spont, column 9), mixing with lexical overlapping improves the low-performance 'SR-O_r' and 'SR-O_{rv}' metrics, at the same time that it causes a significant drop in the high-performance 'DR-O_r' and 'DR-O_{rp}' metrics. Still, the performance of linguistic metrics at the sentence level is under the performance of lexical metrics. This is not surprising. After all, apart from relying on automatic processors, linguistic metrics focus on very partial aspects of quality. However, since they operate at complementary quality dimensions, their scores are suitable for being combined.

4 Conclusions and Future Work

We have presented an empirical study on the robustness of a heterogeneous set of metrics operating at different linguistic levels for the particular case of Chinese-to-English speech translation of basic travel expressions. As an additional contribution, we have presented a novel family of metrics which operate at the semantic level by analyzing discourse representations.

Corroborating previous findings by Giménez and Màrquez (2007), results at the system level, show that metrics guided by deeper linguistic knowledge, either syntactic or semantic, are, in general, more effective and stable than metrics which limit their scope to the lexical dimension.

However, at the sentence level, results indicate that metrics based on deep linguistic analysis are not as reliable overall quality estimators as lexical metrics, at least when applied to low quality translations, as it is the case. This behavior is mainly attributable a drop in recall due to parsing errors. By inspecting particular sentences we have observed that in many cases these metrics are unable to produce any result. In that respect, we have showed that backing off to lexical similarity is a valid and effective strategy so as to improve the performance of these metrics.

But the most remarkable result, in relation to the goal of this work, is that syntactic and semantic metrics exhibit a very robust behavior across the three evaluation subscenarios of decreasing translation quality analyzed. Therefore, sentence ill-formedness is not a limiting factor in the performance of linguistic metrics. The quality drop, when moving from the system to the sentence level, seems, thus, more related to a shift in the application domain.

For future work, we are currently studying the possibility of further improving the sentence-level behavior of present evaluation methods by combining the outcomes of metrics at different linguistic levels into a single measure of quality (citation omitted for the sake of anonymity).

Acknowledgements

This research has been funded by the Spanish Ministry of Education and Science, project OpenMT (TIN2006-15307-C03-02). Our NLP group has been recognized as a Quality Research Group (2005 SGR-00130) by DURSI, the Research Department of the Catalan Government. We are grateful to the SLT Evaluation Campaign organizers and participants for providing such valuable test beds.

References

Enrique Amigó, Julio Gonzalo, Anselmo Pe nas, and Felisa Verdejo. 2005. QARLA: a Framework for the Evaluation of Automatic Sumarization. In *Pro-*

ceedings of the 43rd Annual Meeting of the Association for Computational Linguistics (ACL).

Enrique Amigó, Jesús Giménez, Julio Gonzalo, and Lluís Màrquez. 2006. MT Evaluation: Human-Like vs. Human Acceptable. In *Proceedings of the Joint 21st International Conference on Computational Linguistics and the 44th Annual Meeting of the Association for Computational Linguistics (COLING-ACL)*.

Satanjeev Banerjee and Alon Lavie. 2005. METEOR: An Automatic Metric for MT Evaluation with Improved Correlation with Human Judgments. In *Proceedings of ACL Workshop on Intrinsic and Extrinsic Evaluation Measures for MT and/or Summarization*.

Johan Bos, Stephen Clark, Mark Steedman, James R. Curran, and Julia Hockenmaier. 2004. Wide-Coverage Semantic Representations from a CCG Parser. In *Proceedings of the 20th International Conference on Computational Linguistics (COLING)*, pages 1240–1246.

Johan Bos. 2005. Towards Wide-Coverage Semantic Interpretation. In *Proceedings of the Sixth International Workshop on Computational Semantics*, pages 42–53.

Stephen Clark and James R. Curran. 2004. Parsing the WSJ using CCG and Log-Linear Models. In *Proceedings of the 42nd Annual Meeting of the Association for Computational Linguistics (ACL)*, pages 104–111.

George Doddington. 2002. Automatic Evaluation of Machine Translation Quality Using N-gram Co-Occurrence Statistics. In *Proceedings of the 2nd Internation Conference on Human Language Technology*, pages 138–145.

Jesús Giménez and Lluís Màrquez. 2007. Linguistic Features for Automatic Evaluation of Heterogeneous MT Systems. In *Proceedings of the ACL Workshop on Statistical Machine Translation*, pages 256–264.

Hans Kamp. 1981. A Theory of Truth and Semantic Representation. In J.A.G. Groenendijk, T.M.V. Janssen, , and M.B.J. Stokhof, editors, *Formal Methods in the Study of Language*, pages 277–322, Amsterdam. Mathematisch Centrum.

LDC. 2005. Linguistic Data Annotation Specification: Assessment of Adequacy and Fluency in Translations. Revision 1.5. Technical report, Linguistic Data Consortium. http://www.ldc.upenn.edu/-Projects/TIDES/Translation/TransAssess04.pdf.

Chin-Yew Lin and Franz Josef Och. 2004a. Automatic Evaluation of Machine Translation Quality Using Longest Common Subsequence and Skip-Bigram Statics. In *Proceedings of the 42nd Annual Meeting of the Association for Computational Linguistics (ACL)*.

Chin-Yew Lin and Franz Josef Och. 2004b. ORANGE: a Method for Evaluating Automatic Evaluation Metrics for Machine Translation. In *Proceedings of the 20th International Conference on Computational Linguistics (COLING)*.

Ding Liu and Daniel Gildea. 2005. Syntactic Features for Evaluation of Machine Translation. In *Proceedings of ACL Workshop on Intrinsic and Extrinsic Evaluation Measures for MT and/or Summarization*.

Dennis Mehay and Chris Brew. 2007. BLEUATRE: Flattening Syntactic Dependencies for MT Evaluation. In *Proceedings of the 11th Conference on Theoretical and Methodological Issues in Machine Translation (TMI)*.

I. Dan Melamed, Ryan Green, and Joseph P. Turian. 2003. Precision and Recall of Machine Translation. In *Proceedings of the Joint Conference on Human Language Technology and the North American Chapter of the Association for Computational Linguistics (HLT-NAACL)*.

Sonja Nießen, Franz Josef Och, Gregor Leusch, and Hermann Ney. 2000. An Evaluation Tool for Machine Translation: Fast Evaluation for MT Research. In *Proceedings of the 2nd International Conference on Language Resources and Evaluation*.

Karolina Owczarzak, Josef van Genabith, and Andy Way. 2007. Dependency-Based Automatic Evaluation for Machine Translation. In *Proceedings of SSST, NAACL-HLT/AMTA Workshop on Syntax and Structure in Statistical Translation*, pages 80–87.

Kishore Papineni, Salim Roukos, Todd Ward, and Wei-Jing Zhu. 2001. Bleu: a method for automatic evaluation of machine translation, RC22176. Technical report, IBM T.J. Watson Research Center.

Michael Paul. 2006. Overview of the IWSLT 2006 Evaluation Campaign. In *Proceedings of the International Workshop on Spoken Language Translation*, pages 1–15.

Maja Popovic and Hermann Ney. 2007. Word Error Rates: Decomposition over POS classes and Applications for Error Analysis. In *Proceedings of the Second Workshop on Statistical Machine Translation*, pages 48–55, Prague, Czech Republic, June. Association for Computational Linguistics.

Matthew Snover, Bonnie Dorr, Richard Schwartz, Linnea Micciulla, and John Makhoul. 2006. A Study of Translation Edit Rate with Targeted Human Annotation. In *Proceedings of AMTA*, pages 223–231.

C. Tillmann, S. Vogel, H. Ney, A. Zubiaga, and H. Sawaf. 1997. Accelerated DP based Search for Statistical Translation. In *Proceedings of European Conference on Speech Communication and Technology*.

A Metric Set

Metrics are grouped according to the linguistic dimension at which they operate:

- **Lexical Similarity**

  WER (Nießen et al., 2000).
  PER (Tillmann et al., 1997).
  BLEU (Papineni et al., 2001).
  NIST (Doddington, 2002).
  GTM (Melamed et al., 2003).
  ROUGE (Lin and Och, 2004a).
  METEOR. (Banerjee and Lavie, 2005).
  TER (Snover et al., 2006).
  $\mathbf{O_l}$ (Giménez and Màrquez, 2007). O_l is a short name for lexical overlapping. Automatic and reference translations are considered as unordered sets of lexical items. O_l is computed as the cardinality of the intersection of the two sets divided into the cardinality of their union.

- **Shallow Syntactic Similarity (SP)**

  SP-O_p-$\star$. Average lexical overlapping over parts-of-speech.
  SP-O_c-$\star$. Average lexical overlapping over base phrase chunk types.
  SP-NIST. NIST score over sequences of:
    SP-NIST$_l$ Lemmas.
    SP-NIST$_p$ Parts-of-speech.
    SP-NIST$_c$ Base phrase chunks.
    SP-NIST$_{iob}$ Chunk IOB labels.

- **Syntactic Similarity**

  On Dependency Parsing (DP)

    DP-HWC Head-word chain matching (HWCM), as presented by Liu and Gildea (2005), but slightly modified so as to consider different head-word chain types:
      DP-HWC$_w$ words.
      DP-HWC$_c$ categories.
      DP-HWC$_r$ relations.
    In all cases only chains up to length 4 are considered.
    DP-$O_l|O_c|O_r$ These metrics correspond exactly to the LEVEL, GRAM and TREE metrics introduced by Amigó et al. (2006):
      DP-O_l-$\star$ Average overlapping between words hanging at the same level of the tree.
      DP-O_c-$\star$ Average overlapping between words assigned the same grammatical category.
      DP-O_r-$\star$ Average overlapping between words ruled by the same type of grammatical relations.

  On Constituency Parsing (CP)

    CP-STM Syntactic tree matching (STM), as presented by Liu and Gildea (2005), i.e., limited up to length-4 subtrees.
    CP-O_p-$\star$ Average lexical overlapping over parts-of-speech, similarly to 'SP-O_p-$\star$', except that parts-of-speech are now consistent with the full parsing.
    CP-O_c-$\star$ Average lexical overlapping over phrase constituents. The difference between this metric and 'SP-O_c-$\star$' is in the phrase scope. In contrast to base phrase chunks, constituents allow for phrase embedding and overlapping.

- **Shallow-Semantic Similarity**

  On Semantic Roles (SR)

    SR-O_r-$\star$ Average lexical overlapping between SRs of the same type.
    SR-M_r-$\star$ Average lexical matching between SRs of the same type.
    SR-O_r Overlapping between semantic roles independently from their lexical realization.

  We also consider a more restrictive version of these metrics ('**SR-M_{rv}-$\star$**', '**SR-O_{rv}-$\star$**', and '**SR-O_{rv}**'), which require SRs to be associated to the same verb.

- **Semantic Similarity**

  On Discourse Representations (DR)

    DR-STM Average semantic tree matching considering semantic subtrees up to length 4.
    DR-O_r-$\star$ Average lexical overlapping between DRSs of the same type.
    DR-O_{rp}-$\star$ Average morphosyntactic overlapping between DRSs of the same type.

Fluency, Adequacy, or HTER? Exploring Different Human Judgments with a Tunable MT Metric

Matthew Snover[§], **Nitin Madnani**[§], **Bonnie J. Dorr**[§ †] **& Richard Schwartz**[† ‡]
[§]Laboratory for Computational Linguistics and Information Processing
[§]Institute for Advanced Computer Studies
[§]University of Maryland, College Park
[†]Human Language Technology Center of Excellence
[‡]BBN Technologies
{snover,nmadnani,bonnie}@umiacs.umd.edu schwartz@bbn.com

Abstract

Automatic Machine Translation (MT) evaluation metrics have traditionally been evaluated by the correlation of the scores they assign to MT output with human judgments of translation performance. Different types of human judgments, such as Fluency, Adequacy, and HTER, measure varying aspects of MT performance that can be captured by automatic MT metrics. We explore these differences through the use of a new tunable MT metric: TER-Plus, which extends the Translation Edit Rate evaluation metric with tunable parameters and the incorporation of morphology, synonymy and paraphrases. TER-Plus was shown to be one of the top metrics in NIST's Metrics MATR 2008 Challenge, having the highest average rank in terms of Pearson and Spearman correlation. Optimizing TER-Plus to different types of human judgments yields significantly improved correlations and meaningful changes in the weight of different types of edits, demonstrating significant differences between the types of human judgments.

1 Introduction

Since the introduction of the BLEU metric (Papineni et al., 2002), statistical MT systems have moved away from human evaluation of their performance and towards rapid evaluation using automatic metrics. These automatic metrics are themselves evaluated by their ability to generate scores for MT output that correlate well with human judgments of translation quality. Numerous methods of judging MT output by humans have been used, including *Fluency*, *Adequacy*, and, more recently, Human-mediated Translation Edit Rate (*HTER*) (Snover et al., 2006). Fluency measures whether a translation is fluent, regardless of the correct meaning, while Adequacy measures whether the translation conveys the correct meaning, even if the translation is not fully fluent. Fluency and Adequacy are frequently measured together on a discrete 5 or 7 point scale, with their average being used as a single score of translation quality. HTER is a more complex and semi-automatic measure in which humans do not score translations directly, but rather generate a new reference translation that is closer to the MT output but retains the fluency and meaning of the original reference. This new *targeted* reference is then used as the reference translation when scoring the MT output using Translation Edit Rate (TER) (Snover et al., 2006) or when used with other automatic metrics such as BLEU or METEOR (Banerjee and Lavie, 2005). One of the difficulties in the creation of targeted references is a further requirement that the annotator attempt to minimize the number of edits, as measured by TER, between the MT output and the targeted reference, creating the reference that is as close as possible to the MT output while still being adequate and fluent. In this way, only true errors in the MT output are counted. While HTER has been shown to be more consistent and finer grained than individual human annotators of Fluency and Adequacy, it is much more time consuming and taxing on human annotators than other types of human judgments, making it difficult and expensive to use. In addition, because HTER treats all edits equally, no distinction is made between serious errors (errors in names or missing subjects) and minor edits (such as a difference in verb agreement

Proceedings of the Fourth Workshop on Statistical Machine Translation, pages 259–268,
Athens, Greece, 30 March – 31 March 2009. ©2009 Association for Computational Linguistics

or a missing determinator).

Different types of translation errors vary in importance depending on the type of human judgment being used to evaluate the translation. For example, errors in tense might barely affect the adequacy of a translation but might cause the translation be scored as less fluent. On the other hand, deletion of content words might not lower the fluency of a translation but the adequacy would suffer. In this paper, we examine these differences by taking an automatic evaluation metric and tuning it to these these human judgments and examining the resulting differences in the parameterization of the metric. To study this we introduce a new evaluation metric, TER-Plus (TERp)[1] that improves over the existing Translation Edit Rate (TER) metric (Snover et al., 2006), incorporating morphology, synonymy and paraphrases, as well as tunable costs for different types of errors that allow for easy interpretation of the differences between human judgments.

Section 2 summarizes the TER metric and discusses how TERp improves on it. Correlation results with human judgments, including independent results from the 2008 NIST Metrics MATR evaluation, where TERp was consistently one of the top metrics, are presented in Section 3 to show the utility of TERp as an evaluation metric. The generation of paraphrases, as well as the effect of varying the source of paraphrases, is discussed in Section 4. Section 5 discusses the results of tuning TERp to Fluency, Adequacy and HTER, and how this affects the weights of various edit types.

2 TER and TERp

Both TER and TERp are automatic evaluation metrics for machine translation that score a translation, the *hypothesis*, of a foreign language text, the *source*, against a translation of the source text that was created by a human translator, called a *reference* translation. The set of possible correct translations is very large—possibly infinite—and any single reference translation is just a single point in that space. Usually multiple reference translations, typically 4, are provided to give broader sampling of the space of correct translations. Automatic MT evaluation metrics compare the hypothesis against this set of reference translations and assign a score to the similarity; higher scores are given to hypotheses that are more similar to the references.

In addition to assigning a score to a hypothesis, the TER metric also provides an alignment between the hypothesis and the reference, enabling it to be useful beyond general translation evaluation. While TER has been shown to correlate well with human judgments of translation quality, it has several flaws, including the use of only a single reference translation and the measuring of similarity only by exact word matches between the hypothesis and the reference. The handicap of using a single reference can be addressed by the construction of a lattice of reference translations. Such a technique has been used with TER to combine the output of multiple translation systems (Rosti et al., 2007). TERp does not utilize this methodology[2] and instead focuses on addressing the exact matching flaw of TER. A brief description of TER is presented in Section 2.1, followed by a discussion of how TERp differs from TER in Section 2.2.

2.1 TER

One of the first automatic metrics used to evaluate automatic machine translation (MT) systems was Word Error Rate (WER) (Niessen et al., 2000), which is the standard evaluation metric for Automatic Speech Recognition. WER is computed as the Levenshtein (Levenshtein, 1966) distance between the words of the system output and the words of the reference translation divided by the length of the reference translation. Unlike speech recognition, there are many correct translations for any given foreign sentence. These correct translations differ not only in their word choice but also in the order in which the words occur. WER is generally seen as inadequate for evaluation for machine translation as it fails to combine knowledge from multiple reference translations and also fails to model the reordering of words and phrases in translation.

TER addresses the latter failing of WER by allowing block movement of words, called *shifts*. within the hypothesis. Shifting a phrase has the same edit cost as inserting, deleting or substituting a word, regardless of the number of words being shifted. While a general solution to WER with block movement is NP-Complete (Lopresti

[1]Named after the nickname–"terp"–of the University of Maryland, College Park, mascot: the diamondback terrapin.

[2]The technique of combining references in this fashion has not been evaluated in terms of its benefit when correlating with human judgments. The authors hope to examine and incorporate such a technique in future versions of TERp.

and Tomkins, 1997), TER addresses this by using a greedy search to select the words to be shifted, as well as further constraints on the words to be shifted. These constraints are intended to simulate the way in which a human editor might choose the words to shift. For exact details on these constraints, see Snover et al. (2006). There are other automatic metrics that follow the general formulation as TER but address the complexity of shifting in different ways, such as the CDER evaluation metric (Leusch et al., 2006).

When TER is used with multiple references, it does not combine the references. Instead, it scores the hypothesis against each reference individually. The reference against which the hypothesis has the fewest number of edits is deemed the closet reference, and that number of edits is used as the numerator for calculating the TER score. For the denominator, TER uses the average number of words across all the references.

2.2 TER-Plus

TER-Plus (TERp) is an extension of TER that aligns words in the hypothesis and reference not only when they are exact matches but also when the words share a stem or are synonyms. In addition, it uses probabilistic phrasal substitutions to align phrases in the hypothesis and reference. These phrases are generated by considering possible paraphrases of the reference words. Matching using stems and synonyms (Banerjee and Lavie, 2005) and using paraphrases (Zhou et al., 2006; Kauchak and Barzilay, 2006) have previously been shown to be beneficial for automatic MT evaluation. Paraphrases have also been shown to be useful in expanding the number of references used for parameter tuning (Madnani et al., 2007; Madnani et al., 2008) although they are not used directly in this fashion within TERp. While all edit costs in TER are constant, all edit costs in TERp are optimized to maximize correlation with human judgments. This is because while a set of constant weights might prove adequate for the purpose of measuring translation quality—as evidenced by correlation with human judgments both for TER and HTER—they may not be ideal for maximizing correlation.

TERp uses all the edit operations of TER—Matches, Insertions, Deletions, Substitutions and Shifts—as well as three new edit operations: Stem Matches, Synonym Matches and Phrase Substitutions. TERp identifies words in the hypothesis and reference that share the same stem using the Porter stemming algorithm (Porter, 1980). Two words are determined to be synonyms if they share the same synonym set according to WordNet (Fellbaum, 1998). Sequences of words in the reference are considered to be paraphrases of a sequence of words in the hypothesis if that phrase pair occurs in the TERp phrase table. The TERp phrase table is discussed in more detail in Section 4.

With the exception of the phrase substitutions, the cost for all other edit operations is the same regardless of what the words in question are. That is, once the edit cost of an operation is determined via optimization, that operation costs the same no matter what words are under consideration. The cost of a phrase substitution, on the other hand, is a function of the probability of the paraphrase and the number of edits needed to align the two phrases according to TERp. In effect, the probability of the paraphrase is used to determine how much to discount the alignment of the two phrases. Specifically, the cost of a phrase substitution between the reference phrase, p_1 and the hypothesis phrase p_2 is:

$$\begin{aligned}\text{cost}(p_1, p_2) = &w_1 + \\ &\text{edit}(p_1, p_2) \times \\ &(w_2 \log(\Pr(p_1, p_2)) \\ &+ w_3 \Pr(p_1, p_2) + w_4)\end{aligned}$$

where w_1, w_2, w_3, and w_4 are the 4 free parameters of the edit cost, $\text{edit}(p_1, p_2)$ is the edit cost according to TERp of aligning p_1 to p_2 (excluding phrase substitutions) and $\Pr(p_1, p_2)$ is the probability of paraphrasing p_1 as p_2, obtained from the TERp phrase table. The w parameters of the phrase substitution cost may be negative while still resulting in a positive phrase substitution cost, as w_2 is multiplied by the log probability, which is always a negative number. In practice this term will dominate the phrase substitution edit cost.

This edit cost for phrasal substitutions is, therefore, specified by four parameters, w_1, w_2, w_3 and w_4. Only paraphrases specified in the TERp phrase table are considered for phrase substitutions. In addition, the cost for a phrasal substitution is limited to values greater than or equal to 0, i.e., the substitution cost cannot be negative. In addition, the shifting constraints of TERp are also relaxed to allow shifting of paraphrases, stems, and synonyms.

In total TERp uses 11 parameters out of which four represent the cost of phrasal substitutions. The match cost is held fixed at 0, so that only the 10 other parameters can vary during optimization. All edit costs, except for the phrasal substitution parameters, are also restricted to be positive. A simple hill-climbing search is used to optimize the edit costs by maximizing the correlation of human judgments with the TERp score. These correlations are measured at the sentence, or *segment*, level. Although it was done for the experiments described in this paper, optimization could also be performed to maximize document level correlation – such an optimization would give decreased weight to shorter segments as compared to the segment level optimization.

3 Correlation Results

The optimization of the TERp edit costs, and comparisons against several standard automatic evaluation metrics, using human judgments of Adequacy is first described in Section 3.1. We then summarize, in Section 3.2, results of the NIST Metrics MATR workshop where TERp was evaluated as one of 39 automatic metrics using many test conditions and types of human judgments.

3.1 Optimization of Edit Costs and Correlation Results

As part of the 2008 NIST Metrics MATR workshop (Przybocki et al., 2008), a development subset of translations from eight Arabic-to-English MT systems submitted to NIST's MTEval 2006 was released that had been annotated for Adequacy. We divided this development set into an optimization set and a test set, which we then used to optimize the edit costs of TERp and compare it against other evaluation metrics. TERp was optimized to maximize the segment level Pearson correlation with adequacy on the optimization set. The edit costs determined by this optimization are shown in Table 1.

We can compare TERp with other metrics by comparing their Pearson and Spearman correlations with Adequacy, at the segment, document and system level. Document level Adequacy scores are determined by taking the length weighted average of the segment level scores. System level scores are determined by taking the weighted average of the document level scores in the same manner.

We compare TERp with BLEU (Papineni et al., 2002), METEOR (Banerjee and Lavie, 2005), and TER (Snover et al., 2006). The IBM version of BLEU was used in case insensitive mode with an ngram-size of 4 to calculate the BLEU scores. Case insensitivity was used with BLEU as it was found to have much higher correlation with Adequacy. In addition, we also examined BLEU using an ngram-size of 2 (labeled as *BLEU-2*), instead of the default ngram-size of 4, as it often has a higher correlation with human judgments. When using METEOR, the exact matching, porter stemming matching, and WordNet synonym matching modules were used. TER was also used in case insensitive mode.

We show the Pearson and Spearman correlation numbers of TERp and the other automatic metrics on the optimization set and the test set in Tables 2 and 3. Correlation numbers that are statistically indistinguishable from the highest correlation, using a 95% confidence interval, are shown in bold and numbers that are actually not statistically significant correlations are marked with a †. TERp has the highest Pearson correlation in all conditions, although not all differences are statistically significant. When examining the Spearman correlation, TERp has the highest correlation on the segment and system levels, but performs worse than METEOR on the document level Spearman correlatons.

3.2 NIST Metrics MATR 2008 Results

TERp was one of 39 automatic metrics evaluated in the 2008 NIST Metrics MATR Challenge. In order to evaluate the state of automatic MT evaluation, NIST tested metrics across a number of conditions across 8 test sets. These conditions included segment, document and system level correlations with human judgments of preference, fluency, adequacy and HTER. The test sets included translations from Arabic-to-English, Chinese-to-English, Farsi-to-English, Arabic-to-French, and English-to-French MT systems involved in NIST's MTEval 2008, the GALE (Olive, 2005) Phase 2 and Phrase 2.5 program, Transtac January and July 2007, and CESTA run 1 and run 2, covering multiple genres. The version of TERp submitted to this workshop was optimized as described in Section 3.1. The development data upon which TERp was optimized was not part of the test sets evaluated in the Challenge.

Match	Insert	Deletion	Subst.	Stem	Syn.	Shift	Phrase Substitution w_1	w_2	w_3	w_4
0.0	0.26	1.43	1.56	0.0	0.0	0.56	-0.23	-0.15	-0.08	0.18

Table 1: Optimized TERp Edit Costs

Metric	Optimization Set Seg	Doc	Sys	Test Set Seg	Doc	Sys	Optimization+Test Seg	Doc	Sys
BLEU	0.623	0.867	0.952	0.563	0.852	**0.948**	0.603	0.861	0.954
BLEU-2	0.661	**0.888**	0.946	0.591	**0.876**	**0.953**	0.637	0.883	0.952
METEOR	0.731	**0.894**	0.952	0.751	**0.904**	**0.957**	0.739	**0.898**	0.958
TER	-0.609	-0.864	-0.957	-0.607	-0.860	**-0.959**	-0.609	-0.863	-0.961
TERp	**-0.782**	**-0.912**	**-0.996**	**-0.787**	**-0.918**	**-0.985**	**-0.784**	**-0.914**	**-0.994**

Table 2: Optimization & Test Set Pearson Correlation Results

Due to the wealth of testing conditions, a simple overall view of the official MATR08 results released by NIST is difficult. To facilitate this analysis, we examined the average rank of each metric across all conditions, where the rank was determined by their Pearson and Spearman correlation with human judgments. To incorporate statistical significance, we calculated the 95% confidence interval for each correlation coefficient and found the highest and lowest rank from which the correlation coefficient was statistically indistinguishable, resulting in lower and upper bounds of the rank for each metric in each condition. The average lower bound, actual, and upper bound ranks (where a rank of 1 indicates the highest correlation) of the top metrics, as well as BLEU and TER, are shown in Table 4, sorted by the average upper bound Pearson correlation. Full descriptions of the other metrics[3], the evaluation results, and the test set composition are available from NIST (Przybocki et al., 2008).

This analysis shows that TERp was consistently one of the top metrics across test conditions and had the highest average rank both in terms of Pearson and Spearman correlations. While this analysis is not comprehensive, it does give a general idea of the performance of all metrics by synthesizing the results into a single table. There are striking differences between the Spearman and Pearson correlations for other metrics, in particular the CDER metric (Leusch et al., 2006) had the second highest rank in Spearman correlations (after TERp), but was the sixth ranked metric according to the Pearson correlation. In several cases, TERp was not the best metric (if a metric was the best in all conditions, its average rank would be 1), although it performed well on average. In particular, TERp did significantly better than the TER metric, indicating the benefit of the enhancements made to TER.

4 Paraphrases

TERp uses probabilistic phrasal substitutions to align phrases in the hypothesis with phrases in the reference. It does so by looking up—in a precomputed phrase table—paraphrases of phrases in the reference and using its associated edit cost as the cost of performing a match against the hypothesis. The paraphrases used in TERp were extracted using the pivot-based method as described in (Bannard and Callison-Burch, 2005) with several additional filtering mechanisms to increase the precision. The pivot-based method utilizes the inherent monolingual semantic knowledge from bilingual corpora: we first identify English-to-F phrasal correspondences, then map from English to English by following translation units from English to F and back. For example, if the two English phrases `e1` and `e2` both correspond to the same foreign phrase `f`, then they may be considered to be paraphrases of each other with the following probability:

$$p(e1|e2) \approx p(e1|f) * p(f|e2)$$

If there are several pivot phrases that link the two English phrases, then they are all used in comput-

[3]System description of metrics are also distributed by AMTA: `http://www.amtaweb.org/AMTA2008.html`

Metric	Optimization Set			Test Set			Optimization+Test		
	Seg	Doc	Sys	Seg	Doc	Sys	Seg	Doc	Sys
BLEU	0.635	**0.816**	0.714†	0.550	**0.740**	**0.690**†	0.606	0.794	**0.738**†
BLEU-2	0.643	**0.823**	0.786†	0.558	**0.747**	**0.690**†	0.614	0.799	**0.738**†
METEOR	0.729	0.886	**0.881**	**0.727**	**0.853**	**0.738**†	0.730	**0.876**	**0.922**
TER	-0.630	**-0.794**	-0.810†	-0.630	**-0.797**	**-0.667**†	-0.631	-0.801	**-0.786**†
TERp	**-0.760**	**-0.834**	**-0.976**	**-0.737**	**-0.818**	**-0.881**	**-0.754**	-0.834	**-0.929**

Table 3: MT06 Dev. Optimization & Test Set Spearman Correlation Results

Metric	Average Rank by Pearson	Average Rank by Spearman
TERp	$1.49 \ll 6.07 \ll 17.31$	$1.60 \ll 6.44 \ll 17.76$
METEOR v0.7	$1.82 \ll 7.64 \ll 18.70$	$1.73 \ll 8.21 \ll 19.33$
METEOR ranking	$2.39 \ll 9.45 \ll 19.91$	$2.18 \ll 10.18 \ll 19.67$
METEOR v0.6	$2.42 \ll 10.67 \ll 19.11$	$2.47 \ll 11.27 \ll 19.60$
EDPM	$2.45 \ll 8.21 \ll 20.97$	$2.79 \ll 7.61 \ll 20.52$
CDER	$2.93 \ll 8.53 \ll 19.67$	$1.69 \ll 8.00 \ll 18.80$
BleuSP	$3.67 \ll 9.93 \ll 21.40$	$3.16 \ll 8.29 \ll 20.80$
NIST-v11b	$3.82 \ll 11.13 \ll 21.96$	$4.64 \ll 12.29 \ll 23.38$
BLEU-1 (IBM)	$4.42 \ll 12.47 \ll 22.18$	$4.98 \ll 14.87 \ll 24.00$
BLEU-4 (IBM)	$6.93 \ll 15.40 \ll 24.69$	$6.98 \ll 14.38 \ll 25.11$
TER v0.7.25	$8.87 \ll 16.27 \ll 25.29$	$6.93 \ll 17.33 \ll 24.80$
BLEU-4 v12 (NIST)	$10.16 \ll 18.02 \ll 27.64$	$10.96 \ll 17.82 \ll 28.16$

Table 4: Average Metric Rank in NIST Metrics MATR 2008 Official Results

ing the probability:

$$p(e1|e2) \approx \sum_{f'} p(e1|f') * p(f'|e2)$$

The corpus used for extraction was an Arabic-English newswire bitext containing a million sentences. A few examples of the extracted paraphrase pairs that were actually used in a run of TERp on the Metrics MATR 2008 development set are shown below:

(*brief* → *short*)
(*controversy over* → *polemic about*)
(*by using power* → *by force*)
(*response* → *reaction*)

A discussion of paraphrase quality is presented in Section 4.1, followed by a brief analysis of the effect of varying the pivot corpus used by the automatic paraphrase generation upon the correlation performance of the TERp metric in Section 4.2.

4.1 Analysis of Paraphrase Quality

We analyzed the utility of the paraphrase probability and found that it was not always a very reliable estimate of the degree to which the pair was semantically related. For example, we looked at all paraphrase pairs that had probabilities greater than 0.9, a set that should ideally contain pairs that are paraphrastic to a large degree. In our analysis, we found the following five kinds of paraphrases in this set:

(a) **Lexical Paraphrases.** These paraphrase pairs are not phrasal paraphrases but instead differ in at most one word and may be considered as lexical paraphrases for all practical purposes. While these pairs may not be very valuable for TERp due to the obvious overlap with WordNet, they may help in increasing the coverage of the paraphrastic phenomena that TERp can handle. Here are some examples:

(*2500 polish troops* → *2500 polish soldiers*)
(*accounting firms* → *auditing firms*)
(*armed source* → *military source*)

(b) **Morphological Variants.** These phrasal pairs only differ in the morphological form for one of the words. As the examples show, any knowledge that these pairs may provide is already available to TERp via stemming.

(50 ton → 50 tons)
(caused clouds → causing clouds)
(syria deny → syria denies)

(c) **Approximate Phrasal Paraphrases.** This set included pairs that only shared partial semantic content. Most paraphrases extracted by the pivot method are expected to be of this nature. These pairs are not directly beneficial to TERp since they cannot be substituted for each other in all contexts. However, the fact that they share at least some semantic content does suggest that they may not be entirely useless either. Examples include:

(mutual proposal → suggest)
(them were exiled → them abroad)
(my parents → my father)

(d) **Phrasal Paraphrases.** We did indeed find a large number of pairs in this set that were truly paraphrastic and proved the most useful for TERp. For example:

(agence presse → news agency)
(army roadblock → military barrier)
(staff walked out → team withdrew)

(e) **Noisy Co-occurrences.** There are also pairs that are completely unrelated and happen to be extracted as paraphrases based on the noise inherent in the pivoting process. These pairs are much smaller in number than the four sets described above and are not significantly detrimental to TERp since they are rarely chosen for phrasal substitution. Examples:

(counterpart salam → peace)
(regulation dealing → list)
(recall one → deported)

Given this distribution of the pivot-based paraphrases, we experimented with a variant of TERp that did not use the paraphrase probability at all but instead only used the actual edit distance between the two phrases to determine the final cost of a phrase substitution. The results for this experiment are shown in the second row of Table 5. We can see that this variant works as well as the full version of TERp that utilizes paraphrase probabilities. This confirms our intuition that the probability computed via the pivot-method is not a very useful predictor of semantic equivalence for use in TERp.

4.2 Varying Paraphrase Pivot Corpora

To determine the effect that the pivot language might have on the quality and utility of the extracted paraphrases in TERp, we used paraphrase pairsmade available by Callison-Burch (2008). These paraphrase pairs were extracted from Europarl data using each of 10 European languages (German, Italian, French etc.) as a pivot language separately and then combining the extracted paraphrase pairs. Callison-Burch (2008) also extracted and made available syntactically constrained paraphrase pairs from the same data that are more likely to be semantically related.

We used both sets of paraphrases in TERp as alternatives to the paraphrase pairs that we extracted from the Arabic newswire bitext. The results are shown in the last four rows of Table 5 and show that using a pivot language other than the one that the MT system is actually translating yields results that are almost as good. It also shows that the syntactic constraints imposed by Callison-Burch (2008) on the pivot-based paraphrase extraction process are useful and yield improved results over the baseline pivot-method. The results further support our claim that the pivot paraphrase probability is not a very useful indicator of semantic relatedness.

5 Varying Human Judgments

To evaluate the differences between human judgment types we first align the hypothesis to the references using a fixed set of edit costs, identical to the weights in Table 1, and then optimize the edit costs to maximize the correlation, without realigning. The separation of the edit costs used for alignment from those used for scoring allows us to remove the confusion of edit costs selected for alignment purposes from those selected to increase correlation.

For Adequacy and Fluency judgments, the MTEval 2002 human judgement set[4] was used. This set consists of the output of ten MT systems, 3 Arabic-to-English systems and 7 Chinese-

[4]Distributed to the authors by request from NIST.

Paraphrase Setup	Pearson Seg	Pearson Doc	Pearson Sys	Spearman Seg	Spearman Doc	Spearman Sys
Arabic pivot	**-0.787**	**-0.918**	**-0.985**	**-0.737**	**-0.818**	**-0.881**
Arabic pivot and no prob	**-0.787**	**-0.933**	**-0.986**	**-0.737**	**-0.841**	**-0.881**
Europarl pivot	**-0.775**	**-0.940**	**-0.983**	**-0.738**	**-0.865**	**-0.905**
Europarl pivot and no prob	**-0.775**	**-0.940**	**-0.983**	**-0.737**	**-0.860**	**-0.905**
Europarl pivot and syntactic constraints	**-0.781**	**-0.941**	**-0.985**	**-0.739**	**-0.859**	**-0.881**
Europarl pivot, syntactic constraints and no prob	**-0.779**	**-0.946**	**-0.985**	**-0.737**	**-0.866**	**-0.976**

Table 5: Results on the NIST MATR 2008 test set for several variations of paraphrase usage.

Human Judgment	Match	Insert	Deletion	Subst.	Stem	Syn.	Shift	Phrase Substitution w_1	w_2	w_3	w_4
Alignment	0.0	0.26	1.43	1.56	0.0	0.0	0.56	-0.23	-0.15	-0.08	0.18
Adequacy	0.0	0.18	1.42	1.71	0.0	0.0	0.19	-0.38	-0.03	0.22	0.47
Fluency	0.0	0.12	1.37	1.81	0.0	0.0	0.43	-0.63	-0.07	0.12	0.46
HTER	0.0	0.84	0.76	1.55	0.90	0.75	1.07	-0.03	-0.17	-0.08	-0.09

Table 6: Optimized Edit Costs

to-English systems, consisting of a total, across all systems and both language pairs, of 7,452 segments across 900 documents. To evaluate HTER, the GALE (Olive, 2005) 2007 (Phase 2.0) HTER scores were used. This set consists of the output of 6 MT systems, 3 Arabic-to-English systems and 3 Chinese-to-English systems, although each of the systems in question is the product of system combination. The HTER data consisted of a total, across all systems and language pairs, of 16,267 segments across a total of 1,568 documents. Because HTER annotation is especially expensive and difficult, it is rarely performed, and the only source, to the authors' knowledge, of available HTER annotations is on GALE evaluation data for which no Fluency and Adequacy judgments have been made publicly available.

The edit costs learned for each of these human judgments, along with the alignment edit costs are shown in Table 6. While all three types of human judgements differ from the alignment costs used in alignment, the HTER edit costs differ most significantly. Unlike Adequacy and Fluency which have a low edit cost for insertions and a very high cost for deletions, HTER has a balanced cost for the two edit types. Inserted words are strongly penalized against in HTER, as opposed to in Adequacy and Fluency, where such errors are largely forgiven. Stem and synonym edits are also penalized against while these are considered equivalent to a match for both Adequacy and Fluency. This penalty against stem matches can be attributed to Fluency requirements in HTER that specifically penalize against incorrect morphology. The cost of shifts is also increased in HTER, strongly penalizing the movement of phrases within the hypothesis, while Adequacy and Fluency give a much lower cost to such errors. Some of the differences between HTER and both fluency and adequacy can be attributed to the different systems used. The MT systems evaluated with HTER are all highly performing state of the art systems, while the systems used for adequacy and fluency are older MT systems.

The differences between Adequacy and Fluency are smaller, but there are still significant differences. In particular, the cost of shifts is over twice as high for the fluency optimized system than the adequacy optimized system, indicating that the movement of phrases, as expected, is only slightly penalized when judging meaning, but can be much more harmful to the fluency of a translation. Fluency however favors paraphrases more strongly than the edit costs optimized for adequacy. This might indicate that paraphrases are used to generate a more fluent translation although at the potential loss of meaning.

6 Discussion

We introduced a new evaluation metric, TER-Plus, and showed that it is competitive with state-of-the-art evaluation metrics when its predictions are correlated with human judgments. The inclusion of stem, synonym and paraphrase edits allows TERp to overcome some of the weaknesses of the TER metric and better align hypothesized translations with reference translations. These new edit costs can then be optimized to allow better correlation with human judgments. In addition, we have examined the use of other paraphrasing techniques, and shown that the paraphrase probabilities estimated by the pivot-method may not be fully adequate for judgments of whether a paraphrase in a translation indicates a correct translation. This line of research holds promise as an external evaluation method of various paraphrasing methods.

However promising correlation results for an evaluation metric may be, the evaluation of the final output of an MT system is only a portion of the utility of an automatic translation metric. Optimization of the parameters of an MT system is now done using automatic metrics, primarily BLEU. It is likely that some features that make an evaluation metric good for evaluating the final output of a system would make it a poor metric for use in system tuning. In particular, a metric may have difficulty distinguishing between outputs of an MT system that been optimized for that same metric. BLEU, the metric most frequently used to optimize systems, might therefore perform poorly in evaluation tasks compared to recall oriented metrics such as METEOR and TERp (whose tuning in Table 1 indicates a preference towards recall). Future research into the use of TERp and other metrics as optimization metrics is needed to better understand these metrics and the interaction with parameter optimization.

Finally, we explored the difference between three types of human judgments that are often used to evaluate both MT systems and automatic metrics, by optimizing TERp to these human judgments and examining the resulting edit costs. While this can make no judgement as to the preference of one type of human judgment over another, it indicates differences between these human judgment types, and in particular the difference between HTER and Adequacy and Fluency. This exploration is limited by the the lack of a large amount of diverse data annotated for all human judgment types, as well as the small number of edit types used by TERp. The inclusion of additional more specific edit types could lead to a more detailed understanding of which translation phenomenon and translation errors are most emphasized or ignored by which types of human judgments.

Acknowledgments

This work was supported, in part, by BBN Technologies under the GALE Program, DARPA/IPTO Contract No. HR0011-06-C-0022 and in part by the Human Language Technology Center of Excellence.. TERp is available on the web for download at: http://www.umiacs.umd.edu/~snover/terp/.

References

Satanjeev Banerjee and Alon Lavie. 2005. METEOR: An Automatic Metric for MT Evaluation with Improved Correlation with Human Judgments. In *Proceedings of the ACL 2005 Workshop on Intrinsic and Extrinsic Evaulation Measures for MT and/or Summarization.*

Colin Bannard and Chris Callison-Burch. 2005. Paraphrasing with Bilingual Parallel Corpora. In *Proceedings of the 43rd Annual Meeting of the Association for Computational Linguistics (ACL 2005)*, pages 597–604, Ann Arbor, Michigan, June.

Chris Callison-Burch. 2008. Syntactic constraints on paraphrases extracted from parallel corpora. In *Proceedings of the 2008 Conference on Empirical Methods in Natural Language Processing*, pages 196–205, Honolulu, Hawaii, October. Association for Computational Linguistics.

Christiane Fellbaum. 1998. *WordNet: An Electronic Lexical Database.* MIT Press. http://www.cogsci.princeton.edu/~wn [2000, September 7].

David Kauchak and Regina Barzilay. 2006. Paraphrasing for Automatic Evaluation. In *Proceedings of the Human Language Technology Conference of the North American Chapter of the ACL*, pages 455–462.

Gregor Leusch, Nicola Ueffing, and Hermann Ney. 2006. CDER: Efficient MT Evaluation Using Block Movements. In *Proceedings of the 11th Conferenceof the European Chapter of the Association for Computational Linguistics (EACL 2006).*

V. I. Levenshtein. 1966. Binary Codes Capable of Correcting Deletions, Insertions, and Reversals. *Soviet Physics Doklady*, 10:707–710.

Daniel Lopresti and Andrew Tomkins. 1997. Block edit models for approximate string matching. *Theoretical Computer Science*, 181(1):159–179, July.

Nitin Madnani, Necip Fazil Ayan, Philip Resnik, and Bonnie J. Dorr. 2007. Using paraphrases for parameter tuning in statistical machine translation. In *Proceedings of the Workshop on Statistical Machine Translation*, Prague, Czech Republic, June. Association for Computational Linguistics.

Nitin Madnani, Philip Resnik, Bonnie J. Dorr, and Richard Schwartz. 2008. Are Multiple Reference Translations Necessary? Investigating the Value of Paraphrased Reference Translations in Parameter Optimization. In *Proceedings of the Eighth Conference of the Association for Machine Translation in the Americas*, October.

S. Niessen, F.J. Och, G. Leusch, and H. Ney. 2000. An evaluation tool for machine translation: Fast evaluation for MT research. In *Proceedings of the 2nd International Conference on Language Resources and Evaluation (LREC-2000)*, pages 39–45.

Joseph Olive. 2005. *Global Autonomous Language Exploitation (GALE)*. DARPA/IPTO Proposer Information Pamphlet.

Kishore Papineni, Salim Roukos, Todd Ward, and Wei-Jing Zhu. 2002. Bleu: a Method for Automatic Evaluation of Machine Traslation. In *Proceedings of the 40th Annual Meeting of the Association for Computational Linguistics*.

Martin F. Porter. 1980. An algorithm for suffic stripping. *Program*, 14(3):130–137.

Mark Przybocki, Kay Peterson, and Sebastian Bronsart. 2008. Official results of the NIST 2008 "Metrics for MAchine TRanslation" Challenge (MetricsMATR08). http://nist.gov/speech/tests/metricsmatr/2008/results/, October.

Antti-Veikko Rosti, Spyros Matsoukas, and Richard Schwartz. 2007. Improved word-level system combination for machine translation. In *Proceedings of the 45th Annual Meeting of the Association of Computational Linguistics*, pages 312–319, Prague, Czech Republic, June. Association for Computational Linguistics.

Matthew Snover, Bonnie Dorr, Richard Schwartz, Linnea Micciulla, and John Makhoul. 2006. A Study of Translation Edit Rate with Targeted Human Annotation. In *Proceedings of Association for Machine Translation in the Americas*.

Liang Zhou, Chon-Yew Lin, and Eduard Hovy. 2006. Re-evaluating Machine Translation Results with Paraphrase Support. In *Proceedings of the 2006 Conference on Empirical Methods in Natural Language Processing (EMNLP 2006)*, pages 77–84.

Author Index